BUSINESS DATA NETWORKS AND SECURITY

Ninth Edition

Business Data Networks and Security

Raymond R. Panko
University of Hawai`i at Mānoa

Julia L. Panko
Massachusetts Institute of Technology, Weber State University

PEARSON

Boston   Columbus   Indianapolis   New York   San Francisco   Upper Saddle River
Amsterdam   Cape Town   Dubai   London   Madrid   Milan   Munich   Paris   Montreal   Toronto
Delhi   Mexico City   Sao Paulo   Sydney   Hong Kong   Seoul   Singapore   Taipei   Tokyo

Editor-in-Chief: Stephanie Wall
Executive Editor: Bob Horan
Senior Editorial Project Manager: Kelly Loftus
Editorial Assistant: Ashlee Bradbury
Director of Marketing: Maggie Moylan
Executive Marketing Manager: Anne Fahlgren
Marketing Assistant: Gianna Sandri
Production Manager: Tom Benfatti
Creative Director: Jayne Conte

Cover Designer: Bruce Kenselaar
Cover Image: margouillat/fotolia.com
Full Service Project Management:
   Sudip Sinha, PreMediaGlobal
Composition: PreMediaGlobal
Printer/Binder: Edwards Brothers
Cover Printer: Lehigh-Phoenix Color,
   Hagerstown
Text Font: 10/12 Palatino

Credits and acknowledgments borrowed from other sources and reproduced, with permission, in this textbook appear on the appropriate page within text. All the icons in figures are courtesy to iStockphoto.

Microsoft and/or its respective suppliers make no representations about the suitability of the information contained in the documents and related graphics published as part of the services for any purpose. All such documents and related graphics are provided "as is" without warranty of any kind. Microsoft and/or its respective suppliers hereby disclaim all warranties and conditions with regard to this information, including all warranties and conditions of merchantability, whether express, implied or statutory, fitness for a particular purpose, title and non-infringement. In no event shall Microsoft and/or its respective suppliers be liable for any special, indirect or consequential damages or any damages whatsoever resulting from loss of use, data or profits, whether in an action of contract, negligence or other tortious action, arising out of or in connection with the use or performance of information available from the services. The documents and related graphics contained herein could include technical inaccuracies or typographical errors. Changes are periodically added to the information herein. Microsoft and/or its respective suppliers may make improvements and/or changes in the product(s) and/or the program(s) described herein at any time. Partial screen shots may be viewed in full within the software version specified. Microsoft® and Windows® are registered trademarks of the Microsoft Corporation in the U.S.A. and other countries. This book is not sponsored or endorsed by or affiliated with the Microsoft Corporation.

Library of Congress Cataloging-in-Publication Data
Panko, R. R.
   Business data networks and security/Raymond R. Panko, Julia L. Panko.—9th ed.
        p. cm.
   Rev. ed. of: Business data networks and telecommunications. 8th ed.
   Includes index.
   ISBN-13: 978-0-13-274293-1
   ISBN-10: 0-13-274293-4
   1. Business enterprises—Computer networks—Security measures.   2. Computer networks—Management.   3. Computer networks—Security measures.   4. Computer security.   I. Panko, Julia L.   II. Panko, R. R. Business data networks and telecommunications.   III. Title.
   HD30.37.P36 2013
   005.7'1—dc23

                                                                2012012777

10 9 8 7 6 5 4 3 2 1

ISBN 10:   0-13-274293-4
ISBN 13: 978-0-13-274293-1

To Sal Aurigemma. A great partner in crime in research and teaching.

BRIEF CONTENTS

Online Modules

(available at www.pearsonhighered.com/panko)

CONTENTS

Chapter 4a HANDS-ON: MICROSOFT OFFICE VISIO   171

Applying Concepts and Principles: Up through the Layers

Chapter 5   WIRED ETHERNET LANs   175

Online Modules

(available at www.pearsonhighered.com/panko)

PREFACE FOR STUDENTS

PERSPECTIVE

In the past, information systems (IS) graduates had a single career track: programmer–analyst–database administrator–manager. Today, however, many IS graduates find themselves on the networking/security career track. Both networking and security employment are growing rapidly, and they are exciting to work in. This course is an introduction to the networking/security track.

Even programmers today need a strong understanding of networking. In the past, programmers wrote stand-alone programs that ran on a single computer. Today, however, most programmers write networked applications that work cooperatively with other programs on other computers.

Whichever IT career path you choose, learn as much as you can from each course. Employers do not just look at transcripts. If you make it past initial job interviews, expect to be grilled for hours in subsequent interviews to see what you really know. Employers do not expect perfection, but they demand a high level of knowledge and the retention of that knowledge. Study for mastery and retention.

HOW TO LEARN NETWORKING

Networking and Security Are Different From Programming

Networking is an exciting topic. However, intellectually it is very different from networking and security. In programming, the focus is on creating and running programs. In networking, the critical skills are design, product selection, troubleshooting, and security. These rather abstract skills require a broad and deep knowledge of many concepts. Many IS students have a difficult time adjusting to these cerebral skill requirements. Security is especially a "head game" because we are pitted against intelligent adversaries, not simply difficult choices in complex situations.

How To Study This Book

There are several keys to studying this book:

- Reading chapters once will not be enough. You will need to really *study* the chapters. In the earliest chapters, you will just be developing a mental framework for placing new information into the broader picture. This really hurts retention. You will have to go over things several times to really understand them and to develop the mental framework you will need to absorb additional networking knowledge efficiently.
- Slow down for the hard parts. Some sections will be easy, others difficult. We all have a tendency to go at the same speed through all sections. Also, if you don't get it the first time, work at it. You may be able to get Bs and Cs not knowing the hard stuff, but you won't have the knowledge you need in the workforce.
- When you finish reading a section, immediately do the Test Your Understanding questions. If you don't get one of the questions, go back over the text. The understanding of networking is strongly cumulative, and if you skim over one section,

you will have increasing difficulties with later material. Multiple-choice questions in the test item file are taken entirely from the test-your-understanding questions and the end-of-chapter questions.

- If you can, get together with other students to go over your answers to the Test Your Understanding questions to see if everybody agrees.
- Study the figures. Nearly every key point in each chapter is in the figures. If there is something in a figure you don't understand, you need to study the corresponding section in the chapter. Pretend you are trying to explain the figure to someone else. Also, study the "study figures" that summarize information.
- Key terms are printed in boldface when they are first introduced. Pay special attention. Pay even more attention to material set off with top and bottom borders.
- Network design is about selecting among alternatives. If several concepts are presented in a section or chapter, do not just study them individually. You need to know which one to use in a particular situation, and that requires compare/contrast knowledge. Study the figures that compare concepts, and make your own figures and lists or charts of features if the book does not provide them. Comparing different technologies in order to select the best one for corporate needs is a critical skill for all IT professionals.
- Study the synopsis section at the end of each chapter. The synopsis summarizes key concepts in the chapter. Be very sure that you understand the synopsis very well. You might even study them before beginning the chapter, to get a broad understanding of the material.
- One way to make networking less abstract to you is to do as many hands-on activities as possible.

A Networking/Security Career

If you like the networking course and think you want a networking or security career, an important thing to keep in mind is that both change constantly. This means constant learning and new skills development. On the negative side, this means doing a lot of reading. However, do not underestimate the importance of job variety in your career. Doing the same thing or very similar things every day does not make for a very satisfying career. Networking and security are very satisfying careers.

If you do want to prepare for a networking or security career, there are a number of steps you should take before graduation, even if your school does not have advanced networking or security courses.

- Most importantly, do a networking or security internship. Employers really want workers with job experience—often preferring it to an unwarranted degree over academic preparation.
- Read *networkworld.com* regularly. In fact, read it during this course. You won't understand everything, especially at first, but as your understanding grows, you will find that you can read the professional material in the field. That means that you have a strong background.
- Consider getting one or more industry certifications. In networking, the low-level CompTIA Network+ certification should be obtainable with just a bit more study after you take your core networking course. However, this certification is not highly valued. Cisco's more valuable CCNA (Cisco Certified Network

Associate) certification, which focuses on switching and routing, will require substantially more study. You also have to learn hands-on commands. This will require you to take a class or buy a network simulation program designed for this certification. Microsoft server certification is also valuable, but it focuses more on clients and servers. Employers like certifications, but they know that certifications are no substitutes for job experience. Similarly, the CompTIA Security+ is a relatively low-level certification, while the CISSP is a more impressive certification. Certifications increasingly require several years of work in the field. However, it may be possible to pass the exam to show that you have mastered concepts in the field before you begin working in the field.

ABOUT THE AUTHORS

Ray Panko is a professor of IT management and a Shidler Fellow at the University of Hawai`i's Shidler College of Business. He received his doctorate from Stanford University. His main courses are networking and security. Before coming to the university, he was a project manager at Stanford Research Institute (now SRI International), where he worked for Doug Englebart, the inventor of the mouse. He received his B.S. in physics and his M.B.A. from Seattle University. He received his doctorate from Stanford University, where his dissertation was conducted under contract to the Office of the President of the United States. He has been awarded the Shidler College of Business's Dennis Ching award as the outstanding teacher among senior faculty. His e-mail is Ray@Panko.com.

Julia Panko is doing postdoctoral research at the Massachusetts Institute of Technology. She is also on the faculty of Weber State University. She received her doctorate from the University of California, Santa Barbara. Her research interests include the 20th- and 21st-century novel, the history and theory of information technology, and the digital humanities. Her dissertation focused on the relationship between information culture and modern and contemporary novels. Before the eighth edition, she was the technical editor for the book.

1 | WELCOME TO THE CLOUD

LEARNING OBJECTIVES

By the end of this chapter, you should be able to:

- Discuss why networking and security are converging.
- Describe basic network terminology.
- Describe packet switching as a way to reduce long-distance transmission costs and error retransmissions. Describe physical links and data links.
- Describe the origins of Internet standards and applications, including e-mail.
- Explain why internetworking was needed.
- Explain why Kahn and Cerf's concept for internetworking resulted in duplicated network concepts. Describe the internet and transport layers.
- Explain the five basic layers of standards in the TCP/IP-OSI Hybrid Standards Architecture.
- Describe TCP/IP standards.
- Explain the evolution of the Internet from research network to commercial network.
- List TCP/IP supervisory standards.
- Describe a small home network.

IN THE CLOUDS

Jason Akana

Jason Akana works at the First Bank of Paradise (FBP)[1] in Honolulu, Hawai`i. FBP has 50 branches throughout the state and many more ATMs. Jason helps develop new media campaigns for bank products. His campaigns use Facebook, Twitter, YouTube, e-mail lists, and the bank's website.

Currently, the bank is developing a promotional campaign for its new *AlohaSmart* credit card, which has both a computer chip and a traditional magnetic stripe. Figure 1-1 shows the new card. Cards with computer chips are called **smart cards**. They are common in Europe, and American merchants are beginning to add smart card readers.

---

[1]The "First Bank of Paradise" is a composite of several banks in Hawai`i. Individual banks are obviously reluctant to have specific information about their networking and security made public.

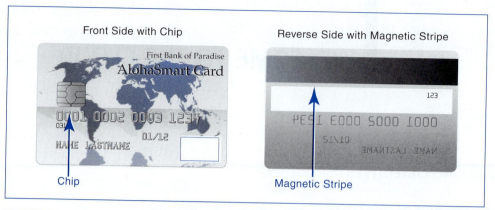

FIGURE 1-1   *AlohaSmart* Credit Card

Source: © omergenc/iStockphoto

The marketing campaign will emphasize the advantages of smart cards over traditional magnetic stripe cards in terms of security and extra services. The card has a slightly higher fee than traditional magnetic stripe cards, so the bank will benefit when customers switch to the new card. Jason has developed a tentative campaign and a PowerPoint presentation to lay out how the bank can use new media to promote the card.

When Jason woke this morning, he opened his tablet and checked his mail. Yesterday, he posted his draft plan and a PowerPoint presentation to everyone in marketing. Three replied with good suggestions for changes. After breakfast, Jason turned on his desktop computer and made the changes to the presentation. He likes to develop new material on his desktop because its large screen allows him to lay out subsidiary material next to the PowerPoint presentation.

Figure 1-2 shows that when Jason finished working on his desktop, his BlueSync software uploaded the PowerPoint presentation to a BlueSync server on the Internet.

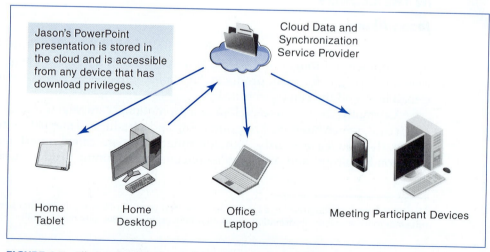

FIGURE 1-2   File Synchronization and Distribution in the Cloud

In more colorful language, it saved the file "to the cloud." Later, when Jason turns on his tablet, it will be available on the tablet. When he turns on his laptop at work, it will be there as well. It will even be available on Jason's smartphone. In fact, on these machines, any file changed on one will be synchronized on the others. For the coming meeting to explain his plan, it will be available to the attendees as well. BlueSync is a **cloud data and synchronization service provider**.

The term *cloud* is used often in networking and other parts of IT today. The **cloud** imagery signifies that users do not have to know what is happening "inside the cloud." The details are taken care of by the organization or by an outside company. BlueSync is one of these external services.

The cloud imagery signifies that users do not have to know what is happening "inside the cloud."

Off to work, Jason rides from his home in Kailua to work in a shared van. It is slower than driving himself, but parking fees are horrendous downtown. On the ride, Jason goes over the presentation several times on his tablet. He also exchanges phone texts with his boss about the presentation.

At home, PowerPoint is installed on his desktop computer. On his tablet, however, Jason uses a cloud version of PowerPoint. It is only downloaded to his tablet when he needs it, and he pays a monthly fee for the service. Figure 1-3 shows that the software is managed by a **cloud software service provider**. This name comes from the fact that software is provided as a service when needed, not on a product to be purchased once and stored on the user's machine like traditional software.

At work, Jason fires up his laptop computer and takes it to the conference room. On this device too, he downloads PowerPoint only when needed. He plugs the laptop into the projector and shows the first slide on the screen. He is ready. Over the next few minutes, four local attendees walk into the room. They exchange small talk, check things on their tablets and laptops, and use their phones to make calls and send texts.

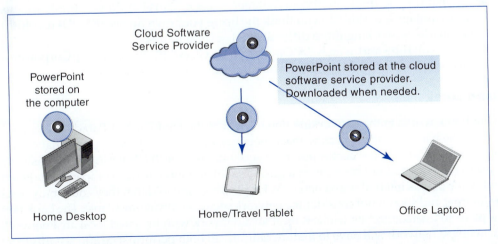

FIGURE 1-3   Software in the Cloud

At 10:00 am, the meeting starts. In addition to being shown on the screen, slide images are on BlueSync, so everybody in the meeting can bring them up on his or her laptops and tablets. Two of the attendees are at a second site. They can see the slides on their computers, and the conference room has an audioconferencing system for voice communication between the attendees at the two sites.

After the overview presentation, Jason goes over Microsoft Word documents, detailing specific aspects of the new media campaign. The group then discusses how to integrate the new media campaign with the bank's traditional media campaign using print, radio, and television. During the discussion, one of the marketing staff members plays a high-definition television ad the department would like to run. With everyone reasonably satisfied, the marketing director gives the green light to both the new media and traditional media campaigns.

Jason's experience is far from unique. Today, user computers span a wide range of sizes. Most of the newest products have been at the small end of the spectrum, with smartphones and tablets growing rapidly. The multi-screen desktop is at the high end today, but in the future, entire tables and walls will be displays.

None of this would be possible without networks to link people to resources locally and over long distances. Networks have been around for many years, and they have always been useful. Today, they are critical. On the negative side of this criticality, if the network fails, even briefly, a great deal of corporate work is disrupted. Networks must work reliably. Networks must also work well; many applications require very high speeds, so networks must be fast, even when they use wireless transmission, which is notoriously finicky. On the positive side, great networks enable the firm to do things like Jason's meeting, which would have been very difficult to do in the past. In general, networks today must be like traditional servants—excellent and invisible.

Test Your Understanding

1. a) Why do you think wireless is such a big concern today in networking and security? (In this book, "do you think" questions require you to go beyond what is in the text. You may not be able to answer them perfectly, but try hard because they are good learning opportunities.) b) Distinguish between cloud data storage and synchronization on the one hand and cloud software service on the other. c) What do you think are the advantages of each? d) What do you think are their disadvantages? e) Why do you think the bring your own device (BYOD) revolution has made networking more difficult? List several issues.

2. Go to YouTube and watch "A Day Made of Glass" by the Corning Corporation. List new ways of displaying information shown in the video.

Claire Lorek

Claire Lorek works in the networking department at the First Bank of Paradise. Her job is to keep the bank's headquarters wireless networking running at peak performance. The bank has over 50 wireless access points to serve its users in the building. Previously, the wireless network had not been given a great deal of attention. It was completely independent of the bank's internal wired network. Employees were told that they could only reach the Internet and should not consider the network secure or always available. The bank now has plans to interconnect its wireless local area network with its wired local area network. The wireless network will have to mature radically in both performance and security.

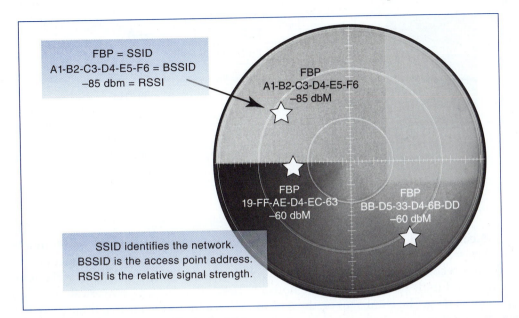

FBP = SSID
A1-B2-C3-D4-E5-F6 = BSSID
−85 dbm = RSSI

FBP
A1-B2-C3-D4-E5-F6
−85 dbM

FBP
19-FF-AE-D4-EC-63
−60 dbM

FBP
BB-D5-33-D4-6B-DD
−60 dbM

SSID identifies the network.
BSSID is the access point address.
RSSI is the relative signal strength.

FIGURE 1-4   The Wireless Sniffer Radar Map

Currently, the bank has no central way to manage its wireless network. Every day and sometimes several times a day, Claire walks around the building with her ultra-portable laptop. At her normal stopping points, she fires up her **wireless sniffer** program. Figure 1-4 shows that the first thing she does is look at the "radar map" which shows the relative directions of nearby access points and their signal strengths.

At this stop, three access points are in range. Each access point has a **service set ID (SSID)**, which is the name of the network. The SSID is FBP, which indicates that this is the bank's network. The access point in the upper left has the **BSSID** A1-B2-C3-D4-E5-F6. This is the address of the specific access point. Note that other access points have different BSSIDs. The **RSSI** value is the relative signal strength indicator, which shows strength in terms of decibel relative to one milliwatt. Everything looks good. The only access points are corporate-approved access points, and signal strengths look good.

Going in more depth, Claire looks at the wireless sniffer details table shown in Figure 1-5. It gives more details about the nearby access points. She checks to make sure that each is properly configured for security. All are using the security methods required by corporate policy. For encryption (so that no one can intercept and read transmissions), all three use AES-CCMP. For authentication (in which a wireless device user proves his or her identity before being allowed to use the access point), the access points all require WPA2/PEAP. We will explain these terms in Chapter 7.

At her next stop, Claire notices a signal strength problem for one of the access points. The problem, she quickly discovers, is that a group of metal filing cabinets were installed yesterday. They are partially blocking the access point's signal. There are other access points available, so this is not a problem, but she makes a note in her daily log.

SSID	FBP	FBP	FBP
BSSID	A1-B2-C3-D4-E5-F6	BB-D5-33-D4-6B-DD	19-FF-AE-D4-EC-63
Signal	−85 dBm	−60 dBm	−60 dBm
Mode	802.11g	802.11n	802.11n
Channel	11	48	44
Encryption	AES-CCMP	AES-CCMP	AES-CCMP
Authentication	WPA2/PEAP	WPA2/PEAP	WPA2/PEAP
Vendor	Cisco	Cisco	Cisco

FIGURE 1-5   Wireless Sniffer Details Table

Near the end of her "walkabout," Claire finds an access point that should not be there. In security terminology, it is a **rogue access point**. Using the map function, she traces it to a conference room. However, the conference room looks clean. She checks in cabinets and finds nothing. Then she notices a network cable and power cable leading up to the ceiling. She climbs up on the table and lifts a tile in the false ceiling. There it is. She disconnects it and turns it off. She will give it to security.

A rogue access point is an unauthorized access point.

The bank will soon be switching over to a centralized wireless management system. Instead of having to walk around, Claire will just check a display. It will give her the information she now collects so laboriously in a single integrated database.

- It will identify rogue access points and access points outside the building automatically, sending her a text when it finds one.
- It will be able to do several things she cannot do now, such as identifying access points that are not operating during one of her walkabouts.
- She will even be able to adjust access point power levels, channels, and other parameters remotely. When she finds a problem, she will usually be able to fix it without wasting time going to the access point.
- She will even be able to adjust the access points when groups of people with smartphones, tablets, and notebooks assemble in a location that was previously quiet.

Claire will need the boost in productivity the wireless management system will bring. Wireless traffic in the building is exploding, and the growth of video applications is requiring her to give increasing attention to error rates and other performance parameters that have not been issues with traditional applications.

Test Your Understandings

3. a) What information could Claire learn about individual access points? b) Distinguish between SSIDs and BSSIDs. c) What is a rogue access point? d) Why do you think rogue access points are dangerous? e) Why is centralized wireless management highly desirable compared to "management by walking around" as Claire does today?

John Lee

John Lee is a member of the First Bank of Paradise IT security staff. Like Claire Lorek, he focuses on the bank's internal wireless LAN. While Claire works to keep the network running, John's job is to keep the users safe (and to keep the bank safe from users).

One of John's projects is to develop security policies for user-owned smartphones and tablets. (There are already security policies for user-owned laptops and desktops.) The main problems that John faces are the diversity of operating systems and the rapid pace of change in technology. There are three major operating systems to keep track of—Apple's iOS, Microsoft's Windows 7 and Windows 8, and Android. Apple and Microsoft keep tight control over their operating systems. The diversity among Android operating system variants, however, is daunting. Just keeping track of security vulnerability reports on these operating systems and variants takes up much of John's day. With the technology changing at dizzying speed, operating systems and hardware are generally maturing, but while each advance seems to bring better security in general, it also brings a few new security problems. John refers to the situation as the **BYOD (bring your own device)** issue.

One issue that concerns John is the loss of smartphones and tablets. Many of these devices are loaded with private customer information, private information about other employees, and trade secrets such as price and customer lists. John wants to find secure encryption and device locking tools that will be strong enough for protection and easy enough to use for phone and tablet users to accept. Right now, however, he can only alert users to the problem and keep his fingers crossed.

Test Your Understanding

4. a) List major wireless LAN security issues. b) Why is BYOD security so difficult today?

The Rogue Access Point

Remember the rogue access point that Claire discovered? John traced it to Albert Gomes, a mid-level manager. Gomes was surprised that his access point had been detected because he had set the access point to "stealth mode." Claire and John replied that their software and hacker software have no problem finding such access points. Gomes replied that he thought stealth mode would keep the company safe.

Claire and John were not interested in making this an inquisition. They asked about the problem that Gomes was trying to solve with his rouge access point. It turns out that he is doing HDTV training in his department and often has two or three people taking training at a time. Claire agreed that the department needed more speed and promised that she would provide it by the next day. She also pointed out that his access point was not capable of implementing quality of service guarantees, which his employees needed for smooth video delivery. Her system would fix that. Greatly relieved and pleased, Albert thanked them enthusiastically. Networking and security had made an important friend and had done their job of using networks to make the company work better.

Networking and Security

Everything is changing in information technology, and it is changing at light speed. Few things are changing more rapidly than networking and security. These are fields for people who do not like boredom, and corporations almost always put these two disciplines near the top of their IT hiring lists.

Although networking and security are technically distinct fields, in practice they are converging rapidly. Networking professionals, who used to be concerned with wires and switches, now find that they need to consider security in everything they do. Security professionals, in turn, find that most of their vexing problems are concerned with networking and require extensive networking knowledge. The title of this book, *Business Data Networks and Security*, reflects this convergence.

Test Your Understanding

5. Why does this book combine networking and security?

BASIC NETWORK TERMINOLOGY

Networks, Hosts, and Applications

In a book on networking, it makes sense to begin by defining what a network is. As a working definition, we will define a **network** as a system that permits applications on different hosts to work together.

As a working definition, a network is a system that permits applications on different hosts to work together.

Figure 1-6 illustrates this working definition.

In Chapter 2, we will extend this working definition into a formal definition using concepts that are not necessary for a broad understanding of networks.

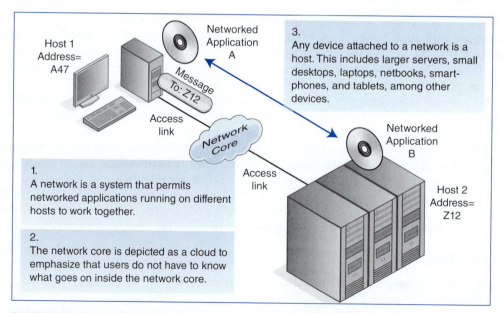

FIGURE 1-6   Basic Network Terminology

NETWORKED APPLICATIONS   Note that the definition focuses on *applications*. Although you will spend most of your time in this course learning the details of how networks operate, our preliminary definition takes the *user's* point of view. Networks are only valuable if they connect the applications that users need to have connected. Users have no desire to know the details of how the network operates. Nor *should* they. They simply want to use their applications as easily as they can. Applications are the only things users care about and should have to know about.

Computer applications existed long before networking. However, as networks began to connect different computers and to do so with greater reliability and speed, there was an explosion in **networked applications**, which require networks to work.

Networked applications are applications that require networks to work.

The 1970s brought the first networked applications, including e-mail for communication and the File Transfer Protocol (FTP) for moving large files. Networked applications continued to evolve steadily, but there was an explosion of applications in the 1990s, driven by the rapid growth and commercialization of the Internet, that brought the World Wide Web (WWW), e-commerce, social networking, and many of the other networked applications we use so extensively today.

This century has brought **Web 2.0** applications, in which users provide the content. In early (Web 1.0) Web applications, the website owner created the content. This was expensive and gave website owners control of what appeared on the World Wide Web. With Web 2.0, these barriers are gone. Users create most or all of the content. Wikipedia is a classic example of a Web 2.0 application. Although Wikipedia has some problems, this "crowd-sourced" application is by far the most comprehensive encyclopedia the world has ever known. On a less august level, there is YouTube.

In Web 2.0 applications, users provide the content.

Included in the Web 2.0 category are **social media applications**, such as Facebook, Twitter, and dating services, which are designed to facilitate relationships. E-mail and other communication applications have long been useful in building relationships, but social media sites have developed specialized tools to enhance social networking. Facebook works on the individual level, connecting a person with several of his or her friends. Other new applications bring together groups of people with common interests.

Social media applications are applications designed to facilitate relationships.

HOSTS AND ADDRESSES   In the definition of networking, it was noted that applications run on devices called *hosts*. We use the term *host* rather than *computer* because not all devices connected to networks are computers in the traditional sense. Smartphones and tablets are good examples of this. In the future, toasters and coffee pots will be connected to networks within individual homes and across the Internet.[2] Formally, we will define a **host** as any device connected to a network.

A host is any device attached to a network.

Each host needs a unique **network address**. When a source host sends a message to a destination host, the source host places the address of the destination host in the message. Based on this address, the network delivers the message to the destination host. The source host does not have to know how the message gets to the destination host—just that it does. Analogously, when you place a call, you simply dial a number and the telephone network invisibly connects you to the other telephone without your knowing how this occurred.

Each host has a unique network address. Based on this address, the network delivers the message to the destination host.

THE NETWORK CORE   For users, a network is simply there. Consequently, Figure 1-6 depicts the **network core**—the central part of the network—as a cloud. Just as you cannot see the inside of a cloud, users do not have to look inside the network.

The network core is the central part of the network.

Of course, as an information systems student, you will need to look *deeply* inside various types of network technologies ranging from the network you may have in your home to the global Internet. Before my grandfather came to America, he was told that the streets of America were paved with gold. When he got here, he found that they were not even paved. Guess who was going to pave them?

Fortunately for you, the network "streets" in corporations today are already reasonably well paved. Your job will be to turn them into true super highways and to help your organization assimilate the ever-growing number of networked applications and novel types of applications that network capabilities will make possible. You will also help users cope with the outpouring of new applications and devices. On the negative side, you will have to deal with a large and rapidly growing number of security threats that threaten the potential benefits of networking.

ACCESS LINKS   Users connect to networks through **access links**, which may use copper wire, optical fiber, or radio transmission. Users typically need to know a little more about access links than about the network core. For example, they may have to plug

---

[2]In fact, there already is an *Internet Coffee Pot Control Protocol* (RFC 2324) for remotely managing coffee brewers. The standard was created on April 1, 1998. In America, the first of April is April Fools' Day, which is a traditional day for pranks. Although the Internet Coffee Pot Control Protocol was a joke standard, the future will hold many similar but serious protocols.

in access link technology, configure it, and troubleshoot simple problems. However, required knowledge should be reduced as far as possible.

Test Your Understanding

6. a) Give the book's definition of *network*. b) What is a networked application? c) What are Web 2.0 applications? d) What are social media applications? e) What is a host? f) Is your laptop PC or desktop PC a host? g) Is a smartphone a host? h) Why is the network core shown as a cloud? i) Why may the user need to know more about his or her access link than about the network cloud?

Application Interactions

Traditionally, programmers wrote applications that ran on a single computer. Today, most programmers need to be able to write applications that work with other applications on other computers on other networks. How to divide the workload between the multiple computers involved in interactions is an important concern.

CLIENT/SERVER PROCESSING   Networked applications on different computers have to interact in a disciplined way. Today, they normally interact through **client/server processing**, in which a **server program** on a **server host** provides service to a **client program** on a **client host**.

In client/server processing, a server program on a server host provides services to a client program on a client host.

You use client/server processing every day because this is how the World Wide Web (WWW) operates. Figure 1-7 illustrates how client/server processing works when you use the Web. Here the application protocol is the Hypertext Transfer Protocol (HTTP). Your PC is the client host, and the webserver is the server host. The webserver host runs webserver application software, while your PC runs a client application program, namely your browser. The webserver application provides service to your browser by sending you the webpages you request.

Although browser–webserver applications are very common, the server is not always a webserver, and the client program is not always a browser. In database

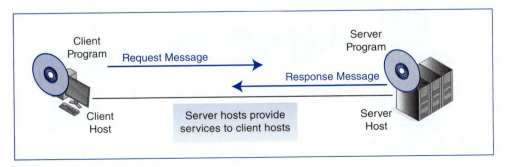

FIGURE 1-7   Client/Server Processing

processing, of course, the server is a database server. The client PC, in turns, often runs a dedicated database client program.

Client/server processing typically operates using a **request–response cycle**. The client sends a **request message** to the server. The server sends back a **response message**. For instance, when you type a URL or click on a link, your browser sends a request message to the webserver. This request message specifies a file to be downloaded. The webserver sends back a response message containing the specified file (or an error message). If the user downloads another webpage a few seconds or minutes later, this is a separate request–response cycle.

Client/server computing is enormously important today, and most programmers will spend much of their careers writing them. Writing client/server programs effectively requires a good understanding of how networks work in order to minimize interaction times and to troubleshoot problems.

PEER-TO-PEER PROCESSING   Although client/server processing is important, it is not the only way to allocate work among computers. An emerging way for applications to interact is **peer-to-peer (P2P) processing**, in which client hosts provide services directly to other client hosts. Figure 1-8 shows a P2P interaction between two nearby mobile phones. In this case, the two phones communicate directly. There is no network between them.

In peer-to-peer (P2P) processing, client hosts provided services directly to other client hosts.

Peer-to-peer processing can also work over a network. Many people illegally share music and movies through P2P services on the Internet, and this has given networked P2P processing a bad name. However, companies are beginning to recognize that their client PC desktops represent an enormous mine of unused processing and storage power. Companies are developing ways to use this power instead of buying more servers. We will look at P2P applications in Chapter 11.

FIGURE 1-8   Peer-to-Peer Computing

Transmission Speed Measurements		
Bits per second (bps)		
Usually not bytes per second (Bps)		
Metric Suffixes		
Kilobits per second	kbps (lowercase k)	1,000 bits per second (not 1,024)
Megabits per second	Mbps	1,000 kbps
Gigabits per second	Gbps	1,000 Mbps
Terabits per second	Tbps	1,000 Gbps

FIGURE 1-9 Transmission Speeds

Speed

The first question people ask about a newborn baby is, "Is it a boy or girl?" The first question people ask about a network is, "How fast is it?" Network speeds[3] are measured in **bits per second (bps)**. Note that this is *bits* per second, not *bytes* per second. Occasionally, when you download files, your software will tell you how many bytes per second are being downloaded. However, that is an exception. In such cases, the B usually is capitalized, so that *bytes per second* is abbreviated as **Bps**.

Network speeds are measured in bits per second (bps), not bytes per second (Bps).

Figure 1-9 shows that, in increasing factors of one thousand, there are **kilobits per second (kbps)**, **megabits per second (Mbps)**, **gigabits per second (Gbps)**, and **terabits per second (Tbps)**.

In the metric system, numbers are expressed in **base units**, such as bps, preceded by a **metric prefix** that multiplies the base unit. Without a metric prefix, five million bits per second would be 5,000,000 bps. With the metric prefix for mega (M), it is 5 Mbps. To give another example, 7.2 kbps without its metric prefix is 7,200 bps.

Note in particular that metric prefixes for speeds increase in factors of 1,000—not 1,024. Factors of 1,024 are used for computer memory and storage.

Note also that the abbreviation for kilobits per second is *kbps*, not *Kbps*. In the metric system, kilo is a lowercase k. (Capital K is for Kelvins, which is a measure of temperature.)

How fast does a network *need* to be? The answer depends upon the sizes of messages transmitted. Figure 1-10 shows download times at various transmission speeds for some applications you might use yourself.

---

[3]Strictly speaking, speed is a poor description because it implies velocity. Signals always travel at the speed of light through propagation media, regardless of how many bits are sent. We really should say rate, which is like the amount of water flowing through a pipe. Looked at another way, velocity is like running faster. More bits per second is like talking faster.

Applications	10 kbps	100 kbps	1 Mbps	5 Mbps	10 Mbps	100 Mbps	1 Gbps
File Transfers							
Text e-mail message (250 words)	1.5 s	0.15 s	0 s	0 s	0 s	0 s	0 s
Photograph (5 MB), E-Mail with 5 MB attachment, or media-rich webpage	83 m	8 m	1 m	10 s	5 s	1 s	0.1 s
Download 1 Hr. HDTV Video (10 Mbps)	42 d	4 d	10 h	2 h	1 h	6 m	36 s
Backup/File Synchronization (10 GB)	116 d	12 d	28 h	6 h	3 h	17 m	2 m
Live or streaming media							
MP3 Song (10 kbps)	OK	OK	OK	OK	OK	OK	OK
Standard-quality TV (2 Mbps)				OK	OK	OK	OK
HDTV (10 Mbps)					OK	OK	OK

FIGURE 1-10   Download Times for Various Applications at Various Throughput Rates

- An e-mail message of 250 words will be downloaded instantly at any current network transmission speed.
- A photograph or e-mail with a large attachment may be 5 GB in size. It is not until 10 Mbps that download becomes only a few seconds, and it even takes a second at 100 Mbps.
- How long will it take to download a one-hour HDTV video? Even at 5 Mbps downstream throughput, it will still take 2 hours to download. In fact, download time does not fall to a reasonable 36 seconds until a gigabit per second.
- We would like to do backup and file synchronization quickly, to encourage people to do it. Assuming 10 GB per backup or synchronization, things are still slow at 100 Mbps and are still 2 minutes at 1 Gbps.
- For an MP3 music file compressed to 10 kbps, all current transmission speeds are sufficient.
- TV requires even faster download speeds. Even with normal-quality television, which requires about 2 Mbps for real-time streaming, transmission speed has to be better than 1 Mbps for good screening.
- For high-definition TV, 10 Mbps is a typical transmission requirement for real-time streaming. Given HDTV's sensitivity to adequate throughput, even faster speeds are important.

How much speed do users need, then? Most applications work well at 1 Mbps, but 10 Mbps or higher is necessary for common downloads or streaming HDTV. For downloading HDTV videos and movies and for very rapid backup and file synchronization, speeds of 100 Mbps to 1 Gbps become highly desirable. Of course, these are speed to individual users. To deliver such speeds, speeds in the network core must be far higher.

Test Your Understanding

7. a) Are network speeds usually measured in bits per second or bytes per second?
  b) How many bits per second (without a metric prefix) is 20 kbps? Use commas.
  c) How many bits per second (without a metric prefix) is 7 Mbps? Use commas.
  d) How many bits per second (without a metric prefix) is 320 kbps? Use commas.
  e) Is the metric prefix for kilo k or K? f) Express 27,560 bps with a metric prefix.

PACKET SWITCHING AND THE ARPANET

So far, we have been looking at networks as they exist today. In this section, we will begin looking at how we got here.

Larry Roberts Has a Burstiness Problem

During the 1960s, the U.S. Department of Defense's **Advanced Research Projects Agency (ARPA)**[4] funded a great deal of basic research across the United States. While some of this research had direct military application, most funding was for basic science and technology.

Dr. Larry Roberts was head of ARPA's Information Processing Technology Office (IPTO). IPTO funded a great deal of software research. In those days, software usually was not portable from one computer to another. If someone needed to use a piece of software, he or she would need a computer terminal and a transmission line to the host computer running the software.

With transmission lines from the telephone company, you have to pay by the minute for service, regardless of whether you are using the line or not. Figure 1-11 shows that this is not a problem for human conversations because long gaps in telephone conversation are rare. Typically, only one side talks at a time, and there are always brief silences. However, normal voice conversations use the capacity of a two-direction telephone line 30 percent to 40 percent of the time.

In contrast to telephone conversations, data transmission is **bursty**, which means that there are brief bursts of traffic followed by long silences. To see this, consider what happens when you visit a website. To download a webpage, you send a request and get back a response containing the webpage. All of this usually takes a second or less. Now, you probably will look at the webpage for about 30 seconds. (Count it sometime!) This means that you are only using one-thirtieth of your circuit—about 3 percent. So while paying by the minute is only somewhat wasteful for voice, it is *very* wasteful for data.

Data transmission is bursty, which means that there are bursts of traffic separated by long silences. This is very wasteful if you are using reserved-capacity circuits.

In addition, Figure 1-11 shows data traffic with large boxes, to indicate that data bursts need to be large. When you download a webpage, you do not want it to dribble

---

[4]Is it ARPA or DARPA? It depends on the year. It was born ARPA in 1958. In 1972, it became DARPA to emphasize its status as a Department of Defense agency. In 1993, it went back to ARPA. Then it went back to DARPA in 1996. DARPA, "ARPA-DARPA: The Name Chronicles," undated. http://www.darpa.mil/About/History/ARPA-DARPA__The_Name_Chronicles.aspx. Last viewed January 2012.

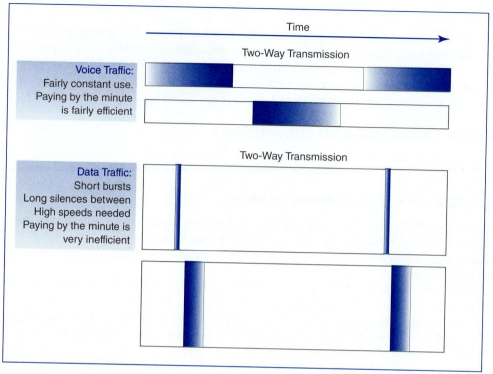

FIGURE 1-11   Data Burstiness

down. You want it right now. This requires a much faster line for data than for voice. Of course, the per-minute cost of a very fast transmission line is much higher per minute than an ordinary voice telephone line. This exacerbates the problem of burstiness.

Test Your Understanding

8. a) Why is paying for a transmission line by the minute not too bad for voice conversations? b) For what two reasons is paying for a transmission line by the minute bad for data transmissions?

Packet Switching Presents a Possible Solution

PACKET SWITCHING   During the 1960s, several researchers identified a solution for the inefficiency of pay-by-the-minute transmission lines for bursty data transmission. This solution was called packet switching. Figure 1-12 shows how packet switching works.

In the figure, an application on Host A wishes to send an application message (Original Message AC) to an application on Host C. The figure shows that Host A fragments the message into many smaller segments and sends each in a separate message called a **packet**. A typical packet is about 100 bytes long. Even sending very brief e-mail messages may require two or three packets. Longer documents, graphics files, audio messages, and video files may be sent in hundreds or thousands of packets. However many packets are sent, the network delivers them to Host C. The destination host reassembles the packets and passes them to the destination application program.

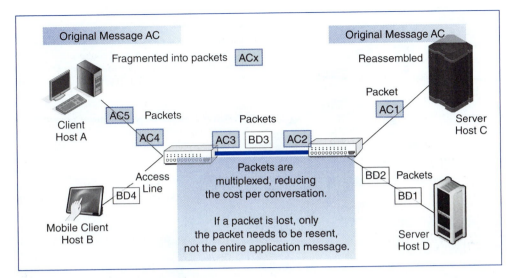

FIGURE 1-12 Packet Switching and Multiplexing

In packet switching the source host fragments the application message into many smaller pieces called packets; the network delivers the packets to the destination host, which reassembles the application message.

Figure 1-12 shows that the packets of multiple conversations can be **multiplexed** (mixed) on long-distance circuits. If each conversation between hosts is using only 3 percent of capacity, then, roughly speaking, about 30 conversations can be multiplexed onto the circuit. Packet switching thus saves money by multiplexing multiple conversations over expensive circuits. Bursty traffic has to pay only for the capacity it actually uses.

Packet switching saves money by multiplexing multiple conversations over expensive circuits.

The figure lists another benefit. If there is a transmission error that destroys a packet, only the lost packet needs to be resent. Early transmission lines had substantial error rates, and when whole messages were sent, messages might have to be resent several times before being received correctly.

PACKET SWITCH SWITCHING DECISIONS   Figure 1-13 looks at the packet switches that make this work. Here, there are six packet switches, imaginatively labeled A through F. The source host transmits a packet to Packet Switch A—the switch to which the source host connects directly. Packet Switch A has to make a **switching decision**. It must decide where to send the packet next. It can either forward the packet to Packet Switch B or send it to Packet Switch C. Packet Switch A decides that Packet Switch B is a better choice for getting the packet to Destination Host Y, so Packet Switch A will forward the packet to Switch B.

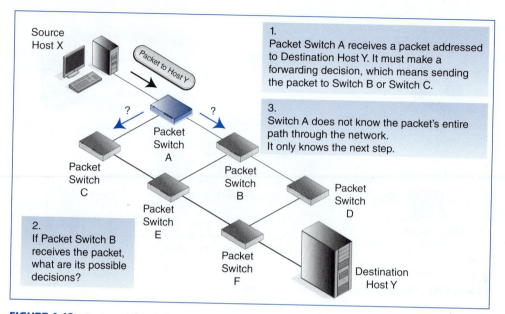

FIGURE 1-13   Sequential Switch Switching Decision

Each packet switch makes a switching decision, which means deciding where to send the packet next.

Now the packet is at Packet Switch B. Packet Switch B has to make its own switching decision. It can forward the packet to Packet Switch D or to Packet Switch E. In this case, it decides to forward the packet to Packet Switch D. Again, it made this decision knowing only about the switches to which it directly connected—Switch D and Switch E.

Note that neither Packet Switch A nor Packet Switch B knows the entire path the packet takes through the network. Each makes a local decision; it only decides where to send the packet *next*. It does not matter how many hops there are across packet switches from the source host to the destination host.

Individual packet switches do not know the packet's entire path through the network. They only make a local switching decision in which they decide where to send the packet next.

Why did Packet Switch A decide to forward the packet to Packet Switch B rather than Packet Switch C? Figure 1-14 gives the answer. It shows that switches have switching tables. Each row specifies a destination host and the next hop for the packet. For Destination Host Y, the next-hop column specifies Packet Switch B. The switch therefore sends the packet on to Packet Switch B.

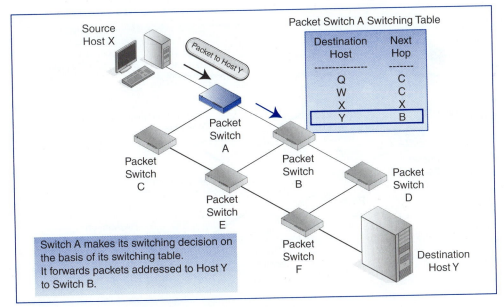

Packet Switch A Switching Table

Destination Host	Next Hop
Q	C
W	C
X	X
Y	B

Source Host X

Packet to Host Y

Packet Switch A

Packet Switch C

Packet Switch B

Packet Switch D

Packet Switch E

Packet Switch F

Destination Host Y

Switch A makes its switching decision on the basis of its switching table. It forwards packets addressed to Host Y to Switch B.

FIGURE 1-14 Address-Based Packet Switch Forwarding Decision

Test Your Understanding

9. a) In packet switching, what does the source host do? b) About how long is a packet? c) Why is fragmentation done? d) Where is reassembly done? e) What are the two benefits of multiplexing? f) When a packet switch receives a packet, what decision does it make? g) Do packet switches know a packet's entire path through a network? h) If Packet Switch A receives a packet addressed to Destination Host W, where will it send the packet?

Physical Links and Data Links

In a packet-switched network, there are two types of links or transmission paths. Figure 1-15 illustrates these links. First, there are **physical links** between hosts and their switches and between switches. These physical links along the path the packet takes between the two hosts may use different technologies.

There also needed to be a name for the path across switches that a packet takes between the source host and the destination host. The term **data link** was selected for this path. When one host transmits a packet to another host, there may be multiple physical links along the way, but there is only one data link.

Test Your Understanding

10. a) In Figure 1-15, how many physical links are there between the source host and the destination host along the indicated data link? b) How many data links are there between the source host and the destination host? c) If a packet passes through eight switches between the source and destination hosts, how many physical links will there be? (Careful!) d) How many data links will there be?

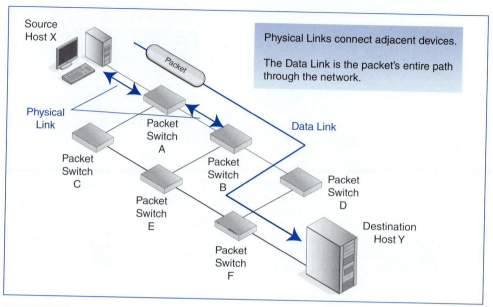

FIGURE 1-15 Physical Links and Data Links

Larry Roberts Builds a Solution

Larry Roberts saw packet switching as a way to reduce the cost of connecting remote terminals to the hosts that ran software funded by ARPA. He also saw it as a research project. Packet switching seemed to have great potential. To see if that potential was real, someone had to build a packet-switched network.

Roberts funded the creation of a packet-switched network called the ARPANET, which Figure 1-16 illustrates. Most of the network chores were handled by minicomputers called **interface message processors (IMPs)**. An IMP received a message from a host attached to it, broke the message into small pieces, and placed each piece in its own packet. The IMPs then acted as packet switches, forwarding the packet to an IMP nearer to the destination host. The final IMP reassembled the original message and passed the message to the destination host. Note in the figure that an IMP can serve multiple hosts. A small team at Bolt Beranek and Newman programmed the IMPs.

Each host ran software called the **Network Control Program (NCP)**. This handled details of host-to-host interactions above the level of packetization, delivery, and reassembly. For instance, if the source host transmitted too rapidly for the destination host to process, the NCP on the destination host could tell the NCP on the source host to slow down.

In 1969, the first two IMPs were installed at UCLA in Los Angeles and at Stanford Research Institute (now called SRI International[5]). As soon as that link was established, the

---

[5]Protests during the Vietnam War caused Stanford University to sever ties with Stanford Research Institute. The institute decided to call itself SRI, but there was already a small consultancy with that name, so Stanford Research Institute became SRI International. However, faculty and graduate students continued to move frequently between the university and the institute. (In one case, a PhD student got a contract worth about $200,000 in today's dollars to do his dissertation.)

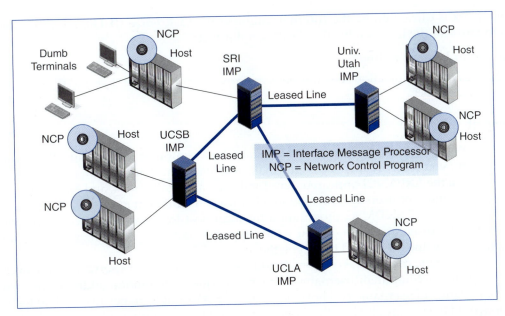

FIGURE 1-16   The ARPANET

University of California at Santa Barbara and the University of Utah were added. When it was clear that NCP and the IMPs were working as intended on these four sites, other sites were added, and some sites began to connect multiple computers to their IMPs.

Although the ARPANET was officially "born" in 1969, its performance was flakey until the early 1970s. More fundamentally, there were no applications at all beyond those that ran on hosts for terminal users. Even in 1973, when the first author used the ARPANET, reliability and services were quite limited. Over time, however, reliability improved and more applications appeared. Users stopped calling the ARPANET the "notwork."

Test Your Understanding

11. a) On the ARPANET, explain the functions of IMPs. b) How is this like what packet switches do today? c) How is it more than packet switches do today?

The Network Working Group

Each of the first four sites had to devise its own way to connect its hosts to its IMP. This had to change. To make the new ARPANET useful, fundamental standards were needed for host–IMP connections. There also needed to be standards for applications, such as e-mail.

Nobody was filling this vacuum for standards, so graduate students from the four initial schools got together to create an informal **Network Working Group**. Led by Steve Crocker at UCLA, the Network Working Group began to create necessary standards. The group had no charter to develop standards, so the group members decided not to call their designs *standards* but rather **Requests for Comment (RFCs)**. Steve Crocker wrote RFC 1 to describe needs for software on two hosts to communicate. Over time, the Network Working Group grew considerably, but it kept its informal flavor. Today, this work is carried on by the **Internet Engineering Task Force (IETF)**, which creates standards for the Internet. It still calls its standards RFCs.

Test Your Understanding

12. a) What organization sets Internet standards today? b) What does the IETF call its standards?

E-Mail

Even before the ARPANET, users on the same host computer had e-mail. When you logged in, you received any messages that other users on that computer had left for you. When the ARPANET appeared, Ray Tomlinson at Bolt, Beranek, and Newman saw the opportunity for users to send mail to other users on different machines. He decided to adapt the local SNDMSG program on his local host for message delivery over the ARPANET. To send a message, you would type SNDMSG and hit Enter. You would then enter a value for To: and then type the body.

On a single computer, your e-mail address was simply your username. However, across multiple computers, usernames were not unique. To be unique, addresses needed a combination of username and host designation. For example, to get an e-mail to Ra3y, you would have to specify that this is a username on the host Office1. Tomlinson looked at his keyboard and saw a character that was hardly ever used. This was the "at" sign, @. So to reach Ray Panko at the Office1 computer at Stanford Research Institute, you sent the mail to Ra3y@Office1.

Now, Tomlinson had to write the e-mail program for host computers. He was not being paid to do this, so he did it on his own time, over a weekend. Networked e-mail was born. However, his program, SNDMSG, was only a message *sending* program. The receiver could only read incoming messages one at a time. One intense early e-mail user was Larry Roberts. He often received dozens of messages per day. Initially, he had to go through his messages one at a time. On his own time, he wrote the first useful e-mail *reading* program, which he called RD. Soon, other ARPANET users created better e-mail reading programs, such as bananard. (It was the 1970s.) This kind of do-it-yourself spirit and an absence of any profit motive made the ARPANET a great development environment.

ARPANET e-mail was also a social networking tool. ARPA funded a great deal of computer science research in the 1960s and early 1970s. People in different organizations funded by ARPA often knew each other well. Individual e-mail messages and computer conferencing message groups increased the cohesion of this research community. For example, the Message Service Group was a mailing list for people who engaged in discussions about issues in e-mail.

In 1974, a young researcher was visiting ARPA. In a meeting, he asked about the cost of an e-mail message. Nobody gave an answer. Later that day, a senior official pulled the visitor into an office and told him to stop asking about the price of e-mail. He said that e-mail's cost was about $60 per message, and e-mail made up 75 percent of the ARPANET's traffic. Government auditors would scream if they knew this, and ARPA would have to come down hard against e-mail use. The researcher said that that $60 per message was impossible. They sat down and poured over the data for several hours. It turned out that the average message cost about as much as a postage stamp to deliver across the network. In the next few months, ARPA's concerns about e-mail relaxed, and ARPA began to advertise its success in connecting people by e-mail.

Test Your Understanding

13. a) How did Ray Tomlinson extend e-mail? b) How did he change e-mail addresses?

THE INTERNET

Bob Kahn Has a Problem

By the early 1970s, the ARPANET was (reasonably) stable. In addition, packet switching was proving itself in wireless environments. The ALOHANET project at the University of Hawai`i demonstrated that packet switching could be done over satellite circuits, despite the long time lags in upward and downward transmission. Terrestrial (earth-bound) packet radio projects also began to appear, using backpack radios.

Dr. Bob Kahn, who was by now in charge of IPTO at ARPA, was happy to see packet switching blossoming. However, he also saw a deep problem. Users on the ARPANET, the PRNET packet radio network, and the SATNET packet-switched satellite network could not communicate with each other. Packet-switched networking was becoming a Tower of Babel.

Test Your Understanding

14. What problem did Bob Kahn face?

Bob Kahn and Vint Cerf Find a Solution

Kahn discussed the problem with a young Stanford professor, Vint Cerf. Together, Kahn and Cerf explored various solutions to the problem of internetworking. Their final solution, which Figure 1-17 illustrates, was to use special devices called **gateways** to connect different networks together into an "internet." Today, we call these devices **routers**.

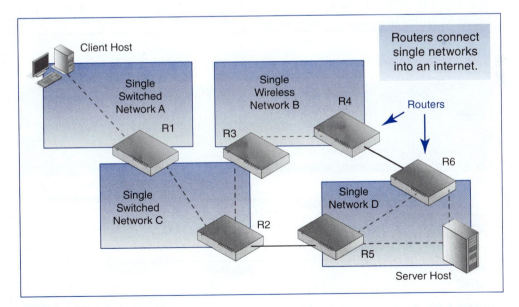

FIGURE 1-17 Internetworking

Routers connect different networks together into an internet.

Test Your Understanding

15. a) What device connects different networks into an internet? b) What is the old name for this device?

A Second Layer of Networking

CAUTION: The following material is difficult because the creation of a second level of networking creates many pairs of concepts that are similar but different.

One problem in connecting different types of networks is that they use incompatible data link technologies. They organize packets in different ways, and they have different and deeply incompatible addressing systems. To overcome such problems, Kahn and Cerf essentially created a higher layer of networking over all of these individual incompatible networks technologies. We will call this higher layer the **internet layer**. Figure 1-18 shows that their solution needed to do more than just create a second layer of networking. It also had to duplicate the concepts of addresses, packet switches, packets, and paths. Unfortunately, this causes a great deal of confusion for students.

Another problem with having two levels of network concepts is that terminology for packet switching matured in confusing ways. Figure 1-18 shows this confused terminology.

WARNING: The following distinctions are critical. If you don't get them down firmly, your life in this class will be absolutely miserable. They are a bit confusing, but they are not at all difficult.

Component	Generic Terminology (Not Used in Actual Networks)	Single Networks	Internets
Addresses		Vary by network technology	32-bit IPv4 Addresses and 128-bit IPv6 Addresses
Packets are called	Packets	Frames	Packets
Packet switches are called	Switches	Switches	Routers
End-to-end routes are called		Data links	Routes

FIGURE 1-18   Two Layers of Networking

- The generic term packet switching, with messages called packets and forwarding devices called switches, is not actually used in real networks.
- In single networks, packets are called frames, and forwarding devices are called switches.
- In internets, packets are called packets, but forwarding devices are called routers.

Overall, then, there are frame switches and packet routers, but there are no packet switches per se in the real world.

POINT OF TERMINOLOGY "Internet" is both a general concept and a name for the largest internet of all, the global Internet. To make distinctions, capitalization will be reserved for the global *Internet* (and of course when internet is capitalized in titles and at the start of sentences). An *internet* (in lowercase) is any internet. Lowercase is also used to refer to the *internet layer*.

Capitalization will be reserved for the global Internet (and of course when internet is capitalized in titles and at the start of sentences). An internet (in lowercase) is any internet. Lowercase is also used to refer to the internet layer.

A SECOND LEVEL OF ADDRESSES Different network technologies use different syntaxes for addresses. For example, Ethernet uses 48-bit MAC addresses, while Frame Relay uses 10-bit DLCI addresses. In addition, these addresses were not always assigned uniquely. Nearly all Frame Relay networks, for example, had a host represented by DLCI 1.

For the second layer of networking, Kahn and Cerf created a new globally unique address, the **Internet Protocol (IP) address**. This address was 32 bits long. Routers work with 32-bit IP addresses directly. However, it is difficult for humans to remember strings of thirty-two 1s and 0s. So for inferior biological entities, IP addresses are usually expressed in **dotted decimal notation**. In this notation, the IP address is broken into four 8-bit segments. Each segment's bits are treated as a binary number and are converted into a decimal number. The four segment decimal numbers are written out with dots (periods) between them. So 128.171.17.13 is a typical IP address in dotted decimal notation.

Computers have no problems dealing with 32-bit strings, so only inferior biological entities use dotted decimal notation as a memory aid.

In a later innovation, a system was given for dividing up the billions of possible IP addresses in a way that would make each IP address globally unique. For example, the University of Hawai`i was given control over all IP addresses beginning with 128.171. This is 16 bits. No other organization could use IP addresses beginning with these bits. The University of Hawai`i then assigned the remaining 16 bits internally in a way that preserved uniqueness. For example, the university assigns one host the IP address 128.171.17.13.

If you think about it, telephone numbers are assigned this way. Each country gets to assign its internal telephone numbers any way it chooses, as long as each phone has a phone number and no two phones have the same number. Countries give non-overlapping blocks of numbers to individual telephone carriers and let the carriers assign them.

IPV4 AND IPV6   In talking about 32-bit Internet Protocol (IP) addresses, we have been describing the address length in the current dominant version of the Internet Protocol, **IP Version 4 (IPv4)**. (There were no Versions 1, 2, and 3.) As we will see in Chapter 2, and later in this book, **IP Version 6 (IPv6)** is beginning to grow in popularity. IPv6 has 128-bit addresses instead of 32-bit addresses. We will see in Chapter 8 that IPv6 uses a much more complex scheme than dotted decimal notation to represent binary addresses for human reading.

A SECOND LEVEL OF PACKETS   Adding a second layer of networking creates of several things besides addresses. We now had two levels of packets: one at the data link layer for single networks and one at the internet layer for internets. In time, terminology emerged to handle these differences. Packets at the data link layer are called **frames**, and packets at the internet layer are called **packets**.

Packets at the data link layer are called frames, and packets at the internet layer are called packets.

THE RELATIONSHIP BETWEEN PACKETS AND FRAMES   Figure 1-19 shows the relationship between packets and frames. Here, there are three networks connected by routers. The packet sent by the source host travels all the way to the destination host. The packet is addressed to the IP address of the destination host. Within each network, however, the packet travels in a frame specific to that network. In other words, packets always travel inside frames. In this case, there is one packet, but there are three frames along the way, one for each network. If 10 networks separated the source host from the destination host, there would have been one packet traveling in 10 different frames.

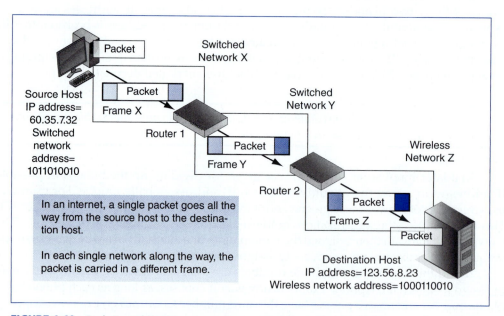

FIGURE 1-19 Packets and Frames

SWITCHES AND ROUTERS   Packet switches are needed at both the network and internet levels. Figure 1-20 shows that at the network level, packet switches are simply called *switches*. It also shows that at the internet layer, packet switches are called *routers*.[6]

PHYSICAL LINKS, DATA LINKS, AND ROUTES   We also need two types of network links above the physical layer. We saw that the path a packet (now called a frame) takes across its single network is called its data link. Figure 1-19 shows that the path that a

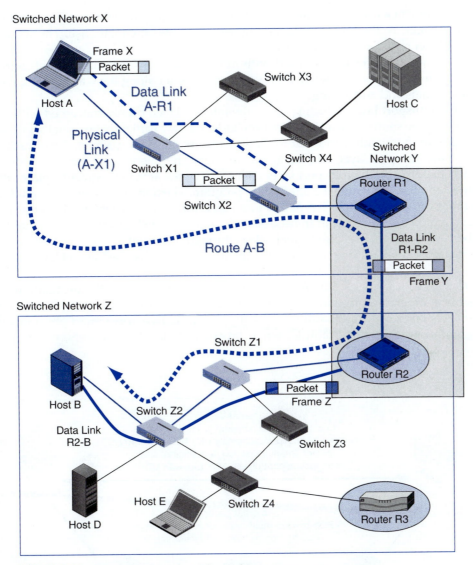

FIGURE 1-20   Physical Links, Data Links, and Routes

---

[6]An odd side effect of this terminology is that you have packet routers and frame switches, but there are no packet switches per se. A really dirty question is, "At what layer do you find packet switches?"

packet takes at the internet layer across an entire internet is called its **route**. If there are 10 networks between the source host and the destination host, there will be 10 data links along the way but only one route.

The path that a packet takes at the internet layer across the entire internet is called its route.

THE TRANSPORT LAYER   Actually, internetworking also required the creation of a fourth level of standards, the **transport layer**. Figure 1-21 shows the relationship between the internet layer and the transport layer.

The internet layer is concerned with moving packets across an internet, across a series of routers. It governs what happens on each router along the way. It also governs packet formats and addressing.

The **transport layer**, which is above the internet layer, is only concerned with what happens on the source host and destination hosts. We saw earlier that original application messages are fragmented and that the fragments are placed in packets. This is actually done at the transport layer, and the application layer fragments are called segments. On the destination host, the transport layer collects all of the arriving segments, places them in order, and passes them to the application program. The transport layer has a number of other functions. For example, it typically provides error correction, which means that packets that are damaged or lost in transmission are retransmitted. Overall, the internet layer is a best-effort service that tries to get packets through but may fail to do so. The transport layer usually is a fix-up layer that supplies the functionality that the internet layer lacks.

THE APPLICATION LAYER   The four lowest layers get a packet to the destination host, possibly with error correction and other services. The fifth layer is the **application layer**. This layer controls communication between the two application programs that are communicating. For example, when browsers talk to webservers, this requires

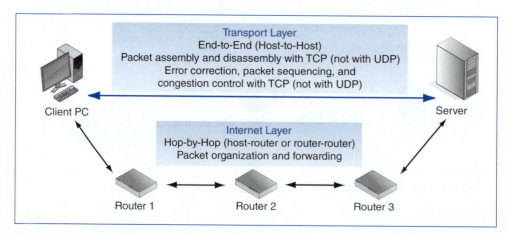

FIGURE 1-21   Internet and Transport Layers

Layer Number	Layer Name	Specific Purpose	Broad Purpose
5	Application	Communication between application programs	Application Communication
4	Transport	Application message fragmentation and reassembly. Ordering of packets, error correction, and congestion reduction	Internet Transmission
3	Internet	Connection across an internet. Defines packet formats and router operation	
2	Data Link	Connection across a single network. Defines frame formats and switch operation	Single-Network Transmission
1	Physical	Physical connections between adjacent devices	

FIGURE 1-22   Five Networking Layers

an application layer standard (HTTP) to specify the communication. There are many applications, and many of them have their own standards. Consequently, there are more application layer standards than there are standards at other layers.

FIVE LAYERS   Overall, network functionality is described fairly well by thinking of the five layers we have seen in this chapter. Figure 1-22 shows that these are the physical layer, data link layer, internet layer, transport layer, and application layer. Each layer provides services to the layer above it. The bottom two layers provide transmission through single networks. The internet and transport layers provide host-to-host transmission through an internet. Finally, the application layer provides application–application communication.

Test Your Understanding

16. a) Distinguish between *internet* with a lowercase i and *Internet* with an uppercase I. b) Why are many networking concepts duplicated in switched networks and internets? c) What are the two levels of addresses? d) How long are IP addresses? e) How are IP addresses usually expressed for humans? f) Distinguish between packets and frames. g) A host transmits a packet that travels through 47 networks. How many packets will be there along the route? h) How many frames will be there along the route? i) Are frames carried inside packets? j) Distinguish between switches and routers. k) Distinguish between physical links, data links, and routes. l) Distinguish between what happens at the internet and transport layers. m) Do IPv4, IPv6, or both use dotted decimal notation for human reading? n) Why are application layer standards needed? o) List the numbers and names of the five layers.

THE INTERNET EVOLVES

The TCP/IP Standards

Kahn and Cerf realized that their new approach would need new standards. Today, these are called the **TCP/IP standards**. As noted earlier, these standards are maintained today by the Internet Engineering Task Force (IETF). Figure 1-23 lists the main TCP/IP standards.

Layer	Standard(s)	
Transport Layer	Transmission Control Protocol (TCP) Fragmentation Error Correction Congestion Control	User Datagram Protocol (UDP) No Fragmentation No Error Correction No Congestion Control
Internet Layer	Internet Protocol (IP) IPv4 and IPv6	

FIGURE 1-23   Core TCP/IP Standards

IPV4 AND IPV6   For the internet layer, the **Internet Protocol (IP)** was created. This layer deals with addresses, so addresses on an internet are called **IP addresses**. As we saw earlier, the dominant version of IP today is Version 4 (IPv4). The emerging version is IPv6.

TRANSMISSION CONTROL PROTOCOL (TCP)   At the transport layer, TCP/IP has two alternatives. For a transport layer protocol with *high functionality*, the transport standard was the **Transmission Control Protocol (TCP)**. TCP fragments application messages. Each fragment is carried in a TCP message, which is called a **TCP segment**. TCP also re-orders information in packets if the packets arrive out of order, corrects errors, and reduces the likelihood of congestion.

USER DATAGRAM PROTOCOL (UDP)   The second transport layer alternative is for applications that do not need or cannot use high transport layer functionality. This is the **User Datagram Protocol (UDP)**. UDP messages are called **datagrams**. UDP does *not* do fragmentation, so the application message must be able to fit inside a single UDP datagram. In addition, UDP does no error correction. If there are any errors, the application program must handle them.

This may not make much sense to you. Why have a layer standard that essentially does nothing? The answer is that while it does nothing, it does so very cheaply. In Chapter 2, we will see that UDP is much simpler than TCP and places a much smaller burden on the network. For applications that do not need the high functionality of TCP, UDP offers lower network costs.

THE TCP/IP STANDARDS   The original standards specified three main protocols: IP, TCP, and UDP. However, they became known collectively as the **TCP/IP standards**. Later, many more standards were created to add functionality missing from TCP, UDP, and IP. However, this growing family of standards usually is still called the TCP/IP standards family. It is the dominant standards family for the Internet.

TCP/IP is a family of standards including IP, TCP, UDP, and many other standards.

Test Your Understanding

17. a) What are the roles of the Internet Protocol? b) What are the roles of the Transmission Control Protocol? c) What are the limitations of the User Datagram Protocol? d) Why is UDP used sometimes? e) What is TCP/IP?

The Internet Is Born—Slowly

When did the ARPANET end and the Internet start? (The equivalent question is when did ARPANET standards end and the TCP/IP standards begin? The TCP/IP standards are the defining feature of the Internet.) The answer is surprisingly difficult because the Internet did not appear all at once. For several years after the TCP/IP standards were created, hosts were allowed to transition gradually from NCP to TCP/IP. During this period, both NCP and TCP/IP standards were supported. Finally, on January 1, 1983, hosts were required to stop using NCP. Although there were a few loud protests,[7] most hosts had long since transitioned TCP/IP. In that sense, the Internet was born on January 1, 1983. At the same time, it had effectively existed for several years.

Test Your Understanding

18. a) In what sense is January 1, 1983, the birthday of the Internet? b) In what sense is it not?

The Internet Goes Commercial

Initially, ARPA funded ARPANET and Internet transmission. In 1986, the National Science Foundation created NSFNET, which two years later became the backbone of the Internet. NSFNET brought higher speeds to the Internet backbone. NSFNET also brought the **Acceptable Use Policy** to the Internet. Basically, the Acceptable Use Policy explicitly forbade the use of the Internet for commercial purposes such as buying, selling, and advertising. The Internet was to be a pure research network, although the e-mail systems of commercial networks were eventually allowed to use the Internet.

On April 30, 1995, the NSF discontinued the NSFNET as the core of the Internet. Before this, a number of companies called Internet Service Providers (ISPs) had formed to connect users to the Internet. These ISPs were also connected to one another. Consequently, when NSF pulled the plug on NSFNET support for the Internet, the Internet continued with no visible change to users.

Figure 1-24 shows today's commercial Internet. Technologically, the Internet is simply a large collection of routers. However, these routers are owned by different ISPs. The ISPs are interconnected at **Network Access Points (NAPs)**, which allow the ISPs to exchange packets.

To use the Internet today, you *must* connect to it via an ISP. The ISP sends your packets into the Internet, to destination hosts. Your ISP also delivers reply packets to you. You need an access line from your home or place of business to your ISP's nearest office. Corporations, which have far larger volumes of Internet traffic than individuals, need much faster access lines.

Who pays for Internet transmission? The answer is that *you* do. You pay money each month to your ISP. Corporations also pay money to their ISPs. While you pay ten to a hundred dollars a month, large corporations pay tens of thousands of dollars per month for service. Given the number of people and corporations on the Internet, there is enough money to pay for all of the Internet's transmission volume.

---

[7]To nudge organizations along, NCP functionality was made nonfunctional for a brief time and then for a slightly longer time as the deadline approached. This was not publicized at the time, but it was effective.

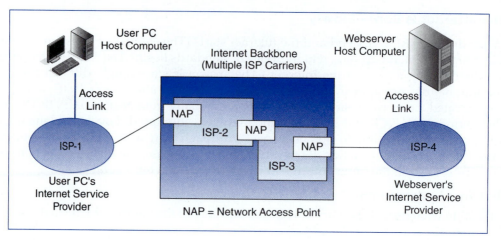

FIGURE 1-24   The Commercial Internet

Although Internet service did not change when the Internet backbone was transferred to commercial ISPs, the vanishing of NSF support led to the vanishing of NSF's acceptable use policy. From that point on, commercial activities were perfectly fine.

The termination of the NSFNET did not come as a surprise to anyone. NSF announced the change far ahead of time, and companies were ready to offer commercial service. Immediately after the NSFNET was disconnected, companies began to offer e-commerce service on a massive scale. In a few months, it was hard to believe that e-commerce was not several years old. Many Internet-only companies began to sell stock through initial public offerings. A vast land rush of dot-com companies appeared, many based on absurd business models. In 2000 and 2001, the bottom dropped out of dot-com stocks. However, e-commerce did not collapse. After one year of stagnant growth in the middle of a recession, e-commerce continued to grow very rapidly.

Most e-commerce activity relied upon the World Wide Web, which was invented at CERN by Tim Berners-Lee. Although he created the HTML and HTTP standards in 1991, WWW protocols were just beginning to reach widespread use on the Internet when commercial activity became possible.

Test Your Understanding

19. a) What was the Acceptable Use Policy in place on the Internet before 1995?
    b) Why did commercial activities on the Internet become acceptable in 1995?
    c) What do we call the carriers that provide Internet service? d) Why do they need to be interconnected? e) At what locations do ISPs interconnect?

Supervisory Applications

TCP, IP, and UDP are sufficient for delivering packets over an internet, but, as noted earlier, the TCP/IP family of standards today is much larger than these three. Many TCP/IP standards are user application standards, such as standards for e-mail and the Web. Many other TCP/IP standards, however, are **supervisory standards** that keep an internet working. We will look at two TCP/IP supervisory application standards in this section. We will see many more throughout this book.

THE DYNAMIC HOST CONFIGURATION PROTOCOL (DHCP)   Servers must have permanent IP addresses. Otherwise, clients could not find them. (Imagine what it would be like if your favorite store kept changing its street address.) Unchanging addresses are called **static IP addresses**.

Client PCs normally get their IP addresses a different way. When a client PC boots up, it realizes that it has no IP address. Figure 1-25 shows that the PC sends[8] a **Dynamic Host Configuration Protocol (DHCP)** request message. This message asks for an IP address.

When the DHCP server receives the message, the server picks an available IP address from its address database. It then sends this IP address in a DHCP response message. The client PC uses that IP address as its IP address. This is called a **dynamic IP address**.

The figure indicates that DHCP does more than give the client PC an IP address. As "Configuration" in the name suggests, it sends general configuration information.

- This includes the IP address of a default router. When the PC needs to send a packet to a host that is not on the same network, it sends the packet to this default router.
- Configuration information also includes the IP addresses of local Domain Name System (DNS) servers, which we will see next.
- It includes other information such as a subnet address mask, which we will see later in this book.

It would be possible to simply enter this information in every corporate PC just once, manually. Afterward, the client PC would not have to use DHCP. However, consider what would happen if the firm later changed the IP addresses of its Domain

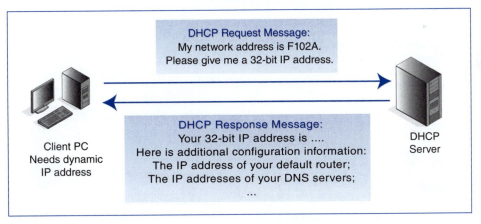

FIGURE 1-25   Dynamic Host Configuration Protocol (DHCP)

---

[8]Actually, it broadcasts the message because it does not know the IP address of the DHCP server. If more than one DHCP server replies, the PC picks one of them.

Name System servers. The firm would have to reconfigure every client PC manually. That would be painfully expensive. With DHCP, every client PC automatically gets hot fresh information every time it boots up. If configuration information changes, all client PCs will be updated automatically.

THE DOMAIN NAME SYSTEM (DNS)   To send a packet to another host, a source host obviously needs to know the IP address of the destination host. However, people are not good at memorizing 32-bit IP addresses, even in dotted decimal notation. Consequently, servers are often given host names, such as Voyager.shidler.hawaii.edu. Host names are much easier to memorize than IP addresses, so when we type URLs, we use host names instead of IP addresses. (In fact, you probably didn't even know that you could use IP addresses instead of host names in URLs.)

For the ARPANET, there was a Network Information Center (NIC) at Stanford Research Institute that maintained a file containing the host names and host ARPANET address of every named host on the ARPANET. The NIC was run by a single person, Elizabeth (Jake) Feinler. When the ARPANET grew, she eventually got an assistant.

As the ARPANET and then the Internet grew, this centralized manual approach to maintaining host names and associated addresses became impossible to continue. Consequently, the IETF created the **Domain Name System (DNS)** in 1984. In this system, each organization with a second-level domain name, such as Panko.com or Hawaii.edu, must maintain one or more DNS servers. ISPs that provide service directly to customers also need to maintain DNS servers for their customers.

Figure 1-26 shows that when a source host needs to know the IP address of a destination host, the source host sends a DNS request message to its local DNS server. The DNS request message contains the host name of the target host.

As the figure shows, the DNS server looks up the IP address associated with the host name in its DNS table. It then sends back a DNS response message that contains the IP address.

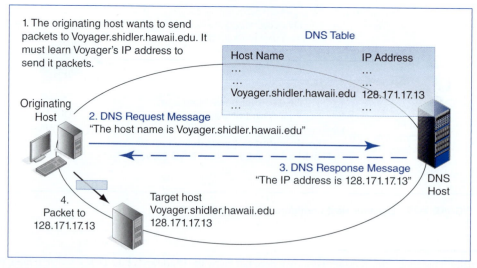

FIGURE 1-26   Domain Name System (DNS) Service

Now the source host knows the IP address of the target host. It has no more need for the DNS server. The source host simply sends packets to the IP address of the target host.

What happens if the local DNS server does not know the IP address of the host name? In that case, the local DNS server will contact other DNS servers until it finds the correct IP address (or until it gives up).

Test Your Understanding

20. a) Why do servers need static IP addresses? b) What protocol provides a client PC with its dynamic IP address? c) What other configuration information does this protocol provide? d) Why should PCs get their configuration information dynamically instead of manually?
21. a) To send packets to a target host, what must the source host know? b) If the source host knows the host name of the target host, how can it get the target host's IP address?
22. Both DHCP servers and DNS servers send a host an IP address. These are the IP addresses of what hosts?

A SMALL HOME NETWORK

We have looked at networking *principles* so far. This box looks at a real, although very small network—a network in a residential home. This is a network on the family's premises, so by definition, it is a local area network. Although this is a small network, it has most of the elements you have studied in this chapter.

Components

Figure 1-27 illustrates the basic hardware devices in a typical home computer network.

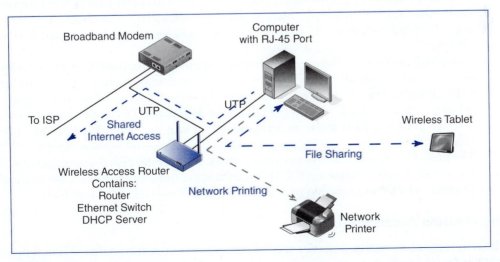

FIGURE 1-27   A Small Home Network

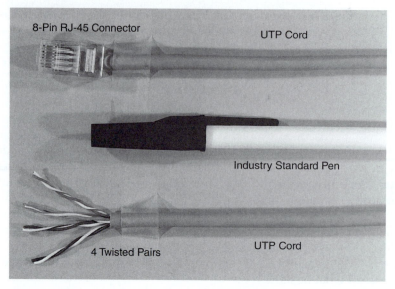

FIGURE 1-28   Unshielded Twisted Pair (UTP) Wiring

Source: Courtesy of Raymond R. Panko

- The heart of the network is a wireless access router. We will look at this device in more detail a little later.
- A broadband modem connects the home network to an Internet Service Provider via a wired connection or a wireless connection. We will look at wired ISP connections in Chapter 10.
- There are two client hosts. One is connected to the wireless access router using a 4-pair unshielded twisted pair (UTP) cable. Figure 1-28 shows that 4-pair UTP consists of eight copper wires arranged in pairs, with each pair twisted around each other several times per inch. 4-pair UTP looks like a fat home telephone wire. It terminates in an RJ-45 connector. We will see more about 4-pair UTP in Chapter 5.
- The other client is a tablet with wireless capability. It connects to the wireless access point via radio signals. With wireless connections, there is no need to buy UTP cables and run them to each computer. However, as we will see in Chapter 7, wireless transmission is not always reliable or as fast as UTP transmission. We will also see in Chapter 7 that the main standard for wireless LAN (WLAN) transmission is 802.11.
- The final element is a wireless **network printer**. This printer also communicates with the wireless access router via 802.11. An increasing number of printers are network printers, which communicate with the access router via UTP, 802.11, or both.

The Wireless Access Router

The **wireless access router** deserves special attention because it contains several important hardware functions.

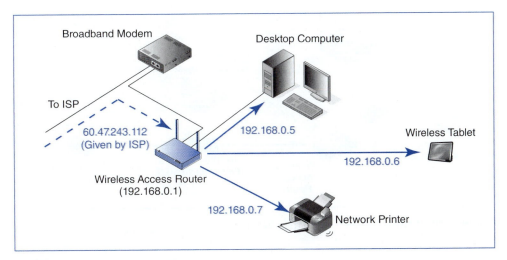

FIGURE 1-29   DHCP in a Small Home Network

- First, although it is more than just a router, the access router really is a router. Routers connect two networks. The access router connects the home network to the network of the ISP that provides Internet access.
- Second, the router has a built-in Ethernet switch. Most home access routers have at least four RJ-45 ports for UTP connections. The router in the figure has another RJ-45 port to connect to the broadband modem.
- The router has a wireless access point to connect by radio to wireless hosts within the house. Not all routers have built-in wireless access points.
- In this chapter, we saw that client PCs get their IP addresses from DHCP servers. Somewhat amazingly, the wireless access router has a built-in DHCP server. Figure 1-29 shows that the DHCP server gives IP addresses to the two clients (192.168.0.5 and 192.168.0.6) and to the network printer (192.168.0.7). The wireless access router's DHCP server also gives the wireless access router its own IP address (192.168.0.1).
- The wireless access router also provides **network address translation (NAT)**, which translates between the internal IP addresses and the single IP address the ISP gives to the household (60.47.243.112). As Figure 1-30 illustrates, the ISP's DHCP server only gives the household a single IP address. When an internal device transmits, NAT converts the IP source addresses in its packets to the ISP's single allocated IP address. It then sends the packet on to the ISP. When packets arrive from the ISP, all have the IP address provided by the ISP as their destination addresses. The NAT function in the wireless access router places the internal IP address of the internal PC or the network printer into the packet's destination IP address field.

Services

Once the network is set up, the users can focus on the services their home network provides. Three of these services dominate today:

- **Shared Internet access** allows the two client PCs to use the Internet simultaneously, as if each was plugged directly into the broadband modem.

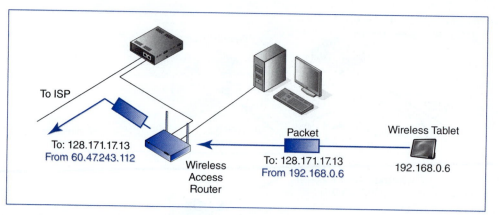

FIGURE 1-30   Network Address Translation (NAT)

- **File sharing** allows the two client PCs to share files on each other's hard drives. For example, one PC may have the family budget. A user at the other PC can access the budget file at any time.[9]
- **Printer sharing** allows either client PC to print to the printer. Both can even print at the same time. If they do, the printer will store one job in the print queue until it finishes printing the other.

Configuration

Shared Internet access is completely automatic and requires no setup. However, file sharing and printer sharing require some setup on each of the client PCs. The process varies between operating systems and between versions of each operating system (e.g., Vista versus Windows 7).

The wireless printer and wireless access point also have to be configured. They do not have displays and keyboards to allow configuration. Consequently, they are configured from one of the PCs. They are first connected to the network. The PC doing the configuration finds them and does the configuration work.

Test Your Understanding

23. a) List the hardware elements in the small home network described in this section. b) For wired connections, what transmission medium is used? c) What is its connector standard? d) What is the standard for wireless PCs and printers to connect to a wireless access point? e) What are the five hardware functions in a wireless access router? f) Why is the DHCP function necessary? g) Why is NAT necessary? h) What three services does this network provide to the desktop PC and the wireless tablet? i) Which devices need to be configured? (List them.)

---

[9]Network hard drives can be attached to the network like a network printer. Networked PCs can access them directly.

HOW THIS BOOK IS ORGANIZED

Figure 1-31 shows how the rest of the book is organized. Chapter 2 looks at network standards in much more depth than we have seen in this chapter. Network standards are critical in networking. They allow products from different vendors to interoperate (work together) regardless of who produced them. Standards create vendor competition with all of the benefits that competition brings in terms of price reductions and the drive to increase features to avoid producing commodity products.

The next two chapters bring us into security. We have not talked about security in this chapter. In fact, in the first two chapters, we will discuss networking as if security was not a problem. Of course, security is a very real and important problem. You can rarely pick up a newspaper or scan the news online today without seeing something about the latest security incident. However, it seems easiest for you to focus on how networks operate in general before looking at how to set up defenses against attackers. To understand network security, you must first understand networks. Just as the networking concepts you will see in the first two chapters will reappear constantly throughout the book, we will look at security concerns in almost everything we cover in the rest of the book.

In this chapter, we introduced the five layers in network standards: the physical, data link, internet layers, transport, and application layers. Beginning in Chapter 5, we will

Chapter	Topics
1	Welcome to the Cloud
1a	Hands-On: Windows Networking
2	Network Standards
2a	Hands-On: Wireshark Packet Capture
3	Network Security
4	Network Management
4a	Hands-On: Microsoft Office Visio
5	Wired Ethernet LANs
5a	Hands-On: Cutting and Connectorizing UTP
5b	Hands-On: Ethernet Switching
6	Wireless LANs I
6a	Hands-On: Using the Xirrus Wi-Fi Inspector
7	Wireless LANs II
8	TCP/IP Internetworking I
9	TCP/IP Internetworking II
10	Wide Area Networks
11	Networked Applications

FIGURE 1-31   Organization of the Book

move up through these five layers, beginning with the lowest layers and moving up to applications in the last chapter. There are three chapters on local area networks (LANs)—one on wired Ethernet LANs and two on the complex world of wireless LANs (WLANs). Chapters 8 and 9 deal with the internet and transport layers and with the TCP/IP standards that dominate at these layers. Chapter 10 discusses the messy but vital world of wide area networks. Finally, Chapter 11 covers how applications work over networks.

The book has several "a" and "b" chapters that provide hands-on exercises in networking. Students tend to like hands-on exercises, but keep in mind that networking is primarily a conceptual game. Anything you learn may be critical in any networking task. In networking, it is the things you don't know that kill you.

CONCLUSION

Synopsis

We began this chapter (and this book) with a look at what user experiences probably will be like in the future. Networking drives all of these innovations, but the network is invisible to the users in this scenario. This is the way it should be. Networking professionals, of course, must understand how networks operate in great detail. Other IT professionals also have to understand networking. For example, programmers increasingly write programs that talk to other programs over networks.

Afterward, we looked at basic network terminology from the user's viewpoint. We defined a network as a system that permits applications running on different hosts to work together. Networked applications, quite simply, are applications that require a network to work (e.g., e-mail). A host, in turn, is any device attached to a network. A host can be a client PC, a server, a laptop, a netbook, a mobile smartphone, a tablet, or any other networked device. The network core is the central part of the network. Access lines connect hosts to the network core. We showed the core of the network as a cloud to indicate that users do not have to "look inside the cloud" to know how it operates.

We then looked at three ways applications can work with each other over networks. In client/server computing, a client program on a client computer receives services from a server program on a server computer. Client/server computing works through a request–response cycle in which the client sends a request to the server and the server sends back a response. Peer-to-peer (P2P) computing, in which client hosts provide service to each other, is growing rapidly. Cloud computing, in which servers, applications, or both are invisible in a cloud, is also beginning to grow.

We noted that speeds are measured in *bits* per second (bps), not *bytes* per second (Bps). Speeds are expressed in the metric system, with kilobits per second (kbps), megabits per second (Mbps), gigabits per second (Gbps), and terabits per second (Tbps). Metric measurements increase in factors of 1,000, not 1,024.

We pay for telephone lines by the minute. This is fine for voice because not too much transmission capacity is needed and because human conversations use telephone lines continuously, wasting little capacity. In contrast, data transmission usually consists of enormous traffic bursts separated by long silences. To pay by the minute for a great deal of capacity and barely use it would not make sense economically.

Packet switching addresses this inefficiency by dividing application messages into small segments and sending each segment in an individual packet. The packets of multiple conversations can share leased line circuits. This is called multiplexing. It uses capacity efficiently. Packet switching also makes error correction easier because only a single packet has to be retransmitted, not the entire original application message.

When a packet arrives at a packet switch, the switch may have several alternatives for forwarding the packet to another packet switch. The switch makes a switching decision and sends the packet on to the next packet switch. That switch makes its own switching decision to another packet switch. These sequential decisions eventually get the packet all the way to the destination host. Links between hosts and packet switches and between pairs of packet switches are called physical links. The path a packet takes across a packet-switched network is called a data link.

The ARPANET was the first major packet-switched network. The first ARPANET standards were created by an informal Network Working Group. This group of graduate students had no formal permission to create standards, so they called their standards requests for comments (RFCs). One of the first applications on the ARPANET was e-mail, but there were soon many more. Later, the job of creating standards for the successor of the ARPANET—the Internet—was taken over by the Internet Engineering Task Force (IETF).

As more networks began to appear, there was a need to interconnect them. Bob Kahn and Vint Cerf came up with an approach for doing this. Their idea was to create internets by connecting individual networks together with routers. They essentially created a second layer of networking. Consequently, internet transmission involves two types of addresses, two types of packet switches (switches and routers), two types of packets (frames and packets), and two types of paths—data links across individual switched networks and routes all the way from the source to the destination address. This is very confusing, but you need to spend the time to understand it clearly or you will have problems throughout the book.

A new set of standards was created for internetworking. These are generically called the TCP/IP standards. The basic work of internetworking was divided into two layers. The internet layer governs packet organization and how packet switches forward packets to their destination. The main standard at this layer is the Internet Protocol (IP). IPv4 addresses are 32 bits long and are often represented as dotted decimal notation, in which there are four numbers separated by dots. An example would be 128.171.17.13. In Chapter 2, we will see that IPv6 addresses are more complex.

The transport layer lies above the internet layer. The TCP standard at the transport layer provides application message fragmentation and reassembly, placing packets in their correct sequence, handling error correction, and bringing congestion avoidance, among other things. The UDP standard at the transport layer does none of these things. UDP is good when an application cannot use the services of TCP.

In addition to these three core protocols, TCP/IP has many application protocols. It also has many supervisory protocols to keep an internet operating (including the global Internet). We briefly looked at two supervisory protocols. DHCP provides your client with an IP address every time you connect to the Internet, as well as other configuration information. DNS allows your computer to learn another computer's IP address if you only know its host name.

The global Internet grew out of the original ARPANET. In 1995, the National Science Foundation stopped paying for the operation of the Internet backbone. Its role was taken over by commercial Internet Service Providers (ISPs), which interconnect at Network Access Points (NAPs). Once government money was no longer used, the Internet could be used for commercial activities. E-commerce was born immediately and grew meteorically.

The chapter closed with a box that looked at a small PC network in a home. These networks are familiar to most students. Although they are small, they encompass most major concepts in networking.

END-OF-CHAPTER QUESTIONS

Thought Questions

1. a) In Figure 1-15, when Host X transmits a packet along the data link shown, how many physical links are there along the data link shown? b) How many data links?
2. a) In Figure 1-20, how many physical links, data links, and routes are there along the way when Host A sends a packet to Host B? b) When Host E sends to Host C? (Assume that hops will be minimized across switches and routers.) c) When Host D sends to Host E? (Assume that hops will be minimized across switches and routers.)
3. In a certain network, there are nine routers between Host R and Host S. a) How many data links will there be along the way when Host R transmits a packet to Host S? (Hint: Draw a picture.) b) How many routes? c) How many frames?
4. Why does it make sense to make only the transport layer reliable? This is not a simple question.
5. a) What does it mean that data transmission is bursty? b) Why is burstiness bad if you pay for a transmission line by the minute?
6. What layer fragments application messages so that each fragment can fit inside an individual packet?

Case Study

1. A friend of yours wishes to open a small business. She will sell microwave slow cookers. She wishes to operate out of her house in a nice residential area. She is thinking of using a wireless LAN to connect her four PCs. What problems is she likely to run into? Explain each as well as you can. Your explanation should be directed to her, not to your teacher. This is not a trivial problem.

Perspective Questions

1. What was the most surprising thing for you in this chapter?
2. What was the most difficult thing for you in this chapter?

1a HANDS-ON: WINDOWS NETWORKING

LEARNING OBJECTIVES

By the end of this chapter, you should be able to:

- Use basic networking commands in Microsoft Windows.
- Discuss network concepts in Chapter 1 with better understanding.

HANDS-ON NETWORKING TOOLS

This chapter introduces you to basic hands-on networking tools in Microsoft Windows. It assumes that you have read Chapter 1.

Binary and Decimal Conversions Using the Microsoft Windows Calculator

It is relatively easy to convert 32-bit IP addresses into dotted decimal notation if you use the Microsoft Windows Calculator. As shown in Figure 1a-1, go to the *Start* button, then to *Programs* or *All Programs*, then to *Accessories*, and then click on *Calculator*. The Windows Calculator will pop up. Initially, it is a very simple calculator. Choose *View* and click on *Scientific* to make Calculator an advanced scientific calculator.

BINARY TO DECIMAL   To convert eight binary bits to decimal, first divide the 32 bits into four 8-bit segments. Click on the *Bin* (binary) radio button and type in the 8-bit binary sequence you wish to convert. Then click on the *Dec* (decimal) radio button. The decimal value for that segment will appear.

Note that you cannot convert the whole 32-bit IP address at one time. You have to do it in four 8-bit segments.

Once you have the four decimal segment values, write them in order with dots between them. It will look something like 128.171.17.13. You have now converted the 32-bit IP address to dotted decimal notation.

DECIMAL TO BINARY   To convert decimal to binary, go to *View* and choose *Scientific* if you have not already done so. Click on *Dec* to indicate that you are entering a decimal number. Type the number. Now click on *Bin* to convert this number to binary.

One subtlety is that Calculator drops initial zeros. So if you convert 17, you get 10001. You must add three initial zeros to make this an 8-bit segment: 00010001.

Another subtlety is that you can convert only one 8-bit segment at a time.

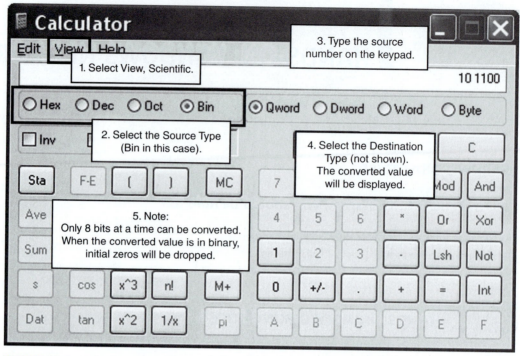

FIGURE 1A-1 Windows Calculator

Source: Screenshot © 2012 by Microsoft Corporation. Used with permission from Microsoft.

1. a) What is 11001010 in decimal? b) Express the following IP address in binary: 128.171.17.13. (*Hint:* 128 is 10000000. Put spaces between each group of 8 bits.) c) Convert the following address in binary to dotted decimal notation: 11110000 10101010 00001111 11100011. (Spaces are added between bytes to make reading easier.) (*Hint:* 11110000 is 240 in decimal.)

Test Your Download Speed

How fast is your Internet connection? Test your download speed at two sites. The following is a list of sites offering free download scans. If you can, test your bandwidth during periods of light and heavy use.

http://www.speakeasy.net/speedtest/

http://reviews.cnet.com/internet-speed-test/

http://www.speedtest.net/

2. a) What kind of connection do you have (telephone modem, cable modem, LAN, etc.)? b) What site did you use for your first test? c) What did you learn? d) What site did you use for your second test? e) Did you get different results?

Working with the Windows Command Line

Windows offers a number of tools from its command line prompt. Network professionals need to learn to work with these commands.

GETTING TO THE COMMAND LINE   To get to the command line, click on the *Start* button and choose *Run*. Type either *cmd* or *command*, depending on your version of Windows, and then hit *OK*.

COMMAND LINE RULES   At the command line, you need to type carefully because even a single-letter error will ruin the command. You also need to hit *Enter* at the end of each line. You can clear the command line screen by typing *cls* and then pressing *Enter*.

3. Go to the command line. Clear the screen.

SEE YOUR CONFIGURATION   In Windows, you can find information about your own computer by typing *ipconfig/all Enter* at the command line. This will give you your IP address, your physical address (your Ethernet address), and other information.

4. Use ipconfig/all or winipconfig. a) What is your computer's IP address? b) What is its Ethernet address? c) What is your default router (gateway)? d) What are the IP addresses of your DNS hosts? e) What is the IP address of your DHCP server? f) When you get a dynamic IP address, you are given a lease specifying how long you may use it. What is the starting time and ending time of your lease?

Ping and Tracert

PING To find out whether you can reach a host and to see how much latency there is when you contact a host, use the **ping** command. You ping an IP address or host name much as a submarine pings a target to see whether it exists and how far away it is. To use the command, type *ping <hostname>* and press *Enter*, or type *ping <IPaddress>* and press *Enter*. Ping may not work if the host is behind a firewall, because firewalls typically block pings.

5. Ping a host whose name you know and that you use frequently. What is the latency? If this process does not work because the host is behind a firewall, try pinging other hosts until you succeed.

PING 127.0.0.1 (PC, CALL HOME)   Ping the address 127.0.0.1. This is your computer's **loopback address**. In effect, the computer's network program sends a ping to itself. If your PC seems to have trouble communicating over the Internet, type *ping 127.0.0.1* and *Enter*. If the ping fails, you know that the problem is internal and you need to focus on your network software's configuration. If the ping succeeds, then your computer is talking to the outside world at least.

6. Ping 127.0.0.1. Did it succeed?

TRACERT   The Windows **tracert** program is like a super ping. It lists not only latency to a target host, but also each router along the way and the latency to that router. Actually, tracert shows three latencies for each router because it tests each router three times. To use tracert, type the *tracert <hostname>* and press *Enter*, or type the tracert *IP address* and press *Enter*. Again, hosts (and routers) behind firewalls will not respond.

7. Do a tracert on a host whose name you know and that you use frequently. You can stop the tracert process by hitting Control-C. a) What is the latency to the

destination host? b) How many routers are there between you and the destination host? If this does not work because the host is behind a firewall, try reaching other hosts until you succeed.

8. Distinguish between the information that ping provides and the data that tracert provides.

Nslookup

The **nslookup** command allows you to send a DNS request message to your local name server. At the command prompt, type *nslookup <hostname>* [*Enter*], where *<hostname>* is a host name for which you wish to know the IP address. The information shown after you type your command is the IP address.

Your local DNS host may send you a non-authoritative IP address. Each DNS server has a group of IP addresses and host names for which it is the authoritative DNS server. For instance, the DNS servers for Hawaii.edu are authoritative for all host names ending in Hawaii.edu. Sometimes, a DNS server will happen to know the IP addresses for host names in other domains. This is a non-authoritative IP address.

9. Find the IP address for Microsoft.com and Apple.com.

RFCs

In networking, you frequently have to look up RFCs. Google, Bing, or other search tools let you do this.

10. a) Look up RFC 1149. b) In layperson's terms, what does this RFC specify? c) What are its sections? (This is a serious question. You should learn how RFCs are structured.) d) On what day was it created?

2 | NETWORK STANDARDS

LEARNING OBJECTIVES

By the end of this chapter, you should be able to:

- Provide the definitions of network; standards and protocols; message syntax, semantics, and order.
- Discuss message ordering in general and in HTTP and TCP.
- Discuss message syntax in general and in Ethernet frames, IP packets, TCP segments, UDP datagrams, and HTTP request and response messages.
- Explain how to encode application messages into bits.
- Explain vertical communication on hosts.
- Discuss major standards architectures: TCP/IP, OSI, and the hybrid TCP/IP–OSI standards architecture.

INTRODUCTION

We looked at network standards briefly in Chapter 1. In this chapter, we will look at standards at a more conceptual level, developing taxonomies of standards types. Much of the rest of this book focuses on specific standards; you will need to understand standards broadly to understand where those specific standards fit into the overall standards picture. This chapter also looks in some detail at the most important standards on the Internet and in corporate networks. These include Ethernet, IP, TCP, UDP, and HTTP.

Standard = Protocol

In this text, we use the terms *standard* and *protocol* to mean the same thing. In fact, standards often have *protocol* in their names. Examples are the Hypertext Transfer Protocol, the Internet Protocol, the Transmission Control Protocol, and the User Datagram Protocol.

Network Standards

WHAT ARE NETWORK STANDARDS? As Figure 2-1 illustrates, **network standards** are rules of operation that govern the exchange of messages between two hardware or software processes. To give a human analogy, in my classes, the standard language is American English. Not all of the first author's students are native English speakers, but we are able to communicate using a standard language.

In this chapter, we will see that network standards govern a number of message characteristics, including semantics, syntax, message order, reliability, and connection orientation.

> *Network standards are rules of operation that govern the exchange of messages between two hardware or software processes. This includes message semantics, syntax, message order, reliability, and connection orientation.*

NETWORK STANDARDS BRING COMPETITION   Standards are important because they allow products from different vendors to **interoperate** (work together). In Figure 2-1, an Internet Explorer browser from Microsoft works with an open-source Apache webserver. Although these software sources are very different and may not even like each other, their products work together because they exchange messages using the Hypertext Transfer Protocol (HTTP) network standard.

With network standards, it is impossible for any company to maintain a monopoly by refusing to allow others to use its proprietary communication protocols. Competition drives down prices. It also spurs companies to add new features so that their products will not be pure commodities that can only compete on price. These new features often appear in the next version of the standard.

Network standards are not only the key to competition. They are also the key to networking in general. To work in networking, you need to understand individual standards so that you can design networks, set up network components, and trouble-shoot problems. Learning networking is heavily about learning standards. In this chapter, we will look broadly at the general characteristics of standards and will also look at some key network standards.

Recap of Chapter 1 Standards Concepts

In Chapter 1, we saw that standards can be described in terms of their layer of operation.

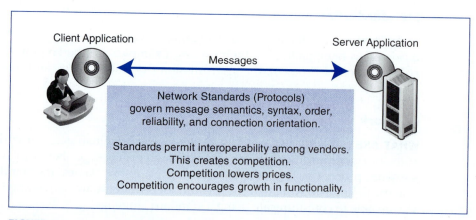

FIGURE 2-1   Network Standards

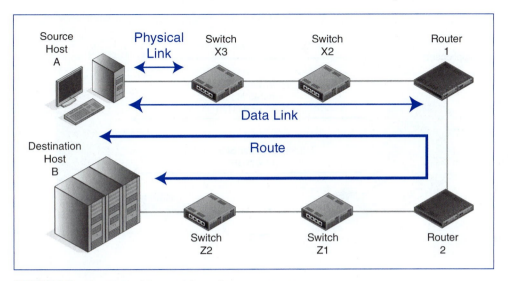

FIGURE 2-2   The Physical, Data Link, and Internet Layers

DELIVERY LAYERS   As Figure 2-2 shows, three layers are involved in the transmission of packets between source hosts and destination hosts.

- Physical links are connections between adjacent devices, such as a host and a switch, two switches, two routers, a host and a switch, and so forth. Physical layer standards are not concerned with messages. Their job is to turn the bits of data link layer messages (frames) into signals.
- Data link layer standards govern the transmission of frames between two hosts, two routers, or a host and a router *across a single switched or wireless network*. The path that a frame takes is called its data link. This layer governs switch operation and frame organization.
- Internet layer standards govern the transmission of packets from the source host to the destination host, across multiple networks in an internet. The path that a packet takes between the two hosts is called its route. This layer governs router operation and packet organization.

A common source of confusion is that concepts are repeated at the data link and internet layers but with different terminology. This occurs because internetworking required the adding of a second layer of standards to those needed for transmission through single networks.

Also, recall that packets are carried inside frames. When a source host sends a packet to a destination host, the packet travels within a frame in each network along the way. If there are 19 single networks on the route between the source and destination hosts, a single packet will travel in 19 different frames.

THE TRANSPORT AND APPLICATION LAYERS   The physical, data link, and internet layers are for standards that move packets along their way between the source host and the

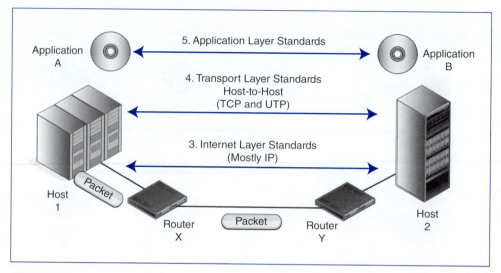

FIGURE 2-3   Transport and Application Processes

destination host. In contrast, Figure 2-3 shows that transport and application processes govern processes that exist only on the two communicating hosts.

- The transport layer supplements the internet layer. Internet layer operation typically is a best-effort service that does not guarantee that packets will be delivered. The transport layer is a "fix-up" layer that can add reliability and other desirable characteristics to transmission across an internet. In addition, the source host transport layer process fragments application messages. These fragments are sent in individual packets. The destination host transport process reassembles the segments and passes the application message to the application.
- The application layer is for application standards. When two e-mail programs need to work together, they use an e-mail application standard. For webservice, HTTP is the application layer standard. There are more application layer standards than there are standards at all other layers combined because there are so many applications and because different applications usually need different application standards.

THE FIVE LAYERS   Figure 2-4 recaps the five layers.

- Speaking broadly, the physical and data link layers govern transmission through single networks.
- Also speaking broadly, the internet and transport layers together govern transmission through an internet. The internet layer governs packet organization and raw packet delivery. The transport layer fixes up problems and does fragmentation and assembly.
- Finally, the application layer governs how two applications work together.

Test Your Understanding

1. a) Give the definition of network standards that this chapter introduced. b) In this book, do *standards* and *protocols* mean the same thing?

Broad Function	Layer	Name	Specific Function
Interoperability of application programs	5	Application	Application layer standards govern how two applications work with each other, even if they are from different vendors.
Transmission across an internet (routed network)	4	Transport	Transport layer standards govern aspects of end-to-end communication between two end hosts that are not handled by the internet layer. These standards also allow hosts to work together even if the two computers are from different vendors or have different internal designs.
	3	Internet	Internet link layer standards govern the transmission of packets across an internet—typically by sending them through several routers along the route. Internet layer standards also govern packet organization, timing constraints, and reliability.
Transmission across a single switched or wireless network	2	Data Link	Data link layer standards govern the transmission of frames across a single switched network—typically by sending them through several switches along the data link. Data link layer standards also govern frame organization, timing constraints, and reliability.
	1	Physical	Physical layer standards govern transmission between adjacent devices connected by a transmission medium.

FIGURE 2-4   Layers Recap

Network Standard Characteristics

Network standards govern communication. Figure 2-5 notes, more specifically, that standards govern five specific things about message exchanges: semantics, syntax, order, reliability, and format. In this section, we will focus on message order, semantics, and syntax, but we will also introduce the concept of whether a standard is reliable.

MESSAGE ORDERING   In medicine and many other fields, a *protocol* is a prescribed series of actions to be performed in a particular order. In cooking, recipes work this way. If you do not put together the ingredients of a cake in the right amounts and prepare them in the right order, the cake is not likely to turn out very well.

In this same way, network standards govern **message ordering**. For the Hypertext Transfer Protocol standard that we saw in Chapter 1, message ordering is very simple. The client sends an HTTP request message, and the server sends back an HTTP response message. Many protocols, including the Transmission Control Protocol (TCP) standard, which we will see in this chapter and in Chapter 9, involve many messages being sent in precise order.

Human beings are intelligent, so message ordering in human conversations tends to be informal and even chaotic. Software is not intelligent, so message ordering in protocols has to be very rigid and exact.

SEMANTICS   To limit the complexity of software, protocols usually define only a few message types, and these types usually have only a few options. Put another way, network protocols greatly limit the **semantics** (meaning) of their messages. For example, the

---

Network Standards

Network standards are rules that govern the exchange of messages between hardware or software processes on different hosts, including messages (ordering, semantics, and syntax), reliability, and connection orientation.

Message Order

Turn taking, order of messages in a complex transaction, who must initiate communication, etc.
In the World Wide Web, the client program sends an HTTP request message
The webserver program sends back an HTTP response message
The client must initiate the interaction
Other network standards have more complex turn-taking; for instance, TCP
Human turn taking is loose and flexible
Message order for network standards must be rigid because computers are not intelligent

Message Semantics

Semantics = the meaning of a message
HTTP request message: "Please give me this file"
HTTP response message: Here is the file. (Or, I could not comply for the following reason.)
Network standards normally have a very limited set of possible message meanings
For example, HTTP requests have only a few possible meanings
GET: Please give me a file
PUT: Store this file (not often used)
A few more

Message Syntax (Organization)

Like human grammar, but more rigid
Header, data field, and trailer (Figure 2-8)
Not all messages have all three parts
Field lengths are measured in bits or bytes
Bytes are also called octets

FIGURE 2-5   Network Standards Concepts

most common HTTP request message is a GET message, which requests a file. There is also a POST request message, which uploads a file to the webserver. Similarly, the HTTP response message is essentially, "Here is the file," or "Sorry, I can't deliver the file."

Semantics is the meaning of a message.

SYNTAX   In addition, while human grammar is very flexible, network messages have very rigid **syntax**, that is, message organization. A little later in this chapter, we will look at the syntaxes of several important protocol messages.

Syntax is how a message is organized.

Test Your Understanding

2. a) What three aspects of message exchanges did we see in this section? b) Give an example not involving networking in which the order in which you do things can make a big difference. c) Distinguish between syntax and semantics.

EXAMPLES OF MESSAGE ORDERING

We will look at two examples of message ordering. We will look first at the very simple message ordering in HTTP. We will then look at the more complex message ordering in TCP.

Message Ordering in HTTP

Figure 2-6 illustrates an HTTP request–response cycle. As we have just noted, the client sends a request, and the server sends a response. Note that the cycle is always initiated by the client, not by the server. The server cannot transmit unless the client has sent it an HTTP request message. This is a very simple type of message ordering.

Message Ordering and Reliability in TCP at the Transport Layer

Many protocols have much more complex rules for message ordering. We will look at the Transmission Control Protocol at the transport layer to see an example of this complexity.

THE SITUATION   Figure 2-7 shows the transport layer processes on Host A and Host B. They are communicating via HTTP at the application layer. The Hypertext Transfer Protocol requires the use of TCP at the transport layer. The figure shows a sample communication session, which is called a connection.

SEGMENTS   In TCP, messages are called **TCP segments** because each carries a segment of an application message (or is a control segment that does not carry application data).

THE THREE-STEP HANDSHAKE OPENING   The communication begins with a **three-step handshake** to begin the communication.

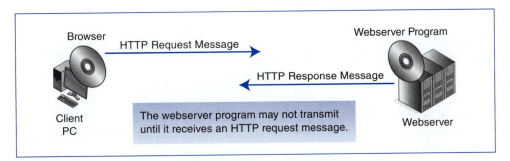

FIGURE 2-6   An HTTP Request–Response Cycle

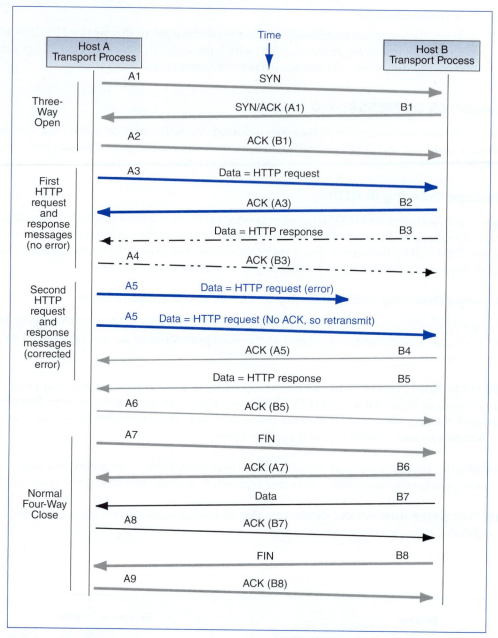

FIGURE 2-7 A TCP Connection

- Host A, which is the client in the HTTP exchanges, initiates the communication. It transmits a TCP SYN segment to Host B. This indicates that Host A wishes to communicate.
- Host B sends back a TCP SYN/ACK segment. The SYN indicates that it also is willing to begin the communication. The ACK part is an acknowledgment of

Host A's SYN message. In TCP, all segments are acknowledged, with the primary exception of pure ACKs. (If pure ACKs had to be acknowledged, there would be an endless series of ACKs.)

- Host A sends back a pure TCP ACK segment. This acknowledges Host B's SYN/ACK.

In TCP, all segments are acknowledged, with the primarily exception of pure ACKs.

CONNECTIONS   TCP creates connections with distinct openings and closings. This is like a telephone call, in which you informally make sure that the other person can talk at the start of a call and mutually agree to end the call. In technical jargon, TCP is a **connection-oriented** protocol.

SEQUENCE NUMBERS   In a connection-oriented protocol, each message is given a sequence number. This allows the receiver to ensure that no message is missing and allows the receiving process to deal with duplicate segments. (It simply discards duplicates.)

Sequence numbers are important because application messages are fragmented and delivered in separate packets. Sequence numbers allow the receiver to place the segments in order and reassemble them.

Note in Figure 2-7 that each side numbers its sequence numbers individually. For simplicity, we have called Host A's sequence numbers A1, A2, A3, and so forth. We have done the same with Host B's messages. So Host A's SYN segment is A1, while Host B's SYN/ACK is B1, and Host A's acknowledgment of the SYN/ACK is A2.

CARRYING APPLICATION DATA   The next four segments (A3, B2, B3, and A4) constitute a request–response cycle.

- A3 carries an HTTP request.
- B2 is an ACK of A3.
- B3 carries the HTTP response message.
- A4 acknowledges the receipt of B3.

Usually, HTTP request messages are small enough to fit in a single TCP segment. However, most HTTP responses are long and must be sent in a number of TCP segments. This does not change the basic picture, however. There would simply be several more exchanges like B3 and A4.

RELIABILITY   TCP is a **reliable** protocol. This means that it corrects errors.

- Segment A5 is sent but never reaches Host B.
- Host B does not send an acknowledgment, because ACKs are only sent when a segment is received correctly.
- Host A realizes that A5 has not been acknowledged. After a certain period of time, it retransmits A5.
- This time, the segment arrives correctly at Host B. Host B sends B4, which is an acknowledgment of A5.
- Finally, Host B sends an HTTP response message (B5) and receives an ACK (A6). Again, sending an HTTP response message tends to take several TCP data/acknowledgment cycles.

In this example, Segment A5 never reached the receiving transport process. What would have happened if A5 had reached the transport process but was damaged during transmission? In this case, the receiving transport process would discard the segment. It would not send an ACK. So there is a simple rule for ACKs. Unless a transport process receives a segment correctly, it does not send an acknowledgment.

Unless a transport process receives a segment correctly, it does not send an acknowledgment.

THE FOUR-STEP HANDSHAKE CLOSING   Host A has no more HTTP request messages to send, so it closes the connection. It does so by sending a FIN segment (A7), which Host B acknowledges (B6). This means that Host A will not send new data. However, it will continue to send ACKs to segments sent by Host B.

- Host B has one more data segment to send, B7. When it sends this segment, Host A's transport process responds with an ACK (A8).
- Now, Host B is finished sending data. It sends its own FIN segment (B8) and receives an acknowledgment (A9).
- The connection is closed.

PERSPECTIVE   TCP is a fairly complex protocol. It uses connections so that it can apply sequence numbers to segments. This allows it to fragment long application messages and deliver the segments with an indication of their order. It also uses connections so that it can provide reliable data to the application layer program above it.

We will see that almost all other protocols are unreliable. Many standards check for errors, but if they find an error, they simply discard the message. Discarded messages never get to the transport process on the other host, so they are never acknowledged. Receiving no acknowledgment, the sender resends them.

Why make only TCP reliable? There are two answers. First, TCP sits just below the application layer. This allows it to send clean data to the application program regardless of errors at lower levels, which are corrected by TCP resends.

Second, as Figure 2-3 shows, only the two hosts have transport layer processes, so error correction is done only once, on the two hosts. It is not done at each packet hop between routers or in each frame hop between switches. Error correction is a resource-consuming process, so it should be done as little as possible. Doing error correction at the transport layer processes on the two hosts accomplishes this.

Test Your Understanding

3. a) Describe the simple message ordering in HTTP. b) In HTTP, can the server transmit if it has not received a request message from the client? c) Describe the three-step handshake in TCP connection openings. d) What kind of message does the destination host send if it does not receive a segment during a TCP connection? e) What kind of message does the destination host send if it receives a segment that has an error during a TCP connection? f) Under what conditions will a source host TCP process retransmit a segment? g) Describe the four-step handshake in TCP connection closes. h) After a side initiates the close of a connection by sending a FIN segment, will it send any more segments? Explain. i) In Figure 2-7, suppose

Host A had already sent A6 before it realized that it would need to resend A5. When it then resent A5, A6 would arrive before A5. How would Host B be able to put the information in the two segments back in order?

EXAMPLES OF MESSAGE SYNTAX

We have just looked at message ordering. Now we will turn to message syntax. In this book, we will be looking at the syntax of many different types of messages. To give you a feeling for message syntax, we will look at the syntax of five important message types.

Syntax: General Message Organization

Figure 2-8 shows that message syntax in general has three parts—a header, a data field, and a trailer.

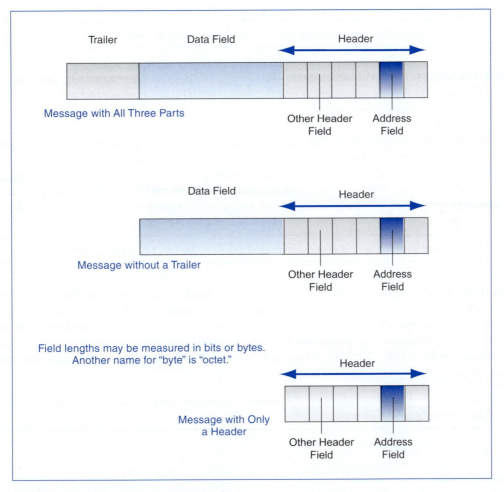

FIGURE 2-8 General Message Organization

DATA FIELD   The **data field** is the heart of the message. It contains the content being delivered by the message. In an HTTP response message, the data field contains the file that the response message is delivering.

The data field contains the content being delivered by a message.

HEADER   The message **header**, quite simply, is everything that comes before the data field.

The message header is everything that comes before the data field.

TRAILER   Some messages also have **trailers**, which consist of everything coming *after* the data field.

The message trailer is everything that comes after the data field.

NOT ALL MESSAGES HAVE ALL THREE PARTS   HTTP messages demonstrate that only a header is present in all messages. Data fields are not always present but are very common. Trailers are not common.

FIELDS IN HEADERS AND TRAILERS   The header and trailer usually contain smaller syntactic sections called **fields**. For example, a frame or packet has a destination address header field, which allows switches or routers along the way to pass on the frame or packet they receive. When we look at network standard messages in this chapter and in later chapters, we will be concerned primarily with header fields and trailer fields.

The header and trailer usually contain smaller syntactic sections called fields.

OCTETS   Field lengths can be measured in bits. Another common measure for field lengths in networking is the octet. An **octet** is a group of 8 bits. Hey, isn't that a byte? Yes, exactly. *Octet* is just another name for *byte*. The term is widely used in networking, however, so you need to become familiar with it. *Octet* actually makes more sense than *byte*, because *oct* means "eight." We have octopuses, octagons, and octogenarians.[1]

An octet is a group of 8 bits.

---

[1]What is the eighth month? (Careful!)

Test Your Understanding

4. a) What are the three general parts of messages? b) What does the data field contain? c) What is the definition of a header? d) Is there always a data field in a message? e) What is the definition of a trailer? f) Are trailers common? g) Distinguish between headers and header fields. h) Distinguish between octets and bytes.

The Ethernet Frame Syntax

Messages at the data link layer are frames. In wired local area networks (LANs), the dominant network standard is Ethernet. Actually, Ethernet, like most "standards," is really a family of standards. Ethernet has many different physical layer protocols from which a company can choose. However, generally speaking, it has a single frame standard, which Figure 2-9 illustrates.

The fields in the frame are delimited by their lengths in octets or bits. The destination host or switch first receives the first bit of the preamble field. It then counts bits until it gets to the next field, the field after it, and so forth. Then it can process the frame.

Ethernet has a complex frame syntax. We will look at its components in more detail in Chapter 5. There are only four fields that we need to emphasize at this time: source and destination address fields, data field packet, and Frame Check Sequence field.

SOURCE AND DESTINATION ADDRESS FIELDS   Ethernet has a destination MAC address field and a source MAC address field. These are like the address and return address on a postal envelope. Switches use the destination MAC address to forward frames.

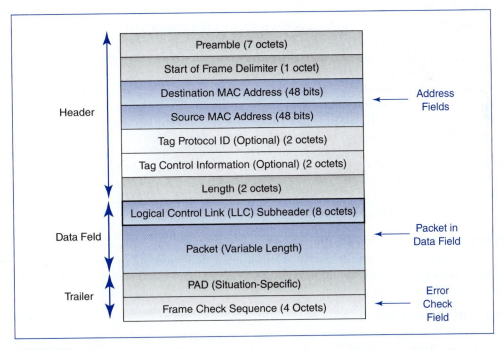

FIGURE 2-9   Ethernet Frame

Note that Ethernet addresses are 48 bits long—not 32 bits long, like IP addresses. Different single network standards have different address lengths. Ethernet addresses are called MAC addresses for reasons we will see in Chapter 6. In that chapter, we will also see that an Ethernet MAC address has six pairs of symbols separated by dashes. An example would be B7-23-DD-6F-C8-AB.

PACKET IN THE DATA FIELD   We saw in Chapter 1 that frames carry packets in their data fields. The figure illustrates how this occurs in Ethernet.

FRAME CHECK SEQUENCE FIELD   The four-octet Frame Check Sequence field is used for error detection. The sending data link layer process computes a number based on other bits in the frame. The receiver recomputes this 32-bit number. If the recomputed number is the same as the number transmitted in the Frame Check Sequence field, then there have been no errors during transmission, and the receiver accepts the frame. If the numbers are different, there was a propagation error and the frame is corrupted. If so, the receiving data link layer process simply discards the frame. This is error detection but not full error correction. Ethernet is not a reliable protocol.

Test Your Understanding

5. a) How long are Ethernet MAC addresses? b) What devices read Ethernet destination MAC addresses? c) If the receiver detects an error on the basis of the value in the Frame Check Sequence field, what does it do? d) Ethernet does error detection but not error correction. Is Ethernet a reliable protocol? Explain.

The Internet Protocol (IP) Packet Syntax

32 BITS PER ROW   Figure 2-10 illustrates the syntax of Internet Protocol (IP) version 4 (IPv4) packets. Later, we will look at the syntax of IP version 6 (IPv6) packets.

An IP packet, like an Ethernet frame, is a long string of bits (1s and 0s). Of course, drawing the packet this way would require a page several meters wide. Instead, Figure 2-10 shows that we usually depict an IP packet as a series of rows with 32 bits per row. In binary counting, the first bit is zero. Consequently, the first row shows bits 0 through 31. The next row shows bits 32 through 63. This is a different way of showing syntax than we saw with the Ethernet frame, but it is a common way of showing syntax in TCP/IP standards, so you need to be familiar with it.

SOURCE AND DESTINATION IP ADDRESS FIELDS   Each IPv4 packet has source and destination IP addresses. Each is 32 bits long, so each has its own row in the header. Routers use destination IP addresses to decide how to forward packets so that they will get closer to their destination.

UNRELIABILITY   The IPv4 **Header Checksum** field is like the Frame Check Sequence field in the Ethernet frame. It also is used for error detection. As in the case of Ethernet frames, incorrect IP packets are simply discarded. There is no retransmission. So like Ethernet, IP is not a reliable protocol.

Test Your Understanding

6. a) How many octets long is an IPv4 header if there are no options? (Look at Figure 2-10.) b) List the first bit number on each IPv4 header row in Figure 2-10,

Internet Protocol Version 4 (IPv4)				
Bit 0				Bit 31
Version Number (4 bits)	Header Length (4 bits)	Diff-Serv (8 bits)	Total Length (16 bits)	
Identification (16 bits)			Flags (3 bits)	Fragment Offset (13 bits)
Time to Live (8 bits)		Protocol (8 bits)	Header Checksum (16 bits)	
Source IP Address (32 bits)				
Destination IP Address (32 bits)				
Options (if any)			Padding	
Data Field (dozens, hundreds, or thousands of bits) Often contains a TCP segment or UDP datagram				

FIGURE 2-10   The Internet Protocol (IP) Packet Syntax in IPv4

not including options. Remember that the first bit in Row 1 is Bit 0. c) What is the bit number of the first bit in the destination address field in IPv4? (Remember that the first bit in binary counting is Bit 0.) d) How long are IPv4 addresses? e) What device in an internet besides the destination host reads the destination IP address? f) What is this device's purpose in doing so? g) Is IP reliable or unreliable? Explain.

Transmission Control Protocol (TCP) Segment Syntax

Earlier, we saw message ordering in the transmission of TCP segments. Now we will look at the syntax of TCP segments.

FIELDS IN TCP/IP SEGMENTS   When IP was created, it was designed to be a very simple "best effort" protocol (although its routing tables are complex). The IETF left more complex internetwork transmission control tasks to TCP. Consequently, network professionals need to understand TCP very well. Figure 2-11 shows the organization of TCP messages, which are called TCP segments.

FLAG FIELDS   TCP has six single-bit fields. Single-bit fields in general are called **flag fields**. If a flag field has the value 1, it is said to be **set**. (If it has the value 0, it is said to be **not set**.) In TCP, flag fields allow the receiving transport process to identify the kind of segment it is receiving. We will look at three of these flag bits:

- If the ACK (acknowledgment) bit is set, then the segment acknowledges another segment. When the ACK bit is set, the acknowledgment field also must be filled in to indicate which message is being acknowledged.
- If the SYN (synchronization) bit is set (has the value 1), then the segment requests a connection opening.
- If the FIN (finish) bit is set, then the segment requests a normal connection closing.

TCP Segment

Bit 0   Bit 31

Source Port Number (16 bits)	Destination Port Number (16 bits)

Sequence Number (32 bits)

Acknowledgment Number (32 bits)

Header Length (4 bits)	Reserved (6 bits)	Flag Fields* (6 bits)	Window Size (16 bits)

TCP Checksum (16 bits)	Urgent Pointer (16 bits)

Options (if any)	Padding

Data Field

*Flag fields are 1-bit fields. They include SYN, ACK, FIN, and RST.

UDP Datagram

Bit 0   Bit 31

Source Port Number (16 bits)	Destination Port Number (16 bits)
UDP Length (16 bits)	UDP Checksum (16 bits)

Data Field

FIGURE 2-11 TCP Segment and UDP Datagram

Single-bit fields are called flag fields. If a flag field has the value 1, it is said to be set. (If it has the value 0, it is said to be not set.)

Earlier, we talked about TCP SYN segments, ACK segments, and FIN segments. These are simply segments in which the SYN, ACK, or FIN bits are set, respectively.

SEQUENCE NUMBERS Each TCP segment has a unique 32-bit **sequence number**. This sequence number increases with each segment. Sequence numbers allow the receiving transport process to put arriving TCP segments in order if IP delivers them out of order.

ACKNOWLEDGMENT NUMBERS   Earlier in this chapter, we saw that TCP uses acknowledgments (ACKs) to achieve reliability. If a transport process receives a TCP segment correctly, it sends back a TCP segment acknowledging the reception. We saw earlier that if the sending transport process does not receive an acknowledgment, it transmits the TCP segment again.

The **acknowledgment number** field indicates which segment is being acknowledged. One might expect that if a segment has sequence number X, then the acknowledgment number in the segment that acknowledges it would have acknowledgment number X. Later in this book, we will see that the situation actually is more complex.

The acknowledgment number indicates which segment is being acknowledged.

Test Your Understanding

7. a) Why was TCP designed to be complex? b) Why is it important for networking professionals to understand TCP? c) What are TCP messages called?
8. a) Why are sequence numbers good? b) What are 1-bit fields called? c) If someone says that a flag field is set, what does this mean? d) If the ACK bit is set, what other field must have a value? e) What is the purpose of the acknowledgment number field?

User Datagram Protocol (UDP) Datagram Syntax

Applications that cannot use the high functionality in TCP or that do not need this functionality can use the **User Datagram Protocol (UDP)** at the transport layer instead of TCP. UDP does not have openings, closings, or acknowledgments, and so it produces substantially less traffic than TCP. UDP messages are called datagrams. Because of UDP's simple operation, the syntax of the UDP datagram shown in Figure 2-11 is very simple. Besides two port number fields, which we will see next in this chapter, there are only two header fields.

- There is a **UDP length** field so that the receiving transport process can know how long the datagram is. The packet in the data field will have variable length, so the UDP datagram will have variable length.
- There also is a **UDP checksum** field that allows the receiver to check for errors in this UDP datagram.[2] If an error is found, however, the UDP datagram is discarded. There is no mechanism for retransmission.

Test Your Understanding

9. a) What are the four fields in a UDP header? b) Describe the third. c) Describe the fourth. d) Is UDP reliable? Explain.

Port Numbers

Both TCP and UDP headers begin with two port number fields, one specifying the sender's port number and one specifying the receiver's port number. Servers and clients use these port number fields differently.

---

[2]If the UDP checksum field has 16 zeroes, error checking is not to be done at all.

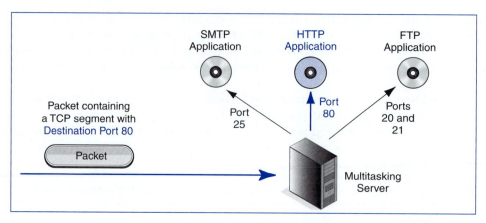

FIGURE 2-12   Server Port Numbers

SERVER PORT NUMBERS   Computers are multitasking machines, which means that they can run several programs at the same time. Figure 2-12 shows a server running **SMTP**, **HTTP**, and **FTP** programs. If a packet arrives, how does the TCP or UDP process know which of the application programs running on the server should receive the message?

The answer is that the TCP or UDP process uses the port number. The port number field contains a number that specifies a specific application running on the server. Port 20 or 21 specifies the FTP (file transfer protocol) program, while Port 25 specifies the SMTP (e-mail) program, and Port 80 specifies the HTTP (World Wide Web) application.

A server administrator can choose any port number for a program, but there are **well-known port numbers** that are normally used to specify particular programs. That is the case for the port numbers used by the server. Most webservers use this port number for the webserver program. The well-known port numbers have a port number range reserved for their use—port numbers 0 through 1023.

CLIENT PORT NUMBERS   Clients use port numbers in a different way. For every conversation a client initiates or accepts, it randomly generates a number in the **ephemeral port number** range. On Windows computers, this is the range from port 1024 to Port 4999. These port numbers are ephemeral, in the sense that they are discarded when a conversation between the client and a particular webserver ends. If the client communicates with the same server program later, the client will generate a new ephemeral port number.

Figure 2-13 shows a client host (60.171.18.22) communicating with a blue server host (1.33.17.13). The server port number is Port 80, indicating that the client is communicating with the HTTP program on the server. The client has generated ephemeral Port 2707. When the client transmits to the server, the source port number field has the value 2707 and the destination port number 80. When the server replies, the source port number is 80 and the destination port number is 2707.

The client is simultaneously connected to an SMTP server (123.30.17.120), which has the well-known port number 25. For this conversation, the client randomly generates ephemeral Port 4400. When the client transmits, the source port number is 4400 and the destination port number is 256.

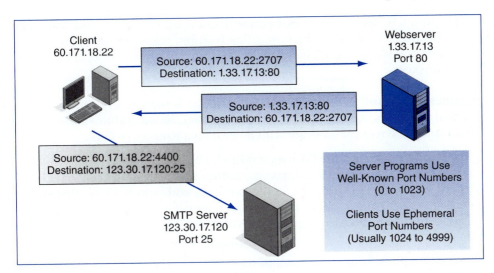

FIGURE 2-13   Client Port Numbers and Sockets

SOCKETS   Figure 2-13 shows that a conversation always involves a source IP address and a source part number, plus a destination IP address and a destination port number. It is common to represent each IP address and port number as a socket, which is simply the IP address, a colon, and the port number. When the client transmits to the webserver, the source socket is 60.171.18.22:2707 and the destination socket is 1.33.17.13:80. When the webserver replies, the source socket is 1.33.17.13:80, and the destination socket is 60.171.18.22:2707.

Test Your Understanding

10. a) What type of port numbers do servers use for common server programs? b) What type of port numbers do clients use when they communicate with server programs? c) What is the range of port numbers for each type of port? d) How are ephemeral port numbers generated? e) Why are they called *ephemeral*?

11. a) What is the syntax of a socket? b) In Figure 2-13, when the client transmits to the server host, what is the source port number? c) What is the destination port number? d) What is the source socket? e) What is the destination socket? f) When the SMTP server transmits to the client host, what is the source port number? g) What is the destination port number? h) What is the source socket? i) What is the destination socket?

HTTP Request and Response Message Syntax

The highest layer is the application layer (Layer 5). Standards at this layer govern how application programs talk to one another. We have used HTTP in most of our examples so far. However, there are many application layer standards—more than there are standards at any other layer. There are application layer standards for e-mail, database queries, and every other application. After network professionals master the network and internetwork standards that this course presents, they spend much of the rest of their careers mastering application standards.

Unfortunately, some students become fixated on examples and lose sight of general principles. At the risk of feeding this fixation, we will look at the syntax for the Hypertext Transfer Protocol. Figure 2-14 illustrates the syntax of HTTP request and response messages.

HTTP REQUEST MESSAGE The HTTP request message is particularly simple. It consists of only two lines of text. Some HTTP request messages have additional lines, but it is rare to see an HTTP request message with more than a handful of lines.

- The first line specifies the GET method (which requests a file retrieval), the location of the file to be retrieved (/panko/home.htm), and the version of HTTP used by the sender (HTTP 1.1). This and other lines end with [CRLF]. This stands for carriage return/line feed. It means to start a new line.
- The second line specifies the host to which this HTTP request message should be sent.

These two lines form the header of the message. The sender is transmitting no data, so there is no data field. Nor is there anything after a data field, so there is no trailer.

HTTP

The application layer is the highest layer.
It has more standards than at any other layer.
HTTP is not the only application layer standard; it is one of many.
Many application layer protocols, such as SMTP for e-mail, are much more complex than HTTP.

HTTP Request Message

GET /panko/home.htm HTTP/1.1[CRLF]
Host: voyager.cba.hawaii.edu

HTTP Response Message

HTTP/1.1 200 OK[CRLF]
Date: Tuesday, 20-MAR-2012 18:32:15 GMT[CRLF]
Server: *name of server software* [CRLF]
MIME-version: 1.0[CRLF]
Content-type: text/plain[CRLF]
[CRLF]
File to be downloaded. A string of bytes that may be text, graphics, sound, video, or other content.

Notes

A relatively old feeling protocol
Fields ended by CRLF, which starts a new line
Based on e-mail (an old protocol) for rapid development

FIGURE 2-14 Hypertext Transfer Protocol Message Syntax

HTTP RESPONSE MESSAGE   Figure 2-14 also shows the syntax of a relatively simple HTTP response message that responds to the HTTP request message we have just seen.

Header   First, there is a header. The header is everything that comes before the data field, which is the file being delivered.

- The first line begins with HTTP/5 to show that it is willing to speak in this version of the standard. The 200 is a code that describes the response. The 200 code states that the message is delivering the requested file. The browser uses the code to know how to react. What about the final OK? The browser ignores it. HTTP is humanly readable, and the "OK" is designed to tell humans, who may not know what the 200 code means, that everything is alright.
- After the first line, other fields in the header have a very specific syntax. There is a keyword, a colon, and then a value for the keyword.
- The Date keyword, for instance, is followed by a colon and the date and time the HTTP response message was sent.
- The Server keyword, to give another example, describes the webserver software sending the response.
- The line containing the [CRLF] is a blank line. It indicates the end of the header.

Data Field   Following the header is the file being sent to the browser. This is a long byte stream that constitutes the text document, photograph, video clip, or other type of file being delivered.

Trailer   As usual, there is no trailer.

A TEXT PROTOCOL   In contrast to the other protocols we have looked at, HTTP is a fairly primitive protocol. It delimits fields with carriage return/line feeds instead of having fields that end at a certain number of bits. Separating the header from the data field with a blank line also seems rather crude. Most application protocols are much more complex than HTTP.

Tim Berners-Lee, who created HTTP, based this standard on e-mail standards. An e-mail header has a number of keywords (e.g., To and From) followed by a colon, the value for the keyword, and a new line. E-mail standards were already very old when HTTP was created, but they got the job done. HTTP also got the job done. In particular, new keywords can be added very easily, given the robust way HTTP has of ending a field and starting a new field.

Test Your Understanding

12. a) Is the application layer standard always HTTP? b) Which layer has the most standards? c) At which layer would you find standards for voice over IP? (The answer is not explicitly in this section.) d) Are all application layer standards simple like HTTP? e) In HTTP response headers, what is the syntax of most lines (which are header fields)? f) In HTTP request and response message, how is the end of a field indicated? g) Do HTTP request messages have headers, data fields, and trailers? h) Do HTTP response messages that deliver files have headers, data fields, and trailers?

CONVERTING APPLICATION MESSAGES INTO BITS

Encoding

One function of application layer programs is to convert messages into bits. This conversion is called **encoding**. At the transport layer and lower layers, all messages consist of bits. Original application layer messages, in contrast, may have text, numbers, graphics images, video clips, and other types of information. It is the application layer's job to convert all of these into bits before putting them in the application layer message.

Test Your Understanding

13. a) What is encoding? b) At what layer is encoding done?

Encoding Text as ASCII

To convert text data to binary, applications use the **ASCII code**, whose individual symbols are each 7 bits long. Seven bits gives 128 possibilities. This is enough for all keys on the keyboard plus some extra control codes.

Figure 2-15 shows some ASCII codes. It shows that uppercase letters and lowercase letters have different ASCII codes. This is necessary because the receiver may need to know whether a character is an uppercase or lowercase letter. ASCII can also encode the digits from 0 through 9, as well as punctuation and other characters. There are even ASCII control codes that tell the receiver what to do. For example, when we looked at HTTP, we saw carriage returns and line feeds. A carriage return is 0101110, and a line feed is 0100000.

For transmission, the 7 bits of each ASCII character are placed in a byte. The eighth bit in the byte is not used today.[3]

Category	Meaning	7-Bit ASCII Code	Eighth Bit in Transmitted Byte
Uppercase Letters	A	1000001	Unused
Lowercase Letters	a	1100001	Unused
Digits (0 through 9)	3	0110011	Unused
Punctuation	Period	0101110	Unused
Punctuation	Space	0100000	Unused
Control Codes	Carriage Return	0001101	Unused
Control Codes	Line Field	0001010	Unused

FIGURE 2-15 Encoding Text as ASCII

---

[3]Early systems used the eighth bit in each byte as a "parity bit" to detect errors in transmission. This could detect a change in a single bit in the byte. At today's high transmission speeds, however, transmission errors normally generate multibit errors rather than single-bit errors. Consequently, parity is useless and is ignored.

Test Your Understanding

14. a) Explain how many bytes it will take to transmit "Hello World!" without the quotation marks. (The correct total is 12.) b) If you go to a search engine, you can easily find converters to represent characters in ASCII. What are the 7-bit ASCII codes for "Hello world" without the quotation marks? (Hint: H is 1001000.)

Whole Binary Numbers

Some application data consists of whole numbers. The sending application program represents whole numbers (integers) as whole **binary numbers**. Figure 2-16 shows how this is done.

With binary numbers, counting begins with 0. This is a source of frequent confusion. In counting, add 1 to each binary number to give the next binary number. There are four simple rules for addition in binary.

- If you add 0 and 0, you get 0.
- If you add 0 and 1 (or 1 and 0), you get 1.
- If you add 1 and 1, you get 10 (carry the one).
- If you add 1, 1, and 1, you get 11 (carry the one).

These rules are simple to use.

- In binary numbers, 8 is 1000.
- The number 9 adds a 1 to the final 0, giving a 1, so 9 is 1001.
- Adding 1 to the final 1 gives us 10, so 10 is 1010.
- The number 11 adds a 1 to the final 0, giving 1011.
- The number 12 adds a 1 to the final 1. With carries, this gives 1100.[4]

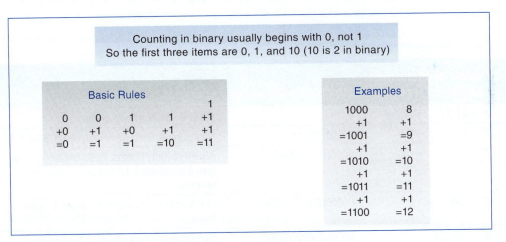

FIGURE 2-16   Binary Representation of Whole Numbers

---

[4]If you read Chapter 1a, you saw how to use the Microsoft Windows Calculator in programmer mode to convert between decimal and binary. You can also use it to check your binary calculations (obviously not on tests). First click on the Bin button to put the calculator in binary mode. Then use the calculator normally. For example, to add two binary numbers, click on Bin, enter the first binary number, hit the plus button, type the second binary number, and click on the equal sign to see the total.

Test Your Understanding

15. a) Does binary counting usually begin at 0 or 1? b) Give the binary representations for 13, 14, 15, 16, and 17 by adding one to successive numbers (12 is 1100).

Encoding Alternatives

Some application data can be expressed as alternatives, such as North, South, East, or West. The application layer process will create a field in the application layer message and represent each alternative as a group of bits. For instance, the four cardinal compass points can be represented by a 2-bit field within the application message. North, South, East, and West can be represented as 00, 01, 10, and 11, respectively. (These are the binary numbers for 0, 1, 2, and 3.) There is no order to the alternatives, so any choice can be represented by any pair of bits.

We just saw that having four alternatives requires a 2-bit field. More generally, if a field has N bits, it can represent 2^N alternatives. We have just seen that a 2-bit field can represent 2^2 alternatives, or 4. What if you need to represent three alternatives? One bit won't do it, because 2^1 is 2, and we need 3. We will have to use a 2-bit field, and one of the alternatives will go unused.

If a field has N bits, it can represent 2^N alternatives.

Figure 2-17 illustrates how alternatives encoding is done for 1-, 2-, 4-, 8-, 16-, and 32-bit fields. It shows that with one bit, you can encode yes or no, male or female, or any other dichotomy. Two bits, as we just saw, are good for the four cardinal compass points. With 4 bits, you can have 16 alternatives. You need 4 bits to represent the top 10 security threats, because 3 bits will encode only eight alternatives. Using 4 bits to

Bits in Field	Number of Alternatives That Can Be Encoded	Possible Bit Sequences	Examples
1	$2^1 = 2$	0, 1	Yes or No, Male or Female, etc.
2	$2^2 = 4$	00, 01, 10, 11	North, South, East, West; Red, Green, Blue, Black
4	$2^4 = 16$	0000, 0001, 0010, …	Top 10 security threats. Three bits would only give 8 alternatives. (With 4 bits, 6 values go unused)
8	$2^8 = 256$	00000000, 00000001, …	One byte per color gives 256 possible color levels
16	$2^{16} = 65,536$	0000000000000000, 0000000000000001, …	Two bytes per color give 65,536 color levels
32	$2^{32} = 4,294,967,296$	000000000000000 0000000000000000, etc.	Number of Internet Protocol Version 4 addresses

If a field has *N* bits, it can represent 2^N alternatives.

FIGURE 2-17 Binary Encoding to Represent a Certain Number of Alternatives

represent 10 threats will waste six alternatives, but this is necessary. With 8 bits, you can represent 256 alternatives.

The 2^N rule is not only used at the application layer. In many layer messages, fields represent alternatives. A one-octet field has 8 bits, so it can represent 2^8 possible alternatives (256).

You should memorize the number of alternatives that can be represented by 4, 8, and 16 bits, because these are common field sizes. Each added bit doubles the number of alternatives, while each bit subtracted cuts the number of alternatives in half. So if 8 bits can represent 256 alternatives, 7 bits can represent 128 alternatives (half as many), while 9 bits can represent 512 alternatives (twice as many). How many alternatives can 6 and 10 bits represent?

Test Your Understanding

16. a) If a field is N bits long, how many alternatives can it represent? b) How many alternatives can you represent with a 4-bit field? c) For each bit you add to an alternatives field, how many additional alternatives can you represent? d) How many alternatives can you represent with a 10-bit field? (With 8 bits, you can represent 256 alternatives). e) If you need to represent 128 alternatives in a field, how many bits long must the field be? f) If you need to represent 18 alternatives in a field, how many bits long must the field be? g) Come up with three examples of things that can be encoded with 3 bits.

Encoding Voice

Increasingly, applications involve voice and even video. Figure 2-18 illustrates how voice encoding is done. Video encoding is done similarly. When you speak into a landline or mobile telephone, your voice loudness rises and falls thousands of times per

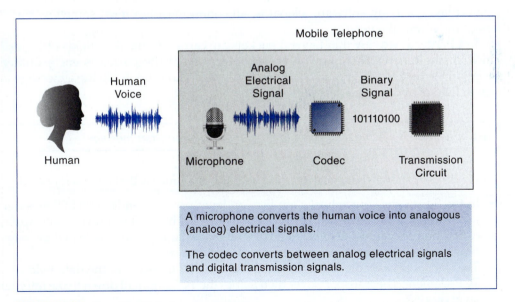

FIGURE 2-18 Encoding Voice

second at different frequencies. This sends pressure waves into your phone's microphone. The microphone converts this into increases and decreases in electricity. The resultant electrical signal rises and falls when your voice loudness rises and falls. To put it another way, the electrical signal is analogous to the voice signal. Therefore, we call this electrical signal an **analog signal**.

The analog signal must be converted into 1s and 0s. This is done by an electrical circuit called a **codec**. Converting outgoing analog signals into digital signals is called *encoding*. Converting incoming digital signals into analog signals to cause the earpiece to vibrate is called *decoding*. Codec is a merciful shortening of these two terms. As we will see in Chapter 11, there are many codec standards. Some specify a higher traffic burden in terms of bits per second; these have higher voice quality. Others are more parsimonious about bandwidth but give lower voice quality.

A codec converts between analog microphone signals and digital transmitted signals.

Test Your Understanding

17. a) Why is the electrical signal generated by a microphone called an analog signal?
b) What two things does a codec do? c) Is there a single codec standard?

VERTICAL COMMUNICATION ON HOSTS

So far, we have talked about what happens at individual layers. For instance, the transport process on the sending host sends TCP segments or UDP datagrams to the transport process on the receiving host.

Obviously, however, there is no direct connection between the two hosts at the transport layer. Barring software telepathy, all communication must somehow travel through the physical layer.

In Chapter 1, we saw that Layer 3 packets are carried in the data fields of Layer 2 frames in single networks. Networking people say that the packet is encapsulated (placed) in the data field of the frame. In general, **encapsulation** is placing a message in the data field of another message.

Encapsulation is placing a message in the data field of another message.

Figure 2-19 shows that encapsulation actually is a process that occurs repeatedly.

- In the figure, the source host's application layer process sends an HTTP message to the application layer process on the destination host. The source host's application process cannot deliver the HTTP message, so it passes the HTTP message down to the transport layer process on the source host.
- The transport layer process encapsulates the HTTP message in the data field of a TCP segment. The transport layer then passes the TCP segment down to the internet layer process.

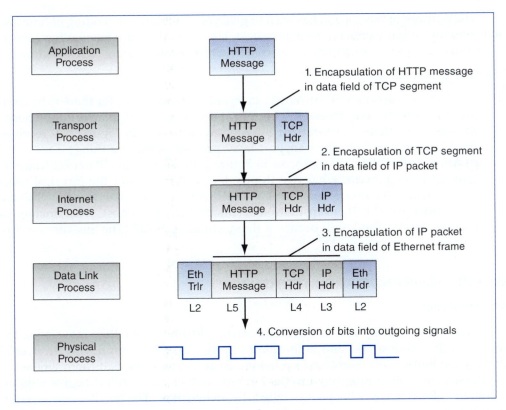

FIGURE 2-19 Layered Communication on the Source Host

- The Internet layer process encapsulates the TCP segment in the data field of an IP packet. It then passes the packet down to the data link layer.
- The data link layer process encapsulates the IP packet in a data link layer frame. If the single network standard is Ethernet, this is an Ethernet frame. If the single network standard is the Point to Point protocol (PPP), this is a PPP frame. The data link layer process may also add a trailer.

The whole process is like a set of Russian nesting dolls. So the frame consists of the following:

- The data link header
- The IP header
- The TCP header
- The application message segment
- The data link trailer if the single network standard has a trailer in its frame standard.

At the physical layer, something very different occurs. When the physical layer process receives the frame from the data link layer process, it does not do encapsulation. It merely converts the bits of the frame into signals and transmits its signal out the physical link connecting it to a switch, router, or host.

The purpose of this section has been to give you a light understanding of how layered communication works on the source host. However, there are many other aspects to vertical communication on source hosts, destination hosts, routers, and switches.

Test Your Understanding

18. a) What is encapsulation? b) Why is encapsulation necessary for there to be communication between processes operating at the same layer but on different hosts, routers, or switches? c) After the internet layer process in Figure 2-19 receives the TCP segment from the transport layer process, what two things does it do? d) After the data link layer process in Figure 2-19 receives the IP packet from the internet layer process, what two things does it do? e) After the physical layer process receives a frame from the data link layer process, what does the physical layer process do? f) If encapsulation occurs on the source host, what analogous process do you think will occur on the destination host? (The answer is not in the text.)

MAJOR STANDARDS ARCHITECTURES

Architectures

When you build a house, you do not design and build a bedroom, then move on to the next room. If you designed and built rooms one at a time, without having an overall plan for the house, you might end up having to go through the bathroom whenever you passed from the dining room to the kitchen. Instead, an architect begins with an overall plan for a house. This plan is called the architecture. The architecture specifies the functions of individual rooms (bedrooms, kitchens, etc.), how many rooms of each type are required, and how the rooms will fit together. Only after the architecture is finished does the architect begin to design individual rooms.

Network standards also need architectures. Network standards architectures break the standards functionality needed for communication into layers and define the functions of each layer. Only after they have done that do they develop individual standards. For instance, the TCP/IP standards architecture shown in Figure 2-20 has four layers. This architecture was created in the late 1970s. Since then, the Internet Engineering Task force has been adding individual standards, beginning with core standards such as IP, TCP, and UDP. It will continue to create individual standards for many years to come.

Network standards architectures break the standards functionality needed for communication into layers and define the functions of each layer. Only after they have done that do they develop individual standards.

Generally, all standards must be taken from the same architecture. For instance, electrical standards architectures in different countries have different voltages, amperages, alternating current cycles per second, plug shapes, and socket shapes. If you took a device built for the U.S. architecture, you could not take it to another country and simply change the plug to fit that country's sockets. Actually you *could* do that

Broad Purpose	TCP/IP	OSI	Hybrid TCP/IP-OSI
Applications	Application	Application (Layer 7)	Application (Layer 5)
		Presentation (Layer 6)	
		Session (Layer 5)	
Internetworking	Transport	Transport (Layer 4)	TCP/IP Transport Layer (Layer 4)
	Internet	Network (Layer 3)	TCP/IP Internet Layer (Layer 3)
Communication within a single switched LAN or WAN	Use OSI Standards Here	Data Link (Layer 2)	Data Link (OSI) Layer (Layer 2)
		Physical (Layer 1)	Physical OSI Layer (Layer 1)

Notes:

The Hybrid TCP/IP-OSI Architecture governs the Internet and dominates internal corporate networks.

OSI standards dominate the physical and data link layers (which govern communication within individual networks) almost exclusively.

TCP/IP dominates the internet and transport layers in internetworking and governs 80% to 90% percent of all corporate traffic above the data link layer.

FIGURE 2-20   The Hybrid TCP/IP–OSI Architecture

physically, but if you plugged the modified device into the wall jack, you should not expect the device to work. You would need a converter that converts between all elements in the U.S. electrical standards architecture and all elements in the foreign electrical architecture.

Although there are several major network standards architectures, two of them dominate actual corporate use: OSI and TCP/IP. Figure 2-20 illustrates layering in both. As you can see, they are quite different. Although it generally is impossible to mix standards for different architectures, this kind of mixing is possible with TCP/IP and OSI. It is possible to use a **hybrid TCP/IP–OSI architecture** that uses TCP/IP standards at some layers and OSI standards at other layers. This hybrid standards architecture is the dominant standards architecture in real corporations.

TCP/IP and OSI are often considered to be competitors. In fact, their standards agencies mostly specialize on different layers. When both are developing standards for a single layer, such as voice over IP standards at the application layer, their standards agencies often work together.

Test Your Understanding

19. a) What does a network standards architecture do? b) In what order are standards and standards architectures developed? c) What are the two dominant network standards architectures? d) What is the dominant network standards architecture in most real firms today? e) Are the two network standards architectures competitors?

The OSI Network Standards Architecture

OSI is an abbreviation for the "Reference Model of Open Systems Interconnection." *Reference model* is another name for *architecture*. An open system is one that is open to communicating with the rest of the world. In any case, OSI is rarely spelled out, which is merciful.

STANDARDS AGENCIES: ISO AND ITU-T   Standards architectures are managed by organizations called **standards agencies**. Figure 2-21 shows that OSI has two standards agencies.

- One is the **International Organization for Standardization (ISO)**, which generally is a strong standards organization for manufacturing, including computer manufacturing. By the way, do not confuse OSI and ISO. OSI is an architecture; ISO is a standards agency.
- The other is the **International Telecommunications Union–Telecommunications Standards Sector (ITU–T)**.[5] Part of the United Nations, the ITU–T oversees international telecommunications standards.

Although ISO or the ITU–T must *ratify* all OSI standards, other organizations frequently *create* standards for inclusion in OSI. For instance, we will see in Chapter 6 that the IEEE creates Ethernet standards. These standards are not official until the ITU–T or ISO ratifies them, although this has always been a mere formality.

OSI'S DOMINANCE AT LOWER LAYERS (PHYSICAL AND DATA LINK)   Although OSI is a seven-layer standards architecture (see Figure 2-22), OSI standards from Layers 3 through 6 are rarely used.

	OSI	TCP/IP
Standards Agency or Agencies	ISO (International Organization for Standardization)	IETF (Internet Engineering Task Force)
	ITU–T (International Telecommunications Union– Telecommunications Standards Sector)	
Dominance	Dominant at physical and data link layers	Dominant at the internet and transport layers
Documents Are Called	Various	Mostly RFCs (requests for comments)
Note:		
Do not confuse OSI (the architecture) with ISO (the organization).		
The acronyms for ISO and ITU–T do not match their names, but these are the official names and acronyms.		

FIGURE 2-21   OSI and TCP/IP

---

[5]No, the names and acronyms do not match for ISO and ITU-T, but these are the official names and acronyms for these two organizations.

Layer Number	OSI Name	Purpose	Use
7	Application	Governs remaining application-specific matters.	Some OSI applications are used
6	Presentation	Designed to handle data formatting differences and data compression and encryption. In practice, a category for general file format standards used in multiple applications.	Rarely used as a layer. However, many file format standards are assigned to this layer.
5	Session	Initiates and maintains a connection between application programs on different computers.	Rarely used
4	Transport	Generally equivalent to the TCP/IP transport layer. However, OSI transport layer standards are not compatible with TCP/IP transport layer standards.	Rarely used
3	Network	Generally equivalent to the TCP/IP internet layer. However, OSI network layer standards are not compatible with TCP/IP internet layer standards.	Rarely used
2	Data Link	End-to-end transmission in a single switched network. Frame organization. Switch operation.	Nearly 100 percent dominant
1	Physical	Physical connections between adjacent devices.	Nearly 100 percent dominant

FIGURE 2-22   OSI Layers

However, at the two lowest layers—the physical and data link layers—corporations use OSI standards almost universally in their networks. These two layers govern transmission within a switched or wireless network. Almost all single networks—both LANs and WANs—follow OSI standards at the physical and data link layers, regardless of what upper-layer standards they use. OSI standards are almost 100 percent dominant at the bottom two layers.

Almost all switched and wireless networks—both LANs and WANs—follow OSI standards at the physical and data link layers, regardless of what upper-layer standards they use.

Other standards agencies, recognizing the dominance of OSI at the physical and data link layers, simply specify the use of OSI standards at these layers. They then create standards only for internetworking and applications.

HIGHER LAYERS IN OSI   The box *Higher Layers in OSI* discusses the higher layers in OSI. Apart from the application layer, the higher layers in OSI are rarely used in networking.

Test Your Understanding

20. a) What standards agencies are responsible for the OSI standards architecture? Just give the acronyms. b) At which layers do OSI standards dominate usage?

The TCP/IP Network Standards Architecture

The **TCP/IP** architecture is mandatory on the Internet at the internet and transport layers. TCP/IP is also widely used at these layers by companies for their internal corporate internets.

The TCP/IP architecture is named after two of its standards, TCP and IP, which we have already seen briefly. However, TCP/IP also has many other standards, including the UDP standard we have already seen. This makes the name TCP/IP rather misleading. Another confusing point about names is that TCP/IP is the *standards architecture*, while TCP and IP are individual *standards* within the architecture.

Note that TCP/IP is the standards architecture, while TCP and IP are individual standards within the architecture.

THE INTERNET ENGINEERING TASK FORCE (IETF) TCP/IP's standards agency is the **Internet Engineering Task Force (IETF)**. Traditionally, the IETF has been viewed as being in competition with ISO and ITU–T for creating standards. However, as noted earlier in this chapter, the IETF and these other organizations have begun to cooperate in standards development. For instance, the IETF is working closely with ITU–T on VoIP transmission standards.

Having evolved from the Network Working Group described in Chapter 1, the IETF historically has been rather informal. Its committees traditionally focus on consensus rather than on voting, and technical expertise is the main source of most power within the organization. Although corporate participation has somewhat "tamed" the IETF, it remains a fascinating organization, although its members might argue that "organization" is too strong a word.

A great deal of the IETF's success is due to the fact that the IETF typically produces simple standards and then adds to their complexity over time. In fact, IETF standards often have the word *simple* in their name, for instance, the Simple Mail Transfer Protocol. Consequently, the IETF develops standards quickly. In addition, vendors can develop TCP/IP-based products quickly and inexpensively because of this speed of development and simplicity. "Inexpensive and fast to market" is almost always a good recipe for success. In contrast, OSI standards often take a very long time to be developed and often are so bloated with functionality that they are uneconomical to implement.

Note that the success of TCP/IP is *not* primarily due to its use on the Internet. Many corporations had already shifted many of their networks to TCP/IP before the Internet became a dominant force in the 1990s.

REQUESTS FOR COMMENTS (RFCs) As we saw in Chapter 1, most documents produced by the IETF have the rather misleading name **requests for comment (RFCs)**. Every few years, the IETF publishes a list of which RFCs are **Official Internet Protocol Standards**. Each list of standards adds some RFCs to the list and deprecates some previously listed standards to indicate that they are no longer official standards.

DOMINANCE AT THE INTERNETWORKING LAYERS (INTERNET AND TRANSPORT)   As noted earlier, physical and data link layer standards govern the transmission of data within a single *switched or wireless network*. We saw that OSI standards are dominant at these layers.

OSI standards are dominant at the physical and data link layers. TCP/IP is dominant at the internet and transport layers.

TCP/IP internet and transport layer standards, in turn, govern transmission across an entire internet, ensuring that any two host computers can communicate. TCP/IP application standards ensure that the two application programs on the two hosts can communicate as well. TCP/IP is dominant in the internetworking layers (internet and transport).[6]

TCP/IP is dominant in corporate networking at the internet and transport layers.

Test Your Understanding

21. a) Which of the following is an architecture: TCP/IP, TCP, or IP? b) Which of the following are standards: TCP/IP, TCP, or IP? c) What is the standards agency for TCP/IP? d) Why have this agency's standards been so successful? e) What are most of this agency's documents called? f) At which layers is TCP/IP dominant?

The Application Layer

OSI is completely dominant at the physical and data link layers, and TCP/IP is very dominant at the internet and transport layers. What about the application layer? The answer here is complex.[7] Overall, it seems best to say that no standards agency or architecture dominates at the application layer, although the IETF is particularly strong, especially for popular standards such as e-mail and file transfer.

Although many applications do not come from the IETF, they almost all run over TCP/IP standards at the internet and transport layers. This is true even for standards created by ISO and ITU–T.

---

[6]A few old legacy systems use other standards architectures at the internet and transport layers, but this is a minor concern in most firms today. The most important of these legacy architectures is IBM's Systems Network Architecture, which links large mainframe computers to terminals.

[7]Many application protocols come from the IETF. These include such popular standards as e-mail protocols (SMTP, POP, IMAP, etc.), the FTP standards, and the Simple Network Management Protocol (SNMP) in network management.

Some application standards come directly from OSI. This is particularly true of graphics file format standards. However, many OSI standards were too complex for widespread use. The IETF then produced simpler versions of these OSI standards. A good example is the Lightweight Directory Access Protocol (LDAP) for access to directory servers. LDAP evolved (devolved?) from the OSI directory access protocol standard.

Other standards agencies also produce application layer standards. HTTP and HTML standards come from the World Wide Web Consortium (W3C), although the IETF is producing some WWW standards. Most confusingly, incompatible Service Oriented Architecture Web services standards are being produced by several competing standards agencies.

At the application layer, as noted earlier, there is growing cooperation between ISO, the ITU–T, and the IETF. In voice over IP, the ITU–T and the IETF have harmonized several key standards. ISO and the IETF, in turn, have been cooperating in file format standards.

Test Your Understanding

22. a) Is any standards architecture dominant at the application layer? b) Do almost all applications, regardless of what standards architecture they come from, run over TCP/IP standards at the internet and transport layers?

TCP/IP *and* OSI: The Hybrid TCP/IP–OSI Standards Architecture

We have noted neither TCP/IP nor OSI dominates at all layers. Consequently, as discussed earlier, the most common standards pattern in organizations is to use OSI standards at the physical and data link layers, TCP/IP standards at the internet and transport layers, and application standards from several sources. This is very important for you to keep in mind because this **hybrid TCP/IP–OSI standards architecture** in Figure 2-18 forms the basis for most of this book.

The most common standards pattern in organizations is to use OSI standards at the physical and data link layers, TCP/IP standards at the internet and transport layers, and application standards from several sources. This is the hybrid TCP/IP–OSI standards architecture.

Test Your Understanding

23. a) Which layers of the hybrid TCP/IP–OSI standards architecture use OSI standards? b) Which layers use TCP/IP standards? c) Do wireless LAN standards come from OSI or TCP/IP? Explain. (The answer is not explicitly in this section.) d) Do switched WAN standards come from OSI or TCP/IP? Explain. (Again, the answer is not explicitly in this section.)

Higher Layers in OSI

In the section on OSI, we noted that OSI standards are dominant at the physical and data link layers but are not widely used at higher layers. This box discusses higher layers in OSI.

OSI Network and Transport Layers

The network layer functionality of OSI corresponds closely to the internet layer functionality of TCP/IP that we saw earlier in this chapter. The transport layer functionality of OSI, in turn, is very similar to the transport layer functionality of TCP/IP. However, while *functionality* may be similar between OSI and TCP at these layers, actual OSI and TCP/IP *standards* at these layers are completely incompatible. More importantly, OSI standards are rarely used at the network or transport layers by real organizations.[8]

OSI Session Layer

The **OSI session layer (OSI Layer 5)** initiates and maintains a connection between application programs on different computers. For instance, suppose that a single transaction requires a number of messages. If there is a connection break, the transmission can begin at the last session layer rollback point instead of restarting at the beginning. For example, if communication fails during a database transaction, the entire transaction does not have to be done over—only the work since the last rollback point. Unfortunately, while this is good for database applications and a few other applications, few applications benefit from the overhead added by the OSI session layer.

OSI Presentation Layer

The **OSI presentation layer (OSI Layer 6)** is *designed* to handle data-formatting differences between the two computers. For example, most computers format character data (letters, digits, and punctuation signs) in the ASCII code. In contrast, IBM mainframes format them in the EBCDIC code. The presentation layer can handle this and other format translations.

The OSI presentation layer also is *designed* to be used for compression and data encryption for application data.

In practice, the presentation layer is rarely used for either data format conversion or compression and encryption. Rather, the presentation layer has become a category for general application file format standards used in multiple applications, including MP3, JPEG, and many other general OSI file format standards.

OSI Application Layer

The **OSI application layer (OSI Layer 7)** governs remaining application-specific matters that are not covered by the session and presentation layers. The OSI application layer, freed from session and presentation matters, focuses on concerns specific to the application in use.

Test Your Understanding

24. a) At which layers do OSI standards dominate usage? b) Name and describe the functions of OSI Layer 5. c) Name and describe the intended use of OSI Layer 6. d) How is the OSI presentation layer actually used? e) Beginning with the physical layer (Layer 1), give the name and number of the OSI layers.

---

[8]Although OSI physical and data link layer standards are dominant, and while many OSI application layer standards are used, almost no systems implement OSI standards at the network, transport, session, or presentation layers. Then why, you may ask, do you need to be able to describe these layers? The answer is that you need to get a job. In a very large percentage of all job interviews, an interviewer noting that you have taken a networking course will ask you to describe the OSI layers. We kid you not.

CONCLUSION

Synopsis

In this chapter, we looked broadly at standards. Most of this book (and the networking profession in general) will focus on standards, which are also called protocols. Standards govern message exchanges. More specifically, they place constraints on message semantics (meaning), message syntax (format), and message order.

Standards are connection-oriented or connectionless. In connection-oriented protocols, there is a distinct opening before content messages are sent and a distinct closing afterward. There also are sequence numbers, which allow fragmentation and are used in supervisory messages (e.g., acknowledgments) to refer to specific messages. In connectionless protocols, there are no such openings and closings. Connectionless protocols are simpler than connection-oriented protocols, but they lose the advantages of sequence numbers.

In turn, reliable protocols do error correction, while unreliable protocols do not. Although unreliable protocols may do error detection without error correction, this does not make them reliable. In general, standards below the transport layer are unreliable in order to reduce costs. The transport standard usually is reliable; this allows error correction processes on just the two hosts to correct errors at the transport layer and at lower layers, giving the application clean data. Figure 2-23 compares the main protocols we have seen in this chapter in terms of connection orientation and reliability.

To discuss message ordering in more detail, we looked at HTTP and TCP. Message ordering in HTTP is trivial. The browser must initiate the communication by sending an HTTP request message; afterward the webserver program may transmit. TCP, in contrast, has complex message ordering. A three-step handshake is needed to open a connection, and four messages are needed to close a connection. Correctly received TCP messages (called segments) are always acknowledged by the receiver. If the sender does not receive an acknowledgment promptly, it retransmits the unacknowledged segment. This gives reliability.

To discuss message syntax in more detail, we looked briefly at the syntax of Ethernet frames, IP packets, TCP segments, UDP datagrams, and HTTP request and response messages. We saw that they represent syntax in three different ways. We will be looking at the syntax of many messages in this course, so you should be familiar with all methods for representing syntax. In the discussion, we saw that octet is another name for byte. We also saw that application programs on multitasking servers are usually

Layer	Protocol	Connection-Oriented or Connectionless?	Reliable or Unreliable?
5 (Application)	HTTP	Connectionless	Unreliable
4 (Transport)	TCP	**Connection-oriented**	**Reliable**
4 (Transport)	UDP	Connectionless	Unreliable
3 (Internet)	IP	Connectionless	Unreliable
2 (Data Link)	Ethernet	Connectionless	Unreliable

FIGURE 2-23 Characteristics of the Protocols Discussed in This Chapter

represented by well-known port numbers, while clients use ephemeral port numbers to represent conversations with servers. A socket consists of an IP address, a colon, and a port number. It represents a particular program (or conversation) on a particular host.

The application layer must convert text, graphics, video, and other application layer content into bits (1s and 0s). In this chapter, we looked at how application programs encode ASCII text, whole numbers, a number of alternatives, and voice and video streams into strings of bits.

We looked at how layer processes work together on the source host. After each layer creates its message, it immediately passes the message down to the next-lower-layer process. The data link, internet, and transport processes take every message they are given and encapsulate it in a message suitable for that layer.

Individual standards are not created in isolation. They are created within broad plans called standards architectures. Only after the broad architecture is designed by specifying the functionality of each layer and ensuring that the architecture overall allows interoperability are individual standards developed.

The TCP/IP architecture has the Internet Engineering Task Force (IETF) as its standards agency. It has a four-layer architecture. The bottom layer basically says, "Use OSI standards for single switched and wireless networks."

The OSI architecture has ISO and ITU–T as its two standards agencies. OSI has a seven-layer architecture. The session layer manages a connection between application programs; if there is an interruption, only communication since the last "rollback point" needs to be repeated. The presentation layer was designed as a layer for converting between application formatting implementations in different operating systems and for providing encryption and compression. In practice, it has become a catch-all category for application standards, such as JPEG.

Most real corporations today use a hybrid TCP/IP–OSI standards architecture that combines layers from TCP/IP and OSI. This architecture, which Figure 2-20 illustrates, will be the focus of this book. At the physical and data link layers, which govern transmission through a single switched or wireless network, OSI standards are almost always used. TCP/IP standards are dominant at the internet and transport layers. Application layer standards come from many sources. OSI and TCP/IP standards agencies frequently collaborate to create application layer standards.

END-OF-CHAPTER QUESTIONS

Thought Questions

1. How do you think TCP would handle the problem if an acknowledgment were lost, so that the sender retransmitted the unacknowledged TCP segment, therefore causing the receiving transport process to receive the same segment twice?

2. a) In Figure 2-13, what will be the value in the destination port number field if a packet arrives for the e-mail application?

   b) When the HTTP program sends an HTTP response message to a client PC, in what field of what message will it place the value 80?

3. Binary for 47 is 101111. Give the binary for 48, 49, and 50.

4. You need to represent 1,026 different city names. How many bits will this take if you give each city a different binary number?

Brainteaser Questions

1. How can you make a connectionless protocol reliable? (You may not be able to answer this question, but try.)
2. Spacecraft exploring the outer planets need reliable data transmission. However, the acknowledgments would take hours to arrive. This makes an ACK-based reliability approach unattractive. Can you think of another way to provide reliable data transmission to spacecraft? (You may not be able to answer this question, but try.)

Perspective Questions

1. What was the most surprising thing you learned in this chapter?
2. What was the most difficult material for you in this chapter?

2a

HANDS-ON: WIRESHARK PACKET CAPTURE

LEARNING OBJECTIVES

By the end of this chapter, you should be able to:

- Use the Wireshark packet capture program at a novice level.
- Capture packets in real time.
- Analyze the packets at a novice level.

INTRODUCTION

A good way to practice what you have learned in this chapter is to look at individual packets. Packet capture programs record packets going into and out of your computer. If you capture a brief webserver interaction, you can look at header fields, TCP three-step connection starts, and other information. There are several good packet capture programs. We will look at Wireshark, which is simple to use, popular, and free to download (at least at the time of this writing).

GETTING WIRESHARK

To get Wireshark, go to wireshark.org. Do *not* go to wireshark.com. Follow the instructions and download the program on your computer.

USING WIRESHARK

Getting Started

After installation, open the Wireshark program. You will see the opening screen. It will look like the screen in Figure 2a-1. There will be controls at the top with a blank area below them. You will soon fill this area with your packet capture.

Starting a Packet Capture

To start a packet capture, click on the *Go* menu item. Then, when the Wireshark: Capture Interfaces dialog appears, as Figure 2a-2 illustrates, select a network interface and click on *Start*.

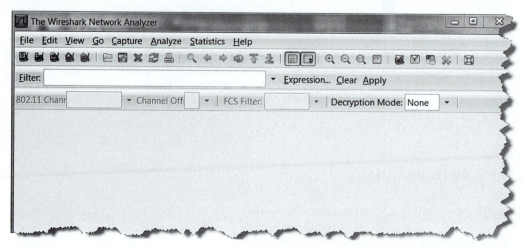

FIGURE 2a-1   Initial Wireshark Screen

Source: Wireshark Foundation.

Getting Data

Your browser should already be open. Switch to your browser and enter a URL. (In this example, the author went to Wikipedia.org.) This creates a flurry of packets between you and the host specified in the URL. These appear on the window below the controls, as shown in Figure 2a-3.

Stopping Data Collection

To stop the data collection, click on the *Capture* menu item, as Figure 2a-4 shows. When the drop-down menu appears, select *Stop.* You now have a packet stream to analyze.

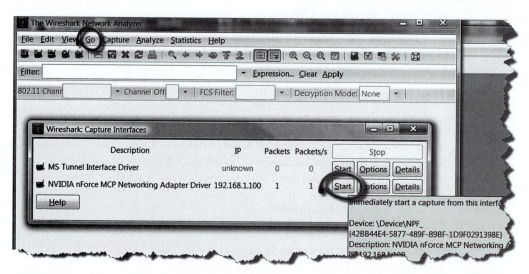

FIGURE 2a-2   Starting a Packet Capture in Wireshark

Source: Wireshark Foundation.

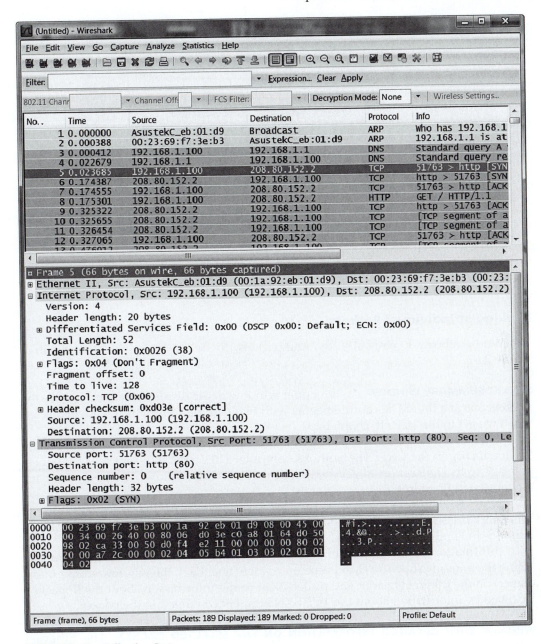

FIGURE 2a-3 Collecting Data

Source: Wireshark Foundation.

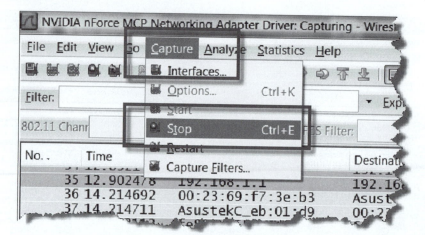

FIGURE 2a-4   Stopping the Data Collection

Source: Wireshark Foundation.

Looking at Individual Packets

Now you can begin looking at individual packets. To see how to do this, look again at Figure 2a-3.

PACKET SUMMARY WINDOW   In the upper window in the display area, you can see the packets one at a time. The capture begins with two ARP packets, which we will discuss when we get to the TCP/IP chapters.

Then come two DNS packets. In the example, the author typed the host name Wikipedia.org in the URL. The author's computer (192.168.1.100) sent a DNS request message to its DNS server to get the IP address for Wikipedia.org. The DNS sent back the requested IP address.

Now, the author's computer opened a connection to 208.80.152.2, which is Wireshark.org's IP address.[1] It first sent a TCP SYN segment to 208.80.152.2. This is Frame 5. In Figure 2a-3, the frame has been selected.

Information about the contents of this particular frame is shown in a window below the window showing each frame on a single line. First, the window shows information on the Ethernet header and trailer. Next comes information about the IP packet, followed by information about the TCP SYN segment contained in the packet.

WINDOW WITH DETAILED INFORMATION ON THE SELECTED PACKET   The Ethernet information has been minimized. Only the source and destination MAC addresses are shown. However, information about the IP packet has been maximized. You can see the values of the individual fields in the selected packet. For example, note that the Time to Live field in this packet had the value 128. In addition, the protocol field value indicates that the data field contains a TCP segment.

---

[1] If you try this, you may get a different IP address. Many firms have multiple physical webservers that they associate with a host name. A DNS response message returns the IP address of one of these physical servers.

The TCP segment information is also expanded, although only the first few fields are shown in the window. Note that the destination port is 80, indicating that the author was contacting the Wireshark.org webserver. Note also that the Flag Fields information says that the SYN bit is set, as one would expect.

To make life easier for you, Wireshark does as much translation as possible. For example, it interprets the information in the protocol field as indicating that there is a TCP segment in the packet's data field. It also indicates that Port 80 is HTTP.

The information on sequence number is highly simplified compared to the discussion in Chapter 2. This is the first TCP segment being sent. It is given the value 0 rather than its complex real value.

HEX WINDOW   The lowest window shows the contents of the packet in hexadecimal (Base 16) format. Hex is difficult for new analysts to interpret, but it is very compact compared to the information in the middle window. Experienced packet analysts quickly learn the positions of important fields and learn to read the hex symbols for that field.

Options

Figure 2a-5 shows that Wireshark capture options allow you to control what packets are captured. If you are connected to multiple external servers simultaneously, this can allow you to capture only packets for a particular connection.

FIGURE 2a-5   Wireshark Options

Source: Wireshark Foundation.

Exercises

1. Do the following:
   - Download Wireshark.
   - Start Wireshark.
   - Turn on Wireshark capture.
   - Type a URL in your browser window (not Wikipedia.org).
   - After a few seconds, stop the capture.
   - Answer the following questions:
     1a. What URL did you use? What was the IP address of the webserver?
     1b. Find the frame in which your PC sent the SYN packet. List the source and destination IP address, the source and destination port numbers, and the header checksum.
     1c. Select the SYN/ACK packet. List the source and destination IP address, the source and destination port numbers, and the header checksum.
     1d. Select the packet that acknowledges the SYN/ACK segment. List the source and destination IP address, the source and destination port numbers, and the header checksum.

2. Change the options so that only packets you send are recorded. Do a capture. Click on the window containing Wireshark and hit *Alt-Enter*. This captures the window to your clipboard. Paste it into your homework.

3

NETWORK SECURITY

LEARNING OBJECTIVES

By the end of this chapter, you should be able to:

- Describe the threat environment, including types of attackers and types of attacks.
- Explain the Plan–Protect–Respond cycle for security management.
- Explain in detail planning principles and policy-based security.
- Describe protection.
  - Evaluate authentication mechanisms, including passwords, smart cards, biometrics, digital certificate authentication, and two-factor authentication.
  - Describe firewall protection, including stateful inspection.
  - Explain in detail the protection of dialogues by cryptography, including symmetric key encryption for confidentiality, electronic signatures, and cryptographic system standards.
- Describe response: Reacting according to plan for successful compromises and disasters.

STEUBEN ARC

Steuben ARC is a nonprofit organization in Bath, New York, that provides care for developmentally disabled adults. In September 2009, cyberthieves stole nearly $200,000 from the company.[1]

The attack began when a cybercriminal sent a fake invoice in an e-mail message to one of the company's accountants. The message had an attachment, dhlinvoice.zip. When the accountant opened the attachment, it installed a very sophisticated keystroke logger on the accountant's computer. This program captured the accountant's username and password on the company's accounting server and sent it to the attacker.

Armed with this information, the thieves transferred the money out of the company's bank accounts in two batches. Instead of sending it to themselves, the thieves had the banks send the money to 20 money mules around the country. These money mules forwarded the money to offshore accounts controlled by the attackers. For each transaction,

[1]Brian Krebs, "Cyber Gangs Hit Healthcare Providers," *Washington Post*, September 28, 2009. voices. washingtonpost.com/securityfix/2009/09/online_bank_robbers_target_hea.html?wprss=securityfix.Mary Pernham, "Alleged cyber-theft: Hackers take $50K from Arc," *The Corning Leader*, October 1, 2009. www. the-leader.com/news/x1699607673/Alleged-cyber-theft-Hackers-take-50K-from-Arc.

the mules received a fee. Using money mules allowed the attackers to avoid shipping the money directly to offshore accounts, which could have raised the bank's suspicions.

The bank actually did become suspicious. It blocked some of the transfers to money mules and by money mules to offshore banks. However, only some of the money was recovered. Overall, it was a successful attack.

Test Your Understanding

1. a) How did the attacker get the credentials for the company's bank account? b) Why were money mules used? c) List indications that this was a sophisticated attack. d) How might the company have been able to avoid this compromise? e) What motivated the attacker? f) What would you say to executives in small companies who believe that they are too little to be attacked?

INTRODUCTION

This is the third of four introductory chapters. The fact that it deals entirely with security tells you how important security has become in networking. In the 1990s, the Internet blossomed, allowing billions of people to reach hundreds of millions of servers around the world. Unfortunately, the Internet also made all of these users potential victims. Security quickly became one of the most important IT management issues.

Figure 3-1 shows security threats and the plan–protect–respond cycle that companies follow to deal with the threat environments. In this chapter, we will begin looking at the threat environment. Sun Tzu's *The Art of War* admonishes defenders to "know your enemy." We will see that the **threat environment**—the attacks and attackers that companies face—is complex and rapidly changing.

The **Plan–Protect–Respond cycle** that companies follow to deal with the threat environment begins with the planning that companies must do to defend against these threats. This is followed by the Protect phase, in which companies implement the

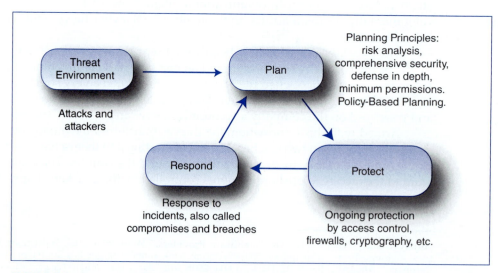

FIGURE 3-1 Threats and the Plan–Protect–Respond Cycle

protections they have planned. The Protect box is larger than the others to emphasize that this phase accounts for most of the work in security. The Respond stage is needed when protections fail and attacks succeed. Successful attacks are called **compromises**, **incidents**, or **breaches**.

The main thing that sets security management apart from other aspects of IT management is that the company must battle against intelligent adversaries, not simply against errors and other forms of unreliability. Companies today are engaged in an escalating arms race with attackers, and security threats and defenses are mutating at a frightening rate.

In this chapter, we will look at security broadly. We will focus on network security, but network security is impossible to separate from general IT security.

Test Your Understanding

2. a) What are the two elements of the threat environment? b) Briefly explain each of the three stages in the plan–protect–respond cycle. c) Which of these three stages consumes the most corporate effort? d) Give three names for *successful attack*. e) What is the main thing that separates security from other aspects of IT?

TYPES OF ATTACKS

As just noted, we will begin by looking at the threat environment that corporations face. In this section, we will look at types of attacks. Later, we will look at the types of attackers.

Malware

    A general name for evil software

Vulnerability-Specific versus Universal Malware

    Vulnerabilities are flaws in specific programs
        Vulnerabilities allow attacks against these specific programs
    Vulnerability-specific malware requires a specific vulnerability to be effective
        Vendors release patches to close vulnerabilities
        However, users do not always install patches promptly or at all and so continue to be vulnerable
        Also, zero-day attacks occur before the patch is released for the vulnerability
    Universal malware does not require a specific vulnerability to be effective
        Universal malware often requires risky human actions

Viruses

    Pieces of code that attach themselves to other programs
        Virus code executes when an infected program executes
        The virus then infects other programs on the computer
    Propagation vectors
        E-mail attachments
        Visits to websites (even legitimate ones)

(continued)

FIGURE 3-2   Malware (Study Figure)

Social networking sites

Many others (USB RAM sticks, peer-to-peer file sharing, etc.)

Stopping viruses

Antivirus programs are needed to scan arriving files for viruses

Antivirus programs also scan for other malware

Patching vulnerabilities may help

Worms

Stand-alone programs that do not need to attach to other programs

Can propagate like viruses through e-mail, etc.

This requires human gullibility, which is slow

Directly-propagating worms jump to victim hosts directly

Can do this if target hosts have a specific vulnerability

Directly-propagating worms can spread with amazing speed

Directly-propagating worms can be thwarted by firewalls and by installing patches

Not by antivirus programs

Mobile Code

HTML webpages can contain scripts

Scripts are snippets of code that are executed when the webpage is displayed in a browser

Scripts enhance the user experience and may be required to see the webpage

Scripts are called mobile code because they are downloaded with the webpage

Scripts are normally benign but may be damaging if the browser has a vulnerability

The script may do damage or download a program to do damage

Payloads

After propagation, viruses and worms execute their payloads

Payloads erase hard disks or send users to pornography sites if they mistype URLs

Often, the payload downloads another program

An attack program with such a payload is called a downloader

Many downloaded programs are Trojan horses

Trojan horses are programs that disguise themselves as system files

Spyware Trojans collect sensitive data and send the data to an attacker

Website activity trackers

Keystroke loggers

Data mining software

Getting Infected

E-mail from infected machines or spammers

Visiting websites

Even normally legitimate websites can be seeded with pages containing mobile malware

Peer-to-peer file transfers

Downloading "free" software

Etc.

FIGURE 3-2 Continued

Malware Attacks

We will begin with malware attacks. **Malware** is a name for any evil software. This includes viruses, worms, Trojan horses, and other dangerous attack software. Malware attacks are the most frequent attacks on companies. Nearly every firm has one or more significant malware compromises each year.

> *Malware is evil software.*

Test Your Understanding

3. What is malware?

VULNERABILITY-SPECIFIC VERSUS UNIVERSAL MALWARE   A **vulnerability** is a flaw in a program that permits a specific attack or set of attacks against this program. If the vulnerability is not present in the program, a **vulnerability-specific** attack aimed at that vulnerability will fail.

> *A vulnerability is a flaw in a program that permits a specific attack or set of attacks against this program.*

When a vulnerability is discovered, the software vendor usually issues a **patch**, which is a small program designed to correct the vulnerability. After patch installation, the program is safe from attacks based on that particular vulnerability. Too often, however, users fail to install patches, and their programs continue to be vulnerable. Even if they do install patches, furthermore, they may delay doing so. This creates a long window of opportunity for attackers.

Of course, if attacks begin before the program vendor creates a patch (or even learns about the attack), the attacks will succeed. A vulnerability-specific attack that occurs before a patch is available is called a **zero-day attack**.

> *A vulnerability-specific attack that occurs before a patch is available is called a zero-day attack.*

Not all malware is vulnerability-specific. **Universal malware** works whether or not the computer has a security vulnerability. In general, universal malware programs require the human victim to do something risky, such as downloading "free" software, pornography, or an electronic greeting card.

Test Your Understanding

4. a) What is a vulnerability? b) How can users eliminate a vulnerability in one of their programs? c) What name do we give to attacks that occur before a patch is available? d) What type of malware does not require a vulnerability?

VIRUSES Pieces of executable code that attach themselves to other programs are called **viruses**. Within a computer, whenever an infected program runs (executes), the virus attaches itself to other programs on that computer.

Viruses are pieces of executable code that attach themselves to other programs on that computer.

Propagation Vectors The virus spreads between computers when an infected program is transferred to another computer via a USB RAM stick, an e-mail attachment, a webpage download, a peer-to-peer file-sharing transfer, a social networking site, or some other **propagation vector** (method for malware to move to a victim computer). Once on another machine, if the infected program is executed, the virus spreads to other programs on that machine.

More than 90 percent of viruses today spread via e-mail. Viruses find addresses in the infected computer's e-mail directories. They then send messages with infected attachments to all of these addresses. If a receiver opens the attachment, the infected program executes, and the receiver's programs become infected.

Another popular propagation vector is visiting a website and having the website download a virus (or other type of malware) to your computer. Obviously, the risk is greatest if you visit a high-risk website, such as a site for "free" software or pornography. However, even if you visit a known legitimate website daily, you may become infected one day if an attacker has planted malware on its webpages. (In 2009, this happened to subscribers who went to the *New York Times* website.) A substantial fraction of all infected websites are legitimate websites.

Social networking sites are already popular with virus writers. By their nature, social networking sites are designed for sharing, and if a malware writer can inject malware into the sharing process, spread can be very rapid. USB RAM sticks and peer-to-peer file transfers are two examples of these other propagation vectors.

Stopping Viruses To stop viruses, a company must protect its computers with **antivirus programs** that scan each arriving e-mail message or file for patterns that identify viruses. Antivirus programs today also scan for other types of malware, but we still call them antivirus programs.

Antivirus programs also scan for other types of malware.

For some viruses (but not for all), it is also useful to patch security vulnerabilities. However, patching does not work for most viruses.

Firewalls are devices that examine each packet passing through a certain part of a network. Client PCs can have firewalls. These firewalls have major benefits, but they do not stop normally propagating worms and viruses.

Test Your Understanding

5. a) What is a propagation vector? b) How do viruses propagate within computers? c) How do viruses propagate between computers? d) In what two ways can viruses be stopped? e) Do firewalls usually stop viruses?

WORMS   Another important type of malware is worms. We have just seen that viruses are pieces of code that must attach themselves to other programs. In contrast, **worms** are full programs that operate by themselves. Both viruses and worms can create mass epidemics that infect hundreds or even millions of computers.

Worms are full programs that operate by themselves.

Worms are capable of propagating, like viruses, through e-mail attachments, USB RAM sticks, and similar propagation vectors. These methods typically require human gullibility to succeed. Although human gullibility is sadly reliable, it is rather slow. Until someone opens an e-mail attachment, inserts an infected USB RAM stick, or takes some other action, nothing happens.

Unlike viruses, some (but not all) worms have another propagation vector. A **directly propagating** worm tries to jump from the infected computer to many other computers. Target computers that have a specific vulnerability will accept the directly propagating worm. They then become sites from which the worm spreads further.

A directly propagating worm tries to jump from the infected computer to many other computers.

Freed from the need for human intervention, directly propagating worms can spread with incredible speed. In 2003, the Blaster worm infested 90 percent of all vulnerable hosts on the entire Internet within 10 minutes. The nightmare scenario for security professionals is the prospect of a fast-spreading worm that exploits a vulnerability in a large percentage of all computers on the Internet.

Antivirus programs do nothing to stop directly propagating worms. However, firewalls and patching vulnerabilities can stop them.

Antivirus programs do nothing to stop directly propagating worms. However, firewalls and patching vulnerabilities can stop them.

Figure 3-3 summarizes the differences between how viruses and worms can be stopped. Note that directly propagating worms cannot be stopped using techniques used to stop traditionally propagating worms.

Propagation Vector	Antivirus Program	Firewall	Patching Vulnerabilities
Normally propagating virus or worm (e-mail, visiting website, etc.)	Yes	No	Sometimes
Directly-propagating worm	No	Yes	Yes

FIGURE 3-3   Stopping Viruses and Worms

Test Your Understanding

6. a) How do viruses and worms differ? b) Distinguish how directly propagating worms and e-mail worms spread. c) Which can spread faster—viruses or directly propagating worms? Explain. d) How can directly propagating worms be stopped? e) Can antivirus programs usually stop directly propagating worms?

MOBILE CODE   An HTML webpage can contain a **script**, which is a group of commands written in a simplified programming language. Scripts are executed when the webpage is loaded. Scripts can enhance the user's experience, and many webpages will not work unless script execution is enabled, which it usually is by default.

Scripts are referred to as **mobile code** because they travel with the downloaded webpage from the webserver to the browser. Mobile code normally is safe and beneficial. However, if the user's browser has a vulnerability, a script may be able to do harm. A script may do damage itself or may download a more complex program to do damage.

Test Your Understanding

7. a) What is a script? b) Are scripts normally bad? c) Under what circumstances are scripts likely to be dangerous? d) Why are scripts on webpages called mobile code?

PAYLOADS   In war, when a bomber aircraft reaches its target, it releases its payload of bombs. Similarly, after they spread, viruses, worms, and other types of malware may execute pieces of code called **payloads**. Malicious payloads can completely erase hard disks and do other significant damage. In some cases, they can take the victim to a pornography site whenever the victim mistypes a URL. In other cases, they can turn the user's computer into a spam generator or a pornography download site. Not all malware has malicious payloads or payloads at all.

TROJAN HORSES   Often, the payload installs another program on the computer. A program that does this is called, as you might suspect, **downloader**.

Often, the downloader retrieves and installs a **Trojan horse**, which is a program that disguises itself as a legitimate system file. This makes it difficult to detect. A Trojan horse cannot spread from one computer to another by itself. Rather, it relies on a virus, worm, hacker, or gullible user to install it on a computer. Once installed, the Trojan horse continues to exploit the user indefinitely.

A Trojan horse cannot spread from one computer to another by itself.

SPYWARE   An especially problematic category of Trojan horses is **spyware**—a name given to Trojan horses that **surreptitiously** (without your knowledge) collect information about you and send this information to the attacker.

- Some spyware Trojans collect information about your Web surfing habits and send this information to advertisers.
- More dangerous are keystroke loggers, which record your keystrokes. Within these keystrokes, they look for passwords, social security numbers, and

other information that can help the person who receives the keystroke logger's data.

- Data mining spyware, in contrast, searches through files on your hard drive for potentially useful information and sends this information to the attacker.

Test Your Understanding

8. a) What are payloads? b) What are Trojan horses? c) How do Trojan horses propagate to computers? d) What is spyware? e) What is a keystroke logger? f) What does data mining software do?

Attacks on Individuals

SOCIAL ENGINEERING   As technical defenses have improved, malware writers have focused more heavily on **social engineering**, which is a fancy name for tricking the victim into doing something against his or her interests. Viruses and worms have long tried to do this with e-mail attachments—say, by telling the user that he or she has won a lottery and needs to open the attachment for the details. The range of social engineering attacks has expanded greatly in the last few years.

Social engineering is tricking the victim into doing something against his or her interests.

SPAM   The most annoying type of malware on a day-in, day-out basis is **spam**,[2] which is unsolicited commercial e-mail. Spammers send the same solicitation e-mail message to millions of e-mail addresses in the hope that a small percentage of all recipients will respond.

Spam is unsolicited commercial e-mail.

FRAUD   Spam is not merely annoying. Attackers use spam to perpetrate damaging attacks. Few spam messages are really designed to sell legitimate products. Most are fraudulent attempts to get someone to send money for "investment opportunities" and goods that will not be delivered or that are effectively worthless. **Fraud** is lying to get victims to do something against their financial self-interest. *Social engineering* is the more general term; fraud is social engineering applied to financial interests.

Fraud is lying to get victims to do something against their financial self-interest.

E-MAIL ATTACHMENTS   Some spam messages have damaging e-mail attachments. For instance, a spam message may say that it is an electronic greeting card. The user is told that a program must be downloaded to read the greeting card. The "reader" program, of course, is malware.

---

[2]Except at the beginnings of sentences, e-mail *spam* is spelled in lowercase. This distinguishes unsolicited commercial e-mail from the Hormel Corporation's meat product, Spam, which should always be capitalized. In addition, Spam is *not* an acronym for "spongy pink animal matter."

Social Engineering

Tricking the victim into doing something against his or her interests

Spam

Unsolicited commercial e-mail

Fraud

Spam often asks the victim to send money for products that will not be delivered
Or for false investment opportunities

E-Mail Attachments
Including a Link to a Website That Has Malware

The website may complete the fraud or download software to the victim

Phishing Attacks

A sophisticated social engineering attack in which an authentic-looking e-mail or website entices the user to enter his or her username, password, or other sensitive information

Credit Card Number Theft

Uses stolen credit card numbers in unauthorized transactions
Performed by carders

Identity Theft

Involves collecting enough data to impersonate the victim in large financial transactions
    Purchase a house or car
    Obtain a loan
    Commit fraud or other crime
Can result in much greater financial harm to the victim than carding
May take a long time to restore the victim's credit rating
In corporate identity theft, the attacker impersonates an entire corporation
    Accept credit cards in the company's name
    Commit other crimes in the name of the firm
    Can seriously harm a company's reputation

FIGURE 3-4 Attacks on Individuals (Study Figure)

INCLUDING A LINK TO A WEBSITE THAT HAS MALWARE Spam can also take victims to dangerous websites. One way for spam to create problems is for messages to include a link to a website. If the receiver clicks on the link, he or she will be taken to a website that will complete the fraud or download malware into the victim's computer.

PHISHING ATTACKS An especially effective form of spam does phishing,[3] which is the use of authentic-looking e-mail or websites to entice the user to send his or her

---

[3]IT attackers often replace *f* with *ph*. For example, *phone freaking* (dialing long-distance numbers illegally) became *phone phreaking* and later just *phreaking*.

username, password, or other sensitive information to the attacker. One typical example of phishing is an e-mail message that appears to be from the person's bank. The message asks the person to "confirm" his or her username and password in a return message. Another typical example is an e-mail message with a link to what appears to be the victim's bank website but that is, in fact, an authentic-looking fake website.

> Phishing is the use of authentic-looking e-mail or websites to entice the user to send his or her username, password, or other sensitive information to the attacker.

CREDIT CARD NUMBER THEFT   In fraudulent spam, the message may convince the user to type a credit card number to purchase goods. The attacker will not deliver the goods. Instead, the **carder** (credit card number thief) will use the credit card number to make unauthorized purchases. Most credit card firms will refund money spent by the carder, but this can be a painful process, and the victim must notify the credit card firm promptly to get a refund.

IDENTITY THEFT   In other cases, thieves collect enough data about a victim (name, address, social security number, driver's license number, date of birth, etc.) to impersonate the victim during complex crimes. This impersonation is called **identity theft**. Thieves commit identity theft in order to purchase expensive goods, take out major loans using the victim's assets as collateral, commit crimes, obtain prescription medicines, get a job, enter the country illegally, and do many other things. Identity theft is more damaging than credit card theft because it can involve large monetary losses and because restoring the victim's credit rating can take months. Some victims have even been arrested for crimes committed by the identity thief.

> In identity theft, thieves collect enough data about a victim to impersonate the victim during complex crimes.

Test Your Understanding

9. a) What is social engineering? b) What is fraud? c) What is the definition of spam? d) How can spam be used to harm people who open spam messages? e) What is phishing? f) Distinguish between credit card number theft and identity theft. g) What are carders? h) Which tends to produce more damage—credit card theft or identity theft? Explain your answer.

Human Break-Ins (Hacking)

A virus or worm typically has a single method. If that method fails, the attack fails. However, human attackers often break into a specific company's computers manually. A human adversary can attack a target company with a variety of approaches until one succeeds. This flexibility makes human break-ins much more likely to succeed than malware break-ins.

WHAT IS HACKING?   **Hacking** is defined as intentionally using a computer resource without authorization or in excess of authorization. The key issue is authorization.[4] If you see a password written on a note attached to a computer screen, this does not mean

Human Break-Ins

Viruses and worms only have a single attack method
Humans can keep trying different approaches until they succeed

Hacking

Informally, hacking is breaking into a computer
Formally, hacking is intentionally using a computer resource without authorization or in excess of authorization

Scanning Phase

Send attack probes to map the network and identify possible victim hosts (Figure 3-6)
Scan for IP addresses with active hosts
Scan IP addresses that reply for programs for which the attacker has an attack method

The Break-In

Uses an exploit—a tailored attack method that is often a program (Figure 3-6)
Normally exploits a vulnerability on the victim computer
The act of breaking in is called an exploit
The hacker tool is also called an exploit

After the Break-In

The hacker downloads a hacker tool kit to automate hacking work
The hacker becomes invisible by deleting log files
The hacker creates a backdoor (way to get back into the computer)
    Backdoor account—account with a known password and full privileges
    Backdoor program—program to allow reentry; usually Trojanized
The hacker can then do damage at his or her leisure
    Download a Trojan horse to continue exploiting the computer after the attacker leaves
    Manually give operating system commands to do damage

FIGURE 3-5 Human Break-Ins (Study Figure)

that you have authorization to use it. Also, note that it is hacking even if a person is given an account but uses the computer for unauthorized purposes.

> *Hacking is intentionally using a computer resource without authorization or in excess of authorization.*

THE SCANNING PHASE   When a hacker attacks a firm, he or she usually begins by **scanning** the network. Figure 3-6 shows that this involves sending **probe packets** into the firm's network. Responses to these probe packets tend to reveal information about the

---

[4]Note also that the unauthorized access must be intentional. Proving intentionality is almost always necessary in criminal prosecution, and hacking is no exception.

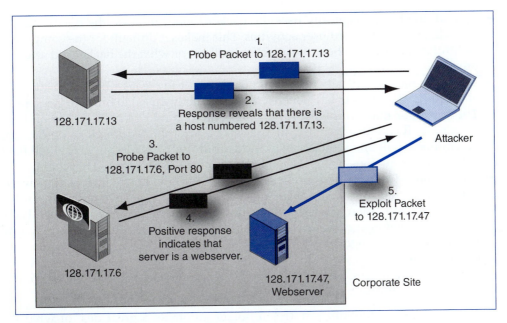

FIGURE 3-6 Scanning Probes and Exploit Packets

firm's general network design and about its individual hosts. Usually there are two phases to these probe attacks.

- The first probe packet in the figure is an IP address probe. It is sent to the IP address 128.171.17.13. If the host at that IP address responds, this means that there is a potential victim at that IP address. The attacker typically probes a large range of IP addresses to get a list of potential victims.
- The attacker then sends port number probes to previously identified IP addresses. This second round of probes is sent to particular ports on these hosts. In the figure, the probe packet is sent to Port 80. As we saw in Chapter 2, this is the well-known port number for webservers. If the server responds, the attacker knows that Host 128.171.17.6 is a webserver.

THE BREAK-IN The colored server is a webserver that the attacker has previously probed. The attacker has an **exploit** (attack method) for webservers. He or she uses this exploit to take over the host by sending exploit packets. Confusingly, the act of breaking into a computer is also called an exploit, as is the program the attacker uses during the break-in.

AFTER THE BREAK-IN After the break-in, the real work begins.

- Typically, the first thing a hacker does is download[5] a **hacker toolkit** to the victim computer. The toolkit is a collection of tools that automate some tasks the hacker will have to perform after the break-in.

---

[5]Some students find the use of the term *download* to be confusing. Look at it this way. The hacker is now logged into the victim computer. So he or she downloads software from a toolkit server to the victim computer and installs the software on the victim computer.

- Second, the hacker typically uses the hacker toolkit to erase the operating system's log files that record user activities. This makes it difficult for the computer's rightful owner to trace how the attacker broke in or what the hacker did after the break-in.
- Third, the hacker typically uses the hacker toolkit to create a **backdoor** that will allow the hacker back in later, even if the vulnerability used to break in is repaired. The backdoor may simply be a new account with a known password and full privileges. It can also be a Trojan horse program that is difficult to detect. The Trojan horse will allow the attacker to log into itself. The Trojan horse will have extensive permissions, which become the attacker's permissions after login.
- Fourth, once invisible and having a way back in, the attacker does damage at leisure by giving commands as a logged-in user with extensive permissions. For long-term exploitation, the hacker may download a Trojan horse, which will continue to cause damage after the hacker leaves. For instance, the Trojan may turn the host into a pornography download site or use the compromised host to attack other computers. Keystroke loggers that collect whatever the user types are also popular Trojan horses. The most dangerous Trojan horses are bots, which we will learn about in the next subsection.

Although hacker toolkits and Trojan horses automate a great deal of what the hacker wishes to do, hackers also work manually. With full access to the computer, the attacker can give ordinary operating system commands to read any file on the computer, change files, delete them, or do anything else that a legitimate user with extensive permissions can do.

Test Your Understanding

10. a) List the three main phases in human break-ins (hacks). b) What is hacking? c) What are the two purposes of probe packets? d) What is an exploit? e) What steps does a hacker usually take immediately after a break-in? f) What software does the hacker download to help him or her do work after compromising a system? g) After breaking in, what does a hacker do to avoid being caught? h) What is a backdoor? i) What are the two types of backdoors?

Denial-of-Service (DoS) Attacks Using Bots

Another type of attack, the denial-of-service attack, does not involve breaking into a computer, infecting it with a virus, or infesting it with a worm. Rather, the goal of **denial-of-service (DoS)** attacks is to make a computer or entire network unavailable to its legitimate users.

The goal of denial-of-service (DoS) attacks is to make a computer or entire network unavailable to its legitimate users.

As Figure 3-7 shows, most DoS attacks involve flooding the victim computer with attack packets. The victim computer becomes so busy processing this flood of attack packets that it cannot process legitimate packets. The overloaded host may even fail.

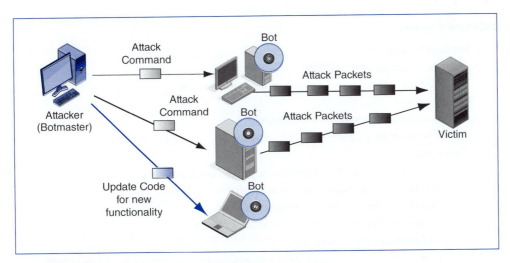

FIGURE 3-7 Distributed Denial-of-Service (DDoS) Attack Using Bots

More specifically, the attack shown in the figure is a **distributed DoS (DDoS)** attack. In this type of DoS attack, the attacker first installs programs called bots on hundreds or thousands of PCs or servers. When the user sends these bots an attack command, they all begin to flood the victim with packets.

Bots are not limited to DDoS attacks. **Bots** are general-purpose exploitation programs that can be remotely controlled after installation. As Figure 3-7 shows, the attacker can send attack commands to the bots and can even upgrade them remotely with new capabilities.

Bots are general-purpose exploitation programs that can be remotely controlled after installation and can even be upgraded remotely with new capabilities.

Bots are extremely dangerous because they can engage in massive attacks that were previously possible only with relatively dumb and inflexible viruses and worms. Through upgrades, bots bring the flexibility of human thought into the attack, making them very dangerous.

Test Your Understanding

11. a) What is the purpose of a denial-of-service attack? b) What are bots? c) What gives bots flexibility? d) How do distributed DoS attacks work?

TYPES OF ATTACKERS

The threat environment consists of types of attacks and types of attackers. As Figure 3-8 shows, there are many different types of attackers facing organizations today.

Traditional Attackers

    Traditional hackers
        Hackers break into computers
        Driven by curiosity, a desire for power, and peer reputation
    Malware writers
        It usually is not a crime to write malware
        It is almost always a crime to release malware
    Script kiddies
        Use attack scripts written by experienced hackers and virus writers
        Scripts usually are easy to use, with graphical user interfaces
        Script kiddies have limited knowledge and abilities
        But large numbers of script kiddies make them dangerous
    Disgruntled employees and ex-employees
        Have extensive access, knowledge of how systems work, and knowledge of how to avoid detection

Criminal Attackers

    Most attacks are now made by criminals
    Crime generates funds that criminal attackers need to increase attack sophistication
    Large and complex black markets for attack programs, attacks for hire services, bot rentals and sales, money laundering, and other activities

On the Horizon

    Cyberterror attacks by terrorists
    Cyberwar by nations
    Potential for massive attacks far larger than conventional attacks

FIGURE 3-8 Types of Attackers

Traditional Attackers

When most people think of attackers, they normally have three pictures in their minds: hackers driven by curiosity, virus writers, and disgruntled employees and ex-employees. Indeed, these used to be the three most important types of attackers.

HACKERS Traditionally, some **hackers** have been motivated primarily by curiosity and the sense of power they get from breaking into computers. In many cases, they are also motivated by a desire to increase their reputation among their hacker peers by boasting about their exploits. This typically is the image of hackers presented in Hollywood movies. However, these are not the typical hackers today.

MALWARE WRITERS **Malware writers**, as the name suggests, create malware. Malware writers appear to enjoy the excitement of seeing their programs spread rapidly. These malware writers tend to be blind to the harm that they do to people.

In most countries, including the United States, it generally is not illegal to *write* malware. These activities are protected under freedom of speech. However, *releasing* malware is illegal in nearly all countries.

SCRIPT KIDDIES Experienced hackers and virus writers often developed small programs, called **scripts**, to automate parts of their attacks. Over time, these programs grew more sophisticated. More importantly, they grew easier to use. Many now have graphical user interfaces and the look, feel, and reliability of commercial programs.

Some hackers and virus writers release or sell their scripts. This has led to the emergence of relatively nontechnical **script kiddie** attackers, who use these scripts developed by more experienced attackers. Although traditional attackers disparage script kiddies for their lack of skills, there are far more script kiddies than traditional hackers and virus writers, and script kiddies collectively represent a serious threat to corporations.

DISGRUNTLED EMPLOYEES AND EX-EMPLOYEES Other traditional types of attackers are **disgruntled employees** and **disgruntled ex-employees** who attack their own or their former firms. Employee attackers tend to do extensive damage when they strike because they typically already have access to systems, have broad knowledge of how the systems work, often know how to avoid detection, and tend to be trusted because they are part of the corporate "family."

The most dangerous employees of all are IT staff members and especially IT security staff members. They typically have far more access than other employees, have much better knowledge of corporate systems, and have extensive knowledge of how to avoid detection. In fact, they may even be in charge of identifying attackers. The ancient Roman question, "Quis custodiet ipsos custodes?" means "Who guards the guardians?" It is a serious question in security.

Criminal Attackers

Today, there are still many traditional attackers of the types we have just seen. However, even collectively they do not make up the majority of attackers today. Today, *most attackers are* **career criminals**, who steal credit card numbers to commit credit card fraud, who extort firms, and who steal trade secrets to sell to competitors.

Today, most *attackers are career criminals.*

Funded by their crimes, many criminals can afford to hire the best hackers and to enhance their own security-breaking skills. Consequently, criminal attacks are not just growing in numbers; they also are growing very rapidly in technical sophistication.

Cyberterrorists and National Governments

On the horizon is the danger of far more massive **cyberterror** attacks by terrorists and even worse **cyberwar** attacks by national governments. These could produce unprecedented damages in the hundreds of billions of dollars.

Cyberwar is not a theory. The United States has acknowledged that it has long had cyberwar capabilities, and it established a consolidated Cyberwar Command in

2009. It is clear that several other countries have these capabilities as well (especially China). Countries could use IT to do espionage to gather intelligence, conduct attacks on opponents' financial and power infrastructures, or destroy enemy command and control facilities during physical attacks.

A 2009 article in the *New York Times*[6] reported that before the 2003 invasion of Iraq, the United States considered an attack that would shut down Iraq's entire financial infrastructure. This attack was not approved, but this was not because it was unfeasible. It was not approved because its impact might have spread beyond Iraq and might even have damaged the U.S. financial system.

Cyberterror is also likely. During physical attacks, terrorists might disable communication systems to thwart first responders and to spread confusion and terror among the population. Cyberterrorists could also conduct purely IT-based attacks. While the United States was afraid of side effects of cyberwar attacks on Iraq, terrorists would have no such qualms.

Test Your Understanding

12. a) Are most attackers today driven by curiosity and a sense of power? b) Is it generally illegal to write malware? c) For what four reasons are employees dangerous? d) What are the most dangerous types of employees? e) What type of attacker are most attackers today? f) What are cyberterror and cyberwar attacks? g) Why are cyberwar and cyberterror serious security concerns?

PLANNING

Security Is a Management Issue

People tend to think of security as a technological issue, but security professionals agree unanimously that security is primarily a management issue. Unless a firm does excellent planning, implementation, and day-to-day execution, the best security technology will be wasted. As Bruce Schneier, a noted security expert, has often said, "Security is a process, not a product."[7] Unless firms have good security processes in place, the most technologically advanced security products will do little good.

Security is primarily a management issue, not a technology issue.

Test Your Understanding

13. Why is security primarily a management issue, not a technology issue?

Planning Principles

Perhaps more than any other aspect of IT, effective security depends on effective planning. Security planning is a complex process that we can discuss only briefly. We will note four key principles that must be used in planning.

---

[6]Markoff, John, and Shanker, Thom, " '03 Plan Displays Cyberwar Risk," *New York Times*, August 1, 2009. www.msnbc.msn.com/id/3032619/%2328368424.

[7]Schneier, Bruce, *Crypto-Gram Newsletter*, May 15, 2000. www.schneier.com/crypto-gram-0005.html.

Security Is a Management Issue, Not a Technical Issue

> Without good management, technology cannot be effective
>
> A company must have good security processes

Security Planning Principles

> Risk analysis
>> Risk analysis is the process of balancing threats and protection costs for individual assets
>>
>> Annual cost of protection should not exceed the expected damage
>>
>> If the probable annual damage is $10,000 and the annual cost is $200,000, the protection is not worth the cost
>>
>> Goal is not to eliminate risk but rather to reduce it in an economically rational level
>
> Comprehensive security
>> An attacker has to find only one weakness
>>
>> A firm needs comprehensive security to close all avenues of attack
>>
>> This requires very good planning
>
> Defense in depth
>> Every protection breaks down sometimes
>>
>> An attacker should have to break through several lines of defense to succeed
>>
>> Providing this protection is called defense in depth
>
> Minimal permissions
>> Access control is limiting who can use resources and limiting their permission while using resources
>>
>> Permissions are things they can do with the resource
>>
>> People should be given minimum permissions—the least they need to do their jobs—so that they cannot do unauthorized things

FIGURE 3-9   Security Planning (Study Figure)

RISK ANALYSIS   In contrast to military security, which often makes massive investments to stop threats, corporate security planners have to ask whether applying a countermeasure against a particular threat is economically justified. For example, if the probable annual loss due to the threat is $10,000 and the security measures needed to thwart the threat will cost $200,000 per year, the firm should not spend the money. Instead, it should accept the probable loss. **Risk analysis** is the process of balancing threats and protection costs for individual assets.

Risk analysis is the process of balancing threats and protection costs for individual assets.

Figure 3-10 shows a simple risk analysis. Without a countermeasure, the damage per successful attack is expected to be $1,000,000, and the annual probability of a successful attack is 20 percent. Therefore, the annual provable damage is $200,000 without a countermeasure. The net annual probable outlay therefore is $200,000.

Countermeasure A is designed to cut the seriousness of a successful attack in half. So the damage per successful attack is expected to be $500,000 instead of a million

Countermeasure	None	A
Damage per successful attack	$1,000,000	$500,000
Annual probability of a successful attack	20 percent	20 percent
Annual probable damage	$200,000	$100,000
Annual cost of countermeasure	$0	$20,000
Net annual probable outlay	$200,000	$120,000
Annual value of countermeasure	$0	$80,000

FIGURE 3-10 Risk Analysis Example

dollars. The countermeasure will not reduce the probability of a successful attack, so that continues to be 20 percent. With Countermeasure A, then, the annual probable damage is reduced to $100,000. However, the countermeasure is not free. It will cost $20,000 per year. So the net annual probable outlay is $120,000 with the countermeasure.

Countermeasure A, then, will reduce the net annual probable outlay from $200,000 to $120,000. The countermeasure has a value of $80,000 per year. This is positive, so Countermeasure A is justified economically.

Note that *the goal of security is not to eliminate risk*. That would be impossible. Despite efforts throughout human history, we still have theft, and we still have murder. Despite strong security efforts, in turn, there will still be some risk of a compromise. People with little to steal who live in gated communities with bars on their windows, expensive alarm systems, and a permanent armed security guard are not doing rational risk analysis. The goal of security is to reduce risk to a degree that is economically rational.

The goal of security is not to eliminate risk. The goal of security is to reduce risk to a degree that is economically rational.

COMPREHENSIVE SECURITY To be safe from attack, a company must close off *all* vectors of attack. In contrast, an attacker only needs to find one unprotected attack vector to succeed. Although it is difficult to achieve **comprehensive security**, in which all avenues of attack are closed off, it is essential to come as close as possible.

Comprehensive security is closing off all avenues of attack.

DEFENSE IN DEPTH Another critical planning principle is defense in depth. Every protection will break down occasionally. If attackers have to break through only one line of defense, they will succeed during these vulnerable periods. However, if an attacker has to break through two, three, or more lines of defense, the breakdown of a single defense technology will not be enough to allow the attacker to succeed. Having successive lines of defense that all must be breached for an attacker to succeed is called **defense in depth**.

Having several lines of defense that all must be breached for an attacker to succeed is called defense in depth.

MINIMUM PERMISSIONS IN ACCESS CONTROL   Security planners constantly worry about access to resources. People who get access to resources can do damage. Not surprisingly, companies work very hard to control access to their resources. **Access control** is limiting who may have access to each resource and limiting his or her permissions when using the resource.

Access control is limiting who may have access to each resource and limiting his or her permissions when using the resource.

One aspect of access control that we will see later is authentication, that is, requiring users requesting access to prove their identity. However, just because you know who someone is does not mean that he or she should have unfettered access to your resources. (There undoubtedly are several people you know who you would not let drive your car.)

Permissions are the actions that a person given access to a resource is allowed to take. For example, although everyone is permitted to view the U.S. Declaration of Independence, no one is allowed to add his or her own signature at the bottom.

Permissions are the actions that a person given access to a resource is allowed to take.

An important principle in assigning permissions is to give each person **minimum permissions**—the least permissions that the user needs to accomplish his or her job. In the case of access to team documents, for example, most team members may be given only read-only access, in which the user can read team documents but not change them. It is far less work to give the user extensive or full permissions so that he or she does not have to be given additional permissions later. However, it is not safe to do so.

Minimum permissions are the least permissions that the user needs to accomplish his or her job.

Test Your Understanding

14. a) List the four major planning principles. b) What is risk analysis? c) Repeat the risk analysis described in this section, this time with Countermeasure B that does not affect damage severity but that reduces the likelihood of an attack by 75 percent. The annual cost of Countermeasure B is $175,000. Show the full table. d) Comment on the statement, "The goal of security is to eliminate risk." e) What is comprehensive security? f) Why is comprehensive security important? g) What is defense in depth? h) Why is defense in depth necessary? i) What is access control? j) What are permissions? k) Why should people get minimum permissions?

Policy-Based Security

POLICIES The heart of security management is the creation and implementation of security policies. Figure 3-11 illustrates how policies should be used. **Policies** are broad statements that specify what should be accomplished. For example, a policy might be, "All information on USB RAM sticks should be encrypted."

Policies are broad statements of what should be accomplished.

POLICY VERSUS IMPLEMENTATION Note that the policy does not specify what encryption technology should be used or other implementation details. Put another way, policies describe *what* (should be done), not *how* (to do it).

Policies describe what (should be done), not how (to do it).

This separation of policy from implementation permits the implementers to implement the policy in the best way possible. Policymakers have the overview knowledge that operational people may not have. For instance, policymakers may know that new laws create serious liability unless USB RAM sticks are encrypted. However, people who do implementation are likely to know more about the specific technologies and the local situation than do policymakers. They have the specific knowledge that policymakers do not, including technical knowledge.

The separation of policy from implementation does not mean that policy is irrelevant to implementation. It is easy to get lost in implementation details. Having a clear

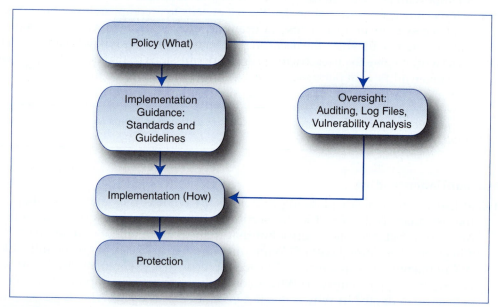

FIGURE 3-11 Policy-Based Security

policy permits everybody involved in implementation to stay synchronized by checking frequently whether what they are doing will lead to the successful implementation of the policy.

IMPLEMENTATION GUIDANCE   In many cases, the policymaker will only specify the policy. However, in some cases, the policymaker will also create some implementation guidance. **Implementation guidance** consists of instructions that are more specific than policies but less specific than implementation.

Implementation guidance consists of instructions that are more specific than policies but less specific than implementation.

For example, after establishing a policy that USB RAM sticks must be encrypted, implementation guidance might be added in the form of a directive that the encryption must be strong encryption. This ensures that implementers will not have the latitude to choose weak encryption that can be defeated by an attacker.

There are two general forms of implementation guidance: standards and guidelines. **Standards** are mandatory directives that *must* be followed. Requiring strong encryption is a standard. It is mandatory for implementers to follow the directive.

Standards are mandatory directives that must *be followed.*

In turn, **guidelines** are directives that *should* be followed but that need not be followed, depending on the context.[8] For example, a directive that security staff members should have three years of security work experience indicates that someone hiring a security staff member must consider that three years of experience is a good indicator of competence. If the person doing the hiring selects someone with only two years of work experience, it would be legitimate to ask the person doing the hiring if he or she felt that less than three years of work experience was acceptable. Following guidelines is optional, but seriously considering guidelines is mandatory.

Guidelines are directives that should *be followed but that need not be followed, depending on the context.*

OVERSIGHT   Figure 3-11 also shows that policymakers cannot merely toss policies and implementation guidance out and ignore how implementation is done. It is essential for management to exercise **oversight**, which is a collection of methods to ensure that policies have been implemented properly.

---

[8]In the *Pirates of the Caribbean* movies, there was a running joke that the Pirate's Code is "more like a guideline, really."

> *Oversight is a collection of methods to ensure that policies have been implemented properly.*

One form of oversight is an audit. An **audit** samples actions taken within the firm to ensure that policies are being implemented properly. Note that an audit only *samples* actions. It does not look at everything, which would be impossible to do. However, if the sampling is done well, the auditor can issue an opinion on whether a policy is being carried out appropriately based on well-considered data.

> *An audit samples actions taken within the firm to ensure that policies are being implemented properly.*

Another form of oversight is reading **log files**. Whenever users take actions, their actions should be recorded in log files. Reading log files can reveal improper behavior. Of course, if these log files are not read, they are useless. Consequently, it is critical to read log files frequently. Important log files should be read daily or even several times each day.

> *Reading log files can reveal improper behavior.*

Another important oversight mechanism is vulnerability testing. Simply put, **vulnerability testing** is attacking your own systems before attackers do, so that you can identify weaknesses and fix them before they are exploited by attackers.

> *Vulnerability testing is attacking your own systems before attackers do, so that you can identify weaknesses and fix them before they are exploited by attackers.*

Note that the policy drives both implementation and oversight. Implementers who attempt to implement the policy must interpret the policy. Auditors and other oversight professionals must also interpret the policy. If the implementers are lax, the auditors should be able to identify this. However, if oversight practitioners and implementers disagree, this may simply mean that they are interpreting the policy differently. Policymakers may find that one or the other has made a poor choice in interpreting the policy. They may also find that the policy itself is ambiguous or simply wrong. The important thing is to identify problems and then resolve them.

> *Policies drive both implementation and oversight.*

EFFECTIVE PROTECTION   Policies certainly do not give protection by themselves. Neither may unexamined implementations. Protection is most likely to be effective when excellent implementation is subject to strong oversight.

Test Your Understanding

15. a) What is a policy? b) Distinguish between policy and implementation. c) Why is it important to separate policies from implementation? d) Why is oversight important? e) Compare the specificity of policies, implementation guidance, and implementation. f) Distinguish between standards and guidelines. g) Must guidelines be considered? h) List the three types of oversight listed in the text. i) What is vulnerability testing, and why is it done? j) Why is it important for policy to drive both implementation and oversight?

AUTHENTICATION

The most complex element of access control is authentication. Figure 3-12 illustrates the main terminology and concepts in authentication. The user trying to prove his or her identity is the **supplicant**. The party requiring the supplicant to prove his or her identity is the **verifier**. The supplicant tries to prove his or her identity by providing **credentials** (proofs of identity) to the verifier.

The type of authentication tool that is used with each resource must be appropriate for the risks to that particular resource. Sensitive personnel information should be protected by very strong authentication methods. However, strong authentication is expensive and inconvenient. For relatively nonsensitive data, weaker but less expensive authentication methods may be sufficient. Strength of authentication, like everything else in security, is a matter of risk management.

Test Your Understanding

16. a) What is authentication? b) Distinguish between the supplicant and the verifier. c) What are credentials? d) Why must authentication be appropriate for risks to an asset?

Reusable Passwords

The most common authentication credential is the **reusable password**, which is a string of characters that a user types to gain access to the resources associated with a certain **username** (account) on a computer. These are called **reusable** passwords because the user will type the password each time he or she needs access to the resource. The reusable password is the weakest form of authentication, and it is appropriate only for the least sensitive assets.

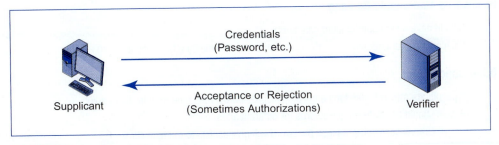

Credentials
(Password, etc.)

Acceptance or Rejection
(Sometimes Authorizations)

Supplicant

Verifier

FIGURE 3-12 Authentication

The reusable password is the weakest form of authentication, and it is appropriate only for the least sensitive assets.

EASE OF USE AND LOW COST The popularity of password authentication is hardly surprising. For users, passwords are familiar and relatively easy to use. For corporate IT departments, passwords add no additional cost because operating systems and many applications have built-in password authentication.

WORD/NAME PASSWORDS AND DICTIONARY ATTACKS The main problem with passwords is that most users pick very weak passwords.

The main problem with passwords is that most users pick very weak passwords.

For example, they often pick ordinary **dictionary words** or the **names** of family members, pets, sports teams, or celebrities. Dictionary-word and name passwords

---

Reusable Passwords

    Passwords are strings of characters
    They are typed to authenticate the use of a username (account) on a computer
    They are used repeatedly and so are called reusable passwords

Benefits

    Ease of use for users (familiar)
    Inexpensive because they are built into operating systems

Often Weak (Easy to Crack)

    Word and name passwords are common
    They can be cracked quickly with dictionary attacks

Passwords Should Be Complex

    Should mix case, digits, and other keyboard characters ($, #, etc.)
    Complex passwords can be cracked only with brute force attacks (trying all possibilities)

Passwords Also Should Be Long

    Should have a minimum of eight characters
    Each added character increases the brute force search time by a factor of about 70

Other Concerns

    If people are forced to use long and complex passwords, they tend to write them down
    People should use different passwords for different sites
        Otherwise, a compromised password will give access to multiple sites

FIGURE 3-13 Password Authentication (Study Figure)

often can be **cracked** (guessed) in a few seconds if the attacker can get a copy of the password file (which contains an encrypted list of account names and passwords). The attacker uses a **dictionary attack**, trying all words or names in a standard or customized dictionary. There are only a few thousand dictionary words and names in any language, so dictionary attacks can crack dictionary-word and name passwords almost instantly.

Dictionary attacks also have **hybrid modes**, in which they look for simple variations on words, such as a word with the first letter capitalized, followed by a single digit (e.g., Dog1). Hybrid word or name passwords are cracked almost as quickly as passwords made of simple words and names.

Names, words, and simple variants of words and names that can be cracked by hybrid mode dictionary attacks are never adequately strong, regardless of how long they are. They can always be cracked too quickly for safety.

Names, words, and simple variants of words and names that can be cracked by hybrid mode dictionary attacks are never adequately strong, regardless of how long they are.

COMPLEX PASSWORDS AND BRUTE FORCE ATTACKS Dictionary and hybrid dictionary attacks fail if passwords are more complex than dictionary words, names, and simple variations. Good complex passwords have all of the following:

- Lowercase letters.
- Uppercase letters, not simply at the start of the password.
- The digits from 0 to 9, not simply at the end of the password.
- Other keyboard symbols, such as & and #, which serve as swear words in cartoons—not simply at the end of the password.

Complex passwords can be cracked only by **brute force attacks** that try all possible combinations of characters. First, all combinations of a single character are tried, all combinations of two characters, all combinations of three characters, and so forth. Brute force attacks take far longer than dictionary attacks.

Unfortunately, complex passwords are difficult for users to remember, so they tend to write them on a sheet of paper that they keep next to their computers. This makes passwords easy to steal so that there is no need to crack them by dictionary or brute force attacks.

COMPLEX PASSWORD LENGTH Increasing **password length** (the number of characters in the password) makes a complex password stronger. If the password has a combination of uppercase and lowercase letters, digits, and other keyboard characters, then each additional character increases cracking time by a factor of about 70.

Given the speed of brute force cracking today, passwords should be complex and at least eight characters long to be considered adequate. Even longer passwords are highly desirable.

Only passwords that are complex and at least eight characters long should be considered to be adequately strong.

Test Your Understanding

17. a) Distinguish between usernames and reusable passwords. b) Why are passwords widely used? c) What types of passwords are susceptible to dictionary attacks? d) What types of passwords are susceptible to dictionary attacks in hybrid mode? e) Can a password that can be broken by a dictionary attack or a dictionary attack in hybrid mode be adequately strong if it is very long? f) What is a brute force attack? g) What types of passwords can be broken only by brute force attacks? h) Why is password length important? i) How long should passwords be?

18. Critique each of the following passwords. First, describe the type of attack that would be used to crack it, justifying your answer. Second, say whether or not it is of adequate strength, justifying your answer. a) velociraptor; b) Viper1; c) NeVeR; d) R7%t&.

Other Forms of Authentication

Companies are beginning to look for stronger types of authentication for most of their resources. This will allow them to replace most or all of their reusable password access systems. We have space to mention only the few types of authentication shown in Figure 3-14.

ACCESS CARDS   To get into your hotel room, you may have to swipe your **access card** through a card reader before being allowed through. For door and computer access, many companies also use these handy access cards, including **proximity access cards** that use radio signals and can be read with a simple tap against a reader. Companies need to control the distribution of access cards, and they need to rapidly disable any access card that has been lost or stolen.

BIOMETRICS   Access cards are easy to use, but if you lose your access card, you cannot get entry. In hotels, of course, you simply walk down to the front desk. They disable the code on your room card reader and give you a new card that will open your room. In corporate environments, the process takes a good deal longer.

In biometrics, in contrast, access control is granted based on something you always have with you—your body. **Biometrics** is the use of body measurements to authenticate you.

Biometrics is the use of body measurements to authenticate you.

There are several types of biometrics that differ in cost, precision, and susceptibility to deception by someone wishing to impersonate a legitimate user.

- At the low end on price, precision, and the ability to reject deception is **fingerprint scanning**, which looks at the loops, whorls, and ridges in your fingerprint. Although fingerprint scanning is not the strongest form of authentication, its low price makes it ideal for low-risk applications. Even for protecting laptop computers and smart phones, fingerprint scanning may be preferred to reusable passwords, given the tendency of people to pick poor passwords and forget them.

Perspective

Goal is to replace reusable passwords

Access Cards

Permit door access

Proximity access cards do not require scanning

Need to control distribution and disable lost or stolen access cards

Biometrics

Biometrics uses body measurements to authenticate you

Vary in cost, precision, and susceptibility to deception

Fingerprint scanning

Inexpensive but poor precision, deceivable

Sufficient for low-risk uses

On a notebook, may be better than requiring a reusable password

Iris scanning

Based on patters in the colored part of your eye

Expensive but precise and difficult to deceive

Facial scanning

Based on facial features

Controversial because can be done surreptitiously—without the supplicant's knowledge

Digital Certificate Authentication

Components

Everyone has a private key that only he or she knows

Everyone also has a public key that is not secret

Public keys are available in unalterable digital certificates

Digital certificates are provided by trusted certificate authorities

Operation

Supplicant does a calculation with his or her private key

Verifier checks this calculation with a public key in a digital certificate

Verifier uses the digital certificate of the true party—the person the supplicant claims to be

If the calculation check works, the supplicant must have the true party's private key, which only the true party should know. The supplicant must be the true party.

Two-Factor Authentication

Supplicant needs two forms of credentials

Example: debit card and pin

Strengthens authentication

Fails if attacker controls user's computer or intercepts authentication communication

FIGURE 3-14 Other Forms of Authentication

- At the high end of the scale on price, precision, and the ability to reject deception is **iris scanning**,[9] which looks at the pattern in the colored part of your eye. Although extremely precise, iris scanners are too expensive to use for computer access. They are normally used for access to sensitive rooms.
- One controversial form of biometrics is **facial scanning**, in which each individual is identified by his or her facial features. This is controversial because facial scanning can be done **surreptitiously**—without the knowledge of the person being scanned. This raises privacy issues.

DIGITAL CERTIFICATE AUTHENTICATION   The strongest form of authentication is digital certificate authentication. Figure 3-15 illustrates this form of authentication.

- In this form of authentication, each person has a secret **private key** that only he or she knows.
- Each person also has a **public key**, which anyone can know.
- A trusted organization called a **certificate authority** distributes the public key of a person in a document called a **digital certificate**. A digital certificate cannot be changed without this change being obvious.

First, the supplicant claims to be someone we will call the **true party**. To prove this claim, the supplicant does a calculation[10] with his or her private key and sends this calculation to the verifier.

Second, the verifier gets the true party's digital certificate, which contains the true party's public key. The verifier tests the calculation with the public key of the true party—the person the supplicant claims to be.[11] If the test works, then the supplicant must know the true party's private key, which only the true party should know. The supplicant must be the true party.

Note that the verifier uses the public key of the true party—not the supplicant's public key. If the verifier used the supplicant's public key, the test would always succeed—even if the supplicant is an impostor.

Note that the verifier uses the public key of the true party—not the supplicant's public key.

TWO-FACTOR AUTHENTICATION   Debit cards are potentially dangerous because if someone finds a lost debit card, the finder might be able to use it to make purchases. So possession of the debit card is not enough to use it. To use a debit card, the user must type a **personal identification number (PIN)**, which usually is four or six digits long. Requiring two credentials for authentication is called **two-factor authentication**. Two-factor authentication increases the strength of authentication.

---

[9]In science fiction movies, eye scanners are depicted as shining light into the supplicant's eye. This does not really happen. Iris scanners merely require the supplicant to look into a camera. In addition, science fiction movies use the term *retinal scanning*. The retina is the back part of the eye and has distinctive vein patterns. Retinal scanning is not used frequently because the supplicant must press his or her face against the scanner.

[10]To be more specific, the verifier sends the supplicant a challenge message that is a random stream of bits. The calculation that the supplicant does is to encrypt the challenge message with the supplicant's private key. The result is the response message, which the supplicant sends to the verifier.

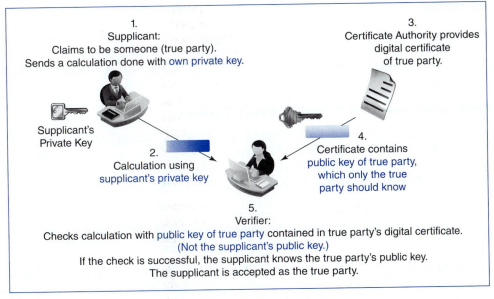

1.
Supplicant:
Claims to be someone (true party).
Sends a calculation done with own private key.

3.
Certificate Authority provides
digital certificate
of true party.

Supplicant's
Private Key

2.
Calculation using
supplicant's private key

4.
Certificate contains
public key of true party,
which only the true
party should know

5.
Verifier:
Checks calculation with public key of true party contained in true party's digital certificate.
(Not the supplicant's public key.)
If the check is successful, the supplicant knows the true party's public key.
The supplicant is accepted as the true party.

FIGURE 3-15   Digital Certificate Authentication

However, if a user's computer is compromised, the attacker typically controls both aspects of communication. Two-factor authentication may also break down if an eavesdropper can intercept authentication communication between the two parties.

Two-factor authentication requires two forms of authentication.

Test Your Understanding

19. a) What security problem do access cards have? b) What is biometrics? c) By what three criteria should biometric methods be judged? d) Why may fingerprint scanning be used to authenticate access to a laptop? e) Why is iris scanning desirable? f) Why is face recognition controversial?

20. a) In digital certificate authentication, what does the supplicant do? b) What does the verifier do? c) Does the verifier use the true party's public key or the supplicant's public key? d) How does the verifier get the public key? e) From what type of organization does the verifier get the digital certificate?

21. a) Why is two-factor authentication desirable? b) Will two-factor authentication still be strong if the attacker controls the supplicant's computer? c) Will two-factor authentication still be strong if the attacker can intercept all authentication communication?

---

[11]To be more specific, the verifier decrypts the response message with the true party's public key. If someone encrypts something with his or her private key, this can be decrypted with the true party's public key. If the supplicant is the true party, the true party's public key will decrypt the response message back to the challenge message. The supplicant will be authenticated as the true party. If the supplicant is an impostor, when the verifier decrypts the response message, the result will not be the challenge message that the verifier originally sent to the supplicant. The supplicant will then be rejected as an impostor.

FIREWALLS

In hostile military environments, travelers must pass through one or more checkpoints. At each checkpoint, their credentials will be examined. If the guard finds the credentials insufficient, the guard will stop the arriving person from proceeding and note the violation in a checkpoint log.

Dropping and Logging Provable Attack Packets

Figure 3-16 shows that firewalls operate in similar ways. Whenever a packet arrives, the **firewall** examines the packet. If the firewall identifies a packet as a **provable attack packet**, the firewall discards it. On the other hand, if the packet is not a provable attack packet, the firewall allows it to pass.

If a firewall identifies a packet as a provable attack packet, the firewall discards it.

The firewall copies information about the discarded packet into a **firewall log file**. Firewall managers should read their firewall log files every day to understand the types of attacks coming against the resources that the firewall is protecting.

Note that firewalls pass *all* packets that are not provable attack packets. Some attack packets will not be provable attack packets. Consequently, some attack packets inevitably get through the firewall to reach internal hosts. It is important to harden all internal hosts against attacks by adding firewalls, adding antivirus programs, installing all patches promptly, and taking other precautions. This chapter focuses on network security, rather than IT host security, so we will not consider host hardening.

Ingress and Egress Filtering

When most people think of firewalls, they think of filtering packets arriving at a network *from the outside*. Figure 3-16 illustrates this **ingress filtering**.

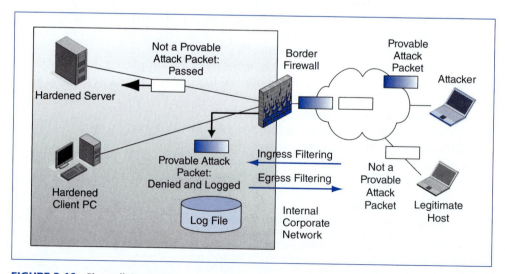

FIGURE 3-16   Firewall Operation

Most firms also do **egress filtering**, that is, they filter packets going from the network *to the outside*. By doing egress filtering, the corporation is acting as a good citizen, ensuring that its computers are not used in attacks against outside firms. Egress filtering also attempts to prevent sensitive corporate information from being sent outside the firm.

Test Your Understanding

22. a) What does a firewall do when a packet arrives? b) Does a firewall drop a packet if it probably is an attack packet? c) Why is it important to read firewall logs daily? d) Distinguish between ingress and egress filtering.

Static Packet Filtering

We have used the term *firewall filtering* up until now without explaining it. We did this because different firewalls use several different **filtering methods**. In this section, we will look at three: static packet filtering, stateful firewall filtering, and deep packet inspection.

Static packet filtering was the first type of filtering used by firewalls. As Figure 3-17 illustrates, static packet filter firewalls examine packets one at a time, in isolation. In addition, they look at only the internet and transport layer fields in the packet.

Despite these limits, static packet filtering can handle many types of packet attacks. For example, in Chapter 2, we saw that TCP segments that have their SYN bit set indicate that the sender wishes to open a connection. In Chapter 8, we will see that the sender sets the FIN bit in a TCP segment to indicate that it wishes to close a connection. Attackers soon discovered that if they set both the SYN bit and the FIN bit in the same segment, they could confuse the receiving transport layer process. Often, the receiving computer would crash. In Chapter 8, we will see that there are many fields in IP, TCP, and UDP headers. Static packet inspection firewalls look for any suspicious patterns in the contents of the field. They can also check for many other things; for instance, if a packet arrives from outside a site that has an address in the range restricted for IP addresses within the site, the static packet filter can drop the packet.

Unfortunately, examining single packets in isolation means that static packet filtering firewalls cannot detect many types of attack. For example, if an incoming

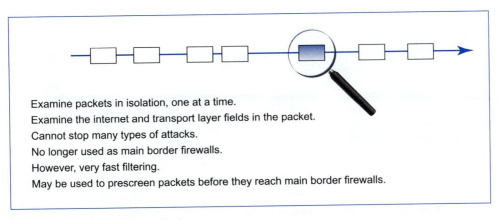

Examine packets in isolation, one at a time.
Examine the internet and transport layer fields in the packet.
Cannot stop many types of attacks.
No longer used as main border firewalls.
However, very fast filtering.
May be used to prescreen packets before they reach main border firewalls.

FIGURE 3-17 Static Packet Filtering

packet has its ACK bit set, this means that it is sending an acknowledgement for a TCP segment from the inside to the outside. However, the static packet filter cannot tell if this is a legitimate acknowledgment because it only examines the packet in isolation. It cannot tell if there was a previous outgoing packet to which this incoming packet is a legitimate acknowledgment.

As a consequence of not being able to stop many types of attacks, static packet filter firewalls are no longer used as main border firewalls in firms. However, static packet filtering is inexpensive to do, so some used static packet firewalls to screen out simple attacks before packets reach the main border firewall.

Test Your Understanding

23. a) What is the limitation of static packet filtering? b) Why is static packet filtering still done despite its weakness, and how is it used?

Stateful Packet Inspection (SPI) Firewalls

The most widely used *firewall filtering method* today is stateful firewall inspection, which treats different types of packets differently, spending the most resources on the most risky packets, which are relatively few, and spending less time on less risky packets.

STATES AND FILTERING INTENSITY When you talk with someone on the telephone, there are two basic stages to your conversation.

- At the beginning of a call, you need to identify the other party and decide whether you are both willing to have a conversation.
- Afterward, if you do decide to talk, you usually don't have to constantly worry about whether the conversation should go on with this person.

The key point here is that you do different things in different stages of a conversation. In the first stage, you have to pay careful attention to identifying the caller and making a decision about whether it is wise to talk. After that, you simply talk and normally do not have to spend much time thinking about whether to talk to the person.

Most firewalls today use **stateful packet inspection (SPI)** filtering, which uses the insight that there are also stages in network conversations and that not all stages require the same amount of firewall attention. At the simplest level, Figure 3-18 shows that

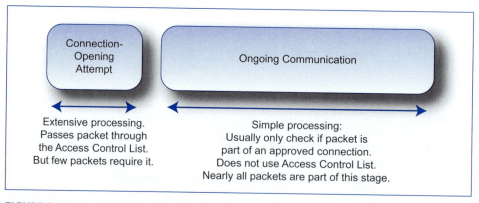

FIGURE 3-18 States in Stateful Packet Inspection (SPI)

Rule	Destination IP Address or Range	Service	Action
1	ALL	25	Allow connection
2	10.47.122.79	80	Allow connection
3	ALL	ALL	Do not allow connection

Note: ACLs are applied only to packets that attempt to open a connection.

FIGURE 3-19   Stateful Inspection Firewall Access Control List (ACL) for Connection-Opening Attempts

there are two stages, which SPI firewalls call **states**: opening a connection (conversation) and ongoing communication.

SPI FILTERING IN THE CONNECTION-OPENING STATE   SPI firewalls focus heavily on the opening state. They have complex rules to tell them whether or not to allow the conversation (connection). If they decide to allow a connection, however, they give minimal attention to packets in the ongoing communication state. This makes sense because the decision to allow a connection is the most complex and dangerous stage in the connection.

For example, suppose that a packet arriving at a firewall contains a TCP SYN segment. This clearly is a connection-opening request to the destination host. So the firewall compares the features of the packet to the rules in its **access control list (ACL)**. Figure 3-19 shows a very simplified access control list. This ACL has only three rules.

- Rule 1 allows connections to all hosts (all IP addresses) on Port 25. We saw in Chapter 2 that Port 25 is the well-known port number for SMTP. This rule permits connections to all internal mail servers.
- Rule 2 permits connections to a single internal host, 10.47.122.79, on Port 80. This rule allows access to a single internal webserver—the webserver at IP address 10.47.122.79. This is safer than Rule 1 because Rule 1 opens the firewall to *every* internal mail server, while Rule 2 opens the firewall only to connections to *a single* server.
- The last rule is the default rule for incoming packets that try to open a connection. (The default is what you get if you do not explicitly specify something else.) This last rule ensures that unless a packet is explicitly allowed by an earlier rule, it is dropped and logged.

Although ACL rules generally are not very complex, there tend to be many of them in real ACLs. Running each connection-opening attempt through the access control list can be fairly time consuming. Fortunately, only a very small percentage of all packets arriving at a firewall are connection-opening attempts.

HANDLING PACKETS DURING ONGOING COMMUNICATION   If a packet does not attempt to open a connection or is not part of a connection-opening attempt, then either the packet must be part of the ongoing communication state of an approved connection or the packet is spurious. When a packet that does not attempt to open a connection arrives, then the stateful firewall does the following (see Figure 3-20).

If the packet does not attempt to open a connection,

> Then if the packet is part of an established connection
>> It is passed without further inspection
>> (However, these packets can be given additional filtering if desired)
> Otherwise, it is dropped and logged

Nearly all packets are not part of connection-opening attempts

> This simplicity makes the cost of processing most packets minimal

---

FIGURE 3-20   Stateful Inspection for Packets That Do Not Attempt to Open a Connection

- If the packet is part of an established connection, it is passed without further inspection. (However, these packets can be further filtered if desired.)
- If the packet is not part of an established connection, then it must be spurious. It is dropped and logged.

These rules for ongoing communication are very simple to implement. Consequently, most packets are handled with very little processing power. This makes stateful firewalls very inexpensive.

PERSPECTIVE   Although the simple operation of stateful inspection makes it inexpensive, stateful filtering provides a great deal of protection against attacks coming from the outside. This combination of low cost and strong security is responsible for the dominance of stateful inspection today.

Test Your Understanding

24. a) Why are states important? b) Why are ACLs needed for stateful firewalls? c) When a packet that is part of an ongoing connection arrives at a stateful inspection firewall, what does the firewall usually do? d) When a packet that is not part of an ongoing connection and that does not attempt to open a connection arrives at a stateful inspection firewall, what does the firewall do? e) Why are stateful firewalls attractive? f) What type of firewalls do most corporations use for their main border firewalls?

25. a) How will an SPI firewall handle a packet containing a TCP segment which is an acknowledgement? b) How will an SPI firewall handle a packet containing a TCP SYN segment? c) How will an SPI firewall handle a packet containing a TCP FIN segment? d) How will the access control list (ACL) in Figure 3-19 handle a packet that attempt to open a connection to an FTP server? Explain.

Deep Inspection Firewalls

There is a relatively new type of firewall inspection method that we will call **deep inspection**. (Different vendors use different terminology.) Figure 3-21 shows that deep inspection firewalls do two things: they examine patterns in *streams* of packets and they look for attack patterns at all layers in a packet, including the application message.

Examine Streams of Messages

Stateful inspection firewalls know packet context (connection-opening or not) but still examine only individual packets.

Deep inspection firewalls look at streams of packets for patterns

For example, reconstruct application messages from TCP segments in different packets

Read All Packet Layers, Including Application Messages

Stateful packet inspection packets do not read application messages in detail

Deep inspection firewalls examine application messages in detail

This allows them to tell when a message to Port 80 is not an HTTP message

These may use Port 80 for illegal file sharing and other attacks

Some deep inspection packets are application-aware, allowing administrators to set up filtering rules for many specific applications

Intrusion Detection Systems (IDSs)

Deep inspection firewalls began as intrusion detection systems (IDSs)

Found suspicious patterns in traffic and notified the firewall administrators

Evolved to the point where there was enough confidence to let them actively stop traffic

Requires Extensive Processing Power

Far more than SPI

Made possible by application-specific integrated circuits (ASICs)

ASICs handle specific deep firewall inspection tasks in specialized hardware, which is very fast

This is finally making deep inspection feasible

FIGURE 3-21 Deep Inspection Firewalls

Although stateful packet inspection firewalls understand the context of each packet (whether or not the packet is a connection-opening attempt), they still only examine individual packets in detail. There are some attacks that are not discoverable unless the firewall can examine a stream of packets to pick out tell-tale patterns indicating that this is an attack stream. Most obviously, a large application message will be fragmented and transmitted in multiple packets. Unless the packets containing the application message fragments are combined, there is no way to discover malicious behavior in the application message. Deep inspection firewalls collect series of packets and analyze their contents as a group.

In addition, SPI firewalls do not read application messages.[12] Instead, they use server port number to be able to create filtering rules for certain applications. For example, a firm may allow all incoming packets with TCP segments with the destination port number 80. This allows all external connections to internal webservers. However, attackers know this, so they often use Port 80 for other purposes, such as illegal file

---

[12]This is a slight lie. They do look for certain things in application messages. For example, in voice over IP, a connection is set up on a particular port number. Once the connection is set up, the voice over IP gateway tells the VoIP client to switch to another port number. Stateful packet inspection firewalls look for such things and allow communicate over the new port number for the duration of the call. Deep inspection firewalls go far beyond such things.

sharing or communicating with bots. Deep inspection firewalls do not have this limitation. They examine the actual application messages in packets to identify the application. For many deep inspection firewalls, the firewall administrators can create filtering rules for individual applications, such as BitTorrent, which is often used for illegal file sharing. Firewalls that do this are called **application-aware firewalls**.

Even when deep inspection firewalls cannot tell beyond a reasonable doubt that a certain conversation is forbidden, they can often classify it as suspicious and warn firewall administrators about the traffic. Deep inspection firewalls that do this are called **intrusion detection systems (IDSs)**. In fact, deep inspection devices were first used exclusively as intrusion detection systems. It was only later that their capabilities were expanded so that they had enough sophistication to be allowed to stop conversations.

If deep inspection sounds expensive, it is. Deep inspection firewalls require far more processing power than stateful packet inspection. They have been feasible to use only recently, thanks to the evolution of application-specific integrated circuits (ASICs). In the past, firewalls had to use general-purpose microprocessors and write programs to do inspection. ASICs are designed for specific purposes, in this case for many deep inspection tasks. ASICs handle these tasks in hardware, which is much faster than handling them in software. This speed advantage has allowed deep inspection firewalls to be useful in many situations today.

Test Your Understanding

26. a) What two things do deep inspection firewalls do that SPI firewalls do not? b) Why is the first useful? c) Why is the second useful? d) What is an application-aware firewall, and how it useful? e) For what type of devices was deep inspection first used? f) What is the main problem with deep inspection firewalls? g) What technology is overcoming this problem, and how is it doing so?

PROTECTING DIALOGUES CRYPTOGRAPHY

We now continue our discussion of the protection phase in the plan–protect–respond cycle by looking at cryptographic protections for dialogues involving the exchange of many messages. Cryptography is the use of mathematics to protect dialogues.

Cryptography is the use of mathematics to protect dialogues.

Symmetric Key Encryption for Confidentiality

ENCRYPTION FOR CONFIDENTIALITY When most people think of cryptographic protection, they think of encryption for confidentiality, which Figure 3-22 illustrates. **Confidentiality** means that an eavesdropper intercepting the message will not be able to read it. The sender uses an encryption method, called a **cipher**, to create a message that an eavesdropper cannot read. However, the receiver **decrypts** the message in order to read it.

SYMMETRIC KEY ENCRYPTION Most encryption for confidentiality uses **symmetric key encryption** ciphers, in which the two sides use the same key to encrypt messages to each other and to decrypt incoming messages. As Figure 3-22 shows, symmetric key encryption ciphers use only a single key for encryption by Party A and decryption by

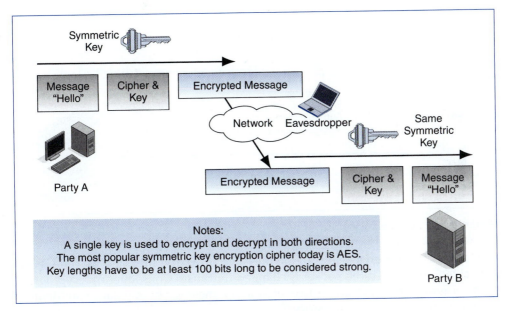

FIGURE 3-22 Symmetric Key Encryption for Confidentiality

Party B. When Party B sends to Party A, in turn, Party B uses the single key to encrypt, while Party A uses the single key to decrypt. The dominant symmetric key encryption cipher today is the **Advanced Encryption Cipher (AES)**.

KEY LENGTH Earlier, we looked at brute force password guessing. Symmetric and keys also can be guessed by the attacker's trying all possible keys. This is called **exhaustive search**. The way to defeat exhaustive key searches is to use long keys, which are merely binary strings. For symmetric key ciphers, symmetric key lengths of 100 bits or greater are considered to be strong. AES supports multiple strong key lengths up to 256 bits.

Keys are long strings of bits.

Test Your Understanding

27. a) What is a cipher? b) What protection does confidentiality provide? c) In two-way dialogues, how many keys are used in symmetric key encryption? d) What is the minimum size for symmetric keys to be considered strong?

Electronic Signatures

AUTHENTICATION AND MESSAGE INTEGRITY In addition to encrypting each packet for confidentiality, cryptographic systems normally add **electronic signatures** to each packet. This is illustrated in Figure 3-23. Electronic signatures are small bit strings that provide message-by-message authentication, much as people use signatures to authenticate individual written letters. An electronic signature allows the receiver to detect a message added to the dialogue by an impostor.

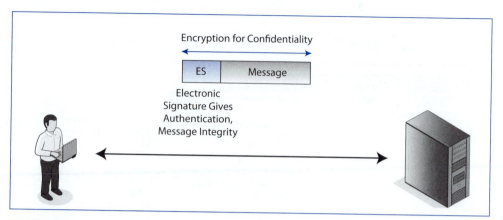

Encryption for Confidentiality

| ES | Message |

Electronic
Signature Gives
Authentication,
Message Integrity

FIGURE 3-23 Electronic Signature

Electronic signatures also provide **message integrity**, meaning that the receiver will be able to detect it if the packet is changed in transit. Consequently, cryptographic systems provide three protections to every packet: message-by-message confidentiality, authentication, and message integrity.[13]

Test Your Understanding

28. What two protections do electronic signatures provide?

RESPONDING

The last stage in the plan–protect–respond cycle is **responding**. Inevitably, some attacks will succeed and will require corrective action. **Response** is reacting to a security incident according to plan. The "according to plan" part is crucial. The amount of damage done in these compromises depends heavily on how quickly and how well the organization responds. Without strong and well-rehearsed response plans, response will take far too long and is likely to be less effective than it should be. For example, the case study at the end of this chapter shows that Walmart has a well-rehearsed response plan for natural disasters. In Hurricane Katrina, while the Federal Emergency Management Agency stumbled badly, Walmart responded quickly and effectively.

> *Response is reacting to a security incident according to plan.*

Stages

There are four general stages in responding to an attack.

DETECTING THE ATTACK The first stage is detecting the attack. Detection can be done by technology or simply by users reporting apparent problems. Obviously, until an attack is detected, the attacker will be able to continue doing damage. Companies need to develop strong procedures for identifying attacks quickly.

---

[13]There are two common types of electronic signatures—digital signatures and key-hashed message authentication codes. Many writers focus on digital signatures, but digital signatures are not very common because they are expensive to implement.

Stages

  Detecting the attack

  Stopping the attack

  Repairing the damage

  Punishing the attacker?

Major Attacks and CSIRTs

  Major incidents are those the on-duty staff cannot handle

  Computer security incident response team (CSIRT)

    Must include members of senior management, the firm's security staff, members of the IT staff, members of functional departments, and the firm's public relations and legal departments

Disasters and Disaster Recovery

  Natural and humanly-made disasters

  IT disaster recovery for IT

    Dedicated backup sites and transferring personnel

    Having two sites that mutually back up each other

  Business continuity recovery

    Getting the whole firm back in operation

    IT is only one player

Rehearsals

  Rehearsals are necessary for speed and accuracy in response

  Time literally is money

FIGURE 3-24 Incident Response (Study Figure)

STOPPING THE ATTACK The second stage is stopping the attack. The longer an attack has to get into the system, the more damage the hacker can do. Reconfiguring corporate firewall ACLs may be able to end the attack. In other cases, attack-specific actions will have to be taken.

REPAIRING THE DAMAGE The third stage is repairing the damage. In some cases, this is as simple as running a cleanup program or restoring files from backup tapes. In other cases, it may involve the reformatting of hard disk drives and the complete reinstallation of software and data.

PUNISHING THE ATTACKER? The fourth general stage is punishing the attacker, but this stage often is skipped. Punishing the attacker is relatively easy if the attacker is an employee. In general, however, attackers are extremely difficult to track down. Even if they are found, prosecution may be difficult or impossible.

  If legal prosecution is to be pursued, it is critical for the company to use proper forensic procedures to capture and retain data. **Forensic** procedures are ways to capture and safeguard data in ways that fit rules of evidence in court proceedings. These rules are very complex, and it is important for the firm to use certified forensics professionals. Even if an employee is fired, it is desirable for the company to use good forensic procedures to avoid a potential lawsuit.

Major Incidents and CSIRTs

Minor attacks can be handled by the on-duty IT and security staff. However, during **major incidents**, such as the theft of thousands of credit card numbers from a corporate host, the company must convene the firm's **computer security incident response team (CSIRT)**, which is trained to handle major incidents.

The key to creating CSIRTs is to have the right mix of talents and viewpoints. Major attacks affect large parts of the firm, so the CSIRT must include members of senior management, the firm's security staff, members of the IT staff, members of functional departments, and the firm's public relations and legal departments.

Disasters and Business Continuity

When natural disasters, terrorist attacks, or other catastrophes occur, the company's basic operations may be halted. This can be extremely expensive. Companies must have active disaster recovery plans to get their systems working quickly.

IT disaster recovery is the reestablishment of information technology operations. Many large firms have dedicated backup sites that can be put into operation very quickly, after data and employees have been moved to the backup site. Another option, if a firm has multiple server sites, is to do continuous data backup across sites. If one site fails, the other site can take over immediately or at least very rapidly.

More broadly, **business continuity recovery** goes beyond IT disasters to deal with events that affect enough of a firm to pause or stop the functioning of the business. IT security is only one player in business continuity recovery teams.

Rehearsals

"Practice makes perfect" is time-honored advice. It certainly is true for major attacks that must be handled by CSIRTs, and it is doubly true for disaster recovery. It is important for the company to establish CSIRT and disaster teams ahead of time and to have them rehearse how they will handle major attacks and disasters. Although practice does not really make perfect, it certainly improves response speed and quality. During the first two or three rehearsals, team members will work together awkwardly, and there will be many mistakes. Rehearsals will also reveal flaws in the company's major incident and disaster response plans. It is important to work through these problems before the firm is in a real crisis.

Test Your Understanding

29. a) What is the definition of response? b) What are the two benefits of a well-rehearsed response plan? c) What are the four response phases when attacks

occur? d) What is the purpose of forensic tools? e) Why are CSIRTs necessary? f) Should the CSIRT be limited to security staff personnel? g) Distinguish between disaster recovery and business continuity recovery. h) Explain how firms use backup sites in disaster recovery.

CONCLUSION

Synopsis

ATTACKS Companies today suffer compromises from many different types of attacks.

- Viruses attach themselves to other programs and need human actions to propagate, most commonly by users opening e-mail attachments that are infected programs. Worms are full programs; they can spread by e-mail, but directly propagating worms can propagate on their own, taking advantage of unpatched vulnerabilities in victim hosts. Some vulnerability-enabled worms can spread through the Internet host population with amazing speed. Many worms and viruses carry damaging payloads. Often, payloads place Trojan horse programs or other types of exploitation software on the victim computer. Malware is the general name for evil software.
- Viruses, worms, and Trojan horses are not the only attacks that are aimed at individuals. Spam deluges the victim with unsolicited commercial e-mail, and messages often are fraudulent. Spyware collects information about users and sends this information to an attacker. Phishing attacks use an official-looking e-mail message or website to trick users into divulging passwords and other special information. Attacks on individuals, including e-mail virus and worm attacks, often depend on social engineering—tricking the victim into doing something against his or her best interests. Two common goals of attacks on individuals are credit card number theft, in which a credit card number is stolen, and identity theft, in which enough private information is stolen to enable the attacker to impersonate the victim in large financial transactions.
- Hacking is the intentional use of a computer resource without authorization or in excess of authorization. Hacking break-ins typically require a prolonged series of probing actions on the part of the attacker.
- Denial-of-service (DoS) attacks overload victim servers so that they cannot serve users. Distributed DOS (DDoS) attacks use bots to carry out the attack. Bots can be updated to take on new functionality.

ATTACKERS Traditionally, most attackers were curiosity-driven hackers and disgruntled employees and ex-employees. Now, criminals dominate the attack world, and the money their crimes generate enables them to invest in new technology and hire top hackers. On the horizon, cyberterror attacks by terrorists and cyberwar attacks by national governments could do unprecedented levels of damage.

SECURITY MANAGEMENT Security is primarily a management issue, not a technical issue. Planning involves risk analysis (balancing the costs and benefits of protections), creating comprehensive security (closing all avenues of attack), using defense in depth (establishing successive lines of defense in case one line of defense fails), and access control using minimum permissions.

We looked at policy-based security in which a high-level policy group creates security policies and lower-level staff members implement the policy. Policies specify what (is to be done). Implementation focuses on how (to do it). This division of labor works because high-level policy people have a broad understanding of security risks and must create policies that will give comprehensive security. Implementation is done by lower-level staff members who know the technology and local situation in detail. Sometimes, the policy group creates intermediate implementation guidance consisting of standards (which must be followed) and guidelines that must be considered, although they do not have to be followed if there is good reason not to.

CONTROL AND AUTHENTICATION Firms need to control access to their assets. Access control normally requires authentication—proving the identity of the person wishing access. The person requesting access is the supplicant, and the device requiring proof of identity is the verifier. The supplicant sends credentials to the verifier to prove the supplicant's identity. For consistency, a central authentication server is used to do the credential checking. There are several common authentication technologies.

- Passwords are inexpensive and easy to use, but users typically choose poor passwords that are easy to crack. Passwords should be used only for low-sensitivity resources.
- Access cards are often used for door entry.
- Biometrics promises to use bodily measurements to authenticate supplicants, replacing other forms of authentication. Concerns with biometrics include cost, error rates, and the effectiveness of deliberate deception by supplicants.
- Digital certificate authentication at the other extreme gives the strongest authentication, but it is complex and expensive to implement.

FIREWALLS Firewalls examine packets passing through the firewall. If a firewall finds provable attack packets, it drops them and records information about them in a log file. If a packet is not a provable attack packet—even if it really is an attack packet—the firewall will not drop it. Ingress filtering examines packets coming into the firm; egress filtering examines packets going out of the firm.

Most firewalls use stateful inspection, which divides communication into stages called states. During the risky connection-opening state, the firewall does extensive work to decide whether to allow connections by passing packets attempting to open a connection. This requires examining every connection-opening packet against rules in an access control list (ACL).

If a packet that does not attempt to open a connection arrives, then it is checked against allowed connections. If it is part of an approved connection, it is passed—usually with little or no additional filtering. If the packet that does not try to open a connection is not part of an approved connection, it is dropped.

Stateful packet inspection firewalls give strong security during the connection-opening state. This is processing intensive, but few packets are parts of connection-opening attempts. For most packets, SPI firewalls do simple inspection, which requires little processing power.

CRYPTOGRAPHIC SYSTEMS Cryptography is the use of mathematics to protect message dialogues. One key protection is encryption for confidentiality, which encrypts messages to prevent attackers from reading any messages that they intercept. Encryption methods are called ciphers. In symmetric key encryption, both sides encrypt and decrypt with a single key. To be strong, a symmetric encryption key needs to be more than 100 bits long.

In addition to providing message-by-message encryption, cryptographic systems also provide message-by-message authentication by adding an electronic signature to each message. Electronic signatures also give message integrity.

Cryptographic protections are organized into cryptographic system standards. SSL/TLS provides medium-strength protection; it is built into all browsers and web-servers. IPsec is a very strong cryptographic system standard. It protects IP packets and encapsulated transport layer and application layer messages.

RESPONSE Protections occasionally break down. Response is reacting to compromises according to plan. The stages in response to attack typically include identifying the attack, stopping the attack, recovering from the attack, and (sometimes) punishing the attacker. Major incidents require the convening of a computer security incident response team (CSIRT). IT disaster recovery requires getting IT back in operation at another site, while business continuity recovery involves getting the entire firm back in operation. It is important for recovery teams to conduct rehearsals before problems occur so that they can respond quickly and correctly.

END-OF-CHAPTER QUESTIONS

Thought Questions

1. a) Suppose that an attack would do $100,000 in damage and has a 15 percent annual probability of success. Spending $9,000 per year on "Measure A" would cut the annual probability of success by 75 percent. Do a risk analysis comparing benefits and costs. Show your work clearly. b) Should the company spend the money? Explain. c) Do another risk analysis if Measure A costs $20,000 per year. Again, show your work. d) Should the company spend the money? Explain.

2. a) What form of authentication would you recommend for relatively unimportant resources? Justify your answer. b) What form of authentication would you recommend for your most sensitive resources?

3. For each of the following passwords, first state the kind of attack that would be necessary to crack it. Justify your answer. Then say whether or not it is an adequate password, again giving specific reasons. a) swordfish; b) Processing1; c) SeAtTLe; d) 3R%t; and e) 4h*6tU9$^l.

4. Keys and passwords must be long. Yet most personal identification numbers (PINs) that you type when you use a debit card are only four or six characters long. Yet this is safe. Why?

5. Revise the ACL in Figure 3-18 to permit access to an FTP server with IP address 10.32.67.112.

6. In digital certificate authentication, the supplicant could impersonate the true party by doing the calculation with the true party's private key. What prevents impostors from doing this?

Online Exercise

1. Go to http://www.cybercrime.gov. Go to the section on computer crimes. Select one of the cases randomly. Describe the type of attacker and the type of attack(s).

Case Study: Patco

In 2009, the Patco Construction Company had $588,000 drained from its bank accounts at Ocean Bank. The theft involved six withdrawals on May 8, May 11, May 12, May 13, May 14, and May 15. The money in each withdrawal was sent to a group of money mules.

After thieves stole all of the company's cash, they continued to make withdrawals. Patco's bank continued to allow withdrawals, covering them with over $200,000 from Patco's line of credit. Although the bank was able to re-cover or block $243,406 in transfers, Patco was still out $345,400. In addition, the bank began charging Patco for interest on the money that had been withdrawn using Patco's line of credit.

Although the transactions were far larger than Patco normally made, Ocean Bank did not inform Patco of any problems until one of the account numbers entered by the thieves was invalid. It sent a notification by mail, and it did not arrive at Patco until several days later. Patco notified the bank of problems the next morning. However, the bank had already sent out $111,963 that day, some of which was recovered.

The bank used account numbers and passwords. For transactions over $1,000, Patco employees had to answer two challenge questions. Most withdrawals were over $1,000, so employees had to answer these same challenge questions many times. Patco believes that these challenge messages were too easy.

The State of Maine has stringent banking laws. The Federal Financial Institutions Examination Council in 2005 required banks to use at least two-factor authentication and specifically noted that usernames and passwords were not enough. Patco sued People's United Bank for its losses, claiming that the challenge questions were nothing more than a second set of passwords and that the bank should have required much stronger credentials.

Patco also claimed that Ocean Bank should have been suspicious when such large unprecedented withdrawals were made and when they were sent to 30 different accounts. Normally, Patco only withdrew money for payrolls on Fridays. Its previous largest single-day withdrawal had been under $37,000. Patco's complaint stated that based on belief and information from the bank, Patco assumed that antifraud monitoring was being done by the bank.

Ocean Bank did not comment on the case, but most banks in a similar situation use the defense that they were not negligent. A bank can be found negligent only if it has lower protections than are the norm in the industry.

CAUTION: The information in this case is based only on Patco's complaint.[14] Consequently, the statements made in the case have not been validated and may be disputed by Ocean Bank as being nonfactual. Analyze the case based on Patco's allegations, but do not draw firm conclusions against the bank.

1. a) According to the information in the case, do you think the bank satisfied the requirement to use two-factor authentication? b) According to the information in the case, do you think the bank was doing antifraud monitoring? c) According to the information in the case, do you think Ocean Bank was negligent? d) According to the information in the case, if you were the head of Ocean Bank, what would you do to prevent the reoccurrence of this problem?

Case Study: Walmart

In 2005, Hurricane Katrina slammed into Louisiana and Mississippi, devastating New Orleans and many other cities along the U.S. Gulf Coast. Shortly afterward, the fourth most intense Atlantic hurricane in history, Rita, added enormously to the destruction. The Federal Emergency Management Agency (FEMA) became notorious for its handling of the crisis, responding belatedly and acting ineptly when it did respond.

Many businesses collapsed because they were poorly prepared for the hurricanes. One company that *did* respond effectively was Walmart.[15] In its Brookhaven, Mississippi, distribution center, the company had 45 trucks loaded and ready for delivery even before Katrina made landfall. The company soon supplied $20 million in cash donations, 100,000 free meals, and 1,900 truckloads full of diapers, toothbrushes, and other emergency supplies to relief centers. The company also supplied flashlights, batteries, ammunition, protective gear, and meals to police and relief workers.

Although the relief effort was impressive, it was merely the visible tip of Walmart's disaster recovery program. Two days before Katrina hit, Walmart activated its business continuity center. Soon, 50 managers and experts in specific areas such as trucking were hard at work. Just before the storm knocked out the company's computer network, the center ordered the Mississippi distribution center to send out recovery merchandise such as bleach and mops to its stores. The company also sent 40 generators to its stores so that stores that lost power could open to serve their customers. It also sent out many security employees to protect stores.

After computer networks failed, the company relied on the telephone to contact its stores and other key constituencies. Most stores came back immediately, and almost all stores were able to serve their customers within a few days. Lines of customers were long, and Walmart engaged local law enforcement to help maintain order.

Walmart was successful because of intensive preparation. The company has a full-time director of business continuity. It also has detailed business continuity plans and clear lines

[14]*Patco Construction Company, Inc., plaintiff, v. People's United Bank*, d/b/a Ocean Bank, defendant. State of Maine, York SS Superior Court Civil Action, Docket No. 09-CV.

[15]Liza Featherstone, "Wal-Mart to the Rescue!" *The Nation*, September 26, 2005. www.thenation.com/doc/20050926/featherstone. Michael Barbaro and Justin Gillis, "Wal-Mart at Forefront of Hurricane Relief," *Washington Post.com*, September 6, 2005. www.washingtonpost.com/wp-dyn/content/article/2005/09/05/AR2005090501598.html. *NewsMax.com*, "Wal-Mart Praised for Hurricane Katrina Response Efforts," www.newsmax.com/archives/ic/2005/9/6/164525.shtml. Ann Zimmerman and Valerie Bauerlein, "At Wal-Mart, Emergency Plan has Big Payoff," *Wall Street Journal*, September 12, 2005, B1.

of responsibility. In fact, while the company was still responding to Katrina and Rita, it was monitoring a hurricane off Japan, preparing to take action there if necessary.

1. a) Why was Walmart able to respond quickly? b) List at least three actions that Walmart took that you might not have thought of.

Perspective Questions

1. What was the most surprising thing you learned in this chapter?

2. What was the most difficult part of this chapter for you?

4 | NETWORK MANAGEMENT

LEARNING OBJECTIVES

By the end of this chapter, you should be able to:

- Explain general concepts in network management, including a focus on the system life cycle, the importance of cost, and strategic network planning.
- Use quality-of-service (QoS) criteria in product selection.
- Do basic design work, including doing traffic analysis with and without redundancy, knowing common topologies, selecting topologies, understanding how to handle momentary traffic peaks, understanding how to reduce capacity needs through traffic shaping and compression, and topologies.
- Evaluate alternatives using multicriteria decision making and specifying costs.
- Describe operational management, including OAM&P, the Simple Network Management Protocol (SNMP), and network management software.

INTRODUCTION

Today, we can build much larger networks than we can manage easily. For example, even a mid-size bank is likely to have 500 Ethernet switches and a similar number of routers. Furthermore, network devices and their users are spread out over large areas—sometimes international areas. While network technology is exciting to talk about and concrete conceptually, network management is where the rubber meets the road.

SDLC versus SLC

In programming and database courses, you focus on the systems development life cycle (SDLC), which looks at your information system from its moment of conception to its implementation. When you think about this, it is rather strange. Teaching the SDLC is like training new doctors in obstetrics and ignoring all training for illnesses after birth. Although the SDLC discusses episodic software maintenance activities, Figure 4-1 shows that the SDLC is far more limited than the **systems life cycle (SLC)**, which lasts from conception until death.

In networking, the creation of new networks and the modification of old networks are important, but the real work of networking professionals is the administration of ongoing networks. While systems administrators who manage servers have a difficult

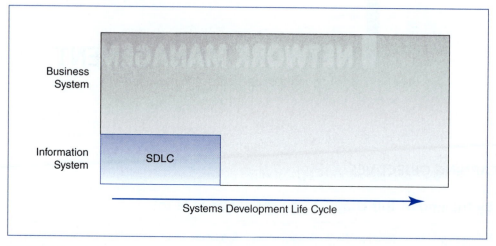

FIGURE 4-1   The Systems Development Life Cycle versus Business Systems and the Systems Life Cycle

job, especially in today's world of virtualization, network administrators face very complex tasks that require a high level of understanding of how networks work. The operational phase of a network after its creation is an enormous part of the network professional's job.

Figure 4-1 also shows that while database and programming professionals have to focus on the information system, the network professional often has to focus on the broader business system in which the information system is embedded. This is particularly true in network security.

Test Your Understanding

1. a) Why must networking professionals be concerned with the SLC rather than the SDLC? b) Why is a focus on information systems insufficient in networking?

Cost

In networking, you can never say, "Cost doesn't matter." Figure 4-2 illustrates that network demand is likely to grow rapidly in the future, just as it has always done in the past. The figure also illustrates that network budgets are growing very slowly (if they are growing at all).

Taken together, these curves mean that network budgets are always stretched thin. If the network staff spends too much money on one project, it will not have enough money left over to do another important project. Although there are many concerns beyond costs, cost is always an important consideration in network management.

Test Your Understanding

2. a) Compare trends in network demand and network budgets. b) What are the implications of these trends?

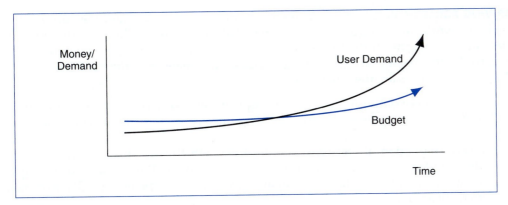

FIGURE 4-2   Network Demand and Budget

Strategic Network Planning

One of the most important things to plan in networking is the technological infrastructure—the firm's arrangement of hardware, software, and transmission lines that allows the network to carry information. Figure 4-3 shows how organizations do strategic network planning.

WHAT-IS ANALYSIS   Planning for changes in the technological infrastructure must begin with the "what is," that is, the current state of the company's network. This may sound like an easy task, but most firms do not have a thorough understanding of their network components and interactions, much less of their trouble spots. What-is analysis begins with an exhaustive inventory of the network's components and their interrelationships. This sounds simple. It is not.

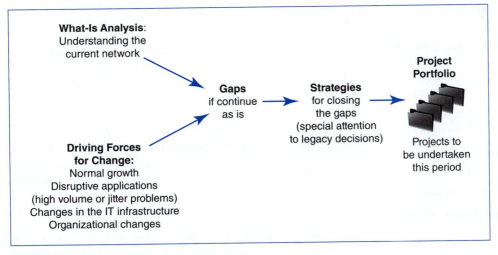

FIGURE 4-3   Strategic Network Planning

DRIVING FORCES FOR CHANGE While it is important to understand the current state of the network, companies must remember that today's technological infrastructure will not be sufficient for the future because many things will change. Companies need to consider the major driving forces that will require changes in the network. Some of these driving forces are the following:

- The normal continuing growth of application traffic demand. In most firms, traffic has been growing at an increasing rate. This will certainly continue in the future.
- The introduction of disruptive applications, which may create major surges in demand far beyond traditional patterns. Voice over IP is an obvious example. However, if video applications begin to grow, capacity planning will become extremely difficult.
- Changes in other elements of the IT technological infrastructure can also require extensive network changes. One long-term trend has been the consolidation of data centers from many to few. This can radically change traffic flows within the corporate network.
- Organizational change can be a major driving force. If a company is adding a site, not only will the site have to be served but communication between different parts of the firm will change, depending on what units are moved there. In fact, all corporate reorganizations are likely to impact network planning. At the extreme are nightmare scenarios that exist if the company is bought out or buys out another firm.

GAPS ANALYSIS Comparing driving forces to the what-is network will create inevitable gaps between what the firm will need and what the current network can provide. These gaps must be identified, characterized, and documented.

STRATEGIES FOR CLOSING THE GAPS The firm then needs to develop strategies for closing the gaps. It must consider multiple technologies and multiple topologies (physical connections) for each gap.

SELECTING A PROJECT PORTFOLIO The network staff will not have the budget to close all gaps satisfactorily. So it is critical for the networking staff to be very selective in how it spends its money. The final stage in strategic planning is to create a **project portfolio**—a selection of projects that the firm will implement during the plan's initial period.

A strong consideration for any project is whether it involves **legacy decisions** that will lock the company into a specific vendor or technology option for several years. Making legacy decisions is not wrong. In fact, making a legacy decision is often necessary. However, because of its implications for the firm, companies need to give special scrutiny to potential projects that require legacy decisions.

Test Your Understanding

3. a) What is what-is analysis? b) List the four driving forces for change. c) For each, give an example not listed in the text. d) What is gaps analysis? e) Why is it

necessary to create a project portfolio? f) What are legacy decisions, and why must projects that involve legacy decisions be judged with great care?

NETWORK QUALITY OF SERVICE (QoS)

In the early days of the ARPANET and the Internet, networked applications amazed new users. However, these users soon said, "Too bad this thing doesn't work better." Today, networking is a mission-critical service for corporations. If the network breaks down, much of the organization comes to a halt. Today, networks must work, and they must work *well*. Companies are concerned with network **quality-of-service (QoS) metrics**, that is, quantitative measures of network performance. Figure 4-4 shows that companies typically use a number of QoS metrics to quantify their quality of service so that they can set targets and determine if they have met those targets.

Test Your Understanding

4. a) What are QoS metrics? (Do not just spell out the acronym.) b) How are QoS metrics used?

Transmission Speed

There are many ways to measure how well a network is working. The most fundamental metric, as we saw in Chapter 1, is speed. While low speeds are fine for text messages, the need for speed becomes very high as large volumes of data must be sent, and video transmission requires extremely high transmission speed.

BITS PER SECOND (BPS) As we saw in Chapter 1, transmission speed[1] normally is measured in bits per second (bps). A bit is either a one or a zero. Obviously, a single bit

---

Quality of Service (QoS) Metric

> Quantifiable measures of network performance

Examples

> Speed
> Availability
> Error rates
> ...

FIGURE 4-4 Network Quality of Service (QoS)

---

[1]Purists correctly point out that *speed* is the wrong word to use to describe transmission rates. At faster transmission rates, bits do not physically travel faster. The sender merely transmits more bits in each second. Transmission rates are like talking faster, not running faster. However, transmission rates are called transmission speeds almost universally, so we will follow that practice in this book.

cannot convey much information. Speeds today range from thousands of bits per second to billions of bits per second. To simplify the writing of transmission speeds, professionals add metric prefixes to the base unit, bps. For example, Figure 4-5 shows that in increasing factors of 1,000 (not 1,024 as with computer memory), we have kilobits per second (kbps), megabits per second (Mbps), gigabits per second (Gbps), and terabits per second (Tbps).

Speeds are measured in factors of 1,000, not 1,024.

Consistent with metric notation, kilo is abbreviated as lowercase k instead of uppercase K. However, megabits per second is Mbps, gigabits per second is Gbps, and terabits per second is Tbps.

Speed

Normally measured in bits per second (bps)
    Not bytes per second
    Metric suffixed in increasing units of 1,000 (not 1,024)
    The metric abbreviation for kilo is lowercase k

Abbreviation	Meaning	Name	Example
1 kbps	1,000 bps	kilobits per second	33 kbps is 33,000 bps
1 Mbps	1,000 kbps	megabits per second	3.4 Mbps is 3,400,000 bps
1 Gbps	1,000 Mbps	gigabits per second	62 Gbps is 62,000,000,000 bps
1 Tbps	1,000 Gbps	terabits per second	

Sometimes speed is measured in bytes per second, Bps, compared to bps
    Bps usually only for file transfers

Expressing Speed in Proper Notation

As Written	Places before Decimal Point	Space between Number and Suffix?	Properly Written
23.72 Mbps	2	Yes	23.72 Mbps
2,300 Mbps	4	No	2.3 Gbps
0.5 Mbps	0 (leading zeros do not count)	No	500 kbps

There must be one to three spaces before the decimal point
    Leading zeros do not count

(continued)

FIGURE 4-5 Transmission Speed

There must be a space between the number and the units

> 12 Mbps is proper; 12Mbps is improper

If the number is decreased by 1,000 (4,523 becomes 4.523), then the suffix must be increased by a thousand (kbps to Mbps)

> 4,523 kbps becomes 4.523 Mbps
>
> (4,523/1000 * kbps * 1000)

If the number is increased by 1,000 (0.45 becomes 450), then the suffix must be decreased by 1,000 (Mbps to kbps)

> 0.45 Mbps becomes 450 kbps

Rated Speed and Throughput

Rated Speed

> The speed a system *should* achieve
>
> According to vendor claims or to the standard that defines the technology

Throughput

> The data transmission speed a system *actually* provides to users

Aggregate versus Rated Throughput on Shared Lines

> The aggregate throughput is the total throughput available to all users
>
> The individual throughput is an individual's share of the aggregate throughput

FIGURE 4-5 Continued

WRITING NUMBERS IN PROPER NOTATION Networking professionals write speeds in a very specific way. The basic rule for writing speeds (and metric numbers in general) in proper notation is that there should be one to three places before the decimal point and that there should be a space between the number and the units. Figure 4-5 illustrates how to write speeds properly.

To write a speed in proper notation, there should be one to three places before the decimal point, and there should be a space between the number and the units.

- Given this rule, 23.72 Mbps is fine (two places before the decimal point and a space between the number and the metric prefix).
- However, 2,300Mbps has four places before the decimal point (2,300.00), so it should be rewritten as 2.3 Gbps (one place). Note that a space has been added between the number and its metric prefix. In turn, 0.5 Mbps has zero places to the left of the decimal point. (Leading zeros do not count.) It should be written as 500 kbps (three places).

When you look at a number in metric notation, remember that if a=b*c, then a also equals b*1000*c/1000 or b/1000*b*1000. Think of the metric prefix k as 1,000 and the metric prefix M as 1,000,000.

Suppose you have the speed 4,523 kbps. To write the number properly, you divide it by 1,000 to get 4.523. If you divide the number by 1,000, then you must multiply the prefix by 1,000. Multiplying kbps by 1,000 gives Mbps, so the number in proper notation becomes 4.523 Mbps.

To give another example, suppose you have 0.45 Mbps. You need to multiply the number by 1,000, getting 450. You then have to divide the prefix (Mbps) by 1,000 to give you kbps. The number in proper notation, then, is 450 kbps.

RATED SPEED VERSUS THROUGHPUT

> **NOTE:** Some students find the distinction between rated speed and throughput difficult to learn. However, we must use this distinction throughout this book, so be sure to take the time to understand it.

Talking about transmission speed can be tricky. A network's **rated speed** is the speed it *should* achieve based on vendor claims or on the standard that defines the technology. For a number of reasons, networks often fail to deliver data at their rated speeds. In contrast to rated speed, a network's **throughput** is the data transmission speed the network *actually* provides to users.

> *Throughput is the data transmission speed a network* actually *provides to users.*

AGGREGATE VERSUS INDIVIDUAL THROUGHPUT   When a transmission line on a network is multiplexed, this means that several conversations between users will share the line's throughput. Consequently, it is important to distinguish between a line's **aggregate throughput**, which is the total it provides to all users who share it, and the **individual throughput** that single users receive as their shares of the aggregate throughput. As you learned as a child, despite what your mother said, sharing is bad.

Test Your Understanding

5. a) In what units is transmission speed normally measured? b) Is speed normally measured in bits per second or bytes per second? c) Give the names and abbreviations for speeds in increasing factors of 1,000. d) What is 55,000,000,000 bps with a metric prefix? e) Write out 100 kbps in bits per second (without a metric prefix). f) Write the following speeds properly: 0.067 Mbps, 23,000 kbps, and 48.62Gbps.
6. a) Distinguish between rated speed and throughput. b) Distinguish between individual and aggregate throughput.

Other Quality-of-Service Metrics

Although network speed is important, it is not enough to provide good quality of service. We will look briefly at other important QoS metric categories.

AVAILABILITY   One of these other metrics is **availability**, which is the percentage of time that the network is available for use. In contrast, **downtime** is the percentage of time that the network is not available.

Ideally, systems would be available 100 percent of the time, but that is impossible in reality. On the Public Switched Telephone Network, the availability target usually is

Availability

The percentage of time a network is available for use

Downtime is the amount of time a network is unavailable (minutes, hours, days, etc.)

Error Rates

Require retransmissions

When an error occurs, TCP assumes there is congestion and slows its rate of transmission

Packet error rate: The percentage of packets that have errors

Bit error rate: The percentage of packets that have error

Latency and Jitter

Latency

Delay, measured in milliseconds

Jitter (Figure 4-7)

Variation in latency between successive packets

Makes voice sound jittery

Application Response Time

The time from when the user hits a key and when the system responds. (Figure 4-8)

Includes the two-way network latency

Includes contributions from the host or application program

Often, configuration problems produce application response time problems

Improvement requires cooperation between networking and host administration

Service Level Agreements

Guarantees for performance

Penalties if the network does not meet its service metrics guarantees

Guarantees specify worst cases (no worse than)

Lowest speed (e.g., no worse than 1 Mbps)

Maximum latency (e.g., no more than 125 ms)

Often written on a percentage basis

No worse than 100 Mbps 99.5% of the time

FIGURE 4-6 Quality of Service II (Study Figure)

99.999 percent. This is known as the "five nines." Data networks generally have lower availability but are under pressure to improve their availability given the cost of network downtime to firms today.[2]

---

[2]On a more detailed basis, availability can be discussed in terms of the mean time to failure (MTTF) and the mean time to repair (MTTR). The former asks how frequently downtime occurs. The latter asks how long service is down after a failure begins. More short failures may be preferable to infrequent but very long outages.

ERROR RATES   Hosts send data in small messages called packets. Ideally, all packets would arrive intact, but this does not always happen. The **packet error rate** is the percentage of packets that are lost or damaged during delivery. The **bit error rate**, in turn, is the percentage of bits that are lost or damaged.

Most networks today have very low average error rates. However, when the network is overloaded, error rates can soar because the network has to drop the packets it cannot handle. Companies must measure error rates when traffic levels are high in order to have a good understanding of error rate risks.

The impact of even small error rates can be surprising. TCP is designed to avoid network congestion by generating TCP segments slowly at the beginning of a connection. If the segments arrive correctly, TCP generates segments more quickly. However, if there is an error or if an acknowledgment is lost, the TCP process assumes that the network is overloaded. It falls back to its initial slow start rate for creating TCP segments. Consequently, even a small error rate can produce a major drop in throughput for applications.

LATENCY AND JITTER   When packets move through the network, they will encounter some delays. The amount of delay is called **latency**. Latency is measured in **milliseconds (ms)**. A millisecond is a thousandth of a second. When latency reaches about 125 milliseconds, turn-taking in telephone conversations becomes difficult.

A related concept is **jitter**, which Figure 4-7 illustrates. Jitter occurs when the latency between successive packets varies. Some packets will come too far apart in time, others too close in time. While jitter does not bother most applications, VoIP and streaming media are highly sensitive to jitter. If the sound is played back without adjustment, it will speed up and slow down. These variations often occur over millisecond time periods, and, as the name suggests, variable latency tends to make voice sound jittery.

Most networks were engineered to carry traditional data such as e-mail and database transmissions. In traditional applications, latency was only slightly important, and jitter was not important at all. However, as voice over IP and video over IP, which are sensitive to jitter and to some extent latency, have grown in importance, companies have begun to worry more about latency and jitter. They are finding that extensive network redesign may be needed to give good control over latency and jitter. This may include fork-lift upgrades for many of its switches and routers.

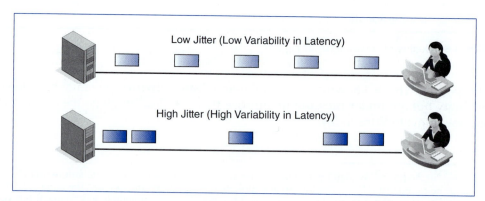

FIGURE 4-7   Jitter

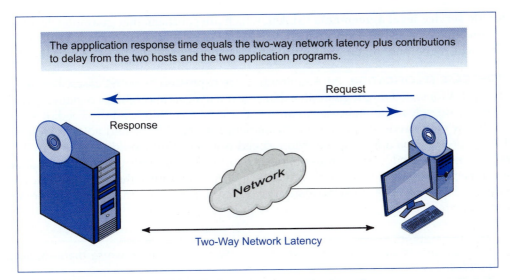

The appplication response time equals the two-way network latency plus contributions to delay from the two hosts and the two application programs.

Request

Response

Network

Two-Way Network Latency

FIGURE 4-8   Application Response Time

APPLICATION RESPONSE TIME   The most challenging QoS metric is **application response time**. This is the duration between the time the user presses a key (or clicks on the page) and the time he or she sees a response. Figure 4-8 shows how application response time is different from network latency.

The figure shows that network latency is only one factor in user response time. Most obviously, the delay at the client and server ends to do processing in the application software is important. However, there can be many other factors in response time. For example, poorly configured networking software in the client or server operating system may add delay. So may firewall filtering, the need for encryption (which is a heavy process), and other security matters.

Application response time planning and execution are complicated by the fact that systems administrators and application professionals often work separately from network professionals. In fact, they often know little about what the other side does. Application response time management requires strong and effective cooperation across these organizational boundaries.

Test Your Understanding

7. a) What is availability? b) What is downtime? c) What are the "five nines"? d) Does corporate network availability usually meet the five-nines expectation of the telephone network? e) What are packets? f) Distinguish between the packet error rate and the bit error rate. g) When should error rates be measured? Why? h) What is latency? i) In what units is latency measured? j) What is jitter? k) For what applications is jitter a problem? l) How does application response time differ from latency? m) Why is application response time difficult to improve?

Service Level Agreements (SLAs)

When you buy some products, you receive a guarantee promising that they will work and specifying penalties if they do not work. In networks, service providers often provide **service level agreements (SLAs)**, which are contracts that guarantee levels of performance for various metrics such as speed and availability. If a service does not meet its SLA guarantees, the service provider must pay a penalty to its customers.

WORST-CASE SPECIFICATION   SLA guarantees are expressed as **worst cases**. For example, an SLA for speed might guarantee that speed will be *no lower* than a certain amount. If you are downloading webpages, you want at least a certain level of speed. If speed falls below your needs, that is a service violation. You certainly would not want a speed SLA to specify a maximum speed. More speed is good. Why would you want to limit the maximum speed? Many students have a difficult time with worst-case thinking. This is because speed is good, so they want the SLA to guarantee them high speed. That is not the SLA's job. SLA is like an insurance policy. It guarantees that speed will not fall below a certain level.

SLA guarantees are expressed as worst cases. *Service will be no worse than a specific number.*

For latency, then, the SLA will require that latency will be *no higher* than a certain value. You might specify an SLA guarantee of 125 ms (milliseconds). This means that you will not get worse latency.

PERCENTAGE-OF-TIME ELEMENTS   In addition, SLAs have percentage-of-time elements. For instance, an SLA on speed might guarantee a speed of at least 480 Mbps 99.9 percent of the time. This means that the speed will nearly always be at least 480 Mbps but may fall below that 0.1 percent of the time without incurring penalties. A smaller exception percentage might be attractive to users, but it would require a more expensive network design. Nothing can be guaranteed to work properly 100 percent of the time.

Test Your Understanding

8. a) What are service level agreements? b) Does an SLA measure the best case or the worst case? c) Would an SLA specify highest latency or lowest latency? d) Would an SLA specify a lowest availability or a highest availability? e) What happens if a carrier does not meet its SLA guarantee? f) If carrier speed falls below its guaranteed speed in an SLA, under what circumstances will the carrier not have to pay a penalty to the customers?

DESIGN

Implementing a network project requires a company to go through all phases of the systems development life cycle. In most cases, these stages are similar to those for other IT projects. One special area in the SDLC is the design of a new network or of a modified network.

Traffic Analysis

Network design always begins with traffic requirements. In network design, traffic analysis asks how much traffic must flow over the network's many individual

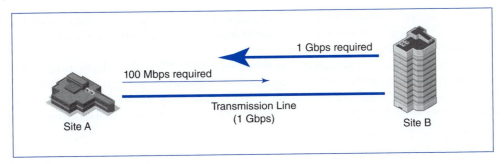

FIGURE 4-9 Two-Site Traffic Analysis

transmission lines. Figure 4-9 shows a trivial traffic analysis. A company only has two sites, A and B. A needs to be able to transmit to B at 100 Mbps. B needs to transmit to A at 1 Gbps. Transmission lines usually are symmetric, meaning that they have the same speed in both directions. Obviously, the company must install a transmission line that can handle 1 Gbps.

As soon as the number of sites becomes larger than two, traffic analysis becomes difficult. Figure 4-10 shows a three-site traffic analysis. For simplicity, we will assume that transmission is symmetric between each pair of sites.

The figure shows that Site Q attaches to Site R, which attaches to Site S. Site Q is 130 meters west of Site R. Site S is 180 meters east of Site R. Site Q needs to be able to communicate with Site R at 45 Mbps. Site R needs to be able to communicate with Site S at 2 Gbps. Site Q needs to be able to communicate with Site S at 300 Mbps.

Are you confused by the last paragraph? Anyone would be. In traffic analysis, it is critical to DTP—draw the picture. Figure 4-10 shows how the three sites are laid out. After laying out the sites, you draw the three required traffic flows.

Note that the line between Q and R must handle both Q–R traffic (45 Mbps) and the Q–S traffic (300 Mbps). It does not handle any of the traffic between R and S, however. Consequently, the line between Q and R must be able to handle 345 Mbps.

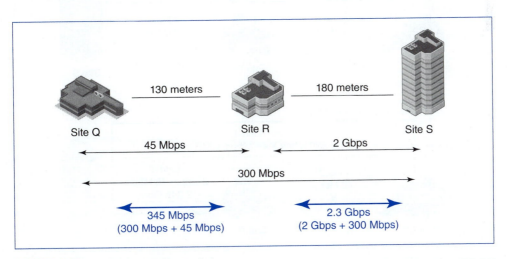

FIGURE 4-10 Three-Site Traffic Analysis

Similarly, the line between R and S must be able to handle R–S traffic (2 Gbps) and Q–S traffic (300 Mbps). This means that the transmission line between R and S must be able to handle 2.3 Gbps.

If a company has many sites rather than just two or three, then doing traffic analysis manually becomes impossible. Companies use simulation programs that determine what site pair traffic will flow over what transmission lines. However, you need to understand what the program is doing, and the way to do that is to work through a few examples with only a few sites.

Test Your Understanding

9. Do a three-site traffic analysis. Site X attaches to Site Y, which attaches to Site Z. Site X is 130 meters east of Site Y. Site Z is 180 meters west of Site Y. Site X needs to be able to communicate with Site Y at 3 Gbps. Site Y needs to be able to communicate with Site Z at 1 Gbps. Site X needs to be able to communicate with Site Z at 700 Mbps. Supply your picture giving the analysis. You may want to do this in Office Visio or Windows Draw and then paste it into your homework. a) What traffic capacity will you need between Sites X and Y? b) Between Y and Z?

Redundancy

Transmission lines sometimes fail. Suppose that the transmission line between R and S in Figure 4-10 failed. Then Q would still be able to talk to R, but Q and R would not be able to talk to S. Obviously, this is highly undesirable.

The solution is to install redundant transmission lines. Redundant transmission lines are extra transmission lines that are not necessary for the system to function but that provide backup paths in case another line fails. For example, Figure 4-11 again shows Sites Q, R, and S. This time, a redundant line has been added between Q and R.

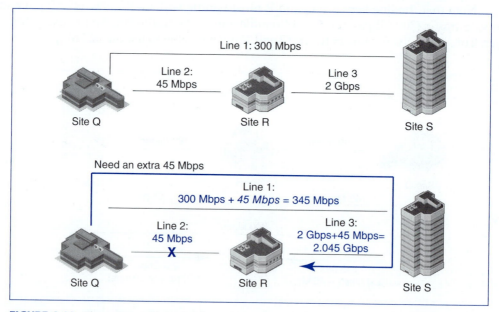

FIGURE 4-11   Three Sites with Redundancy

What happens if the line between Q and R fails? The answer is that Site Q can still talk to Site S through the direct line. Also, Q can still talk to R by sending its transmissions to S, which will send them on to R.

When redundancy is used, lines must be given extra capacity in case of failures. For instance, if the line between Q and R is only 300 Mbps, this will be enough if there are no failures. However, if the line Q–R fails, the line will need another 45 Mbps. So it will need to have 345 Mbps of capacity to handle a Q–R failure. The R–S line will also need 45 Mbps more capacity. It will need 2.045 Gbps of capacity to handle both R–S traffic and Q–R traffic.

Test Your Understanding

10. a) What is the purpose of redundancy in transmission lines? b) If the line between R and S fails in Figure 4-11, how much capacity will the line between Q and S need? c) What about the line between Q and R?

Topology

Network design focuses heavily on network topology. The term **network topology** refers to the physical arrangement of a network's computers, switches, routers, and transmission lines. Topology, then, is a physical layer concept. Different network (and internet) standards specify different physical topologies. Figure 4-12 shows the major "basic" topologies specified by network standards. Real networks often have complex topologies that involve a mixture of these basic topologies.

Network topology is the physical arrangement of a network's computers, switches, routers, and transmission lines. It is a physical layer concept.

POINT-TO-POINT TOPOLOGY   The simplest network topology is the **point-to-point topology**, in which two nodes are connected directly. Although some might say that a point-to-point connection is not a network, companies often connect a pair of sites with a point-to-point private leased line provided by a telephone carrier.

STAR TOPOLOGY AND EXTENDED STAR (HIERARCHY) TOPOLOGY   Modern versions of Ethernet, which is the dominant LAN standard, use the star and extended star topologies. In a simple **star topology**, all wires connect to a single switch. In an **extended star (or hierarchy) topology**, there are multiple layers of switches organized in a hierarchy. We will see Ethernet hierarchies in Chapter 5. An important characteristic of hierarchical standards is that there is only a single possible path between any two end nodes.

MESH TOPOLOGY   In a **mesh topology**, there are many connections among switches or routers, so there are many alternative paths to get from one end of the network to the other. The TCP/IP standards are designed for a mesh router topology.

BUS (BROADCAST) TOPOLOGIES   In a **bus topology**, when a computer transmits, it broadcasts to all other computers. Wireless LANs and WANs, which we will see in Chapters 6 and 7, broadcast their signals and so have bus topologies.

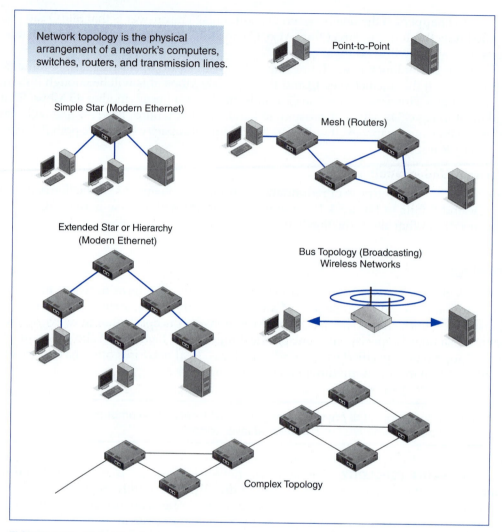

Network topology is the physical arrangement of a network's computers, switches, routers, and transmission lines.

Point-to-Point

Simple Star (Modern Ethernet)

Mesh (Routers)

Extended Star or Hierarchy (Modern Ethernet)

Bus Topology (Broadcasting) Wireless Networks

Complex Topology

FIGURE 4-12 Major Topologies

REAL NETWORK TOPOLOGIES Some network technologies require a pure basic taxonomy. For example, the Ethernet technology we will see in Chapter 5 requires a strict hierarchy. Most networks, however, have **complex topologies** that use different basic topologies in different parts of the network.

Test Your Understanding

11. a) What is a network topology? b) At what layer do we find topologies? c) In what topology are there only two nodes? d) In what topologies is there only a single path between any two end nodes? e) In what topology are there usually many paths between any two end nodes? f) In what topology is broadcasting used? g) What topologies can be used in complex networks?

Leased Line Network Topologies

Figure 4-13 shows that companies have traditionally used leased lines to interconnect their sites. As we will discuss in Chapter 10, leased lines are high-speed, point-to-point, always-on carrier circuits. Because the telephone system only provides raw bandwidth between points, the company must design the overall data network.

FULL-MESH TOPOLOGY   Should many or all pairs of sites be connected to each other, or should there be as few connections as possible? Figure 4-13 shows two topological extremes for building leased line networks.

The first is a **full-mesh topology**, which provides direct connections between every pair of sites. This provides many redundant paths so that if one site or leased line fails, communication can continue unimpeded.

Unfortunately, as the number of sites increases, the cost of a full mesh grows exponentially. For example, if there are N sites, a pure mesh will require $N * (N - 1)/2$ leased lines. So a 5-site pure mesh will require $5 * (5 - 1)/2(10)$ leased lines, a 10-site pure mesh will require 45 leased lines, and a 20-site pure mesh will require 190 leased lines. Full meshes, while reliable, are prohibitively expensive if a company has many sites.

HUB-AND-SPOKE LEASED LINE NETWORKS   The second extreme topology for building leased line networks is the pure **hub-and-spoke topology**. Figure 4-13 also shows this topology. In a pure hub-and-spoke topology, all communication goes through one site. This dramatically reduces the number of leased lines required to connect all sites compared to a full mesh, and so this kind of topology minimizes cost. However, it also reduces reliability. If a line fails, there are no alternative paths for reaching an affected site. More disastrously, if the hub site fails, the entire network goes down.

MIXED DESIGNS   As you might suspect, full meshes and pure hub-and-spoke topologies represent the extremes of cost and reliability. Most real networks use a mix of these two pure topologies. Real networks must trade off reliability against cost.

Test Your Understanding

12. a) What is the advantage of a full-mesh leased line network? b) What is the disadvantage? c) What is the advantage of a pure hub-and-spoke leased line network? d) What is the disadvantage? e) Do most leased line networks use a full-mesh or a pure hub-and-spoke topology? Explain.

13. A company has three sites: Micah, Mallory, and William. Micah and Mallory need 100 Mbps of transmission capacity between them. Mallory and William need 200 Mbps of transmission capacity between them. Micah and William need 300 Mbps of transmission capacity between them. a) Create a hub-and-spoke network with Micah as the hub. What links will there be, and how fast will they need to be? Explain your reasoning. b) For the same situation, create a full-mesh network. What speeds will the links need to have if you are not concerned with redundancy in case of line failure? Explain your reasoning. c) Building on the last part of this question, add redundancy so that a failure of the line between Mallory and William will not bring down the network. (Hint: DTP.)

Full Mesh Topology

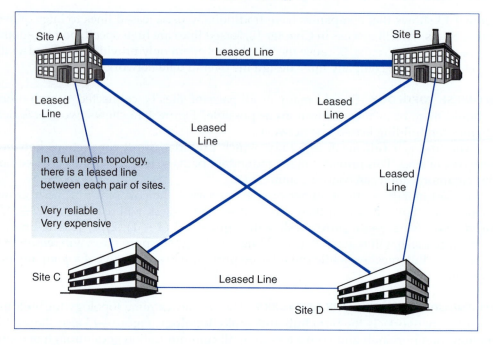

Pure Hub-and-Spoke Topology

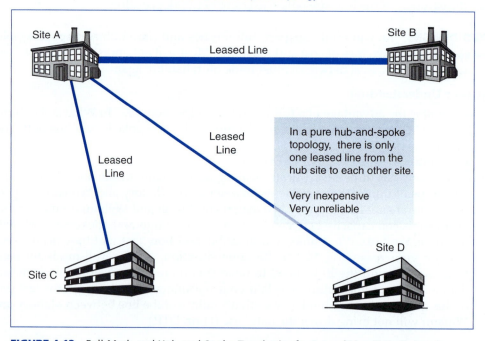

FIGURE 4-13 Full-Mesh and Hub-and-Spoke Topologies for Leased Line Data Networks

Handling Momentary Traffic Peaks

One fact of networking life that can never be ignored in designs is that traffic volume varies widely. Peak periods of traffic can overwhelm the network's switches and transmission lines. Given the statistical nature and high variability of traffic, **momentary traffic peaks** lasting a fraction of a second to a few seconds are bound to occur, and a firm must have a plan for managing momentary traffic peaks. Corporations can use several traditional traffic management methods to respond to momentary traffic peaks, as Figure 4-14 shows. Network planners must select which approach to use in the corporate network or in different parts of the corporate network.

OVERPROVISIONING   One approach is overprovisioning—adding much more switching and transmission line capacity than will be needed most of the time. With overprovisioning, it will be very rare for momentary traffic peaks to exceed capacity. This means that no regular ongoing management is required. The downside of overprovisioning, of course, is that it is wasteful of capacity. Today, the simplicity of overprovisioning and the relatively low cost of overprovisioning on LANs make overprovisioning attractive

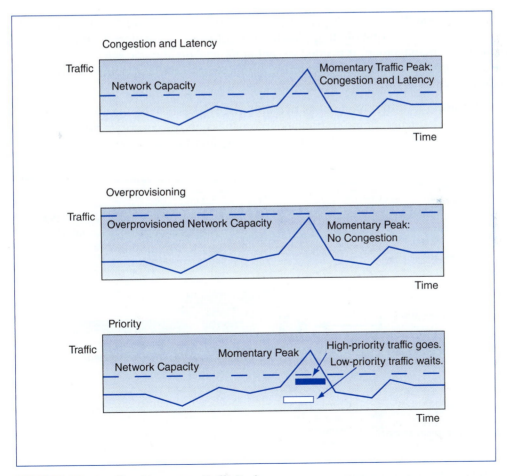

FIGURE 4-14   Handling Momentary Traffic Peaks

on LANs. On WANs, however, where the cost per bit transmitted is very high, overprovisioning is too expensive to consider.

PRIORITY   Priority, in turn, assigns high priority to latency-intolerant applications, such as voice, while giving low priority to latency-tolerant applications, such as e-mail. Whenever congestion occurs, high-priority traffic is sent through without delay. Low-priority traffic must wait until the momentary congestion clears. Priority allows the company to work with lower capacity than overprovisioning but requires more management labor.

QoS GUARANTEES   Quality-of-service guarantees take a step beyond priority, reserving capacity on each switch and transmission line for certain types of traffic. This allows the firm to satisfy QoS service level agreements for selected traffic by providing guarantees for minimum throughput, maximum latency, and even maximum jitter.

QoS guarantees require extremely active management. In addition, traffic with no QoS guarantees gets only whatever capacity is left over after reservations. This may be too little, even for latency-tolerant traffic.

TRAFFIC SHAPING   Even with priority and overprovisioning, sufficient capacity must be provided for the total of all applications apart from momentary traffic peaks. Even more active management is needed to *control the amount of traffic entering the network in the first place*. Restricting traffic entering the network at access points is called **traffic shaping**, which is shown in Figure 4-15.

Filtering   Traffic shaping has two options. The first is *filtering* out unwanted traffic at access switches. Some traffic has no business on the corporate network, such as downloading MP3 and video files, game playing, and illegal file sharing.

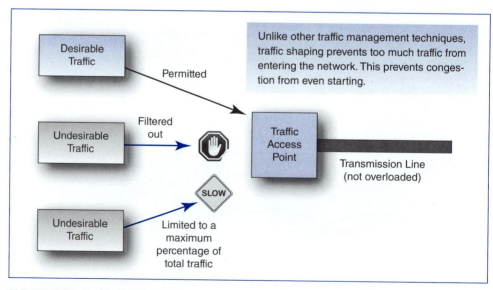

FIGURE 4-15 Traffic Shaping

Capacity Percentages   The second option in traffic shaping is to assign certain **percentages of capacity** to certain applications arriving at access switches. Even if file sharing has legitimate uses within a firm, for instance, the firm may wish to restrict the amount of capacity that file sharing can use. Typically, each application or application category is given a maximum percentage of the network's capacity. If that application attempts to use more than its share of capacity, incoming frames containing the application messages will be rejected.

Perspective on Traffic Shaping   Overprovisioning, priority, and QoS guarantees merely attempt to deal with incoming traffic. Traffic shaping actually reduces the amount of incoming traffic. Only traffic shaping can dramatically reduce network cost.

Although traffic shaping is very economical in terms of transmission capacity, it is highly labor intensive. It is used today primarily on high-cost WAN links. However, as management software costs fall in price and require less labor to operate, traffic shaping should see increasing use.

Another issue that arises when traffic shaping is used is politics. Telling a department that its traffic will be filtered out or limited in volume is not a good way to make friends. Priority and QoS reservations also raise political problems, but in traffic shaping, these problems are particularly bad.

Test Your Understanding

14. a) How long are momentary traffic peaks? b) Distinguish between overprovisioning and priority. c) Distinguish between priority and QoS guarantees. d) What problem can QoS create? e) How is traffic shaping different from traditional approaches to handling momentary traffic overloads? f) In what two ways can traffic shaping reduce traffic?

Reducing Capacity Needs

We have just looked at the design implications of momentary traffic peaks, which usually last only a fraction of a second. More generally, we would like to reduce the overall traffic the network must carry. This would reduce the cost of network services directly.

TRAFFIC SHAPING   Traffic shaping is not just a tool for dealing with momentary traffic peaks. By eliminating some types of traffic entirely and by limiting other types of traffic to small percentages of total network traffic, traffic shaping can substantially reduce the overall traffic a network must handle at all times.

COMPRESSION   Another way to reduce traffic is to compress traffic before it enters a network. **Compression** exploits redundancy in data to recode the data into fewer bits. This means fewer bits to transmit. At the other end, the traffic must be decompressed to put it back in its original form. To give a rough analogy, dehydrated food with water removed is much lighter than normal food. Adding water later reconstitutes the dehydrated food.

Figure 4-16 shows there are two incoming data streams. The first is 3 Gbps. The second is 5 Gbps. This is a total of 8 Gbps. The capacity of the transmission line is only 1 Gbps. We have a problem.

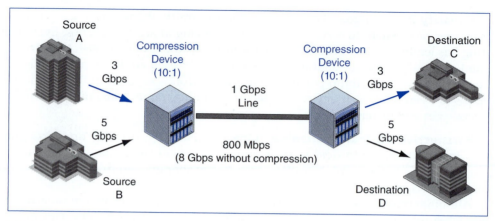

FIGURE 4-16 Compression

Before the incoming data enters the transmission line, however, the data will be compressed by 10:1, which is often possible for typical data streams. This reduces the compressed data streams to 0.3 Gbps (300 Mbps) and 0.5 Gbps (500 Mbps), for a total of only 800 Mbps. This traffic can easily fit on a 1 Gbps line with ample room for other traffic.

At the other end, another device decompresses the data streams. It sends the 3 Gbps data stream to one destination and the 5 Gbps data stream to another destination.

One requirement for compression is that you must have compatible equipment at the two ends of the network. Given a frequent lack of vendor compatibility, compression tends to lock the company into a single vendor's products.

Test Your Understanding

15. a) Why is traffic shaping a more general tool than just being a way to handle momentary traffic peaks? b) Why can compression help in traffic management? c) What makes compression possible?

Natural Designs

We have been discussing general design principles. In many cases, however, designers must choose designs that are natural for their environments. For example, Figure 4-17 shows a natural design for a building LAN. This building has multiple floors. It will simply make everyone's life easier if each floor is given an Ethernet workgroup switch that serves the hosts and wireless access points on that floor. It is also natural to place a core switch in the basement and have all communication between switches go through the core switch. The core switch can then connect to a router that acts as a gateway to the outside world.

Test Your Understanding

16. Why was the design in Figure 4-17 selected?

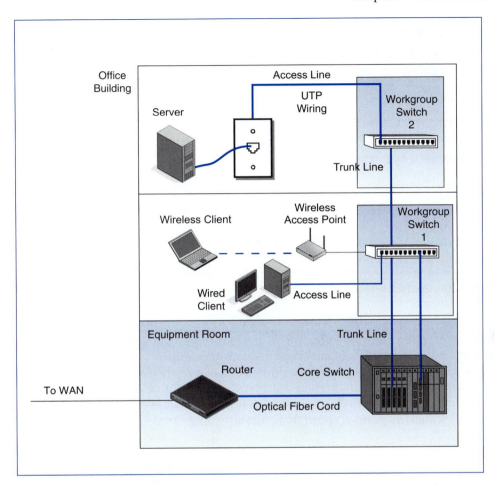

FIGURE 4-17   Natural Design for a Building LAN

EVALUATING ALTERNATIVES

When a design is completed, it is usually necessary to select between products offered by different vendors and perhaps between competing technologies. In much of this book, we will see descriptions of multiple technologies with a special focus on relative strengths and weaknesses. It is not enough to know the individual technologies. You must be able to discuss the pros and cons of competing technologies.

Minimum Requirements

Sometimes there are **minimum requirements** that will exclude a certain product or technology from final consideration. For example, if you need an e-mail server that will support at least 10,000 users in your company, you cannot consider an e-mail server product that will support only 2,000 users—even if it is very inexpensive. If security is

---

Comparing Alternatives

In designs, must select among competing designs and even competing technologies

When learning about technologies, you need to understand pros and cons

Minimum Requirements

Specifications that must be met

Noncompliant products that do not need a minimum requirement cannot be considered

Scalability is a concern (Figure 4-22)

Multicriteria Decision Making

Must look at all aspects of each alternative and evaluate each aspect (Figure 4-23)

Cost

Cost is difficult to measure (Figure 4-24)

FIGURE 4-18 Product Selection (Study Figure)

a high concern, furthermore, you may want to use only a wired technology or routers that require the encryption of supervisory communication.

A special concern is scalability. Some choices simply do not **scale**, meaning that they are not useful beyond a certain traffic volume. As Figure 4-19 shows, a technology may be cost effective when its use is small but may grow too expensive at higher traffic volumes. **Scalable** solutions retain their cost advantage as volume grows.

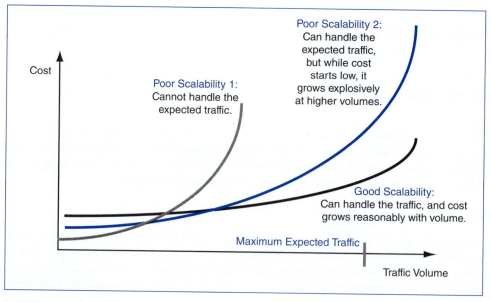

FIGURE 4-19 Scalability

Scalable solutions grow slowly in cost as traffic volume increases.

Another scalability problem is a complete inability to grow enough to meet a company's traffic volume regardless of how much a company spends. The example of the e-mail server that does not meet a minimum requirement is an example of a failure to scale enough.

Test Your Understanding

17. a) Should products that fail to meet minimum requirements be dropped from consideration? b) In what two ways can solutions fail to be scalable?

Product Selection with Multicriteria Decision Making

Once a project is selected and initiated, the network staff must go through the traditional systems development life cycle to implement the project. Given that almost all readers know about the systems development life cycle, we will not discuss it in detail.

In software development projects, there usually is a **make-versus-buy decision**. Should the programming staff create the software itself, or should the company purchase the software? In networking projects, this first option rarely makes sense. User companies like banks and retail stores do not have the technical expertise to make their own switches and routers. Instead, they must *select* and *buy* these technologies. Consequently, in this book, we will look at the factors you need to understand in purchasing decisions that involve different technologies.

When making purchasing decisions, companies tend to use **multicriteria decision making**, which Figure 4-20 illustrates. In this approach, the company decides what product characteristics will be important in making the purchase. Things that are important in the purchasing decision are called **criteria**.

Of course, costs are important, both purchase costs and ongoing costs. However, other decision criteria are also important. In Figure 4-20, the criteria for the product are functionality, availability, cost, ease of management, and electrical efficiency.

Criterion	Criterion Weight (Max: 5)	Product A		Product B	
		Criterion Rating (Max: 10)	Criterion Score	Product Rating (Max: 10)	Criterion Score
Functionality	5	9	45	7	35
Availability	2	7	14	7	14
Cost	5	4	20	9	45
Ease of Management	4	8	32	6	24
Electrical Efficiency	1	9	9	8	8
Total Score			120		126

FIGURE 4-20   Multicriteria Decision Making in Purchase Decisions

Next to each criterion is the **criterion weight**. This weight gives the relative importance of each criterion compared to other criteria. Here, weights range from 1 to 5. Note that cost and functionality have the largest weights (5), emphasizing their importance.

For each product (there are only two in the figure), the evaluation team gives a **rating** for each decision criterion. In this example, the ratings range from 1 to 10, with higher values indicating higher value. More functionality is better, so higher numbers in ratings reflect greater functionality. In contrast, for cost, lower cost is better, so higher rated values must indicate lower cost.

After filling in the ratings on all criteria for all products, the network staff computes the **criterion score** for each product. To do this, the staff multiplies the criterion weight by the rating for that product in that criterion. It then totals the criterion scores into a **total score**.

In Figure 4-20, Product A has a total score of 120, while Product B has a total score of 126. Speaking simplistically, Product B appears to be a better choice. However, the two total scores are very close. Numbers should never drive out thinking. A closer look shows that Product A has very good functionality and ease of management, although its cost is high. Product B has poorer scores on functionality and ease of management. It may be possible to negotiate a lower price on Product A and redo the analysis.

Test Your Understanding

18. a) What is the make-versus-buy decision? b) For routers and switches, do firms usually make or buy? c) We are considering products A, B, and C. Our criteria are price, performance, and reliability with weights of 20 percent, 40 percent, and 40 percent, respectively. Product A's evaluation scores on these three criteria are 8, 6, and 6, respectively. For B, the values are 6, 8, and 8 , respectively. For C, they are 7, 7, and 7 , respectively. Present a multicriteria analysis of the decision problem in tabular form and showing all work. Interpret the table.

Cost Is Difficult to Measure
Systems Development Life Cycle Costs

> Hardware: Full price: base price and necessary components
> Software: Full price: base price and necessary components
> Labor costs: Networking staff and user costs
> Outsourcing development costs
> Total development investment

Systems Life Cycle (SLC) Costs

> System development life cycle versus system life cycle
> Total cost of ownership (TCO)
>> Total cost over entire life cycle
>> SDLC costs plus carrier costs
>>> Carrier pricing is complex and difficult to analyze
>>> Must deal with leases

FIGURE 4-21 Cost (Study Figure)

Cost

Although cost is only one factor in product selection, it is often a critical factor. If you are a mobile phone user, you know how difficult it is to figure your total cost for a month. Figuring the cost of a network alternative is equally complex.

SYSTEMS DEVELOPMENT LIFE CYCLE (SDLC) COSTS   When you begin a project, you need to consider the cost of the system during its development life cycle.

Hardware Costs   Consider what happens when you buy a personal computer. You first have to take hardware into account. When you look at the price of a computer, this may not include a display, and it usually does not include a printer. The **base price** is the price before adding components that will be needed in actual practice. In contrast, the **full price** of the hardware is the price of a complete working system. The distinction between base price and full price is also applicable to network hardware, including the switches and routers we will see later in this term.

Software Costs   After your first computer purchase, you realized that the software can be almost as expensive as the hardware. You have to consider the software you will need very carefully and understand the cost of that software. Individual software products, furthermore, often have misleading base prices that do not include all necessary components. Network product software decisions are similarly complex.

Labor Costs in Development   Although hardware and software costs are complex and difficult to measure, these problems pale beside the problems involved in estimating labor costs in development. Planning, procurement, installation, configuration, testing, programming, and other labor costs can easily exceed hardware and software costs.

User costs should also be considered as an aspect of labor cost because the time that users spend on the system's development during requirements definition and later development states is substantial. This time is not free to the company, any more than network staff time is free.

Outsourcing Development Costs   If the company outsources some or all of the development costs, then outsourcing costs need to be considered in the overall picture.

Total Development Investment   To evaluate potential projects, the networking staff must forecast the total development investment—the total of hardware, software, labor, and outsourcing costs during development. These expenditures truly are investments that should pay off over the life of the project.

SYSTEMS LIFE CYCLE (SLC) COSTS   As noted earlier in this chapter, the systems development life cycle is only part of the overall systems life cycle, which lasts from conception to termination. It is important to consider **systems life cycle costs**, which are costs over a system's entire life, not just during the systems development period. The cost of a system over its entire life cycle is called the **total cost of ownership (TCO)**.

Operating and management costs usually are very important over the system's life cycle. When making equipment and software purchases, it is important to consider how much labor is involved in operating and managing the equipment and software. These costs must be considered very carefully in product selection.

In particular, a new leading-edge technology may give fantastic performance, but leading-edge technologies tend to be immature and tend to create far higher support costs than established technologies.

One new factor in systems life cycle analysis is carrier costs. If you must deal with a communications carrier to carry your signals from one corporate site to another, then you also have to consider carrier pricing. This is rarely easy to do, and it is even harder to compare the prices of alternative carriers offering roughly the same service because of the wording in their contracts. In addition, you usually have to sign equipment leases or service agreements that lock you in for various periods of time, sometimes up to several years.

Test Your Understanding

19. a) What period of a network's life does the SDLC cover? b) Why are hardware and software base prices often misleading? c) List the four categories of SDLC costs. d) Why must user costs in development be considered?

20. a) Distinguish between the systems development life cycle and the systems life cycle. b) What is the total cost of ownership (TCO)? c) Why should operating and management costs be considered in addition to hardware, software, and transmission costs in purchasing decisions? d) What additional cost factor comes into SLC costs, compared to SDLC costs?

Managing the Network as It Provides Service

    The most important (and expensive) part of the systems life cycle
    Tasks described as OAM&P

Operations

    Moment-by-moment traffic management
    Network operations center (NOC)

Maintenance

    Fixing things that go wrong
    Preventative maintenance
    Should be separate from the operations staff

Provisioning (Providing Service)

    Includes physical installation
    Includes setting up user accounts and services
    Reprovisioning when things change
    Deprovisioning when accounts and services are no longer permitted
    Collectively extremely expensive

Administration

    Paying bills, managing contracts, etc.

FIGURE 4-22 Ongoing Management (OAM&P) (Study Figure)

OPERATIONAL MANAGEMENT

In the networking systems life cycle, a great deal of the work takes place after the development finishes. This requires networking professionals to be able to do operational management as well as development.

OAM&P

After a network component is in place, it probably will be used for many years. During its **operational life** (its life after development), there will be substantial labor costs. We will classify these costs in a way that telecommunications carriers have traditionally done—in terms of **operations, administration, maintenance, and provisioning (OAM&P)**

OPERATIONS You probably have seen pictures of **network operations centers (NOCs)** for major telecommunications carriers. These are large rooms with dozens of monitors showing the conditions of various parts of the network. Most corporations also have network operations centers. These corporate NOCs are smaller, usually having only about a half dozen monitors. NOCs manage the network on a moment-by-moment basis.

MAINTENANCE You have undoubtedly seen telephone company maintenance trucks driving on their way to downed transmission lines, broken transformers, or other trouble spots. In addition to fixing equipment failures, telephone companies do preventative maintenance to prevent future failures.

In the same way, companies often have to fix their internal corporate network switches and other physical components. They also have to handle software problems. Although the network operations center can fix some problems remotely, most firms have separate NOC and maintenance staffs. The NOC staff usually is heavily occupied with the moment-by-moment operation of the network, so it makes sense to have other networking professionals focus on maintenance.

PROVISIONING If you get cable television service, the cable company has to **provision** your residence, that is, set up service. This includes physical setup (running the coaxial cable into your home). It also involves setting up your account on the company's computers. The cable company also has to reprovision customers when they change their service by adding channels, dropping optional services, or switching pricing plans.

Within a corporate network, provisioning may involve the installation of additional switches, routers, and transmission lines to serve new users. In networks, every time a new user joins the firm, the company has to provision service for that user. In fact, provisioning has to be done for every user account on every server and access point on the network.

Furthermore, once a user is provisioned for a particular resource, he or she may have to be **reprovisioned** if his or her authorizations change—say, if he or she is upgraded from read-only data access to full read/write access. The user also has to be reprovisioned if he or she changes jobs within a firm, joins project teams, or does many other things. Users also have to be **deprovisioned** when they leave project teams or leave the company entirely. Contractors and other outside organizations also have to be provisioned, reprovisioned, and deprovisioned when they start to work, change the way they work, or stop working with a company. Collectively, provisioning is extremely expensive.

ADMINISTRATION Operations, maintenance, and provisioning involve real-time work to keep the network running. In contrast, administrative work is dominated by such mundane tasks as paying bills to vendors and telephone companies, managing proposals and contracts, doing network budgeting, comparing network budgets to actual costs, and doing other dull but necessary tasks.

Test Your Understanding

21. a) For what is OAM&P an abbreviation in ongoing management? b) Distinguish between operations and maintenance. c) What is provisioning? d) When may reprovisioning be necessary? e) When may deprovisioning be necessary? f) Into which of the four categories would you classify the task of comparing the inventory of parts with the inventory list on the computer?

Network Management Software

Given the complexity of networks, network managers need to turn to **network management software** to support much of their work. Many of these are **network visibility** tools, which help managers comprehend what is going on in their networks.

PING   The oldest network visibility tool is the basic ping command available in all operating systems. If a network is having problems, a network administrator can simply ping a wide range of IP addresses in the company. By analyzing which hosts and routers respond or do not respond, then drawing the unreachable devices on a map, the administrator is likely to be able to see a pattern that indicates the root cause of the problem. Of course, manually pinging a wide range of IP addresses could take a prohibitive amount of time. Fortunately, there are many programs that ping a range of IP addresses and portray the results.

THE SIMPLE NETWORK MANAGEMENT PROTOCOL (SNMP)   Ping can tell you if a host is available. It can also tell you the latency in reaching that host. For remote device management, most network operation centers use more powerful network visualization products based on the **simple network management protocol (SNMP)**, which is illustrated in Figure 4-23. In the NOC, there is a computer that runs a program called the **manager**. This manager manages a large number of **managed devices**, such as switches, routers, servers, and PCs.

Actually, the manager does not talk directly with the managed devices. Rather, each managed device has an **agent**, which is hardware, software, or both. The manager talks to the agent, which in response talks to the managed device. To give an analogy, recording stars have agents who negotiate contracts with studios and performance events. Agents provide a similar service for devices.

The network operations center constantly collects data from the managed devices using SNMP **Get** commands. It places these data in a **management information base (MIB)**. Data in the MIB allows the NOC managers to understand the traffic flowing through the network. This can include failure points, links that are approaching their capacity, or unusual traffic patterns that may indicate attacks on the network.

In addition, the manager can send **Set** commands to the switches and other devices within the network. Set commands can reroute traffic around failed equipment or transmission links, reroute traffic around points of congestion, or turn off expensive transmission links during periods when less expensive links can carry the traffic adequately.

Normally, the manager sends a command and the agent responds. However, if the agent senses a problem, it can send a **trap** command on its own initiative. The trap

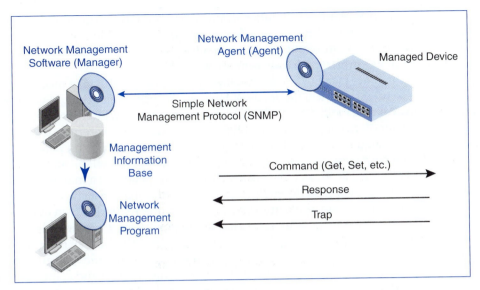

FIGURE 4-23   Network Management Software

command gives details of the problem. There is one more program in the figure—a **network visualization program**. This program takes results from the MIB and interprets the data to display results in maps, finds root causes for problems, and does other tasks. Note that this functionality is *not* included in the simple network management protocol. SNMP simply collects the data in a way that network visualization programs can use. This lack of specification allows network visualization program vendors to innovate without being constrained by standards. What do network visualization programs do?

AUTOMATION   Many other network management chores can be automated to reduce the amount of work that network managers need to spend on minutia. For example, many routers are given a standard corporate configuration when they are installed. Doing this manually can take an hour or more per router. However, it may be possible to create a standard configuration, store it, and simply download it onto new routers. In addition, if corporate standard configurations change or a patch must be installed on all routers, it may be possible simply to "push out" these changes to all routers.

Test Your Understanding

22. a) List the main elements in SNMP. b) Does the manager communicate directly with the managed device? Explain. c) Distinguish between Get and Set commands. d) Where does the manager store the information it receives from Get commands? e) What kinds of messages can agents initiate?

CONCLUSION

Synopsis

This is the last of four introductory chapters. This chapter looked at network management. It began with a discussion of basic concepts, including the need to focus on the systems life cycle, the need to be efficient, and the strategic network planning process.

Strategic network planning includes doing what-is analysis (understanding the current situation), understanding driving forces for change, identifying gaps that will appear if the current system is not changed, creating strategies for closing gaps, and selecting a portfolio of projects to close as many gaps as possible.

Networks must not just work. They must work well. Networks must meet goals for quality-of-service (QoS) metrics. We focused heavily on speed, including how to write speeds properly. We also looked at availability, error rates, latency, jitter, and application response time. After discussing individual QoS metrics, we looked at service level agreements (SLAs), which guarantee levels for certain QoS metrics for a certain percentage of time. Many find it confusing that QoS metrics specify that service will be no worse than certain values. For example, SLAs will specify a minimum speed, not a maximum speed.

There was a long section on design. We looked at traffic analysis, which assesses the traffic that various transmission links must sustain, including redundancy in case of link failures. We looked in detail at a number of alternative topologies, including hierarchical topologies, mesh topologies, and bus (broadcast) topologies. We also looked at the handling of momentary traffic peaks through overprovisioning, priority, and QoS guarantees. Finally, we looked at reducing capacity needs through traffic shaping and compression.

When considering alternatives, it is important to evaluate them systematically. We discussed how to do this with multicriteria decision making. We looked in some detail at estimating costs realistically.

The chapter ended with a discussion of operational management. We looked at the four main traditional elements of network management: operations, administration, maintenance, and provisioning. We looked at the simple network management protocol (SNMP) and saw how important it is in collecting information needed for management and even for doing remote changes on network devices.

END-OF-CHAPTER QUESTIONS

Thought Questions

1. Assume that an average SNMP response message is 100 bytes long. Assume that a manager sends 40 SNMP Get commands each second. a) What percentage of a 100 Mbps LAN link's capacity would the resulting response traffic represent? b) What percentage of a 128 kbps WAN link would the response messages represent? c) What can you conclude from your answers to this question?

2. The telephone network has long boasted that it has the "five nines" (99.999 percent availability). a) How much downtime is this per year? Express downtime in days, hours, minutes, and so on as appropriate. b) How much downtime is there per year with 99 percent availability?

Perspective Questions

1. What was the most surprising thing you learned in this chapter?

2. What was the most difficult part of this chapter for you?

4a | HANDS-ON: MICROSOFT OFFICE VISIO

LEARNING OBJECTIVES

By the end of this chapter, you should be able to:

▪ Create a simple Visio diagram.

WHAT IS VISIO?

Microsoft Office Visio is a drawing program. The professional version has special symbols for drawing network diagrams. Visio is widely used by network professionals to visualize networks they are designing.

USING VISIO

Visio is part of the Microsoft Office family. Installing Visio is like installing any other Office product.

Figure 4a-1 shows how to start a Visio drawing. Of course, this begins by selecting File and then New. In the figure, Network has been selected for the type of drawing. Basic Network Diagram has been selected.

As Figure 4a-2 shows, this brings up a window with a canvas on which you can drag shapes. In the figure, the shape of a generic server has been dragged on to the screen. As you can see, many other network diagramming shapes can be dragged onto the screen.

After you have added the devices you need, it is time to begin showing how they are connected. As Figure 4a-3 shows, there is a connector icon at the top of the screen. Select the connector tool. Then drag between the two icons to connect them. After you have connected them, try dragging one of the connected devices. You will see that the connectors move with them.

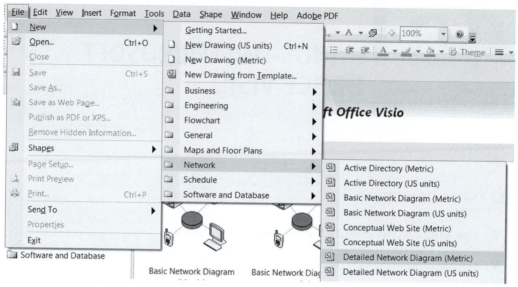

FIGURE 4a-1   Starting a Visio Drawing

Source: Screenshot © 2012 Microsoft Corporation. Used with permission from Microsoft.

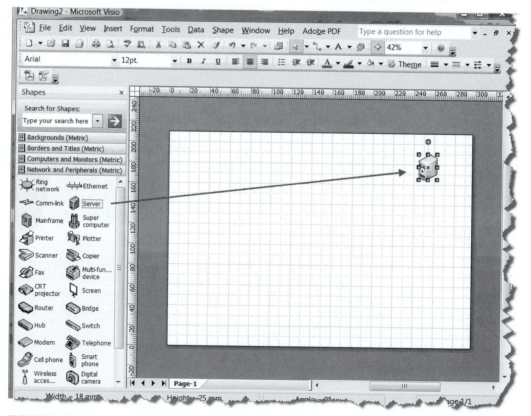

FIGURE 4a-2   Drawing Canvas with Icon Being Dragged

Source: Screenshot © 2012 Microsoft Corporation. Used with permission from Microsoft.

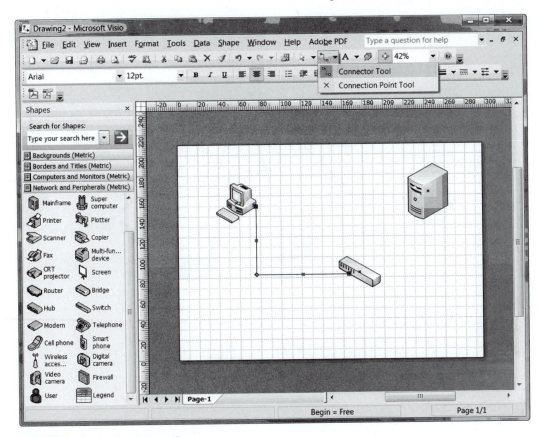

FIGURE 4a-3 Adding Connections

Source: Screenshot © 2012 Microsoft Corporation. Used with permission from Microsoft.

Not shown on the figure, you can double-click on an icon. This adds text below the icon. Visio is not fussy about preventing lines from overlapping text. Overall, Visio diagrams are easy to create but not extremely pretty.

Exercise

In Microsoft Office Visio, create something like the drawing in Figure 4a-4. The drawing has a print server. A print server is a device that allows several users in an office to share a printer. A print server plugs into a printer via a USB port. It also plugs into a switch via a UTP cord.

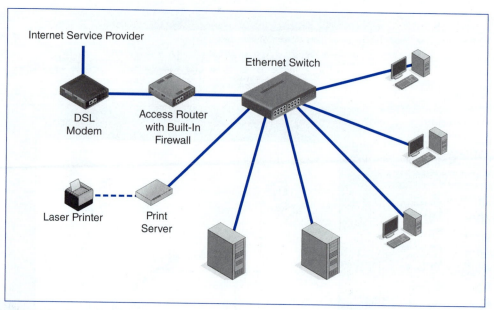

FIGURE 4a-4   Sample Drawing

5

WIRED ETHERNET LANs

LEARNING OBJECTIVES

By the end of this chapter, you should be able to:

- Explain the service and economic differences between LANs and WANs.
- Discuss the concept of Ethernet LANs and explain how they are standardized.
- Describe digital and binary signaling and why they reduce transmission errors.
- Explain the technologies of 4-pair UTP and optical fiber and compare and contrast their relative strengths and weaknesses.
- Be able to design a physical network based on a knowledge of Ethernet standards, including link aggregation.
- Describe the Ethernet frame in detail.
- Explain basic Ethernet data link layer switch operation.
- Explain why the Rapid Spanning Tree Protocol is necessary and how it functions.
- Explain virtual LANs, priority, manageability, and POE in Ethernet LANs.
- Describe security threats to Ethernet LANs and how they are addressed by the 802.1X standard.

INTRODUCTION

In the 19th century, scientists believed that radio waves traveled through an unseen transmission medium called the ether. In the early part of the 20th century, scientists disproved the theory. In the 1970s, a young researcher named Robert Metcalf visited the University of Hawai'i and saw the packet radio experiment being conducted there. Afterward, he designed a wired network technology, which he playfully called **Ethernet**. Today, few are aware of the irony in the name. *Ethernet* has become so common a term that almost nobody thinks about it. Ethernet is simply the way that wired LANs work today. And yes, the fact that it works with wires instead of radio is another piece of irony.

LANs and WANs

ON AND OFF THE CUSTOMER PREMISES There is a fundamental distinction in networking between local area networks and wide area networks. Figure 5-1 compares the two. Most fundamentally, **local area networks (LANs)** operate entirely on the **customer premises**—an office suite, office building, or other property owned by the corporation. A LAN in a corporate headquarters building may connect

Characteristic	Local Area Network (LAN)	Wide Area Network (WAN)
Location	Located entirely on customer's premises	Must carry transmissions beyond customer's premises
Consequence of Location	Owning company operates the LAN	User must contract with a carrier that has rights of way to carry wires between premises
Technology and Service Consequence of Corporate versus Carrier Ownership	Owner can use any technology and service options it wishes	Customer is limited to technologies and service options offered by available carriers
Labor Consequences of Corporate versus Carrier Ownership	Owner must do all operation and maintenance work	Operational and maintenance work is done by the carrier
Economics	Transmission distances are short, so the cost per bit carried is low	Transmission distances are long, so the cost per bit carried is high
Speed Consequences of Economics	Very high speeds are affordable	Customers are content with lower speeds
Design Consequences of Economics	Optimization of transmission capacity is not pressing	Optimization of transmission capacity is critical

FIGURE 5-1   LANs versus WANs

hundreds of hosts throughout the building. (A network you build to connect a few PCs and other devices in your home, apartment, or dorm room is also a LAN.) In this chapter, we will look at wired LANs. In Chapters 6 and 7, you will learn about wireless LANs.

In turn, **wide area networks (WANs)** operate outside the customer premises. While LANs exist within a company's site, WANs connect different sites within an organization or transmit data between organizations. A company might want to receive Internet by running its own wiring through the city to an Internet access point, but it does not have the legal right to lay wires outside its premises. (Imagine what your neighbors would say if you ran wires through their yards.) For transmission beyond its premises, a company must use a transmission **carrier** that has received government **rights of way** to lay wires in public locations or to send radio signals beyond the customer premises. We will look at WANs in Chapter 10, after we have looked at TCP/IP transmission in Chapters 8 and 9.

> Local area networks (LANs) exist within a company's site, while wide area networks (WANs) connect different sites within an organization or transmit data between organizations.

SERVICE IMPLICATIONS   The owner of a LAN can choose any technology and service options it wishes. In addition, it can implement the LAN any way it wishes. On the downside, it also must allocate labor to operate and maintain the network.

In contrast, as we will see in Chapter 10, there are only a few carriers in most communities. In addition, each carrier typically offers only a few technologies and service options. For international networking, countries vary widely in the WAN technologies and services their carriers offer. This makes international corporate network integration difficult. On the positive side, the carrier operates and maintains the WANs, freeing companies of the need to staff the network. Of course, the carrier charges its customers to pay for these services.

ECONOMICS   Another fundamental difference between LANs and WANs stems from economics. You know that if you place a long-distance call, it will cost more than a local call. An international call will cost even more. As distance increases, the price of transmission increases. The cost per bit transmitted therefore is higher in WANs than in LANs.

You know from basic economics that as unit price increases, fewer units are demanded. Or, in normal English, when the price of an item increases, people buy less of it. Consequently, companies tend to purchase lower-speed WAN links than LAN links. Typically, LANs bring 100 Mbps to 1 Gbps of unshared capacity to each desktop. WAN speeds more typically range from 1 Mbps to about 50 Mbps, and these speeds are typically shared by multiple users.

Typically, LANs bring 100 Mbps to 1 Gbps to each desktop. WAN speeds more typically vary from 1 Mbps to about 50 Mbps, and these speeds are typically shared by multiple users.

As a consequence of the higher cost of WAN transmission, companies spend more time optimizing their expensive WAN traffic than their relatively inexpensive LAN traffic. For example, companies may be somewhat tolerant of looking at YouTube videos on LANs, but they almost always clamp down on this type of information on their WAN links. We will see other ways in which companies work to lower their WAN costs in Chapter 10.

Test Your Understanding

1. a) Distinguish between LANs and WANs. b) What are rights of way? c) What are carriers? d) Why do you have more flexibility with LAN service than with WAN service? e) What is the advantage of using carriers?
2. Why are typical WAN speeds slower than typical LAN speeds? Give a clear and complete argument.

Ethernet

The dominant standard for wired LANs today is Ethernet. Although Ethernet was created in the 1970s, it did not become economical until the 1990s. Even then, there were other wired LAN technologies. Over time, however, Ethernet's adequate performance and superior economics completely won the market. Now that Ethernet is the focus of wired LAN development efforts, it continues to grow in speed and sophistication.

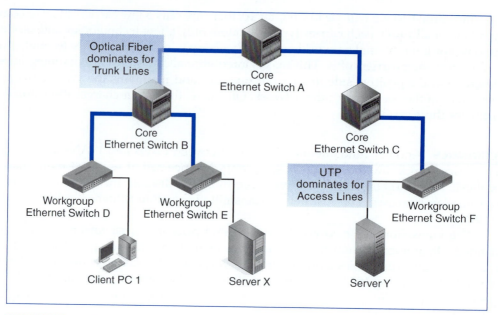

FIGURE 5-2   An Ethernet Network

Figure 5-2 illustrates a simple Ethernet network. At its heart is a collection of Ethernet switches. The switches that connect hosts to the network are called **workgroup switches**. Switches that connect switches to other switches are **core switches**.

Switches that connect hosts to the network are workgroup switches. Switches that connect switches to other switches are core switches.

To connect hosts to switches and switches to other switches, there is a transmission link. As we will see later in this chapter, there are two technologies for transmission links. One is unshielded twisted pair (UTP) copper wire, which we saw briefly in Chapter 1. The other is optical fiber. UTP carries electrical signals over copper wire pairs. Optical fiber carries light signals through very thin glass tubes. Transmission links that connect

FIGURE 5-3   Ethernet Workgroup Switch

Characteristic	Unshielded Twisted Pair	Optical Fiber
Medium	Copper wire	Glass
Signal	Electrical	Light
Maximum Distance in LANs	Usually 100 meters	Usually 200 to 500 meters
Speed	About the same	About the same
Cost	Lower	Higher

FIGURE 5-4   Optical Fiber and UTP

hosts to workgroup switches are called **access links**. Transmission links that connect switches to other switches are called **trunk links**.

> *Transmission links that connect hosts to workgroup switches are called access links. Transmission links that connect switches to other switches are called trunk links.*

Figure 5-4 shows that the main benefit of optical fiber is distance span. While UTP in buildings is normally limited to 100 meters, optical fiber can span distances of 200 to 500 meters. Except at the very highest standardized speeds, which few corporations use, their speeds are comparable. Up to about 10 Gbps today, corporations can use either fiber or UTP. The penalty for greater distance span using fiber is greater cost. Fiber is more expensive to lay than UTP.

Switches in the network core must carry the frames of many conversations, so they must have high processing speeds. Workgroup switches, in contrast, only carry the conversations of the hosts they serve directly. They can operate much more slowly and still give adequate service. Slowness per se is not a virtue, but the low cost that comes with lower operating speeds is a definite virtue.

Test Your Understanding

   3. a) Distinguish between the two types of Ethernet switches in terms of what they connect. b) Distinguish between the two types of Ethernet transmission link technologies in terms of what they connect. c) Why must core switches have more processing power than workgroup switches?

Ethernet Standards Development

Figure 5-5 shows that most LAN and MAN standards are developed by the 802 LAN/MAN standards committee of the IEEE Standards Association. A **MAN** is a **metropolitan area network**; it is a type of WAN limited to a large city and its surrounding communities. Distances are shorter for MANs than for national or international WANs. Constantly MAN prices per bit transmitted are lower than those of WANs with greater geographical scope. Consequently, MAN speeds are higher, although still less than LAN speeds.

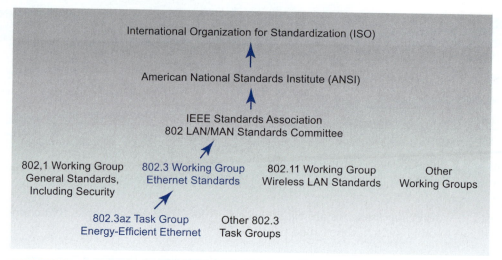

FIGURE 5-5 Ethernet Standards Development

The work of the 802 Committee is done in **working groups**. The 802.3 Working Group creates Ethernet standards, so the terms *Ethernet* and *802.3* are interchangeable. The 802.1 Working Group develops standards used in multiple working groups, for instance, security standards. We will look at the 802.1X security standard in this chapter. The 802.11 Working Group creates the wireless LAN standards, which we will see in Chapters 6 and 7.

The terms Ethernet and 802.3 are interchangeable.

More correctly, the 802.3 Working Group assigns subsets of its members to more specific **task groups**. For instance, the 802.3az Task Group was charged with creating standards for more energy-efficient Ethernet. After a task group completes its assigned work, it passes its results to the 802.3 Working Group, which accepts, rejects, or modifies the work of the task group.

After the 802.3 Working Group ratifies a new standard, it must pass through the 802 Committee and the IEEE Standards Association. From there, it must pass through the **American National Standards Institute (ANSI)**. Finally, because physical and data link layer standards are OSI standards, the standard must pass through ISO. In practice, however, as soon as a standard comes out of the 802.3 Working Group, vendors begin to build products using the standard. Other acceptances are automatic. Sometimes, vendors often begin building products based on draft standards. This sometimes leads to trouble later.

Test Your Understanding

4. a) What is a MAN? b) What standards association creates most LAN standards? c) What is the name of its committee for developing LAN standards? d) What 802 working group creates Ethernet standards? e) What working group is likely to develop security standards to be used by multiple LAN/WAN technologies? f) When do vendors begin to develop products based on new 802.3 standards?

Physical and Data Link Layer Operation

Ethernet networks are single switched networks. Single networks use standards at the physical layer and the data link layer. In the next section, we will look at Ethernet physical layer standards. In the following section, we will look at data link layer standards. After that, we will look at some advanced aspects of Ethernet operation, security, and management.

Single networks use standards at the physical layer and the data link layer.

On hosts, Ethernet physical and data link layer processes are handled in hardware. The circuitry that implements Ethernet is called a **network interface card (NIC)**. It received this name when it was a separate printed circuit board. Today, it is built into the computer's main printed circuit board. Perhaps we should call it the network interface circuit, but the old name has caught on.

Test Your Understanding

5. a) At what layers do single networks require standards? b) Is Ethernet processing executed in hardware or software? c) What circuit implements both of the physical and data link layer processes in Ethernet?

ETHERNET PHYSICAL LAYER STANDARDS

Physical layer standards govern connectors and transmission media. They also govern signaling. We will look at signaling first because it introduces concepts you will need when you look at UTP and optical fiber transmission media.

Test Your Understanding

6. What three things do physical layer standards govern?

Signaling

BITS AND SIGNALS   A frame is a long series of 1s and 0s. To transmit the frame over a physical medium, the sender must convert the 1s and 0s into physical signals. These signals will **propagate** (travel) down the transmission link to the device at the other end of the physical link.

BINARY AND DIGITAL SIGNALING   Figure 5-6 illustrates two popular types of signaling, binary and digital signaling. **Binary signaling** has two **states** (conditions), which may be two voltage levels or light being turned on or off. One state represents a 0. The other state represents a 1. In the figure, a 0 is represented as a high voltage, and a 1 is represented as a low voltage. In optical signaling, a 1 might represent light being turned on, while a 0 might represent light being turned off.

In binary signaling, there are *two* possible states. This makes sense because "bi" is Greek for two. The figure also shows **digital signaling**, in which there are a *few* states (2, 4, 8, etc.). How many "is few?" In some systems, there can be 32 or even 256 states, but the number of states is usually much lower. Also, because each state represents a

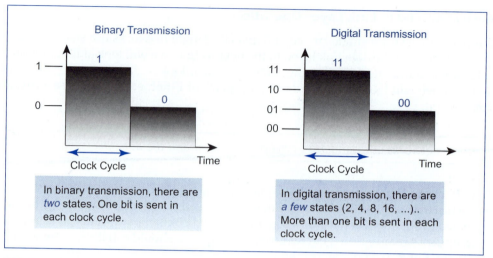

FIGURE 5-6 Binary and Digital Transmission

certain number of bits, the number of states is always a multiple of two—four, eight, sixteen, and so forth.

Note: In binary signaling, there are two possible states. In digital signaling, there are a few possible states (2, 4, 8, etc.).

Having more than two states adds to the complexity and therefore the cost of signaling. However, Figure 5-6 shows that if you have multiple states, you can send multiple bits in a single clock cycle. With two states, you can only represent a single one or a zero. With four states, however, the lowest state might represent 00, the next lowest state might represent 01, the next 10, and the highest 11. With four states, then, you can send two bits at a time.

If "bi" means two, where does "digital" come from? It comes from the fact that we call our 10 fingers *digits*. In fact, some early computer systems operated on Base 10 arithmetic, the same arithmetic that we 10-fingered people use. Very quickly, however, the advantages of building computers and transmission systems that used two or a multiple of two states brought about binary and digital computation and later signaling.

We have talked about binary and digital transmission systems as if they were different. Actually, binary transmission is a subset of digital transmission. In binary transmission, *few* means two. Although binary transmission is the most common form of digital transmission and deserves its own name, all transmission in a typical network can properly be called digital.

Binary transmission is a type of digital signaling. Not all digital signaling, however, is binary signaling.

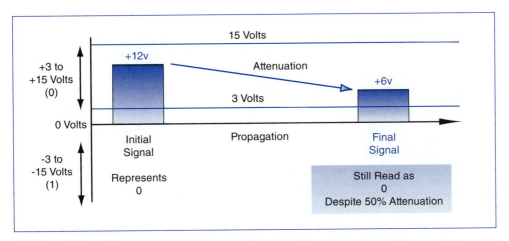

FIGURE 5-7 Error Resistance in Binary and Digital Signaling

ERROR RESISTANCE Why use digital transmission? The answer is that digital transmission is fairly resistant to transmission impairments. In Figure 5-7, a 0 is represented by a signal between 3 and 12 volts, while a 1 is represented by a signal between −3 and −15 volts. This is the signaling scheme used by the serial ports found on older computers. The signaling schemes on newer interfaces are too complex to describe simply.

Suppose that the sender transmits a 12 volt signal. This is clearly a 0. However, as the signal propagates, it will suffer some impairment. For instance, the signal might attenuate to 6 volts. This is 50 percent attenuation, which is a substantial loss. However, the receiver will still correctly record the signal as a 0 because 6 volts is between 3 and 15 volts. The attenuation does not cause an error in reading the signal. This is why binary transmission is error-resistant.

However, think about what happens to error resistance as the number of states increases. Even with four states, a much smaller propagation effect might cause a 11 to be misinterpreted as a 10. In general, as the number of states grows, error resistance declines proportionally. Consequently, there is a strong tendency to use binary signaling in practice. In examples in this book, we will always use binary signaling.

CLOCK CYCLES When a device transmits, it holds the signal constant for a brief period of time called the **clock cycle**. The receiver can read the signal at any time within the clock cycle and read it correctly. In addition, if the sender wishes to send 1111, it will transmit two highest signals in a row. The receiver can tell that this is two signals instead of a single longer signal because the transmission will be two clock cycles long.

To transmit more bits per second, the sender uses either more states or briefer clock cycles. The latter is much easier in practice. Suppose that you are transmitting in binary and the clock cycle is 1/1000th of a second. This means that you can transmit a thousand bits per second. To transmit a gigabit per second with binary signaling, each clock cycle needs to be *one-billionth* of a second long. The limiting factor on transmission speed today is the ability of sending and receiving devices to work properly over every decreasing clock cycle times.

Test Your Understanding

7. a) What must a sender do to send the bits of a frame over a transmission medium? b) Distinguish between binary and digital signaling. c) What is a state? d) Why is binary transmission error-resistant? e) In Figure 5-7, how much could the signal attenuate before it became unreadable? f) Why is binary transmission error-resistant? g) How does error resistance differ in binary and digital signaling? h) Why are clock cycles necessary? i) If the binary transmission rate is 50 Mbps, how long will a clock cycle be?

4-Pair Unshielded Twisted Pair Copper Wiring

THE ORIGINS OF UTP DATA CABLING   In your home, you use copper wiring for electricity. You also use it in your telephone (if you still have a wired telephone). In both cases, a cord contains two wires—a single pair. In contrast, Figure 5-8 shows that type of wiring that businesses had long used before data networking existed. The figure shows that business telephone wiring used four copper wire pairs in each cord. The two wires of each pair are twisted around each other several times per inch. Consequently, this type of wiring is called **4-pair unshielded twisted pair** wiring. Today, we use **4-pair UTP** wiring to carry data in Ethernet. Typically it is just called **UTP.**[1]

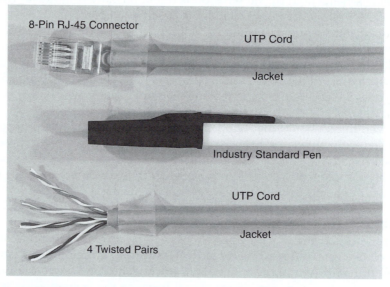

FIGURE 5-8   Four-Pair Unshielded Twisted Pair Wiring

Source: Courtesy of Raymond R. Panko

---

[1]OK, but what about the *unshielded* in the name? This is a hang-over from the early days of twisted pair copper wiring. In some early cases, metal shielding was placed around each wire pair, and more metal shielding was placed around the four shielded pairs. This provided protection from something we will see a little later, electromagnetic interference. However, shielded twisted pair wiring is thick and expensive. In addition, experience showed that it was rarely necessary for electromagnetic interference shielding. Consequently, the copper wiring available in stores is *unshielded* twisted pair wiring.

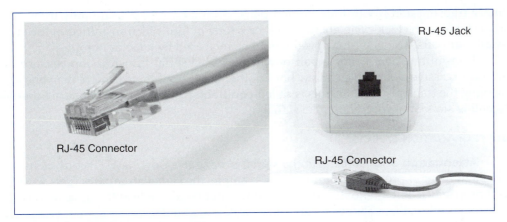

FIGURE 5-9   RJ-45 Connector and Jack

Source: © Rik Kirby/iStockphoto; © Talaj/iStockphoto

RJ-45 CONNECTORS AND JACKS   Your home telephone cord terminates in a snap-in connector at each end. One connector snaps into your wall jack and the other snaps into your telephone. Figure 5-9 shows that 4-pair UTP uses a similar snap-in connector called the **RJ-45 connector**. It looks like your telephone connector, but it is a little wider because it has to terminate eight wires. It snaps into an **RJ-45 jack** in a host or a switch. The figure also shows the RJ-45 jack into which the RJ-45 connector snaps.

SERIAL AND PARALLEL TRANSMISSION   Having four pairs of wires permits faster transmission speeds than having a single pair could provide. Figure 5-10 illustrates this fact. With a single pair of wires, the transmission speed would be limited to a particular value. For simplicity, assume that one bit would be transmitted per clock cycle. (This is

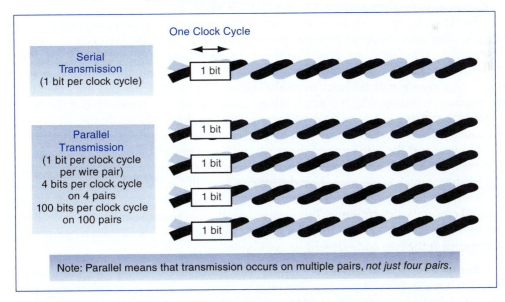

FIGURE 5-10   Serial and Parallel Transmission

binary transmission.) With four twisted pairs, even if each pair could only transmit a single bit in each clock cycle, there would be a total of four bits transmitted in the cycle by all four pairs. Transmission speed would be increased by a factor of four.

Transmitting over a single pair of wires is called **serial transmission** because the bits of successive clock cycles follow one another in series. If there is more than one pair carrying the transmission bits, this is called **parallel transmission**. All modern Ethernet signaling standards specify parallel signaling.

UTP PROPAGATION EFFECTS

Attenuation and Noise   As the signal propagates down a UTP cord, it suffers from a number of propagation effects. For example, the signal **attenuates** (gets weaker) as it propagates. If it attenuates too much, it will not be readable at the destination end.

In addition, there always is random energy, called **noise**, in the copper wires. The noise adds to or subtracts from the signal. The noise is random, so it has occasional high spikes and low valleys. These will cause occasional misreads at the destination end.

The transmitted signal is much stronger than the average noise level. In technical terminology, there is a high **signal-to-noise ratio**. As the signal attenuates, it falls closer to the average noise level, and noise spikes and valleys large enough to cause errors become more likely.

With one exception, which we will see later, the 802.3 Working Group developed its signaling processes so that attenuation and noise will not be significant problems if cord lengths are limited to 100 meters. It is important to obey distance limitations because if attenuation and noise problems become significant, resultant problems can be maddeningly difficult to diagnose.

Interference   UTP wire pairs are essentially long antennas. If there are air conditioners or other nearby devices that generate electromagnetic energy, the energy they generate may be picked up by each wire pair. It will be added to the signal. If this **interference** is large enough, the signal will not be readable, or many errors will occur.

Fortunately, twisting the wires of each pair around each other several times per inch provides almost complete immunity to normal levels of interference. To give you a simplified explanation, suppose that the interference adds to the signal on one half of a twist. The wire in the other half of the twist will be traveling in the opposite direction, so the interference will subtract from the signal. This will cancel out the effect of the interference on the signal. Of course, things do not work this perfectly, but the twisted nature of the wiring keeps normal interference to a negligible level. By the way, the idea of twisting wires to reduce interference was created by Alexander Graham Bell.

However, at the two ends of the cord, the wires must be untwisted to fit into the RJ-45 connectors. This removes their protection against interference, especially **crosstalk interference**, which is generated by the other wire pairs in the same bundle. Crosstalk interference where the wires are untwisted for termination in an RJ-45 jack is called **terminal crosstalk interference**. Terminal crosstalk interference cannot be controlled by wire twisting. However, if the installer untwists the wires no more than a half inch, the interference at the two ends should be negligible.

Recap: Propagation Effects   Figure 5-11 summarizes UTP propagation effects. There are three important propagation effects. There are two simple installation procedures to make these propagation effects negligible.

Propagation Effect(s)	Impact	Installation Discipline
Attenuation	Signal may become too low to be received properly	Limit cord distance to 100 m
Noise	Random electromagnet energy within the wire may occasionally be large enough to produce an error by adding to the signal. Noise is not a problem when the signal-to-noise ratio is large (when the signal is much stronger than the average noise level), but attenuation reduces the signal-to-noise ratio on long cords.	
Terminal crosstalk interference	External interference by other wire pairs in the same bundle is crosstalk interference. Crosstalk interference at the two ends where the wires are untwisted to fit into RJ-45 jacks is terminal crosstalk interference. It can produce errors or make signals unreadable.	Limit the untwisting of the wires in each pair to 1.25 cm (0.5 in.) when placing them in an RJ-45 connector.

FIGURE 5-11   Recap: Propagation Effects

ETHERNET SIGNALING STANDARDS AND UTP QUALITY CATEGORIES   Figure 5-12 shows that Ethernet has several signaling standards for UTP transmission. The **100BASE-TX** signaling standard has a transmission speed of 100 Mbps, while **1000BASE-T** has a transmission speed of 1 Gbps, and **10GBASE-T** has a transmission speed of 10 Gbps.[2] As you might expect, higher speeds require more expensive electronics in the device sending and receiving the Ethernet signals.

Higher transmission speeds require higher-quality cable. Cable quality is indicated by its **category** number. Most of the UTP sold today is **Category 5e** (the *e* stands for enhanced) and **Category 6** UTP. They are almost always referred to simply as *Cat 5e* and *Cat 6*. Both quality categories are sufficient for both 100BASE-TX and 1000BASE-TX. Cat 6 cable is more expensive than Cat 5e cable but cannot carry signals more rapidly.

Cable quality is indicated by its category number.

For 10GBASE-T, which is still rare today, Category 6 wiring is sufficient for distances up to 55 meters. This is below the 100 meter maximum UTP cord runs typically

---

[2]In the three Ethernet signaling standards listed in Figure 5-12, the characters BASE appeared in the name. In fact, all current Ethernet standards have BASE in their names. This refers to the fact that all current standards use baseband signaling, in which the signal is injected directly into the wire. One early Ethernet standard used broadband transmission, in which the signal was sent in a radio channel. The original baseband signal was modulated onto that radio channel. There, it became the broadband signal. Broadband modulation and radios are expensive compared to baseband transmission, so broadband transmission was a dead end for future Ethernet standards. However, broadband transmission is not dead in LANs. The 802.11 wireless LANs we will see in Chapters 6 and 7 all use broadband transmission, although they do not mention this in their names.

Ethernet Signaling Standard	Transmission Speed	UTP Quality Category	Maximum Cord Length
100BASE-TX	100 Mbps	Category 5e, 6, or higher	100 meters
1000BASE-T	1 Gbps	Category 5e, 6, or higher	100 meters
10GBASE-T	10 Gbps	Category 6	55 meters
10GBASE-T	10 Gbps	Category 6A	100 meters

FIGURE 5-12   Ethernet Signaling Standards and UTP Quality Categories

possible in Ethernet. The Cat 6 wiring quality standard was supposed to be sufficient for 100 meter cord runs with 10GBASE-T signaling, so its failure to support 10 Gbps Ethernet with a length of 100 meters was a disappointment and an embarrassment. Consequently, **Category 6A** (advanced) wiring was created. Cat 6A wiring can carry 10GBASE-T signals a full 100 meters.

Test Your Understanding

8. a) What type of copper wiring is widely used in Ethernet? b) How many wires are there in a UTP cord? c) How many pairs? d) What type of connectors and jacks does 4-pair UTP use? e) What is the advantage of parallel transmission compared to serial transmission?

9. a) List the three main propagation effects that can impair a signal travelling through UTP wire. b) List the two ways in which these effects are controlled. c) Which types of propagation effects are controlled by which control method? d) Why is terminal crosstalk interference the main type of interference problem?

10. a) Of what wire characteristic is category a measure? b) What types of UTP wiring can carry signals 100 meters at 1 Gbps? c) What types of UTP wiring can carry signals in 10GBASE-T? d) Which can carry 10Gbps Ethernet 100 meters?

Optical Fiber

CORE AND CLADDING   Figure 5-13 shows that optical fiber carries light signals through a thin strand of glass called the **core**. In fiber's simplest form, light is turned on for a 1 or off for a 0 during a clock cycle.

The figure also shows that the core is surrounded by a thin glass cylinder called the **cladding**. The cladding has a slightly lower index of refraction than the core. Consequently, when a light ray hits the boundary between the core and cladding, it is reflected back into the core with **perfect internal reflection**.[3] Consequently, there is very low attenuation in the light amplitude as the signal travels. Light signals can travel a very long way through LAN fiber—generally from 180 to 550 meters.

OPTICAL FIBER CORDS AND CONNECTORS   Figure 5-14 shows an optical fiber cord. The cord has two **strands** for full duplex transmission, which is the ability to transmit in two directions simultaneously. Each strand carries the signal in one direction.

---

[3]If you remember your physics, this is Snell's Law.

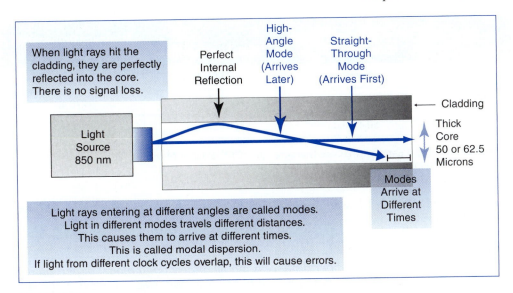

When light rays hit the cladding, they are perfectly reflected into the core. There is no signal loss.

Perfect Internal Reflection

High-Angle Mode (Arrives Later)

Straight-Through Mode (Arrives First)

Cladding

Thick Core 50 or 62.5 Microns

Light Source 850 nm

Modes Arrive at Different Times

Light rays entering at different angles are called modes.
Light in different modes travels different distances.
This causes them to arrive at different times.
This is called modal dispersion.
If light from different clock cycles overlap, this will cause errors.

FIGURE 5-13 Optical Fiber Transmission

Note that the optical fiber cord does not terminate in RJ-45 connectors. UTP only has a single connector standard, but several optical fiber connectors and jacks have been standardized. The cord in Figure 5-14, in fact, has different connectors at each end. One end has a square **SC connector**. The other has a round **ST connector**. This cord would connect a core switch with **SC jacks** with a core switch with **ST jacks**. There is no problem mixing and matching fiber connectors. Optical fibers can be terminated with any type of standard connector.

MODAL DISPERSION AND MODAL BANDWIDTH The limiting factor in LAN fiber distance is modal dispersion. Light rays entering the fiber at different angles are called **modes**. In Figure 5-13, there are two modes. One travels straight down the center of the core. The other bounces repeatedly off the cladding back into the core. Although reflections do not lose noise energy, modes entering the core at higher angles will take longer to travel than the straight mode. This is called **modal dispersion**. If modal dispersion is

Optical Fiber Cord with Two Strands for Full Duplex Communication

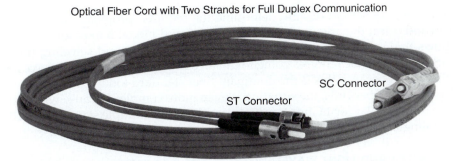

SC Connector

ST Connector

FIGURE 5-14 Optical Fiber Cord and Connectors

Source: © Vitaly Shabalyn/iStockphoto

Wavelength	Core Diameter	Modal Bandwidth	Maximum Propagation Distance
850 nm	62.5 microns	160 MHz-km	220 m
850 nm	62.5 microns	200 MHz-km	270 m
850 nm	50 microns	500 MHz-km	500 m

FIGURE 5-15   Modal Bandwidth, Core Diameter, and Optical Fiber Maximum Cord Length for 1000BASE-SX

too large, parts of the light from sequential light pluses will overlap, making the signal unreadable. Modal dispersion sets a limit on LAN fiber distances.

The limiting factor in LAN fiber distance is modal dispersion. If modal dispersion is too large, parts of the light from sequential light pluses will overlap, making the signal unreadable.

To increase fiber cord length, it is necessary to use higher-quality fiber. Higher-quality LAN fiber has higher **modal bandwidth**, which is a measure of how well the fiber deals with modal dispersion. Modal bandwidth is expressed as **MHz-km**, with higher values being better. Figure 5-15 shows the relationship between modal bandwidth, core diameter, and maximum cord length in LAN fiber. The numbers are for the 1000BASE-SX, which has a signaling speed of 1 Gbps.

Note that quality in UTP is given by category number, and there are discrete categories (5e, Cat 6, etc.). In optical fiber, the situation is more fluid. Modal bandwidth is the measure of quality, and modal bandwidth varies over a wide range, giving the network designer more choices over quality and propagation distance.

Quality in UTP is expressed as a category number. Quality in LAN fiber is expressed as modal bandwidth (MHz-km).

To use Figure 5-15 in design, determine the required propagation distance for a cable run and select the appropriate core diameter and modal bandwidth. Figure 5-15 only shows three combinations. In practice, there are many, and selecting fiber for a **1000BASE-SX** trunk line requires going to catalogs from fiber vendors. We have focused on 1000BASE-SX because this is the dominant fiber standard today.

For 10 Gbps fiber runs, the situation is even more complex because while only the SX standard is popular for 1 Gbps transmission, there are multiple standards of 10 Gbps fiber signaling in Ethernet. They are collectively referred to as 10GBASE-x.

CORE DIAMETER AND LIGHT WAVELENGTH   Figure 5-15 notes that modal bandwidth is not the only thing that affects a cord's maximum propagation distance. Another

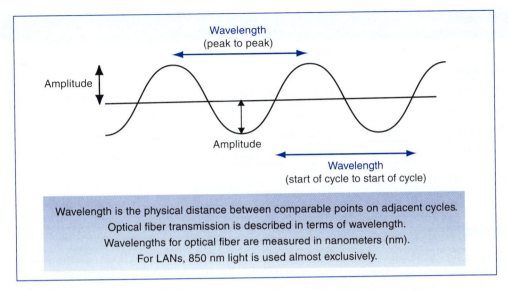

FIGURE 5-16 Light Wavelength

consideration is **core diameter**. In the United States, most companies have standardized on fiber with a core diameter of **62.5 microns**. In Europe, most selected **50 micron** fiber. A smaller diameter allows signals to travel farther. The main reason is that a larger core diameter allows modes to enter at higher angles. Consequently, there is more modal dispersion. In practice, the differences in propagation distances between 50 and 62.5 micron fiber are not great enough to cause corporations to switch standards.

In Figure 5-15, the light wavelength is listed 850 nanometers (nm). As Figure 5-16 shows, light of a single color is a cyclical electromagnetic wave. The distance between successive wave heights, troughs, starts, stops, and so forth is called the **wavelength**. The strength of the signal is called its **amplitude**. If you are familiar with ocean waves, the wavelength is the physical distance between successive waves. Amplitude is how hard the ocean wave will hit you.

No other light wavelength is listed in the table in Figure 5-15. Wavelengths of 1,310 and 1,550 nm give longer propagation distances, but they cost more to generate. For LAN distances, 850 nm light transmitters and receivers are perfectly adequate. In the 1000BASE-SX standard, the *S* stands for short wavelength (800 nm).

Test Your Understanding

11. a) Does the signal travel through the optical fiber core, cladding, or both? b) Why can signals travel very far through optical fiber? c) Why does an optical fiber cord have two strands? d) What is the ability to transmit in both directions simultaneously called? e) Why does modal dispersion happen? f) When will modal dispersion be a problem? g) What is the measure of optical fiber quality? h) In what units is modal bandwidth expressed? i) If you use 1000BASE-SX fiber, what modal bandwidth do you need to transmit a signal 250 meters? j) Will light travel farther in 50 micron fiber or 62.5 micron fiber? k) Of what is wavelength a measure?

Characteristic	LAN Fiber	Carrier WAN Fiber
Required Distance Span	200 to 300 m	1 to 40 m
Light Wavelength	850 nm	1,310 or 1,550 nm
Type of Fiber	Multimode (Thick Core)	Single-Mode (Thin Core)
Core Diameter	50 or 62.5 microns	8.3 microns
Primary Distance Limitation	Modal Dispersion	Absorptive Attenuation
Quality Metric	Modal Bandwidth (MHz-km)	Not Applicable

FIGURE 5-17   LAN Fiber versus Carrier Fiber

Carrier Fiber

We have just seen that optical fiber in LANs uses 850 nm light and core diameters of 50 or 62.5 microns (see Figure 5-17). These options are fine for LAN propagation distances, and they give reasonable cost. Therefore, we have called this type of fiber LAN fiber. Fiber with a core diameter of 50 or 62.5 microns is called **multimode fiber** because, as we saw in Figure 5-13, light modes can enter at various angles.

Telecommunications carriers, in contrast, need much greater propagation distances—10 km to 40 km or more. This requires them to use expensive 1,310 nm or even 1,550 nm light signaling. They also need to use fiber with very tiny cores. A typical diameter for carrier fiber is 8.2 microns instead of 50 or 62.5 microns. Fiber with such a thin core diameter is called **single-mode fiber** because only a single mode—the one traveling straight through the core—can propagate through the core. This completely eliminates modal dispersion, which is the main distance limiter for multimode fiber. This does not mean that signals travel forever in single-mode fiber. The signal still attenuates because it is slightly absorbed by the glass as it propagates. Beyond 10 km or so, the signal becomes too attenuated to be readable. **Absorptive attenuation**, then, is the main distance limiter for carrier fiber.

Test Your Understanding

12. a) Comparing LAN and WAN fiber, what are distance limits? b) What light wavelengths are used? c) What are the two diameters for multimode fiber? d) What is the diameter of single-mode fiber? e) What are the principle distance limiting factors for LAN and carrier fiber? f) Is modal bandwidth a quality measure for LAN fiber, carrier fiber, or both?

Link Aggregation (Bonding)

Ethernet transmission capacity usually increases by a factor of 10. What should you do if you only need somewhat more speed than a certain standard specifies? For instance, suppose that you have gigabit Ethernet switches and need to connect them at 1.5 Gbps?

Figure 5-18 illustrates that a company can use two or more trunk lines to connect a single pair of switches. The IEEE calls this **link aggregation**. Networking professionals also call this **bonding**.

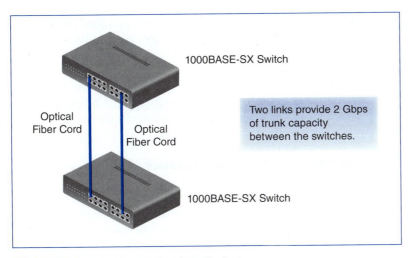

Two links provide 2 Gbps of trunk capacity between the switches.

FIGURE 5-18   Link Aggregation (Bonding)

Link aggregation allows you to increase trunk speed incrementally, by a factor of two or three, instead of by a factor of ten. This incremental growth uses existing ports and usually is inexpensive compared to purchasing new faster switches.

However, after two or three aggregated links, the company should compare the cost of link aggregation with the cost of a tenfold increase in capacity by moving up to the next Ethernet speed. Going to a much faster trunk line will also give more room for growth.

Test Your Understanding

13. a) What is link aggregation? b) What is it also called? c) If you need to connect two 1000BASE-SX switches at 2.5 Gbps, what are your options? d) Why may link aggregation be more desirable than installing a single faster link? e) Why may link aggregation not be desirable if you will need several aggregated links to meet capacity requirements?

Ethernet Physical Layer Standards and Network Design

USING FIGURE 5-12 AND FIGURE 5-15 IN NETWORK DESIGN   Note that if you know the speed you need (100 Mbps, 1 Gbps, etc.) and if you know what distance you need to span, the information in Figure 5-12 and Figure 5-15 will show you what type of transmission link you can use. Because link aggregation is available on all core switches, you have even more choices.

For instance, suppose that you need a speed of 2.5 Gbps between two switches that are 130 meters apart. This is over 100 meters, so you could not use UTP. You would need optical fiber to span this distance.

For speed, 1 Gbps would not be sufficient, and 10 Gbps might be expensive. Your best choice probably would be three bonded 1000BASE-SX links, although you would consider the cost of moving up to a 10 Gbps fiber standard.

Alternatively, if you are designing a network from scratch, say for a new facility, the options presented in Figure 5-12 for UTP and in Figure 5-15 for optical fiber will allow you to consider alternative placements for your switches. With longer physical links, you can place your switches farther apart on average, reducing the total number of switches. This might save money. In the end, of course, you have to consider multiple options and crunch the cost numbers for each.

Although Figure 5-12 is sufficient to consider maximum Ethernet distances, Figure 5-15 only looks at a single transmission speed and a few modal bandwidth levels. There are many more speed/modal bandwidth combinations. For optical fiber, the information in Figure 5-15 is only the beginning.

SWITCHES REGENERATE SIGNALS TO EXTEND DISTANCE   The normal 100-meter Ethernet limit for UTP and the longer distance limits for fiber shown in Figure 5-12 and Figure 5-15 are physical layer standards. Consequently, they only apply to connections *between a single pair of devices*—for example, between a host and a switch, between two switches, or between a switch and a router.

The 100-meter Ethernet limit for UTP and the longer distance limits for fiber shown in Figure 5-12 and Figure 5-15 only apply to physical links between pairs of devices, not to end-to-end data links between hosts across multiple switches.

What should you do if a longer distance separates the source host and the destination host? Figure 5-19 shows a data link with two intermediate switches. In addition to the two 100-meter maximum length UTP access links, there is a 220-meter maximum length 1000BASE-SX optical fiber link (using 62.5/125 micron 160 MHz-km modal bandwidth fiber) between the two switches. This setup can support a data link with a maximum span of 420 meters.

Each switch along the way **regenerates** the signal. If the signal sent by the source host begins as a 1, it is likely to be distorted before it reaches the first switch. The first switch recognizes it as a 1 and generates a clean new 1 signal to send to the second switch. The second switch regenerates the 1 as well.

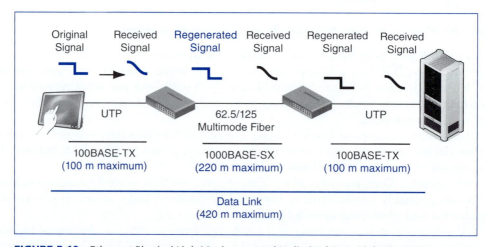

FIGURE 5-19   Ethernet Physical Link Maximums and Unlimited Data Link Distances

The key point again is that Figure 5-12 and Figure 5-15 show maximum distances between *pairs* of devices, not maximum end-to-end transmission distances. To deliver frames over long distances, intermediate switches regenerate the signal. There is no maximum end-to-end distance between pairs of hosts in an Ethernet network. In layer terminology, there are maximum physical link distances, but this does not equate to maximum data link distances.

There is no maximum end-to-end distance (data link distance) between pairs of hosts in an Ethernet network.

Test Your Understanding

14. a) What steps would you go through to use the information in Figure 5-12 and Figure 5-15 in network design? b) If more than one type of Ethernet standard shown in Figure 5-12 and Figure 5-15 can span the distance you need, what would determine which one you choose? c) In Figure 5-12 and Figure 5-15, is the maximum distance the maximum distance for a single physical link or for the data link between two hosts across multiple switches? d) At what layer or layers is the 802.3 100BASE-TX standard defined—physical, data link, or internet? e) How does regeneration allow a firm to create LANs that span very long distances? f) If you need to span 300 meters by using 1000BASE-SX, what options do you have? (Include the possibility of using an intermediate switch.) g) How would you decide which option to choose?

THE ETHERNET FRAME

So far, we have been looking at Ethernet physical layer standards. Now, we will look at Ethernet data link layer standards, beginning with frame organization. The Ethernet frame is called the Ethernet **media access control (MAC)** frame.[4]

The Ethernet Frame's Organization

Figure 5-20 shows the Ethernet MAC layer frame, which we saw briefly in Chapter 2. We will now look at the Ethernet frame in more depth. Recall that an *octet* is a byte.

Preamble and Start of Frame Delimiter Fields

Before a play in American football, the quarterback calls out something like "Hut one, hut two, hut three, hike!" This cadence synchronizes all of the offensive players.

In the Ethernet MAC frame, the **preamble field** (7 octets) and the **start of frame delimiter field** (1 octet) synchronize the receiver's clock to the sender's clock. These fields have a strong rhythm of alternating 1s and 0s. The last bit in this sequence is a 1 instead of the expected 0, to signal that the synchronization is finished.

---

[4]The 802 Committee divided the data link layer into two parts. The lower part was the media access control (MAC) sublayer. This sublayer is different for each technology (802.3, 802.11, etc.). The higher sublayer is the logical link control (LLC) sublayer. The LLC layer does not have planning or management implications, so we will not consider it. It is, however, the reason for the LLC subheader that we will see in the MAC layer frame's data field.

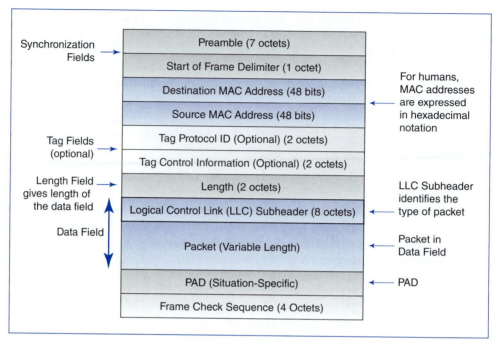

FIGURE 5-20 Ethernet Media Access Control (MAC) Frame Organization

Source and Destination Address Fields

HEX NOTATION We saw in Chapter 2 that the source and destination Ethernet address fields are 48 bits long and that while computers work with this raw 48-bit form, humans normally express these addresses in Base 16 **hexadecimal (hex) notation**. To convert a 48-bit Ethernet address into hex notation, follow these three steps:

- First, divide the 48 bits into twelve 4-bit units, which computer scientists call nibbles.
- Second, convert each nibble into a hexadecimal symbol, using Figure 5-21.
- Third, write the symbols as six pairs with a dash between each pair—for instance, B2-CC-66-0D-5E-BA. (Each pair represents 1 octet.)

To convert a hex address back to binary, change each symbol back to its 8-bit pattern. For example, if the first hex pair is E2, E is 1110, and 2 is 0010. So E2 is equivalent to the octet 11100010. In this conversion, you must keep the two leading zeros in 0010.

MAC ADDRESSES Ethernet addresses exist at the MAC layer, so Ethernet addresses are called **MAC addresses**. They are also called **physical addresses** because physical devices (NICs) implement Ethernet at the physical, MAC, and LLC layers.

Tag Fields

We will look at the two tag fields later in this chapter, when we look at virtual LANs (VLANs). These tag fields are optional and are only used under certain circumstances.

4 Bits	Decimal (Base 10)	Hexadecimal (Base 16)
0000	0	0 hex
0001	1	1 hex
0010	2	2 hex
0011	3	3 hex
0100	4	4 hex
0101	5	5 hex
0110	6	6 hex
0111	7	7 hex

4 Bits	Decimal (Base 10)	Hexadecimal (Base 16)
1000	8	8 hex
1001	9	9 hex
1010	10	A hex
1011	11	B hex
1100	12	C hex
1101	13	D hex
1110	14	E hex
1111	15	F hex

FIGURE 5-21   Hexadecimal Notation

Note: Divide a 48-bit Ethernet address into 12 four-bit "nibbles." (1010, 0001, etc.)
Convert each group of 4 bits into a hex symbol. (A, 1, etc.)
Combine two hex symbols into pairs and place a dash between pairs (A, 1, etc.)
The finished hex expression: A1-36-CD-7B-DF-01 hex.

Length Field

The **length field** contains a binary number that gives the *length of the data field* (not of the entire frame) in octets. The maximum length of the data field is 1,500 octets. There is no minimum length for the data field. However, we will see that if the data field is less than 46 octets long, a PAD field will be added.

The Data Field

The **data field** contains two subfields: the LLC subheader and the packet that the frame is delivering.[5]

LLC SUBHEADER   The **logical link control layer (LLC) subheader** is 8 octets. The purpose of the LLC subheader is to describe the type of packet contained in the data field. For instance, if the LLC subheader ends with the code 08-00 hex (Base 16), then the data field contains an IPv4 packet.[6] Ethernet frames can also carry other types of packets. To give another example, the code 86DD (hex) indicates the presence of an IPv6 packet.

---

[5]Why does the data field have two parts? The answer is that the data field of the MAC layer frame actually is an encapsulated LLC layer frame, which has a header (the LLC subheader) and a data field consisting of the packet being carried in the LLC frame. However, to avoid damaging neurons, it is best simply to think of the MAC layer data field as having two parts.

[6]The LLC subheader has several fields. In the SNAP version of LLC, which is almost always used, the first three octets are always AA-AA-03 hex. The next three octets are almost always 00-00-00 hex. The final two octets constitute the Ethertype field, which specifies the kind of packet in the data field. Common hexadecimal Ethertype values are 0800 (IP), 8137 (IPX), 809B (AppleTalk), 80D5 (SNA services), and 86DD (IP version 6).

THE PACKET The data field also contains the packet that the MAC layer frame is delivering. The packet usually is far longer than all other fields combined.

PAD Field

The **PAD field** is unusual because it does not always exist. Although there is no minimum length for 802.3 MAC layer frame data fields, if the data field is less than 46 octets long, then the sender must add a PAD field so that the total length of the data field and the PAD field is exactly 46 octets long. For instance, if the data field is 26 octets long, the sender will add a 20-octet PAD field. If the data field is 46 octets long or longer, the sender will not add a PAD field.

There is no minimum length for the data field, but if the data field is less than 46 octets long, then a PAD field must be added to bring the total length of the data and pad fields to 46 octets.

How does the receiving NIC know what part of the data field plus the PAD is the data field? Recall that the length field gives the *length of the data field*. Consequently, after reading the LLC header, the remaining number of octets indicated in the length field must be the data field. Everything else beyond the data field that is needed to get the data field and PAD to 46 octets is the PAD field. The receiving NIC ignores the contents of the PAD.

For example, suppose that the length field is 40 octets. This means that the data field is 40 octets. The LLC subheader is 8 octets, so the packet length is 32 octets. The added PAD is 6 octets, because 6 octets must be added to 40 octets to make a total of 46 octets.

Frame Check Sequence Field

The last field in the Ethernet frame is the **Frame Check Sequence Field**, which permits error detection. This is a 4-octet field. The sender does a calculation based on other bits in the frame and places the 32-bit result in the Frame Check Sequence Field. The receiver redoes the calculation and compares its result with the contents of the Frame Check Sequence Field. If the two are different, there is an error in the frame. If there is an error, the receiver simply discards the frame. There is no retransmission of damaged frames.

Test Your Understanding

15. a) What is the purpose of the preamble and start of frame delimiter fields? b) Why are Ethernet addresses called MAC addresses or physical addresses? c) What are the steps in converting 48-bit MAC addresses into hex notation? d) Convert 11000010 to hex. e) Convert 7F hex to binary. f) The length field gives the length of what? g) If the length field is 1020, what is the length of the packet in the data field? h) What are the two components of the Ethernet data field? i) What is the purpose of the LLC subheader? j) What type of packet is usually carried in the data field? k) What is the maximum length of the data field? l) Who adds the PAD field—the sender or the receiver? m) Is there a minimum length for the data field? n) If the data field is 40 octets long, how long a PAD field must the sender add? o) If the data field is 400 octets long, how long a PAD field must the sender add? p) What is the purpose of the Frame Check Sequence Field? q) What happens if the receiver detects an error in a frame?

BASIC ETHERNET DATA LINK LAYER SWITCH OPERATION

In this section, we will discuss the basic data link layer operation of Ethernet switches. This is also governed by the 802.3 MAC layer standard. In the section after this one, we will discuss other aspects of Ethernet switching that a firm may or may not use.

Frame Forwarding

Figure 5-22 shows an Ethernet LAN with three switches. Larger Ethernet LANs have dozens of switches, but the operation of individual switches is the same whether there are a few switches or many. Each individual switch makes a decision about which port to use to send the frame back out to the next switch.

In the figure, Host A1 wishes to send a frame to Host E5. This frame must go to Switch 1, then Switch 2, and then to Switch 3. Switch 3 will send the frame to Host E5.

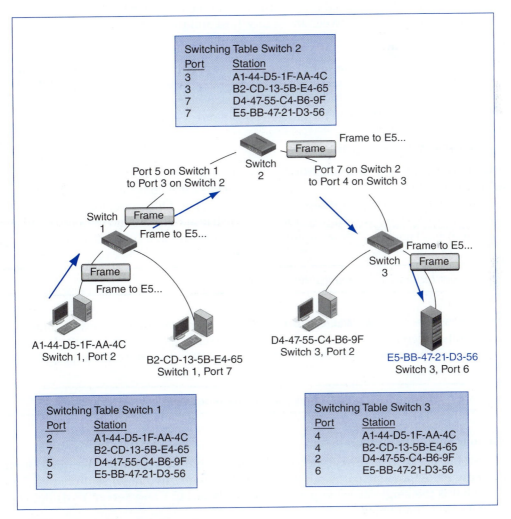

FIGURE 5-22 Multi-Switch Operation

To begin this process, Host A1 puts E5 (later octets dropped for brevity) in the destination address field of the frame. It sends the frame to Switch 1, through Port 2.

- Switch 1 looks up the address E5 in its switching table. It sees that E5 is associated with Port 5, so it sends the frame out Port 5. This is a very simple process, so it requires little processing power. This means that Ethernet switches are inexpensive for the volume of traffic they carry.
- The frame going out Port 5 on Switch 1 goes into Port 3 on Switch 2. Switch 2 now looks up the address E5 in its switching table. This address is associated with Port 7, so Switch 2 sends the frame out Port 7.
- The frame arrives at Switch 3 through Port 4. Switch 3 now looks up the address E5 in the switching table. This time, the address is associated with Port 6. Switch 3 sends the frame out Port 6. This takes it to the destination Host E5.

Note that each switch only knows the information in its switching table. More specifically, it only knows what port to use to send the frame back out. Switches do not know the entire data link between the source host and the destination host.

Test Your Understanding

16. a) Do switches know the entire data link between the source and destination host? b) What does a switch know? c) In Figure 5-22, trace everything that will happen when Host E5 sends a frame to D4. d) Trace everything that will happen when Host E5 sends a frame to B2.

Hierarchical Switch Topology

HIERARCHICAL SWITCH ORGANIZATION   Note that the switches in Figure 5-22 form a **hierarchy**, in which each switch has only one parent switch above it. In fact, the Ethernet standard *requires* a **hierarchical topology** for its switches. Otherwise, loops would exist, causing frames to circulate endlessly from one switch to another around the loop or causing other problems. Figure 5-23 shows a larger switched Ethernet LAN organized in a hierarchy.

Ethernet requires a hierarchical switch hierarchy.

SINGLE POSSIBLE PATH BETWEEN END HOSTS   In a hierarchy, there is only a single possible path between any two end hosts. (To see this, select any two hosts at the bottom of the hierarchy and trace a path between them. You will see that only one path is possible.)

In a hierarchy, there is only a single possible path between any two end hosts.

Test Your Understanding

17. a) How are switches in an Ethernet LAN organized? b) Because of this organization, how many possible paths can there be between any two hosts? c) In Figure 5-23, what is the single possible path between Client PC 1 and Server Y? d) Between Client PC 1 and Server X?

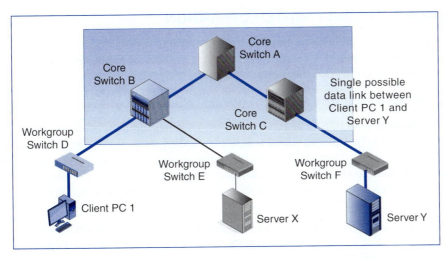

FIGURE 5-23   Hierarchical Switched Ethernet LAN

ONLY ONE POSSIBLE PATH: LOW SWITCHING COST   We have just seen that a hierarchy allows only one possible path between any two hosts. If there is only a single possible path between any two hosts, it follows that, in every switch along the path, the destination address in a frame will appear only once in the switching table—for the specific outgoing port needed to send the frame on its way.

This allows a simple table lookup operation that is very fast and therefore costs little per frame handled. This is what makes Ethernet switches inexpensive. As noted in the introduction, simple switching operation and therefore low cost has led to Ethernet's dominance in LAN technology.

The fact that there is only a single possible path between any two end hosts in an Ethernet hierarchy makes Ethernet switch forwarding simple and therefore inexpensive. This low cost has led to Ethernet's dominance in LAN technology.

In Chapter 8, we will see that routers have to do much more work when a packet arrives because routers are connected in a mesh, so there are multiple alternative routes between any two hosts. Each of these alternative routes appears as a row in the routing table. Therefore, when a packet arrives, a router must first identify all possible routes (rows) and then select the best one—instead of simply finding a single match. This additional work per forwarding decision makes routers very expensive for the traffic load they handle.

Test Your Understanding

18. a) What is the benefit of having a single possible path? Explain in detail. b) Why has Ethernet become the dominant LAN technology? c) Why are routers expensive for the traffic volume they handle?

ADVANCED ETHERNET SWITCH OPERATION

Now that we have discussed basic Ethernet switch operation involved in frame forwarding, we will begin looking at additional aspects of Ethernet switch operation that are important in larger Ethernet networks.

The Rapid Spanning Tree Protocol (RSTP)

SINGLE POINTS OF FAILURE   We have just seen that having only a single possible path between any two hosts allows rapid frame forwarding and, therefore, low switch cost. Unfortunately, having only a single possible path between any two computers also makes Ethernet vulnerable to **single points of failure**, in which the failure of a single component (a switch or a trunk line between switches) can cause widespread disruption.

Having only a single possible path between end hosts in a switched Ethernet network reduces cost, but it creates single points of failure, meaning that a single failure can cause widespread disruption.

To understand this, suppose that Switch 2 in Figure 5-24 fails. Then the hosts connected to Switch 1 will not be able to communicate with hosts connected to Switch 2 or Switch 3. For a second example, suppose that the trunk line between Switch 1 and Switch 2 fails. In this case, too, the network also will be broken into two parts.

Although the two parts of the network might continue to function independently after a failure, many firms put most or all of their servers in a centralized server room. In such firms, clients on the other side of the broken network would lose most of their ability to continue working. For example, in the figure, Client A1-44-D5-1F-AA-4C, which connects to Switch 1, cannot reach Server E5-BB-47-21-D3-56, which connects

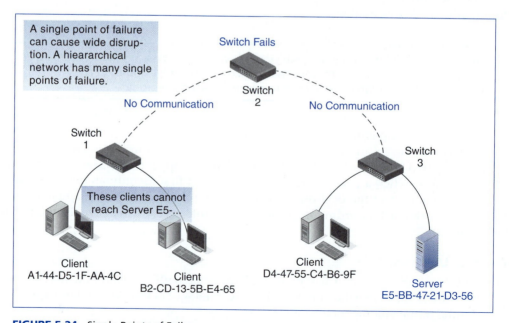

FIGURE 5-24   Single Points of Failure

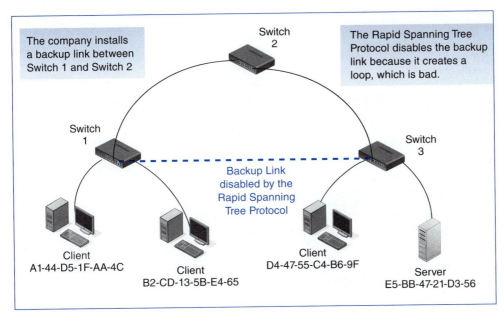

The company installs a backup link between Switch 1 and Switch 2

The Rapid Spanning Tree Protocol disables the backup link because it creates a loop, which is bad.

Switch 2

Switch 1

Switch 3

Backup Link disabled by the Rapid Spanning Tree Protocol

Client
A1-44-D5-1F-AA-4C

Client
B2-CD-13-5B-E4-65

Client
D4-47-55-C4-B6-9F

Server
E5-BB-47-21-D3-56

FIGURE 5-25   Backup Link and the Rapid Spanning Tree Protocol (RSTP)

to Switch 3. External connections also tend to be confined to a single network point for security reasons. Computers on the wrong side of the divide after a breakdown would lose external access.

THE RAPID SPANNING TREE PROTOCOL (RSTP)   The traditional way to deal with single points of failure is to install backup links. This installs **redundancy**, which means that there is more than one way to connect a pair of switches or a pair of hosts. Redundancy increases **reliability**, which is the probability that connections will be made.

In Figure 5-25, the company has installed a transmission link between Switch 1 and Switch 3. As the figure shows, this creates a loop among the three switches. Loops create serious problems in Ethernet. Fortunately, there is a standard to detect and break loops in Ethernet networks. This is the **Rapid Spanning Tree Protocol (RSTP)**, 802.1w.[7] In the figure, RSTP has deactivated the backup link.

What happens if there is a failure? Switches will exchange messages via RSTP. As Figure 5-26 shows, they will agree to disable the links between Switch 2 and the other two switches. They will also agree to reactivate the backup link. Now, the two clients on the left can reach Server E1-… on the right.

Although RSTP was created to detect and break loops, using it to reactivate backup links is rather tricky. When a loop occurs, the switches hold a backup election to pick a root (top level) switch. They then create a hierarchy beneath it. To ensure that the restored hierarchy is the one the company wants to have, the networking staff must "rig the election." It does this by setting certain parameters on each switch. This is easy if there is a single backup link. If there are many backup links, this is very difficult.

---

[7]There was an earlier standard, the Spanning Tree Protocol (802.1D), which is now deprecated because of its slow operation.

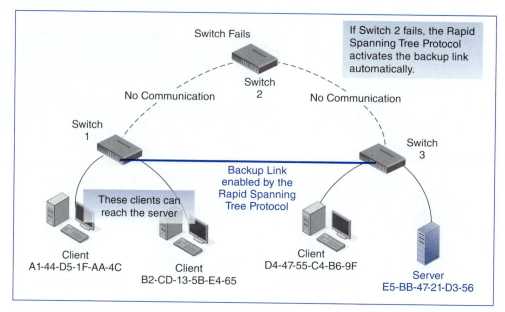

FIGURE 5-26 Reactivating a Backup Link in Ethernet with the Rapid Spanning Tree Protocol

Test Your Understanding

19. a) What is a single point of failure? b) Why is having a single possible path between any two hosts in an Ethernet network dangerous? c) What is the traditional way to address this problem? How does it bring redundancy? How does it improve reliability? d) What standard allows backup links for redundancy in Ethernet networks? e) Is it easy or difficult to create backup links effectively with RSTP?

Virtual LANs and Ethernet Switches

VLANS In a normal Ethernet network, any client can send frames to any server, and any server can reach any client. However, many Ethernet switches can now create virtual LANs. As Figure 5-27 shows, virtual LANs (VLANs) are groups of clients and servers that are allowed to communicate with each other but not with clients or servers on other VLANs.[8] In the figure, clients and servers in VLAN 3 (indicated by blue rectangles) cannot communicate with clients and servers on VLAN 47 (indicated by ellipses).

> *Virtual LANs (VLANs) are groups of clients and servers that are allowed to communicate with each other but not with clients or servers on other VLANs.*

CONGESTION REDUCTION VLANs are used for two main reasons. First, some servers tend to **broadcast** frames to all clients. (One reason for the server to do this is to advertise its availability to its clients every 30 seconds or so.) In a large network, this broadcasting can create a great deal of congestion. With VLANs, however, the server will not flood the entire network with traffic; the frames will go only to the clients on the server's VLAN.

---

[8]What if a client on one VLAN needs to communicate with a server on another VLAN? The client must reach the server through a router. Routers connect different VLANs just as they connect different physical LANs.

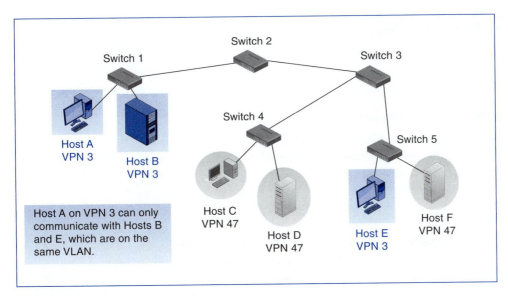

FIGURE 5-27   Virtual LANs (VLANs)

SECURITY   A second reason for using VLANs is security. If clients on one VLAN cannot reach servers on other VLANs, they cannot attack these servers. In addition, if a client becomes infected with a virus, it can only pass the virus on to other clients and servers on its own VLAN.

THE 802.1Q VLAN STANDARDS   To address VLAN standardization, the 802.3 Working Group extended the Ethernet frame through the **802.1Q** standard. This standard adds two optional **tag fields** after the address fields, as shown in Figure 5-20.

802.1Q is the standard for frame tagging.

The first tag field is the **Tag Protocol ID** field, which simply indicates that this is a tagged frame. The second tag field is the **Tag Control Information** field. This field contains a 12-bit VLAN ID that the sender sets to 0 if the firm does not use VLANs. If the firm does use VLANs, the frame is given a VLAN number. With the exclusion of 0 values, there are $2^{12} - 1$ (4,095) possible VLANs. This is sufficient for almost all corporate LANs.

Tagging is used for more than VLANs. The TCI field also has three priority bits. This gives up to eight (2^3) priority levels. Frame tagging is necessary to do priority-based switching in Ethernet.

Test Your Understanding

20. a) What is a VLAN? b) What two benefits do VLANs bring? c) How do VLANs bring security? d) When VLANs or priority is used, what two fields does the 802.1Q standard add to Ethernet frames? e) When VLANs are used, what does the Tag Protocol ID field tell a receiving switch or NIC? f) What information does the tag control information field tell the switch or receiver? g) In Figure 5-27, what server or servers can Host A communicate with? h) In Figure 5-27, what server or servers can Host C communicate with?

Tag Control Information (TCI) Field

> There are 12 bits for VLAN addresses
> There are 3 bits for frame priority
> This permits $2^3 = 8$ different priority values

Momentary Traffic Overloads

> Switches may be overloaded momentarily (usually a fraction of a second)
> During this time, some frames must be stored in a buffer until they can be processed
> Some frames will be lost
> Momentary traffic overloads cause significant delays

Priority Levels

> Higher priority is given to applications that are intolerant of displays
> Voice must have high priority because conversations are easily disrupted by delays
> E-mail can tolerate slight delays and so usually gets low priority

Overprovisioning

> An alternative to using priority is to install much more switch processing speed than needed
> Momentary traffic overloads will be extremely rare
> Overprovisioning is more expensive, but priority requires more labor

---

FIGURE 5-28 Priority and Overprovisioning (Study Figure)

Priority

We have just seen that 12 of the bits in the Tag Control Information field are used for VLANs. Another three bits are used to allow switches to give priority to certain types of traffic. This gives 8 (2^3) possible priority levels. If two frames arrive at a switch at the same time, the frame with the higher **priority** number in the Tag Control Information field will be sent out first.

If the switch has enough capacity to handle all the traffic, priority is not important. However, if the switch is overloaded, it will not have enough capacity to handle all traffic. Each switch has a certain amount of storage called the buffer. During traffic overloads, the frames that cannot be processed will be held in the buffer until they can be processed. Typically, traffic overloads last only fractions of a second, so frames in the buffers are delayed but not lost. However, if the overload lasts too long, the buffer will overflow, and frames will be lost. If applications are using TCP, the lost packet will be retransmitted, but this will add considerable delay. It will also to the congestion.

Frames are given priority levels based on their **delay intolerance**. Voice traffic is intensely intolerant of delay. If there is even slight delay, it will be impossible for the two people to carry on a conversation. Consequently, voice traffic is given very high priority. In contrast, it rarely matters if e-mail is delayed by a few seconds. Consequently, e-mail is usually given low priority.

Priority must be managed, and this increases labor cost. Many firms simply buy much faster Ethernet switches than they will normally need. This is called

overprovisioning. It ensures that traffic overloads will be so rare that they can be ignored. This raises hardware cost but lowers labor cost.

Test Your Understanding

21. a) How many priority levels are possible for Ethernet switches? b) Why does a momentary traffic overload cause delay? Be specific. c) How does priority reduce delay? d) What determines what level of priority a frame will be given? e) What priority would you give to streaming video? Defend your decision. f) What priority would you give to database queries? Defend your decision. g) What is the trade-off between implementing priority and overprovisioning?

Manageability

If there is an Ethernet switch problem, discovering which switch is malfunctioning can be very difficult. Fixing the problem, furthermore, may require traveling to the switch to change its configuration. Switch troubleshooting can be very expensive, especially if the network staff must travel to distant switches to do diagnostics or configuration.

MANAGED SWITCHES AND THE MANAGER   As Figure 5-29 shows, a company can mitigate these problems by using **managed switches**. As the name suggests, these switches have sufficient intelligence to be managed from a central computer called the **manager**. In most cases, management communication uses the Simple Network Management Protocol (SNMP) that we introduced in Chapter 4.

POLLING AND PROBLEM DIAGNOSIS   Every few seconds, the SNMP **manager** polls each managed switch. In the poll, it asks each switch for a certain set of configuration parameters. The manager places all of this information in a **management information base (MIB)**.

   If a problem occurs, the manager can discover quickly which switches are not responding and so can narrow down the source of the problem. In many cases, the configuration data collected from the switches can pinpoint the cause of a problem. Polling uses the **Get** command, which asks for information about the switch.

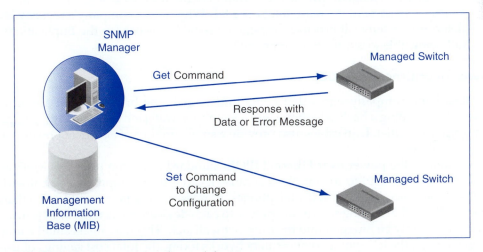

FIGURE 5-29   Managed Switches and the Manager

FIXING SWITCHES REMOTELY In some cases, the network administrator can use the manager to fix switch problems remotely by sending **Set** commands to the switch. The set command tells the switch to change one of its settings. For example, a Set command might tell the switch to turn off a certain port or to test a port that is suspected of malfunctioning. For instance, the manager can command the switch to do a self-test diagnostic. To give another example, the manager can tell the switch to turn off a port suspected of causing problems.

PERFORMANCE SUMMARY DATA At the broadest level, software can search through the SNMP manager's data and can present the status data to the network administrator in summarized form, giving the administrator a good indication of how well the network is functioning and of whether changes will be needed to cope with expected traffic growth.

THE COST SAVINGS OF MANAGEABILITY Managed switches are much more expensive to buy than nonmanaged switches. However, central management slashes network management labor, which is considerable. This labor cost reduction usually far offsets the higher switch purchase costs. The main benefit of network management, then, is to reduce overall costs.

Managed switches are more expensive than nonmanaged switches, but they reduce management labor in large networks enough to more than offset managed switch purchase costs. Managed switches reduce overall costs.

SECURITY A company's security level has a major impact on whether the Set command is used. Set is inherently dangerous because if an attacker can use it, he or she can disable switches and do other damage. In contrast, while Get can help an attacker find information needed for an attack, it is inherently less dangerous than Set because it only supplies information. Unless a company has very strong security, it must disable the Set command on all of its managed switches. This means that it must forgo the cost savings of remote reconfiguration.

Test Your Understanding

22. a) What are managed switches? b) What benefits do they bring? c) Do managed switches increase or decrease total costs? d) Why does a company's security level determine whether it can use the Set command? e) What are the implications of not being able to use the Set command?

Power over Ethernet (POE)

The telephone company wires that come into your home bring a small amount of power. You can plug a basic telephone into a telephone wall jack without having to plug it into a power outlet. USB cables also provide a small amount of electrical power to the devices they connect.

Similarly, the **power over Ethernet (POE)** standard can bring power to RJ-45 wall jacks. POE is important to corporations because it can greatly simplify electrical wiring for installing voice over IP (VoIP) telephones, wireless access points, and surveillance cameras. Instead of having to provide power to each device via electrical wall jacks, the device can simply be plugged into the Ethernet wall jack. This may not seem like much, but given all of the low-power devices in networks today, the total cost savings of using the existing physical Ethernet plant to power many devices is considerable.

Power over Ethernet (POE)

> Switches can supply power to devices connected by UTP
>
> (Wired telephone systems and USB ports already do this)
>
> This may be much less expensive than supplying power separately

Latest POE Standard

> Provides up to 25 Watts to attached devices
>
> Sufficient for most wireless access points
>
> Sufficient for VoIP phones
>
> Sufficient for surveillance cameras
>
> Sufficient for tablets
>
> Not sufficient for desktop or notebook PCs

The Future

> Nonstandard products now supply 60 Watts of power
>
> May become a future standard
>
> Still will not be enough for desktop or notebook PCs

POE switches

> New switches can be purchased with POE
>
> Companies can also add POE equipment to an existing non-POE switch

---

FIGURE 5-30 Power over Ethernet (POE) (Study Figure)

The POE standard currently is limited to 25 Watts of power.[9] Some nonstandard powered switches already raise this to 60 Watts, and these higher power levels may appear in future versions of the POE standard. However, both POE and nonstandard POE are only sufficient for low-power devices. POE does not provide enough power for desktop PCs or even laptop computers.

Companies that wish to supply power through their RJ-45 wall jacks will have to install either new switches compatible with the POE standard or modification kits that can add POE to existing switches.

Test Your Understanding

23. a) What is POE? b) Why is POE attractive to corporations? c) What maximum standard power does the POE standard specify? d) For what types of devices is POE sufficient? e) Is POE sufficient for desktop computers and most notebook computers?

ETHERNET SECURITY

Until recently, few organizations worried about the security of their wired Ethernet networks, presumably because only someone within the site could get access to the network, and security should be strong within the site. Unfortunately, experience has shown that attackers can easily get into sites, especially if a site has public areas. Once

---

[9]Technically, the standard that specifies 25 Watts is POE Plus. The original standard was simply POE.

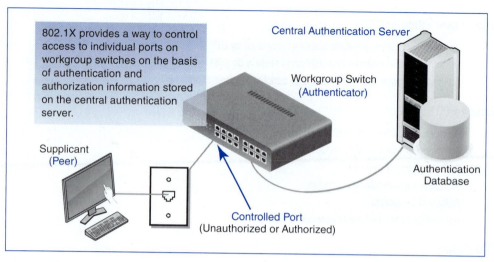

802.1X provides a way to control access to individual ports on workgroup switches on the basis of authentication and authorization information stored on the central authentication server.

Central Authentication Server

Workgroup Switch
(Authenticator)

Supplicant
(Peer)

Authentication
Database

Controlled Port
(Unauthorized or Authorized)

FIGURE 5-31 802.1X Port-Based Access Control on an Ethernet Switch

into the site network, the attacker does not have to worry about the border firewall. He or she is *inside* the border firewall.

Port-Based Access Control (802.1X)

To thwart the ability of attackers to simply plug into the internal network, companies can implement **802.1X**, which is a standard for **Port-Based Access Control** on the workgroup switches that give users access to the network. Quite simply, a switch port will not allow the computer attached to the port to send traffic other than authentication traffic until the computer has authenticated itself.

Figure 5-31 illustrates 802.1X. The workgroup switch is called the **authenticator**. It gets this name because the workgroup switch provides authentication service to the supplicant computer. The 802.1X standard normally also uses a central **authentication server** to do the actual supplicant credentials checking.

When the supplicant host transmits its authentication credentials (password, etc.), the authenticator passes these credentials on to the authentication server. The authentication server checks these credentials against its authentication database. If the authentication server authenticates the credentials, it sends back a confirmation to the workgroup switch. The workgroup switch then allows the supplicant PC to send frames to other devices in the network.

Using a central authentication server provides four benefits.

- *Switch Cost.* First, having the central authentication server check credentials instead of having the switch doing this minimizes the processing power needed in the workgroup switch. Given the large number of workgroup switches, this can produce a major cost saving.
- *Consistency.* Second, having all credentials on the authentication server gives consistency in authentication. An attacker cannot succeed by trying many different workgroup switches until he or she finds one that is misconfigured and gives the attacker access.

- *Reduced Management Cost.* Third, management cost is reduced because credentials only need to be changed on the central authentication server when user authentication information is changed when a user joins the firm, leaves the firm, or needs other credential changes.
- *Rapid Changes.* Fourth, the credentials of individuals who are fired or suspended can be invalidated in seconds, on all workgroup switches.

Security Standards Come from the 802.1 Working Group

Note from its name that the 802.1X standard was created by the *802.1* Working Group, not by the *802.3* Working Group that creates Ethernet standards. The 802.1 Working Group produces standards that cut across all 802 network technologies. This includes security standards.

Test Your Understanding

24. a) What threat does 802.1X address? b) How does the standard address the threat? c) In 802.1X, what device is the authenticator? d) What are the benefits of using a central authentication server instead of having the individual authenticators do all authentication work?

802.3ba: 40 Gbps and 100 Gbps Ethernet

This chapter talked briefly about 40 Gbps and 100 Gbps Ethernet, which were standardized in 2010 as 802.3ba. In this box, we will look at 802.3ba in a little more detail.

For most organizations, 10 Gbps is adequate for their current LAN requirements. However, a few firms are pushing the limits of this technology. Internet service providers (ISPs), which carry the Internet's backbone traffic, are already being squeezed by 10 Gbps speeds. So are some other industry sectors, such as financial services. Most firms, however, are more interested in 802.3ba as a way to reduce costs, especially where link aggregation is being used on trunk links that require multiple 10GBASE-x connections.

The speed of 100 Gbps is a normal expectation based on earlier Ethernet developments, which grew by a factor of 10 with each new standard. The speed of 40 Gbps is used primarily in wide area networking, which we will look at in Chapter 10.

At the data link layer, the IEEE was able to keep everything the same as in earlier standards. This includes the MAC layer frame structure and minimum and maximum frame sizes. At the physical layer, however, the situation is very different.

The 802.3ba standard uses the concept of *lanes*. The **virtual lane** is the entire 100 Gbp or 40 Gbps transmission path. It is called a virtual lane because the physical situation is more complex. Ports on different devices may be connected by multiple optical fiber transmission lines, each being called a **media lane**. In other words, the 100 Gbps virtual lane can consist of several slower media lanes.

For LANs, the most important 100 Gbps standard in the short run is likely to be 100GBASE-SR10. The 100G indicates that the speed is 100 Gbps. The S indicates that short-wavelength light is used (850 nm). The R denotes how the bits are packaged in terms of data and control bits. (We will not look at this issue). Finally, the 10 indicates that there are 10 media lanes.

In practice, 100GBASE-SR10 connects ports on different devices with 24 optical fibers! Ten are used for transmission *in each direction*, with each fiber carrying data at 10 Gbps. In addition, there are an extra two fibers for transmission in each direction. These are called **dark fibers** in the

(continued)

sense that they normally are not used. However, if one of the used fibers goes bad, the sender will turn on one of the two dark fibers going in that direction.

This seems rather unwieldy, but when 24 fibers are packed into a single cord, the resulting cord is still quite thin. In addition, there is only a single connector at each end of the fiber cable. It simply snaps in place like a traditional connector. Of course, the connector is a bit larger than traditional connectors, but it is only about twice as wide. The 24 fibers, being so thin, can be packed closely together in the connector as well as in the cord.

An obvious question is, "Hey, isn't this just trunking in disguise?" The answer is, "Sort of." Both use multiple physical connections for a single logical connection. However, traditional trunking is somewhat costly to manage, and ten 10 Gbps ports are expensive. By requiring only a single port at each end and by automatically handling the virtual lane's multiple media lanes, 100GBASE-SR10 is attractive economically. 100GBASE-SR10 should also reduce power requirements. This will save money both directly in each device and indirectly by lowering air conditional costs for equipment rooms.

It is important to recognize that the physical layer standards that have already been defined should be viewed as "Generation 1" devices. Over time, new options will appear. For example, if each media lane's speed can be increased to 25 Gbps instead of 10 Gbps, only four media lanes would be recovered, so only 10 fibers would be needed, including a dark fiber in each direction. In addition, 100GBASE-SR10 is currently limited to 100 to 125 meters, even over very good optical fiber. Maximum distance is likely to grow in the future.

Test Your Understanding

25. a) What is likely to be the main standard for 100 gigabit per second Ethernet? b) At what speed does 100GBASE-SR10 operate? c) What is the speed of the 100GBASE-SR10 virtual lane? d) What is the speed of an individual 100GBASE-SR10 media lane? e) How many optical fibers does 100GBASE-SR10 require? f) How many connectors does 100GBASE-SR10 require at each device? g) Why is 100GBASE-SR10 better than simply trunking ten 10GBASE-SX connectors on each device? (Explain your answer.) h) How are 100 Gbps standards likely to change for LANs as technology matures?

CONCLUSION

Synopsis

In this chapter, we looked at Ethernet switched wired LANs. In contrast to wide area networks (WANs), LANs are inexpensive per bit transmitted, so organizations can afford to provide extremely high-speed LAN service. There once were several switched wired LAN technologies, but Ethernet, which is standardized by the IEEE 802 Committee's 802.3 Working Group, is the only significant switched wired LAN technology.

All LANs are governed by physical and data link layer standards. We began by looking at physical layer standards—specifically at binary and digital signaling, which give resistance to transmission error. Ethernet uses two major transmission media. Four-pair unshielded twisted pair (4-pair UTP) dominates transmission between hosts and the workgroup switches they connect to. Optical fiber, which can span longer distances, is used primarily to link switches to other switches. LANs use inexpensive multimode fiber, which can span distances up to about 500 meters, which is sufficient for LANs. Carriers use more expensive single-mode fiber. Normally, a single UTP or optical fiber link connects a pair of switches. However, with link aggregation (also called bonding), a pair of switches can be connected by two or more UTP or fiber links. Ethernet has many physical layer standards for both UTP and optical fiber. Standards set both transmission speed and maximum distance. They allow network designer to select media standards for specific media runs within the customer premises. For UTP, quality levels are indicated by category numbers. Today, Category 5e, 6, and 6A wiring are dominant.

We looked in some depth at Ethernet's frame organization. The Ethernet frame has many fields. The first helps synchronize the receiver's clock with the sender's clock. The source and destination MAC addresses are 48 bits long and are expressed for human consumption in hexadecimal notation. The final field is used for error checking. Ethernet does error detection but merely discards incorrect frames. There is no error correction, so Ethernet is an unreliable protocol. The data field has two subfields. The first is the logical link control (LLC) subheader, which specifies the type of packet contained in the data field. The second is the packet itself—usually an IP packet, although other types of packets can be carried. The length field specifies the length of the overall data field. There are two optional tag fields used for priority and virtual LAN operations.

We looked at how Ethernet switches forward frames. Ethernet networks must be organized as a hierarchy, in which there are no loops among the switches. Consequently, there is only a single path between any two hosts. This makes Ethernet switching tables very simple, so Ethernet switches are both fast and inexpensive.

Although basic Ethernet switch forwarding is simple, large Ethernet networks add complications to this basic operation. In a hierarchical LAN, a single point of failure, such as a transmission link or switch, can isolate client hosts from server hosts. Backup links would solve this problem but would create loops that would destroy the strict hierarchy. The Rapid Spanning Tree Protocol allows backup links to be installed but to be activated only if there is a break in the hierarchy.

In a basic Ethernet network, any host can reach any other host. However, advanced Ethernet switches can subdivide the physical LAN into multiple virtual LANs (VLANs) whose hosts can talk to one another but cannot talk to hosts on other VLANs. This provides a measure of security.

Another capability is priority. Different frames can be given different priority levels. If a switch is overloaded, high-priority frames will be sent first. Priority is important for applications that are intolerant of latency (delay). It will allow the frames of these applications to be sent on with minimal delay.

An important capability is switch manageability. Manageable switches can be controlled by a central network manager. This allows the manager to get information from the switches. It also allows the manager to change the configuration of switches. Although managed switches are substantially more expensive than basic switches, they reduce management costs more than enough to offset these purchase costs. Only recent versions of the Simple Network Management Protocol have good security, and even this security can be overcome by lazy network administrators.

When you use a wired telephone at home and the power fails, you can still make and receive calls. This is because the telephone network provides enough power to operate the phone. In an analogous way, the power over Ethernet (POE) standard provides a certain amount of electrical power to each switch port. This allows simple devices such as access points to receive power from the switch instead of requiring a separate power connection, which might be expensive to install.

Ethernet security has not been seen as a major issue in most firms. However, we reviewed the 802.1X standard that requires a host to authenticate itself to a switch port before it is allowed to use the network. This prevents attackers from walking into a firm and simply plugging into any Ethernet wall jack. In 802.1X, the host is called a peer, the switch is the authenticator, and there is a back-end authenticator server that keeps authentication credentials. Having a central authentication server that keeps authentication data and makes authentication decisions reduces the work that must be done by the switch. This minimizes switch cost. Centralizing authentication data and decisions on the authentication server also brings consistency to authentication, reduces management labor, and allows the status of individual users to be changed instantly. Note that this security standard comes from the 802.1 Working Group, not the 802.3 Working Group.

The box at the end of this chapter provided more information on the Ethernet 802.3ba standard for 40 Gbps and 100 Gbps Ethernet. There was an important distinction between the 100 Gbps virtual lane between two devices and the multiple slower media lanes over which the signals are carried. The 802.3ba standard essentially does very elegant and simpler trunking between two devices.

END-OF-CHAPTER QUESTIONS

Thought Questions

1. With power over Ethernet, what is the potential danger to users in having powered switch ports? How do you think this danger might be avoided?

2. When would the optional Tag fields in the Ethernet frame be added?

3. The Length field is 22. a) How long is the combined data field and PAD? b) How long is the PAD?

Design Questions

1. Design an Ethernet network to connect a single client PC to a single server. The two devices are 410 feet apart. They need to communicate at 800 Mbps. Your design will specify the locations of switches and the transmission line between the switches.

2. Add to your design in the previous question. Add another client next to the first client.

This client will also communicate with the server and will also need 800 Mbps in transmission speed. Again, your design will specify the the locations of switches and the transmission line between the switches.

Troubleshooting Question

1. You are connecting two switches in a large Ethernet switch with 32 switches. You are using 4-pair UTP. Suddenly, transmissions cannot travel over the network. What do

you think might have happened? If you cannot come up with a good solution, reread the synopsis and see which points might apply.

Perspective Questions

1. What was the most surprising thing you learned in this chapter?

2. What was the most difficult part of this chapter for you?

5a HANDS-ON: CUTTING AND CONNECTORIZING UTP[1]

INTRODUCTION

Chapter 5 discussed UTP wirsing in general. This chapter discusses how to cut and connectorize (add connectors to) solid UTP wiring.

SOLID AND STRANDED WIRING

Solid-Wire UTP versus Stranded-Wire UTP

The TIA/EIA-568 standard requires that long runs to wall jacks use **solid-wire UTP**, in which each of the eight wires really is a single solid wire.

However, patch cords running from the wall outlet to a NIC usually are **stranded-wire UTP**, in which each of the eight "wires" really is a bundle of thinner wire strands. So stranded-wire UTP has eight bundles of wires, each bundle in its own insulation and acting like a single wire.

Relative Advantages

Solid wire is needed in long cords because it has lower attenuation than stranded wire. In contrast, stranded-wire UTP cords are more flexible than solid-wire cords, making them ideal for patch cords—especially the one running to the desktop—because they can be bent more and still function. They are more durable than solid-wire UTP cords.

Adding Connectors

It is relatively easy to add RJ-45 connectors to solid-wire UTP cords. However, it is very difficult to add RJ-45 connectors to stranded-wire cords. Stranded-wire patch cords should be purchased from the factory precut to desired lengths and preconnectorized.

In addition, when purchasing equipment to connectorize solid-wire UTP, it is important to purchase crimpers designed for solid wire.

CUTTING THE CORD

Solid-wire UTP normally comes in a box or spool containing 50 meters or more of wire. The first step is to cut a length of UTP cord that matches your need. It is good to be a little generous with the length. This way, bad connectorization can be fixed

---

[1]This material is based on the author's lab projects and on the lab project of Professor Harry Reif of James Madison University.

Solid-Wire UTP
> Each of the eight wires is a solid wire
> Low attenuation over long distances
> Easy to connectorize
> Inflexible and stiff—not good for runs to the desktop

Stranded-Wire UTP
> Each of the eight "wires" is itself several thin strands of wire within an insulation tube
> Flexible and durable—good for runs to the desktop
> Impossible to connectorize in the field (bought as patch cords)
> Higher attenuation than solid-wire UTP—Used only in short runs
>> From wall jack to desktop
>> Within a telecommunications closet (see Chapter 3)

FIGURE 5a-1   Solid-Wire and Stranded-Wire UTP (Study Figure)

by cutting off the connector and adding a new connector to the shortened cord. Also, UTP cords should never be subjected to pulls (strain), and adding a little extra length creates some slack.

STRIPPING THE CORD

Now the cord must be stripped at each end using a **stripping tool** such as the one shown in Figure 5a-2. The installer rotates the stripper once around the cord, scoring (cutting into) the cord jacket (but not cutting through it). The installer then pulls off the scored end of the cord, exposing about 5 cm (about 2 in.) of the wire pairs.

It is critical not to score the cord too deeply, or the insulation around the individual wires may be cut. This creates short circuits. A really deep cut also will nick the wire, perhaps causing it to snap immediately or later.

WORKING WITH THE EXPOSED PAIRS

Pair Colors

The four pairs each have a color: orange, green, blue, or brown. One wire of the pair usually is a completely solid color. The other usually is white with stripes of the pair's color. For instance, the orange pair has an orange wire and a white wire with orange stripes.

Untwisting the Pairs

The wires of each pair are twisted around each other several times per inch. These must be untwisted after the end of the cord is stripped.

Ordering the Pairs

The wires now must be placed in their correct order, left to right. Figure 5a-3 shows the location of Pin 1 on the RJ-45 connector and on a wall jack or NIC.

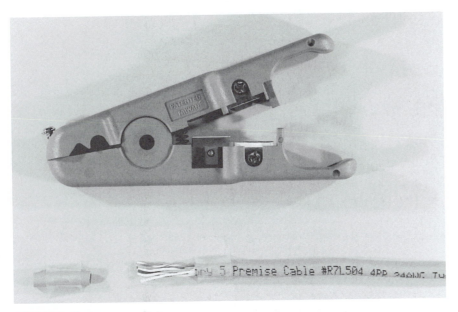

FIGURE 5a-2   Stripping Tool

Source: Courtesy of Raymond R. Panko

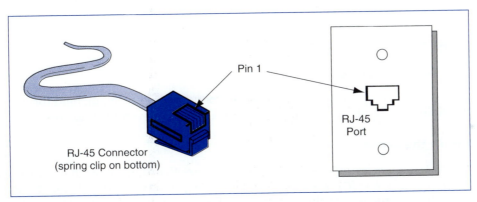

FIGURE 5a-3   Location of Pin 1 on an RJ-45 Connector and Wall Jack or NIC

Which color wire goes into which connector slot? The two standardized patterns are shown in Figure 5a-4. The T568B pattern is much more common in the United States.

The connectors at both ends of the cord use the same pattern. If the white-orange wire goes into Pin 1 of the connector on one end of the cord, it also goes into Pin 1 of the connector at the other end.

Cutting the Wires

The length of the exposed wires must be limited to 1.25 cm (0.5 in.) or slightly less. After the wires have been arranged in the correct order, a cutter should cut across the wires to make them this length. The cut should be made straight across, so that all

Pin*	T568A	T568B
1	White-Green	White-Orange
2	Green	Orange
3	White-Orange	White-Green
4	Blue	Blue
5	White-Blue	White-Blue
6	Orange	Green
7	White-Brown	White-Brown
8	Brown	Brown

Note: Do not confuse T568A and T568B pin colors with the TIA/EIA-568 Standard.

FIGURE 5a-4   T568A and T568B Pin Colors

wires are of equal length. Otherwise, they will not all reach the end of the connector when they are inserted into it. Wires that do not reach the end will not make electrical contact.

ADDING THE CONNECTOR

Holding the Connector

The next step is to place the wires in the RJ-45 connector. In one hand, hold the connector, clip side down, with the opening in the back of the connector facing you.

Sliding in the Wires

Now, slide the wires into the connector, making sure that they are in the correct order (white-orange on your left). There are grooves in the connector that will help. Be sure to push the wires all the way to the end or proper electrical contact will not be made with the pins at the end.

Before you crimp the connector, look down at the top of the connector, holding the tip away from you. The first wire on your left should be mostly white. So should every second wire. If they are not, you have inserted your wires incorrectly.[2]

Some Jacket Inside the Connector

If you have shortened your wires properly, there will be a little bit of jacket inside the RJ-45 connector.

---

[2]Thanks to Jason Okumura, who suggested this way of checking the wires.

CRIMPING

Pressing Down

Get a really good **crimping tool** (see Figure 5a-5). Place the connector with the wires in it into the crimp and push down firmly. Good crimping tools have ratchets to reduce the chance of your pushing down too tightly.

Making Electrical Contact

The front of the connector has eight pins running from the top almost to the bottom (spring clip side). When you **crimp** the connector, you force these eight pins through the insulation around each wire and into the wire itself. This seems like a crude electrical connection, and it is. However, it normally works very well. Your wires are now connected to the connector's pins. By the way, this is called an **insulation displacement connection (IDC)** because it cuts through the insulation.

Strain Relief

When you crimp, the crimper also forces a ridge in the back of the RJ-45 connector into the jacket of the cord. This provides **strain relief**, meaning that if someone pulls on the cord (a bad idea), he or she will be pulling only to the point where the jacket has the ridge forced into it. There will be no strain where the wires connect to the pins.

TESTING

Purchasing the best UTP cabling means nothing unless you install it properly. Wiring errors are common in the field, so you need to test every cord after you install it. Testing is inexpensive compared to troubleshooting subtle wiring problems later.

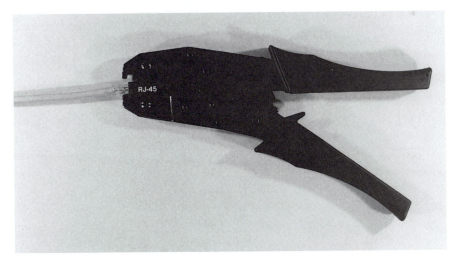

FIGURE 5a-5   Crimping Tool

Source: Courtesy of Raymond R. Panko

Testing with Continuity Testers

The simplest testers are **continuity testers**, which merely test whether the wires are arranged in correct order within the two RJ-45 connectors and are making good electrical contact with the connector. They cost only about $100.

Testing for Signal Quality

Better testers cost $500–$2,000 but are worth the extra money. In addition to testing for continuity problems, they send **test signals** through the cord to determine whether the cord meets TIA/EIA-568 signal-quality requirements. Many include **time domain reflectometry (TDR)**, which sends a signal and listens for echoes in order to measure the length of the UTP cord or to find if and where breaks exist in the cord.

Test Your Understanding

1. a) Explain the technical difference between solid-wire UTP and stranded-wire UTP. b) In what way is solid-wire UTP better? c) In what way is stranded-wire UTP better? d) Where would you use each? e) Which should only be connectorized at the factory?
2. If you have a wire run of 50 meters, should you cut the cord to 50 meters? Explain.
3. Why do you score the jacket of the cord with the stripping tool instead of cutting all the way through the jacket?
4. a) What are the colors of the four pairs? b) If you are following T568B, which wire goes into Pin 3? c) At the other end of the cord, would the same wire go into Pin 3?
5. After you arrange the wires in their correct order and cut them across, how much of the wires should be exposed from the jacket?
6. a) Describe RJ-45's insulation displacement approach. b) Describe its strain relief approach.
7. a) Should you test every cord in the field after installation? b) For what do inexpensive testers test? c) For what do expensive testers test?

5b HANDS-ON: ETHERNET SWITCHING

LEARNING OBJECTIVES

By the end of this chapter, you should be able to:

- Set up a small Ethernet switched network.
- Observe what happens if you create a loop among Ethernet switches.

THE EXERCISE

This is a class exercise rather than an individual exercise. It is rather quick (taking 15 to 20 minutes), but it takes an investment in resources.

What You Will Need

- A number of Ethernet switches. In general, it is good to have one switch for every two to four students, with the low ratio being much better. These can be very cheap switches.
- Enough UTP cords to connect the switches to each other and to the wall jack that bring the campus network into the classroom. Each will need to be 3–6 meters in length, depending on the layout of the classroom. Each student group should have sufficient room to work.
- Each Ethernet switch is powered. You may need to have some power cables so that all of the teams have power for their switches.
- Two notebooks to plug into the network.

Creating the Network

The students should create a network like the one in Figure 5b-1. There should be a top-level switch at the front of the classroom. It should plug into the wall jack that connects the classroom to the campus network.

Below the top-level switch, other switches should be arranged in a hierarchy. I find it is useful to have a simple hierarchy with two columns of switches as shown in the figure. It is important to keep a strict hierarchy among the switches.

After the switches are set up, attach PCs to switches at the end of each column. See if the PCs can connect to the Internet via the classroom wall jack. They should be able to do so.

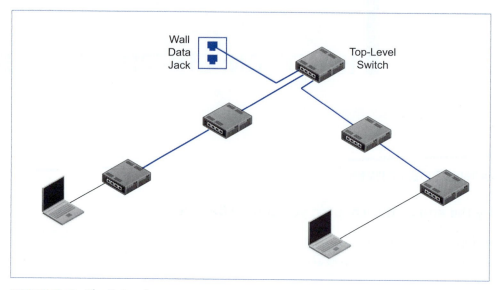

FIGURE 5b-1   The Network

At the end of this exercise, you can see how straightforward it is to set up a hierarchical Ethernet network. The switches are easy to power up, and RJ-45 connectors simply go "snap."

Creating a Loop

Now that the network is working, it is time to create a loop. Loops are not allowed in Ethernet, and you are about to see why. Connect two switches so that a loop is created, as Figure 5b-2 illustrates. Now see if the PCs can still access the Internet. They should not be able to do so.

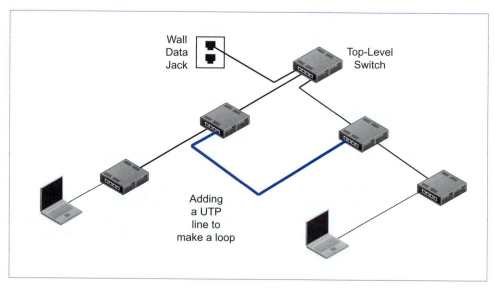

FIGURE 5b-2   Adding a Loop

6
WIRELESS LANs I

LEARNING OBJECTIVES

By the end of this chapter, you should be able to:

- Explain radio signal propagation: frequencies, antennas, and wireless propagation problems.
- Describe wireless LAN technologies.
- Explain radio bands, bandwidth, and channels.
- Distinguish between normal and spread spectrum transmission.
- Describe 802.11 WLAN operation with access points and a switched Ethernet distribution system to link the access points.
- Compare and contrast the 802.11g, 802.11n, 802.11ac, and 802.11ad transmission standards. Discuss emerging trends in 802.11 operation, including channels with much wider bandwidth, MIMO, beamforming, and multiuser MIMO.
- Briefly discuss emerging trends in 802.11 standards. Discuss the key points of Wi-Fi Direct and wireless mesh networking.

CHRISTOPHER LOREK

Two years ago, Christopher Lorek bought his wife a new notebook computer. Claire was pleased with her new computer, but she didn't want to run a new unshielded twisted pair (UTP) line to it from their access router. She wanted mobility. So Christopher bought a new access router with a built-in access point. The new wireless router was inexpensive. It operated in the 2.4 GHz radio band, and it followed the 802.11g standard. Christopher also bought a wireless printer for them to use. It also operated in the 2.4 GHz band using the 802.11g standard.

Although Claire liked the mobility, she found Internet access painfully slow. Christopher downloaded an application to Claire's computer to identify nearby wireless access routers. When he used it, he found that there were only three available channels, and at least one of his neighbors had an access point operating on each channel. The problem, then, appeared to be interference.

Christopher decided to get a router that would operate in the uncrowded 5 GHz band. He was pleased to find that routers that operated in the 5 GHz band also used the 802.11n standard, which is several times faster than 802.11g. The store had two 5 GHz routers. One only operated in the 2.4 GHz band. The other operated in both the 2.4 GHz and 5 GHz bands simultaneously. The one that operated simultaneously in the two bands was more expensive.

Test Your Understanding

1. a) Which terms in this case were unfamiliar to you? b) What do you think Christopher should do? Justify your conclusion.

INTRODUCTION

In Chapter 5, we looked at wired switched networks. Technologies for those networks, for instance, Ethernet, require both physical and data link layer standards. Consequently, they are OSI standards. In this chapter and in Chapter 7, we will look at wireless LAN management and security. Like wired LANs, wireless networks are also single networks, which require physical and data link layer standards. So they too are OSI standards.

Although many people think of wireless transmission as something new and underdeveloped, businesses were already spending more on wireless LANs than wired LANs in 2008. Wireless transmission is the growth sector in networking today and will be for some time to come.

Test Your Understanding

2. a) At what layers do wireless networks operate? b) Are wireless network standards OSI standards or TCP/IP standards? Explain.

BASIC 802.11 WIRELESS LAN (WLAN) OPERATION

Having discussed wireless transmission briefly, we will look at wireless networking's widest application today, wireless local area networks. A **wireless local area network (WLAN)**, like any type of LAN, operates on the customer premises.

Wireless LANs (WLANs) use radio for physical layer transmission on the customer premises.

Wireless LAN Technology

   The dominant WLAN technology today
   Standardized by the 802.11 Working Group

Wireless Computers Connect to Access Points (Figure 6-2 and Figure 6-3)

Supplement Wired LANs

   Access points connect to the corporate LAN
   So that wireless hosts can reach servers on the Ethernet LAN
   So that wireless hosts can reach Internet access routers on the Ethernet LAN

Large 802.11 WLANs

   Organizations can provide coverage throughout a building or a university campus
   By the judicious installation of many access points

FIGURE 6-1   802.11 Wireless LAN (WLAN) Standards (Study Figure)

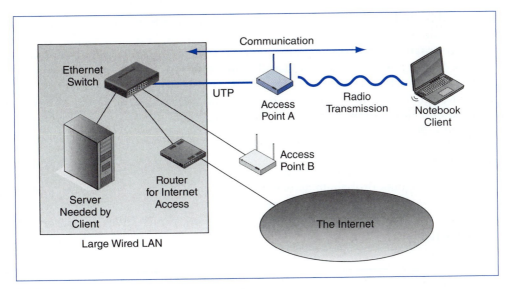

FIGURE 6-2   802.11 Wireless LAN (WLAN) Operation

The most important WLAN standards today are the **802.11** standards, which are created by the **IEEE 802.11 Working Group**. Recall that Ethernet standards are created by a different working group, the 802.3 Working Group.

Rather than being a competitor for wired Ethernet LANs, **802.11 WLANs** today primarily *supplement* wired LANs, but do not replace them. Figure 6-2 shows that mobile users typically connect by radio to devices called **wireless access points**, or, simply, **access points**. These access points link the mobile user to the firm's wired Ethernet LAN.

Why is there normally a connection to the firm's main wired LAN? Quite simply, the servers that mobile host devices need, as well as the firm's Internet access router, usually are on the wired LAN. Wireless hosts need the wired LAN to reach the resources they need. A single 802.11 wireless access point can serve multiple hosts up to 30 to 100 meters away.

In a home, you are likely to have a single access point. Businesses need far larger coverage areas. By placing wireless access points judiciously throughout a building, a company can construct a large 802.11 WLAN "cloud" that can serve mobile users anywhere in the building. We will spend most of this chapter looking at the technology of 802.11 WLANs.

Test Your Understanding

3. a) What 802 working group creates 802.11 standards? b) Why do wireless clients need access to the wired Ethernet LAN? c) How can firms provide WLAN coverage throughout a large building?

RADIO SIGNAL PROPAGATION

Chapter 5 discussed propagation effects in wired transmission media (UTP and optical fiber). Generally speaking, these effects can be well controlled by respecting cord distance limits and taking other installation precautions. This is possible because wired propagation is predictable. If you input a signal, you can estimate fairly precisely what it will be at the other end of a cord.

In contrast, radio propagation is very unreliable. Radio signals bounce off obstacles, fail to pass through walls and filing cabinets, and have other problems we will look at in this section. Consequently, wireless networks, which use radio to deliver signals, are more complex to engineer than wired networks. Therefore, we will spend more time on wireless propagation effects than we did on wired propagation effects.

Frequencies

Wireless radio signals propagate as waves, as we saw in Chapter 5. Figure 6-3 again notes that waves are characterized by amplitude, wavelength, and frequency. While optical fiber waves are given in terms of wavelength, radio waves are described in terms of **frequency**.

Frequency is used to describe the radio waves used in WLANs.

In waves, frequency is the number of complete cycles per second. One cycle per second is one **hertz (Hz)**. Metric designations are used to describe frequencies. In the metric system, frequencies increase by a factor of 1,000, rather than 1,024. The most common radio frequencies for wireless data transmission are about 500 **megahertz (MHz)** to 10 **gigahertz (GHz)**.

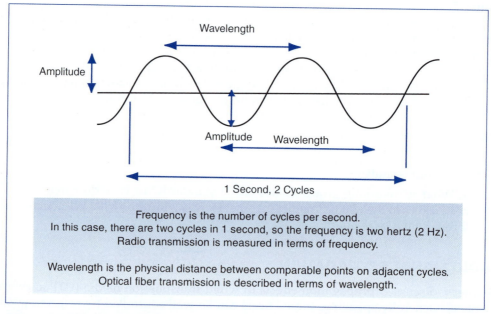

FIGURE 6-3 Electromagnetic Wave

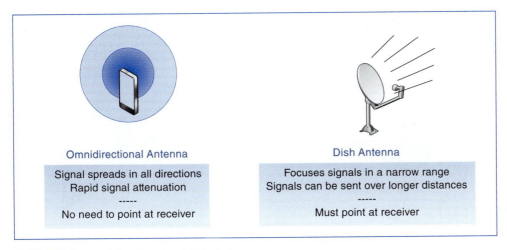

FIGURE 6-4   Omnidirectional and Dish Antennas

Test Your Understanding

4. a) Is wireless radio transmission usually expressed in terms of wavelength or frequency? b) What is a hertz? c) Convert 3.4 MHz to a number without a metric prefix. d) At what range of frequencies do most wireless systems operate?

Antennas

Radio transmission requires an antenna. Figure 6-4 shows that there are two types of radio antennas: omnidirectional antennas and dish antennas.

- **Omnidirectional antennas** transmit signals equally strongly in all directions and receive incoming signals equally well from all directions. Consequently, the antenna does not need to point in the direction of the receiver. However, because the signal spreads in all three dimensions, only a small fraction of the energy transmitted by an omnidirectional antenna reaches the receiver. Omnidirectional antennas are best for short distances, such as those found in a wireless LAN (WLAN) or a cellular metropolitan area network.

- **Dish antennas**, in contrast, point in a particular direction, which allows them to focus stronger outgoing signals in that direction for the same power and to receive weaker incoming signals from that direction. (A dish antenna is like the reflector in a flashlight.) Dish antennas are good for longer distances because of their focusing ability, but users need to know the direction of the other antenna. Also, omnidirectional antennas are easier to use. (Imagine if you had to carry a dish with you whenever you carried your cellular phone. You would not even know where to point the dish!)

Test Your Understanding

5. a) Distinguish between omnidirectional and dish antennas in terms of operation. b) Under what circumstances would you use an omnidirectional antenna? c) Under what circumstances would you use a dish antenna? d) What type of antenna normally is used in WLANs? Why?

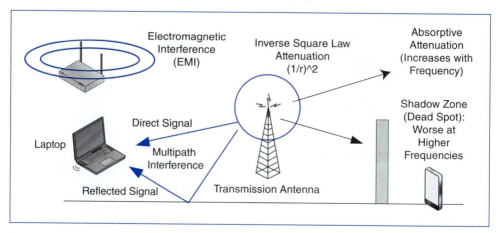

FIGURE 6-5 Wireless Transmission Problems

Wireless Propagation Problems

We have already noted that, although wireless communication gives mobility, wireless transmission is not very predictable, and there often are serious propagation problems. Figure 6-5 illustrates five common wireless propagation problems.

INVERSE SQUARE LAW ATTENUATION Compared with signals sent through wires and optical fiber, radio signals attenuate very rapidly. When a signal spreads out from any kind of antenna, its strength is spread over the area of a sphere. (In omnidirectional antennas, power is spread equally over the sphere, while in dish antennas, power is concentrated primarily in one direction on the sphere.)

The area of a sphere is proportional to the square of its radius, so signal strength in any direction weakens by an **inverse square law** $(1/r^2)$, as Equation 5-1 illustrates. Here, S_1 is the signal strength at distance r_1, and S_2 is the signal strength at a farther distance r_2.

$$S_2 = S_1 * (r_1/r_2)^2 \qquad \text{(Equation 5–1)}$$

To give an example, if you triple the distance $(r_1/r_2 = 1/3)$, the signal strength (S_2) falls to only one-ninth $(1/3^2)$ of its original strength (S_1). With radio propagation, you have to be relatively close to your communication partner unless the signal strength is very high, an omnidirectional antenna is used, or both.

To give a specific example, at 10 meters, the signal strength is 20 milliwatts (mW). How strong will the signal be at 20 meters?

- The distance doubles (so r_1/r_2 is 1/2).
- So we multiply the signal strength at 10 meters by 1/4 (1/2 squared)
- Twenty mW multiplied by 1/4 is 5 mW.
- So the strength of the signal at 10 meters will be 5 mW.

ABSORPTIVE ATTENUATION As a radio signal travels, it is partially absorbed by the air molecules, plants, and other things it passes through. This **absorptive attenuation** is especially bad in moist air, and office plants are the natural enemies of wireless transmission. Absorptive attenuation is especially bad for longer-distance outdoor propagation.

SHADOW ZONES (DEAD SPOTS)   To some extent, radio signals can go through and bend around objects. However, if there is a large or dense object (e.g., a brick wall), blocking the direct path between the sender and the receiver, the receiver may be in a **shadow zone (dead spot)**, where the receiver cannot get the signal. If you have a cellular telephone and often try to use it within buildings, you probably are familiar with this problem.

MULTIPATH INTERFERENCE   In addition, radio waves tend to bounce off walls, floors, ceilings, and other objects. As Figure 6-6 shows, this may mean that a receiver will receive two or more signals—a direct signal and one or more reflected signals. The direct and reflected signals will travel different distances and so may be out of phase when they reach the receiver. For example, one may be at its highest amplitude while the other is at its lowest, giving an average of zero. If so, they will completely cancel out if their amplitudes are the same.

   This **multipath interference** may cause the signal to range from strong to nonexistent within a few centimeters (inches). If the difference in time between the direct and reflected signal is large, some reflected signals may even interfere with the next direct signal. Multipath interference is the most serious propagation problem at WLAN frequencies.

Multipath interference is the most serious propagation problem at WLAN frequencies.

ELECTROMAGNETIC INTERFERENCE (EMI)   A final common propagation problem in wireless communication is **electromagnetic interference (EMI)**. Other devices produce EMI at frequencies used in wireless data communications. Among these

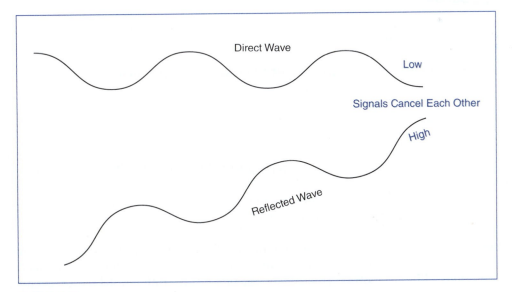

FIGURE 6-6   Multipath Interference

devices are cordless telephones, microwaves, and especially devices in other nearby wireless networks.

FREQUENCY-DEPENDENT PROPAGATION PROBLEMS To complicate matters, two wireless propagation problems are affected by frequency.

- First, higher-frequency waves suffer more rapidly from absorptive attenuation than lower-frequency waves because they are absorbed more rapidly by moisture in the air, leafy vegetation, and other water-bearing obstacles. Consequently, as we will see in this chapter, WLAN signals around 5 GHz attenuate more rapidly than signals around 2.4 GHz.
- Second, shadow zone problems grow worse with frequency. As frequency increases, radio waves become less able to go through and bend around objects.

Test Your Understanding

6. a) Which offers more reliable transmission characteristics—UTP or radio transmission? b) Which attenuates more rapidly with distance—signals sent through wired media or radio signals? c) If the signal strength from an omnidirectional radio source is 8 mW at 30 meters, how strong will it be at 120 meters, ignoring absorptive attenuation? Show your work. d) How are shadow zones (dead spots) created? e) Why is multipath interference very sensitive to location? f) What is the most serious propagation problem in WLANs? g) List some sources of EMI. h) What propagation problems become worse as frequency increases?

RADIO BANDS, BANDWIDTH, AND SPREAD SPECTRUM TRANSMISSION

Radio Bands

Now we can begin looking at new information about radio transmission, beginning with the frequency spectrum, service bands, and channels.

THE FREQUENCY SPECTRUM AND SERVICE BANDS The **frequency spectrum** consists of all possible frequencies from zero hertz to infinity, as Figure 6-7.

SERVICE BANDS The frequency spectrum is divided into contiguous spectrum ranges called **service bands** that are dedicated to specific services. For instance, in the United States, the AM radio service band lies between 535 kHz and 1,705 kHz. The FM radio service band, in turn, lies between 88 MHz and 108 MHz. The 2.4 GHz unlicensed band that we will see later for wireless LANs extends from 2.4000 GHz to 2.4835 GHz. There are also service bands for police and fire departments, amateur radio operators, communication satellites, and many other purposes.

CHANNELS Service bands are subdivided into smaller frequency ranges called **channels**. A different signal can be sent in each channel because signals in different channels do not interfere with one another. This is why you can receive different television channels successfully.

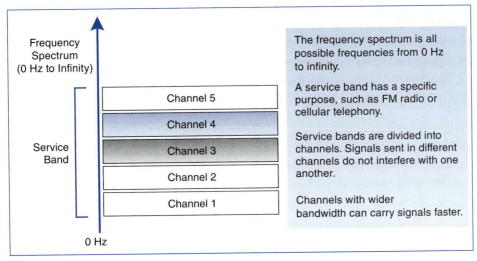

FIGURE 6-7   The Frequency Distribution, Service Bands, and Channels

Test Your Understanding

7. a) Distinguish among the frequency spectrum, service bands, and channels. b) In radio, how can you send multiple signals without the signals interfering with one another?

Signal and Channel Bandwidth

Figure 6-3 showed wave operating at a single frequency. In contrast, Figure 6-9 shows that signals do not operate at a single frequency. Rather, signals spread over a range of frequencies. This range is called the signal's **bandwidth**. Signal bandwidth is measured by subtracting the lowest frequency from the highest frequency.

A channel also has a bandwidth. For instance, if the lowest frequency of an FM channel is 89.0 MHz and the highest frequency is 89.2 MHz, then the **channel bandwidth** is 0.2 MHz (200 kHz). AM radio channels are 10 kHz wide, FM channels have bandwidths of 200 kHz, and television channels are 6 MHz wide.

Why are there such large differences in channel bandwidth across service bands? The answer lies in the relationship between possible transmission speed in a channel and channel bandwidth. Shannon found that the maximum possible transmission speed (C) in bits per second when sending data through a channel is directly proportional to the channel's bandwidth (B) in hertz, as shown in the **Shannon Equation** (Equation 5-2).[1]

$$C = B[\mathrm{Log}_2(1 + S/N)] \qquad \textbf{(Equation 5–2)}$$

The maximum possible speed is directly proportional to bandwidth, so if you double the bandwidth, you can potentially transmit up to twice as fast. However, C is

[1] Claude Shannon, "A Mathematical Theory of Communication," *Bell System Technical Journal*, (July 1938), pp. 379–423, and (October 28, 1938), pp. 623–56.

Signal Bandwidth

Figure 6-4 shows a wave operating at a single frequency
However, most signals are spread over a range of frequencies (Figure 6-10)
The range between the highest and lowest frequencies is the signal's bandwidth
The maximum possible transmission speed increases with bandwidth

Channel Bandwidth

Channel bandwidth is the highest frequency in a channel minus the lowest frequency
An 88.0 MHz to 88.2 MHz channel has a bandwidth of 0.2 MHz (200 kHz)
Higher-speed signals need wider channel bandwidths

Shannon Equation

$C = B [\text{Log}_2 (1+S/N)]$

C = Maximum possible transmission speed in the channel (bps)
B = Bandwidth (Hz)
S/N = Signal-to-noise ratio measured as the power ratio, not as decibels
Note that doubling the bandwidth doubles the maximum possible transmission speed
Multiplying the bandwidth by X multiplies the maximum possible speed by X
Wide bandwidth is the key to fast transmission
Increasing S/N helps slightly, but usually cannot be done to any significant extent

Broadband and Narrowband Channels

Broadband means wide channel bandwidth and therefore high speed
Narrowband means narrow channel bandwidth and therefore low speed
Traditionally, narrowband is below 200 kbps; broadband is above 200 kbps

The Golden Zone

Most organizational radio technologies operate in the golden zone in the 500 MHz to 10 GHz range
Golden zone frequencies are high enough for there to be large total bandwidth
At higher frequencies, there is more available bandwidth
Golden zone frequencies are low enough to allow fairly good propagation characteristics
At lower frequencies, signals propagate better
Growing demand creates intense competition for frequencies in the Golden Zone

FIGURE 6-8 Channel Bandwidth and Transmission Speed (Study Figure)

the *maximum possible speed* for a given bandwidth and signal-to-noise ratio. *Real transmission throughput* will always be less.

To transmit at a given speed, you need a channel wide enough to handle that speed. For example, video signals produce many more bits per second than audio signals, so television uses much wider channels than AM radio (6 MHz versus 10 kHz in AM radio transmission).

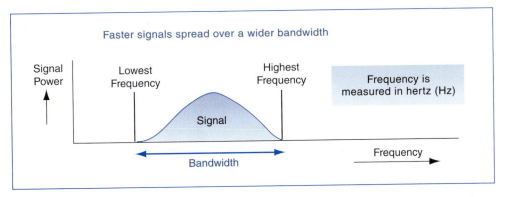

FIGURE 6-9   Signal Bandwidth

The signal-to-noise (S/N) ratio discussed in Chapter 5 is also important, but it is difficult to modify in practice. Radio signal strengths tend to be limited by law, and reducing noise is very difficult without going to super-cooled senders and receivers.

Channels with large bandwidths are called **broadband** channels. They can carry data very quickly. In contrast, channels with small bandwidths, called **narrowband** channels, can carry data only slowly. Although the terms *broadband* and *narrowband* technically refer only to the width of a channel, broadband has come to mean "fast," while narrowband has come to mean "slow."

Transmission systems that are very fast are usually called broadband systems even when they do not use channels.

Test Your Understanding

8. a) Does a signal usually travel at a single frequency, or does it spread over a range of frequencies? b) What is channel bandwidth? c) If the lowest frequency in a channel is 1.22 MHz and the highest frequency is 1.25 MHz, what is the channel bandwidth? (Use proper metric notation.) d) Why is large channel bandwidth desirable? e) What do we call a system whose channels have large bandwidth? f) What other types of system do we call *broadband*?

9. a) Write the Shannon Equation. List what each letter is in the equation. b) What information does C give you? c) What happens to the maximum possible propagation speed in a channel if the bandwidth is tripled while the signal-to-noise ratio remains the same? d) Given their relative bandwidths, about how many times as much data is sent per second in television than in AM radio? (The information to answer this question is in the text.) e) Telephone channels have a bandwidth of about 3.1 kHz. Do the following in Excel. Cut and paste your analyses into your homework. f) If a telephone channel's signal-to-noise ratio is 1,000 (the signal strength is 1,000 times larger than the noise strength), how fast can a telephone channel carry data? (Check figure: Telephone modems operate at about 30 kbps, so your answer should be roughly this speed.)

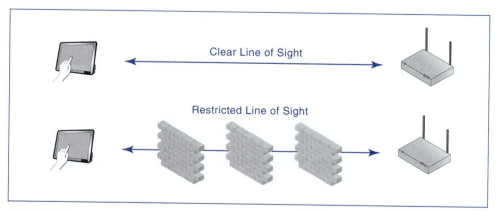

FIGURE 6-10 Line of Sight

The Golden Zone

Commercial mobile services operate in the high-megahertz to low-gigahertz range (approximately 500 MHz to 10 GHz). This is the **golden zone**. At lower frequencies, the spectrum is limited and has been almost entirely assigned. At higher frequencies, radio waves attenuate very rapidly with distance because of absorptive attenuation and cannot flow through or around objects as they do at lower frequencies. Consequently, at frequencies above about 10 GHz, the sender and receiver typically must have a **clear line of sight** (unobstructed direct path) between them. (See Figure 6-10.) Even at the high end of the golden zone, absorption and shadow zone propagation problems are large. The golden zone is limited, and demand for channels and service bands in the golden zone is increasing rapidly. Consequently, there is strong competition for bandwidth in the golden zone.

The golden zone for commercial mobile services is 500 MHz to 10 GHz.

Test Your Understanding

10. a) What is the golden zone in commercial mobile radio transmission? b) Why is the golden zone important? c) What is a clear line-of-sight limitation?

Licensed and Unlicensed Radio Bands

If two radio hosts transmit at the same frequency, their signals will interfere with each other. In the terminology of Chapter 5, this is electromagnetic interference. To prevent such chaos, governments regulate how radio transmission is used. The International Telecommunications Union, which is a branch of the United Nations, creates worldwide rules that define service bands and specify how individual radio service bands are to be used. Individual countries enforce these rules but are given discretion over how to implement controls.

LICENSED RADIO BANDS In licensed radio bands, stations must have a government license to operate. They also need a license change if they move their antennas.

Licensed Radio Bands

> If two nearby radio hosts transmit in the same channel, their signals will interfere
>
> Most radio bands are licensed bands, in which hosts need a license to transmit
>
> The government limits licenses to reduce interference
>
> Television bands, AM radio bands, etc., are licensed
>
> In cellular telephone bands, which are licensed, only the central transceivers are licensed, not the mobile phones

Unlicensed Radio Bands

> Some bands are set aside as unlicensed bands
>
> Hosts do not need to be licensed to be turned on or moved
>
> 802.11 operates in unlicensed radio bands
>
> This allows access points and hosts to be moved freely
>
> However, there is no way to stop interference from other nearby users
>
> Your only recourse is to negotiate with others
>
> At the same time, you may not cause unreasonable interference—for instance, by transmitting at excessive power

FIGURE 6-11   Licensed and Unlicensed Radio Bands (Study Figure)

Commercial television bands are licensed bands, as are AM and FM radio bands. Government agencies control who may have licenses. By doing so, the government limits interference to an acceptable level. In some licensed bands, the rules allow mobile hosts to move about while only central antennas are regulated. This is the case for mobile telephones.

UNLICENSED RADIO BANDS   However, for companies that have wireless access points and mobile computers, even the requirement to license central antennas (in this case, access points) is an impossible burden. Consequently, the government has created a few **unlicensed radio bands**. In these bands, any wireless host can be turned on or moved around without the need for any government approval.

The problem with unlicensed radio bands is that users of unlicensed radio bands must tolerate interference from others. If your neighbor sets up a wireless LAN next door to yours, you have no recourse but to negotiate with him or her over such matters as which channels each of you will use. At the same time, the law prevents you from creating unreasonable interference—for instance, by using illegally high transmission power.

Test Your Understanding

11. a) Do WLANs today use licensed or unlicensed bands? b) What is the advantage of using unlicensed bands? c) What is the disadvantage?

The 2.4 GHz and 5 GHz Unlicensed Bands

It would be impossible for a company to have licenses for all of its access points and wireless hosts, so 802.11 operates in unlicensed radio bands. More specifically, WLANs today use two unlicensed bands. One is the 2.4 GHz band. The other is the 5 GHz band.

The 2.4 GHz Unlicensed Band

Defined the same in almost all countries (2.400 GHz to 2.485 GHz)

Commonality reduces radio costs

Propagation characteristics are good

For 20 MHz 802.11 channels, only three non-overlapping channels are possible

Channels 1, 6, and 11

This creates co-channel interference between nearby access points transmitting in the same 20 MHz channel

Difficult or impossible to put nearby access points on different channels (Figure 6-14)

Also, potential problems from microwave ovens, cordless telephones, etc.

The 5 GHz Unlicensed Band

Radios are expensive because frequencies in different countries are different

Shorter propagation distance because of higher frequencies

Deader shadow zones because of higher frequencies

More bandwidth, so between 11 and 24 non-overlapping channels

Allows different access points to operate on non-overlapping channels

Some access points can operate on two channels to provide faster service

FIGURE 6-12 The 2.4 GHz and 5 GHz Unlicensed Bands (Study Figure)

THE 2.4 GHZ UNLICENSED BAND The **2.4 GHz unlicensed band** is the same in most countries in the world, stretching from 2.40 GHz to 2.4835 GHz. This commonality allows companies to sell generic 2.4 GHz radios, driving down the price of radios. In addition, radio propagation is better in the 2.4 GHz unlicensed band than in the higher-frequency 5 GHz band.

Unfortunately, the 2.4 GHz band is very limited. It has only 83.5 MHz of bandwidth. Traditionally, each 802.11 channel was 20 MHz wide, although 40 MHz bandwidth channels were introduced in 802.11n. Furthermore, due to the way channels are allocated, there are only three possible non-overlapping 20 MHz 802.11 channels, which are centered at Channels 1, 6, and 11.[2] If nearby access points operate in the same channel, their signals will interfere with each other unless the access points are far apart. This interference is called **co-channel interference**. If an 802.11n station finds itself in a crowded area, it will drop back to 20 MHz to reduce the interference it causes.

If you have only three access points that can all hear each other, there is no problem with having only three channels. You simply run each on a different channel, and there will be no co-channel interference. However, when you have multiple access points that can all hear each other, Figure 6-13 shows that there is no way to avoid having some co-channel interference. You can minimize co-channel interference somewhat

---

[2]Channel numbers were defined for the 2.4 GHz band when channels were narrower. A 20 MHz 802.11 channel overlaps several defined channels. Channels 1, 6, and 11 operate in the 2,402 MHz to 2,422 MHz, 2,427 MHz to 2,447 MHz, and 2,452 MHz to 2,472 MHz frequency ranges, respectively. Note that there are 5 MHz unused "guard bands" between the channels to prevent inter-channel interference.

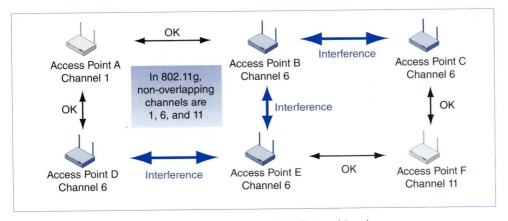

FIGURE 6-13 Co-channel Interference in the 2.4 GHz Unlicensed Band

by giving the shared channel to the two access points that are farthest apart, but this will only reduce interference somewhat.

In addition, the frequencies used in the 2.4 GHz band overlap the frequencies used in microwave ovens, cordless telephones, and Bluetooth equipment. This results in occasional interference that is difficult to diagnose.

THE 5 GHZ UNLICENSED BAND   The 802.11 standard can also operate in the **5 GHz unlicensed band**. There have been two problems with this band. The first is the cost of radios. In the 2.4 GHz band, high sales have allowed manufacturers to ride the learning curve down to lower costs. In addition, while the 2.4 GHz band is standardized through-out most of the world, different countries use different parts of the 5 GHz band. This also makes 5 GHz radios more expensive due to the need to use only those channels permitted within a given country.

Second, because of the 5 GHz band's higher frequencies, signals do not travel as far, and shadow zones are darker. This means that access points have to be placed closer together. It also means that siting access points to avoid dead spots is more difficult.

The big advantage of the 5 GHz band is that it is much wider than the 2.4 GHz band. In contrast to the 2.4 GHz band's mere three channels, the 5 GHz band provides between 11 and 24 non-overlapping 20 MHz channels, depending on the frequencies allocated to unlicensed operation in a country.

Having many channels eliminates the co-channel interference problem because it is easy to assign noninterfering channels to access points even in multi-floor buildings (which introduce interference in three dimensions).

In addition, in the sparsely used 5 GHz service bands, some access points can op-erate simultaneously on two different channels. This doubles the amount of bandwidth available to devices.

The disadvantage of operating in the 5 GHz band is higher radio cost because 5 GHz radios are inherently more expensive and because fewer of them are being produced, raising the cost per unit. However, this cost difference is rather small, and 5 GHz access points and clients are now available on retail shelves at only a modest premium.

Test Your Understanding

12. a) In what two unlicensed bands does 802.11 operate? b) How wide are 802.11 channels usually? c) Which licensed band is defined the same way in most countries around the world? d) Does the 2.4 GHz band or the 5 GHz band allow longer propagation distances for a given level of power? Justify your answer. e) How many non-overlapping channels does the 2.4 GHz band support? f) Why is the number of non-overlapping channels that can be used important? g) How many non-overlapping channels does the 5 GHz band support?

NORMAL AND SPREAD SPECTRUM TRANSMISSION

Why Spread Spectrum Transmission?

At the frequencies used by WLANs, there are numerous and severe propagation problems. In these unlicensed bands, regulators mandate the use of a form of transmission called spread spectrum transmission. Spread spectrum transmission is transmission that uses far wider channels than transmission speed requires.

Spread spectrum transmission is transmission that uses far wider channels than transmission speed requires.

Regulators mandate the use of spread spectrum transmission primarily to minimize propagation problems—especially multipath interference. (If the direct and reflected signals cancel out at some frequencies within the range, they will be double at other frequencies.)

Spread Spectrum Transmission

>   You are required by law to use spread spectrum transmission in unlicensed bands
>   Spread spectrum transmission reduces propagation problems
>   Especially multipath interference
>   Spread spectrum transmission is NOT used for security in WLANs

Normal Transmission versus Spread Spectrum Transmission (See Figure 6-16)

>   Normal transmission uses only the channel bandwidth required by your signaling speed
>   Spread spectrum transmission uses channels much wider than signaling speed requires

Orthogonal Frequency Division Multiplexing (See Figure 6-17)

>   OFDM is the dominant spread spectrum transmission method today
>   It is difficult to transmit in a very wide channel
>   So the sender divides the channel into multiple subchannels called subcarriers
>   Part of the frame is sent in each subcarrier
>   The frame is sent redundantly, so if some subcarriers are lost, the frame is still likely to get through
>   It is much easier to transmit in many smaller-bandwidth subcarriers

---

FIGURE 6-14   Spread Spectrum Transmission (Study Figure)

In commercial transmission, security is *not* a reason for doing spread spectrum transmission. The military uses spread spectrum transmission for security, but it does so by keeping certain parameters of its spread spectrum transmission secret. Commercial spread spectrum transmission methods must make these parameters publicly known in order for two parties to communicate easily.

In wireless LANs, spread spectrum transmission is used to reduce propagation problems and to reduce co-channel interference between nearby hosts transmitting in the same channel, not to provide security.

How wide are spread spectrum channels? Earlier, we saw that 802.11 channel bandwidth was traditionally 20 MHz and may be twice as wide for the 802.11n standard.

Test Your Understanding

13. a) In unlicensed bands, what type of transmission method is required by regulators?
   b) What is the benefit of spread spectrum transmission for business communication?
   c) Is spread spectrum transmission done for security reasons in commercial WLANs?

Spread Spectrum Transmission Methods

NORMAL VERSUS SPREAD SPECTRUM TRANSMISSION   As noted earlier in our discussion of the Shannon Equation, if you need to transmit at a given speed, you must have a channel whose bandwidth is sufficiently wide.

To allow as many channels as possible, channel bandwidths in *normal radio transmission* are limited to the speed requirements of the user's signal, as Figure 6-15 illustrates. For a service that operates at 10 kbps, regulators would permit only enough channel bandwidth to handle this speed.

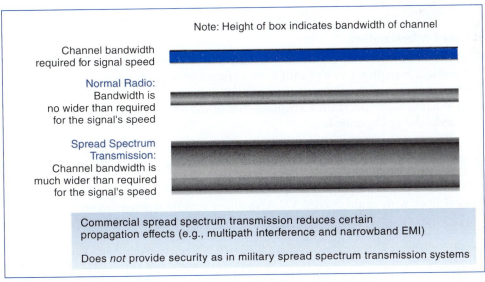

FIGURE 6-15   Normal Radio Transmission and Spread Spectrum Transmission

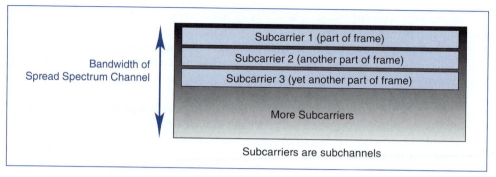

FIGURE 6-16 Orthogonal Frequency Division Multiplexing

In contrast to normal radio transmission, which uses channels just wide enough for transmission speed requirements, **spread spectrum transmission** takes the original signal, called a **baseband signal**, and spreads the signal energy over a much broader channel than is required.

ORTHOGONAL FREQUENCY DIVISION MULTIPLEXING (OFDM)   There are several spread spectrum transmission methods. The 801.11 Working Group's most recent standards, 802.11g and 802.11n, use **orthogonal frequency division multiplexing (OFDM)**, which Figure 6-16 illustrates.

In OFDM, each broadband channel is divided into many smaller subchannels called **subcarriers**. Parts of each frame are transmitted in each subcarrier.[3] OFDM sends data redundantly across the subcarriers, so if there is impairment in one or even a few subcarriers, all of the data usually will still get through.

OFDM is complex and therefore expensive. However, sending data over a single very large channel reliably is difficult. In contrast, OFDM can be used at very high speeds because it is easier to send many slow signals reliably in many small subcarriers than it is to send one signal rapidly over a very wide-bandwidth channel.[4]

Test Your Understanding

14. a) In normal radio operation, how does channel bandwidth usually relate to the bandwidth required to transmit a data stream of a given speed? b) How does this change in spread spectrum transmission?
15. a) What spread spectrum transmission method is used for the most recent 802.11 standards? b) Describe it.

802.11 WLAN OPERATION

As noted at the beginning of this chapter, wireless LANs replace signals in copper wires or optical fiber with radio waves. WLANs allow mobile workers to stay connected to

---

[3] In the 802.11g wireless LAN standard discussed later, each 20 MHz channel is divided into 52 subcarriers, each 312.5 kHz wide. Of the 52 subcarriers, 48 are used to send data and 4 are used to control the transmission.

[4] The ADSL services discussed in Chapter 10 generally also use OFDM, although in ADSL service, OFDM is called discrete multitone (DMT) service.

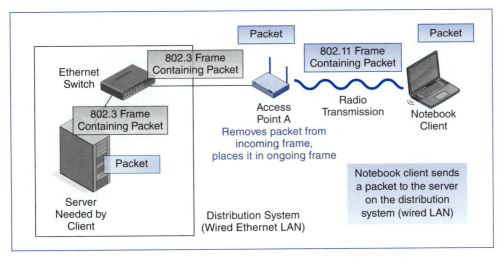

FIGURE 6-17 Typical 802.11 Wireless LAN Operation with Wireless Access Points

the network as they move through a building. In some cases, wireless LANs are less expensive to install than wired LANs, but this certainly is not always the case.

Extending the Wired LAN

As noted at the start of the chapter, and as Figure 6-17 shows, an 802.11 wireless LAN typically is used to connect a small number of mobile devices to a large wired LAN—typically, an Ethernet LAN—because the servers and Internet access routers that mobile hosts need to use usually are on the wired LAN.[5]

In 802.11 terminology, the network to which access points connect is called a **distribution system (DS)**. This typically is an Ethernet network, as we have just discussed. However, it is possible to use any network technology to connect the access points.

The network to which access points connect is called a distribution system (DS).

Test Your Understanding

16. a) List the elements in a typical 802.11 LAN today. b) Why is a wired LAN usually still needed if you have a wireless LAN? c) In the figure, what is the distribution system?

Wireless Access Points

When a wireless host wishes to send a frame to a server, it transmits the frame to a wireless access point.

---

[5] There is a rarely used 802.11 **ad hoc mode**, in which no wireless access point is used. In ad hoc mode, computers communicate directly with other computers. (In contrast, when an access point is used, this is called 802.11 infrastructure mode.) In addition, 802.11 can create point-to-point transmission over longer distances than 802.11 normally supports. This approach, which normally is used to connect nearby buildings, uses dish antennas and higher power levels authorized for this purpose.

As Figure 6-17 shows, when a wireless host transmits to a server on the wired LAN, it places the packet into an 802.11 frame.[6] The wireless access point removes the packet from the 802.11 frame and places the packet in an 802.3 frame. The access point sends this 802.3 frame to the server, via the wired Ethernet LAN. When the server replies, the wireless access point receives the 802.3 frame, removes the packet from the frame, and forwards the packet to the wireless host in an 802.11 frame.[7]

The packet goes all the way from the wireless host to a server. The 802.11 frame travels only between the wireless host and the wireless access point. The 802.3 frame travels only between the wireless host and the server.

The wireless access point also controls hosts. It assigns transmission power levels to hosts within its range and performs a number of other supervisory chores.

Test Your Understanding

17. a) Why must the access point remove an arriving packet from the frame in which the packet arrives and place the packet in a different frame when it sends the packet back out? b) Besides moving packets between wireless clients and the Ethernet network, what other control functions do access points have?

Basic Service Sets (BSSs)

We need to introduce a bit of jargon at this point. First, a **basic service set (BSS)** consists of an access point and the set of hosts it serves. In Figure 6-18, there are two BSSs.

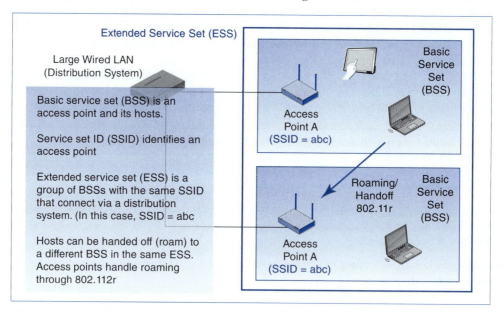

FIGURE 6-18 Basic Service Sets, Extended Service Set, and Roaming

---

[6] Note that 802.11 frames are much more complex than 802.3 Ethernet frames. Much of this complexity is needed to counter wireless propagation problems.

[7] This sounds like what a router does. However, a router can connect any two single networks. Access points are limited to connecting 802.3 and 802.11 networks.

A basic service set (BSS) consists of an access point and the set of hosts it serves

---

The access point in a BSS has an identifier called the **service set identifier (SSID)**. (Note that the term *basic* is not in the name.) Wireless hosts must know the SSID to associate with the access point. Fortunately, this is very easy to do.

Test Your Understanding

18. a) What is a BSS? (Do not just spell out the acronym.) b) What is an SSID? (Do not just spell out the acronym.) c) Does the access point have an SSID? d) Why must wireless devices know the access point's SSID?

Extended Service Sets (ESSS), Handoff, and Roaming

When a mobile host travels too far from a wireless access point, the signal will be too weak to reach the access point. However, if there is a closer access point, the host can be **handed off** to that access point for service. In WLANs, the ability to use handoffs is also called **roaming**.[8]

Roaming requires that both access points belong to the same extended service set. An **extended service set (ESS)** is a group of BSSs that are 1) connected to the same distribution system (network) and 2) have the same SSID.

An extended service set (ESS) is a group of BSSs that are 1) connected to the same distribution system (network) and 2) have the same SSID.

Figure 6-17 shows a wireless client communicating with an internal server. This is the service as users see it. However, access points also need to contact one another via the distribution system. For example, in roaming, they have to exchange information between themselves in order to hand off the client. To do so, they communicate via the **802.11r** standard, which is nicely named because it deals with roaming.

Access points also need to contact one another via the distribution system.

An organization with a single distribution system, like an Ethernet network, may have several different extended service sets. Each ESS will have its own SSID. It is even possible for an access point to be a member of multiple ESSs.

Test Your Understanding

19. a) What is a handoff in 802.11? b) What is the relationship between handoffs and roaming in WLANs? c) What is an ESS? (Do not just spell out the abbreviations.) d) What feature do all access points in an ESS share? e) How can access points communicate with each other? f) What is the purpose of the 802.11r standard?

---

[8] In cellular telephony, which we will see in Chapter 7, the terms *handoff* and *roaming* mean different things.

Sharing a Single Channel

As Figure 6-19 shows, the access point and all of the wireless hosts it serves transmit and receive in a single channel. When a host or the access point transmits, all other devices must wait. (If two devices transmit in the same channel at the same time, their signals will interfere with each other.) As the number of hosts served by an access point increases, individual throughput falls because of this waiting. The box "Controlling 802.11 Transmission" discusses how **media access control (MAC)** methods govern when hosts and access points may transmit so that collisions can be avoided.

Media access control (MAC) methods govern when hosts and access points may transmit so that collisions can be avoided.

The access point and all of the wireless hosts it serves transmit and receive in a single channel. When a host or the access point transmits, all other devices must wait.

Test Your Understanding

20. All wireless hosts and the access point that serves them transmit on the same channel. Why does this cause throughput to fall as the number of wireless hosts increases? Explain why.

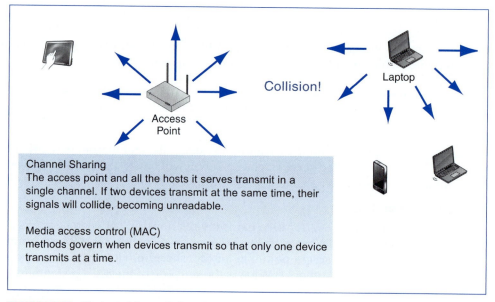

FIGURE 6-19 Hosts and Access Points Transmit on a Single Channel

Controlling 802.11 Transmission

Media Access Control

As noted in the body of the text, the access point and the hosts it serves all transmit in the same channel. If two 802.11 devices (hosts or wireless access points) transmit at the same time, their signals will be jumbled together and will be unreadable. This is called a **collision**.

The 802.11 standard has two mechanisms for **media access control (MAC)**—ensuring that hosts and the access point do not transmit simultaneously. The first, CSMA/CA+ACK, is mandatory. Access points and wireless hosts *must* support it. The second, RTS/CTS, is optional.[9]

Test Your Understanding

21. a) What is a collision? b) Why is it bad? c) What is the purpose of media access control? d) Does media access control limit the actions of wireless hosts, the access point, or both?

CSMA/CA+ACK Media Access Control

CSMA/CA

To reduce the number of collisions, wireless access points and wireless hosts use **carrier sense multiple access with collision avoidance (CSMA/CA)**. Note the focus on collision *avoidance*. Figure 6-20 illustrates CSMA/CA.

CSMA requires that a host refrain from transmitting if it hears traffic. This is a very simple rule. Carrier sensing means listening for traffic. Multiple access means that this is a way of controlling how multiple hosts can access the network to transmit.

CSMA/CA (Carrier Sense Multiple Access with Collision Avoidance)

Sender listens for traffic

Carrier is the signal; sensing is listening

1. If there is traffic, waits
2. If there is no traffic:

    2a. If there has been no traffic for less than the critical time value, waits a random amount of time, then returns to Step 1.

    2b. If there has been no traffic for more than the critical value for time, sends without waiting

    This avoids collision that would result if hosts could transmit as soon as one host finishes transmitting.

ACK (Acknowledgment)

Receiver immediately sends back an acknowledgment

    If sender does not receive the acknowledgment, retransmits using CSMA

CSMA/CA plus ACK is a reliable protocol

FIGURE 6-20   CSMA/CA+ACK in 802.11 Wireless LANs

(continued)

---

[9] Actually, if you have even a single host with older 802.11b equipment connected to an access point, RTS/CTS becomes mandatory. However, 802.11b wireless hosts are almost never encountered anymore.

CSMA requires not transmitting if a device hears traffic. Collision avoidance (CA) is a set of two rules that determine what a host or the access point does if it does *not* hear traffic.

- If the host does not hear traffic, it considers the last time it heard traffic. If the time since the last transmission exceeds a critical value, the host may transmit immediately.
- However, if the time is less than the critical value, the host sets a random timer and waits. If there still is no traffic after the random wait, the host may send.

If the last two points seem odd, note that the goal is to avoid collisions as much as possible. Two hosts are most likely to transmit at the same time if they both have been waiting for another host to finish transmitting. Without the random delay, both will transmit at the same time, causing a collision.

ACK

More specifically, 802.11 uses **CSMA/CA+ACK**. Collisions and other types of signal loss are still possible with CSMA/CA. When a wireless access point receives a frame from a host, or when a host receives a frame from an access point, the receiver *immediately* sends an acknowledgment frame, an **ACK**. A frame that is not acknowledged is retransmitted. Note that there is no wait when transmitting an ACK. This ensures that ACKs get through while other hosts are waiting.

Note also that retransmission makes CSMA/CA+ACK a reliable protocol. We saw in Chapter 2 that very few protocols are reliable because reliability usually costs more than it brings in benefits. The low error rates in wired media simply do not justify implementing reliability in Ethernet and other wired LAN protocols. However, wireless transmission has many errors, so a reliable protocol is required for reasonably good operation.[10]

Thanks to CSMA/CA+ACK, 802.11 is a reliable protocol.

Inefficient Operation

CSMA/CA+ACK works well, but it is inefficient. Waiting before transmission wastes valuable time. Sending ACKs also is time consuming. Overall, an 802.11 LAN can only deliver throughput (actual speed) of about half the rated speed of its standard—that is, the speed published in the standard.

This throughput, furthermore, is aggregate throughput shared by the wireless access point and all of the hosts sharing the channel. Individual host throughput will be substantially lower.

Test Your Understanding

22. a) Describe CSMA/CA+ACK. Do not go into detail about how long a host must wait to transmit if there is no traffic. b) Is CSMA/CA+ACK transmission reliable or unreliable? Explain. c) Why is CSMA/CA+ACK inefficient?

Request to Send/Clear to Send (RTS/CTS)

Although CSMA/CA+ACK is mandatory, there is another control mechanism called **request to send/clear to send (RTS/CTS)**. Figure 6-21 illustrates RTS/CTS. As noted earlier, the RTS/CTS protocol is optional except in one rare case. Avoiding RTS/CTS whenever possible is wise because RTS/CTS is much less efficient, and therefore slower, than CSMA/CA+ACK.

---

[10] In addition, 802.11 uses forward error correction. It adds many redundant (extra) bits to each frame. If there is a small error, the receiver can use these redundant bits to fix the frame. If the receiver can make the repair, it does so and then sends back an ACK. This process makes wireless NICs more expensive than Ethernet NICs, but wireless transmission errors are so common that it makes economic sense to correct errors at the receiver in order to minimize retransmissions.

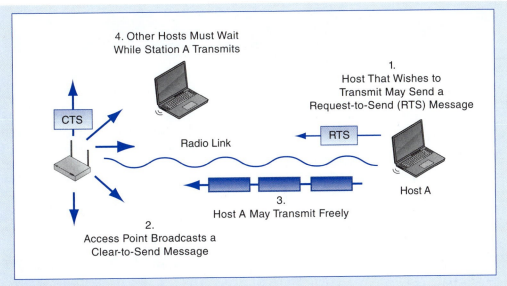

4. Other Hosts Must Wait
While Station A Transmits

1.
Host That Wishes to
Transmit May Send a
Request-to-Send (RTS) Message

CTS

RTS

Radio Link

Host A

3.
Host A May Transmit Freely

2.
Access Point Broadcasts a
Clear-to-Send Message

FIGURE 6-21 Request to Send/Clear to Send

When a host wishes to send and is able to send because of CSMA/CA, the host may send a **request-to-send (RTS)** message to the wireless access point. This message asks the access point for permission to send messages.

If the access point responds by broadcasting a **clear-to-send (CTS)** message, then other hosts must wait. The host sending the RTS may then transmit, ignoring CSMA/CA.

Although RTS/CTS is widely used, keep in mind that it is only an option, while CSMA/CA is mandatory. Also, tests have shown that RTS/CTS reduces throughput when it is used.

RTS/CTS makes sense primarily when two wireless clients can both hear the access point but cannot hear each other. If CSMA/CD+ACK is used, the two stations may transmit at the same time.

Test Your Understanding

23. a) Describe RTS/CTS. b) Is CSMA/CA+ACK required or optional? c) Is RTS/CTS required or optional? d) Which is more efficient, RTS/CTS or CSMA/CA+ACK? e) When does RTS/CTS make sense to use?

802.11 TRANSMISSION STANDARDS

The 802.11 Working Group has created several WLAN transmission standards since 1997. We will look at the most important of these standards today.

Characteristics of 802.11g, 802.11n, 802.11ac, and 802.11ad

Figure 6-22 compares the 802.11g and 802.11n standards that dominate usage today and the 802.11ac and 802.11ad standards that are just entering the market.

Characteristic	802.11g	802.11n Single Band	802.11n Dual Band	802.11ac	802.11ad
Status	Obsolete but widely used	Offers longer speeds and greater distances than 802.11g Growing rapidly in popularity 2.4 GHz band is crowded; often cannot use 40 MHz channel bandwidth	Uses both 2.4 GHz and 5 GHz bands for more total bandwidth Growing rapidly in popularity	Offers much higher speed in the 5 GHz band through wider channels and other technical innovations. Standard is not complete, but vendors are beginning to offer products based on late drafts of the standard.	Offers very high speed over very short distances in the 60 GHz band. Standard is not complete, but vendors are beginning to offer products based on late drafts of the standard.
Spread Spectrum Method	OFDM	OFDM	OFDM	OFDM	OFDM or Single Channel for lower speed
Unlicensed Band(s)	2.4 GHz	2.4 GHz	2.4 GHz and 5 GHz	5 GHz	60 GHz
Channel Bandwidth	20 MHz	40 MHz, but will drop back to 20 MHz if there is interference on the two selected channels	40 MHz, but will drop back to 20 MHz if there is interference on the two selected channels	80 MHz or 160 MHz	2.1 GHz
Number of Non-Overlapping Channels (varies by country)	3	3 in 2.4 GHz band	3 in 2.4 GHz band; 12 in the United States in 5 GHz band The 5 GHz band is still relatively uncrowded.	6 at 80 MHz channel bandwidth and 3 at 160 MHz bandwidth in the United States	3 in the United States, 4 in Europe
MIMO?	No	Yes	Yes	Yes	Yes
Maximum Number of Spatial Streams			4	8	
Multiuser MIMO/ Beamforming?	No	Yes but no single standard	Yes but no single standard	Yes, and only one standard	
Rated Speed	54 Mbps	100 Mbps to 600 Mbps; 300 Mbps common.	100 Mbps to 600 Mbps; 300 Mbps common.	433 Mbps to 6.9 Gbps; 867 Mbps and 1.3 Gbps common.	7 Gbps
Typical Maximum Distance for Rated Speed	30 m (100')	70 m (230')	70 m at 2.4 GHz 50 m at 5 GHz		

FIGURE 6-22   Main 802.11 Standards

- The 802.11g standard is obsolete, but it offers a good rated speed of 54 Mbps up to about 30 meters (100 feet). Even if only a single user is accessing an access point, he or she will only get throughput of about half of that rated speed. The standard has a large installed base of clients and access points that need to continue to be supported.
- The 802.11n standard now dominates sales and will soon dominate the installed base if it has not already done so. By offering wider channels and other technical innovations than 802.11g, and by working in both the 2.4 GHz and 5 GHz bands, 802.11n offers more channels and faster channels than 802.11g. The rated speeds of 802.11n devices are 150 Mbps to 600 Mbps, with 300 Mbps being a common rated speed. In the 2.4 GHz band, the maximum speed is available up to 70 meters (230 feet). In the 5 GHz band, the maximum speed is available up to about 50 meters (160 feet).
- The 802.11ac standard is one of two "gigabit" technologies that are just beginning to reach the market in draft standard form. The 802.11ac standard uses the 5 GHz band along with wider channels than 802.11n and even more technical innovations than 802.11n. It offers rated speeds of 433 Mbps to nearly 7 Gbps, and rated speeds of 433 Mbps to 1.3 Gbps are likely to be common initially.
- The 802.11ad standard is a radical break from earlier standards. Instead of using the 2.4 GHz and 5 GHz bands, it operates in the 60 MHz band. Its rated speed is an enormous 7 Gbps, but absorptive attenuation is so high in the 60 GHz band that distance will be limited to about 10 meters. This will make it ideal for streaming high-definition video, even if multiple HDTV channels are required.

Although gigabit speeds may seem like overkill, it makes new applications possible. In consumer applications, it will make the streaming of multiple simultaneous television signals possible. About a third of all U.S. houses have four or more televisions today, and HD is becoming the norm. For business, data backup and synchronization will become feasible to do wirelessly.

Test Your Understanding

24. a) Of the four 802.11 transmission standards summarized in this section, which are full standards, and which are only draft standards? b) What is the maximum rated speed for each standard? c) Compare maximum speeds for 802.11g and 802.11n and the maximum distances at which each standard can provide these speeds. d) Which can bring gigabit speeds to clients? e) What business application will gigabit transmission speed make feasible to do wirelessly?

Spread Spectrum Method

Figure 6-22 shows that all four standards use OFDM as their main spread spectrum method. The 802.11ad standard has an alternative single-carrier mode, in which the subcarriers of OFDM are not used. The signal is spread across the entire channel. This is simple enough to be implemented on hand-held devices, at the cost of substantially lower speed.

Test Your Understanding

25. What spread spectrum method do all four standards use as their main method?

Bands and Channel Bandwidth

Earlier in this chapter, we saw that transmission speed is highly dependent upon channel bandwidth. Other things being equal, doubling channel bandwidth doubles transmission speed. However, service bands have limited total bandwidth, so wider channels means fewer channels.

802.11G CHANNEL BANDWIDTH   The 802.11g standard operates only in the crowded 2.4 GHz band. With channel bandwidth of 20 MHz, only three 802.11g channels are possible.

802.11N CHANNEL BANDWIDTH   The 802.11n standard operates in both the 2.4 GHz band and the less-crowded and wider 5 GHz band. It also doubles 802.11g bandwidth to 80 MHz. This alone roughly doubles speed. However, early 802.11n products were single-band 802.11n products that operated only in the 2.4 GHz band. In this band, there are already many 802.11g stations operating on 20 MHz channels. To be a good neighbor, when there are stations operating on the three possible channels, 802.11n products will drop back to a 20 MHz channel bandwidth, losing their channel bandwidth advantage. Dual-band 802.11n products operate in both the 2.4 GHz band and the 5 GHz band. In the higher band, 40 MHz channels are widely available. In other words, 802.11n reaches its full expression only in the 5 GHz band.

802.11AC CHANNEL BANDWIDTH   The emerging 802.11ac standard has even wider channels. Support for 80 MHz channels is mandatory, and support for 160 MHz channels is likely to gain quick support. Doubling and quadrupling channel bandwidth compared to 802.11n means roughly a doubling and quadrupling of transmission speeds, other things being equal. Of course, having wider channels means having fewer channels. In the United States, available spectrum capacity in the 5 GHz band can handle twelve 802.11n channels, but it can support only six 80 MHz channels or three 160 MHz channels.

802.11AD CHANNEL BANDWIDTH   The emerging 802.11ad standard, as just noted, uses the 60 GHz band, which has a total bandwidth of about 7 GHz to 9 GHz. (In contrast, the 5 GHz band has less than 1 GHz of bandwidth.) However, 802.11ad channels are an enormous 2.1 GHz wide. In the United States, there are only three non-overlapping 802.11ad channels, while Europe can support four with its wider 60 GHz band spectrum capacity. Fortunately, because 60 GHz signals do not travel far, mutual channel interference should not be a major problem.

Test Your Understanding

26. a) Why is wider channel bandwidth good? What is the downside of wider channel bandwidth? b) What frequency band or bands do 802.11g, 802.11n single band, 802.11n dual band, 802.11ac, and 802.11 ad use? c) For each, compare channel bandwidth and the number of possible channels. d) What are the benefits and problems of transmission in the 60 GHz band?

MIMO

Increasing bandwidth is the easiest way to boost transmission speed, but there are other less brute force way to increase speed without increasing bandwidth. Figure 6-23 notes

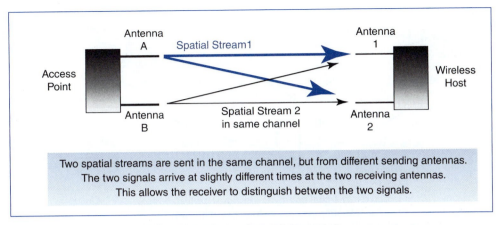

Two spatial streams are sent in the same channel, but from different sending antennas.
The two signals arrive at slightly different times at the two receiving antennas.
This allows the receiver to distinguish between the two signals.

FIGURE 6-23   Multiple Input/Multiple Output (MIMO) Transmission

that standards beyond 802.11g use a technique called **multiple input/multiple output (MIMO)** to achieve speeds far more than increasing bandwidth alone can provide.

The key to higher throughput in MIMO is that the host or access point sends two or more **spatial streams** (radio signals) in the same channel between two or more different antennas on access points and wireless hosts.

In the figure, there are two spatial streams. Transmitting in the same channel, they should interfere with each other. However, the two spatial streams sent by different antennas will arrive at the two receiving antennas at slightly different times. Using detection and separation methods based on differences in arrival times for the two spatial streams, the receiver can separate the two spatial streams in the same channel and so can read them individually.

Even with only spatial streams and two antennas each on the sender and receiver, MIMO can substantially increase throughput. Using more spatial streams and more antennas can increase throughput even more. The MIMO standard will permit two, three, or four antennas on each device and up to four data streams.

With two spatial streams, rated speed in 802.11n with 40 MHz channels is 300 Mbps. Three spatial streams raise the rated speed to 450 Mbps, and four raise it to 600 Mbps. The 802.11n standard requires access points to support four spatial streams, although wireless hosts are only required to support two spatial streams. Typical speeds in 802.11n products today have rated speeds of 150 Mbps to 300 Mbps.

The 802.11ac standard, in addition to doubling or quadrupling channel bandwidth compared to 802.11n, doubles the number of possible spatial streams to eight. The standard offers many possible combinations of bandwidth (80 MHz or 160 MHz) and number of spatial streams (1 to 8). This creates a large number of possible rated speeds, beginning at 433 MHz and extending to 6.93 GHz. Of these, 433 Mbps, 867 Mbps, and 1.3 Gbps are likely to be offered the most when products appear.

Another benefit of MIMO, beyond greater transmission speed, is greater transmission distance. The reasons for this are rather technical, but it is the end result that is important. Greater propagation distances may permit fewer access points to be installed, and this will lower equipment and installation cost.

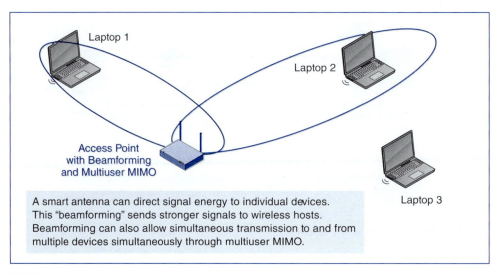

FIGURE 6-24   Beamforming (Multiuser MIMO or Smart Antennas)

Test Your Understanding

27. a) How does MIMO work? b) What is the main benefit of MIMO? What is its other benefit? c) Compare the range of rated speeds possible 802.11g with 40 MHz channels and 802.11ac.

Beamforming and Multiuser MIMO

Another technology to increase propagation and speed is beamforming. By having multiple antennas and changing the phase of waves coming from different antennas, an access point can focus signals toward individual hosts instead of broadcasting them, as Figure 6-24 indicates. This is called **beamforming**. It gives more effective power and therefore a stronger signal to each wireless host. This permits greater propagation distance. Devices that do beamforming are said to have **smart antennas**.

Beamforming can also bring **multiuser MIMO**, which is the possibility of simultaneous transmission in a single channel by multiple devices that are using a single access point.

The 802.11n standard specified multiuser MIMO, but it did not specify a single multiuser MIMO technology. This led to a great deal of market confusion, and multiuser MIMO did not become popular with 802.11n. With 802.11ac, the Technical Group 802.11ac avoided market confusion by specifying a single multiuser MIMO technique. Beamforming is likely to be common in 802.11ac products.

Test Your Understanding

28. a) What is beamforming? b) What two benefits can it bring? c) Distinguish between MIMO and multiuser MIMO. D) What is another name for beamforming?

Speed, Throughput, and Distance

So far, we have been talking about rated speeds. But what throughput—actual speed— can individuals expect to see? The general answer is complicated, but the single most important word is *less*. Individual users will always receive less than rated speeds, often much less.

Rated Speed versus Throughput

Total throughput is substantially lower than rated speed—sometimes 50% lower

Aggregate versus Individual Throughput

Access point throughput is aggregate throughput
This must be shared by all stations currently sending or receiving
Individual throughput can be much lower than aggregate throughput

Throughput versus Distance

As distance from the access point increases, signals get weaker
Wireless hosts must use slower but more reliable transmission processes
This reduces individual throughput

Speed Killers

An 802.11b device connecting to an access point hurts all hosts
Stations far away will transmit more slowly, taking aggregate throughput from other devices

---

FIGURE 6-25   Speed, Throughput, and Distance (Study Figure)

RATED SPEED VERSUS THROUGHPUT   Rated speed is the number of bits that the host or access point will transmit per second. As noted earlier, stations often have to wait to transmit, even if no other station is transmitting. In addition, wireless frames contain many extra bits to improve transmission reliability, even beyond the normal overhead of frame headers. For 802.11g, the highest actual throughput is about half the rated transmission speed. For standards beyond 802.11g, actual throughput is somewhat closer to rated speeds, but throughput of about two-thirds of the rated speed is about the highest possible throughput.

AGGREGATE THROUGHPUT VERSUS INDIVIDUAL THROUGHPUT   In addition, access point throughput is *aggregate* throughput, which is shared by all users of an access point. Suppose that the aggregate throughput is 100 Mbps per second and there are 10 users of an access point. If all 10 transmit or receive simultaneously, then *individual* throughput would be about 10 Mbps (actually somewhat less because of time lost in turn-taking). Of course, it would be rare for all stations to transmit simultaneously. However, even if three are sending and receiving simultaneously, the individual throughput they experience would be about 30 Mbps.

What percentage of time do hosts transmit or receive? It depends entirely on what they are doing. Web downloads occur about every 30 seconds and take only a second or two to download on a fast host. However, streaming video creates an almost continuous data stream, consuming a good deal of the aggregate throughput.

THROUGHPUT VERSUS DISTANCE   Another consideration is that speed is highest when a user is very near an access point. As the user moves away, speed falls. The problem is that at maximum transmission speed, there must be almost perfect propagation characteristics. As a user moves away from an access point, signal strength falls, errors increase, and the access point and host must shift to a less aggressive transmission process that is more forgiving of errors. These less aggressive transmission processes are always slower than the most aggressive processes.

To give an example, suppose that you have an 802.11n host with a 40 MHz channel and two spatial streams. The highest possible rated speed is 300 Mbps. Lower rated speeds that may be necessary at longer distances include 270 Mbps, 240 Mbps, 180 Mbps, 120 Mbps, 90 Mbps, 60 Mbps, and 30 Mbps.

SPEED KILLERS   There are many other factors that will reduce individual throughput. For example, there are still some wireless devices that use the old 802.11b standard, which only has a rated speed of 11 Mbps. If a single 802.11b device associates with a later access point, it will still be served, but everyone's throughput will suffer greatly. Another problem is that if one or more hosts associated with an access point are some distance away, throughput will fall, as just noted. They will take longer to send and receive packets, and this time will be taken away from other users.

IN GENERAL   Overall, it is impossible to say with any certainty what individual throughput a user will receive. A rule of thumb that frequently works is that individual throughput will be a quarter to a third of the rated speed if the access point is not overloaded.

Test Your Understanding

29. a) Distinguish between rated speed, aggregate throughput, and individual throughput. b) What factors influence individual throughput, given a certain level of aggregate throughput? c) Why does transmission speed drop as a computer moves farther from an access point? d) How does the presence of a distant station harm all users of an access point?

Backward Compatibility

When new access points and wireless clients are created, they must be able to work with older equipment. For instance, an 802.11n client must be able to work with an older 802.11g access point. In the same way, an 802.11n access point must be able to work with an older 802.11g access point. Of course, when an 802.11n device works with an 802.11g device, the transmission can take place only at 802.11g speeds. The 802.11n device must drop back to 802.11g operation. This is called **backward compatibility**. Newer devices usually contain multiple radios so that they can work with newer and older devices.

Test Your Understanding

30. a) What is backward compatibility? b) Why do you think it is important? c) When a device designed to use a newer standard must work with a device that only uses an older standard, what standard do they use to communicate?

On the Horizon

Wireless standards are evolving in dog years. Although 802.11ac and 802.11ad are obvious things to consider for the future, there are other issues as well.

In the United States, UHF television channels were required to give up analog operation and relinquish their channels. The Federal Communications Commission

---

White Space Operation

In the United States, broadcasters were required to vacate the UHF spectrum

Some UHF channels have been auctioned off

Unused channels in various bands (called white space) will be made available for unlicensed use

May be used for WLAN operation, but may be reserved for other purposes

Impending Spectrum Scarcity

Traffic has been growing explosively

Governments have made many more service bands available

However, traffic may outstrip capacity

This spectrum scarcity will increase prices and may ultimately limit growth

---

FIGURE 6-26   Trends (Study Figure)

sold some of these channels at auction, but many are unused. The FCC is now considering how equipment can use empty channels (known as **white space**) on an opportunistic basis. This can provide more spectrum capacity for WLAN operation, cellular and similar service, or both. Regulatory agencies around the world are now considering how to allocate white space.

In general, governments have recently made many new blocks of frequency spectrum available to satisfy exploding demands for WLAN operation, cellular telephony, and other wireless data transmission technology. However, demand for spectrum capacity is growing very rapidly, and unless more efficient wireless transmission methods emerge very rapidly, spectrum capacity will place limits on demand growth. Well before that occurs, spectrum scarcity will increase transmission prices.

Test Your Understanding

31. a) What is white space, and why is using it attractive? b) Why may spectrum scarcity be a problem? d) If spectrum scarcity becomes a problem, how will that affect users?

ADVANCED OPERATION

We have been discussing 802.11 WLANs that connect to the corporate wired LAN for backbone transmission. However, two developments will implement 802.11 transmission in different ways.

Wi-Fi Direct

If two 802.11 devices are physically near each other, why go through a wired LAN or even an access point? Figure 6-27 shows that **Wi-Fi Direct**, which is being built into emerging transmission standards, permits direct transmission between two 802.11 devices without using an access point. Although this is a desirable use of 802.11 transmission, two nearby devices can also connect directly through Bluetooth and Near Field Communication (NFC), which we will see in Chapter 7.

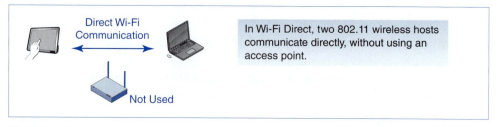

FIGURE 6-27   Wi-Fi Direct

Mesh Networking

A more sophisticated way of not using a wired Ethernet backbone is mesh networking. As Figure 6-28 shows, it is possible for wireless access points and wireless hosts to organize themselves into a mesh, forwarding frames from one to another until they reach the wireless destination host.

The **802.11s** standard for mesh networks exists. However, there are many other subsidiary standards that need to be developed before mesh networking's issues can be resolved sufficiently to be useful in corporations. Standards must address three main issues.

- First, meshes must be self-organizing. If hosts and access points enter and leave the mesh frequently, the amount of processing power consumed in maintaining the routing tables on the access points and wireless hosts must not be substantial.
- Second, it will be difficult to avoid overloading access points near the geographical center of the mesh. (Think of sitting in the middle seat at a table during a Christmas dinner and constantly having to pass food back and forth.) If mesh networking works but does not work well, it will have little value.
- Third, an even bigger issue is security. With no central control, security will have to exist between pairs of devices, many of which will have just entered the mesh and are not well known. This is a recipe for security nightmares.

Test Your Understanding

32. a) How does Wi-Fi Direct differ from the traditional way in which two wireless hosts communicate? b) Can a large Wi-Fi network operate without an Ethernet switched backbone? c) What technology allows this? d) What is the current 802.11 standard for this technology? e) What devices forward frames in a mesh network? f) What three issues must be overcome to make mesh networking acceptable to corporations?

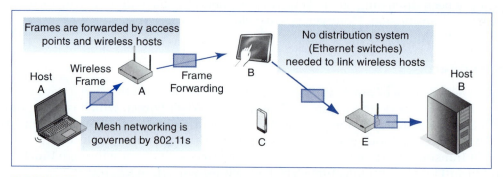

FIGURE 6-28   Wireless Mesh Networking

Standards and Compatibility

We have looked at many standards in this section. However, just because two products are compliant with a particular standard, such as dual-band 802.11n, does not mean that they are equal. This is true because most standards have options. One, for example, is the number of antennas on an 802.11n wireless access point. The standard calls up to four antennas on an access point. In fact, most early 802.11n access points had only two antennas and therefore could only transmit two spatial streams. Today, a growing number of 802.11n access points have three antennas and therefore can transmit three spatial streams. Even if a client has only two antennas, it will be able to receive data faster and more reliably. With three antennas on the access point and two on the client, a typical speed gain in 67%.

Test Your Understanding

33. a) Why can two products that comply with the same standard have different performance? b) What is the advantage of having three antennas rather than two on an access point?

CONCLUSION

Synopsis

Chapter 5 looked at Ethernet switched local area networks. This chapter and Chapter 7 look at wireless LANs (WLANs). All single networks, whether switched or wireless, operate at Layers 1 and 2. OSI standards dominate at those layers, so we can expect all wireless network standards to be OSI standards.

This chapter spends a long time on physical layer propagation. This detail is needed because wireless propagation effects are complex. We can predict what will happen as a signal travels down copper wire or optical fiber, but predicting how strong a radio signal will be where a user is located is far more difficult. We looked at five wireless propagation problems: absorptive attenuation, inverse square law attenuation (yes, there are two types of attenuation), interference, shadow zones, and multipath interference. Multipath interference occurs when the destination device receives multiple signals, with some coming directly from the radio source and some bouncing off walls, ceilings, and other objects. The direct and reflected signals may interfere with each other, making the direct signal unreadable. Multipath interference is the biggest propagation problem in wireless LANs. Absorptive attenuation and shadow zones become worse at higher frequencies.

We looked at two types of antennas—omnidirectional antennas and dish antennas. Wireless LANs use omnidirectional antennas because users would not know where to point a dish antenna and certainly do not want to carry a dish around. Fixed users may use dishes pointing at a distant radio source to have stronger transmission and reception.

We looked at basic radio concepts, including the frequency spectrum that consists of all frequencies from 0 Hz to infinity. (Radio propagation is described by frequency, which is measured in hertz.) Service bands are contiguous chunks of the frequency spectrum that are reserved for particular purposes, such as FM radio, television, or police communication. Service bands are divided into channels. Signals are sent in a single channel, and signals in different channels do not interfere with each other. Most commercial wireless services and corporate WLANs operate in the golden zone, which lies between 500 MHz and 10 GHz. In this golden zone, there is good spectrum capacity plus good propagation characteristics.

Radio signals do not propagate at a single frequency. They spread over a range of frequencies, and the spread increases as signal speed increases. Consequently, to carry fast signals, channels must have wide bandwidth. According to the Shannon Equation, doubling bandwidth should double possible signal speed.

Most radio bands are licensed, meaning that you need a government license to operate and a new license every time you move an antenna. Obviously, that would not work with wireless LAN. Consequently, wireless LANs operate in unlicensed bands. In an unlicensed band, you can set up your network the way you wish. However, you must tolerate interference from nearby WLANs built by others.

Most WLAN technology operates in the 2.4 GHz band, in which radio prices are low and reception is good. However, there are only three non-overlapping channels in this band, so nearby access points often interfere with one another. Some WLAN equipment operates in the 5 GHz unlicensed band, in which there are one or two dozen channels, depending on the country. The 5 GHz band is uncrowded, and the gap between 2.4 GHz prices and 5 GHz prices is narrowing. Consequently, use of the 5 GHz band is beginning to grow rapidly.

In the 2.4 GHz and 5 GHz bands, propagation effects tend to be worse at certain frequencies. This is especially true of multipath interference. Consequently, the government requires the use of spread spectrum transmission, in which the signal is spread far more than it needs to be for its speed. By sending a signal over a much wider range of frequencies, frequency-specific problems tend to be washed out. The two dominant WLAN standards, 802.11g and 802.11n, both use orthogonal frequency division multiplexing (OFDM), in which the channel is broken into much smaller channels called subcarriers. The frame is transmitted redundantly within the subcarriers. WLAN spread spectrum techniques, unlike military spread spectrum techniques, do not provide security.

In 802.11 WLAN operation, access points normally attach to the firm's main wired Ethernet LAN so that wireless clients can access servers and Internet access routers on the wired LAN. When a wireless host transmits, it sends its packet in an 802.11 frame. The access point removes the packet from the 802.11 frame, puts it in an 802.3 frame, and sends the frame to the server or Internet access router. The packet travels all the way; the 802.11 frame does not. We saw that when users move between access points, they can be transferred automatically to the new access point. This is called handoff or roaming. We defined the terms *basic service set*, *service set ID*, and *extended service set*. A BSS is an access point and the wireless stations it serves. The SSID is the name of a radio on an access point. In an ESS, all access points have the same SSID. Among other things, this permits roaming, which is also called being handed off.

The access point and the stations it serves all transmit in a single channel. Media access control is needed to ensure that they take turns transmitting so that their signals do not interfere. Wireless hosts that want to transmit often have to wait their turns. This reduces individual throughput. A box described the two main media access control protocols. CSMA/CA+ACK is mandatory on access points. Request to send/clear to send is optional but sometimes useful.

WLAN products on the market follow one of two 802.11 standards and two 802.11 draft standards. The 802.11g standard allows equipment to be less expensive but has lower speed and distance. The 802.11n standard is much more advanced. Products using 802.11n have higher speeds and longer propagation distances. The 802.11n standard now dominates in terms of sales, although there will be a large installed base of 802.11g products for several years to come. All 802.11n products are backward-compatible with 802.11g, so there is no problem mixing products from the two standards together, although they will all operate with 802.11g performance. Two draft standards are also being used in new equipment sold by vendors. These are 802.11ac and 802.11ad. Both can give gigabit transmission speeds, allowing such tasks as backup and data synchronization to be done in a reasonable amount of time.

Figure 6-22 compares these four 802.11 transmission standards. One consistent theme for newer versions is the use of ever-wider channel bandwidths, which bring ever-higher rated speeds. The 802.11g standard uses 20 MHz-wide channels. The 802.11n standard doubles this, except when there is interference from 802.1g devices in the 2.4 GHz band. The 802.11ac standard beings 80 MHz and 160 MHz channels, and 802.11g brings enormous 2.1 GHz channels. While 802.11g uses the crowded and limited 2.4 GHz band, 802.11n and 802.11ac can take advantage of the wider 5 GHz band's far greater total bandwidth. The 802.11ad standard moves to the ultrawide 60 GHz band, but absorptive attenuation is very high in this band, so 802.11ad signals are limited to about 10 meters.

Another way to boost speed is MIMO, which uses multiple antennas on the sender and receiver. The signals sent by different antennas are called spatial streams. The sender can transmit multiple spatial streams in the same channel, and the receiver will be able to read them. Roughly speaking, transmission speed approximately increases in proportion to the number of spatial streams. The 802.11g standard does not use MIMO. The 802.11n standard uses MIMO and can support up to four spatial streams. The 802.11ac standard can support up to eight.

The 802.11n, 802.11ac, and 802.11ad standards can also use beamforming, which uses smart antennas to direct signals to and from individual devices instead of broadcasting signals omnidirectionally. Beamforming increases distance by focusing more of the sender's power on the receiver. A particularly sophisticated type of beamforming is multiuser MIMO, which allows multiple stations to transmit simultaneously. The access point can use their different spatial streams to separate their signals. If one station is sending, other stations do not have to wait to send. The 802.11n standard did not specify a single beamforming standard, and market confusion has largely left beamforming out of 802.11n technology. The 802.11ac standard specifies a single beamforming standard, and beamforming is likely to be common in 802.11ac products.

It is easy to talk about rated speeds, but actual throughput is more difficult to discuss. Throughput is always slower than rated speed, and this is aggregate throughput shared by all devices transmitting simultaneously. Consequently, individual throughput is always lower. In addition, as a station moves farther from the access point, it must use slower transmission processes, further reducing individual throughput. In addition if a single older 802.11b host connects to an access point, everyone's throughput will suffer, and a single station far from the access point may transmit so slowly that it will take a substantial amount of the total aggregate throughput.

On the horizon, access points may be able to use unused spectrum in bands designated for other purposes. This could help alleviate a likely shortage of total spectrum capacity.

We looked briefly at two 802.11 approaches that do not use a switched Ethernet backbone to connect access points. Wi-Fi Direct allows two 802.11 hosts to communicate directly, without even using an access point. Mesh networks, in turn, use access points and client hosts to forward 802.11 frames wirelessly between two wireless hosts. This forwarding process may require several hops among wireless devices.

In Chapter 7, we will continue to look at 802.11 wireless LANs, focusing on security and management. We will then look at other local wireless technologies, including Bluetooth.

END-OF-CHAPTER QUESTIONS

Thought Questions

1. Reread the Christopher Lorek case. Are any terms still unfamiliar to you? Would you give the same advice? Why or why not?

2. The first letter part in this question was previously asked as a test your understanding question. Telephone channels have a bandwidth of about 3.1 kHz. Do the following in Excel. Cut and paste your analyses into your homework. a) If a telephone channel's signal-to-noise ratio is 1,000 (the signal strength is 1,000 times larger than the noise strength), how fast can a telephone channel carry data? (Check figure: Telephone modems operate at about 30 kbps, so your answer should be roughly this speed.) b) How fast could a telephone channel carry data if the SNR were increased massively, from 1,000 to 10,000? (This would not be realistic in practice.) c) With an SNR of 1,000, how fast could a telephone channel carry data if the bandwidth were increased to 4 kHz? Show your work or no credit. d) What did you learn from these three analyses?

3. A building has four sides that are each 100 meters long. The building is 100 meters tall. Draw a picture. a) If access points have a service radius of 25 meters, how many access points would you need? b) If access points have a range of 33 meters, how many access points would you need. c) What did you learn from your answers?

4. The following matters were not addressed specifically in the text. However, if you understand the concepts of Layer 1 and Layer 2 standards, in each case, give your answer and explain your reasoning. a) Is multipath interference a Layer 1 or Layer 2 concern? b) Is media access control a Layer 1 or Layer 2 concern? c) Is MIMO a Layer 1 or Layer 2 concern? d) Are wireless propagation problems Layer 1 or Layer 2 concerns?

Design Question

1. Consider a one-story building that is a square. It will have an access point in each corner and one in the center of the square. *All access points can hear one another.* a) Assign access point channels to the five access points if you are using 802.11g. Try not to have any access points that can hear each other use the same channel. Available channels are 1, 6, and 11. b) Were you able to eliminate interference between access points? c) Repeat the first two parts of the question, this time using 802.11a. Available channels are 36, 40, 44, 48, 53, 56, 60, 64, 149, 153, 157, and 161, but many NICs and access points only support channels below 100.

Troubleshooting Question

1. When you set up an 802.11g wireless access point in your small business, your aggregate throughput is only about 6 Mbps. a) List at least two possible reasons for this low throughput. b) Describe how you would test each. c) Describe what you would do if each proved to be the problem.

Perspective Questions

1. What was the most surprising thing you learned in this chapter?

2. What was the most difficult part of this chapter for you?

6a

USING XIRRUS WI-FI INSPECTOR

LEARNING OBJECTIVES

By the end of this chapter you should be able to:

- Use Xirrus Wi-Fi Inspector with some facility.
- Interpret output from Wi-Fi Inspector in specific situations.
- Do a site survey.

INTRODUCTION

Wi-Fi analysis programs listen to nearby access points (and sometimes wireless hosts) to determine such things as how strong their signals are, what types of security they use, what their SSIDs and BSSIDs are, and sometimes the directions of the individual access points.

There are many Wi-Fi analysis programs for mobile devices. Many have "stumbler" in their names in homage to one of the first examples, NetStumbler. This chapter looks at *Wi-Fi Inspector* from Xirrus, which runs on Microsoft Windows and which is available as a free download from Xirrus. A comparable Windows Widget that always remains on the desktop is also available from Xirrus.

THE FOUR WINDOWS

Figure 6a-1 shows the ribbon menu and four tiled windows that appear when you bring up Wi-Fi Inspector. This view shows all information in a single Window. This is the default. It is also what you see if you click on Show All in the Layout ribbon.

The Radar Window (Read the Fine Print)

The most obvious window is the radar window, which shows all access points in the vicinity. The access points are spread out across the two-dimensional picture.

RELATIVE DIRECTION (MEANINGLESS)   It appears that the radar window shows the relative directions of the access points, much as an air traffic radar display shows the directions of nearby aircraft. Actually, it does not. The access points are merely spread out

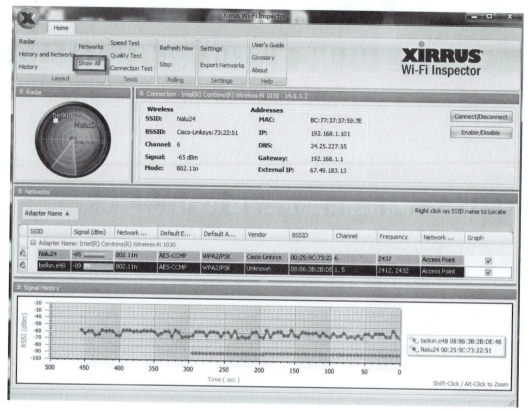

FIGURE 6a-1 Four Windows in Wi-Fi Inspector

Source: © 2012 Xirrus, Inc.

for readability. Direction is meaningless. In this sense, the radar window is misleading. However, it looks cool.

DISTANCE FROM THE CENTER (SIGNAL STRENGTH)   What does distance from the center mean? It looks like it means physical distance, as it would on a physical radar screen. Rather, it means *signal strength*. Access points that are shown closest to the center are the *strongest*, and access points that are the farthest from the center are the *weakest*.

MEASURING SIGNAL STRENGTH   Signal strength gives the RSSI (relative signal strength indicator) for the access point. Smaller negative numbers are better. For example, –60 dBm is a very strong signal, while –87 dBm is a very weak signal. In Figure 6a-1, Nalu24 has a signal strength of –65, which is quite good. Belkin has a signal strength of –89, which is terrible.

FIGURE 6a-2 Expanded Radar Window

Source: © 2012 Xirrus, Inc.

For signal strength, smaller negative numbers are better. (It's a double negative.)

EXPANDING THE RADAR WINDOW The radar window in its normal small form can display only four access points. Under the Layout section of the menu, selecting Radar in the Layout Group will maximize the radar window. This allows up to 10 access point names to be seen. By the way, "network" and "SSID" are synonyms.

Figure 6a-2 shows the expanded radar window. There are only two nearby access points, so there is no need for a large radar window. However, it certainly is easier to read the relative indicated signal strength.

Connection Window

The connection window (in the upper right in Figure 6a-1) shows information about the access point to which the computer running Wi-Fi Inspector is currently connected (Nalu24). It shows the SSID (the network name, in this case, Nalu24),the BSSID (the access point's MAC address, in this case Cisco-Linksys:73:22:51[1]), the channel (6), the signal strength (–65 dBm), and the network mode (802.11n).

In the middle is information about the user's PC. It shows the user's MAC address and configuration information, including the user's IP address, the IP address of the destination server, the IP address of the default gateway (router), and the network's external IP address given to it by the ISP. (This is a home network.) This information does not tell the user about nearby access points, but it can be very useful in assessing connection problems.

On the right is a Connect/Disconnect button. Clicking this button shows a list of potential networks and allows the user's computer to disconnect from the current access point and pick another to connect to. The user can also turn off the computer's wireless adapter.

The Networks Window

The network window shows detailed information about each of the nearby access points. This is what the user goes to when he or she wants detailed information. The row for the access point to which the user is currently connected is shown in orange. Wi-Fi Inspector updates the information in the network window frequently. As Figure 6a-3 shows, the information in this window is detailed.

- SSID. The network name.
- Signal Level in either dBm or percentage. Remember that smaller negative dBm numbers indicate higher strength. Next to the number is a colored bar.
  - Green is for signals of –70 dBm and above (–60 dBm, etc.).
  - Yellow is for signals between –71 dBm and –80 dBm
  - Orange is for signals between –81 dBm and –90 dBm.
  - Red is for –91 dBm and below.
- Network Mode. 802.11g, 802.11n, etc.
- Default Encryption. None, WEP, TKIP (in WPA), or AES (802.11i).
- Default Authentication. Open (none), WPA/PSK, WPA2/PSK, WPA/802.1X, or WPA2/802.1X.
- Vendor. The name of the device manufacturer.
- BSSID. The access point's MAC address.
- Channel. The channel number.
- Frequency. The center frequency of the channel.
- Network Type. Access point or ad hoc (no access point).
- Graph. This is a checkbox that tells Wi-Fi Inspector to graph the signal level over time (checked) or not to do so (unchecked). In the figure, both are checked, so both will be graphed.

In the figure, the access points are listed in terms of declining signal strength. However, the networks table can be sorted by any column heading. The user merely clicks on the column heading.

---

[1] The first two octets in a MAC address identify the company making the network adapter in the access point. Wi-Fi Inspector converts this information into a humanly readable name.

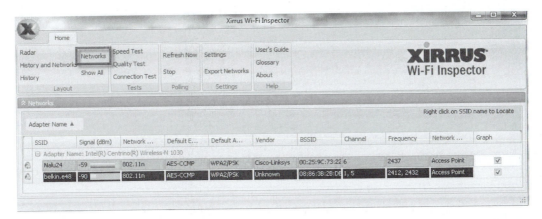

FIGURE 6a-3   Networks Window

Source: © 2012 Xirrus, Inc.

Figure 6a-4 zooms in on the networks window. In the upper right, there are instructions to "Right click on SSID name to Locate." In the section on the radar window, we saw that the window does not give the physical locations of access points. The Locate function under networks addresses this lack of physical location in a limited but interesting way. If you right click on an SSID name such as Nalu24, your computer begins beeping. If you are far away, it will beep slowly. As you approach it, the beeping speed will be increased. Essentially, you are using the network analysis version of a Geiger counter.

Signal History

In the network window, we saw that the user can check or uncheck whether graphing should be done. The Signal History window shows these graphs. The graphs in Figure 6a-5 show that the signal strength for Nalu24 is uniformly excellent, while the signal strength for Belkin is uniformly poor. Major fluctuations would indicate serious problems.

FIGURE 6a-4   Locating an Access Point

Source: © 2012 Xirrus, Inc.

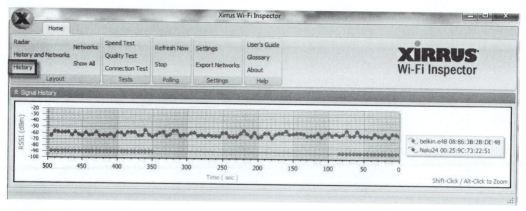

FIGURE 6a-5   Signal History

Source: © 2012 Xirrus, Inc.

Other Groups on the Ribbon

The Layout group on the ribbon is the most-used feature of the Xirrus Wi-Fi Inspector.

HELP GROUP   The Help group provides a user's guide to explain the program's detailed functionality. There is also a helpful glossary of terms.

SETTINGS GROUP   The Settings group allows the user to adjust many settings, for example, expressing RSSI in percentage terms instead of in terms of dBm.

TESTS GROUP   The windows in Wi-Fi Inspector provide information visually. The Tests group allows the user to conduct more detailed tests. These tests are good for troubleshooting.

TESTS

As just noted, the Tests group actively tests the quality of your service. The tests group performs three important tests.

Connection Test

The connection test shows how well you are connected to the outside world and to critical internal devices. Figure 6a-6 shows the results of a connection test. It shows that Wi-Fi Inspector uses ping to test latency to your DNS server, default gateway (router), and a host on the Internet (Internet Reachable). It also does a DNS lookup, in this case for www.google.com.

  The test shows that the user has low latency for the default router and an Internet host. It also shows that the DNS lookup was successful. In color, these are show in green, with the word *Pass*. However, there is relatively high latency to the user's DNS server (152 ms). This is indicated by a yellow bar with the text *Warning: high latency*. However, the latency is not very high. This connection looks good.

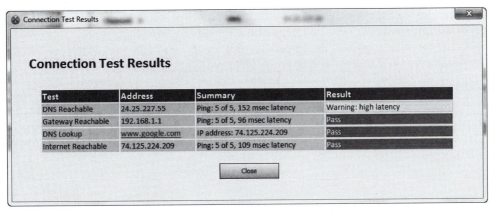

FIGURE 6a-6   Connection Test

Source: © 2012 Xirrus, Inc.

Speed Test

The speed test takes the user to speedtest.net.

Quality Test

The quality test takes you to pingtest.net. When the author ran this test, it gave the user's quality level a B. However, the box on the left notes that the connection should be fine for anything but gaming.

- The ping (latency) averaged 84 ms, which is a little high for games. The server is less than 50 miles away. Connecting to a more distant server would increase latency.
- Jitter, which is variation in latency from packet to packet is 24 ms. This can affect voice and video, for which jitter can result in jittery voice or video.
- There was zero packet loss. The connection appears to be reliable.
- There is a MOS score of 4.33. This is a traditional subjective indicator of voice call quality. A MOS score of 5 indicates toll-call quality on the telephone system. A MOS of 4.33 is quite good.

One caveat is that pingtest.net is a bit "grabby." It tries to sell you its tools and is slightly aggressive. In addition, the site uses Java, which you may have to download. You may also have to give a firewall exception to this Java program.

ACTIVITIES

Questions

1. Why is the radar window's image of a radar scope misleading?
2. How would you locate an access point despite the limitations of the radar window? This will take one to four paragraphs.
3. There is a value of −44 dBm for signal strength. How good is this?

4. How can you sort the networks window?
5. What information does the Connection Test give you?
6. What information does the Speed Test give you?
7. What information does the Quality Test give you?

Activity

   Select a building. Go to at least 10 locations. At each location, record the information in the networks window. Also, do a connection and speed test. Write a brief report what you learned about Wi-Fi service in the building, referring to the data you collected.

7
WIRELESS LANs II

LEARNING OBJECTIVES

By the end of this chapter, you should be able to:

- Explain 802.11 WLAN security.
- Explain 802.11 wireless LAN management.
- Describe other local wireless technologies, including Bluetooth, ultrawideband (UWB) transmission, Zigbee, RFIDs, and software-defined radio.

INTRODUCTION

In Chapter 6, we focused on how 802.11 wireless LANs operate. This chapter continues to look at wireless networks. We will look at 802.11 security and management. We will then turn to other local wireless technologies, including Bluetooth.

Like switched networks, wireless networks are single networks. They are defined by standards at the physical and data link layers. Therefore, they are OSI standards, even if they are created by other organizations, such as the IEEE.

TJX

TJX Companies, Inc. (TJX), is a group of over 2,500 retail stores operating in the United States, Canada, England, Ireland, and several other countries. These companies do business under such names as TJ Maxx and Marshalls. In its literature, TJX describes itself as "the leading off-price retailer of apparel and home fashions in the U.S. and worldwide." With this mission statement, there is strong pressure to minimize costs.

On December 18, 2006, TJX detected "suspicious software" on its computer systems. On December 21, consultants confirmed that an intrusion had actually occurred. The next day, the company informed law enforcement authorities in the United States and Canada. Five days later, the security consultants determined that customer data had been stolen.

The consultants initially determined that the intrusion software had been working for seven months when it was discovered. A few weeks later, the consultants discovered that the company had also been breached several times in 2005. All told, the consultants estimated that 45.7 million customer records had been stolen. This was by far the largest number of personal customer records stolen from any company.

The thieves did not steal these records for the thrill of breaking in or to enhance their reputations among other hackers. They did it to steal information to make fraudulent credit card purchases in the names of the customers whose information had been stolen. These fraudulent purchases based on the stolen information did, in fact, take place.

TJX did not inform customers about the data breach until nearly a month later. The company said that it needed time to beef up its security. The company also said that law enforcement officials had told TJX not to release information about the breach immediately to avoid tipping off the data thieves about the investigation. Of course, the delay also left the customers ignorant of the danger they faced.

How did the breaches occur? When the attackers were caught, it was determined that the data thieves broke into poorly protected wireless networks in some Florida stores to get into the central TJX credit and debit card processing system in Massachusetts.[1] These stores protected their wireless network, but they used the obsolete wired equivalent privacy (WEP) standard instead of newer and better security standards. In Massachusetts, poor firewall protection[2] allowed the data thieves to enter several systems and to install a sniffer that listened to the company's poorly encrypted traffic passing into and out of the processing center. Another problem was that TJX retained some sensitive credit card information that should not have been retained; it is this improperly retained information that the data thieves found valuable.[3]

A number of earlier (and smaller) data breaches had prompted the major credit card companies to create the **Payment Card Industry–Data Security Standard (PCI–DSS)**. Failure to implement PCI–DSS control objectives can result in fines and even the revocation of a company's ability to accept credit card payments.

At the time the data breach was discovered, TJX was far behind in its PCI–DSS compliance program. The company complied with only three of the twelve required control objectives. Internal memos[4] revealed that the company knew that it was in violation of the PCI–DSS requirements, particularly with respect to its weak encryption in retail store wireless networks. However, the company deliberately decided not to move rapidly to fix this problem. In November 2005, a staff member noted prophetically that "saving money and being PCI-compliant is important to us, but equally important is protecting ourselves against intruders. Even though we have some breathing room with PCI, we are still vulnerable with WEP as our security key. It must be a risk we are willing to take for the sake of saving money and hoping we do not get compromised."

When the staff member noted that "we have some breathing room with PCI," he probably was referring to the fact that TJX had been given an extension allowing it to be compliant beyond the standard's specified compliance date.[5] This additional time, ironically, was given after the data breaches had already begun. This extension was dependent upon evaluation of a TJX report on its compliance project by June 2006. It is unknown whether TJX complied with this requirement. The letter that authorized the

[1] Mark Jewel, "Encryption Faulted in TJX hacking," *MSNBC.com*, September 25, 2007.

[2] Ross Kerber, "Details Emerge on TJX Breach," *The Boston Globe*, October 25, 2007.

[3] Mark Jewel, op. cit. www.msnbc.msn.com/id/20979359/.

[4] Evan Schuman, "VISA Fined TJX Processor for Security Breach," *Eweek.com*, October 28, 2007. www.eweek.com/article2/0,1895,2208615,00.asp.

[5] Evan Schuman, "In 2005, Visa Agreed to Give TJX Until 2009 to Get PCI Compliant," *StorefrontBacktalk*, November 9, 2007. storefrontbacktalk.com/story/110907visaletter.

extension was sent by a fraud control vice president for Visa. It ended with, "I appreciate your continued support and commitment to safeguarding the payment industry."

The company quickly became embroiled in commercial lawsuits and government investigations. These lawsuits involved the filing of briefs that shed additional light on the break-ins. For instance, sealed evidence from Visa and MasterCard placed the number of account records stolen at 94 million—roughly double TJX's estimates.[6]

TJX was sued by seven individual banks and bank associations. In December 2007, TJX settled with all but one of these banks, agreeing to pay up to $40.9 million. This would reimburse the banks for the cost of reissuing credit cards and other expenses.

The company also received a large fine from Visa. Actually, Visa could not fine TJX directly but could only fine TJX's merchant bank, the Fifth Third Bank of Ohio. (Merchant banks are financial institutions that serve—and should control—retail organizations that accept credit card payments.) However, merchant banks typically pass on the fine to the retailer, in this case TJX. During the summer of 2007, Visa fined TJX's merchant bank $880,000 and announced that it would continue to impose fines at $100,000/month until TJX had fixed its security problem. However, in the TJX settlement with the seven banks and banking associations, this fine was to be reduced by an undisclosed amount.

In this battle of corporate giants, consumers were handled last. At the time of this writing, TJX has proposed a settlement that would only involve very limited measures such as help with ID theft through insurance and other measures for the roughly 455,000 victims who had given personally identifiable information when they returned goods without a receipt. Other victims would be given a modest voucher or the opportunity to buy TJX merchandise at sale prices.[7]

On August 25, 2008, the Department of Justice charged 11 individuals with conducting the TJX break-in and the subsequent use of the stolen information.[8] Three were Americans, and they were jailed rapidly. Two more were in China. The other six lived in Eastern Europe. Although the three Americans conducted the actual data theft, they fenced the stolen information overseas. Two of the American defendants rapidly entered plea deals to testify against the alleged ringleader, Albert Gonzalez of Miami, Florida. Gonzalez was sentenced in 2010 to 20 years in prison.

One surprising thing about the indictment is that this criminal gang had not only plundered TJX of customer information. Subsequent investigation found that the attackers had repeated the crime with at least a half dozen other major companies.[9] These break-ins also began with the exploitation of WEP security.

Test Your Understanding

1. a) What did the attackers do first to break into TJX and other companies? b) Why do you think TJX failed to upgrade to stronger security than WEP? (There may be more than one consideration.) c) How was the TJX break-in an international crime?

---

[6] Ross Kerber, "Court Filling in TJX Breach Doubles Toll," *The Boston Globe*, October 24, 2007.

[7] John Leyden, "TJX Consumer Settlement Sale Offer Draws Scorn," *TheRegister.com*, November 20, 2007. www.theregister.co.uk/2007/11/20/tjx_settlement_offer_kerfuffle/.

[8] U.S. Department of Justice, "Retail Hacking Ring Charged for Stealing and Distributing Credit and Debit Card Numbers from Major U.S. Retailers," August 5, 2008. www.usdoj.gov/criminal/cybercrime/gonzalez-Indict.pdf.

[9] Ibid.

802.11 WLAN SECURITY

WLAN Security Threats

For most companies, security is the biggest problem with 802.11 wireless LANs. There are several major security threats to 802.11 WLANs:

- Most seriously, **drive-by hackers** park just outside a company's premises and intercept the firm's data transmissions. They can also mount denial-of-service attacks, send malware into the network, and do other mischief. Drive-by hacking software is readily downloadable from the Internet.
- Less importantly, **war drivers** are people who drive around a city looking for working access points that are unprotected. War driving is not illegal. Only if war drivers try to break in do they become drive-by hackers.
- To guard against drive-by hackers, companies can secure their access points using techniques we will see a little later. However, departments or individual employees may set up unauthorized access points. These **rogue access points** often have no security, so they provide entry points for drive-by hackers who could not otherwise break into the network. Even if a company protects all of its official access points very well, a single rogue access point will make the security effort worthless.

Test Your Understanding

2. a) Distinguish between war drivers and drive-by hackers. b) What is a rogue access point?

Drive-by Hackers

Sit outside the corporate premises and read network traffic

Can send malicious traffic into the network

Easily done with readily available downloadable software

War Drivers

Merely discover unprotected access points—become drive-by hackers only if they break in

War driving per se is not illegal

Unprotected Access Points

Drive by hackers can associate with any unprotected access point

They gain access to the local area network without going through the site firewall

Rogue Access Points

Unauthorized access points that are set up by a department or an individual

Often have very poor security, making drive-by hacking easier

Often operate at high power, attracting many hosts to their low-security service

---

FIGURE 7-1 WLAN Security Threats (Study Figure)

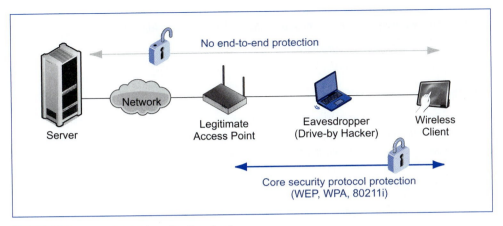

No end-to-end protection

Network

Server

Legitimate
Access Point

Eavesdropper
(Drive-by Hacker)

Wireless
Client

Core security protocol protection
(WEP, WPA, 80211i)

FIGURE 7-2   Core 802.11 Security Standards

802.11 Core Security Standards

Realizing the danger of drive-by hackers, the 802.11 Working Group decided to create a **core security standard** for wireless LANs. As Figure 7-2 shows, 802.11 core security standards provide protection between the wireless access point and the wireless host. This protection includes confidentiality, authentication, and message integrity. A drive-by hacker cannot intercept traffic to read it or send its own messages to the access point.

However, note in the figure that protection only extends between the wireless access point and the wireless host. It does not provide protection end-to-end between the wireless client host and the server host on the wired LAN (or the server host on the Internet). The core security standard has a very limited objective.

The protection provided by 802.11 core security standards only extends between the wireless access point and the wireless host.

Wired Equivalent Privacy (WEP) Security

When the 802.11 Working Group created its first standards in 1997, it only included a very rudimentary core security standard called **Wired Equivalent Privacy (WEP)**.[10] This is the weak security standard that was used by TJX, as we saw at the beginning of this chapter.

With WEP, everyone sharing an access point had to use the same key, and WEP had no automated mechanism for changing this key. In nearly all cases, a firm with many access points and users normally gave all access points the same WEP key. Everybody in the firm knew the WEP key, so many employees thought it was not really secret and often were willing to share the key with unauthorized users. In addition,

---

[10]The WEP specification was only 10 pages long. In contrast, the specification for 802.11i security (discussed later) is 200 pages long.

Provide Security between the Wireless Station and the Wireless Access Point

>   Client (and perhaps server) authentication
>   Encryption of messages for confidentiality

Wired Equivalent Privacy (WEP)

>   Initial rudimentary security provided with 802.11 in 1997
>   Everyone shared the same secret encryption key, and this key could not be changed automatically
>   Because secret key was shared, it does not seem to be secret, users often give out freely
>   Key initially could be cracked in 1–2 hours; now can be cracked in 3–10 minutes using readily available software

Wireless Protected Access (WPA)

>   The Wi-Fi Alliance
>>   Normally certifies interoperability of 802.11 equipment
>>   Created WPA as a stop-gap security standard in 2002 until 802.11i was finished
>   Designed for upgrading old equipment
>>   WPA uses a subset of 802.11i that can run on older wireless NICs and access points
>>   WPA added simpler security algorithms for functions that could not run on older machines
>   Equipment that cannot be upgraded to WPA should be discarded

802.11i (WPA2)

>   Uses AES-CCMP with 128-bit keys for confidentiality and key management
>   Gold standard in 802.11 security
>   But companies have large installed bases of WPA-configured equipment

FIGURE 7-3   802.11 Security Standards (Study Figure)

because there was no automated way to change all of the access point keys when an employee was fired, companies continued to use the same key even when there were clear security threats.

WEP had several other serious design problems. By 2001, software that would crack WEP keys quickly was readily available. Initially, cracking a WEP key with one of these programs took one or two hours. Today, it often takes only about 10 minutes. Many companies began putting the brakes on WLAN implementation, and many pulled out their existing access points.[11]

---

[11]Some companies began taking other steps, like hiding the SSID (Service Set Identifier) of the access point. Users need to know this SSID to use an access point even if WEP is not used. Another common step was to accept only computers whose wireless NICs had registered MAC addresses. (All 802 LANs have 48-bit MAC addresses.) Unfortunately, these measures take a great deal of work, and they are easily cracked by readily available hacking software. They make sense if you are concerned only about unsophisticated but nosy neighbors at home.

Despite problems with WEP, companies continued to use it long after better 802.11 core security standards became available. One company that did so was TJ-MAX in the United States. As we saw at the beginning of this chapter, TJ-MAX made a conscious decision not to upgrade from WEP to a better core security protocol. The result was a disaster. Using a weak core security protocol is a terrible security policy. Although access points and clients usually continue to offer WEP as well as newer security protocols, only the newer security protocols should be used.

Test Your Understanding

3. a) When 802.11 was created, what security protocol did it offer? b) How long does it take to crack WEP today?

WPA (Wireless Protected Access)

The **Wi-Fi Alliance** is an industry trade group that certifies 802.11 products for interoperability. Normally, the Wi-Fi Alliance leaves standards creation to the 802.11 Working Group. However, when WEP's fatal flaws were discovered in 2000 and 2001, the market for wireless products began to falter. Furthermore, the 802.11i security standard being developed by the 802.11 Working Group was going to take years to be ratified.

As a stop-gap measure until 802.11i could be developed, the Wi-Fi Alliance created an interim security standard, **Wireless Protected Access (WPA)**, based on an early draft of the 802.11i core security standard. So that WPA could be used on older wireless access points, the Wi-Fi Alliance watered down the 802.11i draft standard, using weaker security protocols. It announced this standard in 2002 and began certifying products for compliance in early 2003. Despite its weaknesses, WPA was much stronger than WEP. Companies flocked to it.

Test Your Understanding

4. a) Who created WPA? b) What is WPA's disadvantage compared with 802.11i?

802.11i (WPA2)

In 2004, the 802.11 Working Group finally ratified the **802.11i** standard. Most important, the 802.11i standard uses extremely strong **AES-CCMP** encryption. AES-CCMP has 128-bit keys and a key management method for automatically changing keys. In general, for every aspect of security, it uses the strongest security algorithms. Confusingly, the Wi-Fi Alliance refers to the 802.11i standard as **WPA2**.

However, before 802.11i appeared, most companies had already implemented WPA on their access points and wireless hosts. Reconfiguring all of these devices to work with 802.11i can be expensive, and until there were known cracks for WPA, companies were reluctant to make this investment. This changed in 2009, when a partial crack appeared for WPA. Companies that care strongly about WLAN security have transitioned to or are moving rapidly to 802.11i.

Test Your Understanding

5. a) What is the strongest security protocol for 802.11 today? b) What does the Wi-Fi Alliance call 802.11i? c) What encryption method does 802.11i use? d) What is deterring companies from converting from WPA to 802.11i? e) Why is WPA no longer viewed as a safe solution?

802.1X Mode Operation with Added Client–Access Point Security

WPA and 802.11i have two modes of operation. For large firms, the only mode that makes sense is **802.1X mode**. (The Wi-Fi Alliance calls it **enterprise mode**.) In Chapter 5, we saw that 802.1X was created for Ethernet wired networks. Its goal is to prevent attackers from simply walking into a building and plugging a computer into any wall jack or directly into a switch.

Figure 7-5 shows that each workgroup switch acts as an authenticator. The computer wishing access to the Ethernet network connects to the authenticator via UTP. Actual authentication is done by a central authentication server that normally uses the RADIUS protocol.

For Ethernet access, there is no need to have security between the computer seeking access and the workgroup switch that controls access. It is difficult for another person to tap the wired access line between the computer and the switch, and there are easier ways to break into a network. Consequently, as Figure 7-5 shows, there is no security between the wired hosts and the switch that is the 802.1X network access server.

With access points, however, transmissions between a wireless host and the access point are easy to intercept and mimic. The path between the host and the access point needs to be secure. To address this problem, the 802.11 Working Group extended the 802.1X standard by adding security between the access point and the wireless host before 802.1X mode authentication is done. The most common standard for adding this protection is the Protected Extensible Authentication Protocol (PEAP). Other standards for adding this security include EAP-TLS and EAP-TTLS. All of these standards create

---

802.1X Mode (See Figure 8-5)

Uses a central authentication server for consistency

Authentication server also provides key management

Wi-Fi Alliance calls this *enterprise mode*

802.1X standard protects communication with an extensible authentication protocol

    Several EAP versions exist with different security protections

    Firm implementing 802.1X must choose one

    Protected EAP (PEAP) is popular because Microsoft favors it

Pre-Shared Key (PSK) Mode: Stations Share a Key with the Access Point

For networks with a single access point

Access point does all authentication and key management

All users must know an initial pre-shared key (PSK)

Each, however, is later given a unique key

If the pre-shared key is weak, it is easily cracked

Pass phrases that generate key must be at least 20 characters long

Wi-Fi Alliance calls this *personal mode*

FIGURE 7-4   802.11 Security in 802.1X and PSK Modes (Study Figure)

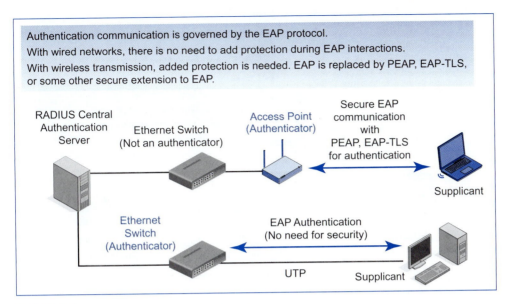

Authentication communication is governed by the EAP protocol.
With wired networks, there is no need to add protection during EAP interactions.
With wireless transmission, added protection is needed. EAP is replaced by PEAP, EAP-TLS, or some other secure extension to EAP.

FIGURE 7-5   802.1X Mode for 802.11i (and WPA)

an SSL/TLS connection between the wireless access point and the wireless client before 802.1X is applied.

Test Your Understanding

6. a) In what mode of 802.11i and WPA operation is a central authentication server used? b) What does the Wi-Fi Alliance call 802.1X mode? c) Why does 802.1X not need security between the authenticator and the computer in Ethernet? d) Why does 802.1X need security between the authenticator and the computer in 802.11 wireless access? e) Why is extra EAP security necessary in 802.11 networks using 802.1X? f) What is the most popular standard for extended 802.1X security?

Pre-Shared Key (PSK) Mode

For homes and small businesses, adding a separate authentication server would be absurd. Consequently, the 802.11 Working Group created a simpler mode of operation beyond 802.1X mode. In this simpler mode, called **pre-shared key mode**, a single access point does all the work to provide a core security protocol. The Wi-Fi Alliance calls this personal mode.

PSK mode in 802.11i and WPA is for homes and small businesses with a single access point.

Figure 7-6 shows that the access points and wireless hosts begin with a shared 64-bit key. Everybody allowed to use the access point is told the shared key. This sounds like WEP, but this shared key is only used in initial authentication. After initial authentication, the wireless access point gives each authenticated user a new unique key to use

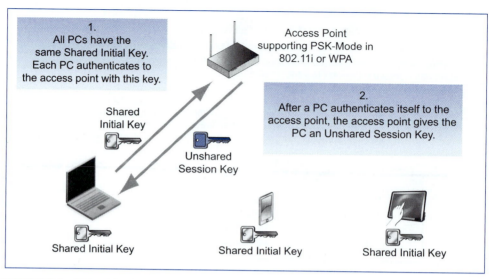

FIGURE 7-6 802.11i (and WPA) in Pre-Shared Key Mode

while on the Internet. It also changes this key frequently. With this approach, too little traffic is created with each key to allow a drive-by hacker to crack the key.

In a home or very small business, having a handful of people know the shared key is not too dangerous. The larger danger is that the household or small business will select a weak key. To create the pre-shared key, the household or company creates a long **pass phrase** (which is much longer than a password) that the access point and each host use to generate the key. This pass phrase must be at least 20 characters long to provide adequate security. If short pass phrases are used, 802.11i and WPA in PSK mode are almost as easy to crack as WEP.

Test Your Understanding

7. a) How does PSK mode differ from 802.1X mode? b) What is a potential weakness of PSK mode? c) How long should pass phrases be with PSK?

Evil Twin Access Points and Virtual Private Networks (VPNs)

Strong core security standards that protect communication between the wireless access point and wireless clients can greatly reduce risks. However, there is one type of attack that can break core security standards. This is the evil twin access point.

EVIL TWIN ACCESS POINTS Figure 7-7 illustrates an evil twin access point attack. Normally, the wireless client shown in the figure will associate with its legitimate access point. The two will establish a core security standard connection between them.

An **evil twin access point** is a notebook computer configured to act like a real access point. The evil twin operates at very high power. If the wireless host is configured to choose the highest-power access point, it will associate with the evil twin access point instead of the legitimate access point. The evil twin will establish a

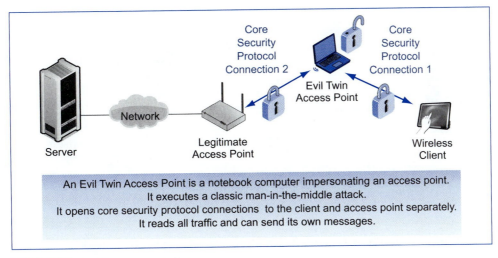

FIGURE 7-7 Evil Twin Access Point

secure connection with the wireless client. This is Core Security Connection 1. Next, the evil twin associates with the legitimate access point, creating Core Security Connection 2.

> *An evil twin access point is a notebook computer configured to act like a real access point.*

The evil twin can now read all traffic flowing between the wireless client and the legitimate wireless access point. When the wireless client sends encrypted frames, the evil twin decrypts them and then re-encrypts them before sending them on to the wireless access point. It does the same with traffic going in the other direction. Neither the wireless client nor the wireless access point knows that this is happening. Both seem to experience a normal secure connection. The wireless client has no problem getting to servers on the main wired LAN or getting to Internet servers.

What damage can an evil twin access point do? Most obviously, it can eavesdrop on the communication between the wireless client and the servers it uses. This allows the evil twin to steal important keys, corporate trade secrets, or personal information transmitted by the client.

The evil twin can also launch attacks against the client or any server attached to the network. On the client, the evil twin may be able to read information on the user's hard drive or plant malware for ongoing exploitation. The evil twin can launch attacks directly against servers, bypassing the company's firewall.

VIRTUAL PRIVATE NETWORKS (VPNS) The evil twin attack is an example of a general class of attacks called man-in-the-middle attacks, in which an attacker intercepts messages and then passes them on. Man-in-the-middle attacks typically are very difficult to defeat. The main way to defeat them is to establish a virtual private

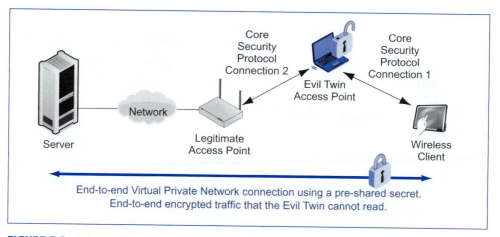

FIGURE 7-8   Using a Virtual Private Network (VPN) to Counter an Evil Twin Attack

network (VPN) connection between the wireless client and the server host it will use, as Figure 7-8 illustrates.

A **virtual private network (VPN)** is nothing more than a cryptographic system connection between a client and a server. A VPN gets its name from the fact that, as far as security is concerned, the client and server seem to have their own private network.

VPNs provide end-to-end protection between the client and the server, including end-to-end authentication. If VPN authentication is based on a pre-shared secret that the client and server know ahead of time, an evil twin will not be able to conduct a man-in-the-middle attack against the client and the server. Although the evil twin can read all wireless transmissions, it cannot intercept the pre-shared secret because this secret is never transmitted. So it will not be able to decrypt the messages passing between the client and the server, and it will not be able to send authenticated attack messages to either.

PERSPECTIVE   Evil twin attacks are not theoretical concerns. They are commonplace, especially in wireless hot spots. Companies should use VPNs whenever clients and servers exchange sensitive communication.

Test Your Understanding

8. a) What is an evil twin access point? b) A company uses 802.11i for its core security protocol. How many 802.11i connections will the evil twin access point set up? c) What does the evil twin do when the client transmits to the legitimate access point? d) Distinguish between evil twin access points and rogue access points. e) How can VPNs defeat evil twin attacks? f) Why must the VPN secret be pre-shared to thwart a VPN attack?

Wi-Fi Protected Setup

One recent problem is a security weakness in **Wi-Fi Protected Setup (WPS)**. This standard is not a creation of the 802.11 Working Group. Rather, it was created by the Wi-Fi

Alliance. The basic idea was a good one. With WPS, it is easy to add a new client to a WPA2 pre-shared key mode access point simply. Unfortunately, if an attacker can use WPS to associate it with an access point illegitimately, he or she then has access to the network. Note that this is only a concern with pre-shared key mode. However, this is a business security concern if employees are using PSK on their home networks.

Part of the WPS process is knowing a secret PIN that is eight digits (the characters from 0 to 9) long. Exhaustive search on such a PIN should take about half of 10^8 or 50,000,000 attempts. This is not practical. However, the Wi-Fi Alliance made a poor decision in its design. It divided the PIN into two 4-digit halves. Then, it unfortunately gave an attacker feedback if the first half was entered correctly correct. Therefore, the attacker only has to try an average of 10^4 or 5,000 attempts to find the first four digits. Once these are known, cracking the second part only takes about half of 10^3 or 500 attempts. Why not half of 10^4? The answer is that one of the last four final numerals is a check digit that can be computed from the other seven. The take away is that by cutting the number of attempts required to learn the secret, PIN is reduced from 50,000,000 attempts to 5,500 attempts. The latter allows Wi-Fi Protected Setup to be broken in a few hours.

What can be done to protect against these weaknesses? For existing access points, the only possibility is to turn off Wi-Fi Protected Setup. Obviously, this means losing easy setup for clients at PSK wireless access points. In addition, it is not even possible to turn off WPS on many wireless routers.

Test Your Understanding

9. a) What does WPS do? b) For what 802.11i mode is it applicable? c) Why is it desirable? d) Why is it dangerous? e) What can be done to reduce the danger of the WPS security weakness?

Denial-of-Service Attacks

A final security concern for 802.11 wireless networks is the possibility of *denial-of-service (DoS)* attacks. In a typical wireless DoS attack, the attacker overloads an access point or causes a client to disassociate from an access point. One approach to DoS attacks is to flood an access point with traffic. This is best done with frames that request association or do something else that requires extensive processing on the access point. Another is to send disassociate frames to a client. This causes a client to disassociate with the access point, breaking the network connection. Wireless attacks are uncommon, and they are usually not effective, but companies must be concerned about that.

Test Your Understanding

10. a) What damage is done by a denial-of-service attack? b) What are the two types of wireless denial-of-service attacks?

802.11 WIRELESS LAN MANAGEMENT

Until recently, the term *WLAN management* was almost an oxymoron. Large WLANs were like major airports without control towers. Companies quickly realized that they needed tools for centralized WLAN management.

Access Point Placement

The first management issue is where to place access points. If placement is not done systematically, there will be many dead spots, interference between many access points, or both.

INITIAL PLANNING The first step is to determine how far signals should travel. In many firms, a good radius is about 30 meters. If the radius is too great, many hosts will be far from their access points. Hosts far from the access point must drop down to lower transmission speeds, and their frames will take longer to send. This will reduce the access point's effective capacity. If the radius is too small, however, the firm will need many more access points to cover the space to be served.

Once an appropriate radius is selected (say 30 meters), the company gets out its building architecture drawings and begins to lay out 30 meter circles with as little overlap as possible. Where there are thick walls or other obstructions, shorter propagation distances must be assumed. And, of course, in a multistory building, this planning must be done in three dimensions.

Access Points Placement in a Building

Must be done carefully for good coverage and to minimize interference between access points

Lay out 30-meter to 50-meter radius circles on blueprints

Adjust for obvious potential problems such as brick walls

In multistory buildings, must consider interference in three dimensions

Install access points and do site surveys to determine signal quality

Adjust placement and signal strength as needed

Remote Access Point Management

The manual labor to manage many access points: can be very high

Centralized management alternatives (See Figure 8-10)

    Smart access points

    Dumb access points, with intelligence in WLAN switches

Desired functionality

    Notify the WLAN administrators of failures immediately

    Support remote access point adjustment

    Should provide continuous transmission quality monitoring

    Allow software updates to be pushed out to all access points or WLAN switches

    Work automatically whenever possible

Desired security functionality

    Notify administrator of rogue access points

    Notify administrator of evil twin access points

    Notify the administrator of flooding denial-of-service attacks

    Notify the administrator of disassociate message denial-of-service attacks

    Instantly deny access to selected stations

FIGURE 7-9 Wireless LAN Management (Study Figure)

Finally, planners assign channels to access point positions. They attempt to minimize interference while doing so.

INSTALLATION AND INITIAL SITE SURVEYS Next, the access points are installed provisionally in the indicated places. However, the implementation work has just begun. When each access point is installed, an **initial site survey** must be done of the area around the access point to discover whether there are any dead spots or other problems. This requires signal analyzer software, which can run on a notebook computer or even a smartphone.

When areas with poor signal strength are found, surrounding access points must be moved appropriately, or their signal strengths must be adjusted until all areas have good signal strength.

ONGOING SITE SURVEYS Although the initial site survey should result in good service, conditions will change constantly. More people may be given desks in a given access point's range, signal obstructions may be put up for business purposes, and other changes must occur. Site surveys must be done periodically to ensure good service. They may also be done in response to specific reports of problems. To address problems, the network staff can adjust the power settings of nearby access points or take other actions.

Test Your Understanding

11. a) Describe the process by which access point locations are selected. b) After access points are installed provisionally, what must be done next?

Remote Management: Smart Access Points versus Wireless Switches

Large organizations have hundreds or even thousands of 802.11 wireless access points. Traveling to each one for manual configuration and troubleshooting would be extremely expensive. To keep management labor costs under control, organizations need to be able to manage access points remotely, from a central management console. Figure 7-10 illustrates two approaches to centralized wireless access point management.

SMART ACCESS POINTS The simplest approach architecturally is to add intelligence to every access point. The central management console can then communicate directly with each of these **smart access points**[12] via the firm's Ethernet wired LAN. However, adding management capacity raises the price of access points considerably. Using smart access points is an expensive strategy.

WIRELESS LAN SWITCHES A second approach illustrated in Figure 7-10 is to use **WLAN switches**. As the figure shows, multiple access points connect to each wireless LAN switch. The management intelligence is placed in the WLAN switch rather than in the

---

[12] Smart access points are also called fat access points.

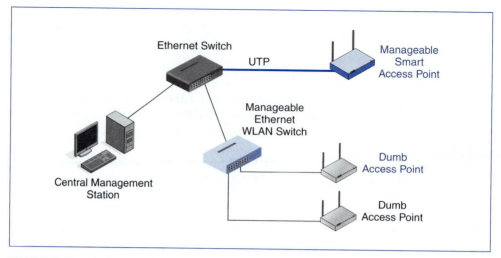

FIGURE 7-10 Wireless Access Point Management Alternatives

access points themselves. Vendors who sell WLAN switches claim that this approach reduces total cost because only inexpensive **dumb access points** are needed. Of course, smart access point vendors dispute these cost comparisons.

WIRELESS LAN MANAGEMENT FUNCTIONALITY Although technological approaches to centralized WLAN management vary, vendors generally agree on the types of functionality these systems should provide.

- These systems should notify the WLAN administrators of failures immediately so that malfunctioning access points can be fixed or replaced rapidly.
- They should provide continuous transmission-quality monitoring at all access points. In effect, they should provide continuous site surveys.
- They should help provide security by detecting rogue access points, evil twin access points, or legitimate access points that have improperly configured security.
- They should allow remote adjustment—for instance, telling nearby access points to increase their power to compensate for an access point failure. Such adjustments are also needed over time as furniture is moved (creating different shadow zones) or as the number of users in an area changes.
- They should allow software updates to be pushed out to all access points or WLAN switches, bypassing the need to install updates manually.
- The management software should be able to work automatically, taking as many actions as possible without human intervention.

WIRELESS MANAGEMENT SECURITY FUNCTIONALITY Centralized wireless LAN management also needs to provide support for detecting and correcting security problems.

- First, the WLAN management system should notify the administrator if a rogue access point appears.

- Second, it should notify the administrator if an evil twin access point appears.
- It should also notify the administrator of jamming denial-of-service attacks that flood an access point with traffic.
- It should notify the administrator of disassociate message that causes a wireless host to drop its connection with an access point.
- Acting on its own, it should instantly deny access to wireless hosts under specified conditions.

Test Your Understanding

12. a) Why is centralized access point management desirable? b) What are the two technologies for remote access point management? c) What functions should remote access point management systems provide?

Expressing Power Ratios in Decibels

In networking, you often need to express the ratio of two signal power levels. For example, you might wish to say that a larger antenna will quadruple the signal power. Or, you might say that signal power at one location is only half as strong as it is at a certain closer location. Or, you might wish to say that the connector between a radio and an antenna reduces power by 30 percent. In each case, percentages and ratios work fine.

Computing Ratios in Decibels

The problem is that radio power ratios often vary by several orders of magnitude, say between 50 Watts and 0.005 Watt. In such cases, ratios expressed as percentages become difficult to read. Instead, it is easier to read ratios expressed in a logarithmic scale. Consequently, relative signal strengths in radio transmission are almost always given in watts. Equation 7-1 shows how to express the ratio between two power levels, P_1 and P_2, in **decibels (dB)**. This looks a bit complicated, but it is easy to do in practice, with the help of a spreadsheet program.

Equation 7–1 Expressing Power Ratios in Decibels

$$L_{db} = 10 * Log_{10}\left(\frac{P_2}{P_1}\right)$$

Computing Ratios

We will discuss the equation backwards, from *right to left*. You first divide the second power level, P_2, in watts, by the first power level, P_1, again in watts. To give an example, if P_1 is 40 W and P_2 is 80 W, the resultant ratio is 80/40 or 2. If the second power level is larger than the first, the ratio will be greater than one. For example, this happens if an antenna boosts a radio's initial power P_1 before sending it out as transmitted power P_2.

If the second power level is larger than the first, the ratio will be greater than one.

In contrast, suppose that P_2 is 40 W and P_1 is 80 W. In that case, the resultant ratio is 40/80 or 0.5. If the second power level is less than the first, the ratio will be smaller than one.

(continued)

This happens if there is a decrease in power, say from attenuation of the signal as it propagates or in case of a power loss in the connector between the radio and the antenna.

If the second power level is larger than the first, the ratio will be less than one.

We have said that both power levels must be measured in watts. Actually, this was a slight lie. As long as both powers are expressed in the same units, for example, milliwatts, it will be fine. However, if one is given in watts and the other in milliwatts, the calculation will not work. You have to put them in the same units.

Expressing Ratios in Decibels

Next, you take the Base 10 logarithm of the ratio. Computing Base 10 logarithms is very difficult. Therefore, you should cheat. Use Excel or some other spreadsheet program. In Excel, the function for Base 10 logarithms is LOG10(). The second column in Equation 7-1 shows Base 10 logarithms for a number of ratios from 100 to –100. This gives the power ratios in Bels, named after Alexander Graham Bell. However, engineers multiply Bels by 10 to give decibels (dB). Decibels prove to be more useful numbers for radio signal measurement. The third column gives this decibel calculation. You now have ratios in decibels. You have mastered Equation 7-1.

Notice the general pattern in Figure 7-11 for decibels. If the ratio is greater than one—that is, if P_2 is larger than P_1, then the number of decibels is positive. In contrast, if the ratio is less than one, that is, if P_2 is smaller than P_1, then the number of decibels is negative. By

Ratio	Bels Log10	Decibels 10 * Log10	Approximately
100	2	20	20
50	1.699	16.990	NA
20	1.301	13.010	13
10	1	10	10
8	0.903	9.031	9
4	0.602	6.021	6
3	0.477	4.771	NA
2	0.301	3.010	3
1	0	0	0
0.5	−0.301	−3.010	−3
0.3333	−0.477	−4.772	NA
0.25	−0.602	−6.021	−6
0.125	−0.903	−9.031	−9
0.1	−1	−10	−10
0.05	−1.301	−13.010	−13
0.01	−2	−20	−20

FIGURE 7-11 Decibel (dB) Calculations for Various Ratios

looking at the sign of the decibel value, you can tell at a glance if the power increased from P_1 to P_2 or if it decreased.[13]

If ratio is greater than one—that is, if P$_2$ is larger than P$_1$, then the number of decibels is positive. In contrast, if the ratio is less than one, that is, if P$_2$ is smaller than P$_1$, then the number of decibels is negative.

Working with Approximations

The fourth column in Figure 7-11 shows that if the ratio is 1, 2, 4, or 8, there are approximations you can use to estimate decibel values without having to compute Equation 7-1. This is useful if you do not have a spreadsheet program readily available or if you just want to get a feel for a number you are given. In the case of powers of two, the estimation rule is that each doubling is an additional 3 decibels. So a ratio of 2 is 3 db, of 4 is 6 db, and of 8 is 9 dB. What would a ratio of 16 be?[14] These are only approximations, but they are very good ones. The true value for each doubling, 3.010, is extremely close to 3.

Each doubling in the power ratio corresponds approximately to 3 dB.

What about ratios less than one? One half is very nearly –3dB, one quarter is nearly –6 dB, and one eighth can be estimated to be –9 dB. What is one sixteenth?[15]

Each halving in the power ratio corresponds approximately to –3 dB.

Things are even easier if ratios are some power of 10. A ratio of 10 is 10 dB. A ratio of 100 is 20 dB. Each multiplication by 10 gives an additional 10 dB. So if the power ratio is 1,000, this is 30 dB. What if the power ratio is 10,000?[16] Going the other way, a ratio of 1/10 is –10 dB, and a ratio of 1/100 is –20 dB. What is a ratio of 1/1,000?[17] These are listed in the table as approximations, but they are really exact. Each increase by a factor of 10 adds exactly 10 dB, and each decrease by a factor of 10 reduces the decibels by a factor of exactly 10.

Each increase by a factor of 10 adds exactly 10 dB, and each decrease by a factor of 10 reduces the decibels by a factor of exactly 10.

These "tricks" for 2 and 10 can be used together. For example, what about a ratio of 20? In this case, you have an increase by a factor of 10 and another by a factor of 2. The order is not important. In power levels, you multiply by 10 and by 2. In logarithms, you *add* the two logarithms. Multiplying by 10 gives 10 db, and multiplying by 2 gives 3 db. Therefore, the decibel

(continued)

---

[13] Of course, if you know the ratio of P_2 to P_1, it is even easier to tell, but if you are just given decibel levels, you can't do this.

[14] Yep, 12 dB.

[15] –12 dB.

[16] Yep, 40 dB.

[17] It is –30 dB. Got it again.

value for a power ratio of 20 should be 10 plus 3 or 13 dB. You can see in Figure 7-11 that this is in fact the case. (The actual value is 13.010 dB.)

What about a ratio of 1/20? Again, you *add* the two approximations. One tenth is −10 dB, and one half is −3 dB. So you get an approximate decibel value of −13 dB.

What about other ratios, like 3:1, 50:1, 1:3, and 1:50? Sorry. There aren't approximations for these. Go to Excel and work it out. You will have to do this for precise calculations anyway, even if you are talking about factors of 2 or ½. Approximations just let you work things out in your head.

At the same time, working with factors of 2 and 10 can give you an approximate range of actual values. For example, what about a ratio of 25? A ratio of 20, which is a little *lower* than 25, would give 13 dB, as we have just seen, so the correct value will be a little *more* than 13 dB. In turn, 32, which is larger than 25, is five doublings or 15 dB. So the value in decibels must be between 13 dB and 15 dB. If you go to Excel and get a number smaller than 13 dB or larger than 15 db, check your work. By the way, the correct answer using Equation 7-1 is 13.98.

dBm

We have looked at expressing ratios in terms of decibels. However, when you look at the power of a radio, you often see it expressed in dBm. This means decibels expressed are relative to one **milliwatt (mW)**, which is one thousandth of a watt.

For example, suppose that your radio has a power of 0.1 Watt. This is 100 milliwatts. So the ratio for the power of the radio compared to one milliwatt is 100. This would give a decibel ratio of 20 dBm. In turn, if the radio had a power of eight milliwatts, this would be a ratio of 8 or 9 dBm. If a radio has a power of 1 Watt, then the ratio compared to one milliwatt is 1,000, and the radio has a power of 30 dBm. If a radio has a power of 10 Watts, then the ratio would be 10,000, and the dBm value would be 40 dBm. A 100 Watts, which would be the power of a light bulb, would have a value of 50 dBm.

One reason that radio engineers like to use dBm is that the ratio is almost always positive. A radio with a power of less than a milliwatt generally will not be able to transmit with any speed or distance.

Perspective: Multiplication versus Addition

One advantage of working with decibels is that while you must multiply with ratios, you can simply add logarithms. For example, suppose that you start with a radio strength of 33 dBm. Also, suppose that the signal strength at a particular location is 1/10 that of the signal strength near the radio. Therefore, you have an attenuation of −10 dB. Finally, suppose that the receiver has a high-gain antenna that will boost the signal by a factor of two (+3 dB). The final signal strength at the receiver will be 33 dBm −10 dB + 3 dB or 26 dBm.

Converting Decibels Back to Power Levels

Sometimes when you are given a decibel value, you wish to know what power ratio this represents. To do this calculation, simply solve Equation 7-1 for P_2/P_1. (Yeah, right.) OK, here is what you get:

Equation 7–2   Converting Decibel Values to Power Levels

$$\frac{P_2}{P_1} = 10^{(L_{dB}/10)}$$

Equation 7-2 looks forbidding, but it is simple. Divide the L_{dB} value by 10. Then raise 10 to that power. Here is how it looks in Excel:

$$(P_2/P_1) = 10^\wedge(L_{db}/10)$$

For example, try an L_{dB} value of 20. Obviously, 20 divided by 10 is 2. Ten squared is 100. So an L_{dB} value of 20 corresponds to a power ratio of 100. Of course, you already knew that.

Test Your Understanding

13. a) Using a spreadsheet program, compute the decibel value for a ratio of 17:1. b) For 1/33. c) Estimate, without using Excel, the decibels for a ratio of 8/1. d) For 1/20. e) For 1/8. f) For 16/1. g) Estimate, without using Excel, the decibels for a ratio of 80/1. h) For 1/40. i) For 1/800. j) For 16,000/1. k) Estimate, without using Excel, the dBm value for 2 mW. l) For a radio with 16 mW. m) For a radio with 2 W. n) For a radio with 0.2 W

14. a) Estimate the final dBm value for a radio if the radio has .1 Watt of power, if there is a 4:1 amplifier before transmission, and if there is attenuation to 1/8 the original signal strength between the sender and receiver. b) Estimate the final dBm value for a radio if the radio has .4 Watt of power, if there is a 10:1 amplifier before transmission, and if there is attenuation to 1/1,000 the original signal strength between the sender and the receiver, and if the receiver's antenna loses half of the signal strength before delivering the signal to the receiver.

15. a) What power ratio does –30 dB represent? b) What power ratio does –21 dB represent? c) What absolute power does 78 dBm represent?

OTHER LOCAL WIRELESS TECHNOLOGIES

The 802.11 Wi-Fi standards were designed to work with Ethernet. In fact, many have called 802.11 "wireless Ethernet." With service radiuses of 30 meters and larger, 802.11 access points can cover the substantial distances required for office-wide communication. In addition, 802.11 access points are designed to work together to cover much larger areas, such as corporate buildings. Their speeds allow them to serve quite a few wireless clients in an area, giving each client fast Internet access, file transfers, video, and other processes that require reasonably high throughput. To serve such long distances, of course, access points consume quite a bit of electrical power. They must be connected to the main electrical lines of the building or to Ethernet switches with power over Ethernet (which we saw in Chapter 5).

Not all local application needs require such large service distances and high speeds. For their more modest requirements, other local wireless technologies have been developed. These technologies offer shorter transmission distances and lower speeds. In compensation, they have much smaller energy requirements. This makes them suitable for even hand-held devices. In this section, we will look at two of these low-performance low-energy technologies, Bluetooth and near field communication (NFC).

Figure 7-12 shows the main characteristics of 802.11, Bluetooth, and NFC. It also gives the main characteristics of ultrawideband (UWB) transmission which has the short distance limitation of Bluetooth but offers far higher speeds (and power consumption).

Characteristic (Typical)	802.11	Bluetooth	Near Field Communication (NFC)	Ultrawideband (UWB)
Use	Typically, infrastructure WLANs linked to Ethernet switches Wi-Fi Direct gives direct communication between two wireless hosts	Personal area networks (PANs) around a desk or a person's body	Very-near communication between two wireless hosts	Extremely high-speed short-distance transmission
Typical Speed	20–300 Mbps	2 Mbps	106, 212, or 424 kbps	100 Mbps
Service Range	30–50 m	10 m	10 cm	10 m
Requires Wall Power	Yes	No	No	Yes
Service Band	2.4 and 5 GHz	2.4 GHz	13.56 kHz	UWB channels typically span multiple entire service bands

FIGURE 7-12   Local Wireless Technologies

In Chapter 6, we saw that newer 802.11 standards allow Wi-Fi Direct communication, in which two wireless hosts communicate peer-to-peer without using an access point. This reduces the difference in scope between 802.11 and Bluetooth.

Bluetooth

If you have a wireless headset for your mobile phone or pocket music player, if you have a wireless mouse and keyboard, or if you have a hands-free cellular system in your car, you may already be using Bluetooth. These are precisely the kinds of short-distance modest-speed applications Bluetooth was created to handle. **Bluetooth** is a short-range radio technology that is designed for **personal area networks (PANs)**—small groups of devices around a person's body or in the area around a desk.

THREE MODES OF OPERATION   How fast is Bluetooth? The answer is that the latest version of the Bluetooth standard, Bluetooth 4.0, has three modes of operation with different transmission speeds and power requirements. Figure 7-13 illustrates these three modes.

Classic Bluetooth   The 802.11 standards are created by the IEEE Standards Association's 802.11 Working Group. In contrast, Bluetooth is created by the **Bluetooth Special Interest Group**, an association of hardware manufacturers and other

	Classic Bluetooth	**High-Speed Bluetooth**	**Low-Energy Bluetooth**
Principal Benefit	Good performance at low power	High-speed transfers available when needed	Ultra-long battery life and ultra-fast setup times
Speed	Up to 3 Mbps	Up to about 24 Mbps	Up to 200 kbps
Expected Duty Cycle	Low to high	Low to high	Very low
Power Required	Low	High	Very low
Distance	~10 m	~30 m	~15 m
Setup Time	< 6 s	Not given	< 3 ms

FIGURE 7-13   Bluetooth Modes of Operation (Study Figure)

organizations. The original version of Bluetooth, created in 1994, has extremely low transmission rates—only 721 kbps in one direction and about one tenth that speed in the other direction. Bluetooth 2.0 through 2.2 introduced what most people think of as the "standard" Bluetooth speed of 2 to 3 Mbps. This is still very slow compared to current versions of 802.11, but it is fast enough for voice communication and even modest-quality video transmission. This is now called **classic Bluetooth**.

High-Speed Bluetooth   In 2009, the Bluetooth SIG introduced Bluetooth 3.0. This introduced a new mode of Bluetooth transmission, **high-speed Bluetooth**. This new mode retains ordinary Bluetooth speeds for most operations. However, for operations that require higher speeds, such as webpage downloads, a Bluetooth device capable of high-speed Bluetooth can turn on a second radio that uses a version of 802.11 limited to peer-to-peer transmission between two devices. In other words, the Bluetooth SIG "borrowed" radio transmission technology from its rival, 802.11. Of course, this requires two radios in the phone—one to implement Layer 1 and Layer 2 of classic Bluetooth and one to implement the same layers in 802.11. High-speed Bluetooth consumes a good deal of power, like regular 802.11. However, high-speed Bluetooth conserves battery power by only using faster speeds when they are needed. In the future, high-speed Bluetooth may be used for other radio transmission standards as well, such as ultra-wideband transmission, which we will see a little later in this section.[18]

Low-Energy Bluetooth   In 2010, the Bluetooth SIG introduced Bluetooth 4.0. In addition to other improvements, this standard introduced a third mode of operation, **low-energy Bluetooth**. Low-energy Bluetooth is for device pairs that have low duty cycles, that is, only communicate with each other a small percentage of the time, such as 0.25 percent. For devices that are used this way, low-energy Bluetooth allows devices with "coin" batteries to work for several years on a single battery. Low-energy Bluetooth also reduces power by restricting transmission speed to about 200 kbps.

---

[18] In general, non-Bluetooth radio transmission alternatives are called alternative mac/phy (AMP).

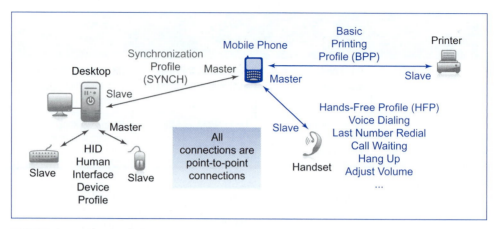

FIGURE 7-14   Bluetooth Operation

As a side benefit low-energy Bluetooth operation, there is an extremely short setup time—less than 3 milliseconds as compared to classic Bluetooth's less than 6 second setup time.

ONE-TO-ONE, MASTER–SLAVE OPERATION   Figure 7-14 shows how several devices communicate through Bluetooth. The device in the top center is a mobile phone. To its right is a printer. The mobile phone user wishes to print a webpage on the mobile's screen. It selects print, chooses the target printer, and prints. In seconds, the user walks up to the printer and picks up the output.

Bluetooth always uses a **one-to-one** connection between a pair of devices. There is no many-to-many networking, as is possible with 802.11 and Ethernet. Reducing operation to one-to-one communication simplifies Bluetooth protocols.

Bluetooth always uses point-to-point communication between a pair of devices.

Bluetooth also uses **master–slave control**. One device is the master, and the other device is the slave. In the printing scenario, the mobile device is the master and the printer is the slave. The mobile phone drives the printing process.

In Bluetooth, one device is the master and the other device is the slave.

Although communication is always one-to-one communication, a master may have multiple slaves. In addition to controlling the printer, the mobile phone in Figure 7-14 also controls the user's hands-free handset. In this case, a single master controls two slaves. However, the operation is still one-to-one. The mobile phone's connections to the two devices are separate Bluetooth connections.

The desktop computer on the left side of the figure also controls two slaves—a keyboard and a mouse. In both of these cases, then, there was one master and two slaves. Can there be more than two slaves, and, if so, how many slaves can a master have? In Bluetooth, a master may have up to seven slaves. A master and its slaves are called, collectively, a **piconet**. A piconet may therefore have up to eight devices—one master and seven slaves. Most masters have only one or two.

> *A master and its slaves are called, collectively, a piconet. A piconet will have a master and up to seven slaves.*

It is even possible for a Bluetooth device to be a master and slave simultaneously. Consider the relationship between the mobile phone and the desktop computer. The two are synchronizing information. The mobile phone is the master, and the desktop is the slave. However, we have just seen that the desktop is master to the keyboard and mouse.

> *A Bluetooth device may be a master of one device and a slave to another device simultaneously.*

Although one device is always the master and the other the slave, they sometimes switch roles during an interaction. For example, when the wearer of a hands-free headpiece initiates a call, the headpiece is the master and the mobile phone is the slave. However, they switch roles afterward, allowing the more powerful mobile phone to control the call interactions.

BLUETOOTH PROFILES   Like 802.11, Bluetooth specifies transmission at the physical and data link layers. The 802.11 Working Group did not have to worry about applications because devices on local area networks have traditionally had many applications.

However, the Bluetooth SIG faced a different situation. Not only were there no transmission standards for short-range one-to-one communication; there also were no application protocols in existence. Consequently, in addition to defining transmission standards, the SIG also defined application profiles, which are called Bluetooth profiles. Profiles govern how devices share information and control messages for various uses.

- In Figure 7-14, the mobile phone communicates with the hands-free handset using the **Hands-Free Profile (HFP)**. This profile governs device–device communication for voice dialing, adjusting volume, hanging up, number redial, call waiting, and other telephone use actions.
- For printing, the mobile phone uses the **Basic Printing Profile (BPP)**. For synchronizing information with the desktop computer, the mobile phone uses the **Synchronization Profile (SYNCH)**.
- The desktop, in turn, uses the **Human Interface Device (HID) profile**. This is probably the most widely used profile.

Peering

When two devices first encounter each other, they must go through a negotiation process

This negotiation process is called peering

It involves the exchange of device information

It may involve authentication

It may also involve one or both of the device owners explicitly deciding if the two devices should be allowed to communicate

Service Discovery Profile (SDP)

Peering uses the Service Discovery Profile (SDP)

Normally, a device is in discoverable mode

If it receives a Service Discovery Protocol request, it will send information about itself:

> Name
>
> Device class
>
> Bluetooth profiles supported
>
> Technical information such as manufacturer's name
>
> …

Binding

After peering is complete, the two devices are bound

They can begin communicating

If they are brought together later, they are still bound

They will begin communication without the peering process

This allows fast setup

The owner of either device can end the binding

FIGURE 7-15 Peering and Binding (Study Figure)

Corporate buyers need to be astute about Bluetooth profiles. In many cases, there are multiple profiles that do roughly the same thing but vary in functionality. For example, the *Bluetooth Headset Profile (HSP)* allows hanging up and volume adjustment. However, it does not support other useful functions that users would like. For that, companies should purchase headsets that implement the *Hands-Free Profile (HFP)*. This profile defines advanced telephone control features such as call waiting and voice dialing.

PEERING AND BINDING For two Bluetooth devices to work together, they must first go through an initial handshaking stage called **peering**. This will require them to exchange information about themselves. It may also involve authentication and requiring each device owner to decide whether to allow the two devices to communicate or not.

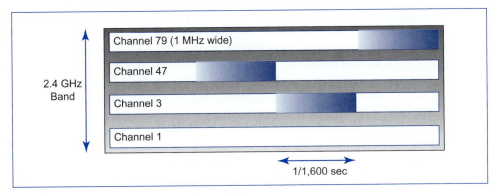

FIGURE 7-16 Frequency Hopping Spread Spectrum

Peering uses the Bluetooth **Service Discovery Profile (SDP)**. Bluetooth devices are normally in discoverable mode. In this mode, when they receive a Service Discovery Profile request, they will transmit information about themselves, including device name, device class, lists of Bluetooth profiles supported, and technical information such as the device's manufacturer and model.

Once two devices have peered, they are said to have been bound. **Binding** is semi-permanent. When the two devices again encounter each other, they do not have to go through peering again. They are bound, so they connect very quickly and without human intervention. Of course, the owner of either of the devices may end the binding at any time.

BLUETOOTH RADIO TRANSMISSION   Bluetooth operates in the same 2.4 GHz band that 802.11 uses. However, 802.11 uses 20 MHz-wide channels, while Bluetooth divides the service band into seventy-nine 1 MHz channels. Up to every 1,600 microseconds, Bluetooth jumps to a different 1 MHz channel. This is called **frequency hopping spread spectrum**. (See Figure 7-16.)

All but the earliest Bluetooth devices avoid channels if they are already carrying traffic. This permits Bluetooth devices to only use free channels, increasing the probability that the Bluetooth communication will get through. This practice also minimizes interference between Bluetooth and 802.11 transmission in the 2.4 GHz unlicensed band.

Test Your Understanding

16. a) What is a PAN? (Do not just spell it out.) b) What organization creates Bluetooth standards? c) Compare the speeds, distances, and duty cycles of classic Bluetooth, high-speed Bluetooth, and low-energy Bluetooth. d) What do these characteristics mean for battery life? e) What is the other benefit of low-energy Bluetooth? f) Would two devices typically use high-speed Bluetooth during their total communication time? Explain.

17. a) What does it mean that Bluetooth uses one-to-one operation? b) Is this even true if a master communicates with four slaves? c) What does master–slave operation mean? d) When you connect a computer to a Bluetooth keyboard and mouse, which devices are masters and slaves? e) At the beginning of a telephone call placed through a Bluetooth headset with the Hands-Free Profile, which device is initially the master? f) What is a piconet, and how many devices may it have? g) Distinguish between peering and bonding. h) If two devices communicate frequently, do they peer each time? i) Name and describe the profile that two devices use to begin peering.

18. a) Why did the Bluetooth SIG have to develop Bluetooth profiles? b) What profile would a Bluetooth-enabled notebook use to print to a nearby printer? c) What profile would a tablet use with a Bluetooth keyboard? d) What *two* profiles might a mobile phone use to communicate with a headset? e) Which is a better profile to use and why? Be specific.

19. a) What service band does Bluetooth use? b) Describe the type of spread spectrum transmission classic Bluetooth uses. c) What other major local wireless technology uses this service band? d) What does Bluetooth do to minimize interference with other wireless technologies in this band?

Near Field Communication (NFC)

REDUCING DISTANCE AND POWER REQUIREMENTS TO THE EXTREME Reducing the service distance between devices reduces transmission power and therefore increases battery power. Taken to the logical extreme, the greatest reduction in transmission power would occur if two devices were physically "bumped" together. In fact, there is a technology that does precisely this. It is called **near field communication (NFC)**. It is governed by the NFC Forum. Figure 7-17 illustrates near field communication.

In NFC, the two devices actually do not have to touch physically. However, they must be within about 4 cm (roughly 2 in.). It is difficult to judge such small distances, so the normal practice is to bump the two devices to ensure communication.

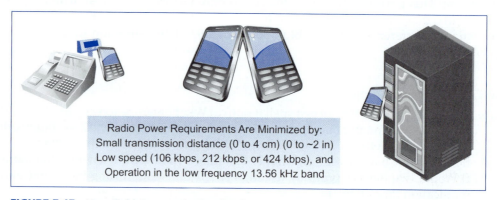

Radio Power Requirements Are Minimized by:
Small transmission distance (0 to 4 cm) (0 to ~2 in)
Low speed (106 kbps, 212 kbps, or 424 kbps), and
Operation in the low frequency 13.56 kHz band

FIGURE 7-17 Near Field Communication (NFC)

Payment of bus fares (already popular in some countries)

Opening car doors

Turning on the ignition

Door entry control

Sharing business cards

Sharing webpages between mobile devices

Retail payments, including loyalty points and coupons (beginning to be popular)

NFC posters with tap points for more communication

Passive Radio Frequency ID (RFID) Tags

FIGURE 7-18   Possible Near Field Communication Applications (Study Figure)

With direct contact or nearly direct contact, transmission distances are small, so transmission power is very low. In addition, the transmission speed is only 106 kbps, 212 kbps, or 424 kbps. Slow transmission also minimizes transmission power. In addition, NFC operates at the 13.56 kHz band. This is a far lower frequency band than the 2.4 GHz and 5 GHz bands. At these lower frequencies, radios use less power than they are at gigahertz frequencies. Overall, NFC devices are very energy efficient. They often use inexpensive "coin" batteries, and these batteries may last for months or even years.

APPLICATIONS   NFC has many possible applications. For example, consider Vishal, who is late to an office meeting. As Vishal leaves his house, he taps his mobile phone against the front door, activating the intruder alarm. He walks to his car and taps the handle with his mobile. This unlocks the car. It also moves the driver's seat to his preferred position. Bumping the ignition with the mobile turns on the car.

At work, Vishal taps his mobile against the building door to gain admittance. To share business cards, he and a visitor tap their phones together. To share a webpage, they do the same.

At the building's convenience store, Vishal bumps his mobile against the reader to pay for a purchase. This also records his loyalty points for the purchase and makes use of any coupons Vishal had loaded onto his mobile last night. On his way out, he sees a poster advertising a new ice cream flavor, chicken ripple. He bumps his phone against a small mark on the poster. This transfers information about the product to his mobile.

RFID TAGS   Many items on the store shelf have small wire arrangements embedded in paper or plastic. These are **passive radio frequency ID (RFID) tags**.[19] When Vishal bumps his mobile against one of these tags, his phone receives the price and some other information about the product. The store uses these passive RFID tags to maintain

---

[19] Active RFID tags contain batteries and can be read from longer distances.

information about its inventory. Using RFID also speeds scanning at checkout. There is no need to line up the item's UPC tag with a laser reader.

The selection of 13.56 kbps as the operating frequency was no accident. This is the frequency that ISO/IEC had already assigned for communication with passive RFID tags. The NFC Forum has defined four tag types with different speed and distance capabilities.

For passive applications, a target device being bumped has no power source at all. When the two devices are brought together, the powered device sends a pulse of radio to the passive device. This provides just enough power for the passive device to generate a reply. This is the same basic process that allows wireless device recharging.

APPLICATIONS IN USE TODAY Although many of the applications we discussed are years away, NFC is already seeing some use. One popular application is to use a card specifically designed to allow someone to use a bus or subway. The user simply taps the card against a reader near the front of the bus. It may not even be necessary to take the card out of the wallet. This application is very popular in Europe and Japan.

Another application with growing popularity is the use of mobile phones as electronic wallets for making purchases. This requires special NFC readers in stores. Several European and Asian countries have experimented with NFC wallets for some time. In 2011, Google released its NFC Google Wallet specification in the United States, and a number of companies such as Starbucks quickly began to implement it.

SECURITY Security is a concern for NFC. For passive devices in particular, cryptographic protections usually are prohibitively power-demanding. It has been said that given the small distances at which passive devices can be read, eavesdroppers would have no chance to read transmissions. However, eavesdroppers may have extremely sensitive highly directional receivers capable of reading transactions at some distance away. NFC communication is also vulnerable to data modification attacks and to jamming denial of service attacks.

Test Your Understanding

20. a) What is the distance limit for near field communication? b) What three factors give NFC low transmission power requirements? c) In what transmission band does NFC operate? d) At what speeds does NFC operate? e) Passive RFID chips have no batteries. How can they transmit when queried? f) How can attackers eavesdrop on NFC transmissions?

Radio frequency ID tags contain information about an item

A passive RFID tag has no internal power source

When read by an NFC device, the power of the reader request gives power for the response

13.56 kHz was specified by ISO/IEC for passive RFID tags long before NFC standards were created

With sensitive antennas, NFC transmission can be eavesdropped upon from a distance

---

FIGURE 7-19 Passive Radio Frequency ID (RFID) Tags (Study Figure)

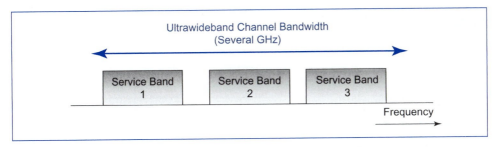

FIGURE 7-20 Ultrawideband (UWB) Transmission

Ultrawideband (UWB)

In 802.11, a channel is 20 MHz or 40 MHz wide. We saw in Chapter 6 that wider wireless transmission channels permit the faster transmission of information. **Ultrawideband (UWB)** transmission channels are far wider than 802.11 channels. Often, UWB channels are several gigahertz wide. They typically are so wide that they cut across multiple service bands (see Figure 7-20).

To avoid interfering with other devices, the power per hertz of bandwidth is very low—far lower than 802.11 power densities. This is necessary because it is important for UWB not to interfere with other transmissions taking place within its enormous bandwidth. In effect, a UWB transmission is like an enormously wide ocean wave arriving at a shore. The total energy is very large, but the wave usually has a gentle effect on each foot of shoreline.

UWB transmission typically produces very high transmission speeds, often 100 Mbps or more. However, it has very short range—about 10 meters, which is the typical distance limit for classic Bluetooth. UWB is likely to be used for local video transmission.

UWB standardization has lagged behind advances in other local wireless technologies. At the time of this writing, UWB is promising, but its standardization is so incomplete that manufacturers are not investing heavily in it. If the standards situation settles out, this could change rapidly.

Test Your Understanding

21. a) How does UWB achieve high data rates? b) How does UWB avoid interfering with other transmissions within its channel bandwidth? c) What is UWB's major limitation?

Security in Emerging Local Wireless Transmission Technologies

Security is a complex situation for emerging local wireless transmission technologies. These technologies face a number of serious threats, including eavesdropping, data modification, impersonation, and denial-of-service attacks.

Some of these technologies have no cryptographic security at all. The classic example is using NFC to read passive RFID tags. Bluetooth probably has the best security among emerging wireless technologies, but its security is still weaker than

Threats

> Eavesdropping
> Data modification
> Impersonation
> Denial-of-service attacks

Cryptological Security

> Some have no cryptological security
> Example: Near field communication for reading passive ID tags
> They rely on short transmission distances to foil eavesdroppers
> Directional antennas and amplifiers can defeat this

Strength of Security

> Some have reasonably good security
> Example: Bluetooth
> However, still not as strong as 802.11i and WPA security

Device Loss or theft

> In this age of bring your own device (BYOD) to work, this is a serious problem
> Most devices are only protected by short PINs

Maturity

> In general, new security technologies take some time to mature
> During this period, they often have vulnerabilities that must be fixed quickly
> User companies must master security for each new technology

FIGURE 7-21 Security in Emerging Wireless Technologies (Study Figure)

802.11i or WPA. In today's world of bring your own device (BYOD) at work, emerging local wireless technologies make a worrisome corporate security situation even more problematic. For example, if devices such as mobile phones are lost or stolen, they are often protected only by brief PINs. Any thief who discovers the PIN may be able to impersonate the owner in significant transactions.

In general, security for new local wireless technologies is simply new. As a general rule, new security technologies tend to have vulnerabilities that take time to discover and protect against. One must hope that technology vendors will be quicker to act than attackers. In any case, companies need to fully understand security for each technology.

Test Your Understanding

22. a) What threats do new wireless transmission technologies face? b) Describe the state of cryptographic security for new transmission standards. c) Why is device theft or loss a serious danger?

CONCLUSION

Synopsis

This chapter continues our discussion of wireless communication. We began with a discussion of 802.11 wireless LAN security threats, including drive-by hackers, war drivers, rogue access points, and evil twin access points.

To address most of these security problems, the 802.11 Working Group created core security standards to protect communication between the wireless client and its nearest wireless access point. Initially, the 802.11 Working Group created WEP as a core security protocol. WEP was badly designed and was soon easily exploited. Later, the 802.11 Working Group created the excellent 802.11i core security standard. Before they did, the Wi-Fi Alliance used an early draft of 802.11i to create a somewhat weaker core security protocol, WPA. They did this because they could develop WPA more quickly, and the industry badly needed something better than WEP. WPA has not been completely cracked, but parts of it have, so companies are advised to upgrade to 802.11i.

The 802.11 Working Group based 802.11i on the 802.1X security standard we saw in Chapter 5. The 802.1X standard uses a central authentication server. However, they needed to extend 802.1X by adding security between the access point and each wireless client during initial authentication, before full 802.1X security is set up. The 802.11i standard also has a pre-shared key mode, which is used for companies that only have a single access point. The wireless clients share a single pre-shared key, which must be kept secret from outsiders. After authentication, however, the wireless access point creates a unique session key for each wireless client.

Evil twin access points impersonate legitimate access points. To avoid being snared by evil twin access points, the clients need to have a virtual private network (VPN) connection to the servers they will use. This connection must use a pre-established secret that is not transmitted during interactions and so cannot be intercepted by the evil twin access point. We also looked at security problems with Wi-Fi Protected Setup (WPS) and looked briefly at the danger of denial-of-service (DoS) attacks.

We discussed wireless LAN management, including strategies for placing access points to give good coverage with a minimum of overlap and with a minimum of interference from nearby access points operating on the same channel. Good access point placement requires initial and ongoing site surveys of signal strength and interference. We also looked at the remote management of access points using smart access points or dumb access points controlled by wireless LAN switches. A central manager can detect rogue access points, allow the remote adjustment of access point power, push software updates out to the access points, and do all this and more automatically, with a minimum of intervention.

We looked at other local wireless technologies, including Bluetooth, which is for personal area networks (PANs) in which all devices are located nearby, often on the same desk or around the body of a person. We then looked at other emerging local wireless technologies, including high-speed, short-distance ultrawideband (UWB) transmission, ZigBee for wireless monitoring systems, and radio frequency ID (RFID) to allow items to be identified within a short distance of a scanner.

END-OF-CHAPTER QUESTION

Essay

1. A friend is interested in installing a wireless LAN in her small business. She has about a dozen employees. She is concerned about security. Write a two-page letter to explain what security threats she is facing and how she can reduce these threats. Remember that you are writing for a friend, not for a teacher. Do not hand in disorganized notes. Double spacing is good.

Perspective Questions

1. What was the most surprising thing you learned in this chapter?

2. What was the most difficult part of this chapter for you?

8
TCP/IP INTERNETWORKING I

LEARNING OBJECTIVES

By the end of this chapter, you should be able to:

- Explain basic TCP/IP, IP, TCP, and UDP concepts.
- Define hierarchical IP addresses, networks and subnets, border and internal routers, and masks.
- Describe router operation when a packet arrives, including ARP. Given a routing table and an arriving packet's destination IP address, be able to predict what the router will do.
- Explain the IPv6 packet header fields and IPv6's use of extension headers. Be able to convert a 128-bit IP address into compressed hexadecimal notation.
- Explain TCP fields and session closings.
- Explain other important TCP/IP standards, including dynamic routing protocols and ICMP.

INTRODUCTION

Switched networks and wireless networks are governed by standards at Layer 1 and Layer 2. We looked at switched wired single networks in Chapter 5. We looked at wireless single networks in Chapters 6 and 7. In this chapter and in Chapter 9, we will discuss internetworking, which is governed by Layer 3 and Layer 4 standards.

We will only look at TCP/IP internetworking because TCP/IP dominates the work of network professionals at the internet and transport layers. However, real-world routers cannot limit themselves to TCP/IP internetworking. They are multiprotocol routers, which can route not only IP packets but also IPX packets, SNA packets, AppleTalk packets, and other types of packets.

TCP/IP RECAP

The TCP/IP Architecture and the IETF

We first looked at TCP/IP in some depth in Chapter 2. Recall from that chapter that the *Internet Engineering Task Force (IETF)* sets TCP/IP standards. TCP/IP is an architecture for setting individual standards. Figure 8-1 shows a few of the standards the IETF has created within this architecture. Some of the standards are shaded in this figure. We will look at these standards in this chapter.

Layer	User Applications			Supervisory Applications		
5 Application	HTTP	SMTP	Many Others	DNS	Dynamic Routing Protocols	Many Others
4 Transport	TCP				UDP	
3 Internet	IP			ICMP		ARP
2 Data Link	None: Use OSI Standards					
1 Physical	None: Use OSI Standards					

FIGURE 8-1 Major TCP/IP Standards

Note: Shaded protocols are discussed in this chapter.

Simple IP at the Internet Layer

Recall also, from Chapter 1, that internetworking operates at two layers. The internet layer moves packets from the source host to the destination host across a series of routers. Figure 8-1 shows that the primary standard at the internet layer is the Internet Protocol (IP). Figure 8-2 shows that IP is a simple (connectionless and unreliable) standard. This simplicity minimizes the work that each router has to do along the way, thereby minimizing routing costs. The internet layer is Layer 3.

Reliable Heavyweight TCP at the Transport Layer

In turn, TCP at the transport layer corrects any errors at the internet layer and lower layers as well. As we saw in Chapter 2, when the transport process on a destination host receives a TCP supervisory or data segment, it sends back an acknowledgment. If the transport process on the source host does not receive an acknowledgment for a TCP segment, it resends the segment. TCP is both connection-oriented and reliable, making it a heavyweight protocol. However, the work of implementing TCP only occurs on the source and destination hosts, not on the many routers between them. This keeps the cost of reliability manageable. The transport layer is Layer 4.

Protocol	Layer	Connection-Oriented/ Connectionless	Reliable/ Unreliable	Lightweight/ Heavyweight
TCP	4 (Transport)	Connection-oriented	Reliable	Heavyweight
UDP	4 (Transport)	Connectionless	Unreliable	Lightweight
IP	3 (Internet)	Connectionless	Unreliable	Lightweight

FIGURE 8-2 IP, TCP, and UDP

Unreliable Lightweight UDP at the Transport Layer

In Chapters 1 and 2, we saw that TCP/IP offers an alternative to heavyweight TCP at the transport layer. This is the User Datagram Protocol (UDP). Like IP, UDP is simple (connectionless and unreliable) and lightweight protocol. This reduces processing requirements on the hosts and also reduces network traffic.

Test Your Understanding

1. a) Compare TCP and IP along the dimensions in Figure 8-2. b) Compare TCP and UDP along the dimensions in Figure 8-2.

IP ROUTING

In this section, we will look at how routers make decisions about forwarding packets— in other words, how a router decides which interface to use to send an arriving packet back out to get it closer to its destination. (In routers, ports are called **interfaces**.)

Router ports are called interfaces.

This forwarding process is called **routing**. Router forwarding decisions are much more complex than the Ethernet switching decisions we saw in Chapter 5. As a consequence of this complexity, routers do more work per arriving packet than switches do per arriving frame. Consequently, routers are more expensive than switches for a given level of traffic. A widely quoted network adage reflects this cost difference: "Switch where you can; route where you must."

When routers forward incoming packets closer to their destination hosts, this is routing.

Hierarchical IP Addressing

To understand the routing of IP packets, it is necessary to understand IP addresses. In Chapter 1, we saw that IP Version 4 (IPv4) addresses are 32 bits long. However, IP addresses are not simple 32-bit strings. They have internal structure, and this internal structure is important in routing.

HIERARCHICAL ADDRESSING   As Figure 8-3 shows, IP addresses are **hierarchical**. They usually consist of three parts that locate a host in progressively smaller parts of the Internet. These are the network, subnet, and host parts. We will see later in this chapter that hierarchical IP addressing simplifies routing tables.

Network Part   First, every IP address has a **network part** which identifies the host's network on the Internet. In this case, *network* is an organizational concept. It is a user organization such as a manufacturing corporation or an ISP. The organization effectively controls part of the Internet.

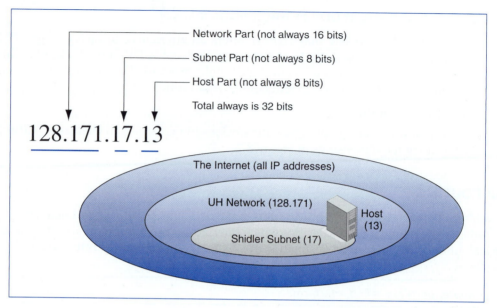

FIGURE 8-3 Hierarchical IPv4 Address

In IP addressing, network is an organizational concept. A network is an organization that controls part of the Internet. It may be a user organization such as a manufacturing corporation or an ISP.

In Figure 8-3, the network part is 128.171. This is two IP segments. Each segment is 89 bits long, so the network part for the University of Hawai`i is 16 bits long. This happens to be the network part for the University of Hawai`i Network on the Internet. All host IP addresses within this network begin with 128.171.

Do not get hung up on the network part being 16 bits. This is only an example. Different organizations have different network parts that range from 8 to 24 bits in length.

Subnet Part   Most large organizations further divide their networks into smaller units called **subnets**. After the network part in an IP address come the bits of the **subnet part**. The subnet part bits specify a particular subnet within the network.

For instance, Figure 8-3 shows that in the IP address 128.171.17.13, the first 16 bits (128.171) correspond to the network part, and the next 8 bits (17) correspond to a subnet on this network. (Subnet 17 is the Shidler College of Business subnet within the University of Hawai`i Network.) All host IP addresses within this subnet begin with 128.171.17.

Again, do not get hung up on the subnet part being 8 bits long. In different organizations, subnet lengths vary widely. Keep clear in your head that the UH Network is only being used as an example.

Host Part   The remaining bits in the 32-bit IP address constitute the **host part**, which identifies a particular host on the subnet. In Figure 8-3, the host part is eight bits long with a value of 13. This corresponds to a particular host, 128.171.17.13, on the Shidler College of Business subnet of the University of Hawai`i Network. Again, host parts in different organizations differ in size.

VARIABLE PART LENGTHS   The IPv4 IP address is 32 bits long. Can you tell just by looking at an IP address what bits correspond to the network, subnet, and host parts? The answer is no. For instance, if you see the IP address 60.47.7.23, you may have an 8-bit network part of 60, an 8-bit subnet part of 47, and a 16-bit host part of 7.23. In fact, parts may not even break conveniently at 8-bit boundaries. The only thing you can tell when looking at an IP address by itself is that it is 32 bits long.

Test Your Understanding

2. a) What is routing? b) What are the three parts of an IP address? c) How long is each part? d) What is the total length of an IP address? e) In the IP address, 10.11.13.13, what is the network part?

Routers, Networks, and Subnets

BORDER ROUTERS CONNECT DIFFERENT NETWORKS   As Figure 8-4 illustrates, networks and subnets are very important in router operation. Here we see a simple site internet. The figure shows that a **border router**'s main job is to connect different networks. This border router connects the 192.168.x.x network within the firm to the 60.x.x.x network of the firm's Internet service provider. Here, the xs are the remaining bits of the IP address, so 192.168 and 60 are the network parts of the two networks.

A border router's main job is to connect different networks.

INTERNAL ROUTERS CONNECT DIFFERENT SUBNETS   The site network also has an internal router. An **internal router**, Figure 8-4 demonstrates, connects different subnets within a firm—in this case, the 192.168.1.x, 192.168.2.x, and 192.168.3.x subnets. Many sites have multiple internal routers to link the site's subnets.

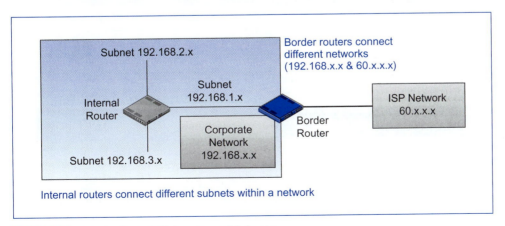

FIGURE 8-4   Border Router, Networks, and Subnets

An internal router only connects different subnets within a firm.

Test Your Understanding

3. Connecting different networks is the main job of what type of router? b) What type of router only connects different subnets?

Network and Subnet Masks

If you know how the University of Hawai'i organizes its IP addresses, you know that the first 16 bits are always the network part, the next 8 are the subnet part, and the final 8 are the host part. However, the sizes of the network, subnet, and host parts differ. Routers need a way to tell the sizes of key parts. The tool that allows them to do it is masks.

32-BIT STRINGS Figure 8-5 illustrates how masks work. A mask is a series of 32 bits like an IP address. However, a mask always begins with a series of 1s, followed by a series of 0s. In a network mask, the bits in the network part of the mask are 1s, while the

---

The Problem

There is no way to tell by looking at an IP address what sizes the network, subnet, and host parts are—only their total of 32 bits

The solution: masks

Series of initial ones followed by series of final zeros for a total of 32 bits

> Example: 255.255.0.0 is 16 ones followed by 16 zeros
>
> In prefix notation, /16
>
> (Decimal 0 is 8 zeros and Decimal 255 is 8 ones)

Result: IP address where mask bits are ones and zeros where the mask bits are zero

Mask Operation

Network Mask	Dotted Decimal Notation
Destination IP address	128.171.17.13
Network mask	255.255. 0. 0
Bits in network part, followed by zeros	128.171. 0 .0

Subnet Mask	Dotted Decimal Notation
Destination IP address	128.171. 17.13
Subnet mask	255.255.255. 0
Bits in network part and subnet parts, followed by zeros	128.171. 17. 0

FIGURE 8-5 IP Network and Subnet Masks

remaining bits are 0s. In subnet masks, the bits of both the network and subnet parts are 1s, and the remaining bits are 0s.

A mask is a 32-bit string of 1s and 0s.
The mask always has a certain number of initial 1s. The remaining bits are always 0s.
In network masks, the initial 1s correspond to the network part.
In subnet masks, the initial 1s correspond to the network and subnet parts.

For example, suppose that the mask is 255.255.0.0. This means that the four 8-bit segments have the values 255, 255, 0, and 0. In dotted decimal notation eight 1s is 255 and eight 0s is 0. So the four segments have, in order, eight 1s, eight 1s, eight 0s, and eight 0s. Putting this together, the mask has sixteen 1s followed by sixteen 0s.

PREFIX NOTATION FOR MASKS   Writing 255.255.255.0 is not very difficult, but networking professionals often use a shortcut called prefix notation. The mask 255.255.255.0 is twenty-four 1s followed by eight 0s. In prefix notation, this mask is represented by /24. Do you see the pattern? In **prefix notation**, a mask is represented by a slash followed by the number of initial 1s in the mask. What about 255.0.0.0? Yes, it is /8. Prefix notation is simpler to write than dotted decimal notation. By the way, we call this prefix notation because it focuses on the first part of the mask—the part that is all 1s.

In prefix notation, a mask is represented by a slash followed by the number of initial 1s in the mask.

Another advantage of prefix notation for a mask is that it is even simple if the number of leading ones is not a multiple of eight. For example, suppose that the mask is eighteen 1s followed by fourteen 0s, the mask in prefix notation is obviously /18. How would you write this in dotted decimal notation? Hmm. Let me get a binary to decimal calculator.

MASKING IP ADDRESSES   Figure 8-5 shows what happens when a mask is applied to an IP address, 128.171.17.13. The mask is 255.255.0.0. Where the mask has one, the result is the original bits of the IP address. For the remaining bits, which are 0s, the result is 0. In this case, the result is 128.171.0.0.

NETWORK MASKS   Routers use two types of masks: network masks and subnet masks. **Network masks** have 1s in the network part and 0s for remaining bits. If the network mask is 255.255.0.0 and the IP address is 128.171.17.13, then the result of masking is 128.171.0.0. This is the network part followed by 0s.

SUBNET MASKS   For **subnet masks**, in contrast, the initial 1s indicate the number of bits in *both* the network and subnet parts. So, if 128.171 is the network part and 17 is the subnet part, then the subnet mask will be 255.255.255.0 (/24). If you mask 128.171.17.13 with /24, you get 128.171.17.0.

Why mark the 1s in both parts in a subnet mask? Think of a network as a state and a subnet as a city. In the United States, there are two major cities named Portland—one in Maine and the other in Oregon. You cannot just say "Portland" to designate a city. You must give both the state and city—analogously, the network and subnet parts. Another way to look at it is that if you only had 1s in the subnet part of a subnet mask, you would break the rule that masks must have a number of leading 1s followed by a number of trailing 0s.

ROUTERS DO NOT CARE Although it is important to understand the difference between network and subnet masks in order to design masks properly, routers do not care about the distinction. To a router, a mask is simply a mask. It gets an IP address and a mask and applies the mask without asking what type of mask it is.

This lack of distinction in router operation is not an accident. Network masks were created first, and routers were designed to use them to mask IP addresses. Later, subnets were created, and the idea of masking was extended to subnet masks. However, routers do not have to know about the type of mask it is applying, so router operation remained unchanged when subnet masks were created. Again, people have to know the distinction to write masks, but routers do not.

Test Your Understanding

4. How many bits are there in a mask? b) What do the 1s in a network mask correspond to in IP addresses? c) What do the 1s in a subnet mask correspond to in IP addresses? d) When a network mask is applied to any IP address on the network, what is the result?

5. a) A mask has eight 1s, followed by 0s. Express this mask in dotted decimal notation. b) Express this mask in prefix notation. c) In prefix notation, a mask is /16. Express this mask in dotted decimal notation. d) Express the mask /18 in dotted decimal notation.

6. Do routers know the difference between network and subnet masks? Who does have to know the difference, and why do they need to know it?

HOW ROUTERS PROCESS PACKETS

Switching versus Routing

In Chapter 5, we saw that Ethernet switching is very simple. Ethernet switches must be organized in a hierarchy. This means that there is only a single possible path between any two hosts across the network. This means that when a packet arrives, there is only one possible port to use to send the frame back out. As Figure 8-6 shows, this means that each Ethernet address only appears in a single row. This row tells the switch which port to send the frame back out. This single row can be found quickly, so an Ethernet switch does little work per frame. This makes Ethernet switching fast and inexpensive.

In contrast, firms organize routers in meshes. This gives more reliability because it allows many possible alternative routes between endpoints. Figure 8-6 shows that in a routing table, each row represents an alternative route for a packet. Consequently, to **route** (forward) a packet, a router must first find all rows representing alternative routes that a particular incoming packet can take. It must then pick the best alternative route from this list. This requires quite a bit of work per packet, making routing more expensive than switching.

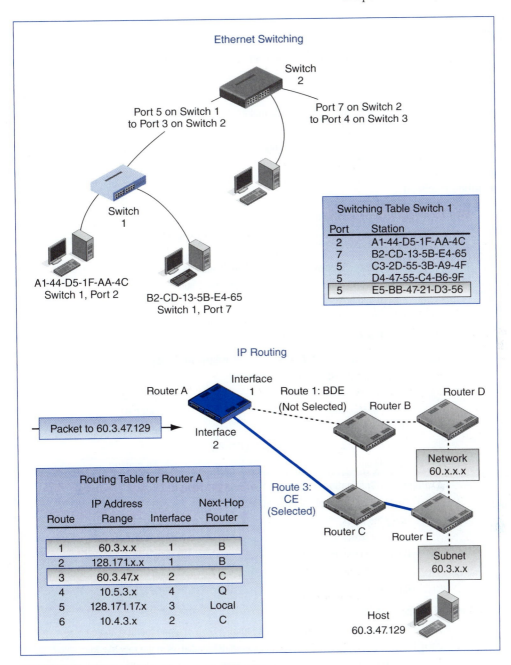

FIGURE 8-6   Ethernet Switching versus IP Routing

Routing

Processing an individual packet and passing it on its way is called routing

The Routing Table

Each router has a routing table that it uses to make routing decisions

Routing Table Rows

Each row represents a route for a range of IP addresses—often packets going to the same a network or subnet

A Routing Decision

Step 1: Finding All Row Matches

The router looks at the destination IP address in an arriving packet

For each row:

Apply the row's mask to the destination IP address in the packet

Compare the result with the row's destination value

If the two match, the row is a match

The router do this to ALL rows because there may be multiple matches

This step ends with a set of matching rows

Example 1: A Destination IP Address that is in NOT the Range

Destination IP Address of Arriving Packet	60.43.7.8
Apply the (Network) Mask	255.255.0.0
Result of Masking	60.43.0.0
Destination Column Value	128.171.0.0
Does Destination Match the Masking Result?	No
Conclusion	Not a match.

Example 2: A Destination IP Address that is in the Range

Destination IP Address of Arriving Packet	128.171.17.13
Apply the Mask	255.255.0.0
Result of Masking	128.171.0.0
Destination Column Value	128.171.0.0
Does Destination Match the Masking Result?	Yes
Conclusion	Row is a match.

Step 2: Find the Best-Match Row

The router examines the matching rows it found in Step 1 to find the best-match row

Basic Rule: It selects the row with the longest match (Initial 1s in the row mask)

Tie-Breaker Rule: If there is a tie on longest match, select among the tie rows based on metric

For cost metric, choose the row with the lowest metric value

For speed metric, choose the row with the highest metric value

FIGURE 8-7   The Routing Process (Study Figure)

Step 3: Send the Packet Back Out

Send the packet out the interface (router port) designated in the best-match row

Address the packet to the IP address in the next-hop router column

If the address says Local, the destination host is out that interface

Sends the packet to the destination IP address in a frame

FIGURE 8-7   Continued

Test Your Understanding

7. Why are routing tables more complex than Ethernet switching tables? Be articulate.

Routing Table

Figure 8-8 shows a routing table. It has a number of rows and columns. We will see how a router uses these rows and columns to make a routing decision—a decision about what to do with an arriving packet.

Rows Are Routes

In the routing table, each row represents a route for all IP addresses within a range of IP addresses—typically a network or subnet. It does not specify the full route, however, only the next step in the route (either the next-hop router to handle the packet next or the destination host).

Row	Destination Network or Subnet	Mask (/Prefix)	Metric (Cost)	Interface	Next-Hop Router
1	128.171.0.0	255.255.0.0 (/16)	47	2	G
2	172.30.33.0	255.255.255.0 (/24)	0	1	Local
3	60.168.6.0	255.255.255.0 (/24)	12	2	G
4	123.0.0.0	255.0.0.0 (/8)	33	2	G
5	172.29.8.0	255.255.255.0 (/24)	34	1	F
6	172.40.6.0	255.255.255.0 (/24)	47	3	H
7	128.171.17.0	255.255.255.0 (/24)	55	3	H
8	172.29.8.0	255.255.255.0 (/24)	20	3	H
9	172.12.6.0	255.255.255.0 (/24)	23	1	F
10	172.30.12.0	255.255.255.0 (/24)	9	2	G
11	172.30.12.0	255.255.255.0 (/24)	3	3	H
12	60.168.0.0	255.255.0.0 (/16)	16	2	G
13	0.0.0.0	0.0.0.0 (/0)	5	3	H

FIGURE 8-8   Routing Table

In the routing table, each row represents a route for all IP addresses within a range of IP addresses—typically a network or subnet.

This is important because the routing table does not need a row for *each IP address* as an Ethernet switching table does. It only needs a row for each *group of IP addresses*. This means that a router needs many fewer rows than an Ethernet switch would need for the same number of addresses.

However, there are many more IP addresses on the Internet than there are Ethernet addresses in an Ethernet network. Even with rows representing groups of IP addresses, core routers in the Internet backbone still have several hundred thousand rows. In addition, while an Ethernet switch only needs to find a single row for each arriving frame, we will see that routers need to look carefully at *all* rows.

ROW NUMBER COLUMN The first column in Figure 8-8 is a route (row) number. Routing tables actually do not have this column. We include it to allow us to refer to specific rows in our discussion. Again, each row specifies a route to a destination.

Test Your Understanding

8. In a routing table, what does a row represent? b) Do Ethernet switches have a row for each individual Ethernet address? c) Do routers have a row for each individual IP address? d) What is the advantage of the answer to the previous subpart of this question?

Step 1: Finding All Row Matches

We will now see how the router uses its routing table to make routing decisions. The first step is to find which of the rows in the routing table match the destination IP address in an arriving packet. Due to the existence of alternative routes in a router mesh, most packets will match more than one row.

ROW MATCHES How does the router know which IP addresses should be governed by a row? The answer is that it uses the *Destination Network or Subnet (destination)* column and the *Mask* column.

Suppose that all IP addresses in the University of Hawai`i (UH) network should be governed by a row. The mask would be the network mask 255.255.0.0, because the UH Network has a 16-bit network part. If this mask is applied to any UH address, the result will be 128.171.0.0. This is the value that will be in the destination column. In fact, this is Row 1 in Figure 8-8.

Let's see how routers use these two fields in Figure 8-8. Suppose that a packet arrives with the IP address 60.43.7.8. The router will look first at Row 1.

- In this row, the router applies the mask 255.255.0.0 to the arriving packet's destination IP address, 60.43.7.8. The result is 60.43.0.0.
- Next, the router compares the masking result, 60.43.0.0, to the destination value in the row, 128.171.0.0. The two are different, so the row is not a match.

However, suppose that a packet arrives with the IP address 128.171.17.13. Now, the situation is different.

- Again, router applies the mask 255.255.0.0 in Row 1 to the destination IP address, 128.171.17.13. The result is 128.171.0.0.
- Next, the router compares 128.171.0.0 to the destination value in the row, 128.171.0.0. The two are identical. Therefore, the row is a match.

MASK AND COMPARE   This may seem like an odd way to see if a row matches. A human can simply look at 60.43.7.8 and see that it does not match 128.171.0.0. However, routers do not possess human pattern-matching abilities.

While routers cannot do sophisticated pattern recognition, routers (and all computers) have specialized circuitry for doing masking and comparing—the two operations that row matching requires. Thanks to this specialized circuitry, routers can blaze through hundreds of thousands of rows in a tiny fraction of a second.

THE DEFAULT ROW   The last row in Figure 8-8 has the destination 0.0.0.0 and the mask 0.0.0.0. This row will match *every* IP address because masking any IP address with 0.0.0.0 will give 0.0.0.0, which is the value in the destination field of Row 13. This row ensures that at least one row will match the destination IP address of every arriving packet. It is called the **default row**. In general, a "default" is something you use if you do not have a more specific choice.

THE NEED TO LOOK AT ALL ROWS   Thanks to their mesh topology, internets have many alternative routes. Consequently, a router cannot stop the first time it finds a row match for each arriving packet because there may be a better match further on. A router has to look at each and every row in the routing table to see which match. So far, we have seen what the router does in Row 1 of Figure 8-8. The router then goes on to Row 2 to see if it is a match by masking and comparing. After this, it goes on to Row 3, Row 4, Row 5, and so on, all the way to the final row (Row 13 in Figure 8-8).

Test Your Understanding

9. In Row 3 of Figure 8-8, how will a router test if the row matches the IP address 60.168.6.7? Show the calculations in the format given in the text. Is the row a match? b) Why is the last row called the default row? c) Why must a router look at all rows in a routing table? d) What rows match 172.30.17.6? e) Which rows match 60.168.7.32? Show your calculations for rows that match. f) Which rows in Figure 8-8 match 128.171.17.13? (Don't forget the default row.) Show your calculations for rows that match.

Step 2: Selecting the Best-Match Row

LIST OF MATCHING ROWS   At the end of Step 1, the mask and compare process, the router has a list of matching rows. For a packet with the destination IP address 128.171.17.13, two rows in Figure 8-8 match. The first is Row 1, as we have already seen. The second is Row 7, with a destination of 128.171.17.0 and a mask of 255.255.255.0. From these, the router must select the **best-match row**, the row that represents the best route for an IP address.

BASIC RULE: LONGEST MATCH RULE How does the router decide whether to follow Row 1 or Row 7? The answer is that it follows the rule of selecting the **longest match**. Row 1 has a mask of 255.255.0.0, which means that it has a 16-bit match. Row 7, in turn, has the prefix /24, meaning that it has a 24-bit match. Row 7 has the longest match, so the router selects it.

Why the longest match rule? The answer is that the closer a route gets a packet to the destination IP address, the better. Row 1 only gets the packet to the UH network, 128.171.x.x, while Row 7 gets the packet all the way to the Shidler College of Business subnet of the University of Hawai`i, 128.171.17.x—the subnet that contains host 128.171.17.13.

TIE-BREAKER RULE: BEST METRIC VALUE The Metric Column for Match Length Ties. What if two rows have the same longest match? For instance, the destination IP address 172.29.8.112 matches both Row 5 and Row 8 in Figure 8-8. Both have a match length of 24 bits—a tie.

In case of a tie for longest match, the tie-breaker rule is to use the **metric** column which describes the "goodness" of a route. For instance, in Figure 8-8, the metric is cost. Row 5 has a cost of 34, while Row 8 has a cost of 20. *Lower cost is better than higher cost*, so the router selects Row 8.

In this case, the row with the *lowest* metric won. However, what would have happened if the metric had been *speed* instead of cost? *More speed is better*, so the router would choose Row 5, with the *higher* speed (34).

Test Your Understanding

10. a) Distinguish between Step 1 and Step 2 in the routing process. b) If any row other than the default row matches an IP address, why will the router never choose the default row? c) Which rows in Figure 8-8 match 128.171.17.13? (Don't forget the default row.) Show your calculations. d) Which of these is the best-match row? Justify your answer. e) What rows match 172.40.17.6? Show your work. f) Which of these is the best-match row? Justify your answer. g) Which rows match 172.30.12.47? Show your work. h) Which of these is the best-match row? Justify your answer. i) How would your previous answer change if the metric had been reliability?

Step 3: Sending the Packet Back Out

In Step 1, the router found all rows that matched the destination IP address of the arriving packet. In Step 2, it found the best-match row. Finally, in Step 3, the router sends the packet back out.

INTERFACE Router ports are called **interfaces**. The fifth column in Figure 8-8 is interface number. If a router selects a row as the best match, the router sends the packet out the interface designated in that row. If Row 1 is selected, the router will send the packet out Interface 2.

Router ports are called interfaces.

NEXT-HOP ROUTER   In a switch, a port connects directly to another switch or to a computer. However, a router interface connects to an entire subnet or network. Therefore, it is not enough to select an interface to send the packet out. It is also necessary to specify *a particular device* on the subnet.

In most cases, the router will send the packet on to another router, called the **next-hop router**. The next-hop router column specifies the router that should receive the packet. It will then be up to that next-hop router to decide what to do next. In Figure 8-8, the next-hop router value is G.[1]

In some cases, however, the destination host will be on the subnet out a particular interface. In that case, the router should send the packet to the destination host instead of to another router. In this case, the next-hop router field will say *local*.

Test Your Understanding

11. a) Distinguish between Step 2 and Step 3 in routing. b) What are router ports called? c) If the router selects Row 13 as the best-match row, what interface will the router send the interface out? d) To what device? e) Why is this router called the default router? (The answer is not in the text.) f) If the router selects Row 2 as the best-match row for packet 172.30.33.6, what interface will the router send the interface out? g) To what device? (Don't say, "the local device.")

Cheating (Decision Caching)

We have discussed what happens when a packet arrives at a router. However, what will the router do if another packet for the same destination IP address arrives immediately afterward? The answer is that the router *should* go through the entire process again. Even if a thousand packets arrive that are going to the same destination IP address, the router should go through the entire three-step process for each of them.

As you might expect, a router might cheat, or as it is euphemistically named, cache (remember) the decision it made for a destination IP address. It will then use this decision for successive IP packets going to the same destination. Using a **decision cache** greatly reduces the work that a router will do for each successive packet.

However, caching is not prescribed in the Internet Protocol. In addition, it is dangerous. The Internet changes constantly as routers come and go and as links between routers change. Consequently, a cached decision that is used too long will result in nonoptimal routing or even routes that will not work and that will effectively send packets into a black hole.

Test Your Understanding

12. a) What should a router do if it receives several packets going to the same destination IP address? b) How would decision caching speed the routing decision for packets after the first one? c) Why is decision caching dangerous?

---

[1] Actually, this column should have the IP address of Router G, rather than its name. However, we include the letter designation rather than the IP address for simplicity of understanding.

Masking When Masks Do Not Break at 8-Bit Boundaries

Masks That Break at 8-Bit Boundaries

All of the masks we have seen up to this point have had their parts broken at 8-bit segment boundaries. For example, at the University of Hawai`i, the network part is 16 bits long, which corresponds to two segments (128.171), the subnet part is 8 bits long (17), and the host part is 8 bits long. All of the masks in Figure 8-8 break also at 8-bit segment boundaries.

Masks that break at 8-bit boundaries are easy for humans to read. In general, you can look at a mask in the table and decide if it matches a particular IP address. For instance, if the mask is 255.255.0.0 (/16), and if the destination column value is 128.171.0.0, this definitely matches the IP address 128.171.45.230.

However, masks do not always break at 8-bit boundaries. For example, suppose that a mask is 11111111 11111000 00000000 00000000 (spaces added for reading). In dotted decimal notation, this is 255.248.0.0, and suppose that the destination address column value is 00000011 10001000 00000000 00000000 (3.264.0.0).

Now suppose that a destination IP address is 3.143.12.12. Does this IP address match the row? There is no way to tell just by looking at the dotted decimal notation versions of the destination, the mask, and the destination IP address. To solve the problem, you go to the raw 32-bit numbers. Figure 8-9 shows that the masked destination IP address matches the destination value in the row, so the row is a match.

IP address: (3.143.12.12)	00000011	10001111	00001100	00001100
Mask: (255.136.0.0)	11111111	11111000	00000000	00000000
Result: (3.136.0.0)	00000011	10001000	00000000	00000000
Destination: (3.264.0.0)	00000011	10001000	00000000	00000000
Match?	Yes	Yes	Yes	Yes

FIGURE 8-9   Using a Mask Whose 1s Do Not Break at an 8-Bit Boundary

Test Your Understanding

13. a) An arriving packet has the destination IP address 128.171.180.13. Row 86 has the destination value 128.171.160.0. The mask is 255.255.224.0. Does this row match the destination IP address? Show your work. You can use the Windows Calculator if you have a Windows PC. In Windows Vista and earlier versions of Windows, choose scientific when you open the calculator. In the Windows 7 calculator, choose programmer mode.

The Address Resolution Protocol

The final step in the routing process for each arriving packet is to send the packet back out another interface, to a next-hop router or the destination host. This seems easy enough, but there is one additional thing that routers must do.

To send a packet to a next-hop router or a destination host, the router's interface must place the packet into a frame and send this frame to the next-hop router or destination host.

To do this, the interface must know the data link layer address of the destination host. Otherwise, the router's interface will not know what to place in the destination address field of the frame.

The router's internet layer process may only know the IP address of the destination host. If the router's interface is to deliver the frame containing the packet, the internet layer process must discover the data link layer address of the destination host. This is called address resolution.

Address Resolution on an Ethernet LAN with ARP

Determining a data link layer address when you know only an IP address is called **address resolution**. Figure 8-10 shows the **Address Resolution Protocol (ARP)**, which provides address resolution on Ethernet LANs. There are other address resolution protocols for other subnet technologies.

ARP Request Message

Suppose that the router receives an IP packet with destination address 10.19.8.17. Suppose also that the router determines from its routing table that it can deliver the packet to a host on one of its Ethernet subnets.

- First, the router's internet layer process creates an ARP request message that essentially says, "Hey, device with IP address 10.19.8.17, what is your 48-bit MAC layer address?" The router then broadcasts this ARP packet to all hosts on the subnet.[2]

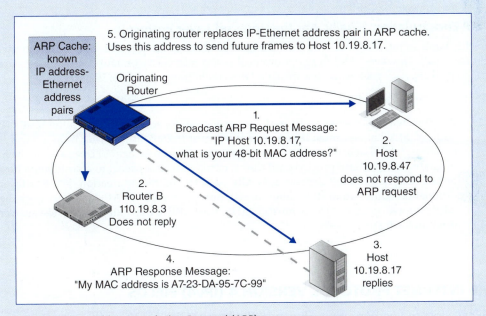

FIGURE 8-10   Address Resolution Protocol (ARP)

(continued)

---

[2]Actually, the router passes the packet down to the data link layer process on the subnet's interface. It tells the data link layer process to broadcast its ARP packet. If the subnet standard is Ethernet, the data link layer process places the packet into a frame with the destination Ethernet address FF-FF-FF-FF-FF-FF (forty-eight 1s). This is the Ethernet broadcast address. Switches will send frames with this broadcast address to all stations, and all stations will accept it as they would a frame addressed to their specific Ethernet address.

- Second, the internet layer process on every host examines the ARP request message. If the target IP address is not that of the host, the host's internet layer process ignores the ARP request message. However, host 10.19.8.17 composes an ARP response message that includes its 48-bit MAC layer address (A7-23-DA-95-7C-99). The target host sends this ARP response message back to the router.
- Third, the router's internet layer process now knows the subnet MAC address associated with the IP address. It will deliver the packet to that host in a frame addressed to A7- . . .

The ARP Cache

ARP is a time-consuming process, and the router does not want to do it for each arriving packet. Consequently, the internet layer process on the router saves the IP address–data link layer address information in its **ARP cache** (section of memory). Afterward, whenever an IP packet comes for this IP destination address, the router will send the IP packet down to its NIC, together with the required MAC address. The NIC's MAC process will deliver the IP packet within a frame containing that MAC destination address.

Using ARP for Next-Hop Routers

We have looked at how routers use ARP when they deliver packets to destination hosts. A router also needs to know the data link layer destination addresses of next-hop routers. Routers use ARP to find the data link layer destination addresses of both destination hosts and other routers.

ARP Encapsulation: Finally, Another Internet Layer Protocol!

In this book so far, we have only seen a single protocol at the internet layer—the Internet Protocol (IP). However, ARP is also a protocol at the internet layer, and ARP messages are called packets. ARP packets are encapsulated directly in frames, just like IP packets.

Test Your Understanding

14. A router wishes to send an IP packet to a host on its subnet. It knows the host's IP address. a) What else must it know? b) Why must it know it? c) What message will it broadcast? d) What device will respond to this broadcast message? e) Does a router have to go through the ARP process each time it needs to send a packet to a destination host or to a next-hop router? Explain. f) Is ARP used to find the destination data link layer destination addresses of destination hosts, routers, or both? g) At what layer does the ARP protocol operate? h) Why must client PCs use ARP to transmit packets? The answer is not in the text.

THE INTERNET PROTOCOL VERSION 4 (IPv4) FIELDS

We have focused on IP routing. However, the Internet Protocol has other properties that networking professionals need to understand.

As noted in Chapter 1, most routers today on the Internet and private internets are governed by the **IP version 4 (IPv4)** standard. (There were no versions 0 through 3.) Figure 8-11 shows the IPv4 packet. Its first four bits contain the value 0100 (binary for 4) to indicate that the packet is formatted according to IPv4. Although we have looked already at some of the fields in IPv4, here we will look at fields that we have not yet seen.

IP Version 4 Packet

Bit 0   Bit 31

Version (4 bits) Value is 4 (0100)	Header Length (4 bits)	Diff-Serv (8 bits)	Total Length (16 bits) length in octets	
Identification (16 bits) Unique value in each original IP packet			Flags (3 bits)	Fragment Offset (13 bits) Octets from start of original IP fragment's data field
Time to Live (8 bits)	Protocol (8 bits) 1 = ICMP, 6 = TCP, 17 = UDP		Header Checksum (16 bits)	
Source IP Address (32 bits)				
Destination IP Address (32 bits)				
Options (if any)				Padding
Data Field				

FIGURE 8-11   IP Version 4 (IPv4) Packet

IP Time to Live (TTL) Field

In the early days of the ARPANET, which was the precursor to the Internet, packets that were misaddressed would circulate endlessly among packet switches in search of their nonexistent destinations. To prevent this, IP added a **time to live (TTL)** field that is given a value by the source host. Different operating systems have different TTL defaults. Most insert TTL values between 64 and 128. Each router along the way decrements the TTL field by 1. A router decrementing the TTL to 0 will discard the packet.

IP Protocol Field

The **protocol field** tells the contents of the data field. If the protocol field value is 1, the IP packet carries an ICMP message in its data field. TCP and UDP have protocol values 6 and 17, respectively. After decapsulation, the internet layer process must pass the packet's data field to another process. The protocol field value designates which process should receive the data field.

IP Identification, Flags, and Fragment Offset Fields

If a router wishes to forward a packet to a particular network and the network's maximum packet size is too small for the packet, the router can fragment the packet into two or more smaller packets. Fragmentation can even happen at multiple routers along the way. The destination host's internet layer process must put the fragments back together.

In practice, fragmentation is rare. In fact, it often indicates an attempt to get around security protections. In any case, most modern operating systems set the "do not fragment" bit in the IP header so that fragmentation cannot occur. Instead, the source host attempts to find the largest packet size that can get through or simply keeps packets to a relatively safe small size.

IP Options

Similarly, **options** are uncommon in IP today and also tend to be used primarily by attackers. If an option does not end at a 32-bit boundary, **padding** is added up to the 32-bit boundary. Although options are uncommon, they cannot be completely avoided. For example, in IPsec security, which is discussed in Chapter 10, the Encapsulating Security Payload header is included as an option.

IP Diff-Serv

The **Diff-Serv** field can be used to label IP packets for priority and other service parameters. Interpretation of this field, unfortunately, has not been widely agreed upon.

Test Your Understanding

15. a) What is the main version of the Internet Protocol in use today? b) What does a router do if it receives a packet with a TTL value of 1? c) What does the protocol field value tell the destination host? d) Under what circumstances would the identification, flags, and fragment offset fields be used in IP? e) Why is IP fragmentation suspicious? f) How can a source host avoid fragmentation? g) Why are IP options suspicious? h) What security standard uses IPv4 options? i) What is the purpose of the Diff-Serv field?

IP VERSION 6 (IPv6)

Outgrowing IPv4

Although IPv4 continues to dominate the Internet's traffic, it has passed its prime. Most seriously, the 32-bit IPv4 address space has proven to be too small. In theory, the 32-bit IPv4 address space permits over four billion IP addresses. Unfortunately, these addresses were given out inefficiently. First, the United States, which originated the architecture, assigned about a third of all IPv4 addresses to itself. Second, and more seriously, IP addresses were only given out in chunks of approximately 256 addresses, 65,536, or 16.8 million addresses.[3] If a firm needed 300 IP addresses, it was bumped up to the next step, 65,536 addresses. In such firms, nearly all of the IP addresses went unused. Although the Internet Assigned Number Authority (IANA) fairly quickly switched to the classless inter-domain routing (CIDR) system, which gave number assignments in smaller increments, assignments were almost always generous to allow room for growth. Overall, only about 14 percent of all IPv4 numbers are actively used.

This limited supply of IPv4 addresses, the rapid Internet growth of economies in Asia, and the explosive growth of mobile devices needing their own IP addresses were

---

[3] A handful of the addresses within each of these three block sizes could not be used for reasons we will see in Chapter 9.

a recipe for disaster. In 2011, the disaster occurred. The IANA gave out the last of its IP addresses to regional registrars. The registrars soon ran out of this last allocation, apart from a few addresses kept in reserve for special purposes.

Test Your Understanding

16. a) What is the main problem with IPv4 that IPv6 addresses? b) What factors combined to cause the exhaustion of IPv4 addresses?

IPv6

The Internet Engineering Task Force had long foreseen this crisis. In its 1994 meeting, it decided to create a new IP version. The IETF gave this new version the designation **IP Version 6 (IPv6)** when the first RFCs (Requests for Comments) were released in 1995. Over the next few years, the IPv6 standards family continued to grow and mature. It was soon ready to be used, and many networking and computer vendors began to build IPv6 into their products.

The most fundamental change in IPv6 is the move from 32-bit addresses to 128-bit addresses. This does not produce merely four times as many addresses. Each additional bit *doubles* the number of addresses. So while there are just under 4.3 billion (4.3×10^9) IPv4 addresses, there are 3.4×10^{38} IPv6 addresses—34 undecillion. To see what this means, there are about seven billion people in the world today. For each person, there are 5×10^{28} IPv6 addresses.

Organizations soon found that using these new equipment capabilities, however, was a great deal more work than simply turning them on. For many years, few organizations saw the need to make the expensive upgrade to IPv6 because they had enough addresses. In addition, Network Address Translation (NAT) greatly extended the use of existing IP addresses in the firm, at the cost of some complexity, but at the gain of some security. IPv6 would have the mandatory inclusion of IPsec security functionality, but IPsec was quickly modified to work with IPv4 as well. Seeing no hard business case for upgrading, few companies did. Now, however, nearly all companies are beginning to at least plan for the implementation of IPv6, and many have already done so. As we will see in Chapter 9, companies have found that IPv6 implementation is a long and complex process. They need employees who understand this new protocol and other "v6" protocols such as ICMPv6 and DHCPv6.

In this chapter, we have focused on IPv4. We will look at IPv6 and its implementation in Chapters 8 and 9.

Test Your Understanding

17. a) What is the designation of the newest version of the Internet Protocol? b) What is its biggest improvement over IPv4? c) Is the conversion from IPv4 to IPv6 relatively inexpensive?

Writing 128-Bit IPv6 Addresses

For IPv4, strings of 32 ones and zeros are difficult for people to write and remember. Therefore, for human use, we write IPv4 addresses in dotted decimal notation—four decimal numbers between 0 and 255 separated by dots. This gives addresses like 128.171.17.13. People can actually remember these addresses.

For the 128-bit addresses of IPv6, we would still like simpler ways to write them, but anything we do will still overload human memory. Consequently, when we write IPv6 addresses for human consumption, we do so only to make the writing easier.

A 128-bit IPv6 address is shown in the following example. This is obviously difficult to write without making a mistake, and it is impossible to read.

---

*10110100010101111011010001010111101101000101011010110100010101111011101000
1010111101101000101011110110100010111111011010001010111*

To simplify this number, IPv6 does not use dotted decimal notation as IPv4 does. Rather, IPv6 uses hexadecimal notation, which we saw in Chapter 5, in the context of Ethernet MAC addresses. Each "nibble" of four bits is converted into a hex symbol from 0 through F. A 128-bit IPv6 address, then, would be translated into 32 hex symbols.

In Ethernet, we write hex symbols in pairs, separating each pair with a dash. This gives addresses like A1-B2-C3-D4-E5-F6. In IPv6, in contrast, we group hex symbols in tetrads (groups of four). Each tetrad is called a **field**. An example of a field is *fe56*. Note that we write the hex symbols in *lowercase* when writing IPv6 addresses. Each symbol is still four bits, so fe56 represents 16 bits. A full IPv6 address will have eight groups of these tetrads, which are separated by *colons* instead of dashes. The following is an IPv6 address written in hexadecimal notation.

2001:0027:fe56:0000:0000:0000:cd3f:0fca

This is still very long. Fortunately, there several rules to help us shorten the writing of addresses a little. The first is that in each field, *any leading zeros are dropped*. This is easy to understand. If the reader sees :27:, this must be :0027:. Note that only *leading* zeros are dropped. If trailing zeros or zeros anywhere were dropped, the reader could not know if :27: was :0027:, :2700:, or 0270:. Dropping leading zeros is also natural because we do that when writing decimal numbers. Here is what the IPv6 address looks like after leading zeros are dropped. This is much shorter.

2001:27:fe56::::cd3f:fca

Note that if a field has four zeros, it will become :: by the first rule. In other words, all four "leading" zeros are dropped, and only the colons remain. A second rule is that if several consecutive fields of zero occur, *one* sequence of *all-zero fields* can be reduced to a simple ::. So if an IPv6 address has a sequence :0000:0000:0000:, this can be replaced by ::. This further simplifies our IPv6 address to the following:

2001:27:fe56::cd3f:fca

These two rules reduce length, but applying them has some subrules that appliers must follow.

- First, address simplification should be done whenever possible. If the two rules can be combined, they should be combined.
- Second, only a *single* group of consecutive zeros may be shortened this way in an IP address. If only one group of zero segments is shortened, then counting the number of fields in a shortened address will tell the reader how many zeros need to be added back in. In the example above, there are five fields, not counting the ::. Therefore, three fields of zeros must be added to bring the total to eight fields.
- Third, the *longest* group of consecutive zero fields should be shortened. This just makes sense. One might as well shorten things as much as possible.
- Fourth, if there are two groups of consecutive zeros of the same length, the *first* group must be shortened. This is not an important rule, but reducing ambiguity is a good thing.

All of these rules can be a little daunting, but it is important to know how to write IPv6 addresses properly. Following these rules means that everyone will write IP addresses the same way. If some people drop some initial zeros while others do not, and if some writers violate the three rules while others do not, the same IP address will be written in different ways by different people. This will make it more difficult to determine if two written addresses are the same or different. It will also make automatic searching in databases and configuration fields far more difficult and error prone.

Test Your Understanding

18. a) Are IPv6 addresses written in uppercase or lowercase letters? b) Are IPv6 addresses written in decimal or hexadecimal symbols? c) How many symbols are there in a field, and how are fields delimited?

19. a) List the rules for simplifying IPv6 addresses. b) Simplify the following IP address: 2001:0ed2:056b:00d3.000c:abcd:0bcd:0fe. c) Simplify the following IP address: 2001:0002:0000:0000:0000:abcd:0bcd:0fe. d) Simplify the following IP address: 2001:0000:0000:00fe:0000:0000:0000:cdef. e) What is the advantage of simplifying IPv6 addresses according to strict rules?

The IPv6 Header

The increase from 32 bits to 128 bits is the most important improvement from IPv4 to IPv6, so we have focused heavily on IPv6 addresses. We will now turn to improvements in the IPv6 header compared to the IPv4 header. Figure 8-12 illustrates both. The most obvious difference is that IPv4 headers are 20 octets long while IPv6 headers are 40 octets long.

The second difference is that the IPv6 header, although longer, is less cluttered, with fewer fields for routers and hosts to consider. This relative simplicity means that routers can actually process longer IPv6 headers faster than they can process IPv4 headers.

VERSION NUMBER FIELD   Both headers begin with a 4-bit **version number** field. For IPv4, the field value is 0100 (four). For IPv6, it is 0110 (six).

TRAFFIC CLASS AND FLOW LABEL FIELDS   In the first row of the IPv6 header, there are an 8-bit type of service field and a 20-bit flow label.[4] The **traffic class field** in IPv6 allows

---

[4] In the original definition of IPv6, these fields were 4 bits and 24 bits, respectively. The change to 8 bits and 20 bits was made in 1998.

IP Version 4 Packet

Bit 0   Bit 31

Version (4 bits) Value is 4 (0100)	Header Length (4 bits)	Diff-Serv (8 bits)	Total Length (16 bits) length in octets
Identification (16 bits) Unique value in each original IP packet		Flags (3 bits)	Fragment Offset (13 bits) Octets from start of original IP fragment's data field
Time to Live (8 bits)	Protocol (8 bits) 1 = ICMP, 6 = TCP, 17 = UDP	Header Checksum (16 bits)	
Source IP Address (32 bits)			
Destination IP Address (32 bits)			
Options (if any)			Padding
Data Field			

IP Version 6 Packet

Bit 0   Bit 31

Version (4 bits) Value is 6 (0110)	Diff-Serv (8 bits)	Flow Label (20 bits) Marks a packet as part of a specific flow
Payload Length (16 bits)	Next Header (8 bits) Name of next header	Hop Limit (8 bits)
Source IP Address (128 bits)		
Destination IP Address (128 bits)		
Next Header or Payload (Data Field)		

FIGURE 8-12 IPv4 and IPv6 Packet Header

up to 256 special handling conditions to be specified. It is almost completely equivalent to the 8-bit type of service field in IPv4.

The **flow label field** allows a stream of packets to be identified as part of a single stream. After the first packet is processed by a router, the router can apply certain processing rules to following packets in the stream, including those in the traffic class field. This further reduces processing time per packet.

Unfortunately, the definitions of these fields are still embryonic, and they are seeing little use currently.

LENGTHS   For IPv4, two fields are used to compute the length of the data field in the IP packet. The header length field gives the length of the header in 32-bit units, while the total length field gives the total length of the packet in octets.

In IPv6, the main packet header is always 40 octets long, so the **payload length field** only needs to give the length of the payload in octets. A router can quickly determine how long the packet is.

The payload length field is 16 bits long, so payloads can be up to 65,536 octets long. IPv6 also has an option for far larger **jumbo headers**. Greater packet length means that routers can handle fewer packets to deliver an application message. This also speeds up router operation.

However, the sending host must limit its packet length so that all of the links between routers along the way can support that packet length. The maximum packet size that can be transmitted without segmentation across a packet's route is called the **maximum transmission unit (MTU)** length. For IPv4, a method for finding the MTU is described in RFC 1191, which was published in 1990. For IPv6, a similar method was published in RFC 1981 (1996). A more robust method for IPv6 MTU discovery was published in RFC 4821 (2007). Without MTU discovery, the maximum packet size must be set to 1,280 octets. All data links are required to support packets of this size.

It should be noted that payload length is not the same as the length of the data field. We will see that an IPv6 packet can have one or more extension headers before the data field. These are included in the payload length.

FRAGMENTATION   In IPv4, routers along a packet's path may be required to fragment a packet so that it can travel through a network with a small MTU. The second row in the IPv4 header allows the destination host to reassemble the fragmented packet. As discussed earlier in the chapter, router fragmentation has become a largely obsolete capability.

IPv6 does not permit routers along the route to fragment packets at all. Therefore, it does not need to have the reassembly information in the IPv4 header. This shortens the IPv6 header by 32 bits.

However, IPv6 does allow a host to fragment a packet *before sending it*. We will see later that there is an extension header to govern packet reassembly on the destination host. This extension header is only added when fragmentation occurs, and routers along the way do not have to consider it.

HOP LIMIT FIELD   IPv4 has a time to live field. As we noted earlier in this chapter, each router along the way decrements this field's value by one. If a router decrements it to zero, the router discards the packet. Internet old timers know that when IPv4 was created, the time to live value was supposed to be an actual clock time. However, this was quickly discovered to be unworkable in practice. The value was then interpreted as the maximum number of hops permitted by the packet.

In IPv6, the corresponding field was the same length as it was in the IPv4 packet header. However, it was renamed the **hop limit field** to more properly identify it. For people not old enough to remember the early definition of time to live, however, it is simply a matter of confusion.

CHECKSUM FIELD. WHAT CHECKSUM FIELD? IPv4 has a checksum field. When IPv4 was created, there was a concern that if packet headers contained errors, they could cause serious problems for the Internet. Experience showed that this concern was overblown. Consequently, IPv6 has no checksum field. The computations needed to check for errors in IPv4 were heavy, even for a 20-octet header. Dropping the checksum field significantly reduces packet handling time on routers.

SOURCE AND DESTINATION IPV6 ADDRESSES Although the IPv6 header has fewer fields than the IPv4 header, the IPv6 source and destination addresses are four times as long as they are in IPv4. Consequently, the IPv6 header is 40 octets long, as opposed to IPv4 header's 20 octets length—assuming no options in the IPv4 header.

Test Your Understanding

20. a) How do the version number fields in IPv4 and IPv6 differ? b) In IPv6, how can the receiver tell the length of packet? c) Does the payload length field include the lengths of any extension headers in the packet? d) What is the maximum possible lengths for ordinary IPv6 payloads? e) What are jumbo packets, and why are they desirable? f) What is the maximum MTU size? g) How is it determined in IPv6? h) If a source host does not do MTU discovery, what is the longest packet it can safely send?

21. a) Compare fragmentation in IPv4 and IPv6. b) How is the hop limit field used? c) Does IPv6 have a header checksum field? d) What are the implications of this? e) What is the general purpose of the traffic class field? f) Of the flow label field?

Extension Headers

The IPv4 packet has an *options* field that allows the sender to add options. Few IPv4 packets have options, but each router must check each packet for options, and this can cost significant time. IPv6 took another approach. In the IPv6 header, there is no options field. Instead, there is a **next-header field**. Instead of having an open-ended options field, the IETF has organized optional information into a series of optional **extension headers**. These extension headers only have to be processed if they are present.

Each extension header has its own next-header field identifying the following extension header. As Figure 8-13 shows, this allows the main header and one or more extension headers to be daisy-chained together.

Figure 8-14 shows that next header values have been defined for particular extension headers. In addition, values have been designed for types of final data fields (upper layer messages) if there are no more extension headers. If these upper layer message values seem familiar, it is because these are the values that are used in the protocol field of the IPv4 header. In essence, the next-header field is an extension of the protocol field in IPv4.

Two of the six currently defined extension headers are the **authentication header** and the **encapsulating security payload (ESP) field**. Both are designed for security. The authentication header allows the packet to validate the sender, but there is no encryption for confidentiality. This has proven to be of little value.

The ESP option, in contrast, gives all of the traditional protections of cryptographic systems, including encryption for confidentiality, authentication, message integrity, and replay protection.

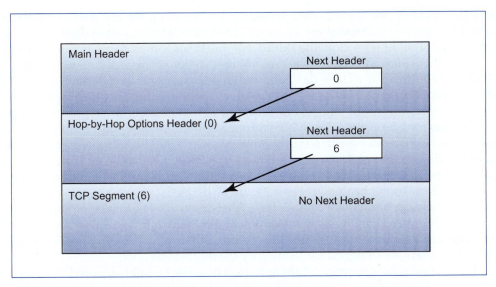

FIGURE 8-13 Next Headers in IPv6 Packet Headers

Header Type	Next Header Code
Extension Headers	
Hop-by-Hop Options	0
Routing Header	43
Fragment Header	44
Authentication Header	51
Encapsulating Security Payload Header	50
Destination Options	60
Mobility Header	135
No Next Header	59
Upper Layer Messages	
TCP	6
UDP	17
ICMPv6	58

FIGURE 8-14 IPv6 Next Header Values

Initially, security was a defining characteristic of IPv6, distinguishing it from IPv4. However, the IETF quickly made the encapsulating security payload (and authentication header) available in IPv4 by allowing their values (50 and 51) to appear in the IPv4 protocol field. In addition, while it is often said that the use of security is mandatory in IPv6, the truth is that providing the *capability* for ESP and authentication header security is mandatory. Their *use* is not mandatory. Consequently, making security an option in IPv4 stole the thunder from IPv6's touted security advantage.

One other extension header has security implications. This is the routing header. This should control how routers deal with routing decisions for the packet. So far, only one type of routing extension header has been released, Routing Heading Type 0. This permits the header to specify the precise sequence of routers that should process it. This capability has long been available in IPv4 through options as loose source routing. Even when IPv6 was being designed, security problems with source routing were being discovered. Today, the use of Routing Type 0 headers is recognized as being risky and was deprecated by RFC 5095 in 2007. However, the routing header as a whole has not been deprecated. New router heading types may still be defined.

Two extension headers for options have been designed. The first is for hop-by-hop options. Each router along the way must look at this header. In fact, this is usually the only extension header the router has to consider, other than a routing header. Other extension headers are designed for reading by the destination host.

The second is for destination host options. These can be safely ignored by routers. In both cases, having specific extension headers for hop by hop and destination host addresses allows options to be handled elegantly if they exist. If there are no hop-by-hop options, hosts do not have to waste any time looking for options.

Test Your Understanding

22. a) Why is handling options the way that IPv4 does undesirable? b) Why is the approach of using optional extension headers desirable? c) Distinguish between protections provided by the authentication header and the encapsulating security payload. d) Are these two security extension headers available in IPv6, IPv4, or both? e) What does it mean that the Routing Header Type 0 has been deprecated? f) What is usually the only extension header that routers normally have to consider? g) What is another they might have to consider? h) How does the last extension header before a UDP datagram indicate that the UDP datagram comes next? (You must infer the answer from the text.) i) If you see 51 in the next header field of a header, what will follow this header? j) If you see 59 in the next header field of a header, what will follow this header?

THE TRANSMISSION CONTROL PROTOCOL (TCP)

Fields in TCP/IP Segments

In Chapter 2, we looked briefly at the syntax of messages (segments) for the **Transmission Control Protocol (TCP)**. In this section, we will look at the syntax of this complex protocol in more depth. When IP was designed, it was made a very simple "best effort" protocol (although its routing tables are complex). The IETF left more complex internetwork transmission control tasks to TCP. Consequently, network professionals need to understand TCP very well. Figure 8-15 shows the organization of TCP messages, which are called TCP segments.

SEQUENCE NUMBERS   TCP can handle messages of almost any length. In Chapter 2, we saw that it does so by fragmenting application messages into many TCP segments and sending each segment in a packet. So that the receiver can put the segments back

TCP Segment

Bit 0   Bit 31

Source Port Number (16 bits)	Destination Port Number (16 bits)
Sequence Number (32 bits)	
Acknowledgment Number (32 bits)	

Header Length (4 bits)	Reserved (6 bits)	Flag Fields (6 bits)	Window Size (16 bits)
TCP Checksum (16 bits)			Urgent Pointer (16 bits)
Options (if any)			Padding
Data Field			

Flag fields are 1-bit fields. They include SYN, ACK, FIN, and RST.

UDP Datagram

Bit 0   Bit 31

Source Port Number (16 bits)	Destination Port Number (16 bits)
UDP Length (16 bits)	UDP Checksum (16 bits)
Data Field	

FIGURE 8-15 TCP Segment and UDP Datagram

in order, each segment has a **sequence number** that gives its position in the stream of segments. The receiving TCP process puts the segments in order of increasing sequence number, creating the full application message. The TCP process then passes the application message up to the correct application process indicated in the port number.[5]

ACKNOWLEDGMENT NUMBERS In Chapter 2, we saw that TCP uses **acknowledgments (ACKs)** to achieve reliability. If a transport process receives a TCP segment correctly,

---

[5] Module A has a detailed discussion of TCP sequence and acknowledgment numbers.

it sends back a TCP segment acknowledging the reception. If the sending transport process does not receive an acknowledgment, it transmits the TCP segment again.

The **acknowledgment number field** indicates which segment is being acknowledged. One might expect that if a segment has sequence number X, then the acknowledgment number in the segment that acknowledges it would also be X. As Module A notes, the situation is more complex, but the acknowledgment number is at least based on the sequence number of the segment being acknowledged.

FLAG FIELDS   As discussed in Chapter 2, TCP has six single-bit fields. Single-bit fields are called flag fields, and if they have the value 1, they are said to be set. These fields allow the receiving transport process to know the kind of segment it is receiving. We saw several uses of these flag bits in Chapter 2.

- If the ACK bit is set, then the segment acknowledges another segment. If the ACK bit is set, the acknowledgment field must be filled in to indicate which message is being acknowledged.
- If the SYN (synchronization) bit is set (has the value 1), then the segment requests a connection opening.
- If the FIN (finish) bit is set, then the segment requests a normal connection closing.

Openings and Abrupt TCP Closes

In Chapter 2, we saw that TCP is a connection-oriented protocol. Connection-oriented protocols have formal openings and closings. Figure 8-16 recaps these openings and closings.

In Chapter 2, we looked at *normal* closings. Just as you do not simply hang up on a telephone call when you want to finish talking if you are polite, a normal TCP close consists of two FIN segments, one in each direction, plus their acknowledgments.

However, Figure 8-16 shows that TCP also permits another type of close. This is an abrupt close. Whenever either side wishes to end a conversation, it can simply send a **TCP reset segment**. This is a segment with the **RST** (reset) flag bit set. This may occur if a problem is encountered during a connection, for security reasons, or for any other reason.

Note in Figure 8-16 that an RST segment is not acknowledged. The side that sent the RST segment is not listening any longer, so acknowledging a reset would be as pointless as saying goodbye after someone has hung up on you. The RST segment is one of two segment types that are not acknowledged. As noted in Chapter 2, a pure acknowledgment is not acknowledged because doing so would create an endless loop of acknowledgments.

Test Your Understanding

23. Why is TCP complex? b) Why is it important for networking professionals to understand TCP? c) What are TCP messages called?
24. Why are sequence numbers good? b) What are 1-bit fields called? c) If someone says that a flag field is set, what does this mean? d) If the ACK bit is set, what other field must have a value? e) What is a FIN segment? f) Distinguish between four-way closes and abrupt resets. g) Why is a reset segment not acknowledged?

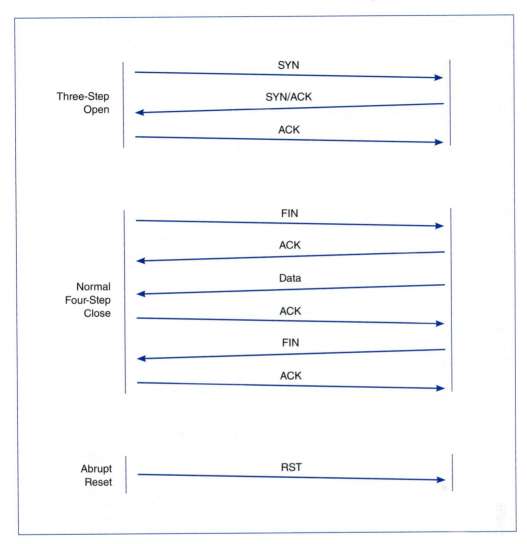

FIGURE 8-16 TCP Session Openings and Closings

THE USER DATAGRAM PROTOCOL (UDP)

We saw UDP in Chapter 2. This is a very simple protocol, so the discussion in that chapter is sufficient except for one point. In the section on TCP, we noted that segmentation and reassembly allows very long application messages—messages far too long to fit into a single packet.

In contrast, UDP cannot do segmentation. It has nothing like sequence numbers or acknowledgment numbers. This means that an application message must fit into a single UDP datagram. The length field in the UDP header is 16 bits long, so the maximum length of the UDP data field, and therefore the maximum length of an application message, is 65,536 octets.

Test Your Understanding

25. a) Why can TCP handle extremely long application messages? b) Can UDP handle extremely long application messages? c) What is the maximum application message size if UDP is used at the transport layer.

OTHER TCP/IP STANDARDS

In this section, we will look briefly at several other important TCP/IP standards that network administrators need to master. We will look at some of these protocols here. Chapter 9 will look more closely at some TCP/IP protocols that are focused on network management.

Dynamic Routing Protocols

How does a router get the information in its routing table? One possibility is to enter routes manually. However, that approach does not scale to large internets. Instead, as Figure 8-17 shows, routers constantly exchange routing table information with one another using **dynamic routing protocols**.

ROUTING   Note that TCP/IP uses the term **routing** in two different but related ways. First, we saw earlier that the process of forwarding arriving packets is called routing. Second, the process of exchanging information for building routing tables is also called routing.

> In TCP/IP, the term **routing** is used in two ways—for packet forwarding and for the exchange of routing table information through dynamic routing protocols.

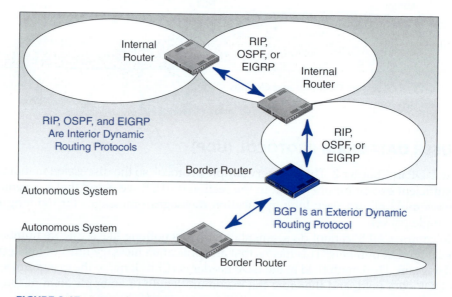

FIGURE 8-17   Internal and External Dynamic Routing Protocols

AUTONOMOUS SYSTEMS AND INTERIOR DYNAMIC ROUTING PROTOCOLS Recall from Chapter 1 that the Internet consists of many networks owned by different organizations. Within an organization's network, which is called an **autonomous system**, the organization owning the network decides which dynamic routing protocol to use among its internal routers, as shown in Figure 8-17. For internal use, the organization is free to choose among available **interior dynamic routing protocols**. There are three popular interior dynamic routing protocols. Each has different strengths and weaknesses.

ROUTING INFORMATION PROTOCOL (RIP) The simplest interior dynamic routing protocol created by the IETF is the **Routing Information Protocol (RIP)**. RIP's simplicity makes it attractive for small internets. Management labor is relatively low. On the negative side, RIP is not very efficient because its metric is merely the number of router hops needed to get to the destination host. However, this is not a serious problem for small internets. The one serious problem with RIP in small internets is poor security. If attackers take over a firm's interior dynamic routing protocol communications, they can maliciously reroute the internet's traffic.

OPEN SHORTEST PATH FIRST (OSPF) For larger autonomous systems, or if security is a serious concern, the IETF created the **Open Shortest Path First (OSPF)** dynamic routing protocol. OSPF is very efficient, having a complex metric based on a mixture of cost, throughput, and traffic delays. It also offers strong security. It costs much more to manage than RIP, but unless a corporate internet is very small, OSPF is the only IETF dynamic routing protocol that makes sense.

EIGRP Cisco Systems is the dominant manufacturer of routers. Cisco has its own proprietary interior dynamic routing protocol for large internets—**Enhanced Interior Gateway Routing Protocol (EIGRP)**. The term **gateway** is another term for *router*. EIGRP's metric is very efficient because it is based on a mixture of interface bandwidth, load on the interface (0 percent to 100 percent of capacity), delay, and reliability (percentage of packets lost). EIGRP is comparable to OSPF, but many companies use

Dynamic Routing Protocol	Interior or Exterior Routing Protocol?	Remarks
RIP (Routing Information Protocol)	Interior	Only for small autonomous systems with low needs for security
OSPF (Open Shortest Path First)	Interior	For large autonomous systems that only use TCP/IP
EIGRP (Enhanced Interior Gateway Routing Protocol)	Interior	Proprietary Cisco Systems protocol. Not limited to TCP/IP routing. Also handles IPX/SPX, SNA, and so forth
BGP (Border Gateway Protocol)	Exterior	Organization cannot choose what exterior routing protocol it will use

FIGURE 8-18 Dynamic Routing Protocols (Study Figure)

it instead of OSPF because it can route SNA and IPX/SPX traffic as well as IP traffic. On the negative side, EIGRP is a proprietary protocol, and using it forces the company to buy only Cisco routers.

EXTERIOR DYNAMIC ROUTING PROTOCOLS For communication outside the organization's network, the organization is no longer in control. It must use whatever **exterior dynamic routing protocol** the external network to which it is connected requires. The almost universal exterior dynamic routing protocol is the **Border Gateway Protocol (BGP)**. BGP is designed specifically for the exchange of routing information between autonomous systems.

Test Your Understanding

26. a) What is the purpose of dynamic routing protocols? b) In what two ways does TCP/IP use the term *routing*? c) What is an autonomous system? d) Within an autonomous system, can the organization choose its interior dynamic routing protocol? e) What are the two TCP/IP interior dynamic routing protocols? f) Which IETF dynamic routing protocol is good for small internets that do not have high security requirements? g) Which IETF dynamic routing protocol is good for large internal internets that have high security requirements? h) What is the main benefit of EIGRP compared to OSPF as an internal dynamic routing protocol? i) When might you use EIGRP as your interior dynamic routing protocol? j) May a company select the routing protocol its border router uses to communicate with the outside world? k) What is the almost universal exterior dynamic routing protocol?

Internet Control Message Protocol (ICMP) for Supervisory Messages at the Internet Layer

SUPERVISORY MESSAGES AT THE INTERNET LAYER IP is only concerned with packet delivery. For supervisory messages at the internet layer, the IETF created the **Internet Control Message Protocol (ICMP)**. IP and ICMP work closely together. As Figure 8-19

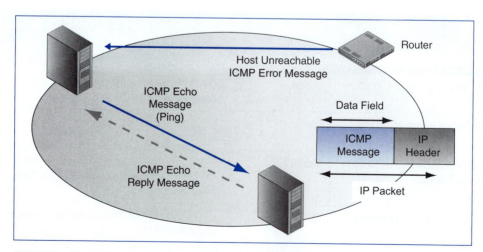

FIGURE 8-19 Internet Control Message Protocol (ICMP) for Supervisory Messages

shows, IP encapsulates ICMP messages in the IP data field, delivering them to their target host or router. There are no higher-layer headers or messages.

ERROR ADVISEMENT   IP is an unreliable protocol. It offers no error correction. If the router or the destination host finds an error, it discards the packet. Although there is no retransmission, the router or host that finds the error may send an **ICMP error message** to the source device to inform it that an error has occurred, as in Figure 8-19. This is **error advisement** (notification) rather than *error correction*. There is no mechanism within IP or ICMP for the retransmission of lost or damaged packets. ICMP error messages are only sent to help the sending process or its human user diagnose problems.

One important subtlety is that sending error advisement messages is not mandatory. For security reasons, many firms do not allow error advisement messages to leave their internal internets because hackers can exploit the information contained in them.

ECHO (PING)   Perhaps the most famous ICMP error message type is the **ICMP echo** message. One host or router can send an echo request message to another. If the target device's internet process is able to do so, it will send back an **ICMP echo reply** message.

Sending an echo request is often called **pinging** the target host, because it is similar to a submarine pinging a ship with sonar to see if it is there. In fact, the most common program for pinging hosts is called **ping**.[6] Echo is a good diagnostic tool because if there are network difficulties, a logical early step in diagnosis is to ping many hosts and routers to see if they can be reached.

Test Your Understanding

27. a) For what general class of messages is ICMP used? b) Explain error advisement in ICMP. c) Explain the purpose of ICMP echo messages. d) Sending an ICMP echo message is called the target host.

CONCLUSION

Synopsis

TCP/IP is a family of standards created by the Internet Engineering Task Force (IETF). IP is TCP/IP's main standard at the internet layer. IP is a lightweight (unreliable and connectionless) protocol. At the transport layer, TCP/IP offers two standards: TCP, which is a heavyweight protocol (reliable and connection-oriented), and UDP, which is a lightweight protocol like IP.

IPv4 addresses are hierarchical. Their 32 bits usually are divided into a network part, a subnet part, and a host part. All three parts vary in length. A network mask tells what bits are in the network part, while a subnet mask tells what bits are in the total of the network or subnet parts. Masks always begin with a certain number of 1s followed

---

[6] The echo reply message also gives the latency for the reply—the number of milliseconds between echo messages and echo reply messages. This is useful in diagnosing problems.

by enough 0s to fill the mask out to 32 bits. For human reading, masks are expressed in dotted decimal notation or prefix notation.

Routers forward packets through an internet. Border routers move packets between the outside world and an internal site network. Internal routers work within sites, moving packets between subnets. Ports in routers are called interfaces. Different interfaces may connect to different types of networks—for instance, Ethernet or Frame Relay networks. Most routers are multiprotocol routers, which can handle not only TCP/IP internetworking protocols, but also internetworking protocols from IPX/SPX, SNA, and other architectures. Routers are designed to work in a mesh topology. This creates alternative routes through the internet. Alternative routes are good for reliability. However, the router has to consider the best route for each arriving packet, and this is time consuming and therefore expensive.

To make a routing decision (deciding which interface to use to send an incoming packet back out), a router uses a routing table. Each row in the routing table represents a route to a particular network or subnet. All packets to that network or subnet are governed by the one row. Each row (route) has destination, mask, metric, interface, and next-hop router fields.

If the destination IP address in an arriving packet is in a row's range, that row is a match. After finding all matches in the routing table, the router finds the best-match row on the basis of match length and, in the case of tied match lengths, on metric values. Once a best-match route (row) is selected, the router sends the packet out a particular interface to the next-hop router specified in that row or to the destination IP address if the destination host is out the interface.

In the examples in the main text, masks broke at 8-bit boundaries, making it easy to specify them with dotted decimal notation. If you read the box "Masking When Masks Do Not Break at 8-Bit Boundaries," you can deal more realistically with the world of masking because masks often do not break at 8-bit boundaries.

If you read the box, "The Address Resolution Protocol (ARP)," you saw that the router must encapsulate the packet in a frame in order to send it out. ARP is a protocol to learn the data link layer destination of the device to which a router or host will send a frame if the router or host only knows the destination host's IP address.

IP version 4 has a number of important fields besides the source and destination address fields. The time to live (TTL) field ensures that packets that are misaddressed do not circulate endlessly around the Internet. The protocol field describes the contents of the data field—ICMP message, TCP segment, UDP datagram, and so forth.

IP version 6 will require networking and security professionals to understand a new approach to expressing addresses. IPv6 addresses are 128 bits long. For human comprehension, they are expressed in hexadecimal notation. In addition, there are certain rules that compress the hex version of the address to reduce its complexity.

The IPv6 header is simpler than the IPv4 header, but because the two address fields are far larger in IPv6 than in IPv4, the IPv6 header is 40 octets long instead of the 20 octet length of IPv4 headers if there are no options. The IPv6 header saves time on each router by not checking for errors and not allowing fragmentation. The IPv6 header has a mechanism for specifying quality-of-service parameters for the packet and for marking the packet as a member of a flow of packets with predefined quality-of-service parameters.

IPv6 does not have options. Instead, it specifies a number of optional extension header for hop-by-hop options, security, and other matters. The next-header field in the main header and each extension header specifies the type of header (or upper layer protocol) that follows this header.

The Transmission Control Protocol (TCP) has sequence numbers that allow the receiving transport process to place arriving TCP segments in order. The TCP header has several flag fields that indicate whether the segment is a SYN, FIN, ACK, or RST segment. Connection openings use a three-step handshake that uses SYN segments. Normal closes involve a four-step message exchange that use FIN segments. Resets close a connection with a single segment (RST) instead of the normal four.

Routers build their routing tables by listening to other routers. Routers frequently exchange messages, giving information stored in their routing tables. These messages are governed by one of several available dynamic routing protocols.

IP itself does not have supervisory messages. For internet layer supervisory messages, hosts and ro uters use the Internet Control Message Protocol (ICMP). We looked at two types of ICMP messages—error advisement messages and echo messages (ping). ICMP messages are carried in the data fields of IP packets.

END-OF-CHAPTER QUESTIONS

Thought Questions

1. How do the postal services use hierarchical sorting? How does this simplify delivery decisions?

2. Give a non-network example of hierarchical addressing, and discuss how it reduces the amount of work needed in physical delivery. Do not use any example in the book, a postal service, or the telephone network.

3. A client PC has two simultaneous connections to the same webserver application program on a webserver. (Yes, this is possible, and in fact, it is rather common.) What will be different between the TCP segments that the client sends on the two connections?

4. A router that has the routing table in Figure 8-8 receives an incoming IPv4 packet. The source IP address is 10.55.72.234. The destination host is 10.4.6.7. The TTL value is 1. The Protocol field value is 6. What will the router do with this packet?

Harder Thought Question

1. For security reasons, many organizations do not allow error reply messages to leave their internal internets. How, specifically, could hackers use information in echo reply messages to learn about the firm's internal hosts? (Hint: Notice that ICMP message are carried in the data fields of IP packets.)

Troubleshooting Question

1. You suspect that the failure of a router or of a transmission line connecting routers has left some of your important servers unavailable to clients at your site. How could you narrow down the location of the problem using what you learned in this chapter?

Perspective Questions

1. What was the most surprising thing you learned in this chapter?

2. What was the most difficult material for you in this chapter?

9

TCP/IP INTERNETWORKING II

LEARNING OBJECTIVES

By the end of this chapter, you should be able to:

■ Explain TCP/IP management: IP subnet planning, Network Address Translation (NAT), Multiprotocol Labor Switching (MPLS), the Domain Name System (DNS), DHCP servers, the Simple Network Management Protocol (SNMP), and IPv6 management.

INTRODUCTION

In Chapter 8, we looked at important TCP concepts. In this chapter, we will focus on the security and management of TCP/IP networks.

CORE TCP/IP MANAGEMENT TASKS

If a firm uses TCP/IP as its internetworking protocol, it must do a considerable amount of work to build and maintain the necessary infrastructure of TCP/IP. While switched networks are (generally) capable of operating for long periods of time without intervention by network managers, TCP/IP internets require constant tuning and support. This results in a need for considerable TCP/IP expertise and management effort. As we saw in Chapter 1, network managers say, "Switch where you can, route where you must."

IP Subnet Planning

As Chapter 8 discussed, IP addresses are 32 bits long. Each organization is assigned a network part. We saw that the University of Hawai`i's network part (128.171) is 16 bits long. There is nothing a firm can do to alter its network part. However, it was up to the university to decide what to do with the remaining 16 bits.

SUBNETTING AT THE UNIVERSITY OF HAWAI`I The University, like most organizations, chose to subnet its IP address space. It divided the 16 bits over which it has discretion into an 8-bit subnet part and an 8-bit host part.

THE $2^N - 2$ RULE With N bits, you can represent 2^N possibilities. Therefore, with 8 bits, one can represent 2^8 (256) possibilities. This would suggest that the university can have

Step	Description				
1	Total size of IP address (bits)	32			
2	Size of network part assigned to firm (bits)	16		8	
3	Remaining bits for firm to assign	16		24	
4	Selected subnet/host part sizes (bits)	8/8	6/10	12/12	8/16
5	Possible number of subnets ($2^N - 2$)	254 $(2^8 - 2)$	62 $(2^6 - 2)$	4,094 $(2^{12} - 2)$	254 $(2^8 - 2)$
6	Possible number of hosts per subnet ($2^N - 2$)	254 $(2^8 - 2)$	1,022 $(2^{10} - 2)$	4,094 $(2^{12} - 2)$	65,534 $(2^{16} - 2)$

FIGURE 9-1   IP Subnetting

256 subnets, each with 256 hosts. However, a network, subnet, or host part cannot be all 0s or all 1s.[1] Therefore, the university can have only 254 (256 – 2) subnets, each with only 254 hosts. Figure 9-1 illustrates these calculations.

In general, if a part is N bits long, it can represent $2^N - 2$ networks, subnets, or hosts. For example, if a subnet part is 9 bits long, there can be $2^9 - 2$, or 510, subnets. Or if a host part is 5 bits long, there can be $2^5 - 2$, or 30, hosts.

In general, if a part is N bits long, it can represent $2^N - 2$ networks, subnets, or hosts.

BALANCING SUBNET AND HOST PART SIZES   The larger the subnet part, the more subnets there will be. However, the larger the subnet part is made, the smaller the host part will be. This will mean fewer hosts per subnet. There is always a trade-off. More subnets mean fewer hosts, and more hosts mean fewer subnets.

The University of Hawai`i's choice of 8-bit network and subnet parts was acceptable for many years because no college needed more than 254 hosts. Its advantage is that its subnet mask (255.255.255.0) was very simple, breaking at 8-bit boundaries. This made it easy to see which hosts were on which subnets. The host at 128.171.17.5, for instance, was the fifth host on the *17th* subnet. If the subnet mask did not break at an 8-bit boundary, you cannot see which subnet a host is on by looking at the address in dotted decimal notation.

However, many colleges in the university now have more than 254 computers, and the limit of 254 hosts required by its subnetting decision has become a serious problem. Several colleges now have two subnets connected by routers. This is expensive and awkward.

The university would have been better served had it selected a smaller subnet part, say 6 bits. As Figure 9-1 shows, this would have allowed 62 college subnets, which probably would have been sufficient. A 6-bit subnet part would give a 10-bit host part, allowing 1,022 hosts per subnet. This would be ample for several years to come.

---

[1]If you have all 1s in an address part, this indicates that broadcasting should be used. All 0s parts are used by computers when they do not know their addresses. As we will see later in this chapter, most client PCs get their IP addresses from DHCP servers. All-zero addresses can only be used in the source addresses of DHCP messages sent from a host to a DHCP server.

A CRITICAL CHOICE   In general, it is critical for corporations to plan their IP subnetting carefully, in order to get the right balance between the sizes of their network and subnet parts.

Test Your Understanding

1. a) Why is IP subnet planning important? b) If you have a subnet part of 9 bits, how many subnets can you have? c) Your firm has an 8-bit network part. If you need at least 250 subnets, what must your subnet size be? d) How many hosts can you have per subnet? e) Your firm has a 20-bit network part. What subnet part would you select to give at least 10 subnets? f) How many hosts can you have per subnet?

Network Address Translation (NAT)

One issue that firms face is whether to allow people outside the corporation to learn their internal addresses. This is a security risk. If attackers know internal IP addresses, this allows them to send attack packets from the outside world. To prevent this, companies

---

NAT

    Sends false external IP addresses that are different from internal IP addresses

NAT Operation (Figure 10-13)

NAT Is Transparent to Internal and External Hosts

Security Reason for Using NAT

    External attackers can put sniffers outside the corporation

    Sniffers can learn IP addresses

    Attackers can send attacks to these addresses

    With NAT, attackers only learn false external IP addresses

Expanding the Number of Available IP Addresses

    Companies may receive a limited number of IP addresses from their ISPs

    There are roughly 4,000 possible ephemeral port numbers for each IP address

    So for each IP address, there can be 4,000 external connections

    If a firm is given 248 IP addresses, there can be roughly one million external connections

    Even if each internal device averages several simultaneously external connections, there should not be a problem providing as many external IP connections as a firm desires

Private IP Addresses

    Can only be used inside firms

    10.x.x.x

    192.168.x.x (most popular)

    172.16.x.x through 172.31.x.s

Protocol Problems with NAT

    IPsec, VoIP, etc.

    Work-arounds must be considered very carefully in product selection

---

FIGURE 9-2   Network Address Translation (NAT) (Study Figure)

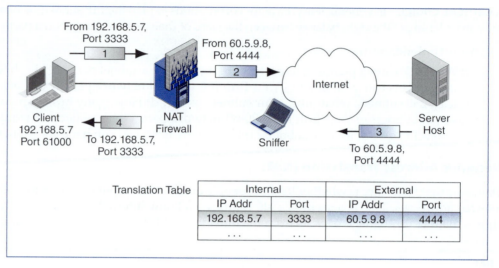

FIGURE 9-3 Network Address Translation (NAT) Operation

can use **network address translation (NAT)**, which presents external IP addresses that are different from internal IP addresses used within the firm.

NAT OPERATION Figure 9-3 shows how NAT works. An internal client host, 192.168.5.7, sends a packet to an external server host. The source address in this packet is 192.168.5.7, of course. The source port number is 3333, which is an ephemeral port number that the source host made up for this connection.

When the NAT firewall at the border receives the packet, it makes up a new row in its translation table. It places the internal IP address and port number in the table. It then generates a new external source IP address and external source port number. These are 60.5.9.8 and 4444, respectively.

When packets arrive from the external host, they have 60.5.9.8 in their destination IP address fields and 4444 in their destination port number fields. The NAT firewall looks these values up in its translation table, replaces the external values with the internal values, and sends them on to the client PC.

TRANSPARENCY NAT is transparent to both internal and external hosts. Hosts do not even know that NAT is happening. Consequently, there is no need to change the ways in which they operate.

SECURITY Figure 9-3 shows how NAT brings security. An attacker may be able to install a **sniffer program** beyond the corporation's NAT firewall. This sniffer will be able to read all packets coming out of the firm. With NAT, an eavesdropper only learns false (external) IP addresses and port numbers. In theory, if an attacker can attack immediately, it can send packets to the external IP addresses and port numbers, and the NAT firewall will pass them on to the internal host. However, this is rarely possible. NAT provides a surprising amount of security despite its simple operation.

EXPANDING THE EFFECTIVE NUMBER OF AVAILABLE IP ADDRESSES An equally important potential reason for using NAT is to permit a firm to have many more internal IP addresses than it is given by its ISP. Suppose that an ISP only gives the firm 254 IP addresses by giving it a host part with 24 bits. Without NAT, a firm can only have 254 PCs simultaneously using the Internet.

However, NAT is really network address translation/port address translation (NAT/*PAT*). With Microsoft Windows, there are almost 4,000 ephemeral port numbers. Even if internal hosts maintained four simultaneous connections to the outside world on average, each IP address could be used by 1,000 client PCs to make outside connections by giving each client PC a different set of port numbers for its connections. If a firm has 254 IP addresses, it can multiply this already large number of connections by 4,000. This could support almost a quarter million PCs using the Internet simultaneously, with each PC having four external connections. While no firm would push the number of connections this far, having 10 to 100 internal hosts for each external IP address is very common.

USING PRIVATE IP ADDRESSES To support NAT, the Internet Assigned Numbers Authority (IANA) has created three sets of **private IP address ranges** that can only be used *within* firms. These are the three ranges:

- 10.x.x.x
- 192.168.x.x
- 172.16.x.x through 172.31.x.x

The 192.168.x.x private IP address range is the most popular because it allows companies to use 255.255.0.0 and 255.255.255.0 network and subnet masks, respectively. These break at convenient 8-bit boundaries. However, the other two private IP address ranges are also widely used.

PROTOCOL PROBLEMS WITH NAT In terms of security and expanding IP effective address ranges, NAT is a simple and effective tool. However, some protocols cannot work across a NAT firewall or can work only with considerable difficulty. These include the popular IPsec cryptographic system in transport mode and several voice over IP (VoIP) protocols. The decision to use NAT must be made only after a careful assessment of protocols.

Test Your Understanding

2. a) What is NAT? (Do not just spell it out.) b) Describe NAT operation. c) What are the two benefits of NAT? d) How does NAT enhance security? e) How does NAT allow a firm to deal with a shortage of IP addresses given to it by its ISP? f) How are private IP address ranges used? g) What are the three ranges of private IP addresses? h) What problems may firms encounter when using NAT?

The Domain Name System (DNS)

As we saw in Chapter 1, if a user types in a target host's host name, the user's PC will contact its local Domain Name System (DNS) server. The DNS server will return the IP address for the target host or will contact other DNS servers to get this information. The user's PC can then send IP packets to the target host. In this chapter, we will look at DNS and its management in more detail.

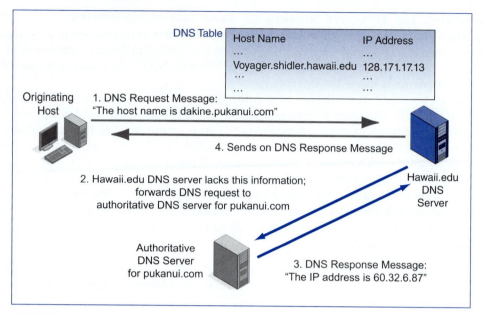

FIGURE 9-4 Domain Name System (DNS) Lookup

Figure 9-4 looks at how a DNS provides IP addresses when a host sends a request message containing a host name. In many cases, as we saw in Chapter 1, the local DNS server will know the IP address and send it back. In other cases, the local DNS host will not know the host's IP address. It must then find the **authoritative DNS server** for the domain in the host name. In the figure, dakine.pukanui.com's authoritative DNS server is authoritative for the pukanui.com domain. This DNS server will send the IP address to the local DNS server, which will pass the address on to the host that sent the DNS request.

WHAT IS A DOMAIN? Figure 9-5 shows that the **Domain Name System (DNS)** and its servers are not limited to providing IP addresses for host names. More generally, DNS is a general system for naming domains. A **domain** is any group of resources (routers, single networks, and hosts) under the control of an organization. The figure shows that domains are hierarchical, with host names being at the bottom of the hierarchy.

> A domain is any group of resources (routers, single networks, and hosts) under the control of an organization.

ROOT The domain name system is organized in a hierarchy. At the top of the DNS hierarchy is the root, which consists of all domain names. The overall control of the root, and therefore of the entire directory tree, is the Internet Corporation for Assigned Names and Numbers (ICAAN). There are 13 **root DNS servers** that keep overview information for the system.

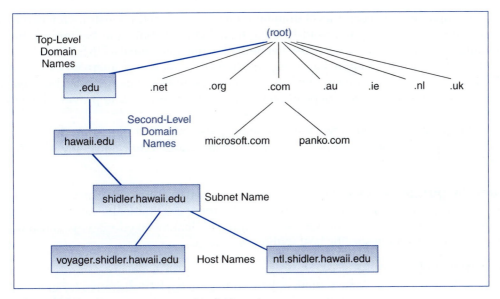

FIGURE 9-5 Domain Name System (DNS) Hierarchy

TOP-LEVEL DOMAINS Under the root are **top-level domains** that categorize the domain in one of two ways.

- **Country top-level domains** specify the country of the domain owner. Examples are .uk, .ca, .ie, .au, .jp, .nl, .tv, .md, and .ch.
- **Generic top-level domains (gTLDs)** specify that the domain is of a particular type. The first gTLDs included .com, .edu, .net, .info, .gov, and .org. Later, several more gTLDs were added, such as .name. In 2012, ICANN opened the naming system, permitting any organization to come forth with new generic top-level domains.

Note the distinction between the root and top-level domains. The root consists of all domains. It is not named as a level, however. If you are familiar with the UNIX operating system, the root directory concept is similar.

Also note that it is common for a domain to have two first-level designations, for instance, AAAA.com.ie. Most organizations, however, tend to use either a country TLD or a generic TLD.

SECOND-LEVEL DOMAINS Under first-level domains are **second-level domains**, which usually specify a particular organization (microsoft.com, hawaii.edu, cnn.com, etc.). Sometimes, however, specific products, such as movies, get their own second-level domain names. Competition for good second-level domain names is fierce. Organizations and individuals compete fiercely to get second-level domains because this is how the public will reach them.

Organizations and individuals compete fiercely to get second-level domains because this is how the public will reach them.

Companies get second-level domain names from domain registrars for nominal fees. However, getting a second-level domain name is only the beginning. Each organization that receives a second-level domain name must have a DNS server to host its domain name information. Large organizations have their own internal DNS servers that contain information on all subnet and host names. Individuals and small businesses that use webhosting services depend on the webhosting company to provide this DNS service.

In addition, a second-level domain name does nothing for the firm until the firm buys or rents a webserver, builds a website, and pays an ISP to connect the website to the Internet.

FURTHER QUALIFICATIONS Domains can be further qualified. For instance, within hawaii.edu, which is the University of Hawai`i, there is a shidler.hawaii.edu domain. This is the Shidler College of Business. Within shidler.hawaii.edu is voyager.shidler.hawaii.edu, which is a specific host within the college.

Test Your Understanding

3. a) Is the Domain Name System only used to send back IP addresses for given host names? Explain. b) What is a domain? c) Distinguish between the DNS root and first-level domains. d) What are the two types of top-level domains? e) Which level of domain name do corporations most wish to have? f) What are DNS root servers? g) How many DNS root servers are there? h) How does a company or individual obtain a second-level domain name? i) Why is getting a second-level domain name only the beginning?

DHCP Servers

In Chapter 1, we saw that client PCs usually get their IP addresses and other configuration information from DHCP servers. This means that they have current configuration information each time they boot up. It also means that they usually get a different IP address each time they boot up. In contrast, servers get static (permanent) IP addresses so that they have the same IP address all the time. This allows clients to find them.

In Chapter 1, we also saw that when a client PC wakes up, it realizes that it has no IP address. It broadcasts a Dynamic Host Configuration Protocol (DHCP) message to all nearby hosts. Only the DHCP server responds.

Figure 9-6 shows that the situation actually is a bit more complex. As the figure shows, there may be multiple DHCP servers, and each will send a response back to the client PC. These initial responses do not carry configuration information. Rather, they are offers of what configuration a DHCP server will provide, including the length of time a PC may use its IP address before surrendering it and starting another DHCP search to get a new IP address.

The user selects among the offers and sends back an acceptance message to the "winning" DHCP server. That server responds with the configuration information. If there is only a single DHCP server, the client PC still goes through the seek–offer–accept–receive cycle. So the DHCP discussion in Chapter 1 was a simplification.

Which of a firm's DHCP servers will respond to an initial DHCP request? The answer is that each DHCP server has a DHCP scope parameter that lists the subnets to which it will respond with an offer.

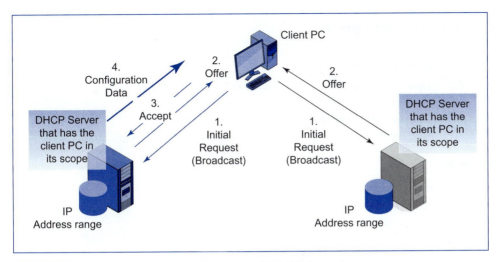

FIGURE 9-6 Dynamic Host Configuration Protocol (DHCP) Operation

The fact that several DHCP servers may respond can provide redundancy and therefore reliability. However, companies must manage each DHCP server's scope and list of available IP addresses carefully.

In addition, when a firm changes its DNS servers to another IP address, changes its subnet masks, or makes any other changes that will affect client PC configuration, it must push these changes out to all DHCP servers.

Test Your Understanding

4. a) What hosts are given static IP addresses? b) Why do these hosts need static IP addresses? c) What are dynamic IP addresses? d) How do clients get dynamic IP addresses? e) Can the client send a DHCP request information to multiple DHCP servers? f) Do DHCP servers update the configuration information they store automatically? g) What are DHCP scopes?

Simple Network Management Protocol (SNMP)

We saw the *Simple Network Management Protocol (SNMP)* in the first chapter and in several chapters since. We will now look at it in a little more detail.

CORE SNMP ELEMENTS   In Chapter 1, we saw that SNMP has several components.

- The network administrator works at a central computer that runs a program called the network management program, or, more simply, the manager.
- The SNMP manager is responsible for many managed devices—devices that need to be administered, such as printers, switches, routers, and other devices.
- Managed devices have pieces of software (and sometimes hardware) called network management agents, or, more simply, agents. SNMP agents communicate with the SNMP manager on behalf of their managed devices. In other words, the manager does not communicate with the managed device directly, but rather with the device's agent.

Core Elements (from Chapter 1)

Manager program

Managed device

Agents (communicate with the manager on behalf of the managed device)

Management information base (MIB)

Stores the retrieved information

"MIB" can refer to either the database on the manager or on the database schema

Messages

Commands

Get

Set

Responses

Traps (alarms sent by agents)

SNMP use UDP at the transport layer to minimize the burden on the network

RMON Probes

Remote monitoring probes

A special type of agent

Collects data for a part of the network

Supplies this information to the manager

Objects (see Figure 10-19)

Information about which information is stored

Number of rows in the routing table

Number of discards caused by lack of resources (indicates a need for an upgrade)

Set Commands

Dangerous if used by attackers

Many firms disable set to thwart such attacks

However, they give up the ability to manage remote resources without travel

SNMPv1: community string shared by the manager and all devices

SNMPv3: each manager–agent pair has a different password

User Functionality

Reports, diagnostics tools, etc. are very important

They are not built into the standard

They are added by SNMP manager vendors

Critical in selection

FIGURE 9-7 Simple Network Management Protocol (SNMP) (Study Figure)

- The manager stores information it receives in a central management information base (MIB). The term *MIB* is somewhat ambiguous because it can refer either to the database itself or to the design (schema) of the database.

To work together, these devices send messages to one another.

- The manager can send commands to the agent, telling the agent what to do. Agents send responses confirming that the command was fulfilled or explaining why it could not be fulfilled.
- *Get* commands ask for a specific piece of information. In practice, the manager constantly polls all of its managed devices, collecting many pieces of data from each in every round of polling.
- *Set* commands tell the agent to change the way the device operates, say by going into self-test mode.
- If an agent detects a problem, it can send a trap (alarm) message to the manager without waiting passively to be asked.
- These commands are sent via UDP to reduce the traffic burden on the network. This leads to occasional errors, but single errors only mean that a few pieces of information are a few seconds or minutes out of date.
- In addition, there is a specialized type of agent called an **RMON probe** (remote monitoring probe). This may be a stand-alone device or software running on a switch or router. An RMON probe collects data on network traffic passing through its location instead of information about the RMON probe itself. The manager can poll the RMON probe to get summarized information about the distribution of packet sizes, the number of various types of errors, the number of packets processed, the 10 most active hosts, and other statistical summaries that may help pinpoint problems. This generates far less network management traffic than polling many devices individually.

The SNMP MIB schema is organized as a hierarchy of **objects** (properties of managed devices). Figure 9-8 shows the basic model for organizing SNMP objects. First, there is the system. This might be a computer, switch, router, or another device. In addition, there are TCP, UDP, IP, and ICMP objects and objects for individual interfaces. Each of these objects has sub-objects under it, and those sub-objects may have further sub-sub-objects.

For example, if a router does not appear to be working properly, the manager can issue **Get** commands to collect appropriate router objects. A first step might be to check if the router is in forwarding mode. If not, it will not route packets. If this does not clarify the problem, the manager can collect more information, including error statistics and general traffic statistics of various types.

The **Set** command is even more powerful. The manager can use a Set command to tell an agent to change the configuration of a managed device. If a router interface seems to be malfunctioning, the manager can have the interface put into testing mode or even turned off. Set commands can also turn off interfaces to avoid using expensive transmission lines when existing less expensive lines can be used. The Set command can send even more detailed commands, for instance, changing how long an interface waits before sending a retransmission because no acknowledgment has been received. By allowing administrators to manage devices remotely, the Set command can save companies a great deal of money by avoiding travel to fix problems.

System Objects

System name
System description
System contact person
System uptime (since last reboot)

IP Objects

Forwarding (for routers). Yes if forwarding (routing), No if not
Subnet mask
Default time to live
Traffic statistics
Number of discards because of resource limitations
Number of discards because could not find route
Number of rows in routing table
Rows discarded because of lack of space
Individual row data

TCP Objects

Maximum/minimum retransmission time
Maximum number of TCP connections allowed
Opens/failed connections/resets
Segments sent
Segments retransmitted
Errors in incoming segments
No open port errors
Data on individual connections (sockets, states)

UDP Objects

Error: no application on requested port
Traffic statistics

ICMP Objects

Number of errors of various types

Interface Objects (One per Interface)

Type (e.g., 69 is 100Base-FX; 71 is 802.11)
Status: up/down/testing
Speed
MTU (maximum transmission unit—the maximum packet size)
Traffic statistics: octets, unicast/broadcast/multicast packets
Errors: discards, unknown protocols, etc.

FIGURE 9-8 SNMP Hierarchical Object Model

SET COMMANDS AND SNMP SECURITY Unfortunately, most firms are very reluctant to use Set commands because of security dangers. If setting is permitted and attackers learn how to send Set commands to managed devices, the results could be catastrophic. Fortunately, SNMP security has improved over time.

- The original version of SNMP, SNMPv1, had almost no authentication at all, making this danger a distinct possibility. The manager and all managed devices merely had to be configured with the same secret **community name**. With hundreds or thousands of devices sharing the same community name, if attackers can learn the community name, they can implement massive attacks. Of course, "everybody" knows the community name, so there is usually little effort to keep it secret.
- SNMPv3 has added passwords for each manager–agent pair, and these pairwise passwords are used to authenticate and encrypt transmissions. This requires a great deal of work to set up, but it is the only way to secure SNMP.

Most products today permit two SNMPv3 passwords for each manager–device pair. One is for *Get* commands and the other is for the more dangerous *Set* commands.

Of course, poor implementation can defeat SNMPv3 security. If a lazy administrator uses the same password for all manager–agent pairs, then this is no better security than community strings.

USER INTERFACE FUNCTIONALITY Collecting data in the MIB is worthless if there is no good way to get it out. All SNMP manager products have the ability to produce reports, diagnose problems, and do many other things that network administrators need to manage networks.

This functionality is not built into the standard. The standard just handles the mechanics of collecting and storing object data from managed devices. User interface functionality is a critical factor in selecting SNMP products.

Test Your Understanding

5. a) List the main elements in a network management system. b) Does the manager communicate directly with the managed device? Explain. c) Explain the difference between managed devices and objects. d) Is the MIB a schema or the actual database? (This is a trick question.) e) Why must user interface functionality for the SNMP manager be considered carefully in selecting SNMP manager products?
6. List one object in each of the following areas: the system, IP, TCP, UDP, ICMP, and an interface.
7. a) In SNMP, which device creates commands? b) Responses? c) Traps? d) Explain the two types of commands. e) What is a trap? f) Why are firms often reluctant to use *Set* commands? g) Describe SNMPv1's poor authentication method. h) Describe SNMPv3's good authentication method.

MULTIPROTOCOL LABEL SWITCHING

Making Routing More Efficient

In Chapter 8, we looked at how routers handle IP packets. They look at an incoming packet's destination IP address. They then compare that IP address to every row in the routing table, select the best match, and send the packet back out a certain port to a

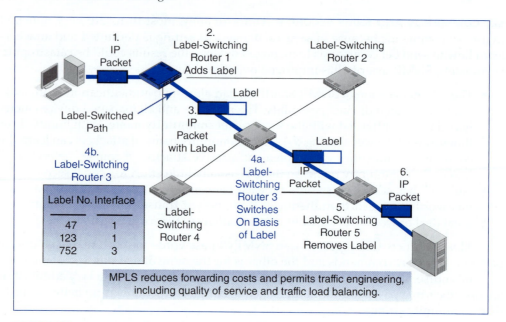

FIGURE 9-9 Multiprotocol Label Switching (MPLS)

certain IP address. The next packet to arrive gets the same treatment—*even if it is going to the same IP address*.

We also noted that many router vendors do decision caching, in which they remember their decisions for certain IP address ranges. We noted that this is somewhat dangerous. Fortunately, there is a more systematic way to avoid having to look at all rows for all packets. This is the **Multiprotocol Label Switching (MPLS)** standard, which Figure 9-9 illustrates.

MPLS Operation

When two hosts begin to communicate, an MPLS network does not immediately send packets. Instead, it determines the best path for the packets. This best path is called the **label-switched path**. This is what gives MPLS its advantages. It may be slow to select a label-switched path at the beginning of a conversation, but we will see that MPLS handles each subsequent packet very quickly.

As Figure 9-9 shows, the source host sends an ordinary IP packet during the rest of the conversation. The router to which the source host connects is a label-switching router. This router places a **label header** in front of the IP header (and after the frame header). Note that this means that there is no need to change either the IP packet syntax or the frame syntax. The label header is simply pushed into place between the frame header and the IP header.

The label header has a **label number** that identifies the label-switched path previously selected for packets in this conversation. The first label-switched router and all others along the label-switching path have a simple MPLS look-up table. This table allows the label-switched router to look up the label number, read the corresponding interface, and send the packet out the indicated interface. For example, if the label number is 47, the router in Figure 9-9 will send it out Interface 1. There is no need to look at many regular routing table rows to select the best interface to send a packet back out. That work was already done when the label-switched path was selected.

Each label-switched router along the way repeats this simple look-up process and forwards the packet on its way. The last label-switched router removes the label, because the destination host does not need it. Note that neither the source host nor the destination host knows that label switching was done.

All packets between two host IP addresses might be assigned the same label number. More likely, all traffic between two *sites* might be assigned a single label number because it would all be going to and from the same site.

Benefits of Label Switching

MPLS offers three major benefits: cost reduction, quality of service, and traffic engineering.

LABEL SWITCHING FOR COST REDUCTION   MPLS is much faster than traditional routing calculations because there is only a single row for each label number. This simplicity dramatically lowers the cost of routing.

QUALITY OF SERVICE   Lowering routing costs is the main attraction of MPLS, but there are other advantages as well. One is quality of service. Traffic flowing between two sites might be assigned different label numbers. One label number might be for VoIP, which is latency-intolerant, and the other might be for latency-tolerant traffic between the sites. For latency-intolerant traffic, it is even possible to reserve capacity at routers along the selected path. This gives full quality of service.

TRAFFIC ENGINEERING   MPLS can also be used for **traffic engineering**, that is, to manage how traffic will travel through the network. One capability is **load balancing**, that is, to move some traffic from a heavily congested link between two routers to an alternative route that uses different and less-congested links. MPLS does this by setting up multiple label-switched routes ahead of time and by sending traffic based on the congestion along different label-switched routes.

MPLS Boundaries

Corporations can use MPLS internally, and most ISPs now use MPLS for their internal traffic, but it is currently impossible to implement MPLS across the entire Internet because of coordination difficulties among the ISPs.

Test Your Understanding

8. a) In MPLS, is selecting the best interface for each packet done when the packet enters the network or before? b) What is the name of the path selected for a particular conversation? c) When a source host first transmits to a destination host, what will happen? d) Do label-switching routers along the MPLS path look at the packet's IP address? Explain your reasoning. e) Why is MPLS decision making fast compared to traditional routing? f) On what does each label-switched router base routing decisions? g) Why is MPLS transparent to the source and destination hosts? h) What is MPLS's main attraction? i) What are its other attractions? j) What is traffic engineering? k) Can MPLS provide traffic load balancing? l) Is it possible to implement MPLS on the entire Internet?

SECURING INTERNET TRANSMISSION

When the Internet was first created, little thought was given to security. As Jon Postel, who edited the main Internet RFCs, explained to the first author, "It just wasn't a problem then, and we were stretched thin." Today, however, Internet security is very much a pressing issue. Companies are beginning to address the security of transmissions across the Internet (and within site networks as well) by using IPsec virtual private networks.

Virtual Private Networks

Figure 9-10 shows that corporations can cryptographically protect traffic flowing between two sites or between a site and a remote user. They can do this by using a **virtual private network (VPN)**, which is a cryptographically secured transmission path through an untrusted environment. Although the firm is using a shared network, it appears to be alone, as far as security is concerned. The Internet is not the only untrusted network, but it is by far the largest.

A virtual private network (VPN) is a cryptographically secured transmission path through an untrusted environment.

Figure 9-10 shows a **remote access VPN** connecting a remote user to a site and a **site-to-site VPN** that connects two corporate sites.

A remote access VPN connects a remote user to a site.

A site-to-site VPN connects two corporate sites.

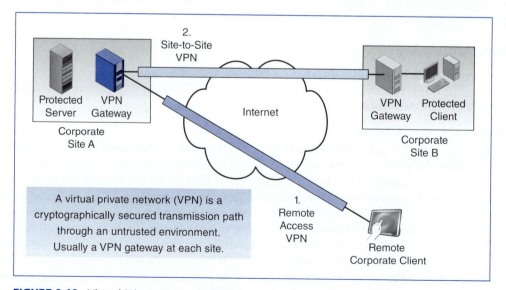

FIGURE 9-10 Virtual Private Networks (VPNs)

- Remote access VPNs are attractive because single hosts trying to connect to a corporate site via the Internet are extremely vulnerable. They are even more vulnerable if they connect to their network wirelessly.
- Site-to-site VPNs protect all traffic flowing between a pair of sites. Typically, sites have heavy traffic between themselves, so site-to-site VPNs tend to carry much more traffic than remote access VPNs.

Both remote-access VPNs and site-to-site VPNs usually terminate in a **VPN gateway** at a site. This VPN gateway handles cryptographic protections when dealing with remote users or a VPN gateway at another site.

IPsec VPNS

For security over the Internet, the Internet Engineering Task force created a family of standards collectively called **IP security (IPsec)**.[2] As its name suggests, IPsec operates at the internet layer. It provides security to all content at the internet, transport, and application layers.[3] This protection is **transparent**, meaning that nothing additional has to be done to protect upper-layer content and that all upper-layer content is protected. By securing packets and their contents, the IETF provided a single mechanism to protect TCP/IP traffic.

IPsec operates at the internet layer. It provides security to all content at the internet, transport, and application layers.

IPsec offers the strongest security and should eventually dominate remote access VPN transmission, site-to-site VPN transmission, and internal site IP transmission. However, IPsec networks are fairly complex to manage and therefore relatively expensive.

IPsec Transport Mode

Figure 9-11 shows IPsec's two modes of operation. In **transport mode**, the two computers that are communicating implement IPsec. This mode gives strong end-to-end security, but it requires IPsec configuration *and* a digital certificate on all machines. Although the cost per machine for configuration and for the digital certificate is small, the large number of computers in a company makes the aggregate cost of transport mode setup high.

IPsec Tunnel Mode

In contrast, in **tunnel mode**, the IPsec connection extends only between *IPsec gateways* at the two sites. This provides no protection within sites, but the use of tunnel mode IPsec gateways offers simple security. The two hosts do not have to implement IPsec

---

[2]*IPsec* is pronounced "eye-pea-sek," with emphasis on the *sek*.
[3]Actuall y, the term *all* is a bit too strong. In transport mode, which is discussed later, attackers can read the IP addresses because the packet is addressed to the destination host instead of to the IPsec gateway server. However, on exams, call it *all*.

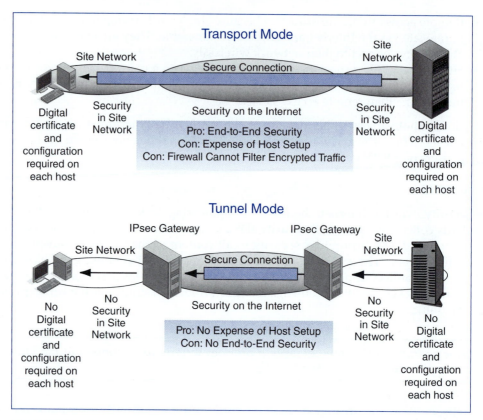

FIGURE 9-11 IPsec in Transport Mode and Tunnel Mode

security and, in fact, do not even have to know that IPsec is being used between the IPsec gateways. Most importantly, there is no need to install digital certificates on individual hosts. Only the two IPsec gateways need to have IPsec configuration and digital certificates. Tunnel mode minimizes costs but provides no protection for the traffic within the sites.

Remote-Access and Site-to-Site VPNs

IPsec is a versatile protocol that can be used simultaneously for both remote-access VPNs and site-to-site VPNs. Coupled with its ability to protect all upper-layer content transparently, IPsec is a general solution for a firm's cryptographic protection needs.

IPsec Security Associations and Policy Servers

One advantage of IPsec as a VPN technology is that it can be centrally managed. Figure 9-12 shows that before two IPsec gateways begin to communicate, they negotiate how they will perform security. The **security associations (SAs)** they negotiate specify what security options they will use.

The figure shows that the gateways implement an association in each direction. If security conditions require it, these SAs can use different security options. For example,

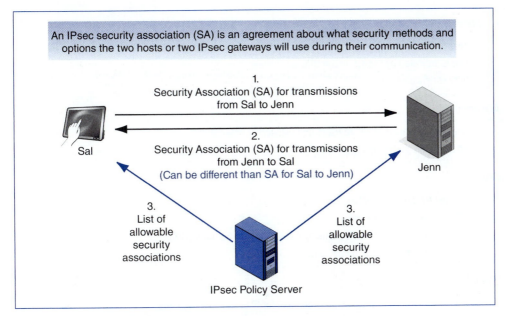

An IPsec security association (SA) is an agreement about what security methods and options the two hosts or two IPsec gateways will use during their communication.

1.
Security Association (SA) for transmissions
from Sal to Jenn

Sal

2.
Security Association (SA) for transmissions
from Jenn to Sal
(Can be different than SA for Sal to Jenn)

Jenn

3.
List of
allowable
security
associations

3.
List of
allowable
security
associations

IPsec Policy Server

FIGURE 9-12   IPsec Security Associations (SAs) and IPsec Policy Servers

for a remote user, a remote access might have a stronger security association from the IPsec gateway to the user than from the user to the IPsec gateway

As we saw in Chapter 3, some security options are very strong. Others may not be. With IPsec, companies can use central **IPsec policy servers**. These servers specify what SA options are allowable for various gateway pairs and what options must not be used. Policy servers are especially important if a firm has many IPsec gateways.

Test Your Understanding

9. a) At what layer does IPsec operate? b) What layers does IPsec protect? c) Does IPsec protect these layers transparently? d) Describe IPsec tunnel mode. e) What is the main advantage of tunnel mode? f) What is the main disadvantage of tunnel mode? g) Describe IPsec transport mode. h) What is the main advantage of transport mode? i) What is the main disadvantage of transport mode? j) In which IPsec mode are clients and servers required to have digital certificates? k) Which IPsec mode does not require clients and servers to have digital certificates? l) Is IPsec used for remote-access VPNs, site-to-site VPNs, or both?

10. a) In IPsec, what are security associations (SAs)? b) Must security associations be the same in the two directions? c) Describe how IPsec gateways can be managed centrally to ensure that weak SAs are not permitted.

SSL/TLS VPNs

Although IPsec is an enormously powerful tool for creating highly secure VPNs, IPsec is expensive to implement. For many networked applications, companies build remote-access VPNs using the SSL/TLS security protocols. These protocols are far less expensive to implement.

Purpose

> To provide a secure connection between a browser to a webserver applications on a webserver host
>
> Use is indicated by https:// in the URL
>
> Very widely used

Attraction

> Universally supported by browsers and webserver applications
>
> So no added cost to use it!

Origin

> Created by Netscape as SSL
>
> IETF took over the standard
>
> IETF changed the standard's name to Transport Layer Security (TLS)
>
> We refer to the standard, generically, as SSL/TLS

Limitations

> Operates at transport layer so no protection for IP or transport headers
>
> Limited to applications written to work with SSL/TLS: HTTP and e-mail, primarily
>
> Cryptographically weaker than IPsec
>
> No policy servers for centralized management

Overall

> Good quality, cheap, and easy security
>
> Only a first step in providing TCP/IP security

FIGURE 9-13 SSL/TLS VPNs (Study Figure)

You have personally used these protocols. In fact, you probably used them today. If you have ever purchased something online, your URL at some point began with https://. The *s* signified that the transaction was secure. It meant that your traffic was secured with the SSL/TLS protocols. In addition, if you use a webmail e-mail service, it is likely that all communication between you and the webserver from which you get your mail is secured by SSL/TLS.

The SSL protocol was developed by Netscape, which produced the first popular browser. Right from the start, the Netscape browser was capable of using SSL. Webservers capable of using SSL merely had to turn on their SSL functionality to be able to work securely with browsers. Soon, all browsers and webserver programs were capable of SSL security. With SSL on all browsers around the world, creating security for a webserver administrator is a simple task that requires brief configuration of the server and no configuration whatsoever on the browser itself. This automaticity makes SSL very inexpensive and simple to use. Many corporations routinely protect all webserver traffic with SSL.

Eventually, Netscape turned over the standardization of SSL to the IETF. The Task Force improved the standard and called its versions Transport Layer Security (TLS). We refer to the standards family generically as SSL/TLS.

Although SSL/TLS works automatically, it is not a substitute for IPsec. As the name Transport Layer Security suggests, SSL/TLS works at the transport layer. It provides no protection for IP packet headers at all. In addition, SSL/TLS only works with some networked applications. It is used almost universally with webservers, and it is used widely by e-mail programs, but there are many applications that are not written to work with SSL/TLS.

In addition, SSL/TLS provides weaker cryptographic security than IPsec. It also has nothing like IPsec policy servers that allows a firm to centrally manage its SSL/TLS security. Overall, SSL/TLS offers good quality, cheap, and easy security. However, most firms view it primarily as a first step in providing general TCP/IP security.

Test Your Understanding

11. a) For what application was SSL/TLS created? b) Why is it attractive? c) Distinguish between SSL and TLS. d) What are its four limitations?

MANAGING IP VERSION 6 (IPV6)

In this chapter, we have looked at managing IPv4. IPv6 has the same management needs. In this section, we will focus on important differences in managing IPv4 and IPv6.

Internet Layer Protocol Stacks

The internet layer sits between the transport layer and the data link layer. As Figure 9-14 illustrates, there has traditionally been a single internet layer process sitting between a host's transport layer process and its data link layer process. The internet layer process is called an **internet layer protocol stack** because it handles more than the internet protocol (IP). For example, it also handles the internet control message protocol (ICMP) and, in the case of IPv4, the address resolution protocol (ARP). It is usually called, simply, the *IP stack*.

Figure 9-14 shows that there was only a single IP stack on hosts originally—the **IPv4 stack**. The coming of IPv6 created two more alternatives.

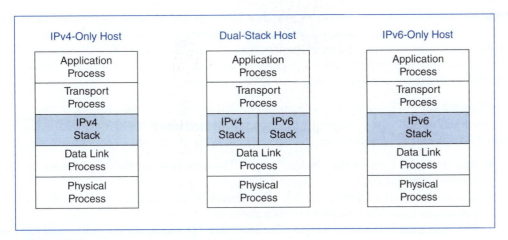

FIGURE 9-14 Internet Layer Protocol Stacks

- One is for hosts to have a single **IPv6 stack** instead of a single IPv4 stack.
- The other is to have a **dual-stack** host with both IPv4 and IPv6 stacks. This allows the host to transmit either IPv4 or IPv6 packets and to execute IPv4 or IPv6 internet layer protocols as needed.

The Internet Engineering Task Force expected that dual-stack implementation would become the norm. This would allow the gradual replacement of IPv4 by IPv6. However, the exhaustion of IPv4 addresses has created a growing number of hosts that have a single IPv6 stack and no IPv4 stack. In addition, although IPv6 was defined in the 1990s, many vendors still sell operating systems that have the IPv46 stack turned off and not trivially turned on, weak IPv6 stacks that cause problems if turned on, and sometimes, as in the case of Apple's Version 6 airport product released in January 2012, no IPv6 stack at all. As we will see in this section, these unexpected developments have caused problems for companies that wish to offer IPv6 service internally and externally.

Test Your Understanding

12. a) What does it mean for a host to have a dual stack for IP? b) Why is it desirable to have a dual stack? c) Why is having only an IPv6 stack problematic?

IPv6 Subnetting

Earlier in this chapter, we looked at IPv4 subnetting. Subnetting in IPv6 is similar, but 128-bit addresses change the situation considerably. Figure 9-15 summarizes some of the key changes.

IPV6 GLOBAL UNICAST ADDRESSES   Earlier in this chapter, we looked at IPv4 addresses. These were really unicast addresses—addresses for packets going from one host to another. We saw that IPv4 unicast addresses have three parts—a host part, a subnet part, and a network part. Although the total length is always 32 bits, the lengths of the three parts are all variable.

These IPv4 addresses are normally public, meaning that they can be used on the Internet. In contrast, private IPv4 addresses can be used only within a corporate site or home network.

GLOBAL ADDRESSES   We will now see that **IPv6 global unicast addresses** are organized in the same way. As noted in Figure 9-15, *global* means that packets with such addresses can be transmitted over the Internet. This is like public IP addresses in IPv4. The term *global unicast IPv6 address* is long, so we will call them, simply, *IPv6 addresses*. Module A discusses some other types of IPv6 addresses.

THE THREE PARTS   Figure 9-15 also illustrates how IPv6 addresses are organized. The figure shows that IPv6 addresses, like IPv4 addresses, are divided into three parts. IPv6 documentation does not use the terms *host part*, *subnet part*, and *network part*, but it uses similar concepts.

- The network part is the *routing prefix*. The **routing prefix** lets routers on the Internet route packets to an organization.
- The subnet part is the *subnet ID*. The **subnet ID** lets routers within a firm route packets to individual subnets within the firm.
- The host part is the *Interface ID*. The **interface ID** identifies an individual host in the firm.

IPv6 Global Unicast Addresses

Like IPv4 public addresses

Terminology

IPv6 Address Part	Corresponding IPv4 Address Part	Length
Routing Prefix	Network Part	Variable
Subnet ID	Subnet Part	Variable
Interface ID	Host Part	64 bits
Total	32 bits	128 bits

Routing Prefix and Subnet ID

Total length is 64 bits

If the routing prefix is 20 bits, the subnet ID must be 44 bits long

A longer routing prefix means a smaller subnet ID and therefore fewer subnets

A shorter routing prefix means a larger subnet ID and therefore more subnets

Creating the 64-Bit Interface ID

MAC addresses are only 48 bits long

Too short for 64-bit interface IDs

The IEEE has defined a way of creating 64-bit extended unique identifiers (EUI-64s) from 48-bit MAC addresses

These can be used as interface IDs

Creating EUI-64s

1. Begin with the MAC in hexadecimal notation
2. Divide the 48 bits into two halves (24 bits each)
3. Insert **fffe** between the two halves
4. Write all three into four-hex groups separated by :s
5. Flip the second-least significant bit in the first octet

FIGURE 9-15   IPv6 Subnetting

The size of the Interface ID in global unicast IPv6 addresses is fixed at 64 bits. It may seem wasteful to "use up" half of all bits in the IPv6 addresses to designate a host. However, with 64 bits left for the routing prefix and the subnet ID, there are still 1.8×10^{19} possibilities for the routing the network and host parts.

The size of the Interface ID in global unicast IPv6 addresses is fixed at 64 bits.

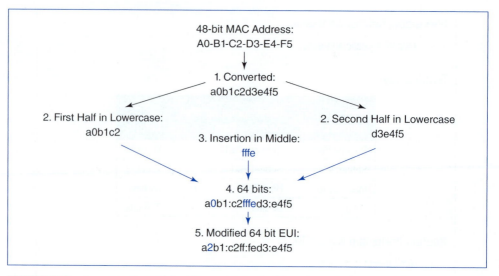

FIGURE 9-16 Converting a MAC address into an EUI-64

ROUTING PREFIX AND SUBNET ID Figure 9-15 indicates that the routing prefix and subnet ID are variable in length, although their total must be 64 bits because the interface ID has already consumed 64 of the 128 bits. To give an example, if the routing prefix is 20 bits, the subnet ID must be 44 bits. If an address registrar gives a firm a small routing prefix, then the company can have a large subnet ID and can therefore have many subnets. Smaller firms, needing fewer subnets, are given a larger routing prefix.

CREATING THE 64-BIT INTERFACE ID It would be nice to be able to use a host's link layer address as the interface ID. However, the most common type of link layer address is the MAC address, which is only 48 bits long. Fortunately, the IEEE 802 Committee has defined a way to create a 64-bit **Extended Unique Identifier (EUI-64)** from a 48-bit MAC address.[4] This EUI-64 can go into the interface ID field.

Creating an EUI-64 from a MAC address requires five steps, which are illustrated in Figure 9-16. These steps are straightforward, and there are good technical reasons for each step. However, without a lot of in-depth knowledge, which frankly is not worth learning for information systems professionals, these five steps can appear to be illogical and weird. Just think of them as a mystical protocol for joining an obscure secret society.

- First, if the MAC address is displayed in hexadecimal notation, the dashes are removed from the MAC address, and the letters are changed to lowercase. So A0-B1-C2-D3-E4-F5 becomes a0b1c2d3e4f5.
- Second, the 48 bits are divided into two half. Each half has 24 bits. In this case, the first half is a0b1c2 and the second half is d3e4f5.

----

[4]The IEEE has actually deprecated the term *MAC address* for the term *extended unique identifier (UI)*. More specifically, the traditional MAC address is called an EUI-48. The 64-bit version is called the EUI-64.

- Third, the hex symbol *fffe* is inserted between the two halves.[5] This gives a0b1c2**fffe**d3e4f5. (The fffe is blue for easier reading in this example).
- Fourth, the first half, the new group, and the second half are written together and regrouped into four fields with four hex symbols apiece. These fields are separated by colons. This gives the result: a0b1:c2ff:fed3:e4f5. Notice that a colon separates the ff and the fe. Use this as a cross-check to make sure you have done things right.
- Fifth, the *second least-significant bit* (the second bit from the right end) in the first octet is inverted. For example, the MAC address in our example begins with A0. These two hex symbols constitute the first octet. In binary, they are 10100000. This must be changed to 10100010 by inverting the *second* least-significant bit.[6] This gives A2 instead of A0. So the final EUI-64 is a2b1:c2ff:fed3:e4f5.

There may be some fields that begin with one or more zeroes. It may be tempting to reduce them now. However, this should not be done until the rest of the IPv6 address is created, including the routing prefix and the interface ID.

Test Your Understanding

13. a) What field in an IPv6 global unicast address corresponds to the network part of a public IPv4 unicast address? b) What field in an IPv6 global unicast address corresponds to the subnet part of a public IPv4 unicast address? c) If the subnet ID is 16 bits long (as it often is), how long is the routing prefix? d) If you are a large company, do you want a large routing prefix or a small routing prefix?

14. a) What field in a global unicast IP address corresponds to the host part of a public unicast IPv4 address? b) How long is this field? c) What are these addresses called? d) Convert the following MAC address to an EUI-64 address: AA-00-00-FF-FF-00. e) Repeat for this MAC address: 9B-E5-33-21-FF-0D.

IPv6 Configuration

When a client host boots up, it needs an IP address to use as its own address. It also needs other configuration information, such as the IP address of its default router. A client with a dual IP stack needs configuration information for each stack.

DHCPv6 AUTOCONFIGURATION An IPv4 client uses a DHCP server to get an IPv4 address and other configuration information. IPv6 clients, in turn, can use DHCPv6 servers to obtain similar configuration information for the IPv6 stack.

STATELESS AUTOCONFIGURATION However, unlike IPv4 clients, IPv6 clients also have a second way to obtain an IPv6 address for themselves. This is **stateless auto-configuration**. In stateless autoconfiguration, the client host creates an IP address by itself. No DHCP server is needed—only a router configured to support stateless autoconfiguration.

There are two phases in stateless autoconfiguration:

---

[5]It just is.
[6]See previous footnote.

Configuration

When a client boots up, it needs an IP address and other configuration information

A client with a dual IP stack needs configuration information for both

DHCPv6 Configuration

IPv4 clients request configuration parameters from DHCP servers

IPv6 clients can do this with DHCPv6 servers

Stateless Autoconfiguration

IPv6 defines another way to do client configuration for the IPv6 stack

The client configures itself, without using a DHCPv6 server

First, the client creases a link-local IPv6 address

Second, the client creates a global unicast IPv6 address

Creating the Link-Local IPv6 Addresses

Link-local IPv6 addresses can be used only within a single network (wireless or switched wired)

If the client does not need a global IP address, the autoconfiguration process can stop here

Creating the link-local address

First create a 64-bit interface ID using the MAC address of the client

Add a routing prefix 111 1110 10 followed by 56 bits of zeroes

This is the link-local IP address: *fe80::x*, where *x* is the octets of the EUI-64

Testing the link-local address

Another host may be using this address

So the client uses the ICMPv6 neighbor discovery protocol to ask if any other host in the single network is using this address

If none reply, the client may use this address within its single network

Creating the Global Unicast IPv6 Address

Needed for communication over the Internet

Begin with the link-local address

Keep the interface ID but get a new routing prefix and subnet ID

Client sends an ICMPv6 *router solicitation* message to the address FFF02::1

Routers respond with IPv6 *router advertisement* messages

The router advisor message may state that autoconfiguration is not allowed

If this is not the case, the message gives the routing prefix and subnet ID

The client now has a global unicast IPv6 address

Limits and Uses

More limited than traditional DHCP autoconfiguration

At a minimum, router advertisement messages give only a routing prefix and subnet ID

Of course, the packet gives the IPv6 address of the router, which becomes the default router

(continued)

FIGURE 9-17 IPv6 Configuration (Study Figure)

Uses

How can a client get other IPv6 configuration information?

If a client is dual-stack client, the IPv4 stack can obtain full configuration information, which the IPv6 stack can use

If the client is not a dual-stack client, it needs at least one more piece of configuration information—the IPv6 addresses of DNS servers

The IETF has extended router advertisement messages to provide the IPv6 addresses of DNS servers

However, this is only an option

Known security weaknesses

An attacker might create an address that does not use its proper EUI-64

An attacker may create an address that uses the EUI-64 of another host to impersonate it

Several operations can be used to create flooding denial-of-service attacks

IPv6 Address Renumbering

Stateless autoconfiguration may be used to renumber all IP addresses in a firm automatically, changing subnet IDs and even routing prefixes

FIGURE 9-17   Continued

- The first is to create a **link-local** IPv6 address, which can be used only within the client's single network (switched wired or wireless). If the client does not have to communicate with hosts outside this single network, the autoconfiguration process can stop here.
- The second is to create a global unicast IPv6 address. This second step requires information from a router. This step is necessary if the client wishes to communicate beyond its single network, even with hosts on different single networks within a firm.

CREATING A LINK-LOCAL UNICAST IPv6 ADDRESS   To create a **link-local** IPv6 address, the client does not have to look outside itself. It creates an EUI-64 from its link address, as discussed earlier in this section. This becomes the final 64 bits of its link-local IPv6 address. For the first 64 bits, the client uses a string created specifically for link-local unicast addresses. The first 10 bits are *1111 1110 10*. The next 54 are *0*s. Therefore, the link local address is *fe80::EUI-64* after the 0s in the middle are taken out.

There is the danger, albeit slight, that another host on the network is already using this address. Therefore, the client should use the ICMPv6 **neighbor discovery protocol** to ask if any other host is using the link-local unicast IPv6 address it has created. If no host replies that it is using this address, the client may use this link-local unicast IP address to communicate with other hosts on its single network.

CREATING A GLOBAL UNICAST IPv6 ADDRESS   If the client wishes to communicate outside its single network, it needs help from a router configured to provide this kind of help.

- The client transmits an ICMPv6 **router solicitation** message to the *FF02::1* multicast address. All routers should read this message.
- One or more routers will respond with an ICMPv6 **router advertisement** message.
- The client reads the router advertisement message to determine if it may use stateless autoconfiguration. (The advertisement message may prohbit this.)
- If stateless autoconfiguration is permitted, the router advertisement gives the client the routing prefix and subnet ID for the client's subnet. The client replaces the fe80:: link-local prefix with the routing prefix and subnet ID it has just received. The client now has an IPv6 global unicast address.

Now that the client has a global unicast IPv6 address, it may communicate with all hosts available on the Internet.

LIMIT AND USES   Although stateless autoconfiguration reduces costs compared to traditional DHCP configuration, it is limited. Most importantly, it offers only very limited configuration information. At a minimum, it provides only two pieces of information. The first is a routing prefix plus subnet ID. The second is the IPv6 address of the router that sent it the router advertisement message. This becomes the IPv6 address of the client's default router.

Stateless autoconfiguration, without options, only provides the client with an IPv6 address and gives the client the IPv6 address of a default router.

How is the client to find DNS servers, network time protocol servers, and other servers it may need? In some cases, the client will *not need additional configuration parameters*. If the client is a dual-stack client, it can begin by doing DHCP configuration for its IPv4 stack. The IPv6 stack has access to this configuration information. In this case, stateless autoconfiguration of the IPv6 stack is fine.

Stateless autoconfiguration is especially attractive for nomadic environments that have many clients coming and going frequently. An example of this is a Wi-Fi hot spot. For some clients, basic IPv6 router advertisement messages will contain all the information they need.

Most, however, will also need another critical piece of configuration information—the IP addresses of DNS servers. Without this, clients cannot browse the Internet and do other things by host name. To address this concern, the IETF has created an option for including DNS server addresses in router advertisement messages. However, this is only an option. Many routers and clients do not implement it yet, and many never will.

In addition, it has known security issues. For instance, a host may decide not to create an EUI-64 based on its link layer address, in order to be anonymous. It may even use an EUI-64 that would allow it to impersonate another client. In addition, several of the interactions in stateless autoconfiguration are susceptible to flooding denial-of-service attacks. Stateless autoconfiguration will have to mature to address these security issues.

IPv6 ADDRESS RENUMBERING   One other use of stateless autoconfiguration is bulk **IPv6 address renumbering**. With traditional IPv6, it is difficult to change the network part or subnet part of all IPv4 clients in a company. However, stateless autoconfiguration supports the changing of all IPv6 addresses in company in a (relatively) simple and rapid way. Each router gives all clients it serves leases (agreements that include a deadline for using its IPv6 routing prefix and subnet ID). In address renumbering, all leases are created to expire at the same time. The IPv6 routers then change all leases, providing new routing information and subnet IDs in the process. There is also a mechanism for telling all routers to change routing prefixes and subnet IDs at the same time. This mechanism includes distributing different subnet IDs to each router.

Test Your Understanding

15. a) Can a client computer use DHCP to get IPv6 configuration information? Explain. b) What other option is available for IPv6 client configuration? c) What are the two phases in IPv6 stateless autoconfiguration? d) What is a link-local IP address? e) For a link-local address, what are the contents of the routing prefix, subnet ID, and interface ID? f) Why must a client use the neighbor discovery protocol after creating a link-local IPv6 address? g) For a global IP address, what are the contents of the routing prefix, subnet ID, and interface ID? h) In what ICMPv6 message are the routing prefix and subnet ID delivered? i) May the router advertisement message forbid the use of stateless autoconfiguration for creating a global IPv6 address?

16. a) At a minimum, what configuration information does a router advertisement message give a client? b) Why is this sufficient for dual-stack clients? c) For single-stack IPv6 clients, what additional piece of configuration information is almost certainly needed? d) How may this information be obtained? e) Is the mechanism for giving the IPv6 addresses of DNS servers mandatory or optional? f) What are the known security weaknesses of IPv6? g) Can stateless autoconfiguration be used to change all routing prefixes and subnet IDs in a firm?

Other IPv6 Standards

In order to make IPv6 work effectively, the Internet Engineering Task Force also had to upgrade a number of support standards. For example, it had to extend ICMP to ICMPv6 with new capabilities. To give an example of this, stateless autoconfiguration needs to use the router solicitation and the router advertisement messages, both of which are ICMPv6 message types.

Another major standard to require changing is DNS, although here the main change is minor. For each host name, a DNS server actually contains multiple records giving information about the particular host using that name.

- **DNS A Record**. The A record contains the IPv4 address for a target host. When your computer sends a DNS message to request the IPv4 address for a particular host name, the DNS server replies with information in the target host's A record.
- **DNS AAAA Record**. For IPv6 addresses, a new address field had to be added. IPv6 addresses are four times as long as IPv4 addresses, so the added record is called the AAAA record.

THE ADDRESS RESOLUTION PROTOCOL (ARP) In IPv4, the address resolution protocol (ARP) did not use IP packets. It had its own packet type. For IPv6, the functionality of ARP was subsumed into ICMPv6, into the **neighbor discovery protocol**, which defines two types of messages. Instead of sending an ARP request message, the sending

---

ICMPv6

Many new types were created for neighbor discovery, stateless autoconfiguration

Domain Name System (DNS)

The DNS information for a host is contained in several records

DNS A Record. The A record contains the IPv4 address for the target host

DNS AAAA Record. For IPv6 addresses, a new address record had to be added. IPv6 addresses are four times as long as IPv4 addresses, so the added record is called the AAAA record.

Address Resolution Protocol (ARP) Messages

In IPv6, handled by the ICMP neighbor discovery protocol, which has two message types

Neighbor solicitation messages ask host to respond

Neighbor advertisement messages give the host's data link address

There is no ARPv6

FIGURE 9-18 Other IPv6 Standards (Study Figure)

host transmits an ICMPv6 **neighbor solicitation** message. The host with the requested IPv6 address sends back an ICMPv6 **neighbor advertisement** message containing the requested data link layer address.

Test Your Understanding

17. a) Does ICMPv6 contain new ICMP message types? b) In the Domain Name System, distinguish between the information contained in the A and AAAA records for a host name. c) What standard replaces the Address Resolution Protocol in IPv6? d) What are the two types of messages in the neighbor discovery protocol? e) What does each contain?

18. a) I type in the host name of an IPv6 host. What does my computer do? I know the IPv6 address of a particular host. b) How can I find its data link layer address so that I can send it frames?

CONCLUSION

Synopsis

Chapter 8 dealt with TCP/IP concepts. This chapter focuses on TCP/IP management. The TCP/IP standards that dominate internetworking require a great deal of management attenuation, both initially and on an ongoing basis. The first step is to develop an IP subnet schema for the firm. This creates a basic trade-off between the number of subnets and the number of hosts per subnet. The firm also has to decide whether or not to use network address translation (NAT). NAT has several benefits, including added security and increasing the effective number of public IP addresses a firm has; but NAT causes problems for certain protocols.

In this chapter, we looked more closely at the Domain Name System (DNS). We saw that the system is a hierarchical system of named domains (collections of resources under the control of an organization). Corporations want second-level domain names, such as pearsonhighered.com. After they get one, they must maintain two or more DNS servers for their second-level domain. We also saw that if a local DNS server does not know the IP address for a host name, it contacts the authoritative DNS server for the domain in the IP address.

We looked in more depth at the Dynamic Host Configuration Protocol, focusing on the need to define scopes for each DHCP servers and to assign IP address groups in a way consistent with the DHCP server's scope.

We have seen the Simple Network Management Protocol (SNMP) repeatedly since we first saw it in Chapter 1. This chapter looked at SNMP operation in a bit more detail, focusing on the concept of objects and the types of objects specified in MIB schemas. We also saw RMON probes.

The Internet is attractive for WAN transmission because it has a very low cost per bit transmitted. However, companies are concerned about security on the Internet. To obtain better security, they use remote-access and site-to-site VPNs.

There are two main VPN protocols. IPsec offers the strongest security. It also offers the important choice between two modes of operation—transport mode and tunnel mode. Most importantly, IPsec offers central manageability.

SSL/TLS can be used for remote-access VPNs. SSL/TLS is attractive because all browsers know how to create a secure SSL/TLS connection with host computers. This means that there is no need to add anything to the client computer. However, there are limitations on the services that SSL/TLS can provide easily.

We ended the chapter with a long discussion on the management of IPv6. Managing IPv6 is similar to managing IPv4, but it is not the same. We began with a discussion of single-stack IPv4-only hosts, single-stack IPv6-only hosts, and dual-stack IPv4/IPv6 hosts. Originally, the IETF believed that dual-stack machines would make the introduction of IPv6 painless. However, implementing IPv6 on dual-stack machines and managing IPv6 traffic proved to be expensive. Now that we have run out of IPv4 addresses, however, single-stack IPv6 hosts are finally driving the introduction of IPv6.

In IPv4, addresses have three parts: network, subnet, and host. In IPv6 global unicast addresses, the comparable parts are called the routing prefix, the subnet ID, and the interface ID. The interface ID is always 64 bits long. It is created from the host's MAC address by a somewhat complex process that we reviewed. This process results in a 64-bit extended unique identifier (EUI-64) that is used as the interface ID. The company is assigned a routing prefix. This sets the size of its subnet ID and determines how many subnets it can have.

For client configuration, DHCPv6 exists. However, IPv6 permits another type of configuration, stateless autoconfiguration, in which the host does its own configuration, without using a DHCPv6 server. First, the host creates a link-local IPv6 address that can be used only within a single network. Second, with the help of an ICMPv6 router advertisement message, it creates a global unicast IPv6 address that can be used on the Internet. For dual-stack devices, the IPv4 stack can obtain configuration information from the DHCP server, so stateless autoconfiguration on the IPv6 stack, which provides only an address for the client host and the IPv6 address of a default router, is sufficient. For single-stack IPv6 computers, the router advertisement message has an optional ability to give the IPv6 addresses of DNS servers. An important feature of stateless autoconfiguration is that it can be used to renumber all hosts in a corporate network.

IPv6 required the extension of existing helper standards. ICMPv6 introduces many new message types, and DHCPv6 can be used for IPv6 configuration. The major change to DNS is the introduction of an AAAA record for host names. This record contains the IPv6 address of the named host. (IPv4 addresses are contained in traditional A records.)

END-OF-CHAPTER QUESTIONS

Thought Questions

1. Both DNS servers and DHCP servers send your client PC an IP address. Distinguish between these two addresses.

2. Assume that an average SNMP response message is 100 bytes long. Assume that a manager sends 40 SNMP *Get* commands each second. a) What percentage of a 100 Mbps LAN link's capacity would the resulting response traffic represent? b) What percentage of a 128 kbps WAN link would the response messages represent? c) What can you conclude from your answers to these questions?

3. A firm is assigned the network part 128.171. It selects an 8-bit subnet part. a) Draw the bits for the four octets of the IP address of the first host on the first subnet. (Hint: Use Windows Calculator.) b) Convert this answer into dotted decimal notation. c) Draw the bits for the second host on the third subnet. (In binary, 2 is 10, while 3 is 11.) d) Convert this into dotted decimal notation. e) Draw the bits for the last host on the third subnet. f) Convert this answer into dotted decimal notation.

4. A firm is assigned the network part 128.171. It selects a 10-bit subnet part. a) Draw the bits for the four octets of the IP address of the first host on the first subnet. (Hint: Use Windows Calculator.) b) Convert this answer into dotted decimal notation. c) Draw the bits for the second host on the third subnet. (In binary, 2 is 10, while 3 is 11.) d) Convert this into dotted decimal notation. e) Draw the bits for the last host on the third subnet. f) Convert this answer into dotted decimal notation.

Troubleshooting Question

1. In your browser, you enter the URL of a website you use daily. After some delay, you receive a DNS error message that the host does not exist. a) What may have happened? Explain your *reasoning. Again, do NOT just come up with one or two possible explanations.* b) How would you logically disconfirm or test each possibility?

Perspective Questions

1. What was the most surprising thing to you about the material in this chapter?

2. What was the most difficult thing for you in the chapter?

10 WIDE AREA NETWORKS

LEARNING OBJECTIVES

By the end of this chapter you should be able to:

- Contrast LANs and WANs in terms of technology diversity, economics, speed, and need for optimization.
- Contrast the technologies of the business and residential local loops of telephone companies. Contrast these technologies with UTP wiring within buildings.
- Distinguish between access lines and leased lines. Discuss the main lower-speed leased lines and bonding. Describe the standards used in leased lines above 50 Mbps.
- Explain the technology used in DSL lines. Explain the differences between residential and business DSL lines.
- Explain the technology used in cable modem service.
- Describe the technologies of leased line networks and public switched data networks. Discuss metropolitan area Ethernet and its attractions. If you read the box, "Virtual Circuits," explain the problem they address and how they address it.
- Explain why it is attractive for companies to use the Internet for WAN service and what issues concern them in using the Internet. Describe how companies can mitigate security concerns. Describe how companies can mitigate performance issues.
- Explain why cellular systems use cells, distinguish between handoffs and roaming in 802.11 and cellular systems. Explain the generations of cellular technology to date. Explain the standards situation today and the direction in which it is moving. Explain why individual throughput is usually far lower than rated speeds. Describe how Wi-Fi and cellular technology are converging.

LANs AND WANs (AND MANs)

One of the most fundamental distinctions in networking is the one between local area networks (LANs) and wide area networks (WANs). Figure 10-1 shows how these two types of networks differ. We will also see how they compare to intermediate-distance networks called metropolitan area networks (MANs).

LANs versus MANs and WANs

ON AND OFF THE CUSTOMER PREMISES Some authors base the difference between LANs and WANs on physical distance. For instance, some say that the dividing line between LANs and WANs is one mile or one kilometer. However, the real distinction appears to be that **local area networks (LANs)** exist within a company's site, while **wide area networks (WANs)** connect different sites within an organization or between organizations.

Category	Local Area Network	Metropolitan Area Network	Wide Area Network
Abbreviation	LAN	MAN	WAN
Service Area	*On customer premises* (home, apartment, office, building, campus, etc.)	*Between sites* in a metropolitan area (city and its suburbs) A Type of WAN	*Between sites* in a region, a country, or around the world.
Implementation	Self	Carrier	Carrier
Ability to Choose Technology	High	Low	Low
Who manages the network?	Self	Carrier	Carrier
Price	Highly related to cost	Based on strategy. Highly unpredictable.	Based on strategy. Highly unpredictable.
Cost per Bit Transmitted	Low	Medium	High
Therefore Typical Transmission Speed	100 Mbps to 1 Gbps or more	10 to 100 Mbps	1 to 50 Mbps
Can Use Switched Technology?	Yes	Yes	Yes
Can Use Routed Technology?	Yes	Yes	Yes

FIGURE 10-1   LANs, MANs, and WANs

Local area networks (LANs) exist within a company's site, while wide area networks (WANs) connect different sites within an organization or between organizations.

For LANs, then, the company owns the property and can do anything it wants. It can choose any LAN technology it wishes, and it can implement it any way it wishes.

There is no such freedom for WANs. A company cannot legally lay wires between two of its sites. (Consider how your neighbors would feel if you started laying wires across their yards.) The government gives certain companies called **carriers**[1] permission (**rights of way**) to lay wires in public areas and offer service to customers. In return, carriers are subject to government regulation.

When you deal with carriers, you can only get the services they offer, and you must pay their prices. Although there may be multiple carriers in an area, the total number of service choices is likely to be quite limited.

On the positive side, you do not need to hire and maintain a large staff to deal with WANs because carriers handle nearly all of the details. In contrast, if you install a LAN, you also have to maintain it. As the old saying goes, anything you own ends up owning you.

---

[1]Carriers were originally called *common carriers*. The name reflected the fact that these carriers were required by law to provide service to anyone or any organization requesting services. Regulation was originally instituted in the railroad industry because many companies that owned railroads also owned other companies and refused to provide services to competitors of these other companies.

ECONOMICS   Another fundamental difference between LANs and WANs stems from economics. You know that if you place a long-distance call, this will cost more than a local call. An international call will cost even more. As distance increases, the price of transmission increases. The cost per bit transmitted therefore is higher in WANs than in LANs.

You know from basic economics that as unit price increases, fewer units are demanded. Or, in normal English, when the price for an item increases, you usually buy less of it. Consequently, companies tend to purchase lower-speed WAN links than LAN links. Typically, LANs bring 100 Mbps to 1 Gbps to each desktop. WAN speeds more typically vary from 256 kbps to about 50 Mbps.

In addition, companies spend more time optimizing their expensive WAN traffic than their relatively inexpensive LAN traffic. For example, companies may be somewhat tolerant of looking at YouTube videos on LANs, but they usually clamp down on this type of information on their WAN links. They also tend to compress data before sending across a WAN so that it can be handled with a lower-capacity WAN link.

Another aspect of economics is pricing. For LANs, you have a good idea of what installing and using a wired or wireless LAN will cost you. In carrier WANs, however, the price of services is only somewhat related to costs. Carriers change their prices strategically, for example, to encourage users to switch from one service to another. Consequently, price changes for WANs are less predictable that they are for customer-owned LAN technology.

TECHNOLOGIES   Another difference between LANs and WANs is that LAN technology has largely settled on two related families of standards—Ethernet (802.3) for wired LANs and Wi-Fi (802.11) for wireless LANs. As we saw in Chapter 6, 802.11 WLANs are primarily used today to extend corporate Ethernet wired LANs to mobile devices.

The technological situation is more complex in wide area networking. Multiple technologies are used, including leased line data networks, public switched data networks, and wireless networks. Within these categories are multiple options. Furthermore, WAN technologies are at different stages in their life cycles, with some increasing rapidly in use and others declining.

Test Your Understanding

1. a) Distinguish between LANs and WANs. b) What are rights of way? c) What are carriers? d) Why do you have more flexibility with LAN service than with WAN service? Why?
2. a) Why are typical WAN speeds slower than typical LAN speeds? Give a clear and complete argument. b) Why are future WAN prices difficult to predict? c) Compare the diversity of technologies in LANs and WANs.

Other Aspects of WANs

METROPOLITAN AREA NETWORKS (MANs)   All WANs connect sites between customer premises and cost more per bit transmitted than LANs. However, WANs differ considerably in the distances they span. Some are international and others span single nations. At the small end, some WANs are **metropolitan area networks (MANs)**, which connect sites in a city and its suburbs.

Technology	LAN	WAN
Can be a single switched or wireless network?	Yes	Yes
Can be an internet?	Yes	Yes

FIGURE 10-2 Single Networks versus Internets

Although MANs are WANs, their relatively short distance span means that the cost per bit transmitted is lower than it is in national and international WANs. Consequently, typical transmission speeds are faster. If you have a smartphone or tablet with 3G or 4G cellular access, then you already use a MAN. Cellular networks almost always span a single MAN or even a single city. However, we will see that wired MANs are important for corporations because site-to-site traffic is large and is more efficiently transmitted over wires.

SINGLE NETWORKS VERSUS INTERNETS   Some people think that LANs are single networks, while WANs are internets. However, as Figure 10-2 shows, that is not the case. Small LANs usually will be single networks, but a larger LAN, such as one on a university campus, is likely to be a local internet.

For WANs, there can also be single networks or internets. Of course, the global Internet is a WAN, and we will see that many companies use it extensively for data transmission among their premises. We will also see that companies also use wide area single switched networks. These are large networks, but they are still switched single networks.

Test Your Understanding

3. a) Why do MANs have higher typical speeds than broader-scope WANs? b) Are LANs single networks or internets? c) Are WANs single networks or internets? d) Is the Internet a WAN?

The Three Basic WAN Components

Figure 10-3 shows that there are three basic components to wide area networks:

- First comes the customer premises with the **customer premises equipment (CPE)** needed to connect to the WAN. With mobile devices, your customer premises is wherever you are, and your mobile device is your customer premises equipment. For connecting corporate sites to wired access lines, the customer premises equipment is likely to be a border router.
- **Access links** connect the customer premises to the network core of the WAN. We will focus on wired access links because they are so prevalent. Later in the chapter, we will look at wireless access links.
- The **network core** connects access links to other access links. Again, we show it as a cloud because customers do not have to understand how it works in detail. The carrier takes care of the network core. Of course, as an IT professional, you have to understand what happens inside the cloud, and we will spend time looking at network core technologies.

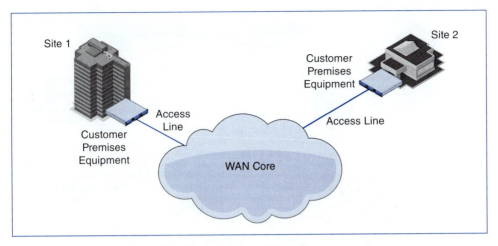

FIGURE 10-3   Components of a Wide Area Network (WAN)

Test Your Understanding

4. a) List the three basic components of wide area networks. b) Are access links wired or wireless? c) What is CPE?

WIRED ACCESS LINKS

We will begin looking at the technology of WANs with wired access links. Although wireless access is common for consumer products, wired access still dominates for corporate and residential access. There are two dominant technologies for access links: public switched telephone network access links and cable modem service. The latter is primarily available within the United States. Later in this chapter, we will look at wireless access links in mobile telephone systems.

Public Switched Telephone Network (PSTN) Access Lines

The traditional wired telephone system is officially the **public switched telephone network (PSTN)**. Although the PSTN was created for voice communication, its lines can carry data as well, and both corporations and private homes use these lines for WANs access.

THE BUSINESS LOCAL LOOP   The access link between the customer premises and the nearest telephone company switch (called the end office switch) is called the **local loop**. Figure 10-4 shows the four main technologies that dominate the PSTN local loop.

Figure 10-5 looks at these technologies in more depth. For perspective, it also compares local loop twisted pair wiring to internal 4-pair UTP, which we saw in Chapter 5.

Two-Pair Data-Grade UTP   Two of these technologies are used to provide leased lines to business. One of these is a type of UTP wiring we have not discussed before.

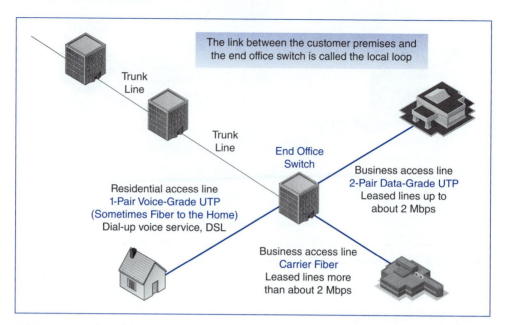

The link between the customer premises and
the end office switch is called the local loop

Trunk
Line

Trunk
Line

End Office
Switch

Business access line
2-Pair Data-Grade UTP
Leased lines up to
about 2 Mbps

Residential access line
1-Pair Voice-Grade UTP
(Sometimes Fiber to the Home)
Dial-up voice service, DSL

Business access line
Carrier Fiber
Leased lines more
than about 2 Mbps

FIGURE 10-4   The Public Switched Telephone Network Local Loop

Purpose	Local Loop Technology	Considerations
Business Local Loop	2-pair data-grade UTP	For leased lines up to about 2 Mbps Must be pulled to the customer premises Not limited to 100 meters
	Optical fiber (carrier fiber)	For leased lines more than about 2 Mbps Must be pulled to the customer premises
Residential Local Loop	1-pair voice-grade UTP	Designed only for voice transmission Can be used for digital subscriber line (DSL) service Not limited to 100 meters Already installed; avoids cost of pulling media
	Optical fiber (carrier fiber)	Fiber to the home New Installed in entire neighborhoods to reduce cost
Internal Data Wiring	4-pair UTP (Category 3-6A)	For inside a site Usually limited to 100 meters
	Multimode optical fiber	Limited to about 300 meters

FIGURE 10-5   Local Loop Technologies

This is **2-pair data-grade UTP**. As the name suggests, this type of UTP wiring uses *two* twisted pairs instead of four. Each pair is for transmission in one direction. *Data grade* means that this wire was designed to carry data instead of voice. Two-pair data-grade UTP is used in the slowest leased lines—those up to about 2 Mbps.

Local loops, of course, are longer than 100 meters. Often, there can be 1 or 2 km between the customer premises and the nearest end office switch. The 100 meter limit on UTP cords that we saw earlier in this chapter is specific to 4-pair UTP and LANs.

The 100 meter limit on UTP cords that we saw earlier in this chapter is specific to 4-pair UTP and LANs. It does not apply to other types of UTP.

Carrier Fiber   Two-pair data-grade UTP is fine for leased lines up to about 2 Mbps. For all faster leased lines, carriers use carrier-grade optical fiber. This means single-mode fiber and higher wavelengths of light—1310 and 1550 nm.

THE RESIDENTIAL LOCAL LOOP

One-Pair Voice-Grade UTP   While businesses needing leased lines may use 2-pair data-grade UTP, the lines running to all residential premises are **1-pair voice-grade UTP**. As its name suggests, this type of wiring was designed to carry voice, not high-speed data. However, it can carry data up to moderate speeds.

Fiber to the Home (FTTH)   Although 1-pair voice-grade UTP can carry data, this is not an ideal medium for transmission. Subscribers want to bring high-definition video into their homes, and they want multiple channels at a time. We cannot do this with digital subscriber lines using 1-pair voice-grade UTP copper wire. To provide extremely high speeds, a number of carriers are beginning to bring **fiber to the home (FTTH)** by running carrier-grade fiber from the end office switch to residential households.

Running new fiber to each household is very expensive, so implementation has been slow. However, by converting entire neighborhoods to FTTH, carriers have been able to lower their per-house installation costs.

LAN VERSUS WAN UTP   We first looked at unshielded twisted pair (UTP) wiring in Chapter 5, in the context of Ethernet LANs. A key point that almost all students remember from that discussion is that Ethernet can normally carry signals over a maximum distance of 100 meters. However, this is an Ethernet limit, not an inherent UTP limit. In the local loop of the telephone system, voice and data signals typically need to travel a kilometer or more. However, while 4-pair UTP with high-category numbers can carry signals over a gigabit per second or more, 1-pair voice-grade UTP and even two-pair data-grade UTP can only carry data signals at much lower speeds.

Test Your Understanding

5. a) What two technologies are used in business local loops? b) What two technologies are used in residential local loops? c) Compare the two local loop UTP technologies in terms of number of pairs and voice-grade versus data-grade wiring quality. d) Compare the types of UTP used in corporate buildings and in low-speed PSTN leased lines. e) Is all UTP wiring limited to 100 meters? Explain.

Business Leased Lines

As Figure 10-6 shows, access lines run from the customer premises to the nearest end office switch. In contrast, leased lines run from one customer premises to another. Leased "lines" are really transmission paths that travel over access lines, through switches, and over trunk lines between switches. They seem like a physical line because there is reserved capacity on each access line, switch, and trunk line along the way. To users, the service is a simple point-to-point connection.

You personally use dial-up connections when you place a call to someone over a landline phone. Leased lines are different from dial-up connections.

- You can dial up any other number, but leased line transmission can only occur between the two customer premises the leased line connects.
- Dial-up connections exist only for the duration of the call. In contrast, leased lines are always-on connections for the duration of the lease.
- You pay for long-distance calls by the minute. In contrast, a leased line has a fixed payment for the term of the lease, typically with an additional cost that depends on use.
- Leased lines are leased. As in mobile telephone service, the lease has a term during which fees must be paid. Installing a leased line is a long-term commitment.
- Leased lines can carry data much faster than residential telephone lines, which require the use of either telephone modems or DSL service (which we saw earlier in this chapter).

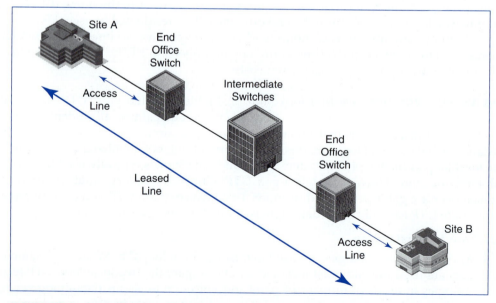

FIGURE 10-6 Access Lines versus Leased Lines

Characteristic	Dial-Up Connections	Leased Lines
Connectivity	Point-to-any-point	Point-to-point
Connection Period	Duration of a call	Duration of lease (always on)
Payment	By the minute for long-distance calls	Flat rate plus per-use changers
Commitment	None (except for cellular plans)	Duration of the lease
Data Transmission Speed	Low to moderate	Moderate to high

FIGURE 10-7 Leased Lines versus Dial-Up Lines (Study Figure)

Test Your Understanding

6. a) Explain the difference between access lines and leased lines. b) Compare dial-up connections with leased line connections along the dimensions shown in Figure 10-7.

Leased Line Speeds

Leased line speeds vary from about one megabit per second to tens of gigabits per second. Figure 10-8 shows that different parts of the world use different standards for leased lines below 50 Mbps. The figure shows lower-speed leased lines in the United States and Europe. There also are differences in other countries.

T1/E1 LEASED LINES The **T1 leased line** in the United States operates at 1.544 Mbps. The comparable European (CEPT) **E1 leased line** operates at 2.048 Mbps.

T1 and E1 lines require 2-pair data-grade UTP access lines. The lines are expensive because when a business needs a T1 or E1 line, the carrier typically must run a new 2-pair data-grade UTP access line to the customer premises.

For faster leased line speeds, optical fiber access links are required. These too typically must be pulled to the customer premise when a new leased line is established.

FRACTIONAL T1/E1 LEASED LINES Many leased line connections do not require T1 or E1 speeds. Many carriers offer **fractional T1/E1** leased lines. Fractional T1 lines typically operate at 128 kbps, 256 kbps, 384 kbps, 512 kbps, or 768 kbps. Fractional T1/E1 lines are slower than full T1/E1 lines, but they are less expensive.

BONDED T1/E1 LINES Sometimes, a firm needs slightly more than a single T1/E1 line but does not need the much higher speed of T3/E3 lines (discussed next). Often, a company can **bond** a few T1/E1 lines, that is, use them as a single connection. This will give a few multiples of 1.544 Mbps or 2.048 Mbps. This is similar to link aggregation in Ethernet, which we saw in Chapter 5. Bonding requires one 2-pair DG access line for each bonded T1 or E1 line.

THE T1/E1 FAMILY IN PERSPECTIVE T1/E1, fractional T1/E1, and bonded T1/E1 lines provide speeds in the range of greatest corporate demand for WAN transmission. Consequently, T1/E1, fractional T1/E1, and bonded T1/E1 lines are the most widely used leased lines.

North American Digital Hierarchy		
Line	Speed	Typical Transmission Medium
T1	1.544 Mbps	2-Pair Data-Grade UTP
Fractional T1	128 kbps, 256 kbps, 384 kbps, 512 kbps, 768 kbps	2-Pair Data-Grade UTP
Bonded T1s (multiple T1s acting as a single line)	Small multiples of 1.544 Mbps	2-Pair Data-Grade UTP
T3	44.736 Mbps	Carrier Optical Fiber
CEPT Hierarchy		
Line	Speed	Typical Transmission Medium
Fractional E1		2-Pair Data-Grade UTP
E1	2.048 Mbps	2-Pair Data-Grade UTP
Bonded E1	Small multiples of 2.048 Mbps	
E3	34.368 Mbps	Carrier Optical Fiber
SONET/SDH Speeds		
Line	Speed (Mbps)	Typical Transmission Medium
OC3/STM1	155.52	Carrier Optical Fiber
OC12/STM4	622.08	Carrier Optical Fiber
OC48/STM16	2,488.32	Carrier Optical Fiber
OC192/STM64	9,953.28	Carrier Optical Fiber
OC768/STM256	39,813.12	Carrier Optical Fiber

FIGURE 10-8   Leased Line Speeds in the United States and Europe

T1/E1, fractional T1/E1, and bonded T1/E1 lines are the most widely used leased lines.

T3/E3 LEASED LINES   The next level of the hierarchy is the T3 line in the United States.[2] It operates at 44.736 Mbps. The comparable E3 line operates at 34.368 Mbps. At this speed, optical fiber access lines are required.

SONET/SDH   Beyond T3/E3 lines, the world has nearly standardized on a single technology or, more correctly, on two compatible technologies. These are **SONET (Synchronous Optical Network)** in North America and **SDH (Synchronous Digital Hierarchy)** in Europe. Other parts of the world select one or the other. As the North American name suggests, SONET/SDH lines all require optical fiber access lines.

SONET/SDH speeds are multiples of 51.84 Mbps, which is close to the speed of a T3/E3 line. Figure 10-8 shows that SONET speeds are given by **OC (optical carrier)** numbers, while SDH speeds are given by **STM (synchronous transfer mode)** numbers.

---

[2]Although there are T2 and E2 standards, they are not offered commercially.

The slowest offered SONET/SDH speed is 155.52 Mbps. From this speed, SONET/SDH speeds range up to several gigabits per second. The SONET speed nearest to 10 Gbps is 9,953.28 Mbps. Ethernet uses this speed for "10 Gbps" WAN usage so that it can transmit data over physical layer SONET lines. (We will see later in this chapter how Ethernet has begun to move outside the corporation.)

Test Your Understanding

7. a) Below what speed are there different leased line standards in different parts of the world? b) What is the exact speed of a T1 line? c) What are the speeds of comparable leased lines in Europe? d) What access link transmission media do T1 and E1 lines use? e) What access link transmission medium do all higher-speed leased lines require? f) Why are fractional T1 and E1 speeds desirable? g) List common fractional T1 speeds. h) What is T1/E1 bonding, and why is it attractive? i) What are the most widely used leased lines?

8. a) What leased line standards are used above 50 Mbps? b) What is the lowest-speed SONET/SDH leased line? c) Why does 10 Gbps Ethernet use a speed of 9,953.28 Mbps on "10 Gbps" WAN links?

Business Digital Subscriber Line (DSL) Service

The problem with T1/E1 lines is that their provisioning typically requires a new pair of data-grade UTP lines to be run from the nearest end office switch to the customer premises. This is expensive. However, until recently, only 2-pair data-grade UTP could carry data signals, so there was no choice.

However, one-pair voice-grade lease lines run to both residential and business locations. They are already in place, so if they could be used for data transmission, there would be no need to run new lines to the customer premises. Potentially, this means that they could offer services similar to leased line services but at a much lower price because there would be no need to pull new 2-pair data-grade UTP lines to the customer premises.

In the past, the inferior 1-pair voice-grade UTP line could only carry voice signals. However, advances in signaling technology allows them to carry data at moderate speed, up to a few tens of megabytes per second. In other words, they can be used for connections that use T1/E1 speeds. Given that 1-pair voice-grade UTP is already installed, they can offer these speeds at prices considerably below those of T1/E1 leased lines. When 1-pair VG UTP lines are used to carry data, carriers call them **digital subscriber lines** because they send and receive digital signals over these traditional subscriber lines designed for non-digital voice signals. Figure 10-9 shows that carriers offer several types of DSL lines.[3]

As discussed in the next subsection, consumers receive asymmetric digital subscriber line service over 1-pair VG UTP lines. The term *asymmetric* means that speeds are different in the two directions (downstream to the subscriber and upstream from the subscribers). Businesses, however, require *symmetric speeds* on their transmission lines—the same speed in both directions. They require *symmetric digital subscriber lines*.

---

[3]OK, "DSL line" technically means "digital subscriber line line." No, it doesn't make grammatical sense, but that's the terminology that people in the field use.

Feature	ADSL	VDSL	HSDL	HSDL2	SHDSL
Name	Asymmetric DSL	Very-High-Bit-Rate DSL	High-Rate Symmetric DSL	High-Rate Symmetric DSL Version 2	Super-High Rate Symmetric DSL
Uses Existing 1-Pair Voice-Grade UTP?	Yes*	Yes	Yes*	Yes*	Yes*
Target Market	Residences	Residences, multi-tenant units	Business	Business	Business
Downstream Rated Speed	Initially, 1.5 Mbps; now up to 12 Mbps	52 to 100 Mbps	768 kbps	1.544 Mbps	192 kbps to 2.3 Mbps
Upstream Rated Speed	Initially, up to 0.5 Mbps; now up to 3.3 Mbps	16 to 100 Mbps	768 kbps	1.544 Mbps	192 kbps to 2.3 Mbps
Speed Symmetry	Asymmetrical	Asymmetric or Symmetric	Symmetrical	Symmetrical	Symmetrical
Quality-of-Service Guarantees?	No	No	Yes	Yes	Yes

*By definition, digital subscriber lines use 1-pair voice-grade UTP.

FIGURE 10-9 Digital Subscriber Lines (DSLs)

Business also needs guarantees that the line will be able to carry these speeds. These guarantees are spelled out in service level agreements (SLAs). If the carrier fails to meet these guarantees for more than a very brief amount of time, the carrier must pay a penalty. Paying a penalty is not attractive, so carriers over-engineer symmetric DSLs for business. As a consequence, while consumer asynchronous DSL lines cost only about $50 per month, business SDSL lines are more expensive.

As Figure 10-9 shows, several business-oriented DSL standards are available. The most popular business DSL is the **high-rate symmetric digital subscriber line (HDSL)**. This standard allows symmetric transmission at 768 kbps (approximately half of a T1's speed) in both directions. A newer version, **HDSL2**, transmits at 1.544 Mbps in both directions. Like all DSLs, both use a single voice-grade twisted pair. Businesses find HDSL and HDSL2 attractively priced compared with T1 and fractional T1 lines.[4]

Growing in popularity is **SHDSL (super-high-rate symmetric DSL)**, which can operate symmetrically over a single voice-grade twisted pair and over a speed range of 384 kbps–2.3 Mbps. In addition to offering a wide range of speeds and a higher top speed than HDSL2, SHDSL also can operate over somewhat longer distances.

Carriers are now beginning to introduce VDSL (Very-High-Rate DSL) and VDSL2 service. VDSL offers downstream speeds up to 52 Mbps and upstream speeds up to 16 Mbps. VDSL2 offers up to 100 Mbps symmetrically. These standards are difficult to

---

[4]In fact, most T1 lines provided to businesses are double-bonded HDSL lines or HDSL2.

categorize because they bridge the asymmetric-symmetric distinction and the business-residential distinction. In addition, although they offer ultrahigh speeds, they require a pristine wiring plant and rather short distances. Even more importantly, many carriers see this as a technology to offer over fiber rather than 1-pair VG UTP. Consequently, it is only a DSL standard in some senses.

Test Your Understanding

9. a) Why are DSL connections likely to be less expensive than traditional leased line connections? b) Are business DSL service speeds symmetric or asymmetric? Explain. c) What are the downstream and upstream speeds of HDSL, HDSL2, and SHDSL? d) Do business, residential, or both DSL services offer quality-of-service guarantees? e) What is the fastest DSL standard? f) Why is VDSL difficult to compare to the other standards?

Residential DSL Service

Most readers are only directly familiar with residential DSL services. As Figure 10-9 shows, these are **asymmetric DSL (ADSL)** services, which means there are different speeds for downloading and uploading. These services have much faster download speed than upload speeds. This is reasonable because website downloading often requires a great deal of speed and because video download and streaming service also need a great deal of speed. Few consumer applications require full two-way high-speed service.

Asymmetric service saves money because upstream speeds are lower and so use a lower-cost transmission technology. In addition, Figure 10-9 shows that residential DSL services do not receive service level agreement guarantees for speed. This means that signaling systems do not have to be over-engineered. This further saves money.

ELEMENTS OF RESIDENTIAL ADSL SERVICE Figure 10-10 shows the main technical elements of ADSL service. The customer needs a DSL modem, which plugs into a wall

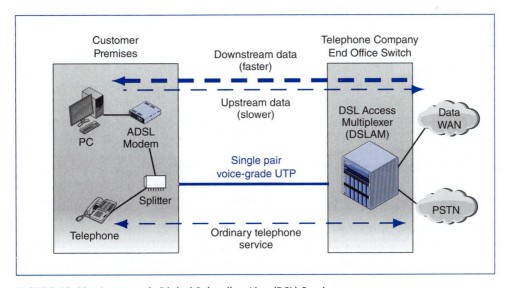

FIGURE 10-10 Asymmetric Digital Subscriber Line (DSL) Service

jack via a home telephone cord. A computer can plug into the DSL modem for digital transmission service. At the same time, the customer can plug his or her telephones into wall jacks and use them while the line is used for data transmission.

To use DSL service effectively, the user must plug a **splitter** into each telephone jack. The splitter separates the voice signal from the data signal so that they cannot interfere with each other. Phones plug into the voice port of a splitter. A DSL modem, if one is present, plugs into the data port on the splitter.

At the telephone company end office switch, the carrier needs to install a **DSL access multiplexer (DSLAM)**. This device separates voice and data traffic. It links voice traffic to the traditional voice part of the public switched telephone network. It links data traffic to a data network.

ADSL SPEED As in most transmission standards, there is a wide gap between ADSL rated speeds and actual throughput. Initially, there were two common ADSL standards. One offered a rated download speed of 1.5 Mbps and a rated upstream speed of 0.5 Mbps and was widely used. By today's standards, it was painfully slow, but compared to a telephone modem limited to 56 kbps downstream and 33 kbps upstream, it was wonderful. Today, the fastest ADSL standard (ADSL2+M) offers a rated download speed of 24 Mbps and a rated upload speed of 3.3 Mbps.

In addition, as we just saw, VDSL can offer far higher speeds to residential customers. Common offerings are 20 to 40 Mbps downstream and 10 to 20 Mbps upstream. VDSL is sufficient for multiple HDTV transmissions to multiple HDTV televisions in a home.

These are not the speeds that users receive. First, there is the usual large gap between rated speeds and throughput under the best of conditions. In addition, remember that all DSL services use existing 1-pair VG UTP access lines that were not designed for high-speed data. Real throughput depends heavily on the quality of the residential wiring plant. It depends even more heavily on the distance between the customer and the central office. Speed starts out fairly high near the central office switch but falls off rapidly with distance. Customers more than 2 km from the central office will receive much lower speeds, and customers more than about 4 km from the central office may not be able to receive service at all.

FIBER TO THE HOME Although DSL speeds today are quite fast, subscribers want to bring high-definition video into their homes, and they want multiple channels at a time. We cannot do this with digital subscriber lines using 1-pair voice-grade UTP copper wire. To provide extremely high speeds (up to about 100 Mbps), a number of carriers are beginning to bring **fiber to the home (FTTH)** by running carrier-grade fiber from the end office switch to residential households.

Running new fiber to each household is very expensive, so implementation has been slow. However, by converting entire neighborhoods to FTTH at one time, carriers have been able to lower their per-house installation costs and offer more reasonable prices.

Test Your Understanding

10. a) Why is asymmetric speed acceptable in residential DSL service? b) What is the benefit of not providing quality-of-service guarantees to residential DSL customers? c) Does residential DSL offer simultaneous voice and data

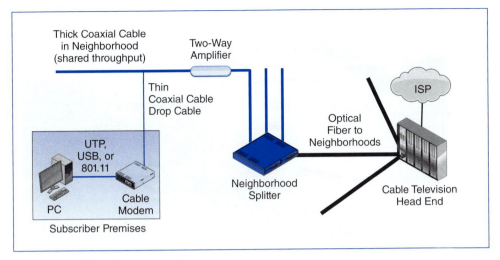

FIGURE 10-11 Cable Modem Service

service? d) What equipment does the customer have to add to his or her home? e) What is the purpose of the DSL access multiplexer? f) Compare rated *downstream* speeds for ADSL initially and today. g) Compare rated *upstream* speeds for ADSL initially and today. h) What three factors reduce actual user throughput? i) Why is fiber to the home attractive? j) Compare fiber to the home installation with pulling optical fiber to firms for high-speed leased lines.

Cable Modem Service

TELEPHONE SERVICE AND CABLE TV In the 1950s, **cable television** companies sprang up in the United States and several other countries, bringing television into the home. Initially, cable only brought over-the-air TV to rural areas. Later, it began to penetrate urban areas by offering far more channels than urban subscribers could receive over the air. In the 1970s, many books and articles forecast a "wired nation" in which two-way cable and the advent of 40-channel cable systems would soon turn cable into an information superhighway. (After all, it would be impossible to fill 40 channels just with television, wouldn't it?) However, available services did not justify the heavy investment to make cable a two-way service until many years later.[5]

Figure 10-11 shows how cable television operates. The cable television operator has a central distribution point, called a **head end**. From the head end, signals travel out to neighborhoods via optical fiber.

From neighborhood splitters, signals travel through coaxial cable. The transmission of an electrical signal always requires *two* conductors. In UTP, the two conductors

[5]This was proven in the dissertation of a Stanford PhD student. The student received a contract from the White House to do the study. Unfortunately, when the study was finished, Richard Nixon was being impeached, and the Executive Office of the President of the United States refused to release the study—despite the fact that the results of the study were already widely known. The study was released a year later, and the student was able to get his PhD.

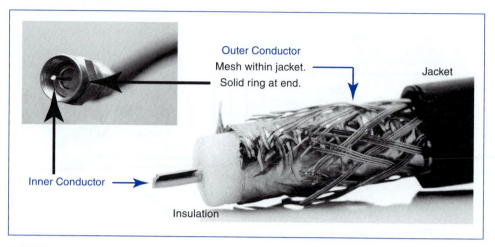

FIGURE 10-12 Coaxial Cable

Source: © Yury Minaev/iStockphoto; © Mark Coffey/iStockphoto

are the two wires in a pair. Figure 10-12 shows that in coaxial cable, the first conductor is a wire running through the center of a coaxial cable. The second conductor is a mesh wire tube running along the cable. The two conductors have the same axis, so the technology is called **coaxial cable**. Before the advent of high-definition HDMI cables, you typically connected your VCR to your television with coaxial cable.

The cable television company runs signals through the neighborhood using *thick coaxial cable* that looks like a garden hose. The access line to individual homes is a *thin coaxial cable* **drop cable**. The resident connects the drop cable to his or her television.

CABLE MODEM SERVICE[6] Cable television companies eventually moved beyond one-way television service to two-way broadband (fast) data service. For television, the repeaters that boost signals periodically along the cable run only had to boost television signals traveling downstream. Data transmission required cable companies to install **two-way amplifiers**, which could carry data in both directions. Although this was expensive, it allowed cable companies to compete in the burgeoning market for broadband service. As in the case of ADSL, cable television service was asymmetric, offering faster downstream speeds than upstream speeds.

Instead of having a DSL modem, the subscriber has a **cable modem**. In general, this cable data service is called **cable modem service**. The coaxial cable drop line goes into the cable modem. The cable modem has a USB port and an Ethernet RJ-45 connector. The subscriber plugs a computer or access router into one of the two ports.

---

[6]Which is better—ADSL service or cable modem service? ADSL services tout the fact that ADSL access lines are not shared, while coaxial cable trunk lines passing through neighborhood are shared. However, DSLAMs are shared in ADSL and often lack full capacity to serve all subscribers simultaneously. In both ADSL and cable modem service, the trunk line leading back to the data network is shared. More importantly, service providers often do not give the highest possible speed at lower monthly prices. In general, cable modem has tended to be somewhat faster and also somewhat more expensive than ADSL service.

At the cable television head end, the cable television company connects to an Internet service provider. This allows subscribers to connect to hosts on the Internet.

Test Your Understanding

11. a) What transmission media do cable television companies use? b) Why is coaxial cable called "coaxial"? c) Distinguish between the coaxial trunk cable and drop cable. d) What types of amplifiers are needed for cable data service? e) What device do customers need for cable modem service?

THE NETWORK CORE

Having looked at wired access links, we will now move on to the network core. In this section, we will look at two traditional methods for providing WAN cores. These are leased lines and public switched data networks. After this section, we will look at a third core WAN technology that is growing in importance—the Internet.

Leased Line Wide Area Networks

LEASED LINE NETWORK TECHNOLOGY   When leased lines appeared in the 1960s, companies realized that they could build their own internal telephone networks to link their sites together. Figure 10-13 shows that companies need two pieces of technology to build leased line WANs.

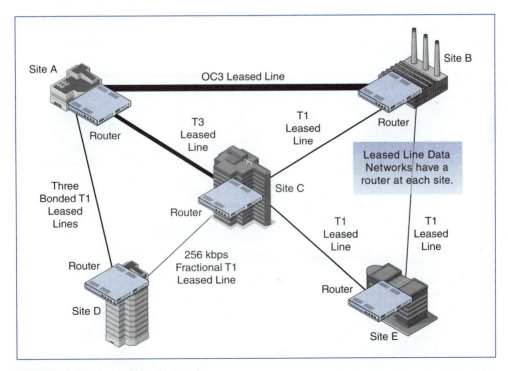

FIGURE 10-13   Leased Line Network

- First, they needed leased lines to connect their sites to one another.
- Second, they needed a router at each site.

LABOR COSTS Designing a leased line network was a considerable task. As Chapter 4 discussed, a firm must first discover the traffic volumes between each pair of sites. In a leased line data WAN, the company must decide which sites to connect and what leased line speeds they need to connect the sites together. It must then contract with the telephone company for leased lines, install the switches, and test the network.

However, the real work begins after the leased line network is installed. Switched data networks in LANs often work with little day-to-day intervention. This is not true for switched WANs. The networking staff in the company must manage the network constantly. The labor costs are substantial.

Test Your Understanding

12. a) What two technologies are needed for leased line switched WANs? b) What are the cost elements in networks of leased lines?

Public Switched Data Network (PSDN)

Companies that build their own leased line WANs must design, install, configure, and manage their leased lines. This is expensive. In contrast, many companies use **public switched data networks (PSDNs)**, which are shown in Figure 10-14. PSDNs allow a company to outsource the work of running a switched data network connecting its sites.

PSDNs allow a company to outsource the work of running a switched data network connecting its sites.

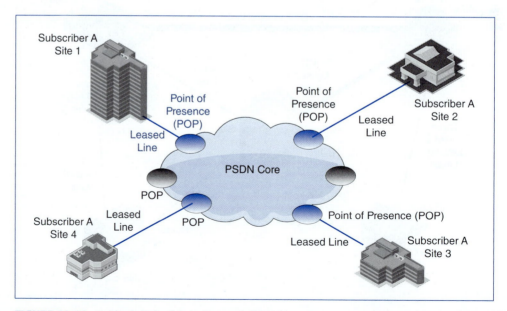

FIGURE 10-14 Public Switched Data Network (PSDN)

PUBLIC SWITCHED DATA NETWORK (PSDN) ACCESS LINES With a PSDN, the corporation needs only one leased line per site. This leased line has to run only from the site to the PSDN's nearest access point. These access points are called **points of presence (POPs)**.

This means that if you have ten sites, you only need ten leased lines. Furthermore, most PSDN carriers have many POPs, so the few leased lines that are needed tend to span only short distances.

THE PSDN CLOUD The PSDN's transport core usually is represented graphically as a **cloud**. This symbolizes the fact that although the PSDN has internal switches and trunk lines, the customer does not have to know how things work inside the PSDN cloud. The PSDN carrier handles almost all of the management work that customers have to do when running their own leased line networks. Customers merely have to send data to and receive data from the PSDN cloud, in the correct format. Although PSDN carrier prices reflect their management costs, there are strong economies of scale in managing very large PSDNs instead of individual corporate leased line networks. Quite simply, it is proportionally cheaper to manage the traffic of many firms than of one firm. There also are very large economies of scale in switching and leased line technologies. These economies of scale allow PSDN prices to remain relatively low.

PSDN STANDARDS There are several standards for PSDN services. They have different speed ranges and also different prices.

X.25 The original PSDN standard was **X.25**. This was a 1970s technology that was slow, expensive, and never widely used. It is completely gone today, but it pioneered PSDN service.

Standard	Characteristics
X.25	Developed in the 1970s Slow, expensive, and very widely used
Frame Relay	Grew rapidly when introduced in the 1990s Speed range of 256 kbps to 40 Mbps In the range of greatest corporate demand for WAN service Aggressive pricing also drives demand Carriers raised Frame Relay prices in the late 1990s and dropped leased line prices Frame Relay is still widely used, but it is now a legacy technology
ATM	Created for the core of the Public Switched Telephone Network Used widely there but also offered to customers Speeds of 1 Mbps to several gigabits per second However expensive in terms of carrier charges and customer management cost Adoption has been limited
Metropolitan Area Ethernet	Extends Ethernet to metropolitan areas 1 Mbps to 100 Mbps at attractive prices Flexible provisioning; customer can get speed increases or decreases in days The only PSDN technology that is growing rapidly

FIGURE 10-15 Public Switched Data Network (PSDN) Standards (Study Figure)

Frame Relay   In the 1990s, **Frame Relay** burst onto the scene. Frame Relay was much less expensive than X.25. Its speed range of 256 kbps to about 40 Mbps was not blindingly fast. However, as noted earlier in this chapter, companies have lower speed requirements for WAN service than for LAN service. Frame Relay had exactly the speed range that corporations needed. In addition, only telephone companies offered leased lines, but new data networking companies could offer Frame Relay service. These new companies offered very low prices.

Frame Relay grew meteorically during the 1990s. Soon, it was used as widely as leased line networks. However, Frame Relay providers had very low profit margins because of their low prices. During the late 1990s, Frame Relay vendors began raising their prices while leased line prices fell precipitously because of improving technology. Frame Relay is still widely used, but it is a now a legacy technology.

ATM   Another PSDN standard is **ATM**.[7] ATM actually was created as a new technology for the entire core of the worldwide Public Switched Telephone Network. In fact, it has already replaced much of the traditional PSTN core, especially on international connections.

ATM offers higher speeds than X.25—from about 1 Mbps up to hundreds of gigabits per second. This makes ATM the fastest PSDN service. However, ATM is extremely expensive in terms of both carrier charges and customer management cost, so ATM prices have also been very high. Consequently, ATM PSDN adoption has been very limited.

Metropolitan Area Ethernet   Ethernet is a switched technology designed for LANs. However, many PSDN carriers have introduced metropolitan area Ethernet to extend Ethernet beyond the LAN. A **metropolitan area network (MAN)** is a WAN that is limited to a metropolitan area, such as a major city and its suburbs. MAN distances are shorter than national and international WAN distances, so MAN prices are lower, and typical speeds are higher. "Metro Ethernet" offers speeds of 1 Mbps to 100 Mbps at a very attractive price.

Metro Ethernet has several attractions beyond high speed and low price. Perhaps the most important is that corporations are already familiar with Ethernet. There is little learning with metro Ethernet compared to Frame Relay or ATM. Many people believe that in the future, companies will primarily use IP over Ethernet for nearly all connections.

Another advantage of metro Ethernet is provisioning. **Provisioning** is providing a service or changing a service. In metro Ethernet, service providers normally can re-provision the speed of a service within a day or so. This is much greater flexibility than companies have traditionally enjoyed with PSDNs.

Provisioning is providing a service or changing a service.

Given the promise of metro Ethernet, it is not surprising that metropolitan area Ethernet is the only PSDN service that is growing rapidly.

---

[7] It stands for Asynchronous Transport Mode. Not very enlightening, is it? Fortunately, nobody ever spells it out.

Test Your Understanding

13. a) List the physical components of PSDN technology. b) Do customers need leased lines if they use PSDNs? c) What is a POP? d) Why do you want a WAN with many POPs? (The answer is not in the text. It requires you to think about POPs.) e) If a company has seven sites, how many leased lines will it need if it uses a PSDN? f) Why are PSDNs fairly inexpensive? g) Why is the PSDN transport core drawn as a cloud?

14. a) What is the speed range of Frame Relay? b) Why is this speed range attractive? c) Why has ATM not been popular? d) What is metro Ethernet? e) For what reasons is it attractive? f) What PSDN service is growing?

Virtual Circuit Operation

Figure 10-16 shows that the PSDN switches that sit inside the cloud are connected in a mesh topology. In any mesh topology, whether partial or full, there are multiple alternative paths for frames to use to go from a source POP to a destination POP.

Selecting Best Possible Paths through Meshes

Selecting the best possible path for each frame through a PSDN mesh would be complex and, therefore, expensive. In fact, if the best possible path had to be computed for each frame at each switch along its path, PSDN switches would have to do so much work that they would be prohibitively expensive.

Virtual Circuits

Instead, most PSDNs select the best possible path between two sites *before transmission begins.* The actual transmission will flow along this path, called the virtual circuit. As Figure 10-16 shows, the switch merely makes a switching decision according to the virtual circuit number

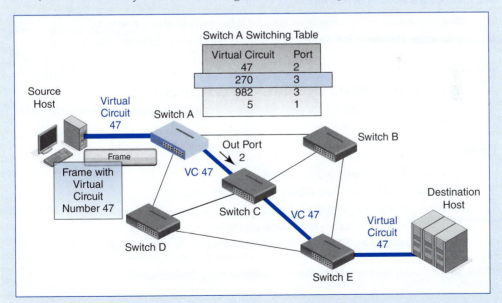

FIGURE 10-16   Virtual Circuit Operation

(continued)

in the frame's header. This virtual circuit lookup is much faster than finding the best alternative path every time a frame arrives at the switch. The "heavy work" of selecting the best alternative path is only done once, before the beginning of communication.

PSDN Frame Headers Have Virtual Circuit Numbers Rather Than Destination Addresses

Note that PSDNs that use virtual circuits do not have destination addresses in their frame headers. Rather, each frame has a virtual circuit number in its header.

This virtual circuit number in Frame Relay is the **Data Link Control Identifier** or **DLCI** (pronounced "DULL-see"). A DLCI typically is 10 bits long.[8] The switch looks up this DLCI in its virtual circuit switching table and sends the frame out through the indicated port.

Test Your Understanding

15. a) Why are virtual circuits used? b) With virtual circuits, on what does a switch base its forwarding decision when a frame arrives? c) Do PSDN frames have destination addresses or virtual circuit numbers in their headers? d) What is the name of the Frame Relay virtual circuit number? e) How long, typically, is a DLCI? f) How many virtual circuits does this number of bits allow? (The answer is not specifically in the text.)

USING THE INTERNET FOR WIDE AREA NETWORKING

The Internet is a wide area network. Many organizations are beginning to use the Internet for some of their WAN traffic. In the future, the Internet is likely to carry most corporate site-to-site traffic and other WAN traffic.

The Internet Is a Wide Area Network

Many corporations are beginning to use the Internet for some part of their WAN traffic.

In the future, the Internet is likely to carry most corporate site-to-site traffic and other WAN traffic.

Attractions

The price per bit transmitted is very low because of large economies of scale

All corporate sites, employees, customers, suppliers, and other business partners are connected to the Internet

Issues

The security of traffic flowing over the Internet

    Addressed by using IPsec virtual private networks (VPNs)

Variable quality of service, with no guarantees

    Addressed by connecting all corporate sites to the same ISP

    Addressed by the ISP (or firm) using Multiprotocol Label Switching (MPLS)

FIGURE 10-17   Using the Internet for Wide Area Networking (Study Figure)

---

[8]Hosts also have true Frame Relay addresses governed by the E.164 standard. These addresses are used to set up virtual circuits. Consequently, if an equipment failure renders a virtual circuit inoperable, a new virtual circuit can be set up using the E.164 addresses.

Attractions and Issues

ATTRACTIONS For wide area networking, corporations would like to use the global Internet because of its very low price per bit transmitted compared to Public Switched Data Networks. The Internet's enormous size creates strong economies of scale. These lead to extremely low costs per bit transmitted compared to other WAN technologies. This alone is driving corporations heavily to the Internet for their WAN traffic.

Another attraction of the Internet is that nearly all of a corporation's sites are already connected to the Internet. So are its sites, employees, buyers, suppliers, and every other firm the company needs to communicate with. In contrast, networks of leased lines can only connect a corporation's sites. Public switched data networks are similarly limited to corporate use, apart from whatever other corporations are using the same PSDN the company uses. There are many PSDNs, and if a company has many other companies to work with, it would have to join many PSDNs, which would be highly uneconomical and unwieldy.

ISSUES However, there are two issues with the Internet. The first is security. The Internet teems with sniffers, hackers, malware, and other threats. These need to be addressed at least in part through cryptographic protections.

The second issue is quality of service. The Internet has always been a best-effort network. For many corporations, this is a serious issue. Companies that depend heavily on the Internet cannot tolerate its variable service quality from day to day.

Test Your Understanding

16. a) What are the two attractions of using the Internet as a WAN? b) What are the two issues that companies must overcome to do so.

Securing the Internet

Securing traffic flowing over the Internet is a complex topic. However, we have already looked at the basics of how to do this in previous chapters.

- In Chapter 3, we saw that it is critical to have a border firewall at each site to inspect incoming traffic for provable attack packets. In addition, intrusion detection systems can often spot traffic that is suspicious and merit further inspection, even if the packets are not provable attack packets.
- In Chapter 9, we saw how IPsec can cryptographically protect traffic passing over the Internet in a general way and how SSL/TLS can cryptographically protect some application traffic. Cryptographically protecting traffic traveling through an untrusted network like the Internet is referred to as having a virtual private network (VPN).
- In Chapter 3, we also saw antivirus (anti-malware) filtering. We will look at this again in Chapter 11.

Test Your Understanding

17. a) List the three protections that can be used to address the lack of security on the Internet. b) Based on what you learned in the first chapter, how can the second approach make the first approach less effective?

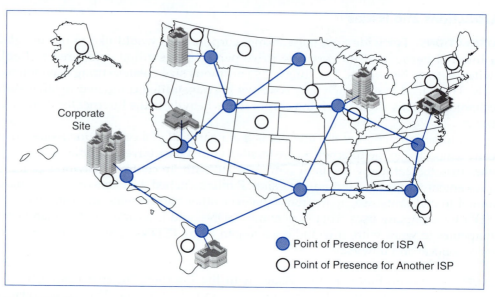

FIGURE 10-18 Connecting All Corporate Sites to a Single ISP

Using a Single ISP

An Internet service provider's network looks like a PSDN, with routers replacing switches. Many ISPs offer nationwide or even worldwide service. This means that a corporation can usually connect all of its sites to a single ISP, as indicated in Figure 10-18.

Why would they do so? The answer is that the Internet, which consists of many ISPs who cooperate to deliver packets, cannot provide quality-of-service guarantees because no one owns or manages the entire Internet. However, individual ISPs do own all of their routers and either own or control the transmission lines connecting each pair of routers. This allows them to control the quality of service they offer to anyone who communicates only through them.

In Chapter 9, we looked at Multiprotocol Label Switching (MPLS). When all routers and transmission lines are under the control of one company, the company can use MPLS to drastically cut costs and to provide quality-of-service guarantees. Most ISPs offer this, as an extra-fee service, to customers who connect all of their sites to the ISP. Connecting all sites to a single ISP that offers quality-of-service guarantees can mitigate service quality problems with the Internet.

Of course, this only provides quality-of-service improvements for traffic between corporate sites. When the firm communicates with a party connected to a different ISP, there are no guarantees.

Test Your Understanding

18. a) How may connecting all of a company's sites to a single ISP mitigate quality-of-service issues for traffic flowing over the Internet? b) What technology do ISPs use to provide quality-of-service guarantees? c) Do these guarantees work for site-to-site traffic within a firm, for traffic with other firms, or both?

CELLULAR DATA SERVICE

Cellular Service

Nearly everybody today is familiar with cellular telephony. In most industrialized countries, well over half of all households now have a cellular telephone.[9] Many people now have *only* a cellular telephone and no traditional *wireline* public switched telephone network phone.

Cells

CELLS AND CELLSITES   Figure 10-19 shows that cellular telephony divides a metropolitan service area into smaller geographical areas called **cells**.

The user has a cellular telephone (also called a **mobile phone**, **mobile**, or **cellphone**). Near the middle of each cell is a **cellsite**, which contains a **transceiver** (transmitter/receiver) to receive mobile phone signals and to send signals out to the mobiles. The cellsite also supervises each mobile phone's operation (setting its power level, initiating calls, terminating calls, and so forth).

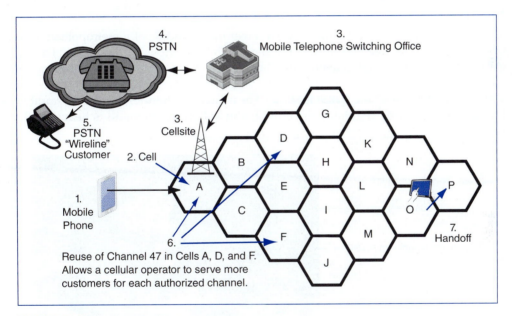

FIGURE 10-19   Cellular Technology

_____

[9]Although cellular telephony was first developed in the United States, the United States has slightly lower market penetration than most other countries. One reason is that normal telephony is inexpensive in the United States, so moving to cellular service is an expensive choice. Another reason is that when someone calls a cellular phone in the United States, the cellular owner receiving the call pays; in most other countries, the caller pays. These two factors increase the relative price of using a cellular phone compared with using a landline phone in the United States. A third factor is that U.S. cellular carriers give inadequate coverage, even in large metropolitan areas. In most other countries, dropped calls and dead spots are rare.

MOBILE TELEPHONE SWITCHING OFFICE (MTSO) All of the cellsites in a cellular system connect to a **mobile telephone switching office (MTSO)**, which connects cellular customers to one another and to wired telephone users.

The MTSO also controls what happens at each of the cellsites. It determines what to do when people move from one cell to another, including deciding which cellsite should handle the transmission when the caller wishes to place a call. (Several cellsites may hear the initial request at different loudness levels; if so, the MTSO selects a service cellsite based on signal loudness—not necessarily based on physical proximity.)

CELLSITE Figure 10-20 shows a typical small cellsite on top of a residential building. The three large "paddles" are cellular antennas. The small round antenna is a microwave antenna. Microwave technology provides point-to-point radio transmission. The antenna is pointed at a similar antenna at the mobile telephone switching office.

Test Your Understanding

19. a) In cellular technology, what is a cell? b) What is a cellsite? c) What are the two functions of the MTSO?

Why Cells?

Why not use just one central transmitter/receiver in the middle of a metropolitan area instead of dividing the area into cells and dealing with the complexity of cellsites? Early precellular phones used a single antenna, and this is much cheaper than using multiple cellsites.

CHANNEL REUSE FOR MORE SUBSCRIBERS The answer is **channel reuse**. The number of channels permitted by regulators is limited, and subscriber demand is heavy. Cellular

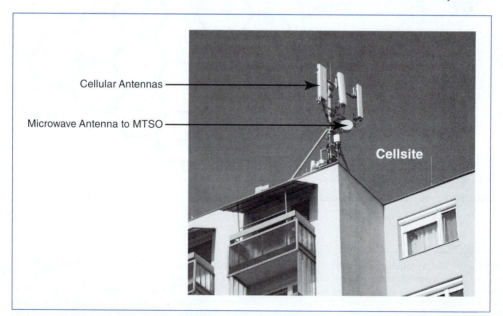

FIGURE 10-20 Cellsite for Mobile Telephones

Source: Courtesy of Raymond R. Panko

telephony uses each channel multiple times, in different cells in the network. This multiplies the effective channel capacity, allowing more subscribers to be served with the limited number of channels available.

Cellular technology is used because it provides channel reuse—the ability to use the same channel in different cells. This allows cellular systems to support more subscribers.

TRADITIONALLY, NO CHANNEL REUSE IN ADJACENT CELLS   There are different mobile technologies. Some allow the use of the same channel in adjacent cells. Others do not to avoid interference from signals "leaking" beyond their cell boundaries. Figure 10-19 illustrates the situation for technology that does not permit the use of the same frequency. Suppose that you use Channel 47 in Cell A. Then you cannot use it in Cells B or C. However, you can use it in D and F. In general, the number of times you can reuse a channel is only about the number of cells, divided by seven. In other words, if you have 20 cells, you can reuse each channel only about three (20/7) times. This is a rough calculation, so "about 2.857 times" makes no sense.

How many cells are there in a city? Later, we will discuss generations of cellular technologies. In the first generation, which appeared in the early 1980s, a mid-size city like Honolulu typically had about a hundred cells. In the second generation, which began in the early 1990s, a city like Honolulu would have a hundred cells. For more recent generations, the number of cells has increased as carriers add many cells to improve channel reuse and also to ensure that not too many customers will be in a cell to allow good service. (Cellsites have high aggregate throughput, but individual throughput falls rapidly as the number of customers served grows.)

CELLS AND WIRELESS LAN ACCESS POINTS   In a sense, enterprise wireless LANs with many access points are like cellular technologies. They allow users to employ the limited number of frequencies available in WLANs many times within a building.

Test Your Understanding

20. a) Why does cellular telephony use cells? b) What is the benefit of channel reuse? c) In Figure 10-19, channels cannot be reused in adjacent cells, and Channel 47 is being used in Cells A, D, and F. What other cells can it be used in? d) Continuing, how many times is Channel 47 used? e) If a city has a hundred cells, how many times can a channel be used without channel reuse? f) Repeat the last two parts if channel reuse is possible in adjacent cells.

Basic Logic

> The same channel can be used in multiple sites
> This allows subscribers to use the same channel if they are in different sites
> Consequently, the carrier can serve more customers per channel

Example

> Without channel reuse: 500 channels, so only 500 simultaneous subscribers can be served
> Channel reuse factor (varies): 20
> Number of simultaneous subscribers: 10,000

FIGURE 10-21   Cells, Channel Reuse, and Number of Subscribers (Study Figure)

	802.11 WLANs	Cellular Telephony
Relationship	*Handoff* and *roaming* mean the same thing	*Handoff* and *roaming* mean different things
Handoffs (means the same in both)	Wireless host travels between access points in an organization	Mobile phone travels between cellsites in the *same* cellular system
Roaming (means different things)	Wireless host travels between access points in an organization	Mobile phone travels to a *different* cellular system

FIGURE 10-22 Handoff and Roaming in 802.11 and Cellular Networks

Handoffs versus Roaming

HANDOFFS   If a subscriber moves from one cell to another within a city, the MTSO will implement a **handoff** from one cellsite to another. For instance, Figure 10-19 shows a handoff from Cell O to Cell P. The mobile phone will change its sending and receiving channels during the handoff, but this occurs too rapidly for users to notice.

ROAMING   In contrast, if a subscriber leaves a metropolitan cellular system and goes to another city or country, this is called **roaming**. Roaming requires the destination cellular system to be technologically compatible with the subscriber's mobile. It also requires administration permission from the destination cellular system. Roaming is as much a business and administrative problem as it is a technical problem.

In cellular telephony, handoffs occur when a subscriber moves between cells in a local cellular system. Roaming occurs when a subscriber moves between cellular systems in different cities or countries.

HANDOFF AND ROAMING IN 802.11 WLANS   Recall from Chapter 6 that *handoff* and *roaming* mean the same thing in 802.11 WLANs. They both mean moving from one access point to another within the same WLAN. In other words, the terms *handoff* and *roaming* are used differently in cellular telephony from the way they are used in WLANs.[10] Figure 10-22 shows how the terms *handoff* and *roaming* are used differently in WLANs and cellular telephony.

Test Your Understanding

21. a) Distinguish between handoffs and roaming in cellular telephony. b) Distinguish between handoffs and roaming in 802.11 wireless LANs.

Using Cellular Telephony for Data Transmission

SMARTPHONES   Originally, mobile phones were just that—telephones that you could carry with you. Today, however, many new mobile phones are **smartphones** that do far more. Most have cameras, and some even have video cameras. Most importantly, all have web browsers to support web access and can download streaming video.

---

[10]Wouldn't it be nice if there were a networking terminology court that could punish this sort of thing?

Generation 1 (1G)

Began in the early 1980s

Analog signaling

Data transmission difficult, limited to 10 kbps

Generation 2 (2G)

Began in the early 1990s

Digital signaling

Data transmission difficult, limited to 10 kbps to 20 kbps

Generation 3 (3G)

Began around 2001

Designed to give at least 2 Mbps download speeds to fixed customers

Designed to give at least 384 kbps download speeds to moving customers

Throughput lower in practice: 100 kbps to 500 kbps initially

Created an explosion in data use

Web surfing, etc., low-quality streaming video, etc.

Generation 4 (4G)

Began around 2010

Performance

> Designed to give at least 1 Gbps download speeds to fixed customers

> Designed to give at least 200 Mbps download speeds to fixed customers

> Throughput lower in practice but generally equal to wired Internet

> Needed for high-definition video

Technology

> MIMO

> Bandwidth of 5 to 20 MHz

> Mandatory to use IP as the transport mechanism

> Strong quality-of-service management

Moving to 4G

The situation today

> HSPA+: rated at 42 Mbps downstream but typically about 7 Mbps down and 1 Mbps up

> LTE (Long-Term Evolution): generally provides 10 Mbps down and 6 Mbps up

> WiMAX: Similar to LTE, but fading in the marketplace

> Overall, LTE is somewhat better, especially in the best systems

> However, HSPA+ has no growth potential

LTE and LTE Advanced

> LTE does not offer speeds anywhere near the 4G requirements

> However, it will, in an evolutionary form called LTE Advanced

> The ITU allows LTE vendors to call their systems 4G anyway, because LTE is a *precursor* 4G technology

> HPSA+ is not a precursor technology to 4G so is only 3G

Carriers are converging on LTE and LTE advanced

FIGURE 10-23 Generations of Cellular Service (Study Figure)

Smartphones are indicative of a trend in cellular service from voice service to voice and data service. Future cellular technologies will primarily be data transmission technology, with voice transmission being a secondary consideration. Applications like web browsing and streaming video require much higher transmission speeds than voice calls, and cellular vendors have been responding with ever-faster service.

FIRST-GENERATION (1G) CELLULAR   The early cellular telephones, which appeared in the early 1980s, could only send and receive data at extremely low speeds and with considerable difficulty. **First-generation (1G)** cellular technology used analog radio transmission and could only send and receive data at speeds below 10 kbps—far slower than even a telephone modem.

SECOND-GENERATION (2G) CELLULAR   **Second-generation (2G)** technology appeared in the early 1990s. It introduced all-digital transmission, but it too was limited to a painfully slow 10 kbps to 20 kbps. This was inadequate for web access, but it was good enough to introduce texting and the exchange of low-quality photographs.

THIRD-GENERATION (3G) CELLULAR   **Third-generation (3G)** technology arrived around the year 2001. Third-generation services were designed to give download speeds of 2 Mbps to stationary customers and 384 kbps to moving customers in cars and busses. (Motion causes serious problems for reading complex radio signals.) Initially, these services only gave speeds of 100 kbps to 500 kbps. This was well below the standard's requirement, but it was a huge leap over 2G speeds. It created an explosion in data use, including web surfing, limited-quality streaming video, file synchronization, and other transmission-intensive tasks. Phones were quickly joined by laptop computers and by eventually tablet computers as consumer devices. Cellular service was not just for phones anymore.

FOURTH-GENERATION (4G) CELLULAR   The next step will be **fourth-generation (4G)** cellular technology. This new generation will be required to give at least 1 Gbps download speeds to stationary users and 200 Mbps to moving customers. This will make wireless as good as or better than wired Internet access. This will be sufficient for heavy web downloading and high-definition streaming video.

Fourth-generation cellular will bring advances in underlying technology. Transmission will be entirely packet-switched using IP. Given the dearth of IPv4 addresses, carriers are specifying that IPv6 must be used. Cellsites and mobiles will use MIMO. Fourth-generation systems will offer scalable bandwidth of 5 to 20 MHz, allowing carriers to provide extremely high speeds or still-high but more economical speeds. There will also be strong quality-of-service management. In general, 4G will be a fully "grown up" technology.

TODAY: CLOSING THE GAP BETWEEN 3G AND 4G   The gap between 3G and 4G is very large, but 3G systems soon began offering speeds much higher than the 3G requirements. As of 2012, three services are dominant.

- **HSPA+** (High Speed Packet Access plus) has a rated speed of 42 Mbps in the best systems (half that in most). Its actual typical speed in the best systems is 7 Mbps down and 1 Mbps up.

- **LTE** (Long-Term Evolution) provides 10 Mbps downstream in good systems and 6 Mbps up.
- **WiMAX** provides service speeds similar to those of LTE. However, WiMAX is falling out of favor with carriers, and most carriers that use it are in the process of switching to LTE. Consequently, we will not discuss it further.

Overall, the two main systems today are HSPA+ and LTE. They are fairly comparable in performance, although LTE is better in most systems and sharply better in the best. In any case, HSPA+ is a dead end for the future with no growth potential. Most HSPA+ vendors are switching to LTE.

PREPARING FOR 4G   Although LTE does not come near ITU specifications for speed, it does embody most of the technology required for 4G systems. It will be extended until it finally reaches full 4G service, at which time it will be called **LTE Advanced**. In 2010, under intense vendor pressure, the ITU allowed systems that are precursors of 4G technology to call themselves 4G. This applies to LTE, which can therefore be called a 4G service. It now appears that nearly all carriers will switch to LTE and LTE Advanced in the near future.

Test Your Understanding

22. a) List the required download speeds for each of the four generations of service. b) With what generation did web surfing become attractive? c) Compare 3G required download speeds with initial 3G actual throughput. d) What throughput do the best 3G services provide today? e) What applications that are difficult or impossible to use with 3G will be easy to use in 4G? f) What are the technical advances required in 4G systems? g) What 4G technology is likely to dominate in the future?
23. a) What generation is HSPA+? b) What generation is LTE in terms of current speed? c) What generation does the ITU allow LTE to be called? Why? d) What is the designation of the version of LTE that will fully meet 4G performance requirements? e) Toward what standards are carriers converging?

Lies, Damned Lies, and Mobile Service Speeds

The speeds we have been discussing were "typical" speeds. However, every 3G user knows that throughputs vary widely by time of day and physical location. In fact, they vary because of several things.

- First, they vary by technology. We have just seen that LTE service is usually faster than HSPA+ service, but cellular technologies have many design options, and these can have a major impact on speed. For instance, most HSPA+ services use 5 MHz channels, while the best use 10 MHz channels. In some technologies, MIMO is possible but optional. Carriers select their specific technology options with an eye toward trade-offs between cost and service speed.
- Second, as noted earlier, cellular throughput is shared by the customers using a cell. As the number of customers increases, service speeds drop roughly linearly with the number of customers. In addition, the presence of even a few very heavy users such as people watching streaming video can reduce individual throughput substantially. The carrier can minimize overcrowding having more cellsites, but this is more expensive for the carrier.

- Third, throughput varies by time of day. During the daytime, there are periods of heavier and lighter use. For example, use tends to increase during commuting time. In addition, use declines an night. Lower use means faster speeds.
- Fourth, throughput varies by location. Not surprisingly, speed are higher at the center of cells and lower at the cells' edges. There may also be buildings or terrain obstructions in certain locations. More subtly, the carrier may have too few cell-sites in some locations, causing overloads that reduce speed.
- Finally, regardless of what the carrier does, the customer cannot have better service than his or her smartphone allows. Most older smartphones cannot handle the latest carrier offerings. In addition, some smartphones are better engineered than others. Better mobiles give faster service than more poor-ly engineered mobiles, even if they have the same technology and options. Overall, users receive the lower of their carrier technology or their cellphone technology.

Actual Customer Throughput Depends on Many Things

Technology Specifics

Standards have many options such as bandwidth per channel

So two carriers using the same basic standard may offer rather different actual speeds

Sharing

Channels are shared

Individual throughput is only a fraction of total throughput

Throughput tends to fall linearly with the number of users

Even a few heavy users such as HTDV viewers can reduce throughput for everybody

Time of Day

There are fewer customers at night, so throughput to individuals tends to be higher then

Commuting times can congest the carrier system

Location

Greater distance from the cell tower reduces throughput

Buildings and terrain obstacles weaken the signal, causing dropbacks to lower speeds

The carrier may have too few cellsites in an area

Customer Smartphone Limits

The customer's smartphone may not be able to use the carrier's best technology

Customers receive the lowest of their carrier technology and the cellphone technology

Some smartphones are simply faster than others for a given standard

---

FIGURE 10-24 Lies, Damned Lies, and Service Speeds (Study Figure)

Test Your Understanding

24. a) List the general categories of conditions that may limit user throughput. b) Which can the carrier do something about? c) What can the vendor do for each of these? d) What category is beyond the vendor's control?

Cellular–Wi-Fi Convergence

We looked at cellular in this chapter and Wi-Fi in Chapters 6 and 7. This makes sense because traditionally there has been a simple dichotomy. Wi-Fi 802.11 systems were used as wired LAN extensions for mobile computers while cellular service was used for telephony and metropolitan area data service. However, this situation is changing. We are seeing increasing convergence between cellular and 802.11 service for data and voice calls.

DATA SERVICE For laptop computers, wireless data service has traditionally meant Wi-Fi. Although a small fraction of users equipped their laptops with cellular service modems, this was too much of a rarity to discuss. For laptops, the main use of wireless technology was to connect the user to the corporate LAN or a public hot spot.

Tablets and smartphones changed this. Although many tablets are still sold with Wi-Fi access only, a large fraction already has cellular service as well. To avoid going over their cellular rate limit, users use Wi-Fi as much as possible. In doing so, they get another benefit. Wi-Fi is much faster than cellular data service today. While low-end "feature phones" often continue to offer data only through cellular carriers, most

---

Data Service

- Laptops
- Smartphones, tablets
- Always provide Wi-Fi access
- Many also offer cellular data access
- Wi-Fi access currently offers much higher speeds
- Cellular access can be used when no accessible Wi-Fi access point is available

Telephone Service

- Traditionally only offered cellular calling
- Some can now offload calling to a Wi-Fi network
- This helps the caller by lowering costs
- This can help the cellular carrier if the customer has a flat-rate plan
- Customers can already receive this benefit if they use Skype or a similar service

Using a Smartphone as an Access Point

- To share the smartphone user's bandwidth

FIGURE 10-25 Cellular–Wi-Fi Convergence (Study Figure)

smartphones have had 802.11 access added. In addition, both tablets and smartphones that can use Wi-Fi notify the user if a Wi-Fi access point is available and whether it is secured. Now laptops—especially highly portable laptops such as ultrabooks—are also beginning to offer integral cellular data service.

VOICE CALLING SERVICE For voice calling, 802.11–cellular convergence has been slower to emerge. For voice calling, a mobile phone would normally use cellular service. However, if the caller was in range of a Wi-Fi access point, the phone would ask the caller if he or she preferred to use the WLAN to place the call. Many callers would welcome this as a way not to use up his or her daytime minutes for calls. In turn, the cellular provider might prefer to offload the customer's traffic from its expensive air network to the less expensive Internet for the path between the customer and the MTSO. Unfortunately, convergence for voice calls is still rare.

Of course, a mobile phone user could install Skype or a similar service on his or her smartphone. If the smartphone has Wi-Fi capabilities, as most do today, then he or she could place a Skype call when near an accessible access point.

USING A SMARTPHONE AS AN ACCESS POINT A third pattern in the convergence of 802.11 and cellular service is that some smartphones can be used as access points. This way, if a user has a laptop or other device that only has Wi-Fi capability, the user can access the Internet when no physical access points are nearby. In fact, several users might share the smartphone acting as an access point. With today's cellular speeds, this arrangement is not too exciting. However, as cellular speeds increase, smartphones that can act as access points will be more attractive.

One drawback of using smartphones as access points is that most carriers charge an additional monthly or usage fees for users doing this. This makes sense when groups share the access because it increases carrier traffic. However, this is a strong impediment to use.

Test Your Understanding

25. a) Why is it attractive to a laptop user to have WLAN access? (This is a simple question.) b) Why is it attractive for a laptop user to have cellular data access? c) Why is it good for users that some smartphones can connect to WLAN access points? d) Why is it good for carriers? e) Why is it attractive to users that some smartphones can act as access points? f) Why is it attractive for a smartphone to act as an access point? g) Why should it be more attractive in the future? h) What is unattractive using a smartphone as an access point today?

VIRTUAL WIDE AREA NETWORKS (VIRTUAL WANs)

An important development in WAN management has been the growing availability and sophistication of virtual WAN software. Most companies today have multiple WAN technology components—leased line connections, PSDNs of various types, Internet WAN transmission, cellular services, and so forth. They also deal with multiple types of access lines.

Traditionally, each of these components has been managed separately. However, traffic between two hosts may pass through multiple components. This makes it dif-

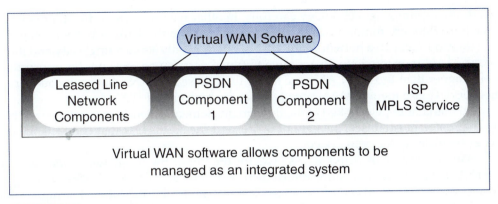

FIGURE 10-26 Virtual WAN

ficult to manage overall performance and efficiency. Optimization is nearly impossible, and it is very difficult to locate the causes of poor transmission quality.

Figure 10-26 shows that virtual WAN technology adds **virtual WAN software** to the corporate network. This software provides overall management of the individual WAN components so that they act as a complete system. This allows overall performance management in terms of efficiency and quality of service.

Once virtual WAN system is in place, it is also relatively easy to change. Individual technology components can be added or dropped with relative ease, and in many systems, the effect of an add or drop can be simulated before the expense of making technological changes is made.

Test Your Understanding

26. a) What technical problem does virtual WAN technology address? b) What must be added to create a corporate virtual WAN? c) What benefits can a virtual WAN system bring?

CONCLUSION

Synopsis

In Chapters 5, 6, and 7, we looked at local area networks. The technology picture was fairly clean. Ethernet dominates for wired LANs, and 802.11 dominates for wireless LANs. We also saw a few niche technologies, such as Bluetooth for personal area networks, but the core technology picture was quite simple.

Now we have switched to wide area networks, which take transmission beyond the customer premises. For WANs, the situation is anything but simple. Most corporations have multiple WAN technologies that must work in an integrated way. In this chapter, we stepped through these technologies, beginning with wired technologies and moving to cellular data transmission in the wireless realm.

LAN transmission distances are short, so the cost per bit transmitted is low. Consequently, companies can afford high transmission speeds and optimization is not an overwhelming concern. In WAN transmission, however, the cost per bit transmitted is relatively high, so companies need to be more frugal, living with lower transmission speeds and optimizing technology carefully. In other words, LAN and WAN managers must have different mindsets. In this chapter, you had to think like a WAN manager.

Metropolitan area networks are WANs, but they only serve a single city and its environs. MAN transmissions do not have to travel very far, so costs per bit transmitted, while higher than those in LANs, are lower than those in WANs that span countries or the world. Consequently, MAN speeds are at the high end of WAN speeds.

In this chapter, we looked at the three main elements of wide area networks. These are the customer premises, the network core, and the access link that connects the customer premises to the network core.

We looked first at wired access links for the Public Switched Telephone Network (PSTN). These access lines are referred to as the local loop. For businesses, 2-pair data-grade UTP lines provide transmission speed up to about 2 Mbps. For higher data speeds, optical fiber is necessary. Typically, the telephone company must run new lines to businesses needing service, and this makes these lines very expensive, leading to high service prices.

Businesses normally receive leased line service over their access lines. Leased lines are high-speed point-to-point lines that are always on. In the United States and Canada, T1 lines have a speed of 1.544 Mbps. In Europe, E1 lines are 2.048 Mbps. T1 and E1 leased lines, fractional T1 and E1 leased lines, and bonded T1 and E1 leased lines dominate leased line usage today. However, companies that need faster leased lines can get them. Above 50 Mbps, leased lines are governed by the SONET/SDH standards. These standards extend to several gigabits per second.

For the residential local loop, 1-pair voice-grade UTP is the norm. These lines were not designed to carry data, but engineers found how to do so. When these lines carry data, they are called digital subscriber lines (DSL lines). Residential customers normally receive asymmetric DSL, with higher downstream speeds than upstream speeds. There is no need to pull new lines to the customer premises. This allows less expensive service. Still, 1-pair VG UTP is not a good data transmission media, and carriers are beginning to serve residential customers with fiber to the home. Businesses also use DSL lines, but they normally receive symmetric speeds and quality-of-service guarantees. These guarantees make business DSL service more expensive than residential DSL service.

In the United States and a few other countries, cable television is widespread. Cable modem service permits the transmission of data over cable television connections. Cable television uses a mixture of optical fiber and coaxial cable, with the final runs to the home consisting of thin coaxial cable. Cable television is a competitor for DSL in most communities. Typically speaking, cable offers somewhat higher throughput at somewhat higher prices.

Access lines connect a company site to the network core at locations called points of presence (POPs). Many companies connect their sites via leased lines, using a router at each site to control the transmission. In addition, carriers offer public switched data networks (PSDNs), which essentially have the customer outsource the work of operating the network core. Customers merely run an access line from each site to the nearest POP. Only metropolitan area Ethernet, which moves Ethernet beyond the LAN, is growing rapidly in use among PSDN technologies.

If you read the box, "Virtual Circuit Operation," you saw how PSDN vendors reduce the work that switches in the network core have to do. These switches are connected in a mesh. This creates alternative routes. As we saw in Chapter 8, this makes routers do a great deal of work for each arriving packet. In virtual circuit operation, the network first establishes a single best path for all frames between two points. Then, when transmission begins, all frames follow that one path.

In the past, leased line networks and PSDNs dominated wide area networking. However, companies are now moving toward use of the Internet as their wide area networking technology. Economies of scale make the Internet inexpensive per bit transmitted. In addition, nearly all suppliers and customers are connected to the Internet.

Unfortunately, the Internet itself has no security. Companies that need to transmit securely across the Internet create virtual private networks (VPNs) using IPsec or SSL/TLS. They also use border firewalls, intrusion detection systems, and antivirus (antimalware) protection.

The Internet also has service quality issues. To address service quality, a company can connect all sites to a single ISP. The ISP can use multiprotocol label switching (MPLS) to control traffic quality and provide quality-of-service guarantees for traffic between corporate sites.

For metropolitan area networks, companies can turn to wireless transmission. Today, that primarily means sending data over cellular networks. In cellular technology, a city is divided into many geographical cells. Each cell has a cellsite with an antenna and radio equipment to communicate with customers within the site. Cellular channels can be reused in cells that are not too near, increasing the number of possible subscribers in a city. (In an analogous way, the many access points in a large wireless LANs permit channel reuse in different areas and therefore service to more 802.11 users.)

One difference between cellular and Wi-Fi networks is the distinction between handoff and roaming. In 802.11, both terms mean moving to another access point in the same wireless network. In cellular terminology, handoff is moving from one cell to another within a city, while roaming is going to a different city.

Cellular technology has gone through three generations of technology and is entering a fourth. Today, service with HSPA+ and LTE can reach 5 to 10 Mbps in downstream speed, although speeds are frequently lower. Normally, LTE is faster. HSPA+ is a 3G technology. LTE only offers 3G speed, but because it is a precursor to LTE Advanced technology, which is a full 4G technology, it may be referred to as 4G. Full 4G service will bring up to a gigabit per second of download speed, although LTE Advanced will undoubtedly offer far lower speeds when it first appears. Cellular throughput for individuals, of course, is limited by many factors, such as the number of simultaneous users in a cell and limits in both carrier and smartphone technology. As they say in television advertisements, your results will vary.

Today, cellular and 802.11 services are quite separate, but they are beginning to converge. Already, many tablets and smartphones can use an access point when they are near one, instead of using up their cellular data limits. They also receive faster transmission speeds. In addition, for voice calls, it may soon be possible to send those through an access point instead of using up cellular calling minutes. In addition, a smartphone using cellular data service can act as an access point to serve one or more 802.11 devices.

At the beginning of this synopsis, we noted that there are many WAN technologies and that most companies use several to serve their needs. A recent trend is the creation of virtual WAN (VWAN) software that manages all WAN transmission as a single integrated system. Even when the technology for a particular need is changed, the VWAN software continues as it has been doing.

END-OF-CHAPTER QUESTIONS

Thought Questions

1. Why was this chapter so difficult?

Hands-On

1. If you have a smartphone, download an app to tell your data transmission throughput. What did you find?

Perspective Questions

1. What was the most surprising thing in this chapter for you?

2. What was the most difficult part of this chapter for you?

11 NETWORKED APPLICATIONS

LEARNING OBJECTIVES

By the end of this chapter, you should be able to:

- Describe the concept and importance of networked applications.
- Describe how taking over an application can give an attacker the ability to control the computer.
- Describe electronic mail standards and security.
- Describe voice over IP (VoIP) operation and standards.
- Describe the World Wide Web in terms of standards and explain how a webpage with text, graphics, and other elements is downloaded.
- Describe cloud computing (including Software as a Service, utility computing, and virtualization, as well as security issues).
- Describe Service-Oriented Architectures, with an emphasis on Web services and SOAP.
- Explain peer-to-peer (P2P) computing (including BitTorrent, Skype, and SETI@home), which, paradoxically, normally uses servers for part of the work.

PAPA MURPHY'S

Papa Murphy's Take 'N' Bake is one of the largest pizza companies in the United States, having more than 1,150 stores in more than 30 states.[1] Many of its stores are franchised. While the company has enjoyed success and expansion, it also faced a problem: how could it create a centralized management system for all of its franchises?

Rather than designing, building, and hosting its own management system, Papa Murphy's decided to outsource the job to Salesforce, a company that provides cloud computing services. According to Papa Murphy's Director of Business Technology, Brian Fisher, "It took less than three months to build what would have taken a year on other platforms."[2] In addition to its quick implementation, the new franchise management system also brought the benefit of mobile access. Since the system is run as an online application, employees can access the information they need from anywhere, via mobile devices. Also, Papa Murphy's is freed from managing the system and the servers it runs on; these IT jobs are taken care of by Salesforce.[3]

---

[1] www.papamurphys.com.
[2] "5 Reasons CIOs are Adopting Cloud Computing in 2009." Salesforce.com white paper. Salesforce.com.
[3] http://www.salesforce.com/customers/distribution-retail/papamurphys.jsp, www.salesforce.com/customers/distribution-retail/papamurphys.jsp.

Test Your Understanding

1. a) What business problem did Papa Murphy's face? b) How did Papa Murphy's resolve this problem? c) What benefits did Papa Murphy's see as a result of its choice to use Salesforce to handle this work? d) Can you think of any risks that are involved in this business choice?

INTRODUCTION

Networked Applications

Applications that require networks to operate are called **networked applications**. The World Wide Web and e-mail are networked applications. So is the Salesforce franchise management application used by Papa Murphy's.

APPLICATION ARCHITECTURES   In this chapter, we will focus on **application architectures**— that is, how application layer functions are spread among computers to deliver service to users. Early PCs used stand-alone operation in which all processing was done on the PC. Today, we have seen that client/server processing is dominant. In this chapter, we will also look at peer-to-peer (P2P) operation.

An application architecture describes how application layer functions are spread among computers to deliver service to users.

Networked Applications

Applications that require a network to operate
World Wide Web, etc.

Application Architectures

How application layer functions are spread among computers to deliver service to users.
Stand-alone operation
Client/server operation
Peer-to-peer (P2P) operation
Service-oriented architecture (SOA) operation

Important Networked Applications

E-mail, voice over IP, the World Wide Web, cloud computing, peer-to-peer (P2P) computing, and mobile applications
Importance of the application layer to users
Contains all of the functionality that users see directly
What happens at lower layers should simply happen

FIGURE 11-1   Basic Networked Application Concepts (Study Figure)

IMPORTANT NETWORKED APPLICATIONS In addition to looking broadly at application architectures, we will look at some of the most important of today's networked applications, including e-mail, voice over IP, the World Wide Web, cloud computing, peer-to-peer (P2P) computing, and mobile applications.

IMPORTANCE OF THE APPLICATION LAYER TO USERS In this chapter, we will focus on the application layer. This is the only layer whose functionality users see directly. When users want e-mail, it is irrelevant what is happening below the application layer, unless there is a failure or performance problem at lower layers.

Test Your Understanding

2. a) What is a networked application? b) What is an application architecture? c) Why do users focus on the application layer?

The Evolution of Client Devices and Networking

Some years ago, the president of the Stanley Works told his Board of Directors, "Last year, we sold 4 million drill bits that nobody wanted." After pausing to let that provacative statement sink in, he went on to explain by saying that, "What they wanted was holes." Drill bits and drills are expensive. They are merely tolerated, despite their expense and difficulty of use, because the customer needs holes. The message he was trying to emphasize is that drills are not the only ways to make holes. The company needed to focus on customer needs, not techology. Of course, although he was fundamentally correct, quite a few customers do like drills, a lot. So technology can to some extent drive demand.

With networked applications—applications that require a network to operate—the same dynamic occurs. Obviously, applications must serve customer needs. However, as client devices and networks have evolved, each step in their evolution has brought new "killer apps" that were impossible before new devices and new networks appeared. Figure 11-2 shows imporant steps in the evolution of client devices.

DUMB TERMINALS When computers were first built, the only way to interact with them was to throw binary switches, rewire boards, and enter programs on punch cards into readers. Then, in the 1960s, remote terminals appeared. People could interact with computers via keyboards and printers (later keyboards and displays). This was before the days of microprocessors, so these devices were dumb terminals. They could merely send keystrokes to the large central computer and send characters from the central computer to the printer or display. In terms of application architecture, all processing had to be done on the large host computer. If the dumb terminal was remote from the large computer, transmission took place at very low speeds over telephone modems. Consequently, the user interface on displays consisted of monochrome text (plain text in a single color against a contrasting color background).

EARLY PERSONAL COMPUTERS In the mid-1970s, the first personal computers appeared. Thanks to microprocessors, they were complete computers. These could be used by average employees in average companies and even homes. There was an explosion in new types of computer applications, including word processing, spreadsheet programs, graphics, and games. A few began to communicate to large computers by emulating (acting like) dumb terminals, but they were primarily stand-alone devices.

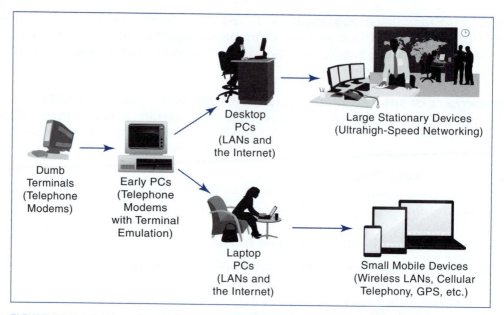

FIGURE 11-2 The Evolution of Client Devices and Networking

DESKTOP AND LAPTOP PCs   In the 1980s, a fundamental divide began between desktop PCs and laptop PCs. For desktop use, the key was processing power, massive amounts of storage, larger screens, and other performance-enhancing technologies. For laptop PCs, the keys were decreasing size and weight while gradually adding processing power. Both categories of PCs benefitted from the growth of local area networks in the 1990s.

In addition, while stand-alone applications were very popular, LANs created a new type of application architecture, client/server processing, which we have seen since the beginning of this book. With PCs growing in performance, client/server processing split the processing work between the client and the large computer. Before PCs, this was not possible. In the 1990s, the Internet caused client/server processing to grow explosively. All computers soon came with browsers, which were initially universal clients for webserver programs. Browsers soon grew beyond this single application to be clients for the file transfer protocol, e-mail, and many other applications. With tremendous economies of scale, the cost of using the Internet fell rapidly. In addition, telephone modem access quickly gave way to broadband access services.

SMALL MOBILE DEVICES   The 21st century expanded the divide between desktop and laptop PCs. Most of the growth to date has come in the category of small mobile devices. New technology has allowed vendors to pack an acceptable amount of processing power and battery life into small hand-held products. Led by Apple, technology companies have introduced a wide variety of small mobile devices. The two fastest-growing segments so far have been tablets and smartphones. Although tablet and smartphone users want faster processing, these devices are now sufficiently powerful to allow direct device–device interactions without a network between them.

Laptops have been undergoing a mobile revolution as well. Laptops, despite their portability, have always been uncomfortably heavy, leading to cases of "jet lug" among travelers. Underpowered netbook PCs enjoyed some growth despite their limitations. Now vendors are offering small laptops that cost more but that come with adequate processing power and usability. Macbook Air computers and Windows ultraportable computers are beginning to gain traction in the market. They are beginning to add multitouch gestures to their trackpads and will soon offer touch screen displays. Nearly all operating system vendors are struggling to create integrated operating systems that will run on devices from notebook computers to smart wristwatches.

Small device technology and wireless networking (including 802.11 WLANs, cellular telephony, and GPS) have combined to create a blizzard of new types of applications. Ever-growing transmission speeds have created rich applications impossible even on large desktop computers only a few years before.

LARGE STATIONARY DEVICES   Small mobile devices are dominating the news on client device evolution. However, working on a small screen can be difficult. Many office workers already have desktop PCs with multiple displays, offering a great deal of "real estate" for laying out windows for multiple applications. In some cases, these are already touch screens. In the future, tables, desks, and walls will themselves be displays and will all be linked together by ultra-high-speed networks. Presumably, these devices too will create a revolution in applications. If history has taught us anything, however, it is that when new computer and networking technologies occur, we always see a flood of startling new applications.

Test Your Understanding

3. Create a table. The first column should be client device (dumb terminal, PC, etc.). The second column should be the technical advance embodied in the client. The third should be networking advances associated with the client. The fourth and last should be new networked applications made possible by the client and networking.

4. What advance made the client/server application architecture possible?

Application Security

In the past, hackers focused primarily on vulnerabilities in the operating system in order to break into computers. Today, however, hackers primarily attack individual applications running on the computer.

The reason for this is shown in Figure 11-3. If a hacker can take over an application, then he or she receives all of the permissions that the operating system gave to the application. Many applications run with root privileges, which means that they can do anything on the computer. Taking over such an application gives the hacker total control over the computer.

If a hacker can take over an application, then he or she receives all of the permissions that the operating system gave to the application.

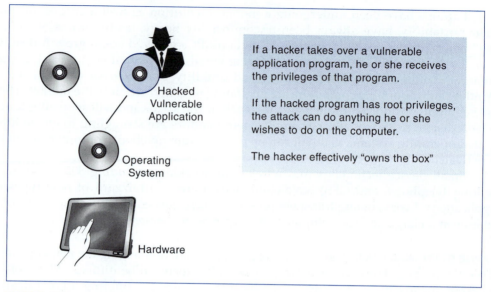

If a hacker takes over a vulnerable application program, he or she receives the privileges of that program.

If the hacked program has root privileges, the attack can do anything he or she wishes to do on the computer.

The hacker effectively "owns the box"

FIGURE 11-3 Application Hacking

Finding a vulnerability in the operating system is increasingly difficult. However, with the many applications running on most computers, and with inconsistent security quality across applications, the probability of finding a vulnerable application on a computer is substantial. Security vulnerabilities in specific applications are listed in many hacker forums that are readily available to attackers.

We are now seeing an explosion in apps created for mobile devices. In addition, we are seeing diversity in mobile operating systems. The newness of mobile operating systems and mobile applications has led many inexperienced developers to create applications with severe vulnerabilities. Coupled with a lack of corporate control over mobile devices, lack of experience has created a flood of application (and operating system) vulnerabilities.

Test Your Understanding

5. a) Why are hackers now focusing on taking over applications? b) What are root privileges? c) Why is the explosion of applications and small mobile devices a particular conern?

ELECTRONIC MAIL (E-MAIL)

Having discussed some factors that are driving new network application, we can now turn to specific networked applications. We will begin with electronic mail (e-mail) which was one of the earliest applications on wide area networks and that is still growing rapidly today.

Importance

A UNIVERSAL SERVICE ON THE INTERNET E-mail has become one of the two "universal" services on the Internet, along with the World Wide Web. E-mail provides mailbox delivery even if the receiver is "off-line" when the message is received. E-mail offers the speed of a fax, plus the ability to store messages in organized files, to send replies, to forward messages to others, and to perform many other actions after message receipt. The telephone offers truly instant communication, but only if the other party is in and can take calls. In addition, e-mail is less intrusive than a phone call.

ATTACHMENTS CAN DELIVER ANYTHING Thanks to attachments, e-mail has also become a general file delivery system. Users can exchange spreadsheet documents, word processing documents, graphics, and any other type of file.

E-Mail Standards

A major driving force behind the wide acceptance of Internet e-mail is standardization. It is rare for users of different systems not to be able to communicate at a technical level—although many companies restrict outgoing and incoming communication using firewalls for security purposes. Consequently, the key issue is application layer standards. Figure 11-4 shows that e-mail uses multiple standards for different aspects of its operation.

MESSAGE BODY STANDARDS Obviously, message bodies have to be standardized, or we would not be able to read arriving messages. In physical mail, message body standards include the language the partners will use (English, etc.), the formality of language, and other matters. Some physical messages are forms, which have highly standardized layouts and fields that require specific information.

RFC 2822 (ORIGINALLY RFC 822) BODIES The initial standard for e-mail bodies (and headers) was **RFC 822**, which has been updated as **RFC 2822**. This is a standard for plain text messages—multiple lines of typewriter-like characters with no boldface, graphics, or other amenities. The extreme simplicity of this approach made it easy to create early client e-mail programs.

HTML BODIES Later, as HTML became widespread on the World Wide Web, most mail venders developed the ability to display **HTML bodies** with richly formatted text and even graphics.

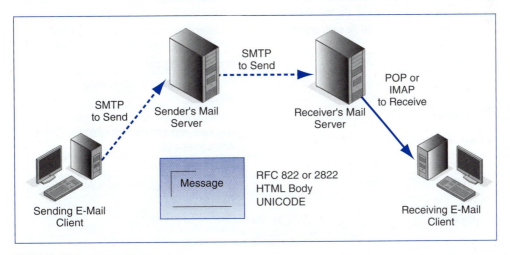

FIGURE 11-4 E-Mail Standards

UNICODE BODIES RFC 822 specified the use of the ASCII code to represent printable characters. Unfortunately, ASCII was developed for English, and even European languages need extra characters. The **UNICODE** standard allows characters of all languages to be represented, although most mail readers cannot display all UNICODE characters well yet.

Simple Mail Transfer Protocol (SMTP)

We also need standards for delivering RFC 2822, HTML, and UNICODE messages. In the postal world, we must have envelopes that present certain information in certain ways, and there are specific ways to post mail for delivery, including putting letters in post office drop boxes and taking them to the post office.

Figure 11-4 shows how e-mail is posted (sent). The e-mail program on the user's PC sends the message to its outgoing mail host, using the **Simple Mail Transfer Protocol (SMTP)**. Figure 11-5 shows the complex series of interactions that SMTP requires between the sender and the receiver before and after mail delivery.

SMTP Process	Command	Explanation
Receiving	220 mail.panko.com Ready	When the sending host establishes a TCP session, the receiver signals that it is ready.
Sending	HELO voyager.shilder .hawaii.edu	Sender asks to begin sending a message. Identifies itself. (Yes, HELO, not HELLO)
Receiving	250 mail.panko.com	Receiver signals it is ready to receive a message.
Sending	MAIL FROM: david@voyager.hawaii.edu	Sender identifies the message author.
Receiving	250 OK	Receiver accepts the message author.
Sending	RCTP TO: ray@panko.com	Sender identifies the first recipient.
Receiving	250 OK	Receiver accepts the first recipient.
Sending	RCTP TO: lee@panko.com	Sender identifies the second recipient.
Receiving	550 No such user here	Receiver rejects the first recipient but will deliver the message to the first recipient.
Sending	DATA	Message will follow.
Receiving	354 Start mail input; end with <CRLF><CRLF>	Gives permission to begin sending the message.
Sending	*When in the course…*	Sender sends the message. Multiple lines of text. Ends with two carriage return/line feeds, which gives a blank line.
Receiving	250 OK	Accepts the message.
Sending	QUIT	Sender requests termination of the SMTP session.
Receiving	221 Mail.Panko.COM Service closing transmission channel	Receiver terminates session.

FIGURE 11-5 Simple Mail Transfer Protocol (SMTP) Interactions

Receiving Mail (POP and IMAP)

Figure 11-4 also shows two standards that are used to *receive* e-mail. These are the **Post Office Protocol (POP)** and the **Internet Message Access Protocol (IMAP)**. IMAP offers more features, but the simpler POP standard is more popular. Programs implementing these standards ask the mail host to download some or all new mail to the user's client e-mail program. Often, users delete new mail from their inbox after downloading new messages. After that, the remaining messages exist only on the user's client PC.

Web-Enabled E-Mail

Almost all client PCs have browsers. Many mail hosts are now Web-enabled, meaning that users only need browsers to interact with them in order to send, receive, and manage their e-mail. As Figure 11-6 showed, all interactions take place via HTTP, and these systems use HTML to render pages on-screen.

Malware Filtering in E-Mail

Although e-mail is tremendously important to corporations, it is a source of intense security headaches. As we learned in Chapter 3, the most widespread security compromises are attacks by malware. Malware enters an organization primarily, although by no means exclusively, through e-mail attachments and (sometimes) through scripts in e-mail bodies. E-mail attachments can also be used to install worms and Trojan horse programs on victim PCs.

ANTIVIRUS SOFTWARE The obvious countermeasure to e-mail-borne viruses is **antivirus software**, which scans incoming messages and attachments for viruses, worms, and Trojan horses. Many companies produce antivirus programs that can run on client PCs.

ANTIVIRUS SCANNING ON USER PCs One problem is that most companies attempt to confront security threats by installing virus scanning on the user PCs. Unfortunately,

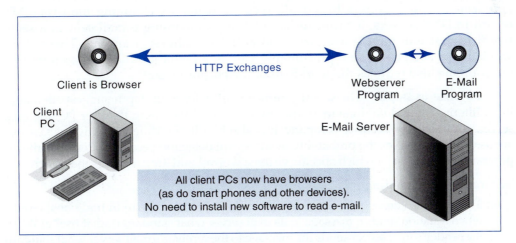

FIGURE 11-6 Web-Enabled E-Mail Operation

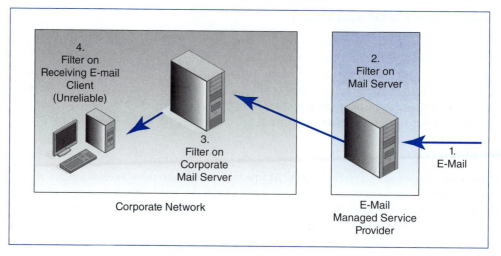

FIGURE 11-7 Scanning Locations for E-Mail Malware

too many users either turn off their antivirus programs if they seem to be interfering with other programs (or appear to slow things down too much) or keep their programs active but fail to update them regularly. In the latter case, newer viruses will not be recognized by the antivirus program.

CENTRALIZED ANTIVIRUS/ANTI-TROJAN HORSE SCANNING Consequently, many companies are beginning to do central scanning for e-mail-borne viruses and Trojan horses. As Figure 11-7 shows, there are several places that this scanning can be done.

Scanning on Mail Servers One popular place to do this is the corporate mail server. Users cannot turn off antivirus filtering on the mail server, and the e-mail staff (hopefully) updates virus definitions on these servers frequently.

Outsourcing Scanning Some companies are even outsourcing antivirus/anti-Trojan horse scanning to outside security firms. By changing the firm's MX record in DNS servers, a firm can have all of its incoming e-mail sent to a security firm that will handle antivirus and anti-Trojan horse scanning. These firms specialize in such tasks and, presumably, can do a better job than the corporation. Outsourcing also reduces the workload of the corporate staff.

Defense in Depth The security principle of defense in depth suggests that antivirus filtering should be done in at least two locations, including the user PC, the mail server, or an external security company. It is also best if two different antivirus vendors are used. This increases the probability of successful detection because different antivirus programs often differ in which specific viruses, worms, and Trojan horses they catch.

Test Your Understanding

6. a) Distinguish among the major standards for e-mail bodies. b) In traditional e-mail, when a station sends a message to its mail server what standard does it use? c) When the sender's mail server sends the message to the receiver's mail server what standard does it use? d) In traditional e-mail, when the receiver's e-mail client downloads new

mail from its mail server what standards are it likely to use? e) What is Web-enabled e-mail? f) What do you think are the advantages of a Web-enabled e-mail system?

7. a) What is the main tool of firms in fighting viruses and Trojan horses in e-mail attachments? b) Why does filtering on the user's PC often not work? c) What options do firms have for where antivirus filtering should be done? d) According to the principle of defense in depth, how should firms do antivirus filtering?

VOICE OVER IP (VOIP)

Another example of the client/server architecture is voice over IP (VoIP). Like e-mail, VoIP is a client/server application in which both the sender and the receiver have their own servers. A major difference between these applications, however, is that, after setting up a connection, the servers in VoIP get out of the way almost completely, and the two clients communicate by sending packets directly to each other until the end of the call.

Basics

One of the newest areas in telephony is **voice over IP (VoIP)**, which is the transmission of telephone signals over IP packet-switched internets (including the Internet) instead of over circuit-switched networks. VoIP offers the promise of reducing telephone costs by moving from traditional telephone transmission which reserved capacity for a call even when neither side was transmitting, to more efficient packet switching, which only charges for information actually sent. This can substantially reduce cost.

Voice over IP (VoIP), which is the transmission of telephone signals over IP packet-switched internets (including the Internet).

CLIENTS   Figure 11-8 illustrates VoIP operation. The figure shows two clients. One is a client PC with multimedia hardware (a microphone and speakers) and VoIP software. The other is a **VoIP telephone**, which has the electronics to encode voice for digital transmission and to handle packets over an IP internet. With VoIP, these two client users can talk with each other.

MEDIA GATEWAY   The figure also shows a media gateway. The **media gateway** connects a VoIP system to the ordinary public switched telephone network. Without a media gateway, VoIP users could talk only to one another. The media gateway translates both signaling and transport transmissions.

The media gateway translates both signaling and transport transmissions.

Test Your Understanding

8. a) What is VoIP? b) What is the promise of VoIP? c) What two devices can be used by VoIP callers? d) What is the purpose of a media gateway? e) Why is having a media gateway in a VoIP system important? f) Does the media gateway translate signaling transmissions or transport transmissions?

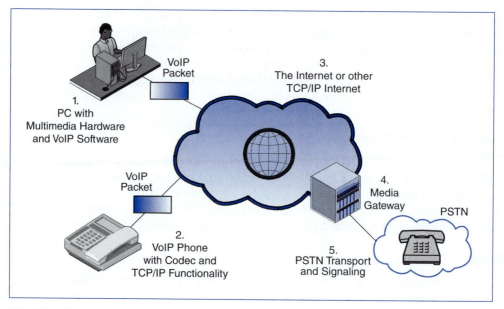

FIGURE 11-8 Voice over IP (VoIP) Operation

VoIP Signaling

In telecommunications, there is a fundamental distinction between signaling and transport. Signaling consists of the communication needed to set up circuits, tear down circuits, handle billing information, and do other supervisory chores. Transport is the actual carriage of voice.

> *In telecommunications, there is a fundamental distinction between signaling and transport. Signaling consists of the communication needed to set up circuits, tear down circuits, handle billing information, and do other supervisory chores. Transport is the actual carriage of voice.*

There are two major VoIP signaling protocols. The first was the ISO **H.323** standard, which was effective, but very complex. More recently, the IETF created the **Session Initiation Protocol (SIP)** standard. Most older VoIP systems use H.323 to control signaling. However, the use of SIP is growing rapidly, and most VoIP systems today use SIP for signaling.

Figure 11-9 illustrates the SIP protocol. Each subscriber has an SIP proxy server. The calling VoIP telephone sends a SIP INVITE message to its SIP proxy server. This message gives the IP address of the receiver. The caller's SIP proxy server then sends the SIP INVITE message to the called party's SIP proxy server. The called party's proxy server sends the SIP INVITE message to the called party's VoIP telephone or multimedia PC.

Test Your Understanding

9. a) What are the two major protocols for VoIP signaling? b) Which of these protocols is growing rapidly? c) Describe how SIP initiates a communication session.

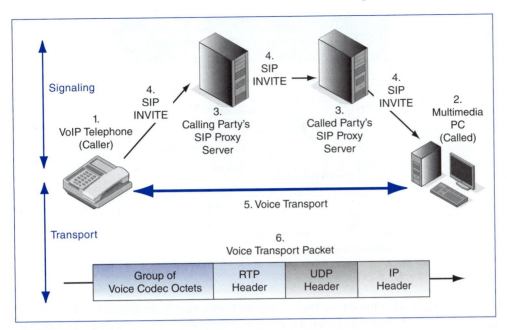

FIGURE 11-9 Voice over IP (VoIP) Signaling and Transport Standards

VoIP Transport

After SIP or H.323 creates a connection, the two VoIP clients begin communicating directly. This is the beginning of transport, which is the transmission of voice between callers. VoIP, as its name suggests, operates over routed IP networks. Therefore, digitized voice has to be carried from the sender to the receiver in packets.

CODECS VoIP telephones and multimedia PCs need codecs to convert analog voice signals into digital voice data streams. VoIP systems can use many different codecs. Figure 11-10 shows that some codecs convert voice streams into bit streams as small as 5.3 kbps. However, the codecs that do the most compression also lose the most voice quality. Selecting codec in a VoIP network means making a trade-off between voice quality and cost reduction.

VOIP TRANSPORT PACKETS As noted in Chapter 1, long application messages have to be fragmented into smaller pieces that can be carried in individual packets. Each packet carries a small part of the application message. In VoIP, packets carry a small snippet of digital voice bytes created by the codec.

   The Application Layer: Codec Bytes Figure 11-9 shows a VoIP transport packet. At the application layer, the application message is a group of voice codec bytes.

   UDP TCP allows reliable application message delivery. However, the retransmission of lost or damaged TCP segments can take a second or two—far too long for voice conversations. Voice needs to be transmitted in real time. Consequently, VoIP transport uses UDP at the transport layer. UDP reduces the processing load on the VoIP

Codec Standard	Bits Transmitted per Second
G.711	64 kbps
G.722	48, 56, or 64 kbps
G.721	32 kbps
G.722.1	24, 32 kbps
G.726	16, 24, 32, 40 kbps
G.728	16 kbps
G.729AB	8 kbps
G.723	5.33, 6.4 kbps
G.7231A	5.3, 6.3 kbps

FIGURE 11-10 Codec Standards

telephones, and it also limits the high network traffic that VoIP generates. If packets are lost, the receiver creates fake noise for the lost codec bytes. It does this by extrapolating between the content of the preceding and following packets.

The Real Time Protocol (RTP) Between UDP and the application message, VoIP adds an additional header, a Real Time Protocol (RTP) header, to make up for two deficiencies of UDP:

- First, UDP does not guarantee that packets will be delivered in order. RTP adds a sequence number so that the application layer can put packets in the proper sequence.
- Second, VoIP is highly sensitive to jitter, which is variable latency in packet delivery. Jitter literally makes the voice sound jittery. RTP contains a time stamp for when its package of octets should be played relative to the octets in the previous packet. This allows the receiver to provide smooth playback.

The IP Header This is a packet, so the IP header comes before the other fields.

Test Your Understanding

10. a) What is the purpose of a VoIP codec? b) Some codecs compress voice more. What do they give up in doing so? c) In a VoIP transport packet, what is the application message? d) Does a VoIP transport packet use UDP or TCP? Explain why. e) What two problems with UDP does RTP fix? f) List the headers and messages in a VoIP transport packet, beginning with the first packet header to arrive at the receiver. (Hint: See Figure 11-9.)

THE WORLD WIDE WEB

HTTP and HTML Standards

We have discussed the World Wide Web throughout this book. Figure 11-11 shows that the Web is based on two primary standards.

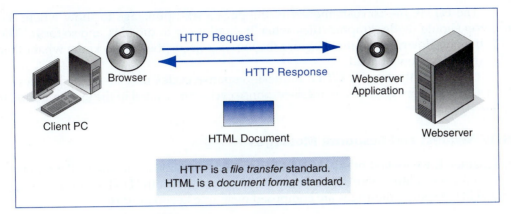

FIGURE 11-11 World Wide Web (WWW) Standards

- First, webpages themselves are created using the **Hypertext Markup Language (HTML)**.
- Second, the transfer of requests and responses uses the **Hypertext Transfer Protocol (HTTP)**.

To give an analogy, an e-mail message may be created using RFC 2822, but it will be delivered using SMTP. Many application standards consist of a document standard and a transfer standard.

Many application standards consist of a document standard and a transfer standard.

Complex Webpages

Actually, most "webpages" really consist of several files—a master text-only HTML file plus graphics files, audio files, and other types of files. Figure 11-12 illustrates the downloading of a webpage with two graphics files.

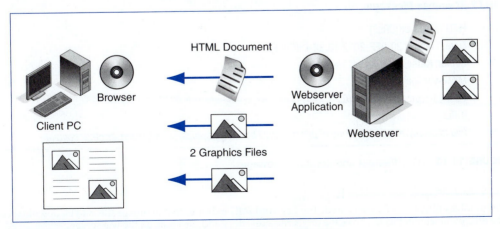

FIGURE 11-12 Downloading a Webpage with Two Graphics Files

The HTML file consists merely of the page's text, plus **tags** to show where the browser should render graphics files, when it should play audio files, and so forth.[4] The HTML file is downloaded first because the browser needs the tags to know what other files should be downloaded.

Consequently, several **HTTP request–response cycles** may be needed to download a single webpage. Three request–response cycles are needed in the example shown in the figure.

HTTP Request and Response Messages

In Chapter 1, we looked briefly at HTTP request and response messages. We will now look at them in a little more detail. Figure 11-13 shows that both HTTP request messages and HTTP response messages are composed of simple keyboard text.

HTTP REQUEST MESSAGES In HTTP request messages, the first line has four elements:

- The line begins with a capitalized method (in this case, GET), which specifies what the requestor wishes the webserver to do. The GET method says that the client wishes to get a file.
- The method is followed by a space and then by the location of the file (in this example, /panko/home.htm). This is home.htm in the panko directory.
- Next comes the version of HTTP that the client browser supports (in this example, HTTP/5).
- The line ends with a carriage return/line feed—a command to start a new line of text.

Each subsequent field is one line long (there is only one in this example). The field consists of a keyword (in this example, Host), a colon (:), a value for the keyword (in this example, voyager.shidler.hawaii.edu), and a carriage return/line feed.

HTTP Request Message

> GET /panko.home.htm HTTP/5[CRLF]
> Host: voyager.shidler.hawaii.edu[CRLF]

HTTP Response Message

> HTTP/5 200 OK[CRLF]
> Date: Tuesday 20-SEP-2012 18:32:15[CRLF]
> Server: Name of server software
> MIME-version 1.0[CRLF]
> Content-type: text/plain [CRLF]
> [CRLF]
> *File to be downloaded. A string of bits that may be text, graphics, sound, video, or other content.*

FIGURE 11-13 HTTP Request and Response Messages

---

[4]For graphics files, the IMG tag is used. The keyword *IMG* indicates that an image file is to be downloaded. The *SRC* parameter in this tag gives the target file's directory and file name on the webserver.

HTTP RESPONSE MESSAGES   HTTP response messages also begin with a four-element first line.

- The webserver responds by giving the version of HTTP it supports.
- This is followed by a space and then a code. A 200 code is good; it indicates that the method was followed successfully. In contrast, codes in the 400 range are bad codes that indicate problems.
- This code is followed by a text expression that states what the code says in humanly readable form. This information ("OK" in this example) is useless to the browser.
- A carriage return/line feed ends this first line.

OTHER FIELDS   Subsequent lines are fields. They have the keyword–colon–value–carriage return/line feed structure we saw in the HTTP request message. In the figure, these fields give a time stamp, the name of the server software (not shown), and two MIME fields. **MIME (Multipurpose Internet Mail Extensions)** is a standard for specifying the format of the file being delivered as the body of the response message. MIME is also used for this purpose in e-mail (as its name suggests) and in some other applications.

- The first MIME field gives the version of MIME the webserver uses (1.0).
- The next line, **content-type** field, specifies that the file being delivered by the webserver is of the text/plain type—simple keyboard characters.

BLANK LINE   After all HTTP response message header fields, there is a blank line (two CR/LFs in a row give a blank line). This is followed by the bytes of the file being sent by the webserver.

Test Your Understanding

11. a) Distinguish between HTTP and HTML. b) You are downloading a webpage that has six graphics and two sound clips. How many request–response cycles will be needed? c) What is the syntax of the first line in an HTTP request message? d) What is the syntax of subsequent fields? e) What is the syntax of the first line in an HTTP response message? f) What do the MIME header fields tell the receiving process? g) Why is this information necessary? h) How is the start of the attached file indicated?

CLOUD COMPUTING

A Shared Project

Figure 11-14 shows Shea and Melinda, who are working to construct a word processing report for their project. Normally, they would use word processing programs stored on their PCs and would exchange versions by storing them as on a corporate server. Their word processing applications are stored locally on their PCs.

This time, however, their manager asks them to use Google Docs for this project, so that they can collaborate remotely more easily. This is illustrated in

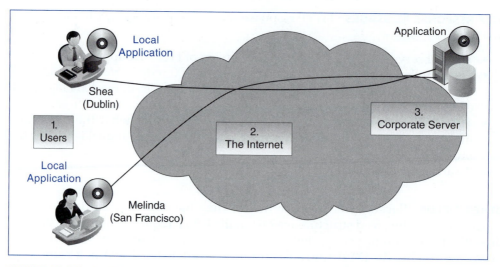

FIGURE 11-14 Traditional Sharing

Figure 11-15. When Shea wants to input information, he logs onto the Google Docs website. The Google Docs website downloads the Google Docs software to his computer. Melinda does the same.

Storing applications on servers for downloading is called **Software as a Service (SaaS)**. The name comes from the fact that the users do not purchase the software, as they do with traditional applications. Instead, they pay a certain amount per month or per use. This is the way people typically pay for services like haircuts, DSL service, and cellular service, hence the term *service*.

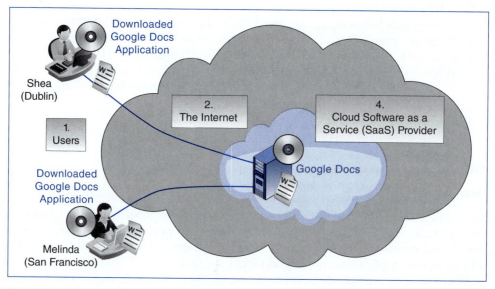

FIGURE 11-15 Software as a Service (SaaS)

Shea uses Google Docs and to draft the report. The draft is stored on the Google Docs servers, rather than on Shea's desktop computer or his company's servers. Shea and Melinda still have the option of downloading documents from the Google servers to their PCs, and they can also upload preexisting documents to the Google Docs servers. The Google Docs servers are backed up frequently, so data loss is much less likely than it is on local PCs.

Afterward, Melinda needs to edit Shea's document, so Shea adds her to the group that has access to it. She uses her browser to access it. She then makes edits and saves the document again. Later, Shea can read the edited document and add his own edits.

Test Your Understanding

12. a) What is software as a service? b) Why is the word *service* in SaaS? c) What do you think are some advantages of storing files on Google Docs services?

Cloud Computing

In Chapter 1, we saw that network users view networks as clouds because users never have to worry about the details of network operation. In Chapter 10, we saw that companies view public switched data networks as clouds because they do not have to understand the internal switching mechanism.

In Figure 11-15, there are two clouds. The broader cloud is the Internet. As users, Shea and Melinda merely connect to the Internet and then ignore it. In addition, Google Docs is shown as another cloud because Shea and Melinda do not have to know how it works or where their documents are stored.

More radically, Google Docs is also a cloud to the company that Shea and Melinda work for. The company does not have to install any software on its employee computers to use Google Docs. Nor does the company have to manage servers and application software on the servers.

Google Docs is just one example of a new trend in computing—cloud computing. In traditional computing, the company had to maintain its servers, server applications, and client PC software. In **cloud computing**, the company outsources some combination of servers, server applications, and client PC software to a **cloud service provider** (a company that provides cloud computing services). If client PC software is outsourced, the client PC only needs a browser. In the case of Google Docs, the company employing Shea and Melinda outsourced all three functions to Google, its cloud service provider.

Cloud computing is a form of computing where the company outsources some combination of servers, server applications, and client PC software to a cloud service provider. If client PC software is outsourced, the client PC only needs a browser.

So far, we have not talked about pricing. Typically, cloud service providers offer **metered service**. In this pay-as-you-go model, the cloud computing customer pays only for the processing capacity that he or she actually uses. A company can buy as little or as much processing capacity as it needs for a given task, rather than having to commit to a monthly service contract that does not match up to its actual needs. This also saves the company from the burden of purchasing servers, software to run on its clients and servers, and annual licenses to use the software.

Test Your Understanding

13. a) What is cloud computing? b) What is an organization that provides cloud services called?

Software as a Service (SaaS)

There are different types of cloud computing services. We will focus on two of the most widely used types: Software as a Service and utility computing. Although both types of service predate cloud computing, each has been enhanced—and has become much more popular—through cloud computing. We will begin by looking at Software as a Service.

DEFINITION   In **Software as a Service (SaaS)**, an application service provider (ASP) supplies an application to customers on demand. SaaS software vendors may host the application on their own webservers or download the application to the consumer device, disabling it after use or after the on-demand contract expires. In **cloud Software as a Service**, the user accesses the software over the Internet, often (although not always) with a browser. If this sounds familiar, Google Docs in Figure 11-15 is an example of cloud SaaS. As with traditional SaaS, the application may either be hosted on the ASP's webservers or downloaded temporarily from the webservers to the consumer device.

SAAS AS A CLOUD COMPUTING MODEL   As just noted, Software as a Service is not a new idea. For example, web-based e-mail has been around for over a decade. What *has* changed with cloud SaaS is that there is a now a very wide range of applications available—everything from word processing and spreadsheet programs to data visualization software that provides real-time analysis of a company's performance, payroll processing, and general accounting, to name just a few.[5] Cloud computing has also made SaaS increasingly popular as a business model. One high-profile example is Salesforce, whose customer relationship management software and other applications have been widely used.[6]

ATTRACTIONS OF CLOUD SAAS   One main attraction of cloud SaaS is that a company can use software on an as-needed basis, which may result in lowered costs and less risk. A company is especially likely to see cost savings if it uses cloud SaaS for an application it uses only occasionally. With cloud SaaS, the company is saved the risk of long-term investment in hardware and management.

A second attraction is that cloud SaaS allows the company to save on personnel resources. Since all of the management of the software is done in the cloud, the company does not have to allocate IT staff to install or manage the application. So a company may be able to save money even if it uses the software heavily.

Mobility is a third attraction. As illustrated in the Google Docs example, because cloud SaaS delivers an application over the Internet, users can access the software from

---

[5] See, for example, Salesforce's Sales Cloud™ datasheet. http://www.salesforce.com/crm/sales-force-automation/analytics-sales-forecasting.
[6] Salesforce.com claims that the Sales Cloud is the world's most popular sales application." http://www.salesforce.com/crm/sales-force-automation/.

anywhere they can access the Internet. This is especially useful for employees who often travel or work from home.

A fourth attraction is collaboration. Most SaaS vendors allow multiple people within a customer company to work on the same information, as in the Google Docs example at the start of this section.

ISSUES FOR CLOUD SAAS   Unfortunately, cloud Software as a Service also raises serious issues that corporations must consider.

- First is the issue of access. A company using cloud SaaS might be unable to access the application for several reasons. If the cloud service provider has a technical problem or is attacked and taken off-line, users will be unable to access the application. Similarly, a cloud service provider may go out of business, leaving users no way to access or recover their stored information, and no way to continue working on a project that required specific software. If software resources on the cloud become inaccessible for any reason, client computers become useless, and companies may be unable to complete time-sensitive projects.
- A second and related concern is that cloud SaaS entails a loss of control. Companies may be locked into proprietary software. They may be unable to migrate their data out of a particular SaaS application, and they may thus be locked into rising costs.
- The third issue is security. If your company's sensitive data is stored in the SaaS application, it may be vulnerable to attackers who target the cloud service provider. A customer can only hope that the cloud service provider has strong security. Similarly, the application software itself may have dangerous vulnerabilities. For example, in 2008, a software bug in Google Docs resulted in some users' documents being inadvertently shared, potentially making corporate data available to parties who should not have had permission to see it.[7]
- A final issue is that legal complications may arise from using cloud SaaS. If a company is required by law or corporate policy to provide regular security audits, what happens if the cloud service provider refuses to be audited? Also, if data stored by the cloud service provider is compromised, who will be held legally liable?

Test Your Understanding

14. a) Describe how Software as a Service (SaaS) works. b) Describe how cloud SaaS works. c) What are the four main attractions of cloud SaaS? d) What are the four issues that cloud SaaS raises?

Cloud Utility Computing

The second main type of cloud computing is cloud utility computing. Like Software as a Service, utility computing predates cloud computing. In fact, utility computing was used as far back as the 1960s. Also like Software as a Service, utility computing has seen a massive increase in popularity since it has been offered as a type of cloud computing.

---

[7]"Google Software Bug Shared Private Online Documents." *Breitbart.com*. March 10, 2008. Accessed November 22, 2009. http://www.breitbart.com/article.php?id=CNG.54c3200989573ae4c9282658f91276df.48 1&show_article.

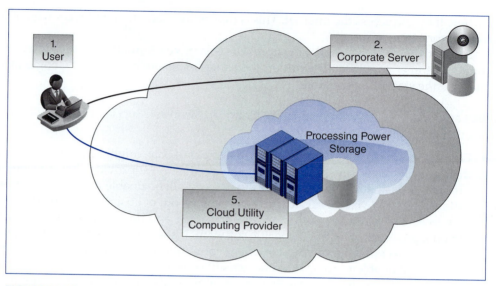

FIGURE 11-16   Cloud Utility Computing

DEFINITION   In **utility computing**, a company offloads server processing work to another company at a remote site. Figure 11-16 shows that in **cloud utility computing** (i.e., utility computing done as a cloud computing model), the company that receives this processing job is a cloud service provider, and the data is sent over the Internet to be processed. Traditional and cloud utility computing are usually offered as pay-as-you-go services. In fact, the name "utility" refers to the fact that public utilities like electricity are typically offered as metered service.

UTILITY COMPUTING   Using cloud utility computing means that a company does not have to run its own data center to do server processing work. Instead, the service provider is in charge of managing the servers and the processing itself. This is a definite change from the traditional model where a company owns its servers. In this traditional model, a company must pay to acquire hardware and install programs, and to hire staff with the expertise to provide ongoing server management. Also, because companies cannot always accurately estimate how much processing capacity they will need for a given task ahead of time, they may opt to buy much more processing power than they will ultimately need. This overprovisioning is expensive and wasteful. Underprovisioning can also be a problem: if a company does not purchase sufficient processing resources, the system may be unable to function. In this case, current and potential users may become dissatisfied with the service, and the company may lose customers.

ATTRACTIONS OF CLOUD UTILITY COMPUTING

- As with cloud Software as a Service, one of the attractions of cloud utility computing is that companies are saved the cost and risk of long-term investment in hardware and management.
- A second shared attraction is that the company does not have to dedicate personnel resources to managing its own data center.

- A third attraction is that this model provides a high level of flexibility. Flexibility is the ability to change capacity dynamically. As we will see later in this section, the use of virtualization allows the cloud service provider to increase or decrease the processing power a user wants by very small increments, on demand. As a result, a cloud user can quickly fine-tune the system so that the processing power used matches the user's requirements much more precisely.
- Fourth, virtualization also makes cloud utility computing highly scalable. As we saw in Chapter 4, scalability is the ability to grow as large as is needed. With virtualization, which we will look at a little later in this section, cloud utility computing can adapt as a firm either grows larger or just needs some extra processing power to handle the Christmas rush.

ISSUES FOR CLOUD UTILITY COMPUTING   The issues facing utility computing are the same as those for Software as a Service: access, loss of control, security, and legal requirements.

Test Your Understanding

15. a) Is utility computing a new phenomenon? b) Describe how utility computing works. c) Why was "utility computing" given this name? d) What provisioning problems might a company face if it runs its own data center?

16. a) What are the four main attractions of cloud utility computing? b) What are the issues facing cloud utility computing?

Why Is Cloud Computing a Hot Topic Now?

In the past several years, cloud computing has become a hot topic in the IT world, with major companies such as Amazon, Microsoft, and Google offering cloud computing services. Yet, as we have seen, utility computing and Software as a Service are the two main types of cloud computing, and neither is itself new. The question thus arises: why has cloud computing become such a hot topic *now*, if we have had the ability to use Software as a Service and utility computing for years?

There are three major factors that have combined to allow cloud computing to take fuller advantage of the potentials of SaaS and utility computing. These are the Internet, Web services, and virtualization. Because of these factors, cloud computing has become very popular.

CLOUD COMPUTING AND THE INTERNET   Although the Internet has existed in some form since the 1960s, in recent years it has become very accessible, very fast, and very reliable. Because of the large increase in wireless coverage, users can now access cloud computing resources from almost everywhere. The speed and reliability of Internet service means that it is feasible for corporations to rely on the cloud to access and process their corporate data.

WEB SERVICES   The existence of Web services has also helped cloud computing become a viable business model. We will look at Web service in more detail later in this chapter, but now we will mention the basics of how it applies to cloud computing. Web services allow one program on one machine to communicate with another program on another machine very easily. Of course, browsers and webservers do this now, for file

Traditional Computer Operation

User	User
	Application Program
Operating System	
Computer Hardware	

Virtualization and Virtual Machines

Virtual Machine (VM) 1		Virtual Machine (VM) 2	
Application 1a	Application 1b	Application 2a	Application 2b
Operating System 1		Operating System 2	
Hypervisor			
Computer Hardware			

FIGURE 11-17   Traditional Computer Operation and Virtualization

downloading. However, Web services allow a program on one machine to send data to a program on another machine; the program on the other machine will do processing, compute a result, and return this result to the calling computer. This ability to call on remote programs for processing service in a general way has greatly expanded the range of programs that are available as cloud computing applications.

VIRTUALIZATION   Figure 11-17 shows a traditional computer. The operating system is designed to hide the details of the hardware from the user and from applications the user runs. It accepts commands from the user or application program and carries them out in hardware. A simple example is deleting a file. This actually is a complex thing to do in hardware. Yet the user merely selects the file in the operating system's graphical user interface and clicks delete. Or, in an application program, the user may open a file. The application program will pass that command to the operating system, which will direct the hardware in the details of retrieving the file.

Figure 11-17 also shows how computers that use virtualization work. In **virtualization**, the real computer's capacity is divided among a number of virtual machines. Each **virtual machine (VM)** acts like a stand-alone computer to its users.

In virtualization, the real computer's capacity is divided among a number of virtual machines.

Each virtual machine (VM) acts like a stand-alone computer to its users.

Note that there is a new layer of software—the hypervisor. The **hypervisor** manages the use of physical computer resources by the virtual machines and communication between each virtual machine and its users. When the operating system of a VM sends a command to hardware, the hypervisor intercepts the command and carries it out on the real hardware beneath the hypervisor.

The hypervisor manages the use of physical computer resources by the virtual machines and communication between each virtual machine and its users.

Advantages   Why is server virtualization done? The first reason is that virtualization provides economies of scale in management cost. Each physical server requires a certain amount of management labor. Reducing the number of physical servers through virtualization greatly reduces management costs. Although virtualized servers require more management labor than actual servers, the net savings in management costs are large.

A second reason is economies of scale in hardware cost. If you compare the prices of two servers, the larger server usually costs substantially less per unit of processing power. So the hardware cost of running many VMs on fewer servers is less than the cost of running many servers without virtualization.

The third reason is the efficient use of server capacity. With non-virtualized servers, the applications running on them often use only a small part of the capacity. With virtualization, each virtual machine gets the capacity it needs and no more. If the hardware becomes overworked, then some of the virtual machines can be moved to other physical servers. Porting a VM from one server to another usually is extremely simple.

A fourth reason is a combination of flexibility and scalability. As mentioned above, flexibility means that if an application suddenly needs considerably more processing capacity—for instance, if there is a major marketing promotion—it can be given more capacity on its real server. Scalability means that if demand for a VM's services grows, the VM can simply be moved to a server with much higher capacity. It may even be possible for the VM to operate across multiple physical machines.

Disadvantages   Of course, virtualization only works well if the systems administrator for the server can give adequate capacity to each VM. If a server becomes overloaded, all VMs will run slowly.

Another disadvantage is that virtualization raises security concerns. Even if a firewall is placed between the physical server and the network, there is a chance that a hacker who gains a foothold on one virtual machine can access another virtual machine on the same server without having to deal with the firewall.

Test Your Understanding

17. a) What three major factors have contributed to the popularity of cloud computing?
    b) How has the Internet contributed to the popularity of cloud computing?
18. Briefly explain how computers that use virtualization work.

Managing Cloud Computing

Many businesses today must ask themselves the question, is cloud computing a sound business choice?

As we have seen, cloud computing has a number of attractions. Using cloud computing often results in cost savings, especially when it comes to capital expenditure. The flexibility and scalability of cloud computing means that a company can rapidly adjust its service as needed, and that the service can grow along with the company. Cloud computing also has the advantage of mobility of access.

Yet cloud computing also involves a fundamental loss of control. Companies may suffer if they lose access to their cloud resources, and they may face security risks and legal complications if their data is stored on the cloud.

When deciding whether to use cloud computing, a company must consider security risk. Of course, this is not unique to cloud computing. As security expert Bruce Schneier says, "IT security is about trust. You have to trust your CPU manufacturer, your hardware, operating system and software vendors—and your ISP."[8] Similarly, a company that uses cloud computing must trust its cloud service provider.

If a company decides to use cloud computing, it should set up safeguards such as service level agreements (SLAs) for reliability, speed, error rates, and other quality-of-service measures. Another important step is to only use cloud service providers that have clearly stated policies about security, data backup, and similar protections, and the execution of these policies should be independently audited. Also, a company must make sure that it understands what its legal liability will be if it uses cloud computing. One final recommendation is that it may be useful to take additional security precautions, such as encrypting data or providing redundancy by using multiple cloud service providers.

Test Your Understanding

19. What major issue must a company consider when deciding whether to use cloud computing?

SERVICE-ORIENTED ARCHITECTURES

The last client/server-based application architecture we will look at is the family of service-oriented architectures, of which Web services is a prominent subcategory.

Traditional Software Architectures and Service-Oriented Architectures (SAAs)

Traditionally, organizations have created applications by writing a single large program or a few programs that interact with each other in a very well-defined way. This works, but it is not very flexible. It is a **program-oriented architecture** because it is a software architecture (plan for providing applications functionality) built on large individual programs.

In contrast, Figure 11-18 shows a **service-oriented architecture (SOA)**. In SOAs, there are many **service objects** instead of a few large programs. Each service object provides one or more **services** to callers. For example, the figure shows Calling Program 1 that contacts Service Object 1 to receive a price quote. The customer's call would contain a part number, the number of units desired, and shipping method. The service object's service would return a message containing the price quote.

Test Your Understanding

20. a) What is a service-oriented architecture? b) What do service objects do?

---

[8]Bruce Schneier, "Be Careful When You Come to Put Your Trust in the Clouds," *The Guardian*, June 2, 2009. www.schneier.com/essay-274.html.

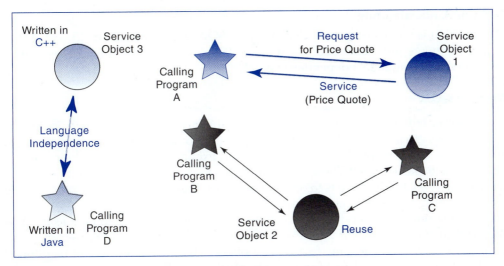

FIGURE 11-18   Service-Oriented Architecture (SOA)

Reuse and Language Independence

REUSE   Compared with traditional application development, the creation of a service-oriented architecture is more difficult. Its value comes through **reuse**. Once a service object is built, other programs can call for its service or services in a very simple standardized way. In Figure 11-18, Service Object 2 is being used simultaneously by two calling programs.

If a service object has frequently needed functionality, it may be used many times by many different applications. A simple example may be a calculator that computes a Fahrenheit temperature for a particular centigrade temperature. If someone creating such a service object can work out payment and trust issues, the object can be in high demand. Eventually, people and organizations may turn to the Internet to find a marketplace for millions of different service objects, each offering specific services.

In the future, applications may consist of small skeletons of commands, with individual groups of commands in the skeleton making calls to service objects to provide certain pieces of information or processing results. This certainly will be a radical way to provide applications.

LANGUAGE INDEPENDENCE   Service objects and calling programs (which may be service objects themselves) exchange formatted messages. The formatting of these messages is independent of the programming language used to create the calling program and the service object. In Figure 11-18, Service Object 3 is written in C++, while the calling program is written in Java. They have no trouble communicating.

This means that calling programs and service objects can be written in any languages, and the two may be written in different languages. This independence of SOA from programming languages is called **language independence**. The entire system is not locked into a single programming language, and new programming languages can be used at any time.

Test Your Understanding

21. a) What is the benefit of reuse? b) Why do SOAs make reuse more likely? c) What is language independence? d) In what sense are SOAs language-independent? e) Why is language independence good?

Web services

Service-oriented architectures, again, consist of large numbers of service objects providing services. These objects are only loosely coupled, meaning that their only interactions come through the messages they exchange. How will their message interactions be structured? There are many ways to do it. One approach to creating a service-oriented architecture is to use Web services. Figure 11-19 emphasizes that Web services is only one way to create an SOA.

Web services use service objects that provide services to customers *using World Wide Web interaction standards*. For example, a user working with a browser may send a Web service request message to a service object. The interaction would be done via HTTP, which is one of the most fundamental WWW standards.

Web services use service objects that provide services to customers using World Wide Web interaction standards.

WEB SERVICE INTERACTIONS USING SOAP MESSAGES ENCODED IN XML   There are many ways to create Web services. One way is to create SOAP messages. This is the only way we will consider. Figure 11-19 emphasizes that just as Web services is only one way to implement a service-oriented architecture, SOAP is only one way to implement Web services.

The body of a SOAP Web service request normally is encoded in XML rather than HTML. In HTML, you cannot create new tags by yourself or within a group. The eXtensible Markup Language is basically an extension of HTML that does allow you to create your

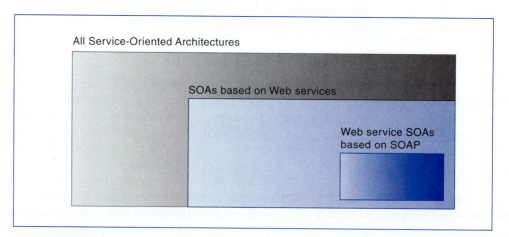

FIGURE 11-19   Service-Oriented Architectures, Web services, and SOAP

SOAP Request Message

```
<SOAP Envelope>
    <SOAP Body>
        <Service=PriceQuote>
            <PartNum>T2000</PartNum>
            <Quantity>47</Quantity>
            <Shipping>Rush</Shipping>
        </Service=PriceQuote>
    </SOAP Body>
</SOAP Envelope>
```

SOAP Response Message

```
<SOAP Envelope>
    <SOAP Body>
        <Service=PriceQuote>
            <Price>$25,892</Price>
        </Service=PriceQuote>
    </SOAP Body>
</SOAP Envelope>
```

FIGURE 11-20   SOAP Messages (Highly Simplified) Encoded in XML

own tags. For instance, a group of companies can create a tag pair, <price> and </price>, to indicate that the value between the two tags is a price. Figure 11-20 shows how new tags can be used in SOAP request and response messages.

XML is a general markup language. It does not describe the logical structure of the message. To impose the structure need to create requests to service objects and create replies, the XML body is organized according to the **Simple Object Access Protocol (SOAP)**, which specifies the syntax of request and response messages. In a SOAP message, there is a SOAP envelope tag pair, and within this there is a SOAP Body tag pair and perhaps a SOAP Header tag pair.

The SOAP Body tag pair contains a request or response. The request indicates parameters the service object needs to know, including PartNum (part number), Quantity (number of units demanded), and shipping type (rush, standard, etc.). With this information, the service object can compute a price. The service object sends this result to the caller in another SOAP message.

The messages in Figure 11-20 are highly simplified. However, they give you a feeling for how Web services may use SOAP-structured messages to communicate. The full syntax of SOAP messages is complex, but this complexity adds nothing to the discussion.

WSDL AND UDDI   For service-oriented architectures to be successful, it is necessary for users to be able to find Web service objects and learn how to use them. Figure 11-21 shows that there are two protocols to serve this purpose for Web services. A **Web Service**

UDDI

Universal Description, Discovery, and Integration

Allows calling program to find a suitable Web service

Like a telephone directory

Yellow pages: find by category of service

White pages: find by name

WSDL

Web Services Description Language

Describes how to use a specific Web service

FIGURE 11-21 UDDI and WSDL (Study Figure)

Description Language (WSDL) response message is like a user's manual for a particular Web service. However, unlike user manuals, WSDL is designed to be read by a software program rather than primarily by a human reader. A WSDL message allows a calling program to understand how to use the Web service object.

If a WSDL message is like a user manual, the **Universal Description, Discovery, and Integration (UDDI)** protocol is like a telephone directory. A UDDI interaction allows a calling program to locate a particular Web service object. This retrieval may be done by name or type of service. These are called, respectively, white pages and yellow pages services.

Test Your Understanding

22. a) What are Web services? b) Distinguish between SOAs and Web services. c) What is the function of SOAP? d) Why are SOAP messages encoded in XML rather than HTML? e) What is the function of WSDL? f) What is the function of UDDI?

Perspective

We have looked at service-oriented architectures very briefly in this section. An SOA is a general architectural strategy for creating many service objects providing the services that other entities need. A Web service architecture is only one type of SOA, albeit a common type. In addition, Web services need to use WWW protocols, but they do not specifically need to use SOAP-formatted messages, WSDL, or UDDI.

Why are service-oriented architectures important in networking? The answer is if they gain wide use, they are likely to change network traffic patterns and characteristics in ways that we can only dimly imagine today. In terms of networking, they have the potential to be desirable but highly disruptive applications.

Test Your Understanding

23. How are service-oriented architectures, Web services, and SOAP related?

PEER-TO-PEER (P2P) APPLICATION ARCHITECTURES

So far, we have examined a number of different application architectures, from traditional terminal–host systems and client/server systems to the new cloud computing model. Another relatively new application architecture is the **peer-to-peer (P2P) architecture**,

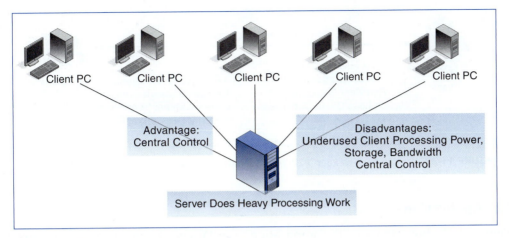

FIGURE 11-22   Traditional Client/Server Applications

in which most or all of the work is done by cooperating user computers, such as desktop PCs. If servers are present at all, they play only facilitating roles and do not control the processing.

In a peer-to-peer (P2P) architecture, most or all of the work is done by cooperating user computers, such as desktop PCs.

Traditional Client/Server Applications

Figure 11-22 shows a traditional client/server application. In this application, all of the clients communicate with the central server for their work.

ADVANTAGE: CENTRAL CONTROL   One advantage of this *server-centric* approach is central control. All communication goes through the central server, so there can be good security and policy-based control over communication.

DISADVANTAGES   Although the use of central service is good in several ways, it does give rise to two problems.

Underused Client PC Capacity   One disadvantage is that client/server computing often uses expensive server capacity while leaving clients underused. Clients normally are modern PCs with considerable processing power, not dumb terminals or early low-powered PCs. Thus, power, storage, and bandwidth are all wasted in this model.

Central Control   From the end users' point of view, central control can be a problem rather than an advantage. Central control limits what end users can do. Just as PCs freed end users from the red tape involved in using mainframe computers, peer-to-peer computing frees end users from the red tape involved in using a server. There is a fundamental clash of interests between central control and end user freedom.

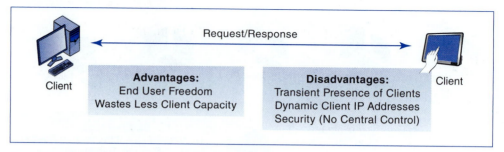

FIGURE 11-23 Simple Peer-to-Peer (P2P) Application

P2P Applications

Figure 11-23 shows that in a P2P application, user PCs work directly with one another, at least for part of their work. In this figure, all of the work involves P2P interactions. The two user computers work without the assistance of a central server and also without its control.

ADVANTAGES   The benefits and problems of P2P computing are the opposite of those of client/server computing. Client users are freed from central control, for better or worse, and less user computer capacity is wasted.

DISADVANTAGES   P2P architectures have a number of unique disadvantages.

Transient Presence   However, P2P computing is not without problems of its own. Most obviously, user PCs have transient presence on the Internet. They are frequently turned off, and even when they are on, users may be away from their machines. There is nothing in P2P like always-present servers.

Dynamic IP Address   Another problem is that each time a user PC connects to the Internet, its DHCP server is likely to assign it a different IP address. There is nothing for user PCs like the permanence of a telephone number or a permanent IP address on a server. Dynamic IP addresses make finding PCs that provide service difficult.

Security Issues   Even if user freedom is a strong goal, there needs to be some kind of security. P2P computing is a great way to spread viruses and other illicit content. Without centralized filtering on servers, security will have to be implemented on all user PCs, or chaos will result.

Test Your Understanding

24. a) What are peer-to-peer (P2P) applications? b) How are P2P applications better than traditional server-centric client/server applications? c) How are they not as good?

P2P File-Sharing Applications: BitTorrent

One particularly popular type of P2P application is file sharing. In P2P file sharing, one client PC downloads a file that it needs from one or more other clients.

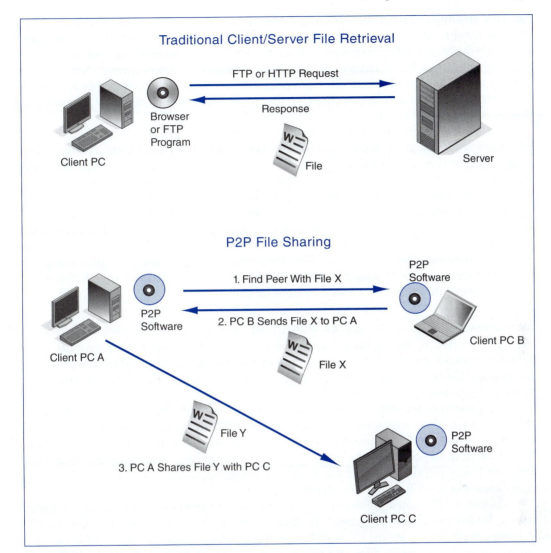

FIGURE 11-24 Traditional Client/Server and Peer-to-Peer (P2P) File Retrieval

TRADITIONAL CLIENT/SERVER FILE RETRIEVAL Traditionally, file retrieval was done as a client/server application, as Figure 11-24 shows. In this model, your computer uses either a browser program or a special FTP program to contact the server where the file that you want is stored. When the server receives your request message, it responds by using a protocol like FTP or HTTP to send a copy of the file to your computer.

Although this model is still dominant in corporations, one problem is that the file server may be overloaded at the moment that you attempt to download a file. This problem is especially common for files that are very large or very popular. If the server is overloaded, download speeds can be prohibitively slow. And, of course, the company providing the files must purchase one or more servers to store and download the files.

P2P FILE SHARING In P2P file sharing, as Figure 11-24 also shows, you download the file you want from another client computer, rather than from a server. Instead of using a Web browser or FTP program to contact a server as you would in client/server file retrieval, you use a P2P software program to find other computers (peers) that have the file you want and download the file from one of them. In turn, you commonly make files available to share from your computer, so that other users of the same P2P network can download the file from you.

In most models of P2P file sharing, your software program searches for and identifies multiple peers that have the file you want; it then contacts a single peer, from which it downloads the file. In other words, while the search is distributed, the download occurs directly from only one peer. The benefit of the P2P model is that it alleviates the overload problem of client/server file retrieval: Since there are multiple peers offering the file rather than a single server, your download speeds are less likely to be slowed down by everyone downloading from the same source. However, since upload speeds are traditionally slower than download speeds, the speed with which you can download the file is limited by the upload speed of the peer providing the file. (As mentioned in Chapter 10, asymmetric download/upload speeds are common whether you are using a cable modem or DSL.)

BITTORRENT Figure 11-25 shows **BitTorrent**, a newer P2P file-sharing protocol that was created to deal with the problem of overloading clients that provide files. BitTorrent uses a slightly different model than traditional P2P. Instead of downloading a complete file from a single peer, you download different parts of the file you want from multiple peers.

Because you are downloading from many peers, you are much less limited by the upload speeds of the peers providing the file. BitTorrent also solves the problem of overloading the client: the burden on individual peers is much lower since each only has to distribute a portion of the file. BitTorrent is especially useful for distributing very large and very popular files, which tend to overwhelm clients providing such files in more common models of P2P file sharing.

Figure 11-25 shows the main steps in BitTorrent operation. First, your computer uses a **BitTorrent client program**. The BitTorrent client program searches for the file it wants, typically by going to an **index website**, which contains .torrent files giving information about specific files and where they are stored (Step 1). Next, the BitTorrent client program contacts a **tracker**, a server that coordinates the actual file transfer (Step 2). Trackers are usually run by independent parties, rather than being directly managed by the BitTorrent company.

To coordinate the file transfer, the tracker program examines all of the computers currently connected to its network to find out which have all or part of the file (Step 3). These computers are called the swarm for that particular file. With the tracker's assistance, the BitTorrent client program begins to download different parts of the same file from multiple computers in the swarm (Step 4). These downloads occur simultaneously. The individual pieces are reassembled on the receiving computer to form the complete file (Step 5).

In order to encourage its users to share files, the BitTorrent system gives faster download speeds to users who opt to make their own files available for others to download. As more users share the same file, the download speeds for that file will become

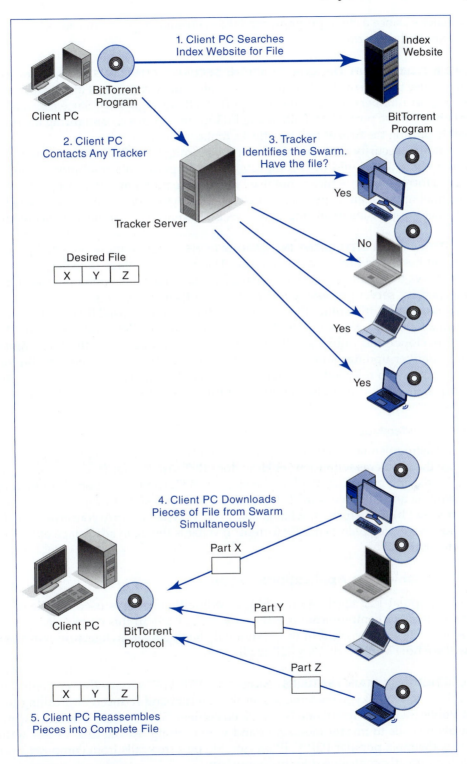

FIGURE 11-25   BitTorrent P2P File Retrieval

even quicker, since a client program can take even smaller pieces of each file from each computer in the swarm.

USING BITTORRENT IN THE CORPORATION: SECURITY CONCERNS   Corporations that decide to use BitTorrent should consider several security concerns. First, BitTorrent uses specific port numbers, usually the TCP ports 6881 through 6889. Since firewalls commonly block these ports by default, using BitTorrent requires reconfiguring the firewall, possibly putting the firm at risk for attacks that exploit these ports.

Another security concern is that employees might use BitTorrent to download an infected file, which could then compromise the corporation's computers. Also, while using BitTorrent to share files is not itself illegal, one problem is that people have used the technology to share copyrighted material. A corporation must consider whether it will be held responsible if an employee uses BitTorrent to distribute illegal content.

BENEFITTING FROM BITTORRENT IN CORPORATIONS   Despite these potential problems, BitTorrent has started to see corporate use. The main advantage of using BitTorrent is that it allows the corporation to use clients (whose capacity is often underused) rather than expensive server processing power. This results in cost savings.

BitTorrent's efficient method of sharing files has been used by broadcasters like Canada's CBC and Norway's NPK to distribute their television programs. Video game developer and publisher Blizzard Entertainment has used the BitTorrent protocol to deliver updates and patches for its World of Warcraft game. The BitTorrent company has also released BitTorrent DNA, a content delivery product designed to aid corporations that want to use BitTorrent to handle large downloads and streaming video.

Test Your Understanding

25. a) Distinguish between client/server file retrieval and P2P file sharing. b) What are the problems with each? c) How does BitTorrent differ from the common P2P file sharing model? d) Explain the steps of BitTorrent operation. e) In BitTorrent, what is an index website? f) What are .torrent files? g) In BitTorrent, what is a tracker? h) In BitTorrent, what is a swarm? i) What security concerns must firms address if they plan to use BitTorrent? j) What is the main advantage of BitTorrent file sharing?

P2P Communication Applications: Skype

Another popular P2P application is Skype. While BitTorrent is used for file sharing, Skype is used for communication between people. Early in this chapter, we saw how voice over IP (VoIP) worked in the traditional client/server architecture. With Skype, we will see how VoIP works as a P2P application.

DESCRIPTION AND MAIN FEATURES   **Skype** is a P2P VoIP service that currently offers free calling among Skype customers over the Internet and reduced-cost calling to and from Public Switched Telephone Network customers. Skype offers a range of features, from phone calls to instant messaging and video calling. At the time of this writing, Skype is the most popular P2P VoIP service. Skype's free calls from computer to computer have greatly contributed to this popularity.

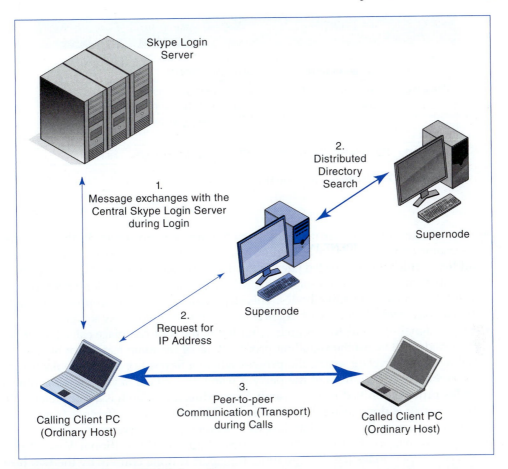

Skype Login
Server

2.
Distributed
Directory
Search

1.
Message exchanges with the
Central Skype Login Server
during Login

Supernode

Supernode

2.
Request for
IP Address

3.
Peer-to-peer
Communication (Transport)
during Calls

Calling Client PC
(Ordinary Host)

Called Client PC
(Ordinary Host)

FIGURE 11-26 Skype P2P VoIP Operation

HOW SKYPE WORKS Figure 11-26 illustrates how Skype probably operates. We have
to say *probably* because Skype has not revealed its protocol and goes to great lengths to
keep its protocol secret. The protocol also changes frequently to get around corporate
screening mechanisms.

MAIN ELEMENTS There are three main elements in the Skype network: the Skype login
server, host nodes, and super nodes.

- The **Skype login server** is a central server managed directly by Skype. It is the
  only centralized component in the Skype network.
- A **host node** is a Skype application that runs on a user's computer.
- A **super node** is a host node that takes on the work of signaling. Any regular host node
  may become a super node if it has enough memory, network bandwidth, and CPU.

OPERATION These elements are involved in the three steps that must occur for a user
to place a call with Skype.

	Traditional VoIP	**Skype**	**Comparison**
Login	Server: user logs into his or her proxy server	Server: User logs into the Skype login server	Similar
Signaling	Server: proxy server manages signaling	Peer-to-Peer: Super nodes manage signaling, using P2P searching governed by a tracker	Major difference
Transport	P2P between the two hosts	P2P between the two hosts	Similar

FIGURE 11-27   Traditional VoIP and Skype

- Step 1 Login. First, a user must log in to the Skype login server. In this step, the username and password are authenticated. The Skype server also notes the user's IP address, which will be needed later, in the directory search process. Login is the only step that involves a central server; the rest of the call process is done peer-to-peer, using host nodes and super nodes. This step is similar to the login process in traditional voice over IP, where each client must log in to its own proxy server.
- Step 2 Signaling/Directory Search. After login, the user can place calls. His or her host node will begin the signaling process. One of the main aspects of Skype signaling is the *directory search*, the process where a Skype application looks up the username and IP address of the party it wants to contact. Skype uses the Global Index protocol for its directory search. Skype directory search is a completely P2P process that is done using the super nodes. This is a major difference from traditional voice over IP, where signaling uses servers (proxy servers).
- Step 3 Transport. Figure 11-27 compares Skype with traditional VoIP. While Skype's super nodes handle signaling, transport is done entirely by the two host nodes involved in the call. In transport, the voice packets are routed completely P2P, from caller to called party and vice versa. This is similar to traditional voice over IP transport, where the two clients also communicate directly.

Because the signaling and transport are done by peers rather than going through a central server, Skype only carries the burden of managing a login server. This greatly reduces Skype's operational costs, resulting in its low-cost calls.

SKYPE SECURITY   Unfortunately, we cannot describe in detail how Skype uses super nodes to provide signaling services because Skype has traditionally been extremely secretive about its operation. In fact, Skype frequently changes the way it operates to prevent attackers from understanding it enough to attack it. Unfortunately, Skype's secretive style means that corporations whose employees use it cannot understand the risks that Skype creates.

Consequently, while Skype is extremely popular among consumers, many corporations ban its use. There are several specific reasons for these bans:

- Skype uses proprietary software and protocols that have not been revealed to security personnel and that change frequently in any case. This causes security professionals to be concerned with the existence of vulnerabilities, backdoors, and other security threats.
- Although Skype uses encryption for confidentiality, its detailed encryption method is unknown.

- A particularly important point is that Skype does not provide adequate proof of a caller's identity. Although Skype authenticates users each time they enter the Skype network, initial registration is open and uncontrolled, so that usernames mean nothing from a security standpoint. An attacker can register other people's names and impersonate them.
- Another problem is that Skype is almost impossible to control at firewalls because the Skype protocol, as just noted, is unknown and changes frequently to avoid analysis. Worse yet, Skype helps users communicate through NAT and firewalls. This is good for the user but bad for corporate security.
- Nor does Skype's file transfer mechanism work with most antivirus products at the time of this writing.

Overall, although most of these Skype concerns are theoretical, the fact that Skype cannot be well controlled by corporate security policies makes it unacceptable in many firms.

In 2011, Skype was purchased by Microsoft. It is now a division within Microsoft, under the direction of Skype's original principals. At the time of this writing, Microsoft has not announced changes in Skype security.

Test Your Understanding

26. a) What is Skype? b) Do you have to pay a fee to make calls using Skype? Explain. c) What is the most popular P2P VoIP service?
27. a) List and define Skype's three main elements. b) Explain how login works in Skype. c) What is a directory search in Skype? d) Which element of the Skype network is in charge of signaling? e) Which element of the Skype network is in charge of transport? f) Which of Skype's three steps is done P2P? g) Compare Skype and traditional voice over IP in terms of whether login, signaling, and transport are P2P or whether they use servers.
28. a) Why is Skype's use of proprietary software problematic? b) What problem is there with Skype's encryption for confidentiality? c) Does Skype control who can register a particular person's name? d) Why do firewalls have a difficult time controlling Skype? e) Does Skype's file transfer mechanism work with most antivirus programs? f) Overall, what is the big problem with Skype?

P2P Processing Applications: SETI@Home

As noted earlier, most PC processors sit idle most of the time. This is even true much of the time when a person is working at his or her keyboard. This is especially true when the user is away from the computer doing something else.

One example of employing P2P processing to use this wasted capacity is **SETI@ home**, which Figure 11-28 illustrates. SETI is the Search for Extraterrestrial Intelligence project. Many volunteers download SETI@home screen savers that really are programs. When the computer is idle, the screen saver awakens, asks the SETI@home server for work to do, and then does the work of processing data. Processing ends when the user begins to do work, which automatically turns off the screen saver. This approach allows SETI to harness the processing power of millions of PCs to do its work. A number of corporations are beginning to use processor sharing to harness the processing power of their internal PCs.

Test Your Understanding

29. How does SETI@home make use of idle capacity on home PCs?

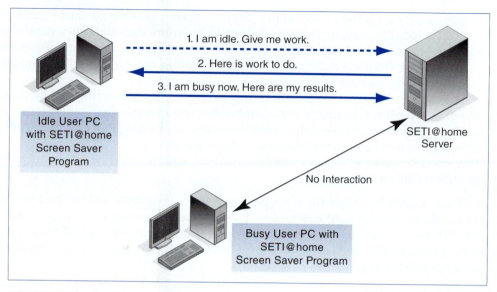

FIGURE 11-28 SETI@home P2P Application Processing

Facilitating Servers and P2P Applications

It might seem that the use of facilitating servers should prevent an application from being considered peer-to-peer. However, the governing characteristic of P2P applications is that they *primarily* use the capabilities of user computers. Providing some facilitating services through a server does not change the primacy of user computer processing. For example, Skype is still considered a P2P application despite its use of a login server. Similarly, SETI is considered P2P even though it uses a server that downloads to and accepts data from the SETI@home users.

> Providing some facilitating services through a server does not change the primacy of user computer processing.

Test Your Understanding

30. Explain how P2P applications may use facilitating servers yet still be called P2P applications.

CONCLUSION

Synopsis

Networked applications are applications that require a network to function. Although IT professionals must understand all layers in networking, users are only concerned with applications. Applications are also critical in terms of security. If an attacker takes over an application, he or she receives all of the application's permissions. In some cases, taking over a single application can allow a hacker to control the computer.

E-mail is extremely important for corporate communication. Thanks to attachments, e-mail also is a general file delivery system. In operation, both the sender and the receiver have mail servers. Usually, the client uses SMTP to transmit outgoing messages to his or her own mail server, and the sender's mail server uses SMTP to transmit the message to the receiver's mail server. The receiver usually downloads mail to his or her client PC by using POP or IMAP. With web-enabled mail service, however, senders and receivers use HTTP to communicate with a webserver interface to their mail servers. Transmissions between mail servers still use SMTP.

Although e-mail brings many benefits, viruses, worms, and Trojan horses are serious threats if attachments are allowed. Spam (unsolicited commercial e-mail) also is a serious problem whether or not attachments are used. Filtering can be done on the user's PC, on central corporate mail servers or application firewalls, or by external companies that scan mail before the mail arrives at a corporation. The problem with filtering on user PCs is that users often turn off their filtering software or at least fail to update these programs with sufficient frequency. Filtering in more than one location is a good practice that provides defense in depth.

Voice over IP (VoIP) is a client/server application in which telephone signals are transmitted over IP packet-switched networks (including the Internet) instead of over circuit-switched networks. There are two major VoIP signaling protocols: the ISO H.323 standard and the Session Initiation Protocol (SIP), which is growing rapidly. While servers are involved in signaling, transport is done directly between the two VoIP clients. Transport packets have an IP header, a UDP header, an RTP header, and a segment of application data.

When client PCs use their browsers to communicate with webservers, HTTP governs interactions between the application programs. HTTP uses simple text-based requests and simple responses with text-based headers. HTTP can download many types of files. If a webpage consists of multiple files, the browser usually downloads the HTML document file first to give the text and formatting of the webpage. It then downloads graphics and other aspects of the webpage. MIME fields are used to describe the format of a downloaded file.

Cloud computing is a popular new trend where the company outsources some combination of servers, server applications, and client PC software to a cloud service provider. It is often offered as a metered service. One major type of cloud computing is cloud Software as a Service, in which an application service provider supplies an application to customers on demand, and the user accesses the software over the Internet. A second major type of cloud computing is cloud utility computing, in which a company offloads server processing work to a cloud service provider, and the data is sent over the Internet to be processed.

An application trend that is potentially very disruptive to network patterns is service-oriented architectures, in which a few large programs are replaced by a large number of service objects that each offers a small, well-defined service or a few services. SOAs are difficult to set up but offer the benefits of reuse and the ability to link service consumers with service providers in a way that is language-independent. One way to implement an SOA is to use Web services in which interactions take place using World Wide Web protocols. In turn, a common way to implement Web services is to use SOAP-formatted messages for requests and responses. SOAP-formatted messages need application-specific tags, such as ProductName. HTML does not allow this, so messages are instead coded in XML, which is similar to HTML but that does permit the creation of application-specific tags.

Most applications today are all client/server applications. In peer-to-peer applications, in contrast, user PCs do most or all of the work. In pure P2P application architectures, no servers are used. However, it often makes sense to use servers to facilitate limited aspects of P2P applications. For instance, Skype is still considered a P2P application despite its use of a login server. Similarly, SETI@home is considered P2P even though it uses a server that downloads to and accepts data from the SETI@home user PCs. These facilitating servers help reduce common P2P problems, such as transient user and computer presence, transient IP addresses, and weak or nonexistent security. However, the application uses peer-to-peer protocols for most of its work—just not all of it.

There are three broad categories of P2P applications: file-sharing applications (such as BitTorrent), communication applications (such as Skype), and processor-sharing applications (such as SETI@home).

END-OF-CHAPTER QUESTIONS

Thought Questions

1. Do you think that pure P2P architectures will be popular in the future? Why or why not?
2. Come up with a list of roles that facilitating servers can play in P2P applications. This will require you to read through the section on P2P applications carefully. You should also try to think of an example not in the text.

Troubleshooting Question

1. You perform a BitTorrent search and get no responses. List several possible causes. Then describe how you would test each.

Perspective Questions

1. What was the most surprising thing for you in the chapter?
2. What was the most difficult material for you in the chapter? Why was it difficult?

GLOSSARY

1000Base-SX: A fiber version of gigabit Ethernet for short wavelengths (transmitting at 850 nm).

1000Base-T: A UTP version of gigabit Ethernet.

1000Base-x: The Ethernet physical layer technology of gigabit Ethernet, used today mainly to connect switches to switches or switches to routers; increasingly being used to connect servers and some desktop PCs to the switches that serve them.

100Base-TX: The dominant Ethernet physical layer 100 Mbps standard brought to desktop computers today. Uses UTP for transmission.

10Base-T: Early Ethernet standard using UTP that could only transmit at 10 Mbps.

1G: See First-Generation Cellular.

1-Pair Voice-Grade UTP: The traditional telephone access lines to individual residences.

2.4 GHz Band: Unlicensed frequency band around 2.4 GHz. Used for Wi-Fi, Bluetooth, and other services.

25-Pair UTP Cord: The cabling used by telephony for vertical wiring that runs within a building.

2G: See Second-Generation Cellular.

2-Pair Data-Grade UTP: The traditional telephone access line for lower-speed leased lines. (Higher-speed leased lines use optical fiber.) Two pairs run out to each customer.

3G: See Third-Generation Cellular.

4G: See Fourth-Generation Cellular.

4-Pair Unshielded Twisted Pair (UTP): The type of wiring typically used in Ethernet networks. 4-pair UTP contains eight copper wires organized as four pairs. Each wire is covered with dielectric insulation, and an outer jacket encloses and protects the four pairs.

5 GHz Band: Unlicensed radio band around 5 GHz. Used for Wi-Fi and other services.

50-micron Fiber: Optical fiber with a core diameter of 50 microns.

50-Pin Octopus Connector: The type of connector in which vertical cords typically terminate.

62.5-micron Fiber: Optical fiber with a core diameter of 62.5 microns.

802 Committee: See 802 LAN/MAN Standards Committee.

802 LAN/MAN Standards Committee: The IEEE committee responsible for Ethernet standards.

802.11 WLAN: Wireless LANs that follow the 802.11 standard.

802.11 Working Group: The IEEE working group that creates wireless LAN standards.

802.11a: Version of the 802.11 WLAN standard that has a rated speed of 54 Mbps and operates in the 5 GHz unlicensed radio band.

802.11b: Version of the 802.11 WLAN standard that has a rated speed of 11 Mbps and operates in the 2.4 GHz unlicensed radio band.

802.11g: Version of the 802.11 WLAN standard that has a rated speed of 54 Mbps and operates in the 2.4 GHz unlicensed radio band.

802.11e: A standard for quality of service in 802.11 WLANs.

802.11i: An advanced form of 802.11 wireless LAN security.

802.11n: Version of the 802.11 WLAN standard that uses MIMO and sometimes doubled bandwidth to achieve a rated speed of 100 Mbps or more and longer range than earlier speed standards.

802.11r: Roaming standard for 802.11 wireless devices.

802.11s: Wi-Fi standard for mesh networking.

802.16: WiMAX. Broadband wireless access standard that competes with 3G and 4G cellular services.

802.16d: WiMAX. Broadband wireless access standard for fixed stations.

802.16e: WiMAX. Broadband wireless access standard for mobile stations.

802.1p: The standard that permits up to eight priority levels.

802.1Q: The standard that extended the Ethernet MAC layer frame to include two optional tag fields.

802.1X: Security standard for both wired and wireless LANs. Mode of operation in 802.11i security.

802.2: The single standard for the logical link control layer in 802 LANs.

802.3 MAC Layer Frame: See Ethernet Frame.

802.3 MAC Layer Standard: The standard that defines Ethernet frame organization and NIC and switch operation.

802.3 Working Group: The 802 Committee's working group that creates Ethernet-specific standards.

802.3ad: Link aggregation protocol standard.

802.3af: Standard for delivering low-wattage electricity from a switch to stations.

900 Number: A number that allows customers to call into a company; callers pay a fee that is much higher than that of a regular toll call.

Absorptive Attenuation: In wireless transmission, the attenuation of a signal but water along the way absorbing its signal power. In optical fiber, attenuation due to the absorption of signal strength as a signal propagates.

Acceptable Use Policy (AUP): An early Internet policy that forbade the use of the Internet for commercial purposes such as buying, selling, and advertising.

Access Card: Small card with a magnetic stripe or microprocessor that gives you access to your computer or to a room.

Access Control: Limiting who may have access to each resource and limiting him or her permissions when using the resource.

Access Control List (ACL): An ordered list of pass/deny rules for a firewall or other device.

Access Control Plan: A plan for controlling access to a resource.

Access Line: 1) In networks, a transmission line that connects a station to a switch. 2) In telephony, the line used by the customer to reach the PSTN's central transport core.

Access Link: Same as Access Line.

Access Point: A bridge between a wireless station and a wired LAN.

Access Router: A router to connect a SOHO network to the Internet. Typically includes a switch, DHCP server, NAT, and other functions beyond routing.

Access System: In telephony, the system by which customers access the PSTN, including access lines and termination equipment in the end office at the edge of the transport core.

Account: An identifiable entity that may own resources on a computer.

ACK: See Acknowledgment.

ACK Bit: The bit in a TCP segment that is set to indicate if the segment contains an acknowledgment.

Acknowledgment (ACK): 1) An acknowledgment message, sent by the receiver when a message is received correctly. 2) An acknowledgment frame, sent by the receiver whenever a frame is received; used in CSMA/CA+ACK in 802.11.

Acknowledgment Bit: A bit in a TCP header. If the bit is set, then the TCP segment contains an acknowledgment.

Acknowledgment Number Field: In TCP, a header field that tells what TCP segment is being acknowledged in a segment.

ACL: See Access Control List.

Active Directory: Microsoft's directory server product.

Active Directory Domain: A group of hosts served by one or more active directory domain controllers.

Active Directory Domain Controller: In an Active Directory domain, one or more hosts that control the other hosts in the domain.

Active Directory Tree: In hierarchy of Active Directory domains.

Address Resolution: A process for determining a host's data link layer address if you know its IP address.

Address Resolution Protocol (ARP): Protocol for address resolution used in Ethernet networks. If a host or router knows a target host's or router's IP address, ARP finds the target's data link layer address.

ADSL: See Asymmetric Digital Subscriber Line.

Advanced Encryption Standard (AES): New symmetric encryption standard that offers 128-bit, 192-bit, or 256-bit encryption efficiently.

Advanced Research Projects Agency (ARPA): An agency within the U.S. Department of Defense that funded the creation of the ARPANET and the Internet.

AES: See Advanced Encryption Standard.

AES-CCMP: AES/Counter Mode with Cipher Block Chaining. The version of AES used in the 802.11i security standard for wireless LANs.

Agent: See Network Management Agent.

Aggregate Throughput: Throughput shared by multiple users; individual users will get a fraction of this throughput.

Alternative Route: In mesh topology, one of several possible routes from one end of the network to the other, made possible by the topology's many connections among switches or routers.

Amplitude: The maximum (or minimum) intensity of a wave. In sound, this corresponds to volume (loudness).

Amplitude Modulation: A simple form of modulation in which a modem transmits one of two analog signals—a high-amplitude (loud) signal or a low-amplitude (soft) signal.

Analog Signal: A signal that rises and falls smoothly in intensity, analogously to the way the voice input signal rises and falls, and that does not have a limited number of states.

Antivirus Program: Program to remove malware from arriving messages and from the computer's disk drive.

Antivirus Software: Software that scans computers to protect them against viruses, worms, and Trojan horses arriving in e-mail attachments and other propagation methods.

Anycast Address: If a packet is sent to this IPv6 address, routers only deliver it to a single host with the anycast address.

Application Architecture: The arrangement of how application layer functions are spread among computers to deliver service to users.

Application-Aware Firewall: A firewall that can identify and manage the application that creates a stream of packets.

Application Layer: The standards layer that governs how two applications communicate with each other; Layer 7 in OSI, Layer 5 in the hybrid TCP/IP–OSI architecture.

Architecture: A broad plan that specifies what is needed in general and the components that will be used to provide that functionality. Applied to standards, networks, and applications.

ARP Cache: Section of memory that stores known pairs of IP addresses and single-network standards.

ARPA: See Advanced Research Projects Agency.

ARPANET: A packet-switched network created by the Advanced Research Projects Agency.

ASCII Code: A code for representing letters, numbers, and punctuation characters in 7-bit binary format.

Asymmetric Digital Subscriber Line (ADSL): The type of DSL designed to go into residential homes, offers high downstream speeds but limited upstream speeds.

Asynchronous Transfer Mode (ATM): The packet-switched network technology, specifically designed to carry voice, used for transmission in the PSTN transport core. ATM offers quality-of-service guarantees for throughput, latency, and jitter.

AT&T: U.S. telecommunications carrier.

ATM: See Asynchronous Transfer Mode.

Attenuate: For a signal's strength to weaken during propagation.

Auditing: Collecting data about events to examine actions after the fact.

AUP: See Acceptable Use Policy.

Authentication: The requirement that someone who requests to use a resource must prove his or her identity.

Authentication Header: In IPsec, a header that protects part or all of the packet with authentication.

Authentication Server: A server that stores data to help the verifier check the credentials of the applicant.

Authenticator: In 802.1X authentication, the device to which the supplicant connects—a workgroup switch or a wireless access point.

Authoritative DNS Server: DNS server that manages host names for a particular domain.

Autonomous System: Internet owned by an organization.

Availability: The ability of a network to serve its users.

Backdoor: A way back into a compromised computer that an attacker leaves open; it may simply be a new account or a special program.

Backward-Compatible: Able to work with all earlier versions of a standard or technology.

Bandpass Filter: A device that filters out all signals below 300 Hz and above about 3.4 kHz.

Bandwidth: The range of frequencies over which a signal is spread.

Baseband: Transmission in which the signal is simply injected into a wire.

Baseband Signal: 1) The original signal in a radio transmission. 2) A signal that is injected directly into a wire for propagation.

Base Unit: In the metric system, the basic unit being measured: bits per second, hertz, meters, and so forth.

Basic Service Set (BSS): An access point and the set of hosts it serves.

Basic Service Set ID (BSSID): The MAC address of the specific access point.

Beamforming: In radio transmission, directing energy toward a wireless device without using a dish antenna.

BER: See bit error rate.

Best-Match Row: In routers, the row that provides the best forwarding option for a particular incoming packet.

BGP: See Border Gateway Protocol.

Binary Data: Data that has only two possible values (1s and 0s).

Binary Numbers: The Base two counting system where 1s and 0s used in combination can represent whole numbers (integers).

Binary Signaling: Digital signaling that uses only two states.

Binary Transmission: Transmission in which there are exactly two states—one state representing a one and the other state representing a zero.

Binding: In Bluetooth, after peering is complete, two devices are bound and may communicate. If they are brought together later, they are still bound and can communicate without peering.

Biometrics: The use of bodily measurements to identify an applicant.

Bit: A single 1 or 0.

Bit Error Rate: The percentage of all transmitted bits that contain errors.

Bit Rate: In digital data transmission, the rate at which information is transmitted; measured in bits per second.

Bits per Second (bps): The measure of network transmission speed.

BitTorrent: A P2P file-sharing protocol where, instead of downloading a complete file from a single peer, you download different parts of the file you want from multiple peers.

Bit Torrent Client: Program that runs on a user host. Allows the user host to participate in a BitTorrent network.

Bluetooth: A wireless networking standard created for personal area networks.

Bluetooth Profile: An application layer standard designed to allow devices to work together automatically, with little or no user intervention.

Bluetooth Special Interest Group: An association of hardware manufacturers and other organizations that sets Bluetooth standards.

Bonding: See Link Aggregation.

Border Gateway Protocol (BGP): The most common exterior routing protocol on the Internet. Recall that gateway is an old term for router.

BorderRouter: A router that sits at the edge of a site to connect the site to the outside world through leased lines, PSDNs, and VPNs.

Bot: A type of malware that can be upgraded remotely by an attacker to fix errors or to give the malware additional functionality.

Bps (bps): See Bits per Second.

Breach: A successful attack.

Bring Your Own Device (BYOD): The phenomenon of employees bringing their own devices (mobile phones, tablets, laptops, etc.) to work and using it for work purposes.

Broadband: 1) Transmission where signals are sent in wide radio channels. 2) Any high-speed transmission system.

Broadcast: To send a message out to all other stations simultaneously.

Brute Force Attack: A password-cracking attack in which an attacker tries to break a password by trying all possible combinations of characters.

BSS: See basic service set.

BSSID: See Basic Service Set ID.

Bursty: Having short, high-speed bursts separated by long silences. Characteristic of data transmission.

Bus Topology: A topology in which one station transmits and has its signals broadcast to all stations.

Business Continuity: A company's ability to continue operations.

Business Continuity Recovery: The reestablishment of a company's ability to continue operations.

BYOD: See Bring Your Own Device.

C7: Telephone supervisory control signaling system used in Europe.

CA: 1) See Certificate Authority. 2) See Collision Avoidance.

Cable Modem: 1) Broadband data transmission service using cable television. 2) The modem used in this service.

Cable Modem Service: Asymmetrical cable data service offered by a cable television company.

Cable Television: Form of television delivery that distributes signals to the home over coaxial cable.

Call Waiting: A service that allows the user to place an original caller on hold if someone else calls the user, shift briefly to the new caller, and then switch back to the original caller.

Caller ID: Service wherein the telephone number of the party calling you is displayed on your phone's small display screen before you pick up the handset; allows the user to screen calls.

Carder: Someone who steals credit card numbers.

Career Criminal: Person who earns money primarily by crime.

Carrier: A transmission service company that has government rights of way.

Carrier Sense Multiple Access with Collision Avoidance and Acknowledgments (CSMA/CA + ACK): A mandatory mechanism used to reduce problems with multiple simultaneous transmissions, which occur in wireless transmission. CSMA/CA+ACK is a media access control discipline, and it uses both collision avoidance and acknowledgment frames.

Cat: A short form for "category" in UTP.

Category: In UTP cabling, a system for measuring wiring quality.

Category (Cat) 5e: Quality type of UTP wiring; required for 100Base-TX and gigabit Ethernet.

Category 6: The newest quality type of UTP wiring being sold; not required for even gigabit Ethernet. Can carry 10 Gbps Ethernet up to 55 feet.

Category 6A: Augmented Category 6 wiring that can carry 10 Gbps Ethernet up to 100 meters.

Cell: In cellular telephony, a small geographical region served by a cellsite.

Cellphone: A cellular telephone, also called a mobile phone or mobile.

Cellsite: In cellular telephony, equipment at a site near the middle of each cell, containing a transceiver and supervising each cellphone's operation.

Cellular Telephone Service: Radio telephone service in which each subscriber in each section of a region is served by a separate cellsite.

Certificate Authority (CA): Organization that provides public key–private key pairs and digital certificates.

Channel: A small frequency range that is a subdivision of a service band.

Channel Bandwidth: The range of frequencies in a channel; determined by subtracting the lowest frequency from the highest frequency.

Channel Reuse: The ability to use each channel multiple times, in different cells in the network.

Cipher: An encryption method.

Cladding: A thick glass cylinder that surrounds the core in optical fiber.

Classic Bluetooth: Early version of Bluetooth that operated at speeds of 2 to 3 Mbps.

Clear Line of Sight: An obstructed radio path between the sender and the receiver.

Clear to Send (CTS): In 802.11, a message broadcast by an access point, which allows only a station that has sent a Request-to-Send message to transmit. All other stations must wait.

CLEC: See Competitive Local Exchange Carrier.

Client Host: In client/server processing, a server program on a server host provides services to a client program on a client host.

Client/Server Processing: The form of client/server computing in which the work is done by programs on two machines.

Clock Cycle: A period of time during which a transmission line's state is held constant.

Cloud: An image that indicates that the user does not need to know what goes on within the problem. A general name for services provided by companies over the Internet.

Cloud Computing: A form of computing where the company outsources some combination of servers, server applications, and client PC software to a cloud service provider.

Cloud Data and Synchronization Service Provider: A company that provides data synchronization from an Internet location.

Cloud Service Provider: A company that provides cloud computing services.

Cloud Software as a Service: Software as a Service where the user accesses the software over the Internet, often (although not always) with a browser.

Cloud Software Service Provider: Software is provided as a service when needed, not on a product to be purchased once and stored on the user's machine like traditional software.

Cloud Utility Computing: Utility computing done as a cloud computing model.

Coaxial Cable: Copper transmission medium in which there is a central wire and a coaxial metal tube as the second connector.

Co-channel Interference: In wireless transmission, interference between two devices transmitting simultaneous in the same channel.

Codec: The device in the end office switch that converts between the analog local loop voice signals and the digital signals of the end office switch.

Collision: When two simultaneous signals use the same shared transmission medium, the signals will add together and become scrambled (unintelligible).

Collision Avoidance (CA): In 802.11, used with CSMA to listen for transmissions, so if a wireless NIC detects a transmission or a very recent transmission, it must not transmit. This avoids collision.

Communication Satellite: Satellite that provides radio communication service.

Community Name: In SNMP Version 1, only devices using the same community name will communicate with each other; very weak security.

Competitive Local Exchange Carrier (CLEC): A competitor to the ILEC.

Complex Topology: A topology wherein different basic topologies are used in different parts of the network.

Comprehensive Security: Security in which all avenues of attack are closed off.

Compression: Reducing the number of bits needed to be transmitted when the traffic has redundancy that can be removed.

Compromise: A successful attack.

Computer Security Incident Response Team (CSIRT): A team convened to handle major security incidents, made up of the firm's security staff, members of the IT staff, and members of functional departments, including the firm's legal department.

Confidentiality: Assurance that interceptors cannot read transmissions.

Connectionless: Type of conversation that does not use explicit openings and closings.

Connection-Oriented: Type of conversation in which there is a formal opening of the interactions, a formal

closing, and maintenance of the conversation in between.

Connectorize: To add connectors to a transmission cord.

Constellation: In quadrature amplitude modulation, the collection of all possible amplitude/phase combinations.

Continuity Testers: UTP tester that ensures that wires are inserted into RJ-45 connectors in the correct order and are making good contact.

Cord: A length of transmission medium—usually UTP or optical fiber but sometimes coaxial cable.

Core: 1) In optical fiber, the very thin tube into which a transmitter injects light. 2) In a switched network, the collection of all core switches.

Core Diameter: In optical fiber, the diameter of the core, through which the light signal propagates. 8.5, 50, or 62.5 microns.

Core Security Standard: In 802.11, a standard that provides protection between the wireless access point and the wireless host.

Core Switch: A switch further up the hierarchy that carries traffic between pairs of switches. May also connect switches to routers.

Country Top-Level Domain: First-level domain name that specifies the owner's country (.UK, .AU, .CN, etc.)

Crack: To guess a password.

Credentials: Proof of identity that a supplicant can present during authentication.

Crimping Tool: Tool used to compress an RJ-45 connector onto the untwisted wires of a UTP cord.

Cross-Connect Device: The device within a wiring closet that vertical cords plug into. Cross-connect devices connect the wires from the riser space to 4-pair UTP cords that span out to the wall jacks on each floor.

Crossover Cable: A UTP cord that allows an NIC in one computer to be connected directly to the NIC in another computer; switches Pins 1 and 2 with Pins 3 and 6.

Crosstalk Interference: Mutual EMI among wire pairs in a UTP cord.

Cryptographic System: A security system that automatically provides a mix of security protections, usually including confidentiality, authentication, message integrity, and replay protection.

Cryptography: Mathematical methods for protecting communication.

CSIRT: See Computer Security Incident Response Team.

CSMA/CA+ACK: See Carrier Sense Multiple Access with Collision Avoidance and Acknowledgments. See definitions of the individual components.

CTS: See Clear to Send.

Customer Premises Equipment (CPE): Equipment owned by the customer, including PBXs, internal vertical and horizontal wiring, and telephone handsets.

Cyberterror: A computer attack made by terrorists.

Cyberwar: A computer attack made by a national government.

Data Field: A field containing the content delivered in a message.

Data Link: The path that a frame takes across a single network (LAN or WAN).

Data Link Control Identifier (DLCI): The virtual circuit number in Frame Relay, normally 10 bits long.

Data Link Layer: The layer that governs transmission within a single network all the way from the source station to the destination station across zero or more switches; Layer 2 in OSI. Governs switch or access point operation and the syntax of frames.

dB: See Decibels.

dBm: Decibels expressed relative to one milliwatt (mW), which is one thousandth of a watt, in the denominator.

DDoS: See Distributed Denial-of-Service attack.

Dead Spot: See Shadow Zone.

Decapsulation: The removing of a message from the data field of another message.

Decibels (dB): A way of expressing the ratio between two power levels, P_1 and P_2 on a logarithmic basis.

Decision Cache: In routing, a list a router keeps of recent routing decisions for specific IP addresses so that it does not have to go through an entire routing decision again if another packet to that IP address arrives. This is nonstandard and somewhat risky.

Decrypt: Conversion of encrypted ciphertext into the original plaintext so an authorized receiver can read an encrypted message.

Deep Inspection: Firewall filtering mechanism that looks at content in all layers of a packet. Typically also looks at streams of packets.

Default Router: The next-hop router that a router will forward a packet to if the routing table does not

have a row that governs the packet's IP address except for the default row.

Default Row: The row of a routing table that will be selected automatically if no other row matches; its value is 0.0.0.0.

Defense in Depth: The use of successive lines of defense.

Delay Intolerance: A delay intolerant application has performance that will suffer unacceptably if there is delay.

Demodulate: To convert digital transmission signals to analog signals.

Denial-of-Service (DoS): The type of attack whose goal is to make a computer or a network unavailable to its users.

Deregulation: Taking away monopoly protections from carriers to encourage competition.

Destination: In a routing table, the column that shows the destination network's network part or subnet's network part plus subnet part, followed by zeroes. This row represents a route to this network or subnet.

DHCP: See Dynamic Host Configuration Protocol.

Dictionary Attack: A password-cracking attack in which an attacker tries to break a password by trying all words in a standard or customized dictionary.

Dictionary Word: A common word, dangerous to use for a password because easily cracked.

Diff-Serv: The field in an IP packet that can be used to label IP packets for priority and other service parameters.

Digital Certificate: A document that gives the name of a true party, that true party's public key, and other information; used in authentication.

Digital Certificate Authentication: Authentication in which each user has a public key and a private key. Authentication depends on the applicant knowing the true party's private key; requires a digital certificate to give the true party's public key.

Digital Signaling: Signaling that uses a few states. Binary (two-state) transmission is a special case of digital transmission.

Digital Signature: A calculation added to a plaintext message to authenticate it.

Digital Subscriber Line (DSL): A technology that provides digital data signaling over the residential customer's existing single-pair UTP voice-grade copper access line.

Direct Distance Dialing: Long distance calls made at the standard long-distance rate.

Directory Server: Server that stores information about an organization's resources hierarchically.

Directly Propagating: A type of worm that tries to jump from the infected computer to many other computers without human intervention.

Disaster Recovery: The reestablishment of information technology operations.

Disgruntled Employee or Ex-employee: Employee who is upset with the firm or an employee and who may take revenge through a computer attack.

Dish Antenna: An antenna that points in a particular direction, allowing it to send stronger outgoing signals in that direction for the same power and to receive weaker incoming signals from that direction.

Distributed Denial-of-Service (DDoS): DOS attack in which the victim is attacked by many computers.

DLCI: See Data Link Control Identifier.

DNS: See Domain Name System.

Domain: 1) In DNS, a group of resources (routers, single networks, and hosts) under the control of an organization. 2) In Microsoft Active Directory, a grouping of resources controlled by one or more Active Directory Servers.

Domain Controller: In Microsoft Active Directory, a computer that manages the computers in a domain.

Domain Name System (DNS): A server that provides IP addresses for users who know only a target host's host name. DNS servers also provide a hierarchical system for naming domains.

Domestic: Telephone service within a country.

DoS: See Denial-of-Service.

Dotted Decimal Notation: The notation used to ease human comprehension and memory in reading IP addresses.

Downlink: Downward transmission path for a communications satellite.

Downloader: Malware that downloads and installs another program on the computer.

Downtime: The percentage of time that the network is not available.

Drive-By Hacker: A hacker who parks outside a firm's premises and eavesdrops on its data transmissions; mounts denial-of-service attacks; inserts viruses, worms, and spam into a network; or does other mischief.

Drop Cable: A thin coaxial cable access line that runs from the cable television company line in a neighborhood to individual homes.

DSL: See Digital Subscriber Line.

DSL Access Multiplexer (DSLAM): A device at the end office of the telephone company that sends voice signals over the ordinary PSTN and sends data over a data network such as an ATM network.

DSLAM: See DSL Access Multiplexer.

Dumb Access Point: Access point that cannot be managed remotely without the use of a wireless LAN switch.

Dumb Terminal: A desktop machine with a keyboard and display but little processing capability; processing is done on a host computer.

Dynamic Host Configuration Protocol (DHCP): The protocol used by DHCP servers, which provide each user PC with a temporary IP address to use each time he or she connects to the Internet.

Dynamic IP Address: A temporary IP address that a client PC receives from a DHCP server.

Dynamic Routing Protocol: A protocol that allows routers to exchange routing table information.

E1 Leased Line: Type of leased line used in Europe. Has a speed of 2.048 Mbps.

EAP: See Extensible Authentication Protocol.

Echo Message: In ICMP, a message that asks the addressed host to send a reply to confirm that it is active and reachable.

Echo Reply Message: In ICMP, a message that responds to an Echo message.

Egress Filtering: The filtering of traffic from inside a site going out.

EIGRP: See Enhanced Interior Gateway Routing Protocol.

Electromagnetic Interference (EMI): Unwanted electrical energy coming from external devices, such as electrical motors, fluorescent lights, and even nearby data transmission wires.

Electronic Signature: A bit string added to a message to provide message-by-message authentication and message integrity.

EMI: See Electromagnetic Interference.

Encapsulation: The placing of a message in the data field of another message.

Encapsulating Security Payload: In IPsec, a header that protects part or all of the packet with confidentiality.

Encoding: The conversation of messages into bits.

Encrypt: To mathematically process a message so that an interceptor cannot read the message.

End Office: Telephone company switch that connects to the customer premises via the local loop.

End Office Switch: The nearest switch of the telephone company to the customer premises.

End-to-End: A layer where communication is governed directly between the transport process on the source host and the transport process on the destination host.

Enhanced Interior Gateway Routing Protocol (EIGRP): Interior routing protocol used by Cisco routers.

Enterprise Mode: In WPA and 802.11i, operating mode that uses 802.1X.

Ephemeral Port Number: The temporary number a client selects whenever it connects to an application program on a server. According to IETF rules, ephemeral port numbers should be between 49153 and 65535.

ESP: See Encapsulating Security Payload.

Ethernet: The dominant wired LAN standard. Now being used for metropolitan and wide area networking.

Ethernet Address: The data link layer address of a host on an Ethernet network. Also called a MAC address.

Error Advisement: In ICMP, a message that advises a host or router that there has been a transmission error.

Error Rate: In biometrics, the normal rate of misidentification when the subject is cooperating.

ESS: See Extended Service Set.

Ethernet Address: The 48-bit address the stations have on an Ethernet network; often written in hexadecimal notation for human reading.

Ethernet Frame: A message at the data link layer in an Ethernet network.

Ethernet Switch: Switch following the Ethernet standard. Notable for speed and low cost per frame sent. Dominates LAN switching.

Evil Twin Access Point: Attacker access point outside a building that attracts clients inside the building to associate with it.

Exhaustive Search: Cracking a key or password by trying all possible keys or passwords.

Exploit: A break-in program or attack method; a program that exploits known vulnerabilities.

Extended Service Set (ESS): A group of BSSs that are 1) connected to the same distribution system (network) and 2) have the same SSID.

Extended Star Topology: The type of topology wherein there are multiple layers of switches organized in a hierarchy, in which each node has only one parent node; used in Ethernet; more commonly called a hierarchical topology.

Extensible Authentication Protocol (EAP): A protocol that authenticates users with authentication data (such as a password or a response to a challenge based on a station's digital certificate) and authentication servers.

Extension Header: In IPv6, a header that follows the main header.

Exterior Dynamic Routing Protocol: Routing protocol used between autonomous systems.

Facilitating Server: A server that solves certain problems in P2P interactions but that allows clients to engage in P2P communication for most of the work.

False Alarm: An apparent incident that proves not to be an attack.

False Positive: A false alarm.

Fiber to the Home (FTTH): Optical fiber brought by carriers to individual homes and businesses.

Field: (1) A subdivision of a message header or trailer. (2) A hexadecimal tetrad in an IPv6 address. Each field represents 16 bits. Fields are separated by colons.

File Sharing: The ability of computer users to share files that reside on their own disk drives or on a dedicated file server.

Filtering Method: A method for examining the content of arriving packets to decide what to do with them.

Fin Bit: One-bit field in a TCP header; indicates that the sender wishes to open a TCP connection.

Fingerprint Scanning: A form of biometric authentication that uses the applicant's fingerprints.

Firewall: A security system that examines each packet passing through it. If the firewall identifies the packet as an attack packet, the firewall discards it and copies information about the discarded packet into a log file.

Firewall Log File: A file that contains summary information about packets dropped by a firewall.

First-Generation Cellular: The initial generation of cellular telephony, introduced in the 1980s. 1G systems were analog, were only given about 50 MHz of spectrum, had large and few cells, and had very limited speeds for data transmission.

Flag Field: A one-bit field.

Flat Rate: Local telephone service in which there is a fixed monthly service charge but no separate fee for individual local calls.

Flow Control: The ability of one side in a conversation to tell the other side to slow or stop its transmission rate.

Flow Label Field: In IPv6, all packets in a stream of packets are given the same flow label number.

Footprint: Area of coverage of a communication satellite's signal.

Forensics: The collection of data in a form suitable for presentation in a legal proceeding.

Format Prefixes: Initial bit sequences in IPv6 addresses.

Forwarding Decision: Decision made by a switch to forward an incoming frame back out through another port to get it closer to the destination host.

Four-Step Close: A normal TCP connection close; requires four messages.

Fourth-Generation Cellular: The emerging generation of cellular telephony, which will provide a download speed of 1 Gbps or even more to stationary hosts and 100 Mbps or more to mobile hosts.

Fractional T1: A type of private line that offers intermediate speeds at intermediate prices; usually operates at one of the following speeds: 128 kbps, 256 kbps, 384 kbps, 512 kbps, or 768 kbps.

Fragment (Fragmentation): To break a message into multiple smaller messages. TCP fragments application layer messages, while IP packets may be fragmented by routers along the packet's route.

Frame: 1) A message at the data link layer. 2) In time division multiplexing, a brief time period, which is further subdivided into slots.

Frame Check Sequence Field: A four-octet field used in error checking in Ethernet. If an error is found, the frame is discarded.

Frame Relay: A popular Public Switched Data Network that operates at speeds of about 256 kbps to 40 Mbps.

Fraud: Lying to get victims to do something against their financial self-interest.

Frequency: The number of complete cycles a radio wave goes through per second. In sound, frequency corresponds to pitch.

Frequency Hopping Spread Spectrum: Form of spread spectrum transmission in which the signal is sent in a narrow band which continuously changes frequency within a wide transmission band.

Frequency Modulation: Modulation in which one frequency is chosen to represent a 1 and another frequency is chosen to represent a 0.

Frequency Spectrum: The range of all possible frequencies from zero hertz to infinity.

FTTH: See Fiber to the Home.

Full-Duplex Communication: A type of communication that supports simultaneous two-way transmission. Almost all communication systems today are full-duplex systems.

Full-Mesh Topology: Topology in which each node is connected to each other node.

Gateway: An obsolete term for "router"; still in use by Microsoft.

Gbps: Gigabit per second.

Generic Top-Level Domain: First-level domain name that specifies the type of organization that owns the domain (.com, .edu, etc.).

GEO: See Geosynchronous Earth Orbit Satellite.

Geosynchronous Earth Orbit Satellite (GEO): The type of satellite most commonly used in fixed wireless access today; orbits the earth at about 36,000 km (22,300 miles).

Get: An SNMP command sent by the manager that tells the agent to retrieve certain information and return this information to the manager.

GHz: See Gigahertz.

Gigabit Ethernet: 1 Gbps version of Ethernet.

Gigabit per Second: One billion bits per second.

Gigahertz (GHz): One billion hertz.

Global System for Mobile Communication (GSM): The cellular telephone technology on which nearly the entire world standardized for 2G service. GSM uses 200 kHz channels and implements TDM.

Global Unicast Addresses: In IPv6, one-to-one addresses that may be used on the Internet. Correspond to public IP addresses in IPv4.

Golden Zone: The portion of the frequency spectrum from the high-megahertz range to the low-gigahertz range, wherein commercial mobile services operate.

Golden Zone: a specific type of resource on a domain.

GSM: See Global System for Mobile communication.

Guideline: A directive that should be followed but that need not be followed, depending on the context.

H.323: In IP telephony, one of the protocols used by signaling gateways.

Hacker: Someone who intentionally uses a computer resource without authorization or in excess of authorization.

Hacker Toolkit: A collection of tools that automate some tasks that the hacker will have to perform after the break-in.

Hacking: The intentional use of a computer resource without authorization or in excess of authorization.

Half-Duplex: The mode of operation wherein two communicating NICs must take turns transmitting.

Handoff: a) In wireless LANs, a change in access points when a user moves to another location. b) In cellular telephony, transfer from one cellsite to another, which occurs when a subscriber moves from one cell to another within a system.

Hands-Free Profile (HFP): In Bluetooth, profile that governs device–device communication for voice dialing, adjusting volume, hanging up, number redial, call waiting, and other telephone use actions.

Hash: The output from hashing.

Hashing: A mathematical process that, when applied to a bit string of any length, produces a value of a fixed length, called the hash.

HDSL: See High-Rate Digital Subscriber Line.

HDSL2: A newer version of HDSL that transmits in both directions at 1.544 Mbps.

Head End: The cable television operator's central distribution point.

Header: The part of a message that comes before the data field.

Header Checksum: The UDP datagram field that allows the receiver to check for errors.

Hertz (Hz): One cycle per second, a measure of frequency.

Hex Notation: See Hexadecimal Notation.

Hexadecimal (Hex) Notation: The Base 16 notation that humans use to represent address 48-bit MAC source and destination addresses.

Hierarchical Topology: A network topology in which all switches are arranged in a hierarchy, in which each switch has only one parent switch above it (the root switch, however, has no parent); used in Ethernet.

Hierarchy: 1) The type of topology wherein there are multiple layers of switches organized in a hierarchy, in which each node has only one parent node; used in Ethernet. 2) In IP addresses, three multiple parts that represent successively more specific locations for a host.

High-Rate Digital Subscriber Line (HDSL): The most popular business DSL, which offers symmetric transmission at 768 kbps in both directions. See also HDSL2.

High-Speed Bluetooth: Bluetooth operating mode that retains ordinary Bluetooth speeds for most operations but that can turn on a second radio that uses a version of 802.11 limited to peer-to-peer transmission between two devices.

Hop Limit Field: In IPv6, the field that limits the number of hops an IPv6 packet may make among routers.

Host: Any computer attached to a network.

Host Computer: 1) In terminal–host computing, the host that provides the processing power. 2) On an internet, any host.

Host Name: An unofficial designation for a host computer.

Host Node: In Skype, an application that runs on a user's computer.

Host Part: The part of an IP address that identifies a particular host on a subnet.

Hot Spot: A public location where anyone can connect to an access point for Internet access.

HSTA+: Form of 3G telephony. Slower than LTE.

HTML: See Hypertext Markup Language.

HTML Body: Body part in a Hypertext Markup Language message.

HTTP: See Hypertext Transfer Protocol.

HTTP Request Message: In HTTP, a message in which a client requests a file or another service from a server.

HTTP Request–Response Cycle: An HTTP client request followed by an HTTP server response.

HTTP Response Message: In HTTP, a message in which a server responds to a client request; contains either a requested file or an error message explaining why the requested file could not be supplied.

Hub-and-Spoke Topology: A topology in which all communication goes through one site.

Human Interface Device (HID) Profile: In Bluetooth, this profile is used for mice, keyboards, and other input devices.

Hybrid Mode: In password cracking, a mode that tries variations on common word passwords.

Hybrid TCP/IP–OSI Standards Architecture: The architecture that uses OSI standards at the physical and data link layers and TCP/IP standards at the internet, transport, and application layers; dominant in corporations today.

Hypertext Markup Language (HTML): The language used to create webpages.

Hypertext Transfer Protocol (HTTP): The protocol that governs interactions between the browser and webserver application program.

Hypervisor: In virtualization, a layer of software that manages the use of physical computer resources by the virtual machines and communication between each virtual machine and its users.

Hz: See Hertz.

ICC: See International Common Carrier.

ICMP: See Internet Control Message Protocol.

ICMP Echo: A message sent by a host or router to another host or router. If the target device's internet process is able to do so, it will send back an echo reply message.

ICMP Error Message: A message sent in error advisement to inform a source device that an error has occurred.

IDC: See insulation displacement connection.

Identity Theft: Stealing enough information about a person to impersonate him or her in large financial transactions.

IEEE: See Institute for Electrical and Electronics Engineers.

IETF: See Internet Engineering Task Force.

ILEC: See Incumbent Local Exchange Carrier.

IMAP: See Internet Message Access Protocol.

Implementation Guidance: Instructions that are more specific than policies but less specific than implementation.

IMP: See Interface Message Processor.

Incident: A successful attack.

Incident Severity: The degree of destruction inflicted by an attack.

Incumbent Local Exchange Carrier (ILEC): The traditional monopoly telephone company within each LATA.

Index Website: In BitTorrent, a website that contains .torrent files giving information about specific files and where they are stored.

Individual Throughput: The actual speed a single user receives (usually much lower than aggregate throughput in a system with shared transmission speed).

Ingress Filtering: The filtering of traffic coming into a site from the outside.

Initial Sequence Number (ISN): The sequence number placed in the first TCP segment a side transmits in a session; selected randomly.

Initial Site Survey: For 802.11 LANs, an electromagnetic field strength survey performed at the beginning of an installation.

Institute for Electrical and Electronics Engineers (IEEE): An international organization whose 802 LAN/MAN Standards Committee creates many LAN standards.

Insulation displacement connection (IDC): A connection in which a metal prong is pushed through insulation into another wire.

Interexchange Carrier (IXC): A telephone carrier that transmits voice traffic between LATAs.

Interface: 1) The router's equivalent of a network interface card; a port on a router that must be designed for the network to which it connects. 2) In webservices, the outlet through which an object communicates with the outside world.

Interface Message Processor (IMP): A minicomputer that handled most of the network chores on the ARPANET.

Interference: See Electromagnetic Interference.

Interior Dynamic Routing Protocol: Routing protocol used within a firm's internet.

Internal Router: A router that connects different LANs within a site.

International Common Carrier (ICC): A telephone carrier that provides international service.

International Organization for Standardization (ISO): A strong standards agency for manufacturing, including computer manufacturing.

International Telecommunications Union–Telecommunications Standards Sector (ITU–T): A standards agency that is part of the United Nations and that oversees international telecommunications.

Internet: 1) A group of networks connected by routers so that any application on any host on any network can communicate with any application on any other host on any other network. 2) A general term for any internetwork (spelled with a lowercase i). 3) The worldwide Internet (spelled with a capital I).

Internet Backbone: The collection of all Internet Service Providers that provide Internet transmission service.

Internet Control Message Protocol (ICMP): The protocol created by the IETF to oversee supervisory messages at the internet layer.

Internet Engineering Task Force (IETF): TCP/IP's standards agency.

Internet Layer: The layer that governs the transmission of a packet across an entire internet.

Internet Message Access Protocol (IMAP): One of the two protocols used to download received e-mail from an e-mail server; offers more features but is less popular than POP.

Internet Protocol (IP): The TCP/IP protocol that governs operations at the internet layer. Governs packet delivery from host to host across a series of routers.

Internet Service Provider (ISP): Carrier that provides Internet access and transmission.

Inverse square law attenuation: Radio signal strength declines with the square of transmission distance.

IP: See Internet Protocol.

IP Address: An Internet Protocol address; the address that every computer needs when it connects to the Internet; IP addresses are 32 bits long.

Ipconfig/all: A command line command to determine the configuration of the user's computer.

IP Security (IPsec): A set of standards that operate at the internet layer and provide security to all upper layer protocols transparently.

IPsec Policy Server: In IP Security, a server that controls IPsec security parameters on a number of hosts.

IP Version 4 (IPv4): The standard that governs most routers on the Internet and private internets.

IP Version 6 (IPv6): A new version of the Internet Protocol.

IPsec: See IP Security.

IPsec Gateway: Border device at a site that converts between internal data traffic into protected data traffic that travels over an untrusted system such as the Internet.

IPv4: See IP Version 4.

IPv6: See IP Version 6.

Iris: The colored part of the eye, used in biometric authentication.

Iris Scanning: A form of biometric authentication that scans the pattern in the colored part of the applicant's eyes.

ISN: See Initial Sequence Number.

ISO: See International Organization for Standardization.

ISO/IEC 11801: European standard for wire and optical fiber media.

ISP: See Internet Service Provider.

IT Disaster Recovery: Recovering from a disaster that damages computer equipment or data.

ITU-T: See International Telecommunications Union–Telecommunications Standards Sector.

IXC: See Interexchange Carrier.

Jacket: The outer plastic covering, made of PVC, that encloses and protects the four pairs of wires in UTP or the core and cladding in optical fiber.

Jitter: Variability in latency.

Jumbo Packet: In IPv6, a packet payload than the 65,536 octets the payload length field normally allows.

kbps: Kilobits per second.

Key: A bit string used with an encryption method to encrypt and decrypt a message. Different keys used with a single encryption method will give different ciphertexts from the same plaintext.

Label Header: In MPLS, the header added to packets before the IP header; contains information that aids and speeds routers in choosing which interface to send the packet back out.

Label Number: In MPLS, number in the label header that aids label-switching routers in packet sending.

Label Switched Path: A path that all packets to a particular address will take across and MPLS label-switched network.

Label-Switching Router: Router that implements MPLS label switching.

Label-Switching Table: In MPLS, the table used by label-switching routers to decide which interface to use to forward a packet.

LAN: See Local Area Network.

Language Independence: In SOAP, the fact that Web service objects do not have to be written in any particular language.

LATA: See Local Access and Transport Area.

Latency: Delay, usually measured in milliseconds.

Latency-Intolerant: An application whose performance is harmed by even slight latency.

Layer 3: See Internet Layer.

Layer 4: See Transport Layer.

Layer 5: See Application Layer.

Leased Line Circuit: A high-speed, point-to-point, always-on circuit.

Legacy Decision: Decision that will lock the company into a specific vendor or technology option for several years.

Legacy Network: A network that uses obsolete technology; may have to be lived with for some time because upgrading all legacy networks at one time is too expensive.

Length Field: 1) The field in an Ethernet MAC frame that gives the length of the data field in octets. 2) The field in a UDP datagram that enables the receiving transport process to process the datagram properly.

LEO: See Low Earth Orbit Satellite.

Licensed Radio Band: Radio band in which stations must have a government license to operate.

Lightweight Directory Access Protocol: Simple protocol for accessing directory servers.

Line of Sight: An unobstructed path between the sender and receiver, necessary for radio transmission at higher frequencies.

Link Aggregation: The use of two or more trunk links between a pair of switches; also known as trunking or bonding.

Link-Local Unicast Addresses: IPv6 address that can only be used within a single link (single switched or wireless network).

LLC: See Logical Link Control.

LLC Subheader: See Logical Link Control Layer Header.

Load Balancing: Dividing traffic across routers in order not to overload any single route.

Local Access and Transport Area (LATA): One of the roughly 200 site regions the United States has been divided into for telephone service.

Local Area Network (LAN): A network within a customer's premises.

Local Calling: Telephone calls placed to a nearby caller; less expensive than long-distance calls.

Local Loop: In telephony, the line used by the customer to reach the PSTN's central transport core.

Log File: A file that contains data on events.

Logical Link Control (LLC) Layer: The layer of functionality for the upper part of the data link layer, now largely ignored.

Logical Link Control Layer (LLC) Header: The header at the start of the data field that describes the type of packet contained in the data field.

Long Distance: A telephone call placed to a distance party; more expensive than a local call.

Long-Term Evolution (LTE) Advanced: Currently, all cellular carriers are planning to use a single transmission standard for 4G, at least initially. This is Long-Term Evolution (LTE) Advanced. Now that there is consensus on technology, 4G service is likely to move forward in a timelier manner. LTE is a slower introductory protocol.

Longest Match: The matching row that matches a packet's destination IP address to the greatest number of bits; chosen by a router when there are multiple matches.

Loopback Address: An IPv6 address that is ::1 (127 0s and a single 1). A packet sent to this address will be delivered back to the sending host.

Low Earth Orbit Satellite (LEO): A type of satellite used in mobile wireless transmission; orbits a few hundred miles or a few hundred kilometers above the earth.

Low-Energy Bluetooth: Bluetooth operating mode in which energy requirements are reduced for devices that do not transmit or receive frequently.

LTE: See Long-Term Evolution.

MAC: See Media Access Control.

MAC Address: See Media Access Control.

Major Incidents: Attack too severe for the on-duty staff to handle; the company must convene the firm's computer security incident response team (CSIRT), which is trained to handle major incidents.

Make-versus-Buy Decision: A decision that a company must make in software development projects, regarding whether the programming staff should create the software itself, or whether the company should purchase the software.

Malware: Software that seeks to cause damage.

Malware Writers: People who create malware. The act of creating malware usually is not a crime.

MAN: See Metropolitan Area Network.

Managed Switch: A switch that has sufficient intelligence to be managed from a central computer (the Manager).

Managed Device: A device that needs to be administered, such as printers, hubs, switches, routers, application programs, user PCs, and other pieces of hardware and software.

Management Information Base (MIB): A specification that defines what objects can exist on each type of managed device and also the specific characteristics of each object; the actual database stored on a manager in SNMP. There are separate MIBs for different types of managed devices; both a schema and a database.

Manager: The central PC or more powerful computer that uses SNMP to collect information from many managed devices.

Mask: A 32-bit string beginning with a series of 1s and ending with a series of 0s; used by routing tables to interpret IP address part sizes. The 1s designate either the network part or the network plus software part.

Master–Slave: Form of transmission in which one host controls the transmission of another host.

Maximum Transmission Unit (MTU): The maximum packet size that can be transmitted without segmentation across a packet's route.

Mbps: Megabits per second.

MD5: A popular hashing method.

Media Access Control (MAC): The process of controlling when stations transmit; also, the lowest part of the data link layer, defining functionality specific to a particular LAN technology.

Media Gateway: A device that connects IP telephone networks to the ordinary public switched telephone network. Media gateways also convert between the signaling formats of the IP telephone system and the PSTN.

Medium Earth Orbit Satellite (MEO): A type of satellite used in mobile wireless transmission; orbits a few thousand miles or a few thousand kilometers above the earth.

Megabits per second: Millions of bits per second.

Megahertz (MHz): One million hertz.

Member Server: In Active Directory, a server that is not a domain controller.

MEO: See Medium Earth Orbit Satellite.

Mesh Networking: A type of networking in which wireless devices route frames without the aid of wired LANs.

Mesh Topology: 1) A topology where there are many connections among switches or routers, so there are many alternative routes for messages to get from one end of the network to the other. 2) In network design, a topology that provides direct connections between every pair of sites.

Message: A discrete communication between hardware or software processes.

Message Integrity: The assurance that a message has not been changed en route; or if a message has been changed, the receiver can tell that it has.

Message Ordering: Controlling when one device in a pair may transmit.

Message Unit: Local telephone service in which a user is charged based on distance and duration.

Metered Service: A pay-as-you-go pricing model where a customer pays only for the service that he or she actually uses.

Metric: A number describing the desirability of a route represented by a certain row in a routing table.

Metric Prefix: In the metric system, a single letter (usually) that multiplies the base unit. For instance, in Mbps, the M stands for mega (million). So Mbps is one million bits per second. This is multiplied by the number before it. So 73.23 kbps is 73,230 bps without a metric prefix.

Metro Ethernet: See Metropolitan Area Ethernet.

Metropolitan Area Ethernet: Ethernet operating at the scale of a metropolitan area network.

Metropolitan Area Network (MAN): A WAN that spans a single urban area.

MHz: See Megahertz.

MHz-km: Measure of modal bandwidth, a measure of multimode fiber quality.

MIB: See Management Information Base.

Micron: Unite of length. One millionth of a meter.

Microwave: Traditional point-to-point radio transmission system.

Microwave Repeater: Transmitter/receiver that extends the distance a microwave link can travel.

Millisecond (ms): The unit in which latency is measured.

Milliwatt (mW): One thousandth of a Watt.

MIME: See Multipurpose Internet Mail Extensions.

MIMO: See Multiple Input/Multiple Output.

Minimum Permissions: The principle of giving each person only the permissions he or she needs to have to do his or her job.

Ministry of Telecommunications: A government-created regulatory body that oversees PTTs.

Mobile Code: Code that travels with a downloaded webpage from the webserver to the browser.

Mobile Phone: See Cellphone.

Mobile Telephone Switching Office (MTSO): A control center that connects cellular customers to one another and to wired telephone users, as well as overseeing all cellular calls (determining what to do when people move from one cell to another, including which cellsite should handle a caller when the caller wishes to place a call).

Modal Bandwidth: The measure of multimode fiber quality.

Modal Dispersion: The main propagation problem for optical fiber; dispersion in which the difference in the arrival times of various modes (permitted light rays) is too large, causing the light rays of adjacent pulses to overlap in their arrival times and rendering the signal unreadable.

Mode: An angle at which light rays are permitted to enter an optical fiber core.

Modem: A device that translates between digital computer signals and analog telephone line signals.

Momentary Traffic Peak: A surplus of traffic that briefly exceeds the network's capacity, happening only occasionally.

MPLS: See Multiprotocol Label Switching.

Ms: See Millisecond.

MTSO: See Mobile Telephone Switching Office.

MTU: See Maximum Transmission Unit.

Multi-User MIMO: A form of MIMO in which multiple users can send and receive in the same channel simultaneously.

Multi-User MIMO: A form of MIMO in which the signals of two or more devices transmitting in the same channel can be distinguished from one another and so can be received correctly.

Multicasting: Simultaneously sending messages to multiple stations but not to all stations.

Multicasting: Address that will be responded to by multiple stations but not to all stations.

Multicriteria Decision Making: An approach wherein the company decides what product characteristics will be important in making a purchase.

Multimode Fiber: The most common type of fiber in LANs, wherein light rays in a pulse can enter a fairly thick core at multiple angles. Inexpensive but can transmit signals over sufficient distance for LAN usage.

Multipath Interference: Interference caused when a receiver receives two or more signals—a direct signal and one or more reflected signals. The multiple signals may interfere with one another.

Multiple Input/Multiple Output (MIMO): A radio transmission method that sends several signals simultaneously in a single radio channel.

Multiplexing: 1) Having the packets of many conversations share trunk lines; reduces trunk line cost. 2) The ability of a protocol to carry messages from multiple next-higher-layer protocols in a single communication session.

Multiplexes: Mixes together, typically to reduce cost through economies of scale.

Multiprotocol: Characterized by implementing many different protocols and products following different architectures.

Multiprotocol Label Switching (MPLS): A traffic management tool used by many ISPs.

Multipurpose Internet Mail Extensions (MIME): A standard for specifying the contents of files.

mW: See Milliwatt.

Nanometer (nm): The measure used for wavelengths; one billionth of a meter (10^{-9} meter).

NAP: See Network Access Point.

Narrowband: 1) A channel with a small bandwidth and, therefore, a low maximum speed. 2) Low-speed transmission.

NAT: See Network Address Translation.

NCP: See Network Control Program.

Near Field Communication (NFC): Form of radio transmission in which devices within about 4 cm (roughly 2 in.) can communicate peer-to-peer.

Network: In IP addressing, an organizational concept: a group of hosts, single networks, and routers owned by a single organization.

Network Access Point (NAP): A site where ISPs interconnect and exchange traffic.

Network Address Translation (NAT): Converting an IP address into another IP address, usually at a border firewall; disguises a host's true IP address from sniffers. Allows more internal addresses to be used than an ISP supplies a firm with external addresses.

Network Control Program (NCP): Software run on an ARPANET host that handles details of host-to-host interactions above the levels of packetization, delivery, and reassembly.

Network Core: The central part of the network.

Network Interface Card (NIC): Printed circuit expansion board for a PC; handles communication with a network; sometimes built into the motherboard.

Network Layer: In OSI, Layer 3; governs internetworking. OSI network layer standards are rarely used.

Network Management Agent (Agent): A piece of software on the managed device that communicates with the manager on behalf of the managed device.

Network Management Program (Manager): A program run by the network administrator on a central computer.

Network Mask: A mask that has 1s in the network part of an IP address and 0s in all other parts.

Network Operations Center (NOC): Central management point for a network.

Network Part: The part of an IP address that identifies the host's network on the Internet.

Network Printer: A printer that connects directly to a network instead of to a computer.

Network Standard: A rule of operation that governs the exchange of messages between two hardware or software processes.

Network Standards Architecture: 1) A broad plan that specifies everything that must be done for two application programs on different networks on an internet to be able to work together effectively. 2) A broad plan for how the firm will connect all of its computers within buildings (LANs), between sites (WANs), and to the Internet; also includes security devices and services.

Network Topology: The order in which a network's nodes are physically connected by transmission lines.

Network Visibility: A type of tool that helps managers comprehend what is going on in their networks.

Networked Application: An application that provides service over a network.

Next Header Field: In an IPv6 main or extension header, the field that specifies the next header's type or specifies that the payload follows the header.

Next-Hop Router: A router to which another router forwards a packet in order to get the packet a step closer to reaching its destination host.

NIC: See Network Interface Card.

Nm (nm): See Nanometer.

NOC: See Network Operations Center.

Node: A client, server, switch, router, or other type of device in a network.

Noise: Random electromagnetic energy within wires; combines with the data signal to make the data signal difficult to read.

Not Set: When a flag's field is given the value 0.

Nslookup (nslookup): A command that allows a PC user to send DNS lookup messages to a DNS server.

OAM&P: Operations, administration, maintenance, and provisioning. The four concerns in ongoing network management.

Object: In SNMP, an aspect of a managed device about which data is kept.

Octet: A collection of 8 bits; same as a byte.

OFDM: See Orthogonal Frequency Division Multiplexing.

Official Internet Protocol Standards: Standards deemed official by the IETF.

Omnidirectional Antenna: An antenna that transmits signals in all directions and receives incoming signals equally well from all directions.

One-to-One: Transmission from one host to another. Unicasting.

One-Pair Voice-Grade UTP: The traditional telephone access lines to individual residences.

Open Shortest Path First (OSPF): Complex but highly scalable interior routing protocol.

Operational Life: The part of the systems development life cycle beyond the systems development life cycle.

Optical Carrier (OC): A number that indicates SONET speeds.

Optical Fiber: Cabling that sends signals as light pulses.

Optical Fiber Cord: A length of optical fiber.

Option: One of several possibilities that a user or technologist can select.

Organizational Unit: In directory servers, a subunit of the Organization node.

Orthogonal Frequency Division Multiplexing (OFDM): A form of spread spectrum transmission that divides each broadband channel into subcarriers and then transmits parts of each frame in each subcarrier.

OSI: The Reference Model of Open Systems Interconnection; the 7-layer network standards architecture created by ISO and ITU-T; dominant at the physical and data link layers, which govern transmission within single networks (LANs or WANs).

OSI Application Layer (Layer 7): The layer that governs application-specific matters not covered by the OSI Presentation Layer or the OSI Session Layer.

OSI Layer 5: See OSI Session Layer.

OSI Layer 6: See OSI Presentation Layer.

OSI Layer 7: See OSI Application Layer.

OSI Presentation Layer (Layer 6): The layer designed to handle data formatting differences between two communicating computers.

OSI Session Layer (Layer 5): The layer that initiates and maintains a connection between application programs on different computers.

OSPF: See Open Shortest Path First.

Overprovision: To install much more capacity in switches and trunk links than will be needed most of the time, so that momentary traffic peaks will not cause problems.

Oversight: A collection of methods to ensure that policies have been implemented properly.

P2P: See Peer-to-Peer.

Packet: A message at the internet layer.

Packet Error Rate: The percentage of packets that are lost or damaged during delivery.

Packet Switching: The breaking of conversations into short messages (typically a few hundred bits long); allows multiplexing on trunk lines to reduce trunk line costs.

PAD Field: A field that the sender adds to an Ethernet frame if the data field is less than 46 octets long (the total length of the PAD plus data field must be exactly 46 octets long).

Padding: In general, adding meaningless binary strings to a meaningful string, in order to make the length of the meaningful and meaningless strings a certain length.

PAN: See Personal Area Network.

Parallel Transmission: A form of transmission that uses multiple wire pairs or other transmission media simultaneously to send a signal; increases transmission speed.

Pass Phrase: A series of words used to generate a key.

Passive radio frequency ID (RFID) Tags: Radio frequency ID tags that do not possess a power source. They are powered by the energy of the radio signal that reads them.

Password: A secret keyboard string only the account holder should know; authenticates user access to an account.

Password Length: The number of characters in a password.

Patch: An addition to a program that will close a security vulnerability in that program.

Payload: 1) In security, a piece of code that can be executed by a virus or worm after it has spread to multiple machines. 2) In IPv6, all of the packet after the main packet header.

Payment Card Industry–Data Security Standard (PCI–DSS): Security standards for companies that accept credit card payments.

Payload Length Field: In IPv6 packets, a field that gives the length of everything following the main header, including subsidiary headers.

PBX: See Private Branch Exchange.

PCI–DSS: See Payment Card Industry–Data Security Standard.

PEAP: See Protected Extensible Authentication Protocol.

Peer-to-Peer Architecture (P2P): The application architecture in which most or all of the work is done by cooperating user computers, such as desktop PCs. If servers are present at all, they serve only facilitating roles and do not control the processing.

Peering: For two Bluetooth devices to work together, they must first go through an initial handshaking stage called peering. This will require them to exchange information about themselves.

Perfect Internal Reflection: When light in optical fiber cabling begins to spread, it hits the cladding and is reflected back into the core so that no light escapes.

Permanent IP Address: An IP address given to a server that the server keeps and uses every single time it connects to the Internet. (This is in contrast to client PCs, which receive a new IP address every time they connect to the Internet.)

Permission: A rule that determines what an account owner can do to a particular resource (file or directory).

Personal Area Network (PAN): A small wireless network used by a single person.

Personal Identification Number (PIN): A four- or six-digit number a cardholder types to authenticate himself or herself.

Personal Mode: Pre-shared Key Mode in WPA or 802.11i.

Phase Modulation: Modulation in which one wave serves as a reference wave or a carrier wave. Another wave varies its phase to represent one or more bits.

Phishing: Social engineering attack that uses an official-looking e-mail message or website.

Physical Address: Data link layer address—not a physical layer address. Given this name because it is the address of the NIC, which is a physical device that implements both the physical and data link layers.

Physical Layer: The standards layer that governs physical transmission between adjacent devices; OSI Layer 1.

Physical Link: A connection linking adjacent devices on a network.

Piconet: In Bluetooth, a personal area network with up to eight devices.

PIN: See Personal Identification Number.

Ping: Sending a message to another host and listening for a response to see if it is active.

Ping 127.0.0.1: Command line command to determine if the computer is set up to talk to the network.

Plan–Protect–Respond Cycle: The basic management cycle in which the three named stages are executed repeatedly.

Planning: In security, developing a broad security strategy that will be appropriate for a firm's security threats.

Plenum: Type of wiring with reduced toxic fumes. Required for runs through air conditioning ducts and other critical airspaces (plenums).

POE: See Power over Ethernet.

Point of Presence (POP): 1) In cellular telephony, a site at which various carriers that provide telephone service are interconnected. 2) In PSDNs, a point of connection for user sites. There must be a private line between the site and the POP.

Point-to-Point Topology: A topology wherein two nodes are connected directly.

Policy: A broad statement that specifies what should be accomplished.

POP: See 1) Point of Presence. 2) Post Office Protocol.

Port: 1) In switching, a point to connect a cord to a switch. 2) In TCP and UDP messages, a header field that designates the application layer process on the server side and a specific connection on the client side.

Port-Based Access Control: Another name for 802.1X.

Port Number: The field in TCP and UDP that tells the transport process what application process sent the data in the data field or should receive the data in the data field.

Post Office Protocol (POP): The most popular protocol used to download e-mail from an e-mail server to an e-mail client.

Power over Ethernet (POE): A standard that can bring electrical power to RJ-45 wall jacks.

Preamble Field: The initial field in an Ethernet MAC frame; synchronizes the receiver's clock to the sender's clock.

Prefix Notation: A way of representing masks. Gives the number of initial 1s in the mask.

Premises: The land and buildings owned by a customer.

Presence Server: A server used in many P2P systems; knows the IP addresses of each user and also whether the user is currently on line and perhaps whether or not the user is willing to chat.

Pre-Shared Key: A mode of operation in WPA and 802.11i in which all stations and an access point share the same initial key.

Presentation Layer: See OSI Presentation Layer.

Printer Sharing: A network service in which multiple users can share a printer over a network.

Priority: Preference given to latency-sensitive traffic, such as voice and video traffic, so that latency-sensitive traffic will go first if there is congestion.

Priority Level: The three-bit field used to give a frame one of eight priority levels from 000 (zero) to 111 (eight).

Private Branch Exchange (PBX): An internal telephone switch.

Private IP Address: An IP address that may be used only within a firm. Private IP addresses have three designated ranges: 10.x.x.x, 192.168.x.x, and 172.16.x.x through 172.31.x.x.

Private Key: A key that only the true party should know. Part of a public key–private key pair.

Probe Packet: A packet sent into a firm's network during scanning; responses to the probe packet tend to reveal information about a firm's general network design and about its individual computers—including its operating systems.

Project Portfolio: A selection of projects that the firm will implement during a plan's initial period.

Propagate: In signals, to travel.

Propagation Effects: Changes in the signal during propagation.

Propagation Vector: A method malware uses to move to a victim computer.

Property: A characteristic of an object.

Protected Extensible Authentication Protocol (PEAP): A version of EAP preferred by Microsoft Windows computers.

Protecting: Implementing a security plan; the most time-consuming stage in the plan–protect–respond management cycle.

Protocol: 1) A standard that governs interactions between hardware and software processes at the same layer but on different hosts. 2) In IP, the header field that describes the content of the data field.

Protocol Field: In IP, a field that designates the protocol of the message in the IP packet's data field.

Provable Attack Packet: A packet that is provably an attack packet.

Provision: To set up service.

Proximity Access Card: Access card that works if it is brought near a reader.

PSDN: See Public Switched Data Network.

PSTN: See Public Switched Telephone Network.

PTT: See Public Telephone and Telegraphy Authority.

Public IP Address: An IP address that must be unique on the Internet.

Public Key: A key that is not kept secret. Part of a public key–private key pair.

Public Key Authentication: Authentication in which each user has a public key and a private key. Authentication depends on the applicant knowing the true party's private key; requires a digital certificate to give the true party's public key.

Public Key Encryption: Encryption in which each side has a public key and a private key, so there are four keys in total for bidirectional communication. The sender encrypts messages with the receiver's public key. The receiver, in turn, decrypts incoming messages with the receiver's own private key.

Public Key Infrastructure (PKI): A total system (infrastructure) for public key encryption.

Public Switched Data Network (PSDN): A carrier WAN that provides data transmission service. The customer only needs to connect to the PSDN by running one private line from each site to the PSDN carrier's nearest POP.

Public Switched Telephone Network (PSTN): The worldwide telephone network.

Public Telephone and Telegraphy Authority (PTT): The traditional title for the traditional monopoly telephone carrier in most countries.

Public Utilities Commission (PUC): In the United States, telecommunications regulatory agency at the state level.

PUC: See Public Utilities Commission.

PVC: See Permanent Virtual Circuit.

QAM: See Quadrature Amplitude Modulation.

QoS: See Quality of Service.

QPSK: See Quadrature Phase Shift Keying.

Quadrature Amplitude Modulation (QAM): Modulation technique that uses two carrier waves—a sine carrier wave and a cosine carrier wave. Each can vary in amplitude.

Quadrature Phase Shift Keying (QPSK): Modulation with four possible phases. Each of the four states represents two bits (00, 01, 10, and 11).

Quality of Service (QoS): Numerical service targets that must be met by networking staff.

Quality-of-Service (QoS) Parameters: In IPv4, service quality parameters applied to all packets with the same TOS field value.

Radio Frequency ID (RFID): A tag that can be read at a distance by a radio transmitter/receiver.

Radio Wave: An electromagnetic wave in the radio range.

RADIUS: A standard for central authentication servers.

Rapid Spanning Tree Protocol (RSTP): A version of the Spanning Tree Protocol that has faster convergence.

Rated Speed: The official standard speed of a technology.

RBOC: See Regional Bell Operating Company.

Real Time Protocol (RTP): The protocol that adds headers that contain sequence numbers to ensure that the UDP datagrams are placed in proper sequence and that they contain time stamps so that jitter can be eliminated.

Redundancy: Duplication of a hardware device in order to enhance reliability.

Regenerate: In a switch or router, to clean up a signal before sending it back out.

Regional Bell Operating Company (RBOC): One of the companies that was created to provide local service when the Bell System (AT&T) was broken up in the early 1980s.

Relative Signal Strength Indicator (RSSI): Signifies the signal strength available to a wireless host, relative to the signal strengths of other access points.

Reliable: A protocol in which errors are corrected by resending lost or damaged messages.

Reliability: The likelihood that a system will work.

Remote Access VPN: Virtual private network that allows a remote host communicate securely with a site.

Remote Monitoring (RMON) Probe: A specialized type of agent that collects data on network traffic passing through its location instead of information about the RMON probe itself.

Request for Comment (RFC): A document produced by the IETF that may become designated as an Official Internet Protocol Standard.

Request to Send: In 802.11 networks, a message sent to an access point when a station wishes to send and is able to send because of CSMA/CA. The station may send when it receives a clear-to-send message.

Request to Send/Clear to Send: A system that uses request-to-send and clear-to-send messages to control transmissions and avoid collisions in wireless transmission.

Request–Response Cycle: A cycle used in client/server processing where a client sends a request message to the server and the server sends back a response message.

Responding: In security, the act of stopping and repairing an attack.

Response: Responding according to plan to security incidents.

Response Message: In Challenge–Response Authentication Protocols, the message that the applicant returns to the verifier.

Response Time: The difference between the time a user types a request to the time the user receives a response.

Reusable Password: Password that is used repeatedly to get access.

RFC: See Request for Comment.

RFC 2822: The standard for e-mail bodies that are plaintext messages.

RFID: See Radio Frequency ID.

Right of Way: Permission to lay wires in public areas; given by government regulators to transmission carriers.

RIP: See Routing Information Protocol.

Risk Analysis: The process of balancing threats and protection costs.

RJ-45 Connector: The connector at the end of a UTP cord, which plugs into an RJ-45 jack.

RJ-45 Jack: The type of jack into which UTP cords RJ-45 connectors may plug.

RMON Probe: See Remote Monitoring Probe.

Roaming: 1) In cellular telephony, the situation when a subscriber leaves a metropolitan cellular system and goes to another city or country. 2) In 802.11, when a wireless host travels from one access point to another.

Rogue Access Point: An unauthorized access point.

Root: 1) The level at the top of a DNS hierarchy, consisting of all domain names. 2) A super account on a Unix server that automatically has full permissions in every directory on the server.

Root DNS Server: One of 13 top-level servers in the Domain Name System (DNS).

Route: The path that a packet takes across an internet.

Router: A device that forwards packets within an internet. Routers connect two or more single networks (subnets).

Routing: 1) The forwarding of IP packets. 2) The exchange of routing protocol information through routing protocols.

Routing Information Protocol (RIP): A simple but limited interior routing protocol.

Routing Protocol: A protocol that allows routers to transmit routing table information to one another.

RSSI: See relative signal strength Indicator.

RST Bit: In a TCP segment, if the RST (reset) bit is set, this tells the other side to end the connection immediately.

RSTP: See Rapid Spanning Tree Protocol.

RTP: See Real Time Protocol.

RTS: See Request to Send.

RTS/CTS: See Request to Send/Clear to Send.

SaaS: See Software as a Service.

SC Connector: A square optical fiber connector, recommended in the TIA/EIA-568 standard for use in new installations.

Scalability: The ability of a technology to handle growth well.

Scale: The ability to handle foreseen traffic increases and to do so without prohibitively rapid cost increases.

Scanning: For attackers, sending probe packets into a network to identify potential victims.

Script: A group of commands written in a simplified programming language.

Script Kiddie: An attacker who possesses only modest skills but uses attack scripts created by experienced hackers; dangerous because there are so many.

SDH: See Synchronous Digital Hierarchy.

Second-Generation Cellular: The second generation of cellular telephony, introduced in the early 1990s. Offers the improvements of digital service, 150 MHz of bandwidth, a higher frequency range of operation, and slightly higher data transmission speeds.

Second-Level Domain: The third level of a DNS hierarchy, which usually specifies an organization (e.g., microsoft.com, hawaii.edu).

Secure Sockets Layer (SSL): The simplest VPN security standard to implement; later renamed Transport Layer Security. Provides a secure connection at the transport layer, protecting any applications above it that are SSL/TLS-aware.

Security Association: An agreement between two parties on the security methods and parameters they will use in their subsequent interactions.

Semantics: In message exchange, the meaning of each message.

Sequence Number Field: In TCP, a header field that tells a TCP segment's order among the multiple TCP segments sent by one side.

Serial Transmission: Ethernet transmission over a single pair in each direction.

Server Host: In client/server processing, a server program on a server host provides services to a client program on a client host.

Service: In a service-oriented architecture (SOA), a service object provides services to calling programs.

Service Band: A subdivision of the frequency spectrum, dedicated to a specific service such as FM radio or cellular telephone service.

Service Control Point: A database of customer information, used in Signaling System 7.

Service Discovery Profile (SDP): When discoverable Bluetooth devices receive a Service Discovery Profile request, they will transmit information about themselves, including device name, device class, lists of Bluetooth profiles supported, and technical information such as the device's manufacturer and model.

Service Level Agreement (SLA): A quality-of-service guarantee for throughput, availability, latency, error rate, and other matters.

Service-Oriented Architecture (SOA): An architecture where there are many service objects instead of a few large programs.

Service Set ID (SSID): On a wireless access point, the name of the network.

Session Initiation Protocol (SIP): Relatively simple signaling protocol for voice over IP.

Session Key: Symmetric key that is used only during a single communication session between two parties.

Session Layer: See OSI Session Layer.

Set: 1) When a flag's field is given the value 1. 2) An SNMP command sent by the manager that tells the agent to change a parameter on the managed device.

SETI@home: A project from the Search for Extraterrestrial Intelligence (SETI), in which volunteers download SETI@home screen savers that are really programs. These programs do work for the SETI@ home server when the volunteer computer is idle. Processing ends when the user begins to do work.

Shadow Zone (Dead Spot): A location where a receiver cannot receive radio transmission, due to an obstruction blocking the direct path between sender and receiver.

Shannon Equation: An equation by Claude Shannon (1938) that shows that the maximum possible transmission speed (C) when sending data through a channel is directly proportional to its bandwidth (B), and depends to a lesser extent on its signal-to-noise ratio (S/N): $C = B \log_2 (1 + S/N)$.

Shared Internet Access: Access that allows two or more client PCs to use the Internet simultaneously, as if each was plugged directly into the broadband modem.

SHDSL: See Super-High-Rate DSL.

Shielded Twisted Pair (STP): A type of twisted-pair wiring that puts a metal foil sheath around each pair and another metal mesh around all pairs.

Signal: An information-carrying disturbance that propagates through a transmission medium.

Signal Bandwidth: The range of frequencies in a signal, determined by subtracting the lowest frequency from the highest frequency.

Signaling: In telephony, the controlling of calling, including setting up a path for a conversation through the transport core, maintaining and terminating the conversation path, collecting billing information, and handling other supervisory functions.

Signaling Gateway: The device that sets up conversations between parties, maintains these conversations, ends them, provides billing information, and does other work.

Signaling System 7: Telephone signaling system in the United States.

Signal-to-Noise Ratio (SNR): The ratio of the signal strength to average noise strength; should be high in order for the signal to be effectively received.

Signing: Encrypting something with the sender's private key.

Simple Mail Transfer Protocol (SMTP): The protocol used to send a message to a user's outgoing mail host and from one mail host to another; requires a complex series of interactions between the sender and the receiver before and after mail delivery.

Simple Network Management Protocol (SNMP): The protocol that allows a general way to collect rich data from various managed devices in a network.

Simple Object Access Protocol (SOAP): A standardized way for a Web service to expose its methods on an interface to the outside world.

Single Point of Failure: When the failure in a single component of a system can cause a system to fail or be seriously degraded.

Single-Mode Fiber: Optical fiber whose core is so thin (usually 8.3 microns in diameter) that only a single mode can propagate, also the one traveling straight along the axis.

SIP: See Session Initiation Protocol.

Site-to-Site VPN: Virtual private network that secures all communication between two sites.

Site Survey: In wireless LANs, a radio survey to help determine where to place access points.

Skype: A P2P VoIP service that currently offers free calling among Skype customers over the Internet and reduced-costs calling to and from Public Switched Telephone Network customers.

Skype Login Server: A central server in the Skype network, managed directly by Skype.

SLA: See Service Level Agreement.

SLC: See Systems Life Cycle.

Sliding Window Protocol: Flow control protocol that tells a receiver how many more bytes it may transmit before receiving another acknowledgment, which will give a longer transmission window.

Slot: A very brief time period used in Time Division Multiplexing; a subdivision of a frame. Carries one sample for one circuit.

Small Form Factor (SFF): A variety of optical fiber connectors; smaller than SC or ST connectors but unfortunately not standardized.

Smart Access Point: An access point that can be managed remotely.

Smart Antenna: Antenna capable of directing energy to and from individual station locations.

Smart Cards: Cards with computer chips.

Smartphone: Cellular telephone that offers many non-telephony functions, such as internet access and running applications.

SMTP: See Simple Mail Transfer Protocol.

Sniffer: In security, a device that intercepts traffic to read it in order to find information useful to an attacker.

SNMP: See Simple Network Management Protocol.

SNR: See Signal-to-Noise Ratio.

SOA: See Service-Oriented Architecture.

SOAP: See Simple Object Access Protocol.

Social Engineering: Tricking people into doing something to get around security protections.

Social Media Applications: Web 2.0 applications that are designed to facilitate relationships.

Socket: The combination of an IP address and a port number, designating a specific connection to a specific application on a specific host. It is written as an IP address, a colon, and a port number, for instance, 128.171.17.13:80.

Software Architecture: A plan for providing applications functionality.

Software as a Service (SaaS): Service in which an application service provider supplies an application to customers on demand.

Software-Defined Radio: Radios that can be changed by software to meet different standards.

Solid-Wire UTP: Type of UTP in which each of the eight wires really is a single solid wire.

SONET: See Synchronous Optical Network.

Spam: Unsolicited commercial e-mail.

Spatial Streams: Radio signals in the same channel between two or more different antennas on access points and wireless hosts.

Speech Codec: See codec.

SPI: See Stateful Packet Inspection.

Splitter: A device that a DSL user plugs into each telephone jack; the splitter separates the voice signal from the data signal so that they cannot interfere with each other.

Spread Spectrum Transmission: A type of radio transmission that takes the original signal and spreads the signal energy over a much broader channel than would be used in normal radio transmission; used in order to reduce propagation problems, not for security.

Spyware: Software that sits on a victim's machine and gathers information about the victim.

SS7: See Signaling System 7.

SSID: See Service Set ID.

SSL: See Secure Sockets Layer.

SSL/TLS: See Secure Sockets Layer and Transport Layer Security.

SSL/TLS-Aware: Modified to work with SSL/TLS.

ST Connector: A cylindrical optical fiber connector, sometimes called a bayonet connector because of the manner in which it pushes into an ST port and then twists to be locked in place.

ST Jack: Port for an ST connector.

Standard: A rule of operation that allows two hardware or software processes to work together. Standards normally govern the exchange of messages between two entities.

Standards Agency: An organization that creates and maintains standards.

Standards Architecture: A family of related standards that collectively allows an application program on one machine on an internet to communicate with another application program on another machine on the internet.

Star Topology: A form of topology in which all wires in a network connect to a single switch.

Start of Frame Delimiter Field: The second field of an Ethernet MAC frame, which synchronizes the receiver's clock to the sender's clock and then signals that the synchronization has ended.

State: In digital physical layer signaling, one of the few line conditions that represent information.

Stateful Packet Inspection Firewall: A firewall whose default behavior is to allow all connections initiated by internal hosts but to block all connections initiated by external hosts. Only passes packets that are part of approved connections.

Stateful Packet Inspection: Firewall filtering mechanism that uses different filtering methods in different states of a conversation.

Static IP Address: An IP address that never changes.

STM: See Synchronous Transfer Mode.

STP: See 802.1D spanning tree protocol out. Shielded Twisted Pair.

Strain Relief: In a UTP connectorization, pressing the RJ-45 connector into the jacket of a UTP cord. This means that even if the cord is pulled, causing strain, the cord will not pull out of the connector.

Strand: In optical fiber, a core surrounded by a cladding. For two-way transmission, two optical fiber strands are needed.

Stranded-Wire UTP: Type of UTP in which each of the eight "wires" really is a collection of wire strands.

Stripping Tool: Tool for stripping the sheath off the end of a UTP cord.

Subcarrier: A channel that is itself a subdivision of a broadband channel, used to transmit frames in OFDM.

Subnet: A small network that is a subdivision of a large organization's network.

Subnet Mask: A mask with 1s in the network and subnet parts and 0s in the host part.

Subnet Part: The part of an IP address that specifies a particular subnet within a network.

Super Node: In Skype, a host node that takes on the work of signaling.

Super-High-Rate DSL (SHDSL): The next step in business DSL, which can operate symmetrically over a single voice-grade twisted pair and over a speed range of 384 kbps to 2.3 Mbps. It can also operate over somewhat longer distances than HDSL2.

Supervisory Standard: A standard that used to keep a network or internet working.

Supplicant: The party trying to prove his or her identity.

Surreptitiously: Done without someone's knowledge, such as surreptitious face recognition scanning.

Switch: A device that forwards frames within a single network.

Symmetric: Speeds that are equal in both directions.

Symmetric Key Encryption: Family of encryption methods in which the two sides use the same key to encrypt messages to each other and to decrypt incoming messages. In bidirectional communication, only a single key is used.

SYN Bit: In TCP, the flags field that is set to indicate if the message is a synchronization message.

Synchronous Digital Hierarchy (SDH): The European version of the technology upon which the world is nearly standardized.

Synchronous Optical Network (SONET): The North American version of the technology upon which the world is nearly standardized.

Synchronous Transfer Mode (STM): A number that indicates SDH speeds.

Syntax: In message exchange, how messages are organized.

System Life Cycle Costs: Costs over a system's entire life.

Systems Life Cycle (SLC): The period between a system's conception and its termination.

Systems Network Architecture (SNA): The standards architecture traditionally used by IBM mainframe computers.

T1 Leased Line: In the North American Digital Hierarchy, a leased line with a speed of 1.544 Mbps.

Tag: An indicator on an HTML file to show where the browser should render graphics files, when it should play audio files, and so forth.

Tag Control Information: The second tag field, which contains a 12-bit VLAN ID that it sets to zero if VLANs are not being implemented. If VLANs are being used, each VLAN will be assigned a different VLAN ID.

Tag Field: One of the two fields added to an Ethernet MAC layer frame by the 802.1Q standard.

Tag Protocol ID: The first tag field used in the Ethernet MAC layer frame. The Tag Protocol ID has the two-octet hexadecimal value 81-00, which indicates that the frame is tagged.

Task Group: In the 802 LAN/MAN Standards Committee, a subgroup of a Working Group.

Tbps: Terabits per second—a thousand billions of bits per second.

TCO: See Total Cost of Ownership.

TCP: See Transmission Control Protocol.

TCP Reset Segment: TCP segment in which the RST flag bit is set.

TCP Segment: A TCP message.

TCP/IP: The Internet Engineering Tasks Force's standards architecture; dominant above the data link layer.

TDM: See Time Division Multiplexing.

TDR: See Time Domain Reflectometry.

Telecommunications: The transmission of voice and video, as opposed to data.

Telecommunications Closet: The location on each floor of a building where cords coming up from the basement are connected to cords that span out horizontally to telephones and computers on that floor.

Terabits per Second: Trillions of bits per second.

Terminal Crosstalk Interference: Crosstalk interference at the ends of a UTP cord, where wires are untwisted to fit into the connector. To control terminal crosstalk interference, wires should not be untwisted more than a half inch to fit into connectors.

Termination Equipment: Equipment that connects a site's internal telephone system to the local exchange carrier.

Terrestrial: Earth-bound transmissions.

Test Signals: Signal sent by a high-quality UTP tester through a UTP cord to check signal quality parameters.

Texting: In cellular telephony, the transmission of text messages.

Third-Generation Cellular: The newest generation of cellular telephony, able to carry data at much higher speeds than 2G systems.

Threat Environment: The threats that face the company.

Three-Party Call: A call in which three people can take part in a conversation.

Three-Step Handshake: A three-message exchange that opens a connection in TCP.

Throughput: The transmission speed that users *actually* get. Usually lower than a transmission system's rated speed.

Time Division Multiplexing (TDM): A technology used by telephone carriers to provide reserved capacity on trunk lines between switches. In TDM, time is first divided into frames, each of which are divided into slots; a circuit is given the same slot in every frame.

Time Domain Reflectometry (TDR): A testing system for UTP that can detect breaks in the wire.

Time to Live (TTL): The field added to a packet and given a value by a source host, usually between 64 and 128. Each router along the way decrements the TTL field by one. A router decrementing the TTL to zero will discard the packet; this prevents misaddressed packets from circulating endlessly among packet switches in search of their nonexistent destinations.

TLS: See Transport Layer Security.

Toll Call: Long-distance call pricing in which the price depends on distance and duration.

Toll-Free Number Service: Service in which anyone can call into a company, usually without being charged. Area codes are 800, 888, 877, 866, and 855.

Top-Level Domain: The second level of a DNS hierarchy, which categorizes the domain by organization type (e.g., .com, .net, .edu, .biz, .info) or by country (e.g., .uk, .ca, .ie, .au, .jp, .ch).

Topology: The way in which nodes are linked together by transmission lines.

Total Cost of Ownership (TCO): The total cost of an entire system over its expected lifespan.

Tracert: A command line command to list the routers between the computer and the destination host and to list average latency to each router along the way.

Tracert (tracert): A Windows program that shows latencies to every router along a route and to the destination host.

Tracker: In BitTorrent, a server that coordinates the file transfer.

Traffic Class Field: An IPv6 field for specifying special handing for a packet.

Traffic Engineering: Designing and managing traffic on a network.

Traffic Shaping: Limiting access to a network based on type of traffic.

Trailer: The part of a message that comes after the data field.

Transceiver: A transmitter/receiver.

Transmission Control Protocol (TCP): The most common TCP/IP protocol at the transport layer. Connection-oriented and reliable.

Transparently: Without having a need to implement modifications.

Transport: In telephony, transmission; taking voice signals from one subscriber's access line and delivering them to another customer's access line.

Transport Core: The switches and transmission lines that carry voice signals from one subscriber's access line and delivering them to another customer's access line.

Transport Layer: The layer that governs communication between two hosts; Layer 4 in both OSI and TCP/IP.

Transport Layer Security (TLS): The simplest VPN security standard to implement; originally named Secure Sockets Layer. Provides a secure connection at the transport layer, protecting any applications above it that are SSL/TLS-aware.

Transport Mode: One of IPsec's two modes of operation, in which the two computers that are communicating implement IPsec. Transport mode gives strong end-to-end security between the computers, but it requires IPsec configuration and a digital certificate on all machines.

Traps: The type of message that an agent sends if it detects a condition that it thinks the manager should know about.

Trojan Horse: A program that looks like an ordinary system file, but continues to exploit the user indefinitely.

True Party: In authentication, the person the supplicant says that he or she is.

Trunk Line: A type of transmission line that links switches to each other, routers to each other, or a router to a switch.

Trunking: See Link Aggregation.

TTL: See Time to Live.

Tunnel Mode: One of IPsec's two modes of operation, in which the IPsec connection extends only between IPsec gateways at the two sites. Tunnel mode provides no protection within sites, but it offers transparent security.

Twisted-Pair Wiring: Wiring in which each pair's wires are twisted around each other several times per inch, reducing EMI.

Two-Factor Authentication: A type of authentication that requires two forms of credentials.

Two-Way Amplifier: In cable television, an amplifier that amplifies signals traveling in both directions.

U: The standard unit for measuring the height of switches. One U is 1.75 in. (4.4 cm) in height. Most switches, although not all, are multiples of U.

UDDI: See Universal Description, Discovery, and Integration.

UDDI Yellow Pages: The UDDI search option that allows users to search for Web services by function, such as accounting, much like telephone yellow pages.

UDP: See User Datagram Protocol.

UDP Checksum: Field in the UDP header that the receiver uses to check for errors. If the receiving transport process finds an error, it drops the UDP datagram.

UDP Length: Field in the UDP header that gives the length of the UDP data field in octets.

Ultrawideband (UWB): Spread spectrum transmission system that has extremely wide channels.

Unicasting: Transmission to a single other host.

UNICODE: The standard that allows characters of all languages to be represented.

Universal Description, Discovery, and Integration (UDDI): A protocol that is a distributed database that helps users find appropriate Web services.

Universal Malware: Malware that works whether or not the target computer has a security vulnerability.

Unlicensed Radio Band: A radio band that does not require each station using it to have a license.

Unreliable: (Of a protocol) not doing error correction.

Unshielded Twisted Pair (UTP): Network cord that contains four twisted pairs of wire within a sheath. Each wire is covered with insulation.

Uplink: In satellites, transmission from the Earth to a communication satellite.

User Datagram Protocol (UDP): Unreliable transport-layer protocol in TCP/IP.

Username: An alias that signifies the account that the account holder will be using.

Utility Computing: A model of computing where a company offloads server processing work to another company at a remote site.

UTP: See Unshielded Twisted Pair.

UWB: See Ultrawideband.

Verifier: The party requiring the supplicant to prove his or her identity.

Version Control: Field in an IP packet header that indicates whether the packet is an IPv4 or IPv6 packet.

Vertical Riser: Space between the floors of a building that telephone and data cabling go through to get to the building's upper floor.

Very Small Aperture Terminal (VSAT): Communication satellite earthstation that has a small-diameter antenna.

Virtual Circuit: A transmission path between two sites or devices; selected before transmission begins.

Virtual LAN (VLAN): A closed collection of servers and the clients they serve. Broadcast signals go only to computers in the same VLAN.

Virtual Machine (VM): One of multiple logical machines in a real machine; to its users, it appears to be a real machine.

Virtual Private Network (VPN): A network that uses the Internet or a wireless network with added security for data transmission.

Virtual WAN Software: Software that treats various types of WAN transmission in a firm as a single network.

Virtualization: A process where the real computer's capacity is divided among a number of virtual machines.

Virus: A piece of executable code that attaches itself to programs or data files. When the program is executed or the data file opened, the virus spreads to other programs or data files.

VLAN: See Virtual LAN.

VM: See Virtual Machine.

Voice Mail: A service that allows people to leave a message if the user does not answer his or her phone.

Voice over IP (VoIP): The transmission of voice signals over an IP network.

Voice-Grade: Wire of a quality designed for transmitting voice signals in the PSTN.

VoIP: See Voice over IP.

VoIP Telephone: A telephone that has the electronics to encode voice for digital transmission and to handle packets over an IP internet.

VPN: See Virtual Private Network.

VSAT: See Very Small Aperture Terminal.

Vulnerability: A security weakness found in software.

Vulnerability-Specific: A type of attack aimed at a particular vulnerability.

Vulnerability Testing: Testing after protections have been configured, in which a company or a consultant attacks protections in the way a determined attacker would and notes which attacks that should have been stopped actually succeeded.

WAN: See Wide Area Network.

War Driver: Someone who travels around looking for unprotected wireless access points.

WATS: See Wide Area Telephone Service.

Wavelength: The physical distance between comparable points (e.g., from peak to peak) in successive cycles of a wave.

WDSL: See Webservice Description Language.

Web 2.0: A category of applications in which users provide the content.

Webservice: A type of service-oriented architecture based on World Wide Web standards.

Webservice Description Language (WSDL): A Webservice Description Language (WSDL) response message is like a user's manual for a particular webservice. However, unlike user manuals, WSDL is designed to be read by a software program rather than primarily by a human reader. A WSDL message allows a calling program to understand how to use the Web service object.

Well-Known Port Number: Standard port number of a major application that is usually (but not always) used. For example, the well-known TCP port number for HTTP is 80. Well-known port numbers range from 0 through 1023.

WEP: See Wired Equivalent Privacy.

White Space: Unused radio frequencies that may be able to be used opportunistically.

Wide Area Network (WAN): A network that links different sites together.

Wide Area Telephone Service (WATS): Service that allows a company to place outgoing long-distance calls at per-minute prices lower than those of directly dialed calls.

Wi-Fi Alliance: Trade group created to create interoperability tests of 802.11 LANs; actually produced the WPA standard.

Wi-Fi Direct: Standard that permits direct transmission between two 802.11 devices without using an access point.

WiMAX: Broadband wireless access method. Standardized as 802.16.

WiMAX Forum: The WiMAX Forum has developed a wireless metropolitan area network service called WiMAX. WiMAX is designed for carriers who want to provide metropolitan area networking. Its signals can easily reach all customers in a metropolitan area.

Window Size Field: TCP header field that is used for flow control. It tells the station that receives the segment how many more octets that station may transmit before getting another acknowledgment message that will allow it to send more octets.

Wired Equivalent Privacy (WEP): A weak security mechanism for 802.11.

Wireless Access Point: Devices that control wireless clients and that bridge wireless clients to servers and routers on the firm's main wired LAN.

Wireless LAN (WLAN): A local area network that uses radio transmission instead of cabling to connect devices.

Wireless LAN Switch: An Ethernet switch to which multiple wireless access points connect; manages the access points.

Wireless Networking: Networking that uses radio transmission instead of wires to connect devices.

Wireless NIC: 802.11 network interface card.

Wireless Protected Access (WPA): The 802.11 security method created as a stopgap between WEP and 802.11i.

Wireless Protected Access 2 (WPA2): Another name for 802.11 security.

Wireless Sniffer: Program that provides information about nearby access points and perhaps other wireless devices.

WLAN: See Wireless LAN.

Work-Around: A process of making manual changes to eliminate a vulnerability instead of just installing a software patch.

Workgroup: A logical network. On a physical network, only PCs in the same workgroup can communicate.

Workgroup Switch: A switch to which stations connect directly.

Working Group: A specific subgroup of the 802 Committee, in charge of developing a specific group of standards. For instance, the 802.3 Working Group creates Ethernet standards.

Worm: An attack program that propagates on its own by seeking out other computers, jumping to them, and installing itself.

Worst Case: In service-level agreements, the worst service a customer will receive without the service provider paying a penalty. The worst case for speed would be a certain *minimum* speed.

WPA: See Wireless Protected Access.

WPA2: See Wireless Protected Access 2.

X.25: The original PSDN standard. Relatively slow because it did error correction.

Zero-Day Attack: Attack that takes advantage of a vulnerability for which no patch or other work-around has been released.

INDEX

Page numbers in **bold** type indicate where terms are defined or characterized; page numbers in *italics* indicate tables or figures; page numbers with an "n" indicate a footnote.